Management Accounting

AN INTEGRATIVE APPROACH

DEDICATED TO:

To Cyndi, who at her first job interview for accounting asked, "What answer do you want?" While there are better or worse answers, her spirit will always live on.

—C.J.

To my wife, Gail Worth Merchant.

—KENNETH

Management Accounting

For information about this title or to order other books and/or electronic media, contact the publisher:
IMA
10 Paragon Drive, Suite 1
Montvale, NJ 07645-1760
(800)638-4427 or +1 (201) 573-9000
www.imanet.org

ISBN: 978-0-9967293-5-2

Printed in the United States of America
Cover and Interior design: 1106 Design

About IMA® (Institute Of Management Accountants)

IMA, the association of accountants and financial professionals in business, is one of the largest and most respected associations focused exclusively on advancing the management accounting profession. Globally, IMA supports the profession through research, the CMA® (Certified Management Accountant) program, continuing education, networking, and advocacy of the highest ethical business practices. IMA has a global network of more than 85,000 members in 140 countries and more than 300 professional and student chapters. Headquartered in Montvale, N.J., USA, IMA provides localized services through its four global regions: The Americas, Asia/Pacific, Europe, and Middle East/India. For more information about IMA, please visit www.imanet.org.

About the CMA® (Certified Management Accountant)

IMA's globally recognized CMA® (Certified Management Accountant) is the leading certification for management accountants and financial professionals in business. Earning the CMA requires a mastery of advanced-level knowledge in four critical areas: financial planning, analysis, control, and decision support. For more information about the CMA certification program, please visit www.imanet.org/cma-certification.

About the Authors

C.J. MCNAIR-CONNOLLY, PH.D., CMA, is known for her innovative work in cost management and control systems. Based on a multitude of field studies conducted over almost 35 years, plus a lifetime of working in practical settings, she brings a common-sense perspective that emphasizes how management accounting is applied by modern organizations. Dr. McNair-Connolly has published extensively on such topics as performance management, capacity cost management, lean/process management, and strategic cost management.

KENNETH A. MERCHANT, PH.D., CPA, is the Deloitte & Touche LLP Chair of Accountancy at the University of Southern California where he previously served as the Dean of the Leventhal School of Accounting. He previously taught at Harvard University and the University of California, Berkeley. His research interests span the areas of management accounting, management control systems, accounting ethics, and corporate governance, and, on those topics, he has written 11 books and more than 80 articles.

Acknowledgements

REVIEWERS

Many thanks to the following individuals who generously volunteered their time and expertise.

George Joseph, University of Massachusetts Lowell; Lorenzo Patelli, University of Denver; Mohammad Nurunnabi, Prince Sultan University; Dennis J. George, University of Dubuque; Diane Miller, Central Christian College of Kansas; Deron Adam Watanabe du Pon, Virginia Polytechnic Institute & State University; Todd A. Shawver, Bloomsburg University of Pennsylvania; Cathy Margolin, University of Phoenix; Karen Mattison, Presbyterian College; Sajay Samuel, Penn State; Bruce R. Neumann, University of Colorado Denver; Steven A. Hirsch, Metropolitan State University; Joshua Zender, Humboldt State University; B. Douglas Clinton, Northern Illinois University; Christopher P. Aquino, Niagara University; Gregory L. Davis, University of Illinois at Urbana-Champaign.

CONTENTS

CHAPTER ONE

Business Planning and Analysis: An Integrative Framework for Management Accounting

The culminating point of administration is to know well how much power, great or small, we ought to use in all circumstances.

MONTESQUIEU[1]

CHAPTER ROADMAP

1. The World of Management: An Overview
   - ➤ *What Is a Manager?*
   - ➤ *Types of Managerial Work*
2. The Management Process and the Role of Management Accounting
3. What Is Business Planning and Analysis?
   - ➤ *BPA as a Tool to Integrate Management Accounting Practices*
   - ➤ *A Financial vs. Managerial Perspective*
4. The BPA Integrated Framework and Management Accounting
   - ➤ *The BPA Database*
   - ➤ *The Decision Domains*
5. Management Accounting: Real World—Real Issues
   - ➤ *Analyzing Performance*
   - ➤ *Management Accounting in Action*
6. *IMA Statement of Ethical Professional Practice*
7. The Management Accounting Professional

LEARNING OBJECTIVES

After studying this chapter, you should be able to:

1. Explain the basic nature of managerial work.
2. Discuss the management process and describe how management accounting supports these efforts.
3. Describe how a BPA lens affects management accounting practices and how these differ from financial accounting.
4. Identify the primary types of information in a management accounting database and analyze the concept of a decision domain and how it is applied to organizations.
5. Illustrate how measurements influence decision making and behavior in organizations.
6. Interpret the *IMA Statement of Ethical Professional Practice* that guides the use and presentation of information within organizations.
7. Describe the various career paths open to management accounting professionals.

1 *The Forbes Scrapbook of Thoughts on the Business of Life*, Chicago: Triumph Books, 1992: p. 182.

SUCCESS IN BUSINESS BOILS DOWN TO MANAGERS MAKING GOOD DECIsions. Behind every such decision lies a management accounting database supported by an information network that either formally (for example, with rules or policies) or informally (for instance, the culture of an organization) links the organization's people and progress across space and time. This network of information, and the data that flows through this network, defines and shapes the practice of management accounting, which is the focus of this textbook.

This book is built around three unique features:

1. An integrative framework that uses a business planning and analysis perspective to emphasize the relationship between management accounting and management decision making, control, and information.
2. Three Excel-based databases that illustrate how organizations use information to complete the management accounting processes of planning, decision making, and control.
3. Three industry settings (an airline, a kitchen cabinet manufacturer, and an automobile dealership) to help you understand management accounting in action.

The overriding objective is to improve your existing critical thinking skills by helping you learn to analyze and respond to the challenges faced every day by organizations and the managers who run them.

The World of Management: An Overview

This chapter introduces the **management process**—*what managers do to ensure that their organization achieves its objectives*. We will approach management accounting from a business planning and analysis (BPA) perspective, which, when applied to management accounting issues, includes all of the activities in which managers use information, whether for planning, decision making, or control.

OBJECTIVE 1
Explain the basic nature of managerial work.

Information lies at the center of the management process. Information is data that has been organized to meet a specific need during decision making and analysis. It is the lifeblood of any organization, essential to the effective decision making and actions of management. A key focus of this book is to illustrate and explain what types of information are used during the various stages of the management process. This chapter focuses on understanding the basic elements of the integrative management accounting framework and how it relates to the work done by business managers. Attention then turns to how management accounting informs BPA, the key differences between a management accounting vs. a financial accounting perspective, and what career options exist for the management accounting professional.

Let us begin by taking a look at the role of management in organizations and how management accounting serves the organizations' information and decision-making needs. As the "In Context" discussion of Easy Air suggests, these needs span the gamut of a business, from strategic decisions such as what markets and customers to serve, to basic operational details (for example, what food to serve on a specific flight). The "In Context" discussions are used throughout the text to help illustrate the role of management accounting in a realistic business setting.

IN CONTEXT ➤ Easy Air: Confronting the Problem

Easy Air Chief Operating Officer (COO) Fran Conte stared out of the window of her office. Lying open on the desk behind her were the most recent figures from the finance department. Profits were down for the third quarter in a row, lost and damaged baggage claims were soaring, and Easy Air's on-time arrival and departure performance was abysmal. The trends were troubling, and it was Fran's job to change them. In the 20 years since she and Frank Russo founded Easy Air, they had faced constant challenges. But at the end of the day, they had always found a way to improve performance and make money at the same time—until now.

Easy Air, headquartered in the Midwest, flies only one type of plane, the Airbus 321. This means one kind of spare parts and one maintenance routine, which greatly simplifies Easy Air's operations. Each plane has the same seating configuration, making it quite simple to switch aircraft (or "tails") between routes and flights. Easy Air offers only one class of service—no-frills coach seating—and only one fare for each flight. No matter when or how the passengers for a specific flight book and pay for their travel, they pay the same price.

Emphasizing point-to-point service, Easy Air flies directly between secondary airports located near major cities and population centers. Initially a regional carrier serving the Chicago/Milwaukee/Indianapolis market, the company has grown steadily over the last 20 years to become the 10th largest air carrier in the United States, serving all major cities from Kansas City, Kan., to the eastern seaboard.

With this growth, operations have become increasingly complex. Corporate headquarters has been relocated five times, each time to a significantly larger space. Flight operations, once housed in a single room, now has its own dedicated wing. Advertising, initially run by Frank, now has more than 150 employees who coordinate ad campaigns, design promotions, and manage a wide-ranging set of corporate programs. While Frank still has the first chair he bought for himself when Easy Air was founded, the company bears little resemblance to the fledgling airline of its early years.

Unfortunately, some of the differences between the Easy Air of the past and today's company are not as positive. Easy Air built its reputation on hassle-free, on-time, dependable air travel. But with growth has come a rapid decline in performance, as the most recent financial and operational reports so clearly demonstrate. Fran's challenge is to determine what Easy Air can do to reverse these trends. How can profits be improved without increasing fares or reducing the level of service Easy Air provides to its customers? Should some routes be cut, or should new ones be added? Would it be better to lower fares to fill empty seats, or raise them to increase the revenue earned per passenger mile flown?

Before she could answer these questions, Fran knew she needed more information in order to properly analyze the current situation, identify options for improvement, make choices, and track the impact of any changes made. For this, she would have to call upon her management accounting systems and analysts.

WHAT IS A MANAGER?

An organization is the sum of the skills and efforts of its people. Every individual is an essential part of the complex web of actions and relationships that define and shape the modern business organization. The coordinated effort of these actions and relationships results in products and services that customers are willing to buy.

In an effective business organization, individuals have different roles and responsibilities. Not everyone makes the product or calls on customers to secure sales of these products. Some individuals are directly involved in producing the firm's goods and services, while others support these efforts. Some perform the tasks they are assigned, while others—the managers—determine what should be done.

Managers *are those individuals in an organization who are responsible for the work performed by one or more other people.* Managers define the goals and objectives for those under their direction. They organize the work so that the team, or work group, can achieve these objectives. Managers also take on the responsibility for ensuring that the efforts of the work group yield the desired outcomes. This includes securing and mobilizing needed resources, evaluating progress towards defined goals, and making adjustments to both plans and individual or group actions when needed.

TYPES OF MANAGERIAL WORK

As Table 1.1 shows, there are many different types and levels of managers in organizations. Management accounting supports each level of management, providing the specific type of information needed to make strategic, tactical, and operational decisions; control operations at all levels; and make adjustments to how work is done.

The lowest level of management is the **operational manager,** *who structures, manages, and directly participates in the day-to-day activities that result in the production or support of the products and services offered by the firm.* Also known as a "supervisor," the operational manager is only one step removed from the actual daily work of the organization. Work at this level is organized along two primary dimensions: horizontal (process-based) or vertical (function-based). Management accounting supports analysis and decision making across both dimensions.

Functional managers *translate organizational objectives into practical goals, establish performance evaluation criteria, ensure that leading-edge practices are applied, and assign individuals to purposeful tasks and activities.* They focus on a specific type of work, such as finance, marketing, or manufacturing. For example, when you choose a major in college, you are making the choice of a "function" or type of work that you will do when you graduate. A functional manager oversees the "vertical" or top-to-bottom flow of work, information, relevant objectives, and decisions in an organization.

TABLE 1.1 MANAGEMENT LEVELS AND ACTIVITIES

Management Level	Types of Activities Performed
Top Management Team	Establish the vision for the organization.
	Develop strategy and key objectives.
	Secure required capital and other key resources.
	Define the organizational structure.
	Assign responsibility for decision making and results.
	Establish expectations and criteria for evaluation performance.
	Set the tone for management and the organizational culture.
Process Managers	Establish effective relationships with key customers and suppliers of process output.
	Define standards of performance for activities within the process.
	Coordinate individual and group efforts to optimize performance and minimize disruptions, variance, and errors.
	Effectively negotiate for and obtain needed process resources.
	Identify and implement best practices.
	Create and execute continuous improvement initiatives.
Functional Managers	Translate organizational objectives into functional goals and objectives.
	Identify key activities and performance requirements.
	Organize and assign operational managers to specific activities and functional goals and objectives.
	Establish performance evaluation criteria for the operational managers and their work groups.
	Negotiate and obtain required resources.
	Ensure that leading-edge practices are implemented.
Operational Managers	Translate functional and process objectives into key activity and task goals to guide their employees' efforts.
	Organize and assign individuals to specific activities.
	Assign specific goals and evaluate resulting progress.
	Negotiate and secure needed resources.
	Identify and resolve operational problems.
	Ensure coordination with other work groups.
	Support learning and continuous improvement within the work group.
	Report results and problems to affected managers.

Process managers, on the other hand, *define standards of performance, establish relationships with key customers and suppliers, and coordinate individual and group efforts to achieve objectives*. They oversee specific clusters or chains of activities—in other words, how the efforts of individuals, teams, and functional groups are linked together to produce products and services for the firm's customers. A process manager emphasizes the organization's "horizontal" or cross-functional efforts. Process and functional managers jointly oversee the work of operational managers.

The top management team *establishes the vision; sets the strategy; secures required capital and key resources needed to produce, deliver, and support the firm's products and services; builds the culture of the organization; defines the organization's structure; and assigns responsibility for achieving organizational objectives.* Like an army general, top management either directly or indirectly performs command and control activities that shape the efforts of every individual in the organization. Responsible for the performance of the entire organization, the top management's vision shapes the organization's potential and performance.

LOOKING BACK ➤ The Five Basic Tasks of a Manager

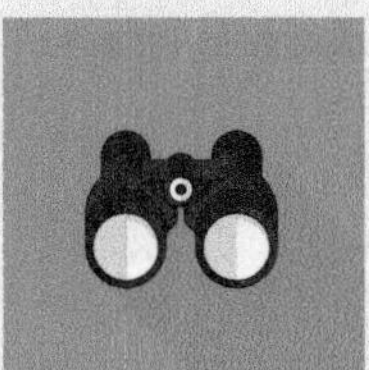

More than 60 years ago, Peter Drucker published his first major book on the work of managers in organizations. It is as pertinent today as it was then.

The manager has the task of creating an organization that is larger than the sum of its working parts, making it a productive entity that turns out more output than the sum of the resources used to produce this output. The task of organizing the entity to be productive requires the manager to make effective use of whatever benefits there are available in his resources—especially in the human resources—and neutralize whatever weaknesses are discovered.

There are five basic activities that comprise the work of the manager:

1. Managers **set objectives** for their employees and determine what needs to be done to reach these objectives. Through effective communication of these objectives to the workforce, managers optimize organizational actions.
2. Managers **organize** the activities of the organization. They analyze the activities, decisions, and relations needed to get work done and then select the people who will manage the work and ensure that it is done effectively and efficiently.
3. Managers **motivate and communicate** with their employees. Using effective team-building approaches, they ensure the smooth functioning of work units.
4. Managers **measure outcomes**. By analyzing outcomes using accurate and effective measurements, they ensure that the workforce understands what needs to be done and why each activity and outcome is important. A manager analyzes performance, appraises it, and interprets it.
5. Managers **develop people**. Based on the way that they deal with their workforce, managers either improve or destroy employee motivation, focusing their attention on either the right or wrong things. They bring out what is

best in each individual, or what is worst in them. All of this is done based on the manner in which the manager deals with the workforce.

All managers perform these activities when they manage—whether they are conscious of these facts or not. They may do them well, or they may do them quite poorly, but they always do them.

Peter Drucker, *The Practice of Management*, New York: Harper & Row Publishers, 1954: pp. 341-344.

The Management Process and the Role of Management Accounting

OBJECTIVE 2

Discuss the management process and describe how management accounting supports these efforts.

Managers work in all parts of the organization, overseeing everything from the processing of an invoice to the development of new products and services. Even so, the work that managers do has a common structure, as Peter Drucker suggests. This structure reflects key management work of setting objectives, organizing work flows, motivating and communicating, measuring, and developing their staff so they are better able to do their work. We call this structure the **management process,** *a continuous cycle of effort, action, achievement, target setting, and growth that underlies all managerial work*. It has four primary components: Plan, Do, Check, and Adjust; it is often referred to in organizations and management literature as PDCA. It uses resources to accomplish organizational goals and is illustrated in Figure 1.1. Managers are responsible for planning how the resources will be deployed. They also provide leadership, making sure that the work their subordinates do is well-organized and controlled. With a constant eye on the targeted objectives, effective managers coordinate, support, and direct the efforts of their work group to achieve desired results.

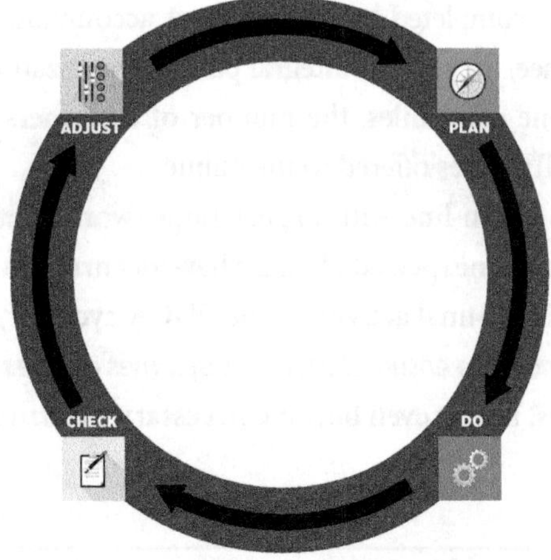

FIGURE 1.1 THE MANAGEMENT PROCESS

The first PDCA component—**"plan"**—*requires making a decision about something that has not yet happened*. When managers plan, they are projecting into the future, thinking through the many different paths and potential pitfalls that may lie ahead. Like an explorer in a new world, the manager is constantly scanning the environment, looking for clues and confirmation that the path being followed will lead to the desired goal—maximizing the value the organization creates for its stakeholders.[2]

Let us think about the various plans an organization might make. For instance, a cell phone producer such as Apple or Motorola has to determine what features it wants to offer in its various models. It has to plan on the size of the phone, its weight, the features it will provide, and the service providers with which it wants to partner. Should the cell phone have a built-in keyboard like a BlackBerry, or have one that digitally "pops up" like an iPhone? How big should the screen be? These are all decisions that are made during the planning phase of the management process.

Manufacturers must consider a variety of options when designing their products. In this case, the decision revolves around the options that cell phone manufacturers must take into account when designing new models or versions. Color, size, weight, options, battery life, and type of display screen are just a few of the issues that have to be considered.

Unfortunately, there is no one right way or one right approach for an organization—just a series of better-or-worse options. The manager uses various types of tools and techniques to identify and compare, and then chooses among these options. After the required choices are made, *actions are set in motion to achieve the desired results. The actions that are taken make up the* **"do"** *that is the primary purpose of an organization*. "Do" is the basis for satisfying customers and earning revenues. The decisions the cell phone developer makes during the planning stage define what needs to be done to bring the phone to the market.

As events unfold and actions are taken, it becomes important for managers to measure progress toward the organization's goal. A **measure** *is a quantification of the dimensions, size, or capacity of any object of interest based on comparing it to a standard or defined scale or measurement system*. Measures are used both to keep track of ongoing operations and to assess progress toward defined goals. **"Check"** *describes the comparison of actual results to the original plan.* Managers can use many different tools to complete this part of the process, including variance analysis, trend analysis, and profitability analysis. These are all part of the basic tool set that shapes the analysis completed by management accountants. You will learn more about these tools in Chapter 5. As you will see, they are an integral part of organizational and management learning and improvement. For the cell phone companies, the number of customers who choose their various models define the profitability of the cell phones offered to the public.

If the measured outcomes are in line with expectations, work continues. On the other hand, if outcomes are not acceptable or if any unexpected changes have occurred in the situation, managers may need to make adjustments. "Adjust" is the final activity in the PDCA cycle, or the management process. *The goal of the* **"check and adjust"** *sequence is to ensure that good outcomes can be repeated and bad ones eliminated, or at least minimized.* In some cases, it may even become necessary to change the defined goals and objectives

---

2 A *stakeholder* is anyone who has an interest in, or is affected by, the performance of an organization. A customer is a stakeholder. Other stakeholders include the owners, employees, and organization's business partners.

to address new challenges or opportunities. For our cell phone example, Apple might find problems like it did with the placement of the antenna on the iPhone 4. This problem led to adjustments in how the model was designed in order to improve the phone's network connectivity.

The management process, therefore, includes all of the activities and actions taken to keep the organization on track[3]—to check on outcomes and then make adjustments to improve performance against goals. Managing an organization is a dynamic process of planning and control, action, and adjustment. An effective management accounting system has to be equally dynamic. It has to be designed to fit the unique needs of the organization, reflect the goals and objectives being pursued, and change as conditions or organizational needs evolve over time. When we merge the structures, objectives, and tenets of the management process with the measurements, analytical approaches, and focus of the management accounting system, we are adopting an integrated approach that is the essence of all business planning and analysis.

What Is Business Planning and Analysis?

OBJECTIVE 3

Describe how a BPA lens affects management accounting practices and how these differ from financial accounting.

Business planning and analysis (BPA) is a discipline that can trace its roots back to the earliest days of the "managed" organization: management accounting.[4] BPA is, in fact, the application and extension of the focus and practices that define management accounting. The resulting integrated approach emphasizes how resources are used to complete work in the organization, and how plans, analysis of results and potential opportunities, and evaluation of performance are developed.

BPA AS A TOOL TO INTEGRATE MANAGEMENT ACCOUNTING PRACTICES

BPA and management accounting have the same roots in effective management practice, but BPA moves beyond traditional management accounting logic and analysis in several ways:

1. BPA emphasizes the entire management process, while traditional management accounting tends to focus more on cost and profitability analysis.

3 This definition was first developed and presented in the context of management control in Kenneth A. Merchant, *Control in Business Organizations*, Boston: Pitman Publishing, 1985. In this text, the control function is presented as an integral part of the management process, not as a separate management function.

4 In much of the early management writing in the 20th Century, the term "cost accounting" was used in place of, or interchangeably with, "management accounting." By the mid-1950s, these two terms had taken on quite different meanings, with cost accounting defined as an extension of financial accounting that emphasized inventory valuation issues. At this point, management accounting became the dominant term used to describe the use of financial information in planning, decision making, and control.

2. BPA creates an integrated analytical approach, underscoring the fact that management accounting analysis is based upon a logical set of tools, techniques, and concepts all focused on understanding and improving organizational performance and decision making.
3. Management accounting based on the BPA framework utilizes an integrated database in its analysis. Organizations today rely heavily on databases, often called data warehouses, to support analysis of potential projects or outputs, decision making, and comparison of actual results with the planned outcomes.

A FINANCIAL VS. MANAGERIAL PERSPECTIVE

While BPA is a logical extension of traditional management accounting that reflects and meets the needs of today's management team, this integrated approach has a less explicit tie to the field of financial accounting. In many ways, management accounting precedes financial accounting in the life of an organization. Financial accounting takes a historical perspective, effectively "tallying up" the results of prior periods with an eye toward entity performance. Management accounting develops a set of potential activities, projects, and outputs, supports the decision-making process, aids in the negotiations that result in the deployment of firm capital and resources to specific uses, and provides the information that is used to evaluate and reward performance.

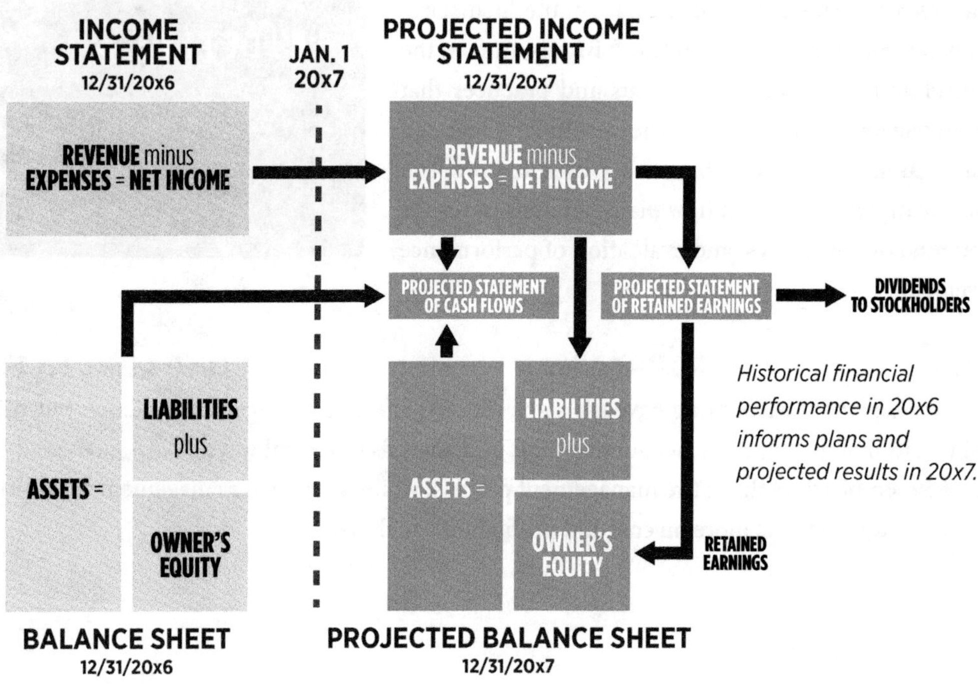

FIGURE 1.2 TYPICAL FINANCIAL ACCOUNTING STATEMENTS

The output of financial accounting is a set of financial statements that includes a balance sheet, income statement, and statement of cash flows as illustrated in Figure 1.2. It is designed to meet the information needs of a wide range of external users, such as investors and taxing authorities. In order to ensure that these outside parties can rely on the data in the published financial statements, and compare these results to those of other firms, financial accounting has to rely on a large number of rules and regulations. We call these rules and regulations GAAP, or Generally Accepted Accounting Principles.

As we consider the problems and challenges managers face, we become less focused on rules and more concerned with developing decision-relevant information. By definition, information developed for management's use in planning has to be ex ante, or pre-decision, in nature. This information includes creating estimates, building scenarios, and predicting results rather than compiling and summarizing prior events.

In management accounting, ex post, or historical, results are used in decision analysis and choice to allow the comparison of actual results to what was planned, but the goal of these comparisons is to create new plans and make adjustments to current processes and procedures, not solely to judge past results. Past results are just one part of the complete set of information used during the management process to explore opportunities and solve problems at all levels of the organization.

Financial and management accounting should be mirror images of each other in a well-run organization. Where management accounting and analysis emphasize the future, financial accounting shines light on the outcomes of past actions. Where financial accounting looks outward to external users, management accounting applications focus on meeting internal information needs. Each organization has unique forms and uses for management accounting information, but financial accounting presents a comparable set of data and reports for external use by adhering to a defined body of rules and regulations. The better the management accounting analytics and resulting information systems are, the more accurately management can predict and shape future results. Management accounting, as informed by BPA, hands off key information to financial accounting using budgets (formal business plans) and performance targets. They are complementary, not competing, information systems.

The BPA Integrated Framework and Management Accounting

OBJECTIVE 4

Identify the primary types of information in a management accounting database and analyze the concept of a decision domain and how it is applied to organizations.

As you are beginning to see, management accounting using a BPA framework encompasses the vast range of issues and objectives and questions and answers that are part of the everyday life of a manager. It is not a "subject" one learns, but rather a set of tools and techniques that are part of every decision, every action, and every evaluation made within an organization.

In other words, the integration of management accounting and BPA provides information to help managers identify and understand the options available to their organization (plan), choose a future course of action (do), and then ensure that the actions taken achieve the desired ends (check and adjust). The complete integrated framework is illustrated in Figure 1.3.

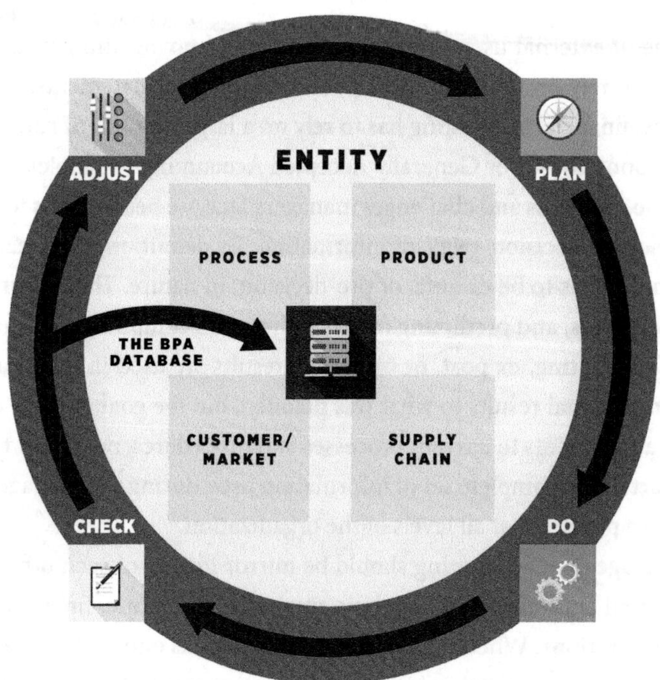

FIGURE 1.3 THE INTEGRATED FRAMEWORK

The integration of management accounting and BPA provides managers with the tools needed to make decisions and act on and evaluate them. There are three primary parts that comprise the BPA integrated framework:

1. The *databases* that contain information about the financial and nonfinancial resources and results of the management process.
2. The *management process* that identifies the Plan-Do-Check-Adjust sequence that helps the organization achieve its goals.
3. The five *decision domains* around which the discussion about the application of the integrated framework within organizations is organized.

The integrated framework is more than a learning or organizational tool. It encapsulates the essence of the work done by managers in organizations—the dynamic give-and-take, action and reaction, and plan and adjust that make the world of business so exciting. We have already discussed the management process in some depth, so we now turn our attention to the remaining two parts of the integrative framework: the management accounting database and the decision domains.

THE BPA DATABASE

Information is the lifeblood of any organization. It is the basis for planning, or providing a baseline of knowledge upon which to build future plans. Information provides insights into current trends in customer requirements, competitive structures, and the general economic conditions facing the organization. Information also serves as the basis for analyzing and evaluating results. Throughout the management process, information is both used and created.

Information *is data that is imbued with a purpose.* In management accounting, we focus on data that captures key characteristics of the organization and its performance. This data comes from a number of sources, such as the general ledger of the organization, where data from financial transactions is recorded. Data is also collected about the production of the firm's goods and services. Figure 1.4 shows the six primary sources of data that make up the BPA integrated database: economic trend data, financial accounting, management accounting, operations data, marketing data, and supply chain information.

The management process is defined and constrained by the data available within an organization. This data is built up over time using the combined inputs of the organization's financial results (for example, revenues, costs, and profits) and nonfinancial performance metrics that capture operational and strategic efforts and results (such as market share, quality, and customer satisfaction). Data is transformed into information during the management process, and it is then used to analyze issues across the five decision domains.

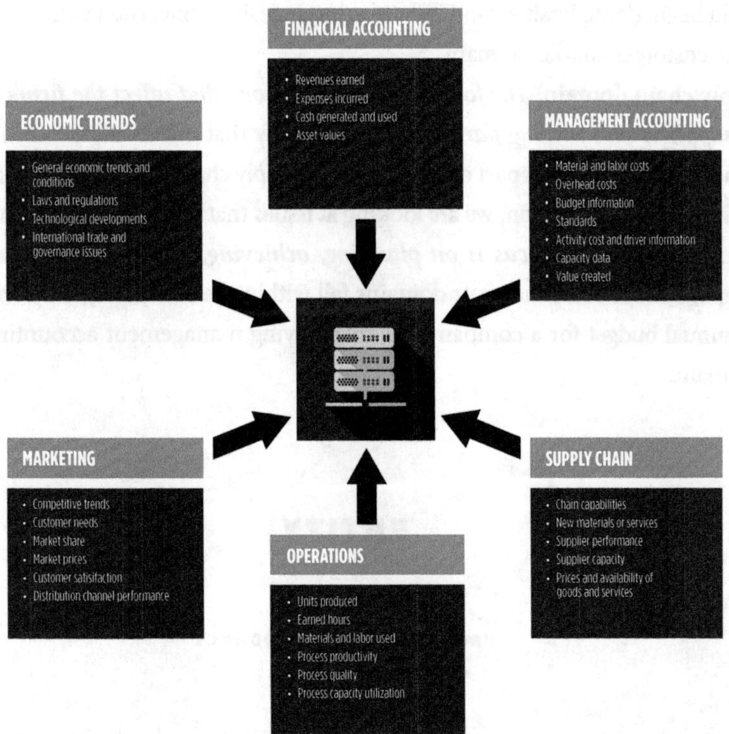

FIGURE 1.4 THE SIX PRIMARY SOURCES OF DATA THAT COMPRISE THE BPA DATABASE

THE DECISION DOMAINS

While the management process is relatively stable, it is applied in a vast number of unique situations. At any given time, attention can be focused on specific business processes, products, customers or markets, the entire organization, or external relationships (for instance, the organization's supply chain). These different situations, or decision domains, are clusters of decisions that are made by the same type and level of manager or address a similar set of opportunities and issues. They present unique opportunities and challenges to the company and the people who work in it.

As suggested in Figure 1.5, organizations have five primary decision domains:

1. **The process domain:** ***The focus is on how work is done.*** A process is the *linked set of actions and outcomes that are used to meet customer expectations on an ongoing basis.* When you choose your classes at school, you are using your school's registration process.
2. **The product domain:** ***The focus is on all of the decisions and activities that directly or indirectly support the products or services offered by an organization to its customers.*** In the product domain, *what* is accomplished with an organization's resources is emphasized. A question about how much it costs to make one pair of blue jeans is answered in the product domain.
3. **The customer/market domain:** ***The focus is on the decisions and activities that affect a specific part, or segment, of the firm's customers or markets.*** This includes all of the analysis and decisions that tie to a specific customer or market segment. If a company is trying to decide if it should begin doing business in China, for instance, it is concerned with an issue that falls within the customer/market domain.
4. **The supply chain domain:** ***The focus is on the decisions that affect the firm's relationships with its suppliers and trading partners.*** The company that makes the denim fabric used in making a pair of blue jeans is part of the industry's supply chain. When we look outside of the boundaries of the organization, we are looking at issues that fall in the supply chain domain.
5. **The entity domain:** ***The focus is on planning, achieving, and evaluating results for the entire organization.*** The other four domains fall within the entity domain. When we calculate the annual budget for a company, we are applying management accounting within the entity domain.

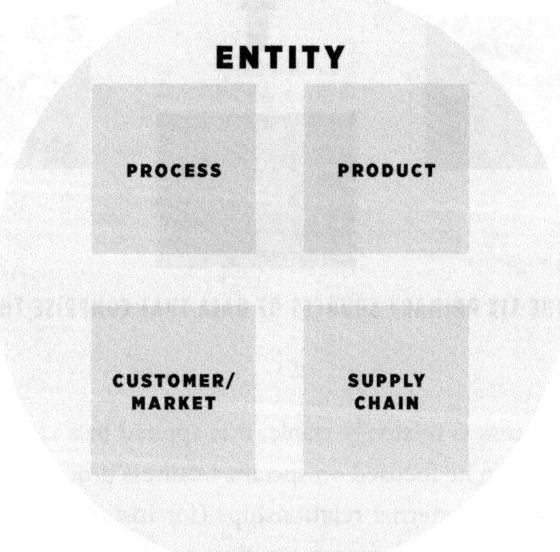

FIGURE 1.5 THE DECISION DOMAINS

The decision domains are used to organize the tools, techniques, and topics that make up modern management accounting practice. In each domain, the same concepts, logic, and analytical tools are used, but are just applied to a different set of problems. In other words, while there are many different issues that arise in the course of doing business and many different questions that managers must answer on any given day in an organization, the underlying flow of the management process remains relatively stable. It begins with identifying opportunities and challenges, and gathering information about the issue. Analysis and decision making follow, setting in motion the actions that managers believe will help them accomplish the organization's goals.

One of the hardest things for organizations to implement is the sharing of decision making throughout the organization. This is especially true in entrepreneurial firms. Often the entrepreneur does not want to let go of the reins. It is a wise entrepreneur who realizes he or she cannot be an expert at everything. One such entrepreneur was Dane Miller, founder of Biomet, one of the world's largest manufacturers of medical equipment. Facing problems managing the growth of the firm, Dane agreed to a merger with Zimmer, another company in the orthopedic market. Trained as a biomechanical engineer, he was very gifted when it came to inventing complicated new medical equipment, but he knew he did not know it all.

When it came time to buy half a million dollars' worth of computer equipment, he turned to those individuals in the organization who would know the right thing to do—he moved the decision into the right decision domain: the process domain. In all matters, Dane forced decisions down to the level where they could be best made. While that is not always easy in a culture that defers to senior management, Dane credited this delegation of decisions to the individuals skilled in the various domains as the reason for his company's growth from a start-up to its subsequent merger to form Zimmer Biomet in 2015, a firm that now has estimated net assets in excess of $27.2 million. The merger was formally approved on February 16, 2015, six days after Dane passed away. The culture of delegation and trust that Dane built lives on in the company.

Management Accounting: Real World—Real Issues

In order to help you understand the concept of decision domains and decision making, it is useful to first get a better understanding of the environment in which a company operates. Since the company being focused on in this chapter is Easy Air, let us take a look at the challenges it faces.

The airline industry is one of the most highly regulated and highly taxed industries in the United States. In 1914, the first commercial airline operation was started to transport passengers from Tampa to St. Petersburg, Fla., using a Benoist seaplane.[5] While this first flight was not subject to federal regulations,

5 Teo Ozdener, "Quality Management Systems and the Aviation Regulatory Environment," *Handbook of Airline Operations*, G.F. Butler and M.R. Keller, eds., New York: Aviation Week/McGraw-Hill, 2000: pp. 19-20.

within weeks, the U.S. Army Signal Corps established the Aircraft Production Board to control quality and schedules in the aviation industry. As Table 1.2 suggests, this was only the tip of the iceberg in terms of aviation regulations.

TABLE 1.2 REGULATIONS AND THE AIRLINE INDUSTRY

Date	Agency or Act	Focus
1914	**Aircraft Production Board**	Controls quality and scheduling within the aviation industry.
1915	**National Advisory Committee for Aeronautics**	Provides recommendations and oversight for aeronautic activities; became the National Aeronautics and Space Administration (NASA) in 1958.
1926	**Air Commerce Act**	Focuses on licensing, air traffic control, accident investigation, and the testing of aircraft and engines; it is the foundation for all aviation regulations.
1936	**Air Transport Association of America formed**	Represents the airline industry; it is still the only aviation trade association for the principal U.S. airlines.
1938	**Civil Aeronautics Act**	Creates Civil Aeronautics Authority (CAA), which is responsible for all civil aviation.
1940	**Civil Aeronautics Board**	Establishes the CAB, an offshoot of the CAA, to oversee airline industry routes, rates, and antitrust and business practices.
1958	**Federal Aviation Act**	Creates the Federal Aviation Agency (FAA) and mandates, through statutes, the improvement of air traffic control and other aspects of air safety; today, the FAA controls all navigable U.S. airspace.
1966	**The Department of Transportation created**	Creates the National Transportation Safety Board (NTSB) to investigate accidents; FAA also moved into this department; renamed the Federal Aviation Administration in 1967.
1974	**Independent Safety Board Act**	Makes NTSB an independent agency charged with investigating all transportation accidents.
1997	**Aerospace Basic Quality System Standard**	Sets an industry quality standard for aircraft manufacture and maintenance; developed by the FAA, Department of Defense, and NASA.
2001	**Transportation Security Act**	Makes broad-sweeping changes to the security systems in U.S. airports on the heels of the 9/11 terrorist attacks; the administrative bureau created by this act continues to issue regulations that affect every traveler every day.
2009-2012	**Enhancing Airline Passenger Protections Acts**	Focuses on preventing excessive tarmac delays, increasing information availability on flight reliability, and fare structures; as of 2012, these two major acts (EAPPs), created under this umbrella legislation, are projected to impose major compliance costs on airlines.
Ongoing	All of these organizations, along with Congress and state bodies, continue to create new regulations and requirements for the airline industry. The FAA periodically issues Federal Aviation Requirements (FARs) to control the design, manufacturing, and certification of airline engines, as well as certify airlines, pilots, mechanics, and related functions. While the FARs only mandate inspections, the FAA Advisory Circulars emphasize internal audits and the use of specific corrective or preventive actions.	

Federal Aviation Requirements impose operational requirements on airlines, including several mandatory management positions: director of operations, director of maintenance, chief inspector, and chief pilot. Most airlines also have specific positions for in-flight and dispatch operations, all of which report to the vice president of operations, as detailed in Figure 1.6.

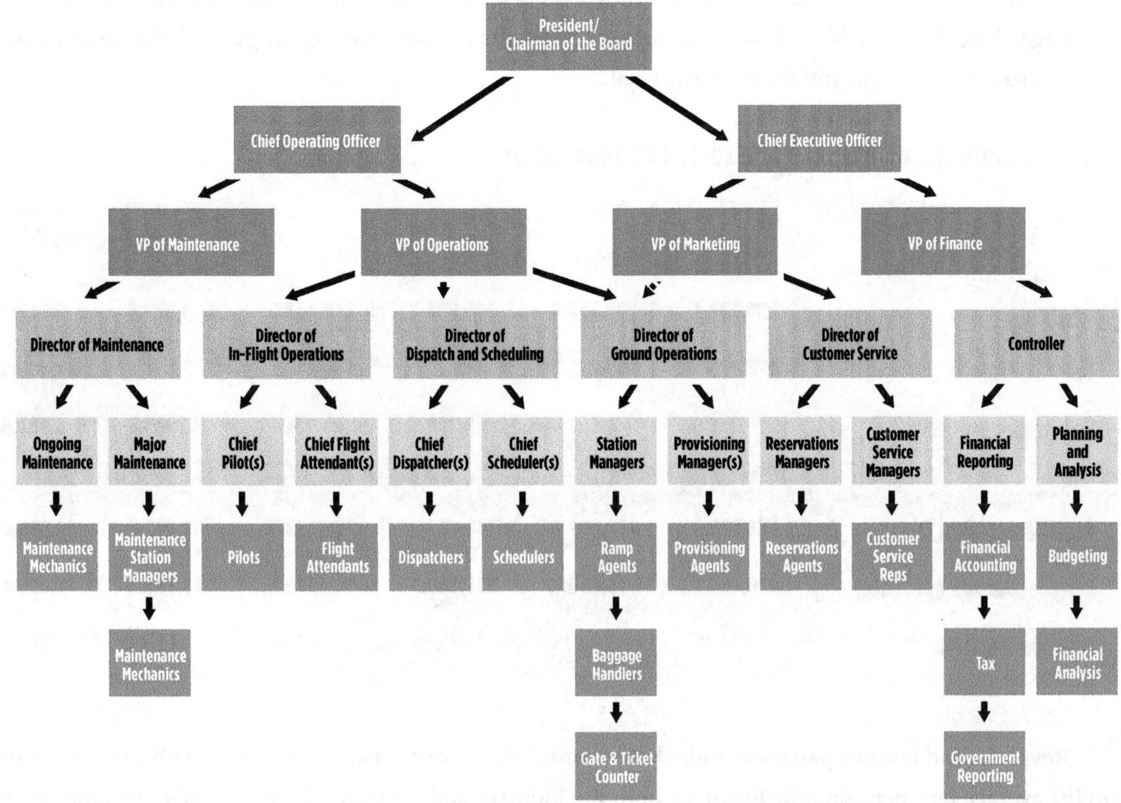

FIGURE 1.6 BASIC AIRLINE ORGANIZATIONAL STRUCTURE

ANALYZING PERFORMANCE

It is in this complex environment that Fran and her management team at Easy Air have to successfully and profitably compete. Although Easy Air posted profits during most of its years of operations, it has become very difficult to make money in the era after the aircraft-based bombings of the World Trade Center and the Pentagon on September 11, 2001, with its environment of increased taxes, heightened fare-based competition, and major additions to the body of FAA regulations governing airline operations. All of these challenges have been enhanced by concerns with terrorism and its impact on the flying public. In addition, Easy Air must deal with a traveler who accepts fewer frills but expects more convenience and reliability than passengers did in the 1990s. Air travel is no longer a luxury, enjoyed by few, but the

OBJECTIVE 5

Illustrate how measurements influence decision making and behavior in organizations.

central means of travel the majority of Americans use. Today, airplanes are to modern travel what buses and trains were to travelers in earlier eras.[6]

The airline industry uses many traditional measures of profitability, such as operating revenue, operating profit, and net income. There are also many measures of performance and profits that are unique to the industry, including revenue passenger miles, available seat miles (an industry capacity measure), and passenger load factor. Table 1.3 summarizes recent results for the industry in general, for large national carriers such as Easy Air, and for Easy Air itself.

TABLE 1.3 SUMMARY OF OPERATING RESULTS FOR 20x4-20x5[7]

Measures	Airline Industry		National Carriers		Easy Air	
($s stated in millions)	20x5	20x4	20x5	20x4	20x5	20x4
Operating revenues	$ 205,133.4	$ 207,713.9	$ 145,834.1	$ 146,753.9	$ 9,522.0	$ 9,112.7
Operating expenses	$ 178,735.5	$ 199,211.9	$ 124,609.6	$ 136,232.1	$ 8,536.5	$ 7,430.9
Operating income (loss)	$ 26,397.9	$ 8,502.0	$ 21,224.5	$ 10,521.8	$ 985.5	$ 1,781.8
Available seat miles ('000)	1,568,525.6	1,472,592.7	742,617.5	705,373.0	62,993.5	53,986.0
Revenue passenger miles ('000)	1,296,884.1	1,271,650.7	631,100.3	598,970.2	53,796.4	48,215.4
Passenger load factor	82.7%	82.7%	85.0%	84.5%	85.4%	85.1%

Revenues and revenue passenger miles both trended down for the two-year period, with a similar impact on the average fare-per-seat mile flown for both the industry and for Easy Air. Specifically, the industry as a whole earned $0.163342 per seat mile flown in 20x4 (that is, $207,713.90 in operating revenues divided by 1,271,650.7 revenue passenger miles) down to $0.158174 per seat mile in 20x5, a drop of more than 7%.

Many of the questions that arise from these numbers involve the ***product domain***—the cost and profit of flying passengers. Specifically, what are the costs to serve one passenger on one flight? How many passengers are needed to **break even,** *the point in operations where the total costs to meet customer needs exactly match the revenue earned from these activities*, which in this case would mean to meet the unavoidable costs of one flight? One route? Are some routes more profitable than others? Why or why not?

To begin to understand these issues, Fran asked Sanjiv Dugal, one of her senior financial analysts, to develop a cost estimate for operating a flight and serving a specific customer, along with summary statistics for Easy Air for the period 20x4 to 20x6. Table 1.4 presents the results of Sanjiv's initial work.

---

6 Throughout the first five chapters, heavy reliance is placed on the report "Consumer Regulation and Taxation of the U.S. Airline Industry: Estimating the Burden for Airlines and the Local Impact," by Darryl Jenkins, Joshua Marks, and Michael Miller, Bethesda, Md.: The American Aviation Institute, 2011.

7 The source for these statistics is the U.S. Transportation Department Bureau of Statistics, specifically www.transtats.bts.gov, obtained on August 28, 2016.

TABLE 1.4 SUMMARY OF EASY AIR'S PERFORMANCE 20x4-20x6

Perfomance Indicator	20x6	20x5	20x4
Total flights flown	3,575,240	3,489,434	3,297,515
Total passengers flown	373,369,464	363,557,175	342,354,639
Total revenue seat miles flown (in thousands)	54,405,612	53,796,413	48,215,413
Available seat miles (in thousands)	63,557,958	62,993,458	56,657,360
Average miles per passenger flight	265	260	233
Number of stations	120	112	106
Total operating revenue (in thousands)	$ 9,303,359.7	$ 9,521,965.1	$ 9,112,713.1
Total operating expenses (in thousands)	$ 8,899,038.1	$ 8,536,503.9	$ 7,430,858.9
Operating profit (in thousands)	$ 404,321.6	$ 985,461.2	$ 1,681,854.1
Average revenue per revenue seat mile flown	$ 0.171	$ 0.177	$ 0.189
Average expense per revenue seat mile flown	$ 0.164	$ 0.159	$ 0.154
Average profit per revenue seat mile flown	$ 0.007	$ 0.018	$ 0.035
Average load factor (% seats filled per flight)	85.6%	85.4%	85.1%
Average on-time performance rating	88.5%	92.5%	95.3%
Number of baggage claims	250,200	179,100	155,800
Number of customer complaints	380,100	295,300	245,500
Number of ground/gate delays	3,800	2,100	1,800
Number of canceled flights	1,425	950	600
Number of purchase orders	800,000	765,000	725,000
Number of deplane/enplane events	7,150,480	6,978,868	6,595,031
Number of bags handled	298,695,571	290,845,740	273,883,711
Number of tickets issued	410,706,410	399,912,892	376,590,103
Number of reservations	466,711,830	454,466,468	427,943,299
Number of ads placed	1,675,000	1,273,000	1,527,600

For Easy Air, the story was even worse than it was for the industry as a whole and for other national carriers, with average fare per revenue seat mile dropping from $0.189 in 20x4 to $0.177 in 20x5, or a drop of 6.3%. Unless things changed, the average fare for 20x7 would drop to $0.171, or another 3.4%.

Easy Air had run a series of promotions in 20x6 to boost its load factor, offering "buy one, get one free" deals for any passenger booking two or more flights at one time. The multiple flights applied to one person traveling multiple times between two cities, or for two or more people traveling on the same plane. While looking at these results, it is easy to understand why Fran is so concerned about Easy Air's performance. Revenues are down while passenger miles flown have increased—the gains have come at the cost of profits. Full planes that come close to losing money are not a good idea if Easy Air wants to remain in business.

Knowing these results and measurements is clearly important, but what Fran needs to know is how Easy Air can reverse these negative trends. The information we have so far shows us the results of the work done by the company. To change these results, however, Fran and her team have to turn their attention inward to gain a better understanding of Easy Air's processes, costs, and capabilities. Performance improvements, such as those needed at Easy Air, require analysis and decision making across all five of the decision domains.

Revenues and the number of passengers flown climbed over the past three years, but profits actually dropped. Looking at the cost picture, there was a small increase in the average expenses per passenger flight, but given the related increase in average miles flown, it appears that these costs actually held fairly steady. Using the information in Table 1.4, we can begin to develop an idea of the profit Easy Air made per passenger. Specifically:

Estimated revenue per passenger mile flown—20x7	$	0.171
Less: average cost per passenger mile flown	–	0.164
Average profit per passenger mile flown in 20x7	$	0.007
Times: average nautical miles per flight	×	265
Estimated profit per passenger per flight in 20x7	$	1.855

It appears that one of the problems facing the airline industry is that average revenue and operating profit per mile flown are quite low. The industry results for 20x5, for instance, were $0.158174 of revenue per passenger mile flown (as calculated from Table 1.3). It would appear that even though this metric is declining at Easy Air, the firm is still well-positioned in the industry. That said, far too little is being earned per revenue passenger mile. If the company raises prices, however, it will likely reduce the number of passengers who opt to fly Easy Air because of the high elasticity (-1.4[8]) in the industry with respect to fares. In other words, Easy Air would face a rapid drop in demand for its air travel if the price

8 Source of elasticity metric is http://www.iata.org/publications/economic-briefings/air_travel_demand.pdf obtained on January 19, 2017.

of air travel increases. The good news is that Easy Air did post an operating profit over this period due to its lower administrative costs. However, it would not take much of a drop in average fares or number of passengers flown to put Easy Air in the unhappy position of posting a loss.

As we can see from the nonfinancial information in Table 1.4, while the passenger load factors increased steadily over the past three years, there is also a less than desirable increase in problems. Baggage claims are up, on-time arrival performance is slipping, and complaints are growing. Armed with this information about the challenges facing Easy Air, let us rejoin Fran as she meets with Sanjiv to discuss his findings.

IN CONTEXT ➤ Easy Air: Compiling the Data

"Sanjiv, if I'm reading these numbers correctly, we are barely breaking even on a passenger's flight. Even worse, it seems that as we're getting busier, our passengers are becoming less and less happy with us. Neither of these trends is very good."

"Are you really surprised? I thought everyone knew that baggage problems are on the rise. The hum in ground ops is that we can't seem to turn around a plane as fast as we once did. They'd like us to increase the time we give them to deplane a flight, clean the plane, and then reboard new passengers by 10 minutes. That would improve the on-time performance, at least in their view. I think we just have to loosen our standards a bit and we'll be okay!"

"I know we have problems, Sanjiv, but I don't think we have enough information to come up with an answer yet," Fran replied. "Ground ops may want more time, but that's not the answer. Actually, wouldn't that just create more problems? How could we service our existing routes and flights if we spend 50% more time on the ground than we do today? Do you have a Plan B?"

"Not right off the top of my head, but I'm sure there are other options," Sanjiv replied.

"Great! To get us started, then, I want you to pull together some backup information, starting with the nonfinancial performance issues, such as baggage claims. What's happening? Why? What would it take to fix the problems apart from spending a gazillion dollars, which we clearly can't do?

"Ask Sherry Patterson and Rudy Mendez to help you hunt down the information. What I would like to be able to see is a recap of the issues, some explanation of why we're having these problems, and what you think we can do to fix them. Can we get together again next week and discuss your progress? And, thank you in advance!"

"That sounds like a good plan, Fran. See you next week, same time, same place, better information."

As Sanjiv left, Fran's thoughts turned to the past. What had happened to make Easy Air's performance falter so? Where had they lost their way, and what was to be done? Was their strategy flawed? Before the week was up, she would need to speak with Vince Rosman, Easy Air's chief executive officer and one of her oldest and most trusted friends. Easy Air needed to make some changes—that was clear—but exactly what those changes were was far less obvious.

Finding answers to questions such as those Fran at Easy Air raises is one of the primary goals of a modern management accounting professional. Using information from a variety of sources, both financial and nonfinancial, analyses are created that explore the impact of different assumptions and scenarios on a firm's profits and performance. Management accounting is not a static exercise with clearly defined boundaries and results, but rather a way of thinking about a problem. It is a set of analytical tools that are used to explore a wide variety of potential outcomes, looking for the approach that will provide the greatest benefit to the company's stakeholders per dollar and effort expended. There is no one right answer in management accounting, but rather better or worse ways to analyze a problem.

While there are very few rules guiding management accounting analysis in practice, there are criteria and guidelines that influence how information is used and analysis completed. We will be discussing these issues throughout the text.

MANAGEMENT ACCOUNTING IN ACTION

Management accounting practice is based upon measurement. Cost is a measure of the economic value of the resources consumed by different types of work. Quality is a measure of a product's or service's inherent value—its degree of perfection. Timeliness metrics have to do with such things as the reliable meeting of a schedule, the timely arrival of a product, and so on. In fact, we often talk about wanting the right product, at the right price, the right time, and the right place as the basis for successful competition in the marketplace.

We measure in order to understand what is happening and to learn how to improve performance. Within an organization, however, the role of measurement extends beyond these basic objectives to include the use of measurements to influence individual and group behavior. When an event or outcome is measured, it takes on an additional level of meaning in an organization. Because something is measured, it is seen as being more important than other events or outcomes that are not measured.

Measurement has another unique feature: It creates **visibility**, or *the ability to see and act upon a specific result or event*. When we measure, therefore, we draw attention to a specific event or outcome. For instance, Fran now knows that baggage-handling problems have increased significantly over the past year. She is aware of that fact because baggage-handling claims are one of the key measurements used by management to track the performance of Easy Air. In other words, this measure makes the baggage-handling problems visible, which creates the basis for analysis and action. If the baggage claim measure is also used in the evaluation of the affected operational managers, their behavior is likely to change. Being held accountable for results directs attention to a key performance criteria and underscores the fact that current conditions are no longer acceptable. In other words, management gets what it measures and rewards.

The use of measurement by organizations impacts behavior in many different ways. As the previous example suggests, a measure can be used to draw attention to an undesirable situation and encourage individuals to search for solutions to the problem. A measure can be used to motivate an individual to achieve a specific objective, such as reducing the baggage claim frequency to no more than one error per thousand bags handled.

If a specific measure is used by management to evaluate and reward performance, individuals will likely "move mountains" to make sure they perform well on the measured criterion. Unfortunately, not every action taken by individuals to meet their goals or score well on a specific measure is equally good for the organization. Some measures can actually create dysfunctional behavior on the part of the individual or group.

The role of measurement is so important in management accounting that two chapters are devoted to the topic. Specifically, Chapter 2 takes a broad view of measurement, spanning the full range of financial and nonfinancial metrics used in modern organizations and the behavioral issues they raise. In Chapter 3, attention is focused on different measures of cost, or resource consumption, within an organization.

One of your first goals in this course should be to gain a better understanding of the different types of measurements we use in a BPA-driven management accounting system, including their relative strengths and weaknesses. Once these basics are mastered, you will be better able to apply these metrics to analyze different decisions and opportunities.

IMA Statement of Ethical Professional Practice

OBJECTIVE 6

Interpret the IMA Statement of Ethical Professional Practice *that guides the use and presentation of information within organizations.*

There are very few formal rules that management accounting follows. Unlike its financial accounting cousin, management accounting is not defined by a rigid set of regulations or procedures. Different numbers are used for different purposes, with experience and common sense serving as the primary guides to the choice of specific measures and decision models. Even though there is no one right way to complete an analysis of a problem or estimate the potential impact of a decision, a series of ethical guidelines has been developed to reduce the potential for distortion and fraudulent practices among management accountants and related business professionals.[9] IMA® (Institute of Management Accountants) has developed a set of ethical guidelines, called the *IMA Statement of Ethical Professional Practice*, to assist in the practice of management accounting (see Figure 1.7). These guidelines are very important given that there are very few rules or regulations guiding the development of internal information. Internal auditing does provide some guidance, but, in many settings, the only rules available to guide why, what, where, when, and how analysis and measurement are applied are the ethics of the management accountant.

The decision to falsify information, whether about a company or your own record, is unethical, and, in the extreme, illegal. The *IMA Statement* focuses on the specific issues faced by professionals who develop, maintain, and manage the use and disclosure of financial information, but its message applies to every manager.

9 The *IMA Statement* was developed for management accounting, but actually serves as a set of guidelines that should be followed by any individual who prepares information for use in any manner in or outside the organization.

The objective of the *IMA Statement* (Figure 1.7) is to establish clear responsibilities and expectations for the preparation of unbiased information and analysis within an organization. Avoiding conflicts of interest is one way that bias can be reduced. For instance, it is probably not a good idea for the manager who is responsible for awarding bonuses for sales performance to be eligible to receive such a bonus. The temptation to award a bonus to oneself might be an overpowering incentive to manipulate reported results.

IMA STATEMENT OF ETHICAL PROFESSIONAL PRACTICE

Members of IMA shall behave ethically. A commitment to ethical professional practice includes overarching principles that express our values and standards that guide member conduct.

PRINCIPLES

IMA's overarching ethical principles include: Honesty, Fairness, Objectivity, and Responsibility. Members shall act in accordance with these principles and shall encourage others within their organizations to adhere to them.

STANDARDS

IMA members have a responsibility to comply with and uphold the standards of Competence, Confidentiality, Integrity, and Credibility. Failure to comply may result in disciplinary action.

I. COMPETENCE

1. Maintain an appropriate level of professional leadership and expertise by enhancing knowledge and skills.
2. Perform professional duties in accordance with relevant laws, regulations, and technical standards.
3. Provide decision support information and recommendations that are accurate, clear, concise, and timely. Recognize and help manage risk.

II. CONFIDENTIALITY

1. Keep information confidential except when disclosure is authorized or legally required.
2. Inform all relevant parties regarding appropriate use of confidential information. Monitor to ensure compliance.
3. Refrain from using confidential information for unethical or illegal advantage.

III. INTEGRITY

1. Mitigate actual conflicts of interest. Regularly communicate with business associates to avoid apparent conflicts of interest. Advise all parties of any potential conflicts of interest.

2. Refrain from engaging in any conduct that would prejudice carrying out duties ethically.
3. Abstain from engaging in or supporting any activity that might discredit the profession.
4. Contribute to a positive ethical culture and place integrity of the profession above personal interests.

IV. CREDIBILITY

1. Communicate information fairly and objectively.
2. Provide all relevant information that could reasonably be expected to influence an intended user's understanding of the reports, analyses, or recommendations.
3. Report any delays or deficiencies in information, timeliness, processing, or internal controls in conformance with organization policy and/or applicable law.
4. Communicate professional limitations or other constraints that would preclude responsible judgment or successful performance of an activity.

RESOLVING ETHICAL ISSUES

In applying the Standards of Ethical Professional Practice, the member may encounter unethical issues or behavior. In these situations, the member should not ignore them, but rather should actively seek resolution of the issue. In determining which steps to follow, the member should consider all risks involved and whether protections exist against retaliation.

When faced with unethical issues, the member should follow the established policies of his or her organization, including use of an anonymous reporting system if available.

If the organization does not have established policies, the member should consider the following courses of action:

- The resolution process could include a discussion with the member's immediate supervisor. If the supervisor appears to be involved, the issue could be presented to the next level of management.
- IMA offers an anonymous helpline that the member may call to request how key elements of the *IMA Statement of Ethical Professional Practice* could be applied to the ethical issue.
- The member should consider consulting his or her own attorney to learn of any legal obligations, rights, and risks concerning the issue.

If resolution efforts are not successful, the member may wish to consider disassociating from the organization.

IMA Ethics Helpline Number for callers in the U.S. and Canada: (800) 245-1383

In other countries, dial the AT&T USA Direct Access Number from www.att.com/esupport/traveler.jsp?tab=3, then the above number.

FIGURE 1.7 *IMA STATEMENT OF ETHICAL PROFESSIONAL PRACTICE*

While paying an unearned bonus would not be desirable, the real problem that this type of misconduct causes falls downstream when another manager or group uses the falsified information to make other decisions. Once false data enters into the organization's information system, it can create unanticipated problems and crises. Information plays such a central role in modern organizations that protecting its validity and reliability is critical.

The *IMA Statement* was originally designed for management accountants, but a careful reading of its content suggests that these are rules that should be followed by everyone in an organization. Whether a manager is completing financial analysis for use by others in the organization, defining a marketing strategy, or evaluating the productivity of a production plant or service location, the work that is done must be completed with competence, respecting confidentiality, reflecting personal integrity, and ensuring objectivity. These are the rules that define ethical business practice, no matter where or when these activities take place.

The Management Accounting Professional

Management accounting is more than a set of tools and techniques; it is a unique management perspective that emphasizes decision making and control within organizations. It is an approach that is used, either explicitly or implicitly, by every manager, every day.

OBJECTIVE 7

Describe the various career paths open to management accounting professionals.

Even though management accounting is a specific analytical approach to planning, decision making, and control, it is clear that not everyone in an organization has the same level of expertise in completing the analysis and data collection that lies at the heart of the discipline. Some individuals will merely draw upon the results of the management accounting analysis. Others, who we refer to as **management accounting professionals,** *create the data, systems, and analysis that make up the management accounting integrated framework*, which is used in decision making in all types of organizations. In many organizations, the title of financial or business analyst may be used, but the activities and analytics that are used remain the same.

There are many different career paths that can be pursued by someone with advanced management accounting skills. Some of the positions held by management accounting professionals include business analyst, financial analyst, management consultant, controller, chief budget officer, and accountant general. The combination of financial and analytical business skills makes a powerful, flexible combination of talents that opens doors and provides the basis for a challenging, dynamic career.

IN THE NEWS ➤ Lessons in Ethics

Unfortunately, there always seem to be fresh examples of individuals or organizations caught doing something unethical.

In October 2015, short seller Andrew Left accused drug company Valeant of using specialty pharmaceutical company Philidor to artificially inflate its sales. Valeant denied the charges. But because Valeant had never discussed its close ties to Philidor, it raised questions about Valeant's and Philidor's sales practices. It also shook investors' confidence in Valeant, which had racked up debt as it acquired companies.

If Philidor broke any laws, Valeant might be on the hook. Valeant employees appear to have worked at Philidor under aliases to hide their identities. More importantly, Valeant had paid $100 million for an undisclosed option to acquire Philidor without further payment whenever it wanted, essentially giving Valeant ownership of the company.

Valeant has appointed a special committee of its board and an outside investigator to look into the company's ties to Philidor, but it has yet to report its findings. Valeant said that Philidor sales never amounted to more than 7% of its total sales.

In the wake of these revelations, Valeant's shares fell 75% to just over $70 from a high of $260. Further contributing to the stock's fall was the accusation in summer 2016 that Valeant was price gouging, buying the rights to drugs and rapidly raising their prices. Members of Congress have called for an investigation into the company's drug pricing practices. And in early October, the company confirmed that it had received a federal subpoena.

Many well-known hedge funders, including Bill Ackman, who had defended the company, suffered big losses in the wake of the scandal.

Source: www.fortune.com/2015/12/27/biggest-corporate-scandals-2015/ accessed on August 28, 2016.

Summary

Managers are responsible for the work performed by one or more other persons. They define the goals and objectives for their work group, organize and assign tasks and activities, mobilize resources to attain objectives, and evaluate and adjust activities and performance to ensure that goals are met. There are many different levels of managers in organizations, including operational, functional, process, and top management positions.

The work that managers do has a common structure, which we call the management process. The management process has four primary components: plan, do, check, and adjust.

Business planning and analysis (BPA) includes all of the activities and actions taken to keep the organization on track—to check and then make adjustments to improve performance. The BPA-based management accounting approach is a modern version of a discipline that can trace its roots back to the earliest days of the "managed" organization. This modern version of management accounting has a larger scope and greater emphasis on the management process than its predecessors.

The integrated management accounting database, the management process, and the decision domains make up the integrated framework that defines this book and the way in which common management issues are addressed through the BPA-based management accounting techniques and analysis. The integrated framework serves to organize your learning experience around the "Plan-Do-Check-Adjust" cycle that defines management work. Six primary sources of data make up the integrated database: economic trend data, financial accounting data and metrics, management accounting analysis and metrics, operations data, marketing data, and supply chain information.

While the management process is relatively stable in nature, it is applied in a vast number of unique situations. These different situations, or decision domains, are clusters of decisions that are made by managers of the same type and level or address a similar set of opportunities and issues. There are five primary decision domains in organizations: product, process, customer/market, supply chain, and entity. We use the decision domains to organize the tools, techniques, and topics that make up modern management accounting practice.

The product domain includes all of the decisions and events tied to the full set of products and services offered by an organization to its customers. In the process domain, we focus on how work is done. The customer/market domain includes all of the analysis and decisions that tie to a specific customer or market segment. The supply chain domain emphasizes the relationships between a firm and its primary trading partners (such as suppliers and customers). Within the entity domain, our attention centers on planning and achieving results for the entire organization.

Measurement puts subjective words and concepts into objective terms. We measure in order to understand what is happening and to learn how to improve performance. Measurement has another unique feature—it makes an outcome or event visible. The use of measurement by organizations impacts behavior in many different ways.

The *IMA Statement of Ethical Professional Practice* requires that individuals who develop and use information should strive to meet the principles of competence, confidentiality, integrity, and objectivity. Finally, there are many different career paths that can be pursued by someone with advanced management accounting skills, among them are business analyst, financial analyst, management consultant, controller, chief budget officer, and accountant general.

Key Terms

Adjust: a change in the current work to improve performance and the potential to reach the firm's objectives.

Breakeven: the point in operations in which the total costs to meet customer needs exactly matches the revenue earned from these activities.

Business planning and analysis: what managers do to ensure that an organization reaches its objectives.

Check: the comparison of current results to the plan.

Cost: the economic value of the resources consumed in completing activities, products, and services.

Customer/market domain: the area of an organization that focuses on the decisions and activities that affect a specific part, or segment, of the firm's customers or markets.

Decision domain: a cluster of decisions that address a similar set of opportunities or issues.

Do: the coordinated set of goal-directed actions that facilitate how the products and services of the firm are manufactured and supported.

Functional managers: individuals who translate organizational objectives into practical goals, establish performance evaluation criteria, ensure that leading-edge practices are applied, and assign individuals to purposeful tasks and activities.

Information: data that is instilled with a purpose.

Manager: the individual who is responsible for the work performed by one or more other people.

Management accounting professional: one who creates the data, systems, and analysis that make up the management accounting integrated framework.

Management process: a continuous cycle of effort and action that underlies all managerial work. It is made up of four key activities: plan, do, check, and adjust.

Nonfinancial data: information that focuses on various aspects of performance, such as the quality of the firm's activities, products, or services.

Operational managers: individuals who structure, manage, and directly participate in the day-to-day activities that result in the production or support of the products and services offered by the firm.

Planning: "decision making in advance"; involves setting objectives and then determining what needs to be done to reach them.

Process domain: the area in organizations focused on how work is done.

Process managers: individuals who define standards of performance, establish relationships with key customers and suppliers, and coordinate individual and group efforts to achieve goals.

Product domain: the area in organizations that determines all of the decisions and activities that directly or indirectly support the products or services offered to its customers.

Supply chain domain: the area that covers the decisions that affect the firm's relationships with its suppliers and trading partners.

Top management team: the group that establishes the vision; sets the strategy; secures required capital and key resources needed to produce, deliver, and support the firm's products and services; builds the culture of the organization; defines the organization's structure; and assigns responsibility for achieving organizational objectives.

Visibility: the ability to be seen; when we measure, we draw attention to a specific event or outcome.

Questions

1. What are the primary differences between management accounting and financial accounting?
2. How does the BPA perspective influence the practice of management accounting?
3. What is the key attribute that changes data into information?
4. Where do costs occur in organizations?
5. What is the management process?
6. What are the five decision domains? What are the responsibilities of each?
7. What are the primary types of managers in an organization? How do their tasks differ?
8. What are the four components of the *IMA Statement of Ethical Professional Practice*? Why do we need an ethical code in this area of management?

Exercises

1. **LEVELS OF MANAGEMENT.** Using the following list of tasks, identify the type of manager who would have responsibility for the task's planning and completion. Use "T" for top management, "P" for process managers, "F" for functional managers, and finally "O" for operational managers. If a task is done by more than one type of manager, include all of the relevant letters.

   a. Establish strategic objectives
   b. Develop financial statements
   c. Coordinate individual and group efforts
   d. Assign specific individuals to tasks
   e. Negotiate for needed resources
   f. Define organizational structure
   g. Create continuous improvement initiatives

2. **LEVELS OF MANAGEMENT.** Using the following list of tasks, identify the type of manager who would have responsibility for the task's planning and completion. Use "T" for top management, "P" for process managers, "F" for functional managers, and finally

"O" for operational managers. If a task is done by more than one type of manager, include all of the relevant letters.

a. Assign operational managers to key activities
b. Assign specific goals and evaluate performance
c. Identify and implement best practices
d. Oversee the production of product from raw materials through shipping
e. Establish performance requirements for other managers
f. Set tone for organizational culture
g. Define standards of performance for activities in a process

3. **DECISION DOMAINS.** For the following list of decisions and activities, please identify which domain is affected. Specifically, use "P" for process, "R" for product, "C" for customer/markets, "S" for supply chain, and "E" for entity domains. Only one domain is responsible for each decision.

a. Setting the price for a firm's services
b. Deciding to compete in a specific market segment
c. Developing an annual plan for the organization
d. Developing the sequence of production activities
e. Determining which features to offer on different models of products
f. Negotiating contracts with raw material suppliers
g. Evaluating top management's performance

4. **DECISION DOMAINS.** For the following list of decisions and activities, please identify which domain is affected. Specifically, use "P" for process, "R" for product, "C" for customer/markets, "S" for supply chain, and "E" for entity domains. Only one domain is responsible for each decision.

a. Setting up a distribution channel for a series of products
b. Creating a strategy for a specific customer segment
c. Developing the plan to create a strong culture
d. Implementing continuous improvement of activities
e. Developing a product marketing plan
f. Directing the work of many functions
g. Reporting to company stakeholders

5. **MANAGEMENT PROCESS.** Reorganize the activities in the following sequences so that they match the four stages of the management process. Put "plan" activities first, followed by "do" activities, then "check" activities, and finally "adjust" activities.

a. Change objectives, complete products, set objectives, analyze results
b. Establish market price, put "sale" price on product, sell product, check sales figures
c. Reset production goals, make production plan, inventory products made, make products
d. Evaluate performance, assign objectives to managers, develop strategic plan, develop a new strategic plan
e. Complete financial statements, set financial reporting goals, complete analysis of performance shortfalls, change financial objectives
f. Set daily output goals, assign workers to activities, change work assignments, verify output achieved
g. Evaluate supplier performance, negotiate supplier agreements, accept materials from supplier, find a new supplier

6. **MANAGEMENT PROCESS.** For the following list of activities, identify whether it is a "P" or "plan" activity, "D" or "do" activity, "C" or "check" activity, or an A or "adjust" activity. Only one letter should be assigned to each activity.

a. Create strategic plans
b. Analyze performance reports
c. Provide a service
d. Renegotiate supplier contracts
e. Check actual output against plan
f. Complete financial statements
g. Sell products
h. Develop a marketing strategy
i. Coordinate activities between functions
j. Complete a performance evaluation
k. Change employee goals
l. Create annual performance goals for employees
m. Hire new employees
n. Renegotiate labor contracts

7. ***IMA STATEMENT OF ETHICAL PROFESSIONAL PRACTICE.*** For each of the following activities, identify what aspect of the *IMA Statement* is being violated. Use "C" for competence, "N" for confidentiality, "O" for objectivity, and "I" for integrity. You may use more than one letter if you feel the activity affects more than one area.

a. Issue false financial statements
b. Take money for work you did not complete properly
c. Change results to make a manager look better to his or her boss
d. Agree to do a job for which you have no expertise
e. Have someone else complete your homework
f. Talk about the new products your company is making to your friends
g. Agree to develop the performance metrics for a job that will impact your own annual bonus

8. ***IMA STATEMENT OF ETHICAL PROFESSIONAL PRACTICE.*** For each of the following activities, identify what aspect of the *IMA Statement* is being violated. Use "C" for competence, "N" for confidentiality, "O" for objectivity, and "I" for integrity. You may use more than one letter if you feel the activity affects more than one area.

   a. Sell your product's secret formula to a competitor
   b. Change how you calculate a performance measure for marketing without telling anyone
   c. Fail to attend a refresher course
   d. Let a friend copy your company's budget for a school project
   e. Fail to check the tax laws before completing your firm's tax returns
   f. Neglect to tell your teacher that you were given too many points on a test
   g. Call your friends to let them know what was on this week's quiz

Problems

1. **MAGNITUDE OF CHANGE.** Bill Larkin, president of LM Landscaping, has recently completed a course in BPA, giving him new skills with which to analyze his company. He pulls together the following information.

Measure	20x6	20x5	20x4
Annual profits	$225,500	$198,875	$150,250
Number of employees	15	12	8
Number of customers	250	175	100

REQUIRED:

a. You have agreed to help Bill by calculating the absolute size, or magnitude, of change in each of these categories.
b. What do the numbers suggest?

A HELPING HAND

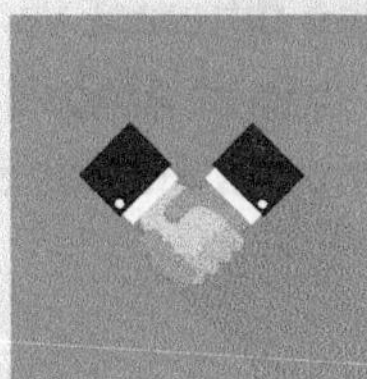

In the problem above, we have learned how to calculate the magnitude of change in a specific measure, a critical concept in BPA. Let us look a bit more carefully at the concept before we move on to more problems. When we calculate change, we have to choose a starting point and then calculate the actual change in that measure from one point to another, such as between the years 20x6 and 20x5. We then take this amount of change and divide it by our **basis** or first number in our change equation to derive the percentage change. Let us try it with formulas:

Magnitude of change: Value at Point (b) less Value at Point (a), or

$$(b - a)$$

Percentage change: Degree of change divided by Value at Point (a), or

$$\frac{(b - a)}{a}$$

We can use any point in a range of numbers as our basis point. In other words, we could hold 20x4 as the constant basis, or (a), in all of our equations and then looked at the change across the years. We could just as easily have chosen 20x6 and worked backwards in time. As you may guess, what baseline you choose will change your numerical results. Rule of thumb? If you want to gauge improvement over time, use the oldest date as the baseline. Want to assess loss? Use the most current date. In the problem below, we will also look at percentage change year by year. These are different pieces of information, both of which can have value in decision making. Let us try this now focusing on the percentage change in LM Landscaping's key metrics.

2. **PERCENTAGE CHANGE.** Now that Bill has gotten another class under his belt, he wants to understand the relative impact, in percentage terms, of the changes in his business. So using the data from Problem 1 above:

REQUIRED:

a. **Calculate the percentage change in each of Bill's three key variables. Start with 20x6 and work backwards.**
b. **Decide what you would suggest to Bill now.**

3. **MAGNITUDE OF CHANGE.** Amos Bundy runs a small convenience store. His sales are booming, but he is not quite sure why. He offers three main services: basic grocery sales, ready-to-eat sandwiches, pastries, and coffee, and pizza in three different varieties (cheese, cheese and sausage, and cheese and pepperoni). Since you stop at Amos's store almost every day for coffee, you offer to help him look at his sales numbers. He has pulled the following information together for you.

Sales Item	January	February	March	April
Grocery sales	$1,525.00	$1,385.00	$1,250.00	$1,100.00
Deli and coffee	$950.00	$850.00	$675.00	$550.00
Pizza	$895.00	$975.00	$1,200.00	$1,675.00

REQUIRED:

a. Calculate the absolute change in each category of sales items across the four months of this year.
b. What do the numbers suggest?

4. **PERCENTAGE CHANGE.** You decide to take the analysis a bit further. Using the results you obtained in Problem 3 and the lessons you have learned about percentage change, do the following:

REQUIRED:

a. Calculate the percentage change by offering for Bundy's store. Start with April and work backward to January.
b. What do these percentages suggest? Does it differ from the information you got when you only used the amount of change in your original analysis? Why or why not?

5. **DEGREE OF CHANGE.** Darby Computer Associates provides computer services to both small businesses and individuals. It has faced changing conditions in the marketplace, one characterized by constant changes in both hardware and software. Add to that the seemingly endless viruses, and Darby Computer faces a major challenge to the business to stay current and focused on where attention needs to be. The following data summarizes key business statistics for the last four years.

Measure	20x6	20x5	20x4	20x3
Businesses served	125	135	153	189
Individual customers	988	885	825	725
Classes attended	35	27	22	18
Average hours to complete a job	10.5	9.0	8.25	7.75
Average monthly profits	$25,323	$26,619	$28,555	$32,683

Phil Darby, the owner of Darby Computer Associates, is concerned. It seems he and his team are working harder all of the time, but as the numbers suggest, profits are not following effort. He needs your help to answer the following questions. Note that Phil charges business customers a flat monthly rate, while individuals are charged by the hour.

REQUIRED:

a. Calculate the absolute change for each measurement across the four years. Do this focusing on the change from year to year, working from 20x6 backward to 20x3.

b. Looking only at the magnitude of change, what would you suggest to Phil? Specifically, where should he place his attention?

c. Now let us get a bit fancier and calculate percentage change from one year to the next. To do this, take the amount of change you calculated in requirement (a) above and divide it by the actual measurement for the latest year in your calculations. In other words, there are 36 fewer business customers between 20x3 and 20x6. If you divide 36 by 153, the number of business customers in 20x4, you will get the percentage change between the two years, or -23.5% (rounded). Do this calculation for the remaining measurements across the four years.

d. Given these results, what looks like Phil's biggest problem now? Do you feel the change you calculated in (a) or the percentage change you did in (c) has more relevance to Phil? Why?

e. What would you recommend Phil do? Write a one- or two-paragraph recommendation using the numbers you have calculated.

6. **DEGREE OF CHANGE.** Rontell, Inc., is a medium-sized producer of latex balloons that are filled by helium and given on special occasions. It distributes its balloons in many styles and colors to the tri-state region surrounding Chicago, Ill. Martha Rontell, owner of Rontell, Inc., is trying to understand what type of balloons sells best so she can invest more artist time crafting unique balloons in that category. Always customer-oriented, Martha will test the new designs with a customer panel before beginning production. That said, she needs to make sure the effort is going to the best-selling products as creating new art and testing its effectiveness with customers is costly. The following table lists the sales over the past four years for the different types of balloons.

Balloon Type	20x6 Sales	20x5 Sales	20x4 Sales	20x3 Sales
Happy Birthday	1,525,500	1,377,250	1,250,750	1,200,600
Welcome Home	950,300	980,200	995,500	998,750

Balloon Type	20x6 Sales	20x5 Sales	20x4 Sales	20x3 Sales
Get Well Soon	750,300	600,250	525,500	495,600
Happy Retirement	650,000	500,250	430,500	395,600
Happy Anniversary	225,000	215,000	203,500	201,750

REQUIRED:

a. Calculate the actual amount of change between years, starting with 20x6 and working backward. Do this for each type of balloon.

b. Based on these results and the overall sales patterns, where would you recommend Martha put her time, artist effort, and money?

c. Now calculate the percentage change in each of the categories. Once again, start with 20x6 and work your way back year by year. Remember, when you move from 20x6 to 20x5 as your basis year, you must change your denominator to the 20x5 value. Be careful here!

d. Recalculate the percentage change, now using 20x6 as the basis year across all of the categories and calculations of change. You will still calculate the difference from one year to the next, but, this time, always use 20x6 as your basis year.

e. Finally, do one calculation for each category. Specifically, subtract the 20x3 value from the 20x6 value and then divide by the 20x6 value. What does this information tell you?

f. Out of all of the numbers you have calculated, which do you feel is most useful to making the decision facing Martha? Why?

g. Looking at all of your calculations, draft a simple one- to two-paragraph memo to Martha with your suggestions for where she would get the most benefit from enhancing a specific product line.

---

7. ***IMA STATEMENT OF ETHICAL PROFESSIONAL PRACTICE.*** You have taken a job for the summer. One day you come across some data that just does not seem to make sense. You go to your supervisor, who tells you that the data is fine and to return to work. You are bothered, however, so you start digging and soon discover that falsified data has been entered into the system. What ethical violation has your supervisor asked you to commit? What should you do to address the problem? Why?

---

8. ***IMA STATEMENT OF ETHICAL PROFESSIONAL PRACTICE.*** You recently enrolled in an advanced class in accounting, where you are expected to work on your own for many of the assignments. The professor relies on the honor code and makes you submit a signed

honor code statement with every assignment you turn in. Recently he assigned a major project that would require at least eight hours to complete. Late on the night before the assignment is due (yours is done, of course), a classmate comes to see you. He asks if he can look at what you have done so he can have a better idea of how to approach the problem. He asks to borrow your assignment for half an hour, after which he will return it and ask nothing more of you.

REQUIRED:

a. **Should you agree to this request? Why or why not?**

b. **Does this request violate an element of the *IMA Statement*? If so, which one?**

Cases

CASE 1.1 TREND ANALYSIS. The Coffee Palace just had its third business anniversary. Alice Cornwell, the company's owner, has recently become concerned. Early in the year, she increased her prices to bring in more revenue, adding $0.25 per cup to the regular and decaffeinated coffees she sells and reducing the price of novelty coffees to increase demand for them. Now she is busier than ever, but the sales volume of each category has changed, as suggested in the following table.

Product Type	Current Price in $	Last Year's Price in $	Current Volume	Last Year's Volume
Regular coffee	$1.75	$1.50	4,500	8,000
Decaffeinated coffee	$1.75	$1.50	4,000	5,800
Flavored coffees	$2.00	$1.75	4,000	6,000
Cappuccino	$3.00	$3.25	3,000	2,000
Mochaccino	$3.00	$3.25	2,500	1,800
Iced Cappuccino	$3.25	$3.50	1,800	1,200
Iced Mochaccino	$3.25	$3.25	3,500	2,600
Regular Latte	$2.50	$2.75	4,500	3,000
Flavored Latte	$2.75	$3.00	3,000	2,100

Alice is worried because a lot more labor goes into making the novelty drinks than simply pouring a cup of regular coffee. Specifically, materials to make specialty coffees average $1.25 a cup, while the cost for materials for regular coffee (the cup, a lid, and the coffee itself) is only

$0.50. Labor for the novelty drinks is three minutes at $10 per hour, while labor for regular coffee drinks is only one minute.

Learning that you are taking a course at college that deals specifically with trends in costs and profits, Alice enlists your help in exchange for free coffee (regular) for the year. To help Alice, you do the following:

a. Calculate the total direct costs (labor and materials) for each type of product Alice makes. Your table should look like:

Product Type	Materials (1)	Labor Costs (2)	Total Cost per Cup (1) + (2)

b. Complete a table that determines the profit made per type of product sold by Alice. It should look like this:

Product Type	Price (1)	Direct Costs (2)	Profit per Cup (1) - (2)

Do this for both years of data you have. You should end up with two tables.

c. With profit per cup in hand, you can now calculate how much profit Alice makes for each different type of product by year. This table should look like:

Product Type	Profit per Cup (1)	Volume Sold (2)	Total Profit (1) x (2)

Once again, calculate these numbers for two years.

d. Now do a trend analysis for profitability over the two years. Your table should look like this:

Product Type	Profit This Year (1)	Profit Last Year (2)	Change in Profit (3) = (1) - (2)	Percentage Change (4) = (3) / (2)

e. Now determine how much sales volume has changed. Your table should look like this:

Product Type	Volume This Year (1)	Volume Last Year (2)	Change in Volume (3) = (1) - (2)	Percentage Change (4) = (3) / (2)

f. Using all of this data, draft a one- to two-paragraph memo to Alice explaining what is happening and making recommendations to help her plan the next year.

CASE 1.2 *IMA STATEMENT OF ETHICAL PROFESSIONAL PRACTICE*. Tim Carswell has recently graduated from his state university, majoring in accounting. He has taken a job with a medium-sized firm that offers financial accounting, audit, and consulting services to retailing firms across the United States. The company, Howard & Partners, is well-respected in its niche field, so its percentage of consulting is a significant and profitable aspect of its overall business model.

Tim has been assigned to help on the audit of one of the firm's major customers, Charlie's Electronics. Charlie's has grown from a single store 10 years ago to more than 50 retail outlets in the Northeast U.S. today. Charlie's has used Howard & Partners as both financial accountant and auditor. Howard & Partners cannot be a formal consultant to the company due to federal regulations arising out of the Sarbanes-Oxley Act.

Late one afternoon, Tim watches the manager on the job as he is called into Charlie's office. Charlie does not pull out any of the company's financial statements, but instead seems intent on asking specific questions of the manager, Perry Cartwright. Tim then sees Perry come back to his computer and pull up some consulting files that were used at one of Charlie's competitors for a job Tim was on just a week ago. Perry walks back into Charlie's office and spends the rest of the day going over the consulting report with Charlie.

Tim is very concerned, but when he asks Perry about it, Perry replies, "We've been doing this for Charlie for years now. It is just part of the extras we provide him. We're not breaking any laws because we're not directly doing consulting for him, we're just providing a little informal input to help him make better decisions as he expands the chain. It's a win-win situation, so don't worry about it."

REQUIRED:

Analyze the situation Tim is facing based on the *IMA Statement*. Even though Tim is doing financial accounting work today, he also does consulting so the *IMA Statement* applies to him every day. Is what Perry is doing wrong? Why? What recommendations would you make to Tim in this situation?

CHAPTER TWO

Measuring and Evaluating Performance

I keep six honest serving men
They taught me all I knew
Their names are What and Why and When
And How and Where and Who.

RUDYARD KIPLING[1]

CHAPTER ROADMAP

1. **Measurement: A Matter of Perspective**
   - ➤ *Financial Accounting vs. Management Accounting Measurements*
2. **Measurement: A Strategic View**
   - ➤ *Good Measures, Bad Measures*
   - ➤ *A System of Measurements—McDonald's-Style*
3. **Measurement and the Management Process**
   - ➤ *Measurement and Planning*
4. **Action and Measurement**
5. **Using Measures to Check Progress**
   - ➤ *Using Measurements to Adjust Performance*
   - ➤ *The Behavioral Impact of Performance Measurement*
6. **Results, Action, and Personnel/Cultural Controls**
   - ➤ *Control in a Continuous Improvement Setting*
7. **The Potential for Dysfunctional Consequences**

LEARNING OBJECTIVES

After studying this chapter, you should be able to:

1. **Describe the differences between financial accounting and management accounting performance measurements.**
2. **Develop a basic set of measurements that reflect a firm's objectives and critical success factors.**
3. **Define the role of measurement in the management process.**
4. **Describe the various forms of measures used at the point of action.**
5. **Create a basic trend, gap, and variance analysis of performance results.**
6. **Define and describe key differences between results, action, and personnel/cultural controls.**
7. **Understand the dysfunctional consequences of measurement and suggest methods for minimizing them.**

---

1 Laurence J. Peter, *Peter's Quotations*, New York: Bantam Books, 1977: p. 436.

IN CONTEXT ➤ Easy Air: Defining the Problem

It was 8:45 a.m. on Monday. Sanjiv had commandeered Sherry Patterson and Rudy Mendez from the finance group to help him with Fran's project. This was the first of what would become many meetings and discussions about different ways to measure and evaluate Easy Air's performance.

Sanjiv began, "Sherry, Rudy...thanks for being here on time and ready to go. As you know, our profits and performance are off, even though we are flying more passengers than ever before. Our revenues went down by $219 million last year, but our profits actually dropped by 59% from $985 million to $404 million. At the same time, total revenue passenger miles increased as did passenger load, which went from 85.4% to 85.6%. That means we're flying lots of people to lots of places, in planes that are 85.6% full, and not making a lot of money doing it. I know you know this—it's on the intranet—but the brass needs to know more than we do before they can fix it, and we've been asked to analyze the problem and suggest solutions."

Silence. Not a good start. Sanjiv tried again.

"I know you're probably as overwhelmed by this assignment as I am, but I really need your help. Fran says you two are the best...So do Jennifer Oscarson [finance V.P.] and Bryant Richardson [the corporate controller]. So what do you think? Any suggestions for where we should begin? I know this won't be easy. If the answers were easy, Fran would do this herself. She knows this company better than anyone. But it's not easy—Easy Air has major problems that don't have easy answers. The old solutions aren't working, and the latest 'new' solution seems to be doing more harm than good."

"You mean the new marketing blitz, right?" Sherry eased her way into the conversation.

"Yup. If the only goal was to fly more revenue miles, it worked, but that wasn't the only goal. The profit on these new fares is lower than we were making. If trends continue, and more and more people opt to fly on 'cheap seats,' we could end up *really* busy and losing money at the same time. To paraphrase my old accounting professor, 'If you lose money on every passenger you fly, you're not going to make it up on volume.' More low-fare passengers will increase the loss, not fix it. And, to make matters worse, when you add the required $59 tax, our low fares don't look all that low!"

"Sherry, haven't you been down this path before on a project you did for Bryant?" Rudy asked.

"Actually, yes. That was when we were facing really stiff competition in the Milwaukee market a few years back. We reduced regional fares to meet the threat, and I estimated the impact on profits for the market and the company. Unlike this, that was a localized situation. Our competitor went out of business shortly thereafter—apparently, the low fares were a desperation move on their part." As she answered, Sherry clicked away on her computer.

"I've got it! Sanjiv, this is the analysis I did then. I don't know if it helps, but here's what we did," Sherry said.

"Let's see, you estimated the loss in revenue if we reduced the fares and compared it to the loss that would probably occur if the passengers switched airlines to take advantage of the competition. Interesting, and well done, but you're right. It was a different situation, and I'm not sure that's what we need here, where we need to decide whether to add or drop a market, or to change our fares. Fran wants us to dig deeper than we usually do, and measure things we don't now measure because we need to find information that will help us pinpoint the root causes of the decline in profitability and performance. That means she'll also want suggestions for how we can improve performance—and fast!

"She knows the power of information—especially financial information—to create the momentum needed for change. It's a challenge I think we can meet, and an opportunity too good to pass up."

Sanjiv knew he had gotten past the first hurdle and had motivated the team, but they had a long way to go. In his mind, it was an adventure.

Measurement: A Matter of Perspective

UNDERSTANDING WHAT MAKES A GOOD MEASURE VS. A BAD ONE, AND how certain types of measurements impact people's perceptions and behavior, is the focus of this chapter. We will look at the different types of measurements companies use, how we can combine measures to get a better understanding of a problem or to evaluate performance, and how the nature of the measurement itself impacts outcomes and events. Let us start by looking at the basic concepts surrounding measurement in modern organizations.

Measurements are used to direct attention, suggest action, and shape behavior in organizations. That said, there are many different ways that measurements can be developed and used by managers and their firms. The value of a measure, in fact, is determined by how well it meets the needs of the individual or group that is using it. A measure that is relevant to one group, such as people thinking about investing in a company, may be much less relevant to a manager who is trying to decide whether or not to outsource the company's accounts payable function. One measure does not fit all. For instance, potential investors in Easy Air are likely to be interested in the number of new routes added in the preceding 12 months, while a manager at Easy Air might be interested in the current and projected cost of jet fuel.

OBJECTIVE 1

Describe the differences between financial accounting and management accounting performance measures.

FINANCIAL ACCOUNTING VS. MANAGEMENT ACCOUNTING MEASUREMENTS

In management accounting, we measure many more aspects of an organization than are measured in financial accounting, and at many more points in the management process (see Table 2.1). Where financial accounting emphasizes transactions with the external environment, management accounting stresses internal activities. Where financial accounting focuses on the outcomes of the firm's actions, management accounting provides information to support decision making *before* any actions are taken. The measurements used by management accounting encompass a broad range of issues, events, features, and activities in modern organizations.

TABLE 2.1 MEASUREMENT: FINANCIAL ACCOUNTING VS. MANAGEMENT ACCOUNTING

	Financial Accounting Perspective	Management Accounting Perspective
What managers measure	Financial transactions	Critical success factors, key performance indicators, process, and individual performance
Why managers measure	To summarize the outcome of the firm's activities for owners and external users of the information	To direct attention, objectify key events, communicate current status, analyze trends and outcomes, and motivate desired behavior
When managers measure	When an economic transaction is completed; summaries done monthly, quarterly, and annually	Before, during, and after the completion of key activities
How managers measure	In monetary units	Using a broad number of integrated financial and nonfinancial metrics
Where managers measure	Wherever a completed financial transaction is identified	Across and within all key processes, from the value chain through to individual levels of analysis; vertically from the bottom to the top of the organization
Who managers measure	Business units and entity performance	Individuals, managers, work groups, suppliers, and other key process partners

In management accounting, therefore, measurements are used to focus attention and support decision making before, during, and after the completion of the firm's key activities. What you choose to measure directly impacts the type of analysis that can be completed. Why? Because the measurements used help managers focus on specific "Plan-Do-Check-Adjust" activities, helping them communicate more precisely what is wanted and how well the existing goals and objectives are being met. For instance, if the measurements used emphasize how well Easy Air is doing against specific customer satisfaction measures, such as effectiveness of baggage handling and on-time performance, then the company's managers will focus on these measures when assessing whether or not changes to the way operations are managed should be made.

We also draw from a broad range of potential measurements in management accounting to develop an integrated set of financial and nonfinancial measures, defined in both quantitative and qualitative terms. For instance, Easy Air has developed measurements that focus on quality, delivery (on-time and safely), cost, and productivity. For quality, one measurement used is customer satisfaction, which ranges from "very satisfied" to "very dissatisfied." This is a qualitative measure because it cannot be added, divided, or otherwise manipulated mathematically. In addition, the company measures the number of customer complaints by type. This complementary measure is quantitative as it provides a precise understanding of how many such events occur, and it can be analyzed mathematically for trends, percentage change, and so forth. This diversity in what and how we measure helps us see the organization from many different perspectives. That said, we clearly need to limit the number of measures we use to ensure that management can spot key trends and track progress against its primary goals. In other words, we need to choose among the almost limitless set of measures that could be used, picking those measures that will be most useful to management. These choices are driven by the firm's strategy.

Measurement: A Strategic View

OBJECTIVE 2
Develop a basic set of measurements that reflect a firm's objectives and critical success factors.

A firm's values, strategies, and progress are all reflected in both what it chooses to measure and how those measures are used to influence behavior. These measurements link the past, present, and future of the organization into a cohesive whole.

The choice of specific measurements for each of the key elements of the organization is based upon the firm's defined critical success factors. A **critical success factor (CSF)** *is a key strategic or operational goal or objective that captures an aspect of performance vital to the firm's success*. Limited in number, CSFs should emphasize the activities and processes that will have the greatest impact on the firm's overall performance. Some typical CSFs used by business organizations include:

- Designing new products quickly
- Keeping the cost of a product or service low
- Responding quickly to customer requests
- Producing products and services that meet customer expectations for quality and performance

As you can tell from this brief list of CSFs, it would be very hard for employees to know exactly what is expected of them on a daily basis if there were no other information available to guide them. What is needed by individuals is a more concrete, quantifiable statement of the firm's goals and objectives—a set of **key performance indicators (KPIs),** *a simple and accurate gauge of an employee's or unit's progress or results against a CSF*. KPIs make the CSFs actionable and understandable. They allow the firm, and its managers, to monitor and communicate performance against its goals and desired results on an ongoing basis. Timeliness, quality, and cost are three common KPIs used by companies to track the firm's and/or a process's progress against strategic objectives.

When we put a specific definition around a KPI, it becomes a **measure,** *a KPI that has a specific definition, unit, or quantity*. For instance, we might define timeliness for Easy Air in terms of the percentage of flights that *depart* the gate at their scheduled time. Another definition for timeliness might be the number of flights that *arrive* at their destination at the scheduled time. The former would measure *performance at the beginning* of the **value-creating process,** *the sequence of activities and outcomes that are focused on meeting or exceeding customer expectations*; it is the basis for competitive positioning and success. The latter measure would measure performance *at the end* of the value-creating process. Clearly, Easy Air would choose the measure that most closely corresponds to the customers' definition of a successful flight. It is quite likely arriving on time will matter more to the customers who are taking several flights in a day because they may need to make tight connections.

In a related manner, Easy Air could measure its quality in terms of the number of lost or misplaced bags, while cost could be captured in terms of the cost per passenger flown on a specific flight. In other words, *we have to measure many different aspects of the organization to ensure that its strategic objectives are met.* We cannot focus on just one dimension, such as net income or on-time performance. Why? If we only measure one dimension, everyone's attention will be directed solely on that dimension of performance *to the exclusion of other, equally important, actions and results.* Unless one thing—and only one thing—needs to go right for the firm to succeed, we have to measure at many different points to ensure that key trade-offs are identified and effectively balanced by the firm's managers.

GOOD MEASURES, BAD MEASURES

Measures capture a diversity of experiences and events, from many different perspectives. That said, not all measures are created equal. Some are more accurate than others, while others may be more objective. When we use measures, therefore, we need to be concerned with their basic features. As suggested by Table 2.2, there are many different ways we can evaluate the "goodness" of a measure.

TABLE 2.2 BASIC CHARACTERISTICS OF EFFECTIVE MEASURES

Feature	Description
Objectivity	The measure lacks bias; it provides the same reading, or signal, no matter who or what is being measured, or who is doing the measuring.
Reliability	The measure provides the same information, or signal, every time a specific event takes place. The reading on a thermostat is a reliable indication of the temperature of the outside air.
Accuracy	The measure is clear, precise, and consistent; it provides the right signal within an acceptable level of measurement error.
Ambiguity	The measure is unambiguous and free of distortion; what is being measured is explicitly and uniquely defined.
Cost-Effectiveness	The measure should provide more value to its users than it costs to develop and maintain it. The cost/benefit rule is a basic concept that is used throughout management accounting.
Consistency	The measure is conducive to most forms of linear transformation (for example, addition). A centimeter is always 1/100th of a meter. Its value is "scaled" or based on a defined measure of length.

Feature	Description
Sensitivity	The measure signals changes in key conditions or assumptions before action is needed.
Functionality	The measures chosen create desired behaviors. In other words, we "get what we measure and reward."

While Table 2.2 may seem a bit overwhelming at first glance, in reality many of its ideas are common sense. When we measure, we are trying to learn more about an organization, event, or outcome. If a measure is unreliable or inaccurate, it will not provide a very solid basis for decision making or control.

When a measure is qualitative (stated in words) rather than quantitative (stated in numbers), it only provides directional information. When Easy Air measures customer satisfaction solely in words, its managers will have some understanding of how well it is meeting customer expectations. If they wanted to make improvements in performance, however, they would need more precise information. For example, they might want to look at the complaints Easy Air is receiving from its customers, categorize them to identify the types of problems customers are facing, then trend the results over several time periods, such as weeks or months. This more precise measure of performance trends would help Easy Air's management team focus improvement efforts in those areas that would result in the greatest reduction of customer complaints. Good measures provide the information needed to make good decisions.

Throughout this textbook, we will be developing and using measurements to understand and evaluate the performance of people, products, processes, entities, and supply chains. Whenever a measure is presented, you should stop and ask yourself, "How objective is this measure? How accurate? What kind of behavior might be triggered by using it?" We need to be constantly aware of the fact that what we measure, and how we reward performance based on these measurements, shapes the actions individuals take in organizations. Let us look a bit more closely at the basic types of measurements used by organizations to motivate individual and group performance.

A SYSTEM OF MEASUREMENTS—MCDONALD'S-STYLE

To illustrate these issues, let us think about a company that most of us have experience with—McDonald's. If we think about what is important for McDonald's to succeed as a company, it is clear that meeting customer expectations has to be very high on its list of CSFs. In fact, the strategic objectives for McDonald's are centered on one core message—its journey toward "good." The areas it was concerned with for 2016[2] include sustainability priorities, good food, good sourcing, good planet, good people, and good community. These six areas are the focus of all of its operations, its measures, and its definition of success. Operating more than 36,000 restaurants in more than 100 countries, it is clear these strategic objectives need to be translated into specific measures of performance at all levels of the organization, from the boardroom to the drive-through window at a specific restaurant.

---

2 www.mcdonalds.com/us/en-us/about-us/values-in-action.html

Let us extend the example a bit further. We might want to think about a set of specific KPIs that might help McDonald's management focus employee attention in a specific restaurant on outcomes that can be measured, communicated, and evaluated. What areas would these measurements focus on? As indicated on the McDonald's website, there are currently six areas of concern, which are listed above. Translating these high-level strategic objectives into measures that can guide the actions taken by individual employees and franchisees is critical to the success of the organization.

Let us return to our discussion of the need to develop performance measures that focus employees' attention on taking actions and achieving outcomes that support the strategic objectives of the firm. You can see that while most of the hypothetical measures for McDonald's in Table 2.3 are quantitative (measured in numerical terms)—such as the average customer wait time—many others are qualitative or non-numerical in nature—such as customer satisfaction with current service or food quality. Also, you can see that very few of these measures are defined in purely financial terms. Strong financial results are the outcome of good management and good performance—not their cause.

TABLE 2.3 A SET OF HYPOTHETICAL MEASURES MCDONALD'S MIGHT USE

Key Performance Indicator	Performance Measurement
Recycling efforts	Amount of materials recycled per week
	Percentage of packaging items made with recycled materials
Quality of dining experience	Number of complaints about dining room cleanliness or appearance
	Number of "eat-in" patrons as a percentage of total customers
Quality of service	Average time required to fill a counter order
	Average time required to fill a drive-through order
	Number of complaints about service quality, speed, or attitude of employees
Quality of food: tasty, hot, and easy to eat	Average time between cooking and selling menu item
	Customer complaints or satisfied comments about food quality
	Number of customer cleaning bills resulting from problems with how the food is served
Satisfied employees	Employee turnover
	Employee satisfaction rating
	Average length of employment
Community involvement	Number of charity events sponsored per month
	Total monthly donations to Ronald McDonald House
	Percentage of employees volunteering time or money to local nonprofit organizations

Let us now turn our attention to how we develop and use measurements to support the management process. Before we do this, however, it might be useful to revisit the Easy Air team and see how they are dealing with Fran's most recent requests.

IN CONTEXT ➤ Easy Air: Digging into the Data

The team was now into its fourth day and had not yet come up with anything to show to Fran. She had given Sanjiv a week to come up with a recap of the issues, an explanation of why nothing was working right, and suggestions for what to do to turn things around.

Rudy was running a ton of different variances to dig below the surface but kept hitting compatibility problems, which made it hard to do "apples-to-apples" comparisons. He was frustrated. "We have loads of financial data available, but not much of it provides answers to Fran's questions. How can that be? How can we have so much data, but so little management information? My prof used to say that the traditional accounting system really isn't set up to answer management questions—it provides a summary of what has happened, at least the past according to GAAP [Generally Accepted Accounting Principles]—but it looks backward, not forward. Fran wants help figuring out what to do next; we're not going to get that from the financial accounting records."

"Yes," Sherry chimed in. "It just shows that our internal information needs are just as important as the external ones. Not more important—just as important. Maybe Fran's request will finally get us to build a solid management accounting system. For now, though, we have to try to put the pieces together the best we can."

Sanjiv turned to Rudy and said, "I'm impressed with what you've put together. How did you know to combine the financial and nonfinancial data like this? You've made more progress than you think in helping us understand the issues."

"All I've done so far is to try to split the profitability issue into its pieces. And, as we all thought, reducing our average fare per passenger mile flown is the culprit," Rudy said. "If my figures are right, we actually were much more efficient this year than last, but the fare cuts wiped out all of those gains. It's a good thing the ops people were able to reduce costs, or we might have redlined!"

Sherry, looking over Rudy's shoulder, was puzzled. "How can we be flying more passengers more miles at lower cost, and have a 59.2% reduction in average profit per revenue mile flown?"

"It appears our cost per flight increased by $243.12, while the fare cuts combined with increased load factors earned on average per flight $67.25 additional revenue," Rudy said. "So our costs are in the hole by 5.2% per flight, and that's without looking at other things. We know flight operations aren't the cause, so where's the money going? Something about the trends also bother me. I think we need to look at these numbers in a couple of different ways before Sanjiv meets with Fran."

"Actually, I'd like both of you to go with me to that meeting. You're doing the work, and have come up with great insights. I want everyone to know that you're doing great work!" Sanjiv said.

Measurement and the Management Process

Just as managers undertake different types of work, they need and use measurements for many different purposes. A measure that is useful during the planning stage of the management process might not be as useful during the "check" or "adjust" activities. In some cases, the differences may be simply due to timing. For instance, we may use an estimate of the potential cost of an activity during the planning stage of a project, while the actual cost will be used to evaluate how efficiently and effectively the activity was completed. During the "adjust" phase, our attention might turn to the amount of change we can expect in our costs if we modify how the activity is done. In other words, measures are related across the four aspects of the management process, but how the measure is developed and used will vary based on the type of decision or analysis being completed. For instance, if Easy Air is trying to understand how to increase profitability without increasing fares, it would look to the cost side of operations. Could ground operations reduce the cost to service a plane after landing? Could check-in procedures utilize more efficient technologies that would reduce the cost to service a passenger? If price is assumed a given, as it is in most competitive settings, then solutions to profitability problems have to come from the cost side. To help us understand these issues, let us look at what information is needed at each stage of the management process.

OBJECTIVE 3

Define the role of measurement in the management process.

MEASUREMENT AND PLANNING

During the planning phase of the management process, attention is directed toward establishing goals and defining individual and group performance objectives. The syllabus you receive at the beginning of a semester is one example of a planning document. It helps you understand what is expected of you and when you will be "held accountable" for demonstrating your progress, and defines how the course will be focused. It also defines the material that will be covered and the guidelines for earning your grade.

Within an organization, planning is shaped by a vision statement as embodied in the firm's strategic, tactical, and operational objectives. A **vision statement** *describes the basic goals, characteristics, and philosophies that shape the strategic direction of the firm.*[3] When you want to really know what a company is about,

3 Statement on Management Accounting (SMA) #4DD, *Tools and Techniques for Implementing Integrated Performance Management Systems*, Montvale, N.J.: IMA® (Institute of Management Accountants), 1998: p. 15.

you look at its vision statement. It provides direction to employees when they face difficult decisions, and it helps everyone involved with the firm understand how it intends to create value for its stakeholders.

Easy Air's vision is *to be the airline of choice for business travelers in the point-to-point market.* This vision is translated into concrete terms via a **mission statement,** *which identifies the key customer needs an organization intends to meet*. Easy Air has a specific mission. It is:

...to provide hassle-free, low-cost, dependable air service using point-to-point lines of flight through secondary airports with one fare basis for all passengers regardless of when or where they purchase their tickets.

The mission statement captures more than the firm's promise to its customers—it serves as the basis for developing its strategies, shaping its culture, and providing a clear signal to employees and other stakeholders about the firm's focus. It embodies the primary elements of the firm, as illustrated in Figure 2.1.

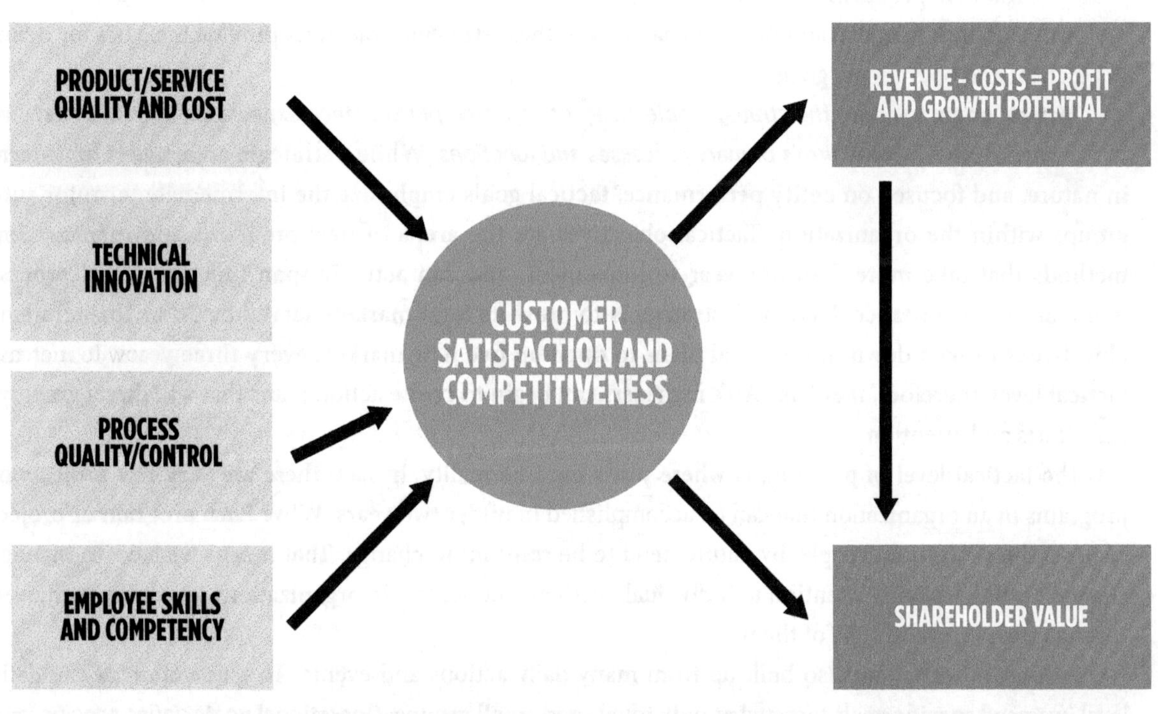

FIGURE 2.1 GENERIC MODEL OF A BUSINESS

The vision, mission, and strategy of an organization have to take each of the key dimensions of the business into account: product quality and cost, technical innovation, process quality and cost, and employee skills and competencies. Value is created for the firm's owners through the effective combination of these primary elements, which, if completed effectively, will result in revenues, and if cost-controlled, profit. If a firm focuses solely on only one or two elements in its plans, measurements, or actions, it will not prosper in the long run. Good management is a tapestry of plans and actions and goals and results that begins with a clear vision and mission.

A firm's mission statement shapes its strategic objectives. **Strategic objectives** *provide structure to the firm's vision, translating it into specific, actionable elements; they focus on the long run*, defining the firm's focus for the coming five to 10 years.

Specific strategic objectives set the tone for action, serving as the basis for identifying a firm's CSFs. And as we saw earlier in this chapter, CSFs are the basis for developing specific measurements.

At Easy Air, the strategic objectives for the current five-to-10-year period include the following:

- Grow the number of markets served by 20%
- Become the recognized leader in point-to-point travel
- Increase customer satisfaction
- Develop and retain a superior workforce
- Increase market share in markets served by 10%
- Increase revenues by 100%
- Improve profitability by 200%

A mix of both financial and nonfinancial targets, these strategic objectives provide the basis for defining tactical and operational goals.

Tactical goals *translate the strategic objectives into specific performance expectations for the next two to five years for each of the firm's primary processes and functions.* While a strategic objective is long-term in nature, and focused on entity performance, tactical goals emphasize the intermediate term for subgroups within the organization. Tactical objectives are the arena of new programs and management methods that take more than one year to implement, and can actually span functional and process boundaries. For instance, Easy Air's strategy is to grow its total markets served by 20%. This strategic objective is broken down into tactical plans to open up five new markets every three years. It is at the tactical level, therefore, that Easy Air's managers can begin to create action plans that will direct employees' efforts and attention.

The tactical level of planning is where plans become reality. In fact, there are very few projects or programs in an organization that can be accomplished in under two years. Why? Each program or project changes the status quo. People, by nature, tend to be resistant to change. That means we have to manage change carefully, paying attention to individual needs and concerns. In organizations, results are achieved through people, not in spite of them.

Results, however, are also built up from many daily actions and events. To guide effort at the daily level, we need specific goals targeted at individuals and small groups. **Operational goals** *define specific individual and group performance expectations for the coming day, month, or year.* Short-term in nature, operational goals provide the basis for evaluating individual performance.

Sanjiv has been given an operational goal by Fran—to analyze the recent trends in Easy Air's financial and nonfinancial performance. These are contained in Table 2.4. He has been asked to develop new measures where necessary, and to dig underneath the surface of existing measures and methods to provide more detailed information. Fran will use this information to reshape Easy Air's tactical objectives in order to improve the chances that its overall strategic objectives are met.

TABLE 2.4 PERCENTAGE CHANGE IN EASY AIR'S PLANNED PERFORMANCE

Performance Indicator	20x7 Plan	20x6 Actuals	Percentage Change
Total flights flown	3,932,764	3,575,240	10.00%
Total passengers flown	410,706,410	373,369,464	10.00%
Total revenue seat miles flown (in thousands)	62,566,454	54,405,612	15.00%
Average miles per passenger flight	270	265	1.89%
Total operating revenue (in thousands)	$10,419,762.8	$9,303,359.7	12.00%
Total operating expenses (in thousands)	$9,877,932.3	$8,899,038.1	11.00%
Operating profit (in thousands)	$541,830.5	$404,321.6	27.35%
Average revenue per revenue seat mile flown	$0.167	$0.171	-2.33%
Average expense per revenue seat mile flown	$0.158	$0.164	-3.15%
Average profit per revenue seat mile flown	$0.009	$0.007	10.19%
Average revenue per flight	$2,649.48	$2,602.16	1.82%
Average expense per flight	$2,511.70	$2,489.07	0.91%
Average profit per flight	$137.77	$113.09	15.77%
Average load factor (% seats filled per flight)	85.70%	85.6%	0.12%
Average on-time performance rating	95%	88.5%	7.34%
Number of baggage claims	187,650	250,200	-25.00%
Number of customer complaints	228,060	380,100	-40.00%
Number of ground/gate delays	2,280	3,800	-40.00%
Number of canceled flights	1,069	1,425	-25.00%

Throughout the planning process, therefore, we use measurements to define expectations, establish performance standards and benchmarks, and create guidelines for individual action. Without measurement, the vision and mission of the firm are unlikely to become a reality. Measurement helps us anchor the mission in concrete ways to the daily activities of individuals across the organization. It is how we transform plans into action—the "do" of the management process.

Action and Measurement

OBJECTIVE 4

Describe the various forms of measures used at the point of action.

If we think about what is going on every day in our lives, we can see that we constantly use measurements to describe current conditions and to make minor shifts in our activities. In one respect, these minor changes are part of the "adjust" cycle of the management process. But, when the changes are small or no one is holding us "accountable" for a specific outcome, a measure is a much more personal signal of our progress.

For a measure to guide our actions, it needs to be available on a "real-time" basis. In modern organizations, many of these measures are embedded in the process itself. For instance, a production process can be structured to include a bell or a light that a worker can activate as soon as a problem is spotted. In a continuous improvement setting, these signals go by the name of andon lights. Another example of an action-shaping measurement would be the fuel gauge on a car or in the cockpit of one of Easy Air's planes. Action-shaping measures help us judge current conditions and focus our attention on problems before they become a crisis.

While financial measures are not normally considered to be useful at the action level, in reality we can use a cost estimate to put an event in financial terms. For instance, at some companies, a "waste meter" is kept at various stages on the production line. The waste meter restates the current defect rate into dollars and cents of foregone profit (see Figure 2.2). When a line worker is trying to decide how to handle a defective unit or raw material, it is very useful for them to know the economic impact of their decision to scrap vs. salvage the part or unit. If it is an inexpensive part, it makes the most sense to scrap it because the cost to salvage or repair it would exceed the cost faced if the part is scrapped. On the other hand, if it is an expensive part or the product is close to completion, salvage becomes a more logical and economically justifiable action.

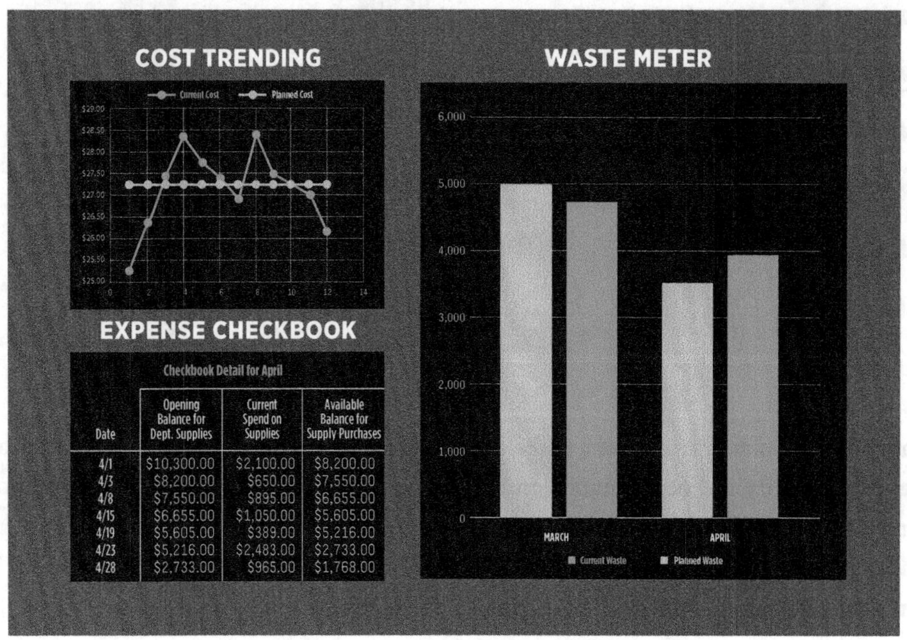

Checkbook Detail for April

Date	Opening Balance for Dept. Supplies	Current Spend on Supplies	Available Balance for Supply Purchases
4/1	$10,300.00	$2,100.00	$8,200.00
4/3	$8,200.00	$650.00	$7,550.00
4/8	$7,550.00	$895.00	$6,655.00
4/15	$6,655.00	$1,050.00	$5,605.00
4/19	$5,605.00	$389.00	$5,216.00
4/23	$5,216.00	$2,483.00	$2,733.00
4/28	$2,733.00	$965.00	$1,768.00

FIGURE 2.2 "REAL-TIME" FINANCIAL MEASURES

Other companies use a "checkbook" to help line supervisors control their area's spending. Each time materials or support activities are requested by the supervisor, he or she writes a check against a "balance" of funds that have been "deposited" to reflect the anticipated costs of direct production and ongoing maintenance and related expenses. If the checking account gets overdrawn, the supervisor has to go to management and request more funds. In this way, the company's management helps its first-line supervisors understand the economic impact of their decisions and action in real time, not at the end of a month or year.

Cost trending is yet another way that various companies can bring financial information into real time. On an hourly or daily basis, the average cost of producing a good unit is calculated and trended against the planned costs. In many cases, the cost graphs are combined with scrap, schedule attainment, and units-per-hour graphs that are posted and maintained somewhere on the production line.

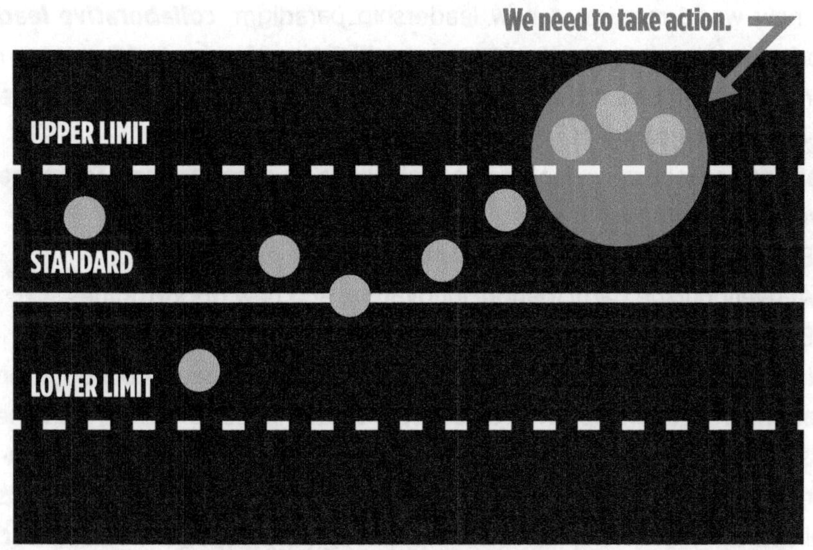

FIGURE 2.3 SHEWHART CONTROL CHART

One of the more common ways that we use measurements at the point of action is with **Shewhart control charts**, *which are quality control tools used to verify that a process is operating within its control limits*. (Figure 2.3) A Shewhart chart is maintained on the line. An individual worker samples the output and takes measurements on one or more key features, such as the item's weight or its size. These measures are then plotted on a chart that has been designed to include the expected, or standard, for the feature as well as an "acceptable range" above and below the standard. When one or more of the samples falls outside of the acceptable range, work is discontinued until the underlying process problem can be fixed. Originally designed in the early 1900s, Shewhart charts continue to be used because they effectively focus measurement at the point of action.

The goal of measurement at the point of action is simple: to help individuals gain knowledge on how their decisions and actions impact company performance. Placing its emphasis on learning, not evaluation, measurements at the *point of action* transform everyone into a manager and decision maker. It includes them in the continuous process of improving performance against customer expectations—a game that underlies business management in practice.

IN THE NEWS ➤ Every Employee a Decision Maker

Powerful shifts have been taking place in the world as more individuals are demanding a say about the institutions and situations that impact them. Customers are determining what a company's brand is, for instance, while employees are taking an ever-more active role in organizational decision making. It is an exciting revolution, and many organizations are responding with new ways of working. For example, many hospitals are involving patients in decisions from what range of food options should be offered to how nurses and support staff are scheduled and managed. Other organizations are leveraging social media to reach out to potential customers, offering to co-design and fund products with them.

This new world requires a new leadership paradigm: ***collaborative leadership***. This style works because it is less top-down, enabling employees to have very real involvement in making their organization succeed. In other words, collaborative leadership makes employees business partners.

What does collaborative leadership look like in an organization? There are four essential activities that comprise this approach to management:

- Engage employee teams to define objectives and set goals
- Actively pursue participation, innovation, and new opportunities
- Empower team members to take ownership of actions and results
- Implement a culture, and control system, that will enable collaboration

Collaborative leadership involves actively taking steps to ensure that the right technology is readily available so that all employees can be involved in decision making and taking action, can work collaboratively, and can share their knowledge and insights in real time. Collaborative leadership also requires that specific management approaches, such as the setting of collaboration guidelines for team members, the implementation of new skills training, and ensuring that required knowledge about organizational and process strategies and objectives, are available to team members. Only by investing in the necessary infrastructure can the organization be assured that it will be able to reap the benefits of collaborative leadership.

Clearly, developing a collaborative leadership-based culture takes time and dedication. However, with commitment, strong sponsorship and leadership, and investment in the necessary tools, technology, training, and skills, an organization can transform itself to succeed, and thrive, in today's global economy. The result—more engaged and empowered employees—will produce better results for all stakeholders.

This insert is an adaptation of the article "Why employees must be at the decision-making table" by Sandy Richardson, first published in the Globe and Mail on Tuesday, September 30, 2014, 7 p.m. EDT. It is part of the Globe Careers' Leadership Lab series, where executives and experts share their views and advice about leadership and management and can be found at www.theglobeandmail.com/report-on-business/careers/leadership-lab/how-.to-get-employees-involved-at-the-decision-making-table/article20861105/.

Using Measures to Check Progress

OBJECTIVE 5

Create a basic trend, gap, and variance analysis of performance results.

Individuals and groups use measurements to continuously monitor their own progress and performance. When this information becomes summarized and added to the entity's information system, we have moved from the "do" to the "check" facet of the management process. Measurements now become used in a much more formal way to communicate information across management levels and across functional and process boundaries. Attention turns away from guiding action to evaluating results.

There are many different techniques used by companies to complete the "check" activity. For instance, if we have set a standard for the cost of material in a product, we might want to compare actual results to this standard. If the focus is on the size of the difference between actual and plan, we might complete a **gap analysis,** *which emphasizes the cumulative impact of events and outcomes to determine if any significant performance problems exist*. In other situations, we might be more concerned with the improvement (or lack of it) compared to prior periods. In that event, we might do a **trend analysis,** *which tracks changes over time in KPIs such as net profits, revenues, number of defective units produced, on-time performance, and workforce productivity*. In yet a third case, we might want to analyze the causes of any difference, which would be a **variance analysis,** *which isolates the cause of differences in a measure by focusing on one variable at a time to better understand the reasons for performance shortfall*. If the goal is to direct attention to the total change in a measure, however, gap analysis and variance analysis would yield the same result.

Let us look at an example to get a better feeling for what these analyses mean. Sam Underwood runs a moderately successful golf pro shop. He has completed an MBA, so he understands how important it is to measure the activities in his pro shop if he is to steadily improve performance and profits. At the beginning of the year, Sam put together a plan for the business. It is now year's end and he wants to see how close he came to his projections (Table 2.5).

TABLE 2.5 PLAN VS. ACTUAL

Sam's Golf Pro Shop		
Measure	**Plan**	**Actual**
Total revenues from merchandise	$40,750.00	$38,650.00
Total revenues from instruction	23,200.00	23,750.00
Total revenues from driving range	32,500.00	40,000.00
Total cost of goods sold	(22,445.00)	(27,055.00)
Total operating costs	(38,580.00)	(35,840.00)
Operating Profit	$35,425.00	$39,505.00

Just looking at the raw numbers, we see that merchandise revenues were lower than Sam expected, but instructional and driving range revenues exceeded expectations. The net impact on profit was very favorable, but by exactly how much? We can take a simple gap analysis approach to see in absolute terms exactly how much Sam has either achieved or failed to meet his goals (Table 2.6). By adding the terms "favorable" for situations in which Sam's results exceeded expectations and "unfavorable" where he fell short of goal, we are beginning to add variance analysis logic to our tool kit.

TABLE 2.6 ANALYZING SAM'S RESULTS

Measure	Plan	Actual	Gap	Favorable or Unfavorable
Total revenues from merchandise	$40,750.00	$38,650.00	$(2,100.00)	**Unfavorable**
Total revenues from instruction	$23,200.00	$23,750.00	$550.00	**Favorable**
Total revenues from driving range	$32,500.00	$40,000.00	$7,500.00	**Favorable**
Total cost of goods sold	$22,445.00	$27,055.00	$4,610.00	**Unfavorable**
Total operating costs	$38,580.00	$35,840.00	$(2,740.00)	**Favorable**
Operating Profit	$35,425.00	$39,505.00	$4,080.00	**Favorable**

Looking at the "favorable" and "unfavorable" tags above, we start to see something very specific about completing the various analyses. When we are talking about revenue, profit, or unit sales metrics, if the company does better than plan, this is clearly a good thing—we would mark this difference as "favorable." When we talk about the cost side of the equation, however (remember, revenue minus costs is profit), if actual is greater than plan it is "unfavorable." As we will see in Chapter 5, variance analysis is a bit more complicated when we start to break out individual causes for the performance gap, but, for now, let us follow the simple rules:

- **Rule #1:** If revenue, sales, or profit actual results are greater than plan, this is favorable for the company. If they are less than plan, this is unfavorable.
- **Rule #2:** If actual costs are greater than plan, this is unfavorable for the company. When these costs are less than plan, all other things being equal, it is a favorable result.

We might want to plot these changes on a graph, which would give us another perspective that might clarify the results. This is done for Sam's business in Figure 2.4. Since Sam did a pretty good job of predicting his activities, the comparison of plan and actual is not as dramatic as it would be if Sam's plans had been less accurate.

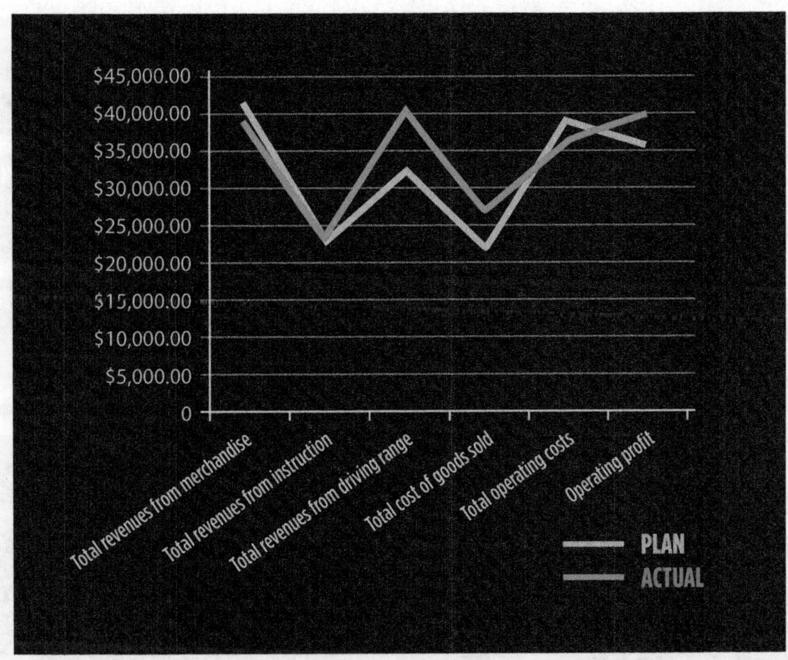

FIGURE 2.4 ACTUAL VS. PLANNED OUTCOMES

What Sam might want to do in the future, however, is evaluate his performance using only the three revenue measures to get a better understanding of how the mix of business is changing. We have done that for you in Table 2.7 and Figure 2.5.

TABLE 2.7 ANALYSIS OF REVENUE TRENDS

Sam's Golf Pro Shop Analysis of Revenue Trends				
Measure	**20x3**	**20x4**	**20x5**	**20x6**
Total revenues from merchandise	$42,500.00	$41,000.00	$39,500.00	$38,650.00
Total revenues from instruction	$18,250.00	$29,000.00	$20,500.00	$23,750.00
Total revenues from driving range	$32,500.00	$35,000.00	$37,000.00	$40,000.00

What we see even in absolute terms is that merchandise sales have steadily fallen while instruction and driving range revenues are on the rise. This is a problem for Sam because he is doing as many golf clinics as he has time to do. If he is to gain further increases in this area of the business, he is going to have to hire more help, which will drive up his operating costs. But if he hires a golf pro, he might be able to jump-start not only his instructional revenues, but possibly reverse the trend on merchandise (more lessons means more golf tees and gloves, as well as more driving range time).

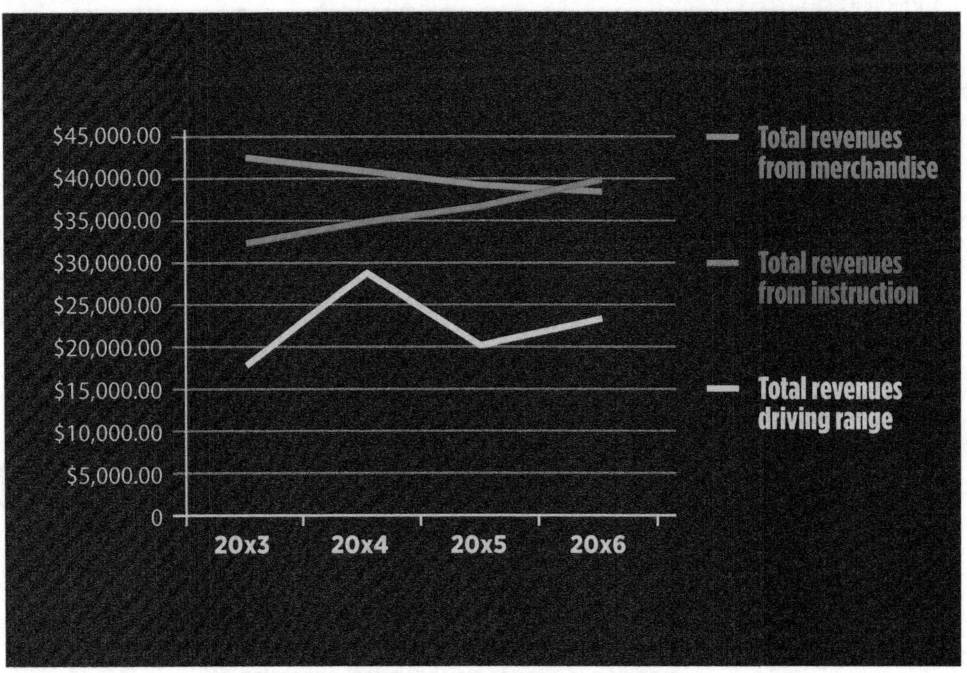

FIGURE 2.5 REVENUE TRENDS

The gap we have looked at in Sam's basic analysis (Table 2.5) represents *actual* results less *planned* results. Let us call actual results (b) and planned results (a), so the equation for the performance gap is (b – a). In the last chapter's problems, we learned how to create a percentage-based trend analysis to help us better understand what is happening. Since we want to compare the percentage change in actual to plan, the percentage change formula becomes (see Table 2.8):

$$\frac{(b - a)}{a}, \text{ or } (b - a) \text{ divided by } (a)$$

Looking at the problem in terms of percentages, we see the largest increase in revenue streams is traceable to instruction activities. This trend suggests that Sam might be well-advised to hire a golf pro to help boost his capacity in this vital area of growth. Since the revenue from instruction is closely followed by an increase in the revenue from the selling of buckets of balls at the driving range, Sam needs to put major thought into expanding this part of his business if he is to continue to see growth. He might even have to add some teeing areas to his driving range!

TABLE 2.8 PERCENTAGE DIFFERENCE IN PLANNED VS. ACTUAL RESULTS

Sam's Golf Pro Shop			
Measure	**Plan**	**Actual**	**% Change**
Total revenues from merchandise	$40,750.00	$38,650.00	-5.2%
Total revenues from instruction	$23,200.00	$23,750.00	2.4%
Total revenues from driving range	$32,500.00	$40,000.00	23.1%
Total cost of goods sold	$22,445.00	$27,055.00	20.5%
Total operating costs	$38,580.00	$35,840.00	-7.1%
Operating Profit	$35,425.00	$39,505.00	11.5%

We will revisit this type of analysis in more depth in Chapter 5. For now, let us leave Sam pondering how best to grow his business without having costs spiral out of control.

USING MEASUREMENTS TO ADJUST PERFORMANCE

When we have completed our "check" activities, it is often necessary to make adjustments to either our plans or our actions. We now need measurements to help us analyze the impact of potential *changes* on future performance. For instance, returning to the situation facing Easy Air, if the number of passengers flown can be increased 10% if prices are dropped 5%, will this have a positive or negative impact on the firm? What will happen to profitability and performance if Easy Air outsources its ticketing and reservation activities to another firm? Should Easy Air contract for its baggage-handling services at the local level, or should this continue to be a company-controlled activity? These are just a few of the possible changes that Fran might want to examine in more depth.

There are several common management accounting tools we use to analyze potential changes to an organization's activities or key features: cost-volume-profit analysis, incremental analysis, and the development of a business case. We will only briefly introduce these topics at the conceptual level here, spending much more time on the concepts in Chapters 3 and 5.

Cost-volume-profit analysis (CVP) *is a tool used to analyze the impact of price, cost, or volume changes on company profitability.* When this tool is used, attention is placed on the *flow* of work through the process. In other words, in CVP analysis, the *structure* of the company or process is left unchanged. The focus is instead placed on how much work is being done with available resources. In many ways, CVP is a "stop and go" light approach to analyzing the impact of changing conditions on company performance. It can give us a general idea of whether or not we will increase profits if we make changes to price, cost, or volume sold. CVP analysis takes a simple approach to the economics of the firm, separating all costs into only one of two buckets: ones that change at an even rate with changes in volume vs. those that are the same no matter how much work we do. As we will see in Chapter 3, we can learn a lot from CVP analysis, but it also leaves many questions unanswered.

In **incremental analysis,** *which examines the impact of complex changes, such as structural changes, on a firm's performance*, we are able to focus our analysis of potential changes on many different issues and many different dimensions of performance. Moving away from the simple world of CVP analysis, we look at the impact of changes in the underlying structure or nature of the work that is done by a company. For instance, if Easy Air wants to understand the impact of having an outside firm handle its reservation system, what types of things would Fran want to consider?

- The total cost of the outsourced service
- How many of the current resources used to complete the reservation activity could be outsourced, and what really would be eliminated
- The potential impact on customer service if the reservation process is outsourced
- The potential loss of contact with customers and their changing demands if the reservation activity is outsourced
- Increased or decreased customer satisfaction if the change is made
- Impact on employee morale if the reservation department is eliminated
- Impact on overall business risk if outsourcing is pursued
- Impact on company flexibility and responsiveness if reservation activities are outsourced

The outsourcing option would require that Fran look at many different aspects of the business, using a multitude of measures. A potential change might look very good in terms of its impact on the company's operating profits, but if it reduces customer satisfaction, increases business risk, or negatively impacts overall morale and employee retention, it may not be a good idea.

There are a number of measurements, and measurement issues, that we want to consider during incremental analysis, as we will see in Chapter 5. As noted above, we will probably want both financial and nonfinancial measures that focus on internal and external factors. In using these measures, we will need to pay careful attention to the timing of an event, the magnitude of change, the interdependence of one event to another, and so on. The measurement issues we will be concerned with include objectivity (freedom from bias), stability, reliability, and relevance to the decision at hand.

The results of incremental analysis are combined with other information in a document called a **business case,** *which is a complete analysis of the impact of a proposed change on the company's structure, processes, or products, including financial and nonfinancial metrics, an assessment of business risk and implementation concerns, and an examination of the sensitivity of the suggested course of action to changes in assumptions*. One of the primary skills you will gain in this course is the ability to develop a business case to effectively communicate the pros and cons of different types of change on a company's performance. In making a case for change, you will want to be as thorough as you can be, looking at the financial, operational, and strategic implications of a decision.

Throughout this textbook, we will look at a variety of potential changes to the way a company is operated. With the help of the various databases, you will be able to test your understanding of the tools and techniques that underlie management accounting practice. Incremental analysis and the subsequent development of a business case will play major roles in each of these cases. They provide us with the most comprehensive means to explore the impact of change on overall performance. Using the existing operations as a benchmark for the "as is" setting, we will explore the impact of changes in the structure of a company's processes, the products it makes, the services it provides, whether or not it "makes or buys" part of its products or its activities, and so on.

Before leaving this chapter, however, let us look at one more key feature of management accounting measurements: how they influence behavior in organizations.

THE BEHAVIORAL IMPACT OF PERFORMANCE MEASUREMENT

While the word "control" often is perceived in negative ways, in reality any time a person sets out to influence the behavior of another person, they are undertaking a control activity. In organizations, this effort is called **management control**—*all of the efforts of an organization to influence individual performance, including all of the rules, regulations, measures, and behavioral tools and techniques used to influence employee behavior in order to achieve desired results*. In the majority of cases, the reason for any form of control is positive. For instance, if you stop friends from doing something that could harm them, you are trying to control them.

Whenever a company creates a measure, puts in place a policy, or defines its expectations to its employees, it is engaging in a control activity. Clearly, an organization has to have controls in place to remain viable. Why? Because people are not always inclined to do what is best for the organization when they take actions or make decisions. There are three main reasons why people may not always act the way the firm's owners might want them to: lack of direction, motivational problems, and personal limitations.

Whether measures are used to help employees understand what is expected (provide direction), motivate them to do what is best for the firm, or help them gain new knowledge and new skills (address personal limitations), the objective of measurement remains the same: to ensure that people will act in desired ways. For it is people who make things happen in organizations, for better or for worse.[4]

Different measures create different types of behavioral responses in people. When coupled with a variety of incentive and risk-reducing systems—such as bonuses for reaching a sales quota—measurements can drive a whole host of behavioral responses—some good, some not so good. For instance, if the sales quota objective is met by booking sales to a friendly customer on the last day of a quarter, with the understanding that when the order is delivered, it will be rejected, the salesman is gaming the system. When measures increase the tendency of individuals to do what the organization needs them to do, we say that the measures increase **goal congruence,** *meaning the firm, its other key stakeholders, and its employees have compatible goals and objectives*. The flip side, which we call **dysfunctional behavior,** *captures the unintended negative consequences of measures used by an organization*. In this situation, the measurements used to control behavior actually create incentives for individuals to do things the organization does not want them to do. To understand these issues a bit better, let us look at measurement from a control perspective.

---

4 This section is an updated discussion of concepts that originally appeared in Kenneth A. Merchant, *Control in Business Organizations*, Boston: Pitman Publishing Company, 1985.

Results, Action, and Personnel/Cultural Controls

OBJECTIVE 6

Define and describe key differences between results, action, and personnel/cultural controls.

When we set out to measure performance, we have to make many different choices. One of these choices revolves around where we focus our measures in the flow of activities that underlie daily work in organizations: at the end (results control), in the midst of the flow (action control), or through the people who make it all happen (personnel/cultural control).

Results control *is the most common form of control used in organizations; emphasis is placed on what is accomplished, not on how the outcomes are achieved.* This is the type of measurement we have used in this chapter. Placing the emphasis on what is accomplished, not how it is accomplished, results controls treat the flow of activities leading up to the result as a black box: It is the ends attained that are defined, measured, and evaluated—not the means. When a salesman receives a bonus for reaching a sales goal, it is a results control. Your grade on an exam or for a course is a results control. As long as we know what results are wanted, and that these results can be measured as well as controlled by the person being held accountable for them, results controls can be used.

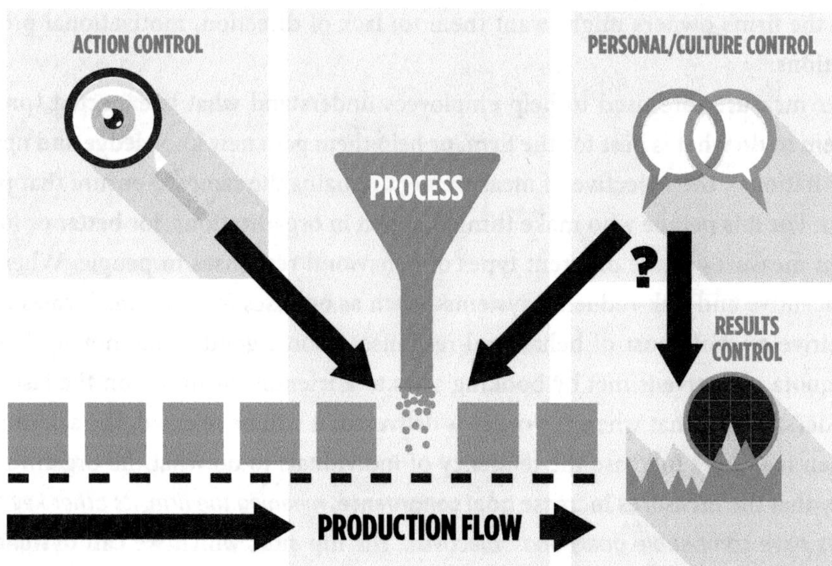

FIGURE 2.6 ORGANIZATIONAL CONTROL: RELATIONSHIP AMONG RESULTS, ACTION, AND PERSONNEL/CULTURAL CONTROLS

Action control *focuses on how work is done; it looks inside the black box to the activities that lead to results.* In modern organizations, there are two main ways we use action controls: 1) to define the sequence of steps that must be followed to complete a task; and 2) to monitor the progress and quality of the work completed up to the control point. The former use of action control is most often called a **standard operating procedure (SOP),** *an action control that requires work be done in a specific manner and sequence*. When it is very important that work be completed in exactly the same way, each and every time, SOPs are used. The sequence of steps and checks that must be completed before a space shuttle is launched, or those used to control the operation of a nuclear power plant, are just two examples of situations where SOPs are applied.

In **personnel/cultural control,** *the emphasis is on the role that individual and group dynamics play in influencing behavior in organizations*. This last form of control has its source in the people that make up the organization. Personnel controls have two primary components: an individual's self-control and the pressure exerted by groups on individuals to conform to established norms or standards of behavior, which can include the organizational culture. When an individual is self-motivated, external forms of control are simply not needed. The individual will do what is needed because they want to, not because they have to.

In other situations, the pressure peers place on each other can be leveraged to improve the performance of the organization. As suggested in Figure 2.6, team meetings that explore why actual results do not meet process goals are one form of personnel control. The best-run companies in the world rely on group-based personnel controls—on the culture of their firm—to help them outperform their competitors. Southwest Airlines, for instance, is known for placing more emphasis in its hiring process on the attitudes and personality of a candidate than on that individual's technical skills. The value placed on its employees is so high that Southwest refused to lay off any of its workforce after the events of September 11, 2001. It is a policy that has paid handsome dividends for the firm and its stakeholders ever since.

As you might imagine, the strongest form of control we can enact in an organization is personnel/cultural control. When people do what is needed and expected because they want to, management can turn its attention away from "controlling" behavior to finding the most effective ways to channel its human resources into activities that create the most value for the firm's customers. This shift in management focus and practice is the subject of the collaborative leadership approach described in the "In the News" discussion in this chapter. Unfortunately, there is a downside to personnel control—it is not very robust. Personnel control is based on mutual trust between the individual and one or more other individuals in the organization. When this trust is lost, so is the effectiveness of personnel controls.

Clearly, when Southwest Airlines refused to lay off employees, it was concerned with keeping its trust in the company and its management. It is no coincidence, therefore, that Southwest was the only airline to ride out the devastating events of late 2001 into 2002 with its profits, and customer base, relatively intact. In fact, in Providence, R.I., Southwest posted a 1% increase in passenger traffic during the last quarter of 2001 while rivals posted up to a 24% reduction in passengers flown during the same period over similar routes. Southwest Airlines surged as the airline industry in general was experiencing significant reductions in overall passenger traffic. As this example suggests, people are at the heart of every well-run company.

CONTROL IN A CONTINUOUS IMPROVEMENT SETTING

Since the mid-1990s, the second form of action control has become more common: ***control at the point of action***. The examination of why there is a gap in units flowing across the production line in Figure 2.6 reflects this approach to action controls. Control at the point of action is usually driven by the implementation of **total quality management (TQM),** *a management technique that seeks to eliminate defects and unnecessary variation from processes, products, and services*, and the **continuous improvement philosophy (CIP),** *a way of thinking that encourages individuals and organizations to seek out ways to constantly improve performance by eliminating waste and finding better methods, materials, or machines to complete work*. CIP is the basis for many modern management techniques. Both TQM and CIP empower line personnel to make process decisions, such as stopping a production line to fix a machine or quality problem without direct management intervention. Techniques such as statistical process control (which can use Shewhart charts), kanban, poka-yoke, andon lights, control boards, and jidoka are all examples of control at the point of action. Table 2.9 contains definitions of each of these tools and techniques, which help those who do the work monitor and control the process in real time.

TABLE 2.9 CONTINUOUS IMPROVEMENT-BASED ACTION CONTROLS

Type of Action Control	Definition
Statistical process control	The use of in-process measurements and sampling to determine if a machine or process is operating within established performance limits; Shewhart charts make statistical process controls visible
Kanban	An in-process inventory control technique that keeps a line in balance and serves as a visual signal of problem spots that may occur during production
Poka-yoke	A foolproof mechanism that prevents defects or machine stoppages by preventing errors at their source; the USB connectors on your computer that can only be inserted in one way are an example of this type of control.
Andon lights	Lights used to visually signal trouble spots on a production line; they bring immediate attention to bear on problems, such as a lack of materials at a key assembly station.
Control boards	Visually show the progress being made against preset goals or schedules; they make discrepancies between actual vs. plan visible to everyone.
Jidoka	Provides a machine with the independent ability to use "judgment" or intercede in the flow of production; literally defined as "autonomation"; an example would be a traffic light that "senses" if there is any cross traffic waiting in the intersection, and then "judges" it is time to change the signal from red to green.

These are just a few of the more common types of what we will call "point of action" controls. Many of these techniques originated in Japan, serving as vital parts of the Toyota manufacturing system. What these tools do is allow the process to be self-regulating, while increasing the probability that errors, defects, and problems will be detected before they are passed down the line to the customer.

LOOKING BACK ➤ Formal vs. Informal Controls

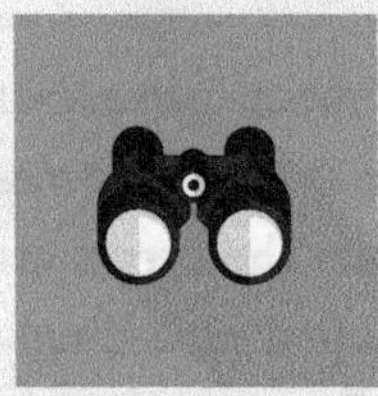

An obvious and yet basic fact about organizations is that they are built by and around people. A manager's primary task is to get these people to accomplish specific results without using undesirable methods to attain them...it would be quite inappropriate to examine the preparation and use of any form of control in an organization without understanding and addressing the needs, desires, and feelings of the people who will be affected.

A management accounting system may be very well-designed, conforming to best practice guidelines, but this system is of no use to a manager unless it motivates desired actions and results achieved by the people who make up the organization.

It is easy to place too much emphasis on results controls and to miss entirely, or place too little emphasis on, personnel controls. Management control tools such as budgets, accounting records, progress reports, and the analysis of actual results vs. plan are visible tools that are tangible. What type of information is provided by them, the accuracy of this information, who has prepared specific reports, and who has received this information is readily known. It is far more difficult to evaluate the impact of personnel controls, since these may consist of such unquantifiable things as random face-to-face conversations or a specific individual's interpretation of a casual glance or tone of voice. Management control is most effective when all of the available tools are skillfully blended into a consistent and effective whole. That said, personnel controls are quite likely more effective in defining and achieving organizational goals than are the vast array of written records.

Adapted from Robert N. Anthony, *Management Controls in Industrial Research Organizations*; Boston: Harvard University, 1952: pp. 45-47.

The Potential for Dysfunctional Consequences

OBJECTIVE 7
Understand the dysfunctional consequences of measurement and suggest methods for minimizing them.

Before leaving the topic of measurement and management control, it is important to deal with the fact that control brings with it the potential for **dysfunctional consequences,** *or undesirable side effects, which occur when measurements actually create incentives for individuals to do things the organization does not want them to do*. You do not have to go very far to see the negative impact controls can have on behavior—just think back to your own years as a teenager and the various ways you "got around" the rules set down by your parents. A natural part of maturing, this resistance to being controlled by someone or something is an integral part of the human makeup. People will resist control efforts, or find ways around the control mechanisms, in order to do what they want to do. Whether it is called "free will" or simply a stubborn desire to be independent and in charge of our fate, the fact remains that what and how we measure can trigger a mild-to-extreme case of "rebellion" from those we are trying to influence with our measurements.

Some common types of dysfunctional behavior include behavioral displacement, gamesmanship, operating delays, and negative attitudes. **Behavioral displacement** *refers to situations in which the measures actually encourage people to do things that are not consistent with the firm's objectives.* The events at Wells Fargo are one example of behavioral displacement. Its sales associates, seeking to open exceedingly high numbers of new customer accounts (checking, savings, and credit cards), opened large numbers of new accounts without the customers' knowledge or permission. The incentives in place, such as bonuses for opening more accounts than budgeted, led sales associates to undertake fraudulent transactions that affected customers' credit ratings and overinflated Wells Fargo's reports to key stakeholders. Having paid a substantial fine, the company has discontinued the use of this incentive system, offered to compensate affected customers, and undertaken new efforts to directly contact any customer who opens any type of new account. While it may have made sense to create incentives to grow the number of accounts and customers the bank serviced, how this desired result was communicated to sales associates and incentivized led to behavioral displacement—achieving desired results through undesirable means.

Behavioral displacement can be the outcome of an incorrect or incomplete definition of the firm's goals or of expected behavior. Another cause can be the excessive reliance on quantifiable measures, which can shift attention away from what is actually going on. Peter Drucker, a well-known management expert, poignantly described this problem when he noted that whenever a measure is put in place, it tends to draw more attention, and create more action, than is intended. Measures are visible signals that can make management feel that things are under control, but when the dysfunctional consequences of any specific measure is considered, there may actually be little or no control at all.[5]

Behavioral displacement can take place regardless of the form of control that is being used. For instance, action controls can lead individuals to pay more attention to what they do (the means) than what they are supposed to accomplish (the ends). In a related fashion, action controls can create rigid, non-adaptive behavior. Anyone who has tried to "argue" with a government bureaucrat has faced this problem.

If the list of dysfunctional consequences of using measurements for control stopped with behavioral displacement, it would cause us concern. Unfortunately, other unanticipated and undesirable situations can occur when we develop and use measures in organizations—gamesmanship, negative attitudes, and operating delays. Let us look at each of these briefly to round out this chapter's discussion on the use of measurements in organizations.

Gamesmanship *occurs when people undertake actions that are intended to improve their measured performance, but which are not necessarily in the best interest of the organization.* When the actions do not produce any positive economic effects, we say that the person is "gaming" the system. Two of the more common types of gamesmanship are **creation of slack resources,** *which occurs when more resources are requested than are needed to do the job*, and **data manipulation,** *which occurs when managers distort or change their reported*

5 Peter F. Drucker, "Controls, Control and Management," in *Management Controls: New Dimensions in Basic Research*, Charles P. Bonini, Robert K. Jaedicke, and Harvey M. Wagner, eds., New York: McGraw-Hill Publishing, 1964: p. 294.

performance results. In the former situation, a manager will ask for more resources than are really needed to do a job. Similarly, if the results or action control measure is focused on a specific performance target, a manager will often attempt to have that measure set as low as possible.

For example, if a sales representative is asked to set a sales goal for the next year, he or she will try to set this goal low enough so that it is relatively certain the goal can be attained easily. If the firm provides bonuses for sales above the agreed-upon sales target, there is even greater incentive for the sales representative to "lowball" the sales estimate. It is, in fact, quite rational for a manager to build this buffer, which is called slack, into performance targets. Rational or not, however, slack resources translate into waste, and waste translates into lost profits. To whatever extent possible, therefore, we should try to develop measures that minimize the amount of excess slack in the system.

Data manipulation is a much more troubling form of gamesmanship. In this case, managers actually "fudge" the numbers that they report in order to make their performance look better than it actually is. Managers can either falsify their reported results or attempt to "smooth out" variation in their reported results by manipulating *when* an event is reported. For instance, the manager of a regional sales office may hold back a number of new orders received during the last few days of this month until next month because the current month's sales goals have already been met. Once the new reporting period starts, the orders are placed, providing an increased chance that sales goals will once again be met. Timely delivery of the ordered items is negatively affected, which in turn could lead to a dissatisfied customer. But? The regional sales manager will likely get a bonus, raise, or promotion for a job well done. This type of practice is known as **smoothing,** *a form of data manipulation to improve current performance by shifting when something is reported.*

If, on the other hand, the action taken by the sales manager is similar to those undertaken by Wells Fargo employees, namely that fictitious orders are entered during the last few days of the month and "canceled" at the beginning of the next month, then falsification has taken place. Why? The sale, and its associated revenues, never really existed. Records were falsified to allow the manager to record an increase in monthly sales revenues for the region, and a decrease in related inventories, when no real sale had been made. While this situation is serious enough, it is clear that falsification can be much more damaging than this simple example. One of the primary reasons companies develop internal controls is to try to detect and prevent data manipulation and related forms of undesirable behavior.

Operating delays *are waits that occur when the control measures prevent the completion of a key task or activity.* For instance, we might want to limit the access to a company's stockroom to reduce the potential for theft and inventory shrinkage. If we restrict access, then it is quite likely that somewhere downstream, a part is going to be needed when no one with the right clearances is available to get it. That means everyone will have to wait, including the customer. We have to always be aware of the fact that if we put some form of results or action control in place, it can actually make it harder for people to get their work done. Sometimes this is an unavoidable situation, in which case all attempts should be made to minimize the potential for delay. If there is another way to achieve the desired control over the process, however, it should be used. In the highly competitive global market, a company that cannot meet its customers' delivery needs may not be able to secure enough orders to survive.

Negative attitudes *are a serious dysfunctional consequence in response to an organizational control.* They can result in absenteeism, high turnover, behavior problems, sabotage, and other problems. At first it may actually seem a bit amusing to think of all of the ways that people can exhibit a negative attitude when they dislike a measure or a specific type of control. In reality, however, negative attitudes translate into inefficiencies at the least, and the potential for sabotage or worse in their extreme. People can develop a "bad attitude" when they feel the measures are imprecise or unfair, the stated goals unrealistic, or that they are being held accountable for events and outcomes they really cannot control. Once negative attitudes are created, any number of problems can arise, including the loss of key employees and damage to the firm.

Does this long list of potential side effects mean we should not use measurements in organizations, or that we should not attempt to set goals and motivate individuals to achieve them? Clearly, this is not the case. In fact, measures are essential to learning and to collaborative effort in general. What we want to do, however, is to always be aware of the fact that at the end of the day, the measures we develop will have an impact on the behavior of people. Every time we develop a measure, we should ask ourselves a very simple question: "If someone used this measure to evaluate me, what would I do and how would I feel?" While every person is clearly different, if you know that you would be tempted to do undesirable things because of the measure or how it is used, it is likely others will respond the same way. We cannot avoid all of the dysfunctional consequences of measurement, but being aware of these potential problems can help us find ways to reduce their effect.

Let us now return to Easy Air and see how Sanjiv's meeting with Fran is going before turning our attention to one specific type of measure—a cost estimate—in Chapter 3.

IN CONTEXT ➤ Easy Air: Analyzing the Results

"Fran, as you can see from Rudy's calculations, we're really looking at a mixed set of results. Revenue seat miles are up, but the remaining trends look pretty dismal. It appears that this is one of those situations where the pennies add up to a big number." Sanjiv spoke for the team.

"Rudy, although you've run some trend and variance analyses of our financial results, I still don't really understand what's happening here," Fran said. "The simple answer, of course, is that the fares are too low. On the other hand, we've attracted a lot of new customers, which is a plus if they stick with us.

"What I'd really like to know is the relationship between our costs and our operations. If we fill a plane, what is the plus and minus in terms of costs and revenues? What would happen to passenger volume if we bump our prices back up a bit? Is there waste in our system that we could eliminate to reduce costs even further and let us keep the low fares? If we had to choose, should we raise fares or cut passenger amenities? And, what does it *really* cost us to fly one more passenger? This average cost number is...well, an average that is only right if volume doesn't change...correct?"

"I don't have the answers to all those questions, Fran, but what you're implying makes sense. Sanjiv and Sherry have been working on some of those issues—right, guys?" (Rudy wanted off the hot seat, and fast.)

"Right," Sanjiv jumped in. "Sherry has been tackling the problem using incremental analysis. I've been concentrating on the nonfinancial measures, such as our on-time arrival rate problems, increases in baggage claims, and so on. You have our summary statements on these issues. We've got an interesting challenge. Our success seems to be the cause of our failures—we're running so 'hot' right now that we are making mistakes. I've documented the most common causes, and they all seem to come back to the fact that the new pricing policies have led to more transfer passengers. They are linking flights—something we never intended to support—and our processes aren't up to the challenge."

"These nonfinancial results are interesting, Sanjiv, but I think we need to look at our costs *before* we can craft a solution," Fran said.

Sherry stepped into the discussion. "Fran, we know what you mean, but we're having a hard time getting the information we need from our accounting system. In fact, I think we're going into uncharted territory here, because to answer your questions, we need to look at the interrelationships between financial and nonfinancial measures. That said, I do have some preliminary numbers."

With that, all four heads turned toward the screen on Sherry's laptop as she explained how they could break down the financials to get a better idea of how costs and profits would be affected by changes in operations, passenger volume, and fares. They decided that next week, the team would focus its attention on costs, leaving the other performance measures aside for a bit. Fran, for now, wanted an answer to what had seemed like a simple question: *How could they help Easy Air make more money?*

Summary

Measurement is one of the major ways we learn how to influence the behavior of individuals in organizations. We use measurements to learn about the firm and its goals and to track performance over time. They also help us gauge the potential impact of changes to the strategy, structure, processes, or products an organization provides to its customers. Measurements create the basis for communication of knowledge and observations, providing the foundation for the coordinated action that defines an organization.

Measurements are created to reflect a firm's vision, mission, strategy, and critical success factors (CSFs). An effective linkage between the key performance indicators (KPIs), or primary measurements, and the firm's strategy is a delimiting feature of its potential to create value for its customers and other stakeholders. Measurements convey to the individuals who work in the firm not only what is expected of them, but how their actions and efforts impact the organization as a whole.

We use measurements at all phases of the management process, from the development of initial plans through the adjustment phase. While the demands placed on a firm's measurements at each stage of the management process differ, it is important that the measures used be effectively integrated into a comprehensive set of metrics. Each measure should bear some relationship to a primary goal, or feature of the organization, that has been deemed critical to its success. Each should capture as objectively and accurately as possible the current status of the firm, as well as changes that take place over time.

We combine measurements into a series of analyses. Some of these focus on trends in performance, while others emphasize the gap between actual and planned results. It is also possible to separate the different causal factors for a performance gap using an extended variance analysis. We will get more information on detailed variance analysis in Chapter 5. For now, it is simply important to know that it is one of our key analytic tools in management accounting.

There are three main ways we can categorize a measurement: financial vs. nonfinancial; quantitative vs. qualitative; and based on whether it emphasizes action, results, or personnel controls. Regardless of what we measure, and how, there remains a strong possibility that our measurements will create various forms of dysfunctional consequences, including gamesmanship, data manipulation, operating delays, and negative attitudes. What we measure becomes visible—perceptually more important—than what is left unmeasured. Whenever we develop a measure, whether it is stated in dollars or in some other type of scale, we have to be aware that what, how, and when we measure shapes the behavior of people.

Key Terms

Action control: how work is done; it looks inside the black box to activities that lead to results.

Andon lights: visually signal trouble spots on a production line, and bring immediate attention to bear on problems, such as a lack of materials at a key assembly station.

Behavioral displacement: situations where the measures actually encourage people to do things that are not consistent with the firm's objectives.

Business case: a complete analysis of a proposed change to the company's structure, processes, or products, including financial and nonfinancial metrics, an assessment of business risk and implementation concerns, and an examination of the sensitivity of the suggested course of action to changes in assumptions.

Continuous improvement philosophy: a way of thinking that encourages individuals and organizations to seek out ways to constantly improve performance by eliminating waste and finding better methods, materials, or machines to complete work.

Control boards: visually show the progress being made against preset goals or schedules; they make discrepancies between actual vs. plan visible to everyone.

Cost-volume-profit analysis: a tool used to analyze the impact of price, cost, or volume changes on company profitability.

Creation of slack resources: a form of gamesmanship that occurs when more resources are requested than are needed to do the job.

Critical success factor: an operational or strategic objective that captures an aspect of performance vital to the firm's success.

Data manipulation: a form of gamesmanship where managers actually distort or change their reported performance results.

Dysfunctional consequences: undesirable behavior; the unintended consequence of measures taken by an organization.

Gamesmanship: when people undertake actions that are intended to improve their measured performance but that are not necessarily in the best interest of the organization.

Gap analysis: emphasizes the cumulative impact of events and outcomes to determine if any significant performance problems exist.

Goal congruence: when the firm, its other key stakeholders, and its employees have compatible goals and objectives.

Incremental analysis: examines the impact complex changes, such as structural changes, have on a firm's performance.

Jidoka: providing a machine with the independent ability to use "judgment" or intercede in the flow; defined as "autonomation."

Kanban: an in-process inventory control technique that keeps a line in balance and serves as a visual signal of problem spots that may occur during production.

Key performance indicator: a way to simply and accurately measure an individual's or unit's progress or results against a critical success factor.

Management control: all of the efforts of an organization to influence individual performance, including all of the rules, regulations, measures, and behavioral tools and techniques used to influence employee behavior in order to achieve desired results.

Management process: the continuous cycle of effort that underlies all management work; it is made up of four key activities: plan, do, check, and adjust.

Measure: a key performance indicator that has been assigned a specific definition, unit, or quantity.

Mission statement: identifies the key customer needs an organization intends to meet.

Negative attitudes: a serious dysfunctional consequence in response to an organizational control.

Operating delays: waits that occur when the control measures prevent the completion of a key task or activity.

Operational goals: define specific individual and group performance expectations for the coming day, month, or year.

Personnel/cultural controls: emphasize the role that individual and group dynamics play in influencing behavior in organizations.

Poka-yoke: a foolproof mechanism that prevents defects or machine stoppages by preventing errors at their source.

Results control: the most common form of control used in organizations; it emphasizes what is accomplished, not on how the outcomes are achieved.

Shewhart control charts: quality control tools used to verify that a process is operating within its control limits.

Smoothing: a form of data manipulation used to improve current performance by shifting when something is reported.

Standard operating procedures: action controls; work must be done in a very specific manner and sequence.

Statistical process control: uses of in-process measurements and samplings to determine whether or not a machine or process is operating within established performance limits.

Strategic objectives: provide structure to the firm's vision, translating it into specific, actionable elements; they are long-run in nature.

Tactical goals: translate strategic objectives into specific performance expectations for the next two to five years for each of the firm's primary processes and functions.

Total quality management: a management technique that seeks to eliminate defects and unnecessary variation from processes, products, and services.

Trend analysis: used to track changes over time in key performance indicators, such as net profits, revenues, number of defective units produced, on-time performance, and workforce productivity.

Variance analysis: isolates the cause of differences in a measure by focusing on one variable at a time to better understand the reasons for performance shortfalls.

Vision statement: describes the basic goals, characteristics, and philosophies that shape the strategic direction of the firm.

Questions

1. What are the primary differences between financial accounting measures and the managerial accounting measures? What is a CSF?
2. What is a KPI? How does it differ from a CSF?
3. What are the eight basic characteristics of an effective measurement?
4. How are measurements used in the management process?
5. What is a vision statement? How does it differ from a mission statement?
6. What are the three levels of objectives used by a firm and how do they differ?
7. What are the various types of action controls an organization can use? Please be as specific as you can.
8. What are the primary differences between gap analysis, trend analysis, and variance analysis?
9. What does it mean to have goal congruence in a firm?
10. What are the three different types of controls we use in business planning and analysis (BPA)?
11. Please list the various types of continuous improvement-based action controls and provide a brief description of them.
12. What does "dysfunctional consequences" mean in BPA?
13. Please list the key dysfunctional consequences of control and provide an example of each that reflects what might happen during the course of a semester.

Exercises

1. **TYPE OF CONTROL MEASURE.** Go back to the table of proposed measures for McDonald's in Table 2.3. What type of control measures are these? Please list them by type in your answer.

2. **TYPE OF CONTROL MEASURE.** For the following list of control measures, please note whether it is an action (A), results (R), or personnel (P) control.

   a. Number of exams given
   b. Instructions on how a case should be written
   c. The personality of a teacher
   d. Self-grading of quizzes
   e. The dynamics in a group project team
   f. Grades
   g. Questions at the end of chapters
   h. School spirit
   i. Directions in a problem

3. **GAP ANALYSIS.** Ernesto's Sub Shop offers six different kinds of sandwiches. Using the data below, perform a simple gap analysis of Ernesto's sales.

Type of Sub Sandwich	Planned Sales (a)	Actual Sales (b)
Italian meats	100	125
Meatball	250	300
Salami	50	25
Turkey	350	300
Tuna	300	275
Roast beef	150	200

REQUIRED:
Perform a simple gap analysis of Ernesto's sales.

4. **TREND ANALYSIS.** Using the data in Exercise 3, perform a percentage change, or trend analysis, of Ernesto's sales.

5. **GAP ANALYSIS.** Angie's Repair Shop does custom sewing repairs for customers, including sewing on buttons and putting in new zippers. Angie went to business school, so she knows that she needs to keep an eye on her sales trends. Results for October through December are listed below.

Type of Job	October Units	November Units	December Units
Sew on buttons	250	400	500
Put in new zipper	100	125	150
Hem pants	200	175	200
Hem skirt	100	80	75
Take in waistband	50	40	30
Let out waistband	50	75	100

REQUIRED:

Perform a simple gap analysis of Angie's sales.

6. **TREND ANALYSIS.** Using the data in Exercise 5, perform a percentage change, or trend analysis, of Angie's sales. Do you spot any patterns in sales?

7. **GAP ANALYSIS.** You have been hired by C&L Tools to evaluate its sales performance. You are given the following numbers for the company's four salespeople:

Salesperson	20x4	20x5	20x6
Sam Spade	$52,500	$50,500	$47,500
Lisa Williams	$65,000	$59,000	$45,000
Frank Hustler	$125,000	$115,000	$125,000
Gene Frank	$29,500	$35,000	$52,300

Perform a gap analysis for these four salespeople, using 20x6 as the starting point of your gap analysis. What would you recommend to management?

8. **DYSFUNCTIONAL CONSEQUENCES.** Adam Smith, owner of PB Manufacturing, uses one performance measure—units sold—to evaluate his sales staff. Recently he has noted that while units sold are increasing, he is actually making far less money (operating profit). What do you think is happening at PB Manufacturing? What type of dysfunctional consequence is occurring?

9. **DYSFUNCTIONAL CONSEQUENCES.** Tom Perdy works at the local insurance company, South County Insurers. The company only uses results controls. Increasingly, Sam has noticed other salespeople making special deals with customers or even cutting corners. What type of dysfunctional consequence is happening here?

10. **DYSFUNCTIONAL CONSEQUENCES.** For the following list of undesirable outcomes, please note whether it is an example of behavioral displacement (B), gamesmanship (G), operating delays (O), or negative attitudes (N).

    a. Salesman ships excess goods to a regular customer.
    b. Accounting changes the amount sold for a specific customer to get them the quantity discount.
    c. An employee sabotages the database by entering a string of fictitious customers.
    d. Employees stop in the middle of doing a job to have personal conversations.
    e. You are in a restaurant, and employees are more focused on their own conversations than on you, so you sit waiting to put in your order.
    f. A local sales manager suggests he can only sell 100 units to a customer when he knows the customer needs 150.
    g. You are in your school's records office but cannot get them to change your address because there is no procedure set up for doing so.
    h. When a hamburger is returned because it is too rare, the grill cook makes sure he burns it before it goes back out to the customer's table.

Problems

1. **VARIANCE ANALYSIS.** Using the data in the following table, do a simple variance analysis for Don's pizza shop for March. Make sure to mark your variances as favorable or unfavorable.

Measure	Plan	Actual
Number of pizzas sold	500	525
Number of grinders sold	150	120
Number of sodas sold	1,000	800
Total revenue	$8,700	$8,845
Total operating costs	$5,525	$5,600

REQUIRED:

a. What appears to be the best explanation for Don's performance?
b. What recommendations could you make to Don to help him continue to grow his business?

2. **VARIANCE ANALYSIS—PROFIT.** Eastern Productions is a medium-sized maker of promotional films and advertisements for the beverage industry. It has six salespeople on payroll. The following table shows the results against plan on two key variables: total sales and number of jobs sold. The company usually makes more money off of its larger clients as it can make multiple film clips off of the same basic footage shot. Small clients are usually "one-up" advertisements, so the entire cost of a shoot has to be absorbed in one advertisement, tending to make the job less profitable over all.

Eastern Productions				
Salesperson	Planned Dollar Sales	Actual Dollar Sales	Planned Jobs Sold	Actual Jobs Sold
Sam Sneed	$500,000	$465,000	50	75
Wendy Silversmith	$450,000	$500,000	45	40
Anne Conlon	$475,000	$525,000	50	60
James Burke	$600,000	$585,000	60	50
Frederick Thompson	$550,000	$600,000	55	45
Susan Coyle	$500,000	$575,000	50	80
Company Total	$3,075,000	$3,250,000	310	350

REQUIRED:

a. Complete a variance analysis for each salesperson in terms of dollar sales. Be sure to mark the variance as favorable or unfavorable. Who is the best performer this year? The worst performer? Why?

b. Now do a variance analysis for the number of actual vs. planned jobs sold. Given that profitability of a large job is normally greater than that of a small job, who looks like the best performer now? The worst performer? Why?
c. Divide the planned sales revenue for each salesperson by the planned number of jobs. What size job is the company targeting on average?
d. Now divide actual sales revenue for each salesperson by the actual number of jobs. Who looks like they are bringing in the more profitable jobs from this calculation? Least profitable? Why?
e. Can you easily assign favorable or unfavorable ratings to the number of jobs sold? Why or why not? In other words, how does the size and profitability of different jobs affect your answer?

3. **VARIANCE ANALYSIS—COST.** Arthur Treidmont owns a small landscaping business in the Deep South. He can work most of the year, although in summer, his workforce slows down in response to the heat index—it is simply too hot. Arthur just hired you to look at his labor costs and profits on the six jobs his company recently finished. Three of these big jobs were done in May, the other three in July and August. Use the following information to complete your analysis for Arthur.

Treidmont Landscaping				
Job Number	Month of Job	Revenue from Job	Labor Costs for Job	Other Costs for Job
15	April-May	$7,500	$3,750	$1,875
20	May	$5,000	$2,550	$1,250
23	May	$3,500	$1,925	$875
35	June	$8,000	$4,800	$2,000
38	July	$4,000	$2,800	$1,000
42	August	$2,500	$1,875	$625

REQUIRED:

a. Calculate the percentage of labor cost for each job.
b. Calculate the percentage of other costs for each job.
c. Calculate the profit per job (revenue minus costs) in dollar terms and as a percent of the total revenue.
d. What does this information tell you?

e. When Arthur plans a job, he estimates labor to be 55% of the total job cost with other costs accounting for 20%, leaving him with an expected profit of 25% of the job's revenue. Would you recommend Arthur make some changes to his planning for each job given the results of your analysis? What changes would you recommend? Why?

f. Landscaping is a very competitive business. If your answer to part (d) was to raise prices, are you at all concerned that Arthur may lose more business? In other words, are there other things he could do to ensure profitability on a job?

4. **VARIANCE ANALYSIS—COST.** Free and Easy, a local window-cleaning operation, has been having trouble maintaining its profitability. The company president, June Williams, has asked you to come in and help her identify why she is missing her profit goals. She plans for labor to be 50% of the job's cost, supplies 15%, and "overhead" (the ladders, and so forth) at 5%, leaving her with a 20% profit per job. She gives you the following information on her six representative jobs:

Free and Easy Window Cleaning				
Job Number	**Job Price**	**Labor**	**Supplies**	**Overhead**
15	$500.00	$255.00	$75.00	$27.50
18	$375.00	$225.00	$52.50	$20.63
25	$250.00	$155.00	$30.00	$13.75
32	$300.00	$174.00	$39.00	$16.50
35	$450.00	$234.00	$67.50	$24.75
40	$600.00	$288.00	$108.00	$33.00

REQUIRED:

a. Calculate the percentage of labor cost for each job.
b. Calculate the percentage of supply costs for each job.
c. Calculate the percentage of actual overhead for each job.
d. Calculate the profit per job (revenue minus costs) in dollar terms and as a percent of the total revenue.
e. What does this information tell you?
f. What would you recommend to June? Is her answer in changing her prices or changing how she runs her business? Why?

5. **SHEWHART CONTROL CHARTS.** Basic Manufacturing, a maker of hose fittings, uses point of action controls on the plant floor to help its workforce stay on target to continuously improve performance. Two measures are made for each hose fitting made: circumference of fitting and thickness of the threads, which screw on to a hose to make a leakproof fitting. The circumference is targeted for 1.25 inches with an upper allowable size of 1.3 inches and a lower allowable size of 1.2 inches. The thickness of the threads is targeted for 0.2 inches with an upper limit of 0.21 inches and a lower limit of 0.19 inches. The table below has the actual measured circumference and thread thickness for the day's production.

Basic Manufacturing		
Circumference of Fitting		
Time of Sampling	**Circumference of Fitting**	**Size of Fitting Threads**
7:55 a.m.	1.250	0.213
9 a.m.	1.275	0.202
10:15 a.m.	1.283	0.201
12 p.m.	1.357	0.195
12:45 p.m.	1.262	0.201
1:30 p.m.	1.215	0.205
2:30 p.m.	1.191	0.211

REQUIRED:

a. Make a Shewhart control chart for the circumference variable. Plot each of the observations on your control chart by time.

b. Make a Shewhart control chart for the size of the threads variable. Again, plot each observation by time.

c. Right now, Basic only resets the calibration on its machines at the start of the day and at lunchtime. Given the results from your control charts, do you feel it should recalibrate the machines more regularly or stop the line whenever the observation falls out of range to adjust the machines? Why?

6. **SHEWHART CONTROL CHARTS.** Singleterry Products makes rods and piston housings for various types of motors. Having a perfect fit is critical if an engine is going to work properly and not leak oil. If it is too tight a fit, the rod will wear down the piston housing, causing early failure (freezing up) of the engine. If the fit is too loose, oil leaks and

compression is lost. For one model of rod and piston housing, the circumference of the rod needs to be 0.495 inches, while the circumference of the piston housing needs to be 0.5 inches to ensure a perfect fit. These measures can only vary by 0.005 or leaving a gap of 0.005 between the rod and piston housing circumferences. The gap can only be between 0.004 and 0.007 before problems occur. The company uses Shewhart control charts to keep track of this vital characteristic of its rods and pistons. The data collected on the line yesterday is contained in the table below.

Singleterry Products			
Time of Sample	**Rod Circumference**	**Piston Housing Circumference**	**Gap**
7 a.m.	0.495	0.500	0.005
8 a.m.	0.495	0.502	0.007
9 a.m.	0.496	0.508	0.012
10 a.m.	0.498	0.512	0.014
11 a.m.	0.495	0.495	0.000
12:30 p.m.	0.494	0.505	0.011
1:30 p.m.	0.487	0.512	0.025
2:30 p.m.	0.482	0.515	0.033

REQUIRED:

a. Make a Shewhart control chart for the circumference variable. Plot each of the observations on your control chart by time.
b. Make a Shewhart control chart for the size of the piston housing circumference variable. Again plot each observation by time.
c. Make a Shewhart control chart for the size of the gap, again plotting each observation by time.
d. When should Singleterry shut down the line and make adjustments? Specifically, should it focus on only one of these metrics, and if so, which one is critical? Why?

7. **TYPES OF MEASUREMENTS.** Ajax Programming does freelance programming jobs, including blog and website design, for a wide variety of businesses and individual consumers. The company has grown from a simple start-up with only its two founders, Jim and Kenny Phillips, to a firm of more than 20 full-time employees. Recently it has noticed that the profitability of jobs is falling off and that individual customers are beginning to

complain about the attitudes of the firm's employees. To date, Ajax has used no type of control outside of trusting its employees to do the right thing. Now, however, it looks like it needs help if it is to get the business back on track.

REQUIRED:

a. What type of measurement is the company relying on right now to run the business?
b. Can you develop several action controls that might help the company out?
c. On the other hand, results measures might be more useful. Can you suggest two or three potential results measures?
d. Is it a foregone conclusion that the bigger a firm gets, the more it needs results controls? Why or why not?
e. What would you recommend to Jim and Kenny as they ponder the next wave of growth in their business? Please draft a one- to two-paragraph memo to Jim and Kenny with your recommendations.

8. **TYPE OF MEASUREMENTS.** Rapid Car Wash is a franchiser of car wash companies across the northeastern United States. It has grown from simply owning one car wash to now having more than 100 franchisees. Lately, top management has been getting complaints from customers about the cleanliness of their cars after the car wash, the cost of the car wash, and the attitude of employees. Rapid does not directly own 99 of the 100 shops bearing its name, but these results can clearly damage the reputation of the franchise and hurt good and bad franchisees alike.

Robert Kingsley, owner of Rapid Car Wash, has asked you to come in and make some recommendations about how he can use different types of controls to ensure more consistent performance. He does not have a vision or mission statement, so you are going to have to dig deep to help him out.

REQUIRED:

a. What type of measurement is the company relying on right now to run the business?
b. Can you develop several action controls that might help the company?
c. On the other hand, results measures might be more useful. Can you suggest two or three potential results measures?
d. Do you think Rapid Car Wash is too large to rely on personnel and action controls? Why or why not?
e. What would you recommend to Robert as he thinks about the next wave of growth in his business? In other words, do you think he can continue on without a

mission statement, vision statement, and strategic plan even though he does not directly own and operate 99% of the business? Please draft a one- to two-paragraph memo to Robert with your recommendations.

9. **DYSFUNCTIONAL CONSEQUENCES.** Janice Dean teaches several accounting classes at Blankton State University. She has always relied on her syllabus and its honor code to regulate the behavior of her students. Over the past few years, however, Janice has faced greater and greater obstacles and problems, including student collusion on assignments, attempted hacking of her computer to get at the grading files, and in general poor performance against her preset learning goals. Janice is not very detail-oriented when it comes to writing instructions for individual assignments and exams, but she always states her expectations when she starts the semester. She has also been known to lose her temper with students and classes when they do not meet her expectations.

REQUIRED:

a. What type of controls is Janice using in her class?
b. What types of dysfunctional behavior is resulting?
c. What other types of problems may Janice face moving forward given how she is handling her classes?
d. What would you recommend that Janice do to change the dynamics of her classroom and regain control (for example, achievement of learning objectives)?

10. **DYSFUNCTIONAL CONSEQUENCES.** Bryan Owens is a part-time manager at Rusty's Steak House. The owner of Rusty's spends his time split between Rusty's and three other restaurants he owns, so he has to rely on his managers to keep his restaurants operating successfully. To keep track of things, Rusty uses the same set of monthly performance measures for every manager. They are:

Goal	Measure
Profitable operations	Sales per hour
Growth in total customers	Total customers served
Minimal customer complaints	Number of customer complaints
High average order size	Average size of bill
High % repeat customers	Number of customers known by name

Lately, Bryan has noticed that the other managers are leaving him with a messy restaurant and kitchen. Bryan is very conscientious, so he ends up having his employees spending more time cleaning than performing some of the other "jobs" around the restaurant, such as chatting with customers. He knows it is important to have customer loyalty, but he just cannot stand a dirty restaurant. The other managers are doing far better on profitability, number of customers served, high bills, and repeat customers. Bryan is doing better on complaints.

REQUIRED:

a. **Analyze the operations at Rusty's Steak House. What type of measurements is he using?**
b. **What dysfunctional consequences are present in the company?**
c. **What would you recommend Rusty do to ensure that all five measures are met by all of his managers? In other words, should he fire Bryan or promote him?**

Database Problems

For database templates, worksheets, and workbooks, go to MAdownloads.imanet.org

DB 2.1 PROFITABILITY USING VARIOUS METRICS. In Chapters 1 and 2, we have only had Easy Air's profits in terms of revenue miles flown. Now we would like to expand this analysis to look at profitability both in terms of number of passengers flown and number of flights flown. To do this, let us use the Easy Air database and solution templates.

Using the Excel worksheet titled Summary Easy Air and Template for DB 2.1.

- First, fill in the first three rows of the template by calculating the average revenue, expense, and profit based on revenue per passenger miles flown for the years 20x4 to 20x6.
- Repeat these calculations for the next three rows of the worksheet using the number of flights as your divisor.
- For the last three rows of the worksheet, repeat the calculation of average revenue, expense, and profit using the number of passengers flown as your divisor.

REQUIRED:

a. **Turn in your worksheet to your instructor.**
b. **Given this information, do you see any trends in overall profitability? What are they?**
c. **Which of these measures do you like the best? Why?**

DB 2.2 EVALUATING PLANNED PERFORMANCE. Easy Air has put in place some very difficult or "stretch" goals for the upcoming year, as the table recreated from the chapter indicates.

Performance Indicator	20x7 Plan	20x6 Actuals
Total flights flown	3,932,764	3,575,240
Total passengers flown	410,706,410	373,369,464
Total revenue seat miles flown (in thousands)	62,566,454	54,405,612
Average miles per passenger flight	270	265
Total operating revenue (in thousands)	$10,419,762.8	$9,303,359.7
Total operating expenses (in thousands)	$9,877,932.3	$8,899,038.1
Operating profit (in thousands)	$541,830.5	$404,321.6
Average revenue per revenue seat mile flown	$0.167	$0.171
Average expense per revenue seat mile flown	$0.158	$0.164
Average profit per revenue seat mile flown	$0.009	$0.007
Average revenue per flight	$2,649.48	$2,602.16
Average expense per flight	$2,511.70	$2,489.07
Average profit per flight	$137.77	$113.09
Average load factor (% seats filled per flight)	85.70%	85.6%
Average on-time performance rating	95%	88.5%
Number of baggage claims	187,650	250,200
Number of customer complaints	228,060	380,100
Number of ground/gate delays	2,280	3,800
Number of canceled flights	1,069	1,425

REQUIRED:

a. Using the data above, as recreated for you in the Easy Air template titled DB 2.2, calculate the absolute (for example, actual size) of change in performance expected.

b. Now use your results from (a) to calculate the percentage change. Remember to use 20x6 as the denominator in your Excel equation.

Turn in your completed worksheets and also answer the following two questions.

c. Do you think all of these planned results are attainable? Specifically, which ones do you think they can meet and which look difficult if not impossible to attain?

d. For those you feel are difficult to attain, please explain why you feel this way.

DB 2.3 DEGREE OF CHANGE. You have just been hired as an intern by Easy Air and have been assigned to Sanjiv to help him with the major analysis of Easy Air's operational and profit performance. As a first part of the task, Sanjiv asks you to do a trend (for example, degree of change, both magnitude and percentage) for all of the performance measurements in Easy Air's database. These figures are included in the following table (see Summary Easy Air facts and solution template DB 2.3a and DB 2.3b in the workbook for this problem):

Summary of Easy Air's Performance 20x4-20x6

Performance Indicator	20x6	20x5	20x4
Total flights flown	3,575,240	3,489,434	3,297,515
Total passengers flown	373,369,464	363,557,175	342,354,639
Total revenue seat miles flown (in thousands)	54,405,612	53,796,413	48,215,413
Available seat miles (in thousands)	$63,557,958	$62,993,458	$56,657,360
Average miles per passenger flight	265	260	233
Number of stations	120	112	106
Total operating revenue (in thousands)	$9,303,359.7	$9,521,965.1	$9,112,713.1
Total operating expenses (in thousands)	$8,899,038.1	$8,536,503.9	$7,430,858.9
Operating profit (in thousands)	$404,321.6	$985,461.2	$1,681,854.1
Average revenue per revenue seat mile flown	$0.171	$0.177	$0.189
Average expense per revenue seat mile flown	$0.164	$0.159	$0.154
Average profit per revenue seat mile flown	$0.007	$0.018	$0.035
Average load factor (% seats filled per flight)	85.6%	85.4%	85.1%

Summary of Easy Air's Performance 20x4-20x6			
Performance Indicator	**20x6**	**20x5**	**20x4**
Average on-time performance rating	88.5%	92.5%	95.3%
Number of baggage claims	250,200	179,100	155,800
Number of customer complaints	380,100	295,300	245,500
Number of ground/gate delays	3,800	2,100	1,800
Number of canceled flights	1,425	950	600

REQUIRED:

a. Using the Easy Air database templates for this problem, calculate the magnitude of change for each of Easy Air's performance measures.
b. Using the corresponding worksheet titled DB 2.3 template, calculate the percentage change for each year. Make 20x6 your base year and work backward in time.
c. Turn in your completed worksheets and then answer the following three questions:
d. What do the trend numbers suggest? Make sure to pay attention to both the magnitude and percentage change numbers in crafting your answer.
e. What would you recommend to Sanjiv? Why?
f. What other information would you like to have? Why?

Cases

CASE 2.1 EVALUATING ACTUAL AND PLANNED PERFORMANCE. Returning to Sam's Golf Pro Shop in the chapter, Sam really wants to hone in on what part of his sales package is working and what is not. In talking about it, Sam notes, "The easiest solution would be to hire a golf pro and put in a few more tees on the driving range. But these are costs it won't be easy to justify if I don't get both individual and group classes going strong. I also have to use the push from these activities to make sure that I get more merchandise sales, because a pro shop with dusty, out-of-date merchandise won't help anyone out. I need a more comprehensive plan."

To help do further analysis, Sam has pulled together actual unit sales in each of the categories of revenue (merchandise sales, instructional sales, driving range revenues) that he relies upon to make his business grow. These numbers are in the following table.

Sam's Golf Pro Shop		
Measure	**Plan**	**Actual**
Number of sets of golf clubs sold	50	40
Number of packages of golf balls sold	1,000	1,200
Number of golf gloves sold	250	225
Number of bags of tees sold	1,500	1,600
Number of hours of private instruction	320	400
Number of golf classes given	80	65
Number of golf sweaters sold	75	100
Number of golf jackets sold	40	50
Number of driving range buckets of balls sold	6,500	8,000
Total revenues from merchandise	$40,750.00	$38,650.00
Total revenues from instruction	$23,200.00	$23,750.00
Total revenues from driving range	$32,500.00	$40,000.00
Total cost of goods sold	$22,445.00	$27,055.00
Total operating costs	$38,580.00	$35,840.00
Operating profit	$35,425.00	$39,505.00

Sam needs some help in analyzing his results. Specifically, he wants to try to separate the causes for his gains and losses in the various categories of value-creating efforts he makes for his clients.

REQUIRED:

a. **Complete a total gap and trend analysis for Sam's business. Pay particular attention to sales trends that fall in the same revenue category but move in different ways.**
b. **What would you recommend to Sam?**
c. **Craft a two- to three-paragraph recommendation to Sam, including your views on whether he should hire a golf pro that would cost him $60,000 a year if this golf pro could improve both individual and group class quantities and all of the related merchandise and driving range revenues. Remember, if he hires a golf pro, he will have to add more tees to his driving range at the cost of $500 per tee. Factor these tees, which last a long time, into your assessed impact on Sam's**

business this year. Assume that merchandise sales will go up by 20%, number of private instruction hours will increase to 1,000, number of classes taught will increase to 250, and number of buckets of golf balls sold will increase by 40%. He will need to add six tees to the driving range if he hires the pro.

CASE 2.2 DYSFUNCTIONAL CONSEQUENCES. Marty Smith recently graduated from college. He has been hired by Stevenson Associates as a sales associate. Stevenson provides payroll services for a broad range of manufacturing and service companies throughout the southeastern United States.

Marty has never set his own sales goals, but, regardless of his inexperience, management expects him to do so. Specifically, he has to estimate both the number of new jobs he will attain for the company as well as the total revenue these clients will represent over a year's time frame.

Unclear about what to do, Marty turns for help to Sam White, one of the younger sales associates. Sam shares with Marty his own plan for the year, noting that he derived it by looking at last year's sales and then adding the minimum amount he thought he could get by with as a sales increase. Marty decides that sounds reasonable, but decides that since he is new, he will make some estimates off of Marty's sales from last year. Marty really needs the bonus he will get if he does better than his sales projections, so he does not want to set the bar too high.

After all of the sales associates have put in their projections, managers compile the data to see what the total sales of the company will be. When they are done, they are not happy. Even though they have hired three new sales associates over the last year, the total increase in sales is minimal. They know that the results need to be better than this if the firm is to make its growth goals, so they send a memo to all of the sales associates asking them to raise their projections by 5% and resubmit their sales plan.

Marty is worried because he does not really know how much he can sell. He does not want to add the 5%, but since he went low in his first estimates, he decides he really does not have a choice. That said, he manipulates the figures in such a way that he still feels he can make the goals by focusing on getting smaller jobs, so he can beat at least the number of new clients goal. He knows bigger jobs are more profitable for Stevenson Associates, but, after all, it is his bonus that matters most to him.

Listening at the lunch table, Marty finds out all of the sales associates are unhappy with the need to raise their goals 5%. Most worried of all is Sam White, who used last year's record actual sales as the baseline to set new sales goals. The older sales associates simply smile, telling Marty to never use his best year as the baseline, as he will have a very difficult time beating these aggressive goals and getting his bonus. Mark Williams goes so far as to say that he put off reporting some December sales so he could keep this year's goals lower and have a cushion to start the year. Marty is amazed at the number of ways the older associates have found to keep their goals down and bonuses up. It gives him a lot to think about, and worry about, since he used Sam's sales as a starting point.

REQUIRED:

Discuss the various types of dysfunctional behavior that are taking place at Stevenson Associates. What should management do to change these dynamics?

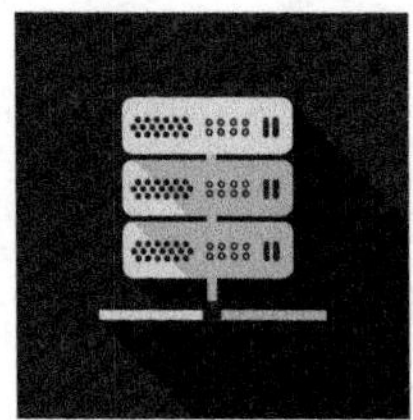

Defining and Using Cost Estimates

All business proceeds on beliefs, or judgments of probabilities, and not on certainties.
CHARLES ELIOT[1]

CHAPTER ROADMAP

1. **Cost Measurement: Basic Concepts**
   - *Direct and Indirect Costs*
   - *Different Costs for Different Purposes*
2. **The Behavior of Costs**
   - *Fixed, Variable, and Mixed Costs*
   - *Estimating Average Costs*
   - *Stepped Costs and the Relevant Range*
3. **Cost-Volume-Profit Analysis**
   - *The Basic CVP Formula*
   - *The Variable Cost Income Statement and Operating Leverage*
   - *Using CVP to Improve Profit Performance*
   - *Expanding the Basic CVP Formula*
   - *Multiple Product CVP*
4. **Building an Effective Business Case**

LEARNING OBJECTIVES

After studying this chapter, you should be able to:

1. **Understand the basic concept of cost.**
2. **Describe and apply the four basic forms of cost behavior and use them to build a variable cost income statement.**
3. **Apply CVP to identify the impact of potential changes in price, costs, or volume on a firm's profitability.**
4. **Explain how to build an effective business case.**

1 *The Forbes Scrapbook of Thoughts on the Business of Life*, Chicago: Triumph Books, 1992: p. 25.

IN CONTEXT ➤ Developing and Using Cost Estimates at Easy Air—Part 1

Sanjiv and the business analysis team were getting a lot done. They had met Fran's first set of demands for information on nonfinancial performance measures and related problems a week ago, only to have her insist that they also get a handle on current financial results (or lack of same) and the implications of various changes on these results. They needed to develop a complete set of cost estimates.

Looking up from her computer, Sherry said, "I'm trying to set up some worksheets to get us started."

"What have you got? Fran wants to know what it costs us to serve a customer. I think we could just divide the major expenses by the number of passengers and be done with it, but you don't seem to think so. So, what's the alternative?" Rudy asked.

"Rudy, you know as well as I do that an average cost doesn't tell us very much," Sherry said. "If the information we provide is going to help Fran and the management group make decisions, we must have some idea of how much our costs will change if we have more or fewer passengers, or more or less flights. Not all of our operating costs will change if we make adjustments. Some will, some won't...don't you think?"

"I do, but how are we going to figure that out? I know our general ledger inside and out, and it's not going to help us," Rudy said. "We can see *what we spent* on different resources, but *not why we spent it*. And, if the total expense for something, fuel for example, changes, we can't really tell if that was because prices went up, usage went up, or both."

"Sanjiv, didn't you tell us yesterday that Fritz Mueller has been collecting some new kinds of financial information that looks at issues like these?" Sherry asked. "Since one definition of insanity is 'doing the same thing over and over and expecting different results,' it might be a good idea to meet with him and see what he's doing."

"Okay, I'll give Fritz a call," said Sanjiv. "Fran said we could use anyone we needed, and it'll be good to get a new set of eyes on the issues. I'll call him now and see when he can meet with us."

COST IS AN INTERESTING CONCEPT. WE ALL USE THE TERM, ASSUMING THAT everyone knows what we mean. In one respect they do—anyone hearing us say the word "cost" conjures up a picture of someone paying money to purchase a product or service. In fact, the dictionary states that a cost is "the price paid or charged for something."[2] In a business, **cost** *is the economic value of resources consumed in making a product, process, or completing an activity*. Cost provides the basis for understanding the relationship between the resources used to provide a product or

2 *The New Webster's Dictionary of the English Language*, New York: Delair Publishing Co., Inc., 1981: p. 361.

service to customers and the value placed on this output by customers. It plays a key role in defining both the price and profit the product or service commands in the competitive marketplace. **Value** *is the worth of the product or service to the customer.* If the value to the customer is less than the cost of making the product or providing the service, then no viable business opportunity exists. **Price** *is what a seller charges the customer.* The seller will make a **profit** *when the price is greater than the cost*. Value sets an upper bound on the price that can be charged because no customer will be willing to pay more for a product than what it is worth to them.

Some people assume that costs and prices are closely linked. Here are some common quotations: "Prices can be cut if you cut cost," "Prices are controlled by what it costs to make a product, and this changes regularly," and "Lowering costs helps lower prices, which is important in fighting off competition."[3]

In competitive markets, there is the potential for a linkage between cost and price. If costs rise, then prices might also rise if the companies selling in that market wish to continue making a profit. But this generally accepted relationship between cost and price may not be accurate in all cases. What is increasingly evident is that customers *do not care* what it costs a company to make a product or provide a service. They are willing to buy a product or use a service if it is available at a price at or below the value they place on it.

Companies are able to choose what products or services they will offer customers, what features these products or services will have, and what type and amount of resources they will use to provide these product or service features. Customers decide whether or not they will buy the product or service offered to them at the stated price. Even if a company is a price setter in its industry, it is going to have to know its costs and keep them below its customer-defined market price if it wants to make a profit.

A price setter either has a large market share advantage over competitors or provides a highly differentiated product that is hard to duplicate. OPEC serves as a price setter for crude oil, using production output as a competitive weapon to manipulate world oil supply and pricing. As oil prices rose in 2014 and 2015, non-OPEC companies began using new methods such as fracking to produce more oil domestically in the United States. Faced with this challenge to its dominant role in the crude oil marketplace, OPEC radically increased production in late 2015 and early 2016, flooding the market with its high-quality crude oil and driving the price per barrel down to a low of $26.50 in January 2016. Comparatively, barrel prices in October 2015 and October 2016 were $45.02 and $47.87, respectively. This aggressive action by OPEC effectively made fracking unprofitable, reducing the viability of this technology.

While understanding cost does not equate to making a profit, companies that have a solid understanding of the relationship between their costs, prices, and profits consistently outperform those that lack this basic knowledge. Southwest Airlines is a good example of a company that has been able to turn a profit even in the face of national and economic crises in the early 21st Century. Knowing its costs, Southwest Airlines established its routes to maximize customer load, which allowed the company to offer reduced fares, free checked baggage, and great customer service. Figure 3.1 details the routes served by Southwest in 2016. Carefully chosen and managed to maximize overall profitability, Southwest constantly

3 Joe Griffith, *Speaker's Library of Business Stories, Anecdotes and Humor*, Englewood Cliffs, N.J.: Prentice-Hall, 1990: p. 270.

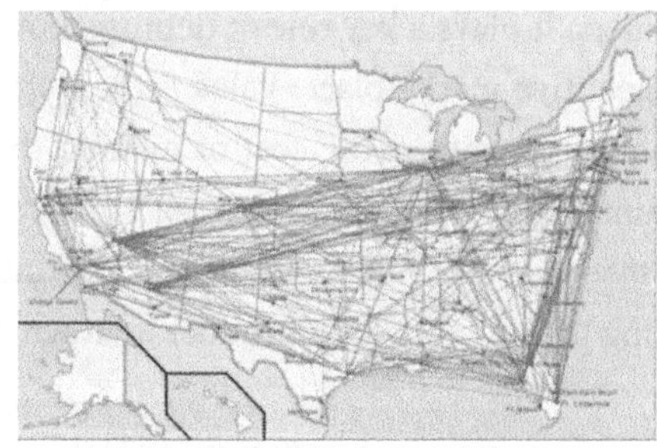

FIGURE 3.1 SOUTHWEST AIRLINES ROUTE MAP: ROUTES WERE DESIGNED TO INCREASE PROFITABILITY

reviews both the routes flown as well as the number and frequency of flights on each route. With a sound understanding of the cost to operate a single flight, including both ground operations and the cost of the flight itself (airplane, crew, fuel, and snack service), Southwest is able to set and manage prices to ensure both high ridership and sustainable profitability.

In this chapter, we will explore the basic issues that shape our concepts of what a cost is. As we will see, it can be quite challenging to define and measure cost in the dynamic, interdependent world of modern business.

Cost Measurement: Basic Concepts

OBJECTIVE 1
Understand the basic concept of cost.

One of the key elements in gaining an understanding of cost management is getting comfortable with developing a reasonably accurate and reliable **cost estimate,** *the evaluation of the resources used in providing a product or service*. There are no hard or fast rules—only common sense—to guide this effort. At its very heart, however, costing comes down to one simple formula that compares the resources a firm uses with the outcomes those resources produce. This relationship is captured in the basic equation:

$$\text{Cost} = \frac{\text{Dollars}}{\text{Activity}}$$

An example of an activity that might be used in a cost estimate is the number of revenue miles flown (RSM) in a year by an airline, such as Southwest Airlines. RSM is one of the most common output measures reported by all airlines in their annual report and filings to the Bureau of Transportation. While it might seem logical to use cost per passenger, in reality the majority of costs for operating an airplane, such as fuel, are driven by the miles flown. The cost per RSM, therefore, is one way we can use the basic cost formula to gain an understanding of an airline's cost performance. This calculation is captured in Table 3.1 for Southwest Airlines for 2012 to 2015. The cost equation, therefore, results in a performance measure that can be used to:

- Understand the efficiency and effectiveness of an organization
- Project future resource requirements and profitability

- Assess the desirability of different options and alternative solutions to business opportunities and challenges
- Evaluate performance

Typically this formula is used to develop an estimate of costs. A cost estimate is a number that is seen as having more relevance and merit than an opinion or judgment because it is stated in precise, measurable terms. As any knowledgeable cost analyst will attest, however, a cost estimate is just that: a calculation that is based on assumptions and beliefs that may be as much fiction as fact.

TABLE 3.1 COST PER REVENUE MILE FLOWN FOR SOUTHWEST AIRLINES

	2015	2014	2013	2012
Operating Expenses (millions)	$15,704.00	$16,380.00	$16,421.00	$16,465.00
Revenue Passenger Miles (RPM; millions)*	117,499.88	108,035.13	104,348.22	102,874.98
Operating Cost per RPM	$0.134	$0.152	$0.157	$0.160

*RPM is the number of miles the airline flew its fare-paying passengers in a year. It is a standard measure of output activity in the airline industry. The data in this table was reported in Southwest Airlines' published annual report for 2015.

When we develop a cost estimate, our goal is to define and populate the basic cost equation in such a way that it provides an accurate snapshot of the organization and the way it consumes resources in the process of creating value for its customers. While simple in concept, the underlying dynamics of creating a reliable cost estimate can prove to be quite challenging. The challenge begins with the first step we take in developing a cost estimate: tying the use of resources to the activities and outputs that consume them.

DIRECT AND INDIRECT COSTS

Costing practices are shaped by the needs of the organization and its decision makers, but constrained by the nature of the resources it has at its command. Attaching resources to activities and outcomes is relatively straightforward when there is a direct link between the resource and its use. For instance, when a bakery makes a loaf of bread, the eggs, yeast, and flour are all resources that are used specifically to make that loaf of bread and no others. When this clear relationship between a resource and an outcome exists, it is called a **direct cost,** *a cost that can be uniquely assigned to a specific outcome or activity*.

If you think about Southwest Airlines, what resources do you think are *direct* to serving one passenger? The snacks and beverages consumed in flight are an example of a direct cost, as are a small amount of fuel (based on the passenger's weight), a boarding pass, and possibly a baggage tag. If we tally up all of these direct resource costs, we still would not have accounted for very much of Southwest's total costs. In fact, Southwest Airlines, like most organizations, has far more shared resources than direct ones.

When a resource is shared by two or more activities or outcomes, it is called an **indirect cost,** *a cost that is not traceable to a specific output or activity, but is shared by two or more outcomes or activities*. The airplane itself is an indirect cost in the context of serving one passenger, as are the flight attendants, the pilots, and the airport services such as checking in passengers, enplaning and deplaning passengers, fueling the plane, and handling baggage. We may be able to estimate some portion of baggage handling, for instance, as direct to one bag (the labor involved), but the carts that are used to move the bags around on the tarmac are indirect costs because they are shared many times over by multiple customers.

DIFFERENT COSTS FOR DIFFERENT PURPOSES

We have looked at cost from the standpoint of how the underlying resources are consumed. There is another way to look at resource costs—in terms of how they are used by organizations, as suggested by J.M. Clark in this chapter's "Looking Back" feature.

LOOKING BACK ➤ Demystifying the Terminology of Cost

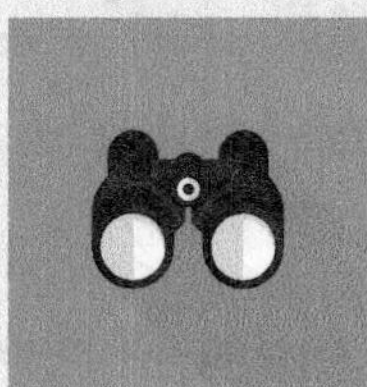

J.M. Clark, an economist in the early 1900s, had a good handle on the phenomenon we call cost, as the following quotations suggest.

"We may start with the general proposition that the terminology of costs is in a state of much confusion and that it is impossible to solve this confusion by discovering and adopting the one correct usage, because there is no one correct usage, usage being governed by the varying needs of varying business situations and problems..."

"...To sum up, the demands made upon cost accounting may be roughly catalogued under the following ten functions: (1) to help determine a normal or satisfactory price for goods sold; (2) to help fix a minimum limit on price-cutting; (3) to determine which goods are most profitable and which are unprofitable; (4) to control inventory; (5) to set a value on inventory; (6) to test the efficiency of different processes; (7) to test the efficiency of different departments; (8) to detect losses, wastes, and pilfering; (9) to separate the 'cost of idleness' from the cost of producing goods; and (10) to 'tie in' with the financial accounts."

"...It is apparent...that the purposes of cost analysis require a number of different conceptions and measures of cost, and the natural result is a plea for the development of a sufficiently varied technique to satisfy these quite independent requirements."

J.M. Clark, *The Economics of Overhead Costs*, Chicago: The University of Chicago Press, 1935: pp. 175, 234, 257.

Direct and indirect costs are one of the major categories of cost. That said, there are actually a significant number of adjectives we can put in front of the word "cost" that shift the focus and, at times, meaning of this basic term. Table 3.2 offers some simple definitions of some of the more common cost categories.

TABLE 3.2 RESOURCE COSTS AND HOW THEY ARE USED

Type of Cost	Definition
Product cost	A cost that can be directly tied to making a product—it is a cost that can be used to place a value on finished goods inventory.
Period cost	A cost that is incurred every period (normally per month) regardless of whether or not the company is open for business. It is a resource that is depleted over time; for example, the rent for an office building is a period expense.
Manufacturing cost	A cost incurred in manufacturing companies that can be directly tied to making the product they sell.
Nonmanufacturing cost	A cost incurred in manufacturing companies that cannot be directly tied to making the product.
Material costs	The costs for the raw materials used in making a product.
Labor costs	All of the labor expenses directly traceable to making a product or providing a service.
Overhead cost	The sum of all of the indirect costs of making a product or providing a service; for example, the salary paid to the plant or office manager.

Table 3.3 details the product costs for a typical airline, such as Southwest Airlines, for one customer. As you see, even in an airline, the total cost incurred to serve one customer on a specific flight includes materials, labor, and overhead costs.

TABLE 3.3 ESTIMATED COSTS PER CUSTOMER FLOWN

Cost Element	Materials	Labor	Overhead
Baggage tag	$0.03 per passenger		
Boarding passes	$0.05 per passenger		
Peanuts	$0.05 per passenger		
Beverages	$0.20 per passenger		
Baggage handling		$5.00 per passenger	
Check-in activities		$5.00 per passenger	
Boarding/deplaning aircraft		$1.50 per passenger	
Serving beverages and snacks		$1.00 per passenger	
Other flight attendant activities		$4.00 per passenger	
Pilot and co-pilot		$7.50 per passenger	

Cost Element	Materials	Labor	Overhead
Jet fuel		$8.00 per passenger	$7,500 per flight
Plane depreciation			$1,250 per flight
Takeoff and landing fees			$1,500 per flight
Gate charges			$500 per flight
Airport security surcharges			$1,250 per flight
TOTAL	**$0.33 per Passenger**	**$32.00 per Passenger**	**$12,000 per Flight**

Assuming one checked bag per passenger, we see materials amounting to $0.33 per passenger, labor costing $32 per passenger, and overhead, which we cannot charge directly to a passenger, at $12,000 per flight. The materials and labor can be charged directly to a passenger, while overhead is indirect to each passenger. Overhead is caused by the fact that we fly the plane, not how many passengers are on it. We see one cost—fuel—which has both a direct part based on passenger weight and an indirect part due to the weight of the plane and the activities required for it to fly. Many resource costs are split in this manner. The goal is to trace as many dollars of cost into direct costs as possible. Overhead is more difficult to control as it has many causes and many people responsible for incurring and controlling this element cost.

We can combine these product costs together to get two more types of cost: **prime cost,** *the sum of materials and labor used to make a product*, and **conversion cost,** *the total direct labor and overhead costs used to turn raw materials into finished goods*. These are useful numbers when we are trying to find the best overhead approach, because, once we calculate it, we can shift our focus to the impact of the various methods available for calculating overhead costs per unit made or service provided. Why do we use all of these terms? Because they make the costing exercise clearer—we know why we are summing certain costs together. It is truly a situation where we use different definitions of resource costs for different types of purposes.

For instance, Southwest Airlines would use one definition of baggage handling costs, specifically direct cost, when it is estimating the costs to service one passenger using existing employees, materials, methods, and equipment. On the other hand, if Southwest Airlines was doing an analysis of a potential decision to implement a bar coding system for baggage handling that would reduce errors, the focus would not be on the direct cost per passenger, but rather the **incremental costs,** *the new costs caused by the decision*. Would the decision to implement bar coding for baggage handling ultimately affect the direct cost per customer served? It would, but the impact would have to also be analyzed incrementally, including both the costs of the bar coding system, disposal costs for any equipment or material that would no longer be needed, the potential reduction in baggage handling labor costs, the reduction in all of the costs caused by dealing with lost baggage and customer complaints, and the potential improvement in the number of passengers choosing to fly Southwest because it has improved this important component of its service.

So when we say that we use different costs for different purposes, we are drawing attention to the fact that as we change the decision or analysis that we are doing, the costs that are relevant to us change correspondingly. While we would include the cost for dealing with lost baggage if we are deciding whether or not to implement a bar coding system because these costs are affected by the decision, we would not bundle these costs in our estimate for how much it costs, on average, to correctly handle one customer's bag. In the former case, lost baggage costs are relevant to the decision; in the latter case, they are irrelevant because they will not be changed by correctly servicing one passenger more or less.

The Behavior of Costs

OBJECTIVE 2

Describe and apply the four basic forms of cost behavior and use them to build a variable cost income statement.

When J.M. Clark talked about different costs for different purposes, therefore, he was suggesting that, as we change the questions we ask, we change the relevance of one resource cost estimate vs. another. Understanding the impact on a resource cost estimate of changing assumptions about the amount of work that needs to be done or the way the work is completed is an integral part of the notion of "different costs for different purposes." We now turn our attention to this question of how costs respond when we change the amount of work that is being done.

FIXED, VARIABLE, AND MIXED COSTS

There are two primary ways that we think about changes in costs: variability and avoidability. **Cost variability** *is how costs change in response to changes in the volume of work.* **Cost avoidability** *is focused on whether one or more costs will go away totally if we discontinue making a specific product or providing a specific service.* Let us see how these types of costs respond to the decisions made in a very common type of company—a bakery that sells a variety of breads and pastries.

In a bakery, there are costs, like the milk, that "go away" if the bread is not made at all. For this decision, the costs that can be avoided, or are actionable, are fairly straightforward. In all likelihood, however, though easy to estimate, these costs will only include the materials used to make the bread and perhaps a small amount of power if the oven can be turned off. Labor probably will not change, nor will the equipment, baking pans, and supplies, or the other major costs for making, displaying, and selling products to customers, like the cost of the display counters. They are **unavoidable costs,** *costs that remain regardless of actions or decisions of management.*

There are some costs that fall in the middle. For example, if the number of loaves made drops, some of the cost goes away, or is avoided, but not all of it. Yeast falls into this category. Some costs are hard to put an exact cost behavior on. The bakery has to have electricity, for instance. According to the summary of costs in Table 3.4, this bakery spends about $10,800 per year on electricity, but how do we trace this cost to one loaf of bread? And how many loaves can be baked before the oven has to be replaced? As we can see, it is not easy to estimate something as simple as the cost of a loaf of bread.

Divisible resources, such as the flour used in making bread, *can be used a little at a time*. Their cost is very responsive to changes in the amount of work that is done, while the cost of resources that are not divisible will be far less unresponsive to changes in demand. An example of this type of resource would be the oven in the bakery. We can avoid the electricity cost if we do not turn the oven on, but the oven itself is a fixed cost of doing business—if we bake one or many loaves of bread at one time, the cost of the oven is unchanged. The responsiveness of a resource cost to changes in the volume of work that is done—its variability—is captured by the following equation:

$$\text{Cost Variability} = \frac{\text{Change in Cost}}{\text{Change in Volume}}$$

To help you understand this concept, let us take a closer look at Table 3.4, a simple example that details some of the information Tim Perkins, owner of Best Bread Bakery, has developed to answer several basic questions about the trends in the company's profitability. Using the resources needed to make an average loaf of white bread, we see that some of the resource costs change as the number of loaves made change, such as the amount of flour used; while others, like the cost of the oven, do not change directly based on the number of loaves baked.

TABLE 3.4 BEST BREAD BAKERY OPERATING COSTS

Best Bread Bakery			
Resource Costs	Purchase Costs	Conversion Factor	Cost per Unit
Flour—White	$ 0.300 per pound	4.5 cups per pound	$ 0.067 per cup
Flour—Whole wheat	$ 0.400 per pound	4.5 cups per pound	$ 0.089 per cup
Sugar	$ 1.890 per pound	38.4 Tbsp per pound	$ 0.049 per Tbsp
Eggs	$ 2.400 per dozen	12 eggs per dozen	$ 0.200 per egg
Butter	$ 3.200 per pound	32 Tbsp per pound	$ 0.100 per Tbsp
Salt	$ 2.000 per pound	80 Tbsp per pound	$ 0.025 per Tbsp
Yeast	$ 0.750 per packet	1 packet	$ 0.750 per packet
Shortening	$ 0.089 per ounce	2 Tbsp per ounce	$ 0.045 per Tbsp
Milk	$ 6.400 per gallon	16 cups per gallon	$ 0.400 per cup
Plastic bag	$ 0.023 per bag	N/A	$ 0.023 per loaf

Best Bread Bakery						
Resource Costs	Purchase Costs		Conversion Factor		Cost per Unit	
Twist tie	$ 0.001	per twist tie	N/A		$ 0.001	per loaf
Baker	$ 24,000.000	per year	120,000	minutes per year	$ 0.200	per minute
Loaf pan	$ 500.0000	25 pans	N/A			
Electricity	$ 10,800.000	per year	N/A			
Telephone	$ 3,000.000	per year	N/A			
Water	$ 1,200.000	per year	N/A			
Oven	$ 40,000.000	each	N/A			
Bread Slicer	$ 1,500.000	each	N/A			
Oven stands/shelves	$ 2,500.000	each	N/A			
Display counters	$ 5,000.000	each	N/A			
Building	$ 30,000.000	per year	N/A			

To get a better handle on his costs, Tim can use a recipe, such as the one that follows in Figure 3.2, to make six loaves of his popular white bread to assign some of the costs directly to a loaf.

Recipe for a Six Loaves of White Bread

Ingredients:

6 (.25 ounce) packages active dry yeast	10 tablespoons white sugar
7 1/2 cups warm water (110 degrees F)	3 tablespoons salt
10 tablespoons lard, softened	20 cups bread flour

Directions:

In a large bowl, dissolve yeast and sugar in warm water. Stir in lard, salt and six cups of the flour. Stir in the remaining flour, 1 cup at a time, beating well after each addition. When the dough has pulled together, turn it out onto a lightly floured surface and knead until smooth and elastic, about 8 minutes.

Lightly oil a large bowl, place the dough in the bowl and turn to coat with oil. Cover with a damp cloth and let rise in a warm place until doubled in volume, about 1 hour.

Deflate the dough and turn it out onto a lightly floured surface. Divide the dough into six equal pieces and form into loaves. Place the loaves into six lightly greased 9x5 inch loaf pans. Cover the loaves with a damp cloth and let rise until doubled in volume, about 40 minutes.

Preheat oven to 375 degrees F.

Bake for about 30 minutes or until the tops are golden brown and the bottom of a loaf sounds hollow when tapped.

FIGURE 3.2 RECIPE FOR WHITE BREAD

It takes roughly 10 minutes for a baker to do all of the work associated with mixing up the six-loaf batch of bread. The dough sits idle while it rises after which it will bake for roughly 30 minutes. When cooled, each loaf is sliced, and then packaged for sale. Each loaf will use one plastic bag and one twist tie. So based on these facts, Tim can estimate for the batch of six loaves both the total direct costs for all six loaves, and with a simple division, estimate the cost for one loaf. Table 3.5 details these calculations.

TABLE 3.5 DIRECT COSTS OF THE BREAD

Best Bread Bakery			
Direct Costs for White Bread			
Ingredient	Amount used	Cost per unit	Total Cost
Water	7 1/2 cups	FREE	-
Lard	10 Tbsp	0.045	$ 0.446
Sugar	10 Tbsp	0.049	$ 0.492
Salt	3 Tbsp	0.025	$ 0.075
Yeast	6 packets	0.250	$ 1.500
Flour	20 cups	0.067	$ 1.333
Plastic bag	6 each	0.023	$ 0.138
Twist tie	6 each	0.001	$ 0.004
Baker	10 minutes	0.200	$ 2.00
Total Cost for Six-Loaf Batch			$ 5.988
Cost per Loaf (Batch Cost / 6)			$ 0.998

Note: Columns are rounded.

These are all costs we can calculate on a per-loaf basis. Because these costs will change based on how many loaves of bread Tim makes, we call this type of cost pattern a **variable cost,** *a cost that changes a constant amount in direct response to changes in volume*. For all of the costs except Tim, the baker, there are no costs at all if we do not bake a loaf of bread. These resources behave as pure variable costs. Tim works on an ongoing basis, so while we can assign his cost to the batch of bread based on how much time is used, we have to *translate* or estimate the cost per loaf. So, while it looks variable, the underlying cost is actually much less responsive than flour costs are for making one more loaf of bread. This reflects the resource's **divisibility,** *the degree to which a resource can be subdivided into smaller consumption units*, and **storability,** *the ability of a resource to be held for future use without a loss of its value-creating ability*.

Looking at the costs for the loaf pans, oven, bread slicer, and so forth, we see just the opposite situation. No matter how many loaves we make this month, Best Bread will have the same level of cost for these resources. We call these types of costs **fixed costs**, or *costs that do not change with changes in volume*. Not all fixed costs are indirect. Some may be directly traceable to making product. It is important that we do not mix up the terms direct/indirect and fixed/variable as they capture different aspects of our costing exercise.

Some of Best Bread's costs, such as electricity and water, change as volume changes, but do not totally go away even when the bakery is closed. There is a flat fee of $1,200 per month for electricity for the refrigerators, security lights, and temperature control. There is also an additional electricity cost for every hour we run the oven (25 kilowatt hours per hour of use, or $3.75 per hour at $0.15 per kilowatt hour). Telephone hookups require paying a fixed rate each month, in addition to a variable charge for the number of minutes of long-distance calls used. These types of resource costs are called **mixed costs**, or *costs that have both fixed and variable components*.

What are the total fixed costs for running the bakery? To have a useful number for this calculation, Tim now has to make some estimates of how much of the useful life of the oven, pans, mixers, and other fixed costs get used up in a year. We have done this in Table 3.6 based on information Tim has compiled on how long his assets will last.

TABLE 3.6 TOTAL FIXED COSTS

Best Bread Bakery			
Resource	**Cost**	**Years of Useful Life**	**Cost per Year**
Baking sheets and pans	$ 1,200.00	5	$ 240.00
Electricity	$ 10,800.00	1	$ 10,800.00
Telephone system	$ 3,000.00	1	$ 3,000.00
Mixers	$ 3,250.00	5	$ 650.00
Refrigerator unit	$ 6,500.00	10	$ 650.00
Water	$ 1,200.00	1	$ 1,200.00
Oven	$ 40,000.00	10	$ 4,000.00
Bread slicer	$ 1,500.00	5	$ 300.00
Flour/sugar/spice racks	$ 2,400.00	10	$ 240.00
Oven stands/shelves	$ 2,500.00	10	$ 250.00
Display counters	$ 6,000.00	5	$ 1,200.00
Building rental and maintenance	$ 30,000.00	1	$ 30,000.00
		Total	$ 52,530.00

All of these fixed costs are indirect to the activity of making a loaf of bread. These total indirect costs make up the category of cost that is called overhead. Overhead can have both fixed and variable components. In our simple example, they all happen to be fixed, but this is the exception rather than the rule.

We can now combine the information about the variable and fixed costs at Best Bread to get a **total cost formula,** *variable cost per unit times volume sold plus fixed costs*. Specifically, if we use the estimate above of the **total fixed costs (TFC),** *the sum of all of the firm's fixed costs*, for one year plus our information on what it costs to make one loaf, or $0.998 times the number of loaves we sell (V), we can estimate Tim's operating costs for a year.

Total Cost = (Variable Cost per Unit x Volume Sold) + Total Fixed Costs

or

TC = (VC x V) + TFC

Where: TC is the total cost
VC is the variable cost per unit
V is the volume of bread sold
TFC is the total fixed costs

For Best Bread, the formula becomes:

TC = $0.998(V) + $ 52,530.00

In other words, the total costs we estimate for Tim's bakery is $0.998 per loaf of white bread sold plus $52,530.00 in fixed overhead costs.

Given this formula, we can now estimate how much it is going to cost Tim to run his business based on the estimated number of loaves of bread sold per year. Table 3.7 contains some examples of these total costs of operation.

TABLE 3.7 TOTAL COST OF OPERATION

Best Bread Bakery				
Variable Cost per Loaf	Loaves Sold	Total Variable Costs	Total Fixed Costs	Total Costs
$ 0.998	1,000	$ 998	$ 52,530	$ 53,528
$ 0.998	5,000	$ 4,990	$ 52,530	$ 57,520
$ 0.998	10,000	$ 9,980	$ 52,530	$ 62,510
$ 0.998	15,000	$ 14,970	$ 52,530	$ 67,500
$ 0.998	20,000	$ 19,961	$ 52,530	$ 72,491
$ 0.998	25,000	$ 24,951	$ 52,530	$ 77,481
$ 0.998	50,000	$ 49,902	$ 52,530	$ 102,432
$ 0.998	100,000	$ 99,803	$ 52,530	$ 152,333

This is very useful information, but we can also derive these results by using a change in cost approach that works backward from a total cost number to derive the variable portion of a cost by using the cost change formula. Specifically, we can look at how much the costs change as we move from one volume to the next, as follows:

$$\frac{\textbf{Change in Cost}}{\textbf{Change in Volume}} = \textbf{Variable Cost per Unit}$$

or

$$\frac{\$\ 57{,}520 - 53{,}528}{5{,}000 - 1{,}000} = \frac{\$\ 3{,}992}{4{,}000} = \$\ 0.998 \text{ per loaf}$$

The change in cost for every loaf of bread that is made is $0.998, the variable cost per loaf of bread. We find this basic formula very useful when we are trying to get a general feeling for how much it costs us to do business. It is an estimate only because we made some assumptions to derive it and "overlooked" some of the costs that were difficult to pin down, because, although they appear to vary with the number of loaves made, they do not necessarily have a direct correlation with them. For instance, there is no reason to believe the number of minutes of long-distance calling will go down just because we make fewer loaves of bread. Thus, our estimate is only a starting point, but a useful one, one we will rely on throughout this textbook.

As we will see, we can actually use this information to look at the impact of different prices and varying conditions on Best Bread's profitability. We call this type of analysis cost-volume-profit analysis (CVP). Before we turn to this issue, however, we need to deal with two more issues: average costs and stepped costs.

IN THE NEWS ➤ Variable Cost Business Models Lead to Rise in Number of Small Businesses

Variable cost business models are having a major impact on the small business sector by greatly increasing the viability of niche markets by:

1. ***Lowering the capital costs*** required to enter and serve niche markets. Lower capital costs also reduce the risk of serving niche markets.
2. ***Providing cost advantages*** to niche producers relative to their larger competitors.

Customers are increasingly looking for goods and services that meet their specific needs. The internet has allowed niche producers and customers to find one another more easily, and technology is lowering the costs of serving niche markets.

Combined, these trends are making more and more niche markets economically viable. And we are seeing more and more examples of small businesses using innovative variable cost business models to exploit niche markets and outmaneuver larger competitors.

Source: www.typepad.com, Sept. 16, 2013.

ESTIMATING AVERAGE COSTS

The total costs faced by Best Bread for making its standard loaf of white bread varies based on how many loaves are made. This is valuable information for Tim to have, but he might also want to know what it costs, on average, to make a loaf. In other words, Tim might want to see how much his fixed costs add to the direct costs of one loaf. To develop this cost estimate, we divide the total costs by the number of loaves made, as follows:

$$\textbf{Average Cost Per Loaf} = \frac{\textbf{Total Costs of Operations}}{\textbf{Total Loaves Made}}$$

Table 3.8 develops an estimate of the **average cost per loaf**, or *the total cost per loaf given a specific level of output*, as the volume of loaves made per year changes. As you can see, as we increase the number of loaves that are made, the average cost per loaf drops. In other words, our **marginal cost**, or *the cost to make one more unit* or additional loaf of bread, drops as we spread out the fixed costs over more units. Looking at the next column, we see that this change *exactly matches* the change in the **average fixed cost,** *the total fixed costs divided by the units sold or made*; in this case, per loaf made.

$$\textbf{Average Fixed Cost} = \frac{\textbf{Total Fixed Costs of Operations}}{\textbf{Total Loaves Made}}$$

What we also see is that the difference between our average cost (AC) and average fixed cost (AFC) is our variable cost per loaf. The formula for this relationship is:

Average Cost - Average Fixed Cost = Variable Cost per Unit

In other words, all of the change in our average cost is due to the impact of changing volumes on the average fixed cost per unit.

TABLE 3.8 AVERAGE COSTS

Best Bread Bakery							
Loaves Made (1)	Total Costs (2)	Average Total Costs (AC), or (3) = (2)/(1)	Decrease in Average Total Cost	Total Fixed Costs (4)	Average Fixed Cost (AFC), or (5) = (4)/(1)	Decrease in Average Fixed Cost	Difference in AC and AFC, or (3) - (5)
1,000	$ 53,528	$ 53.528	-	$ 52,530	$ 52.530	-	$ 0.998
5,000	$ 57,520	$ 11.504	$ 42.024	$ 52,530	$ 10.506	$ 42.024	$ 0.998
10,000	$ 62,510	$ 6.251	$ 5.253	$ 52,530	$ 5.253	$ 5.253	$ 0.998
15,000	$ 67,500	$ 4.500	$ 1.751	$ 52,530	$ 3.502	$ 1.751	$ 0.998
20,000	$ 72,491	$ 3.625	$ 0.878	$ 52,530	$ 2.627	$ 0.875	$ 0.998
25,000	$ 77,481	$ 3.099	$ 0.526	$ 52,530	$ 2.101	$ 0.526	$ 0.998
50,000	$ 102,432	$ 2.049	$ 1.050	$ 52,530	$ 1.051	$ 1.050	$ 0.998
100,000	$ 152,333	$ 1.523	$ 0.526	$ 52,530	$ 0.525	$ 0.526	$ 0.998

The pattern we have uncovered in this analysis is the basis for what is called **economies of scale**, where the *fixed cost per unit made or sold drops as a result of spreading fixed costs over more output units*. Simply put, our average costs drop as our volumes increase because we are *spreading our fixed costs over more units*. To put it another way, as we increase the amount of value we create with our fixed resources, we actually are reducing the amount of our fixed resources that are being wasted. We know that Tim is limited to 72,000 loaves per year if he is the only employee. That is because there are 2,000 hours (or 120,000 minutes) in an average work year. To make each loaf takes 1.67 minutes (10 minutes divided by six loaves) in total elapsed time, so 120,000 minutes divided by 1.67 minutes is 72,000 loaves. This is the bakery's current production **capacity,** *the amount of work a resource is capable of supporting before it must be replenished*. Tim could clearly work more hours per week, but there is a limit to how hard we can push one person.

Looking further at the information in Table 3.8, we also see that the difference between the estimated **average total cost**, or *total fixed cost divided by the number of units produced*, and average fixed cost is always $0.998. You may recall, this is *exactly* the amount of variable cost per loaf made that we derived earlier. Is this just a coincidence? No, it is not. Our variable cost per unit remains the same no matter how many loaves we make. It is always $0.998 per loaf. **Average variable cost**, or *total variable cost divided by the number of units produced*, is a constant and is always equal to the total variable cost per unit.

At Easy Air, it normally costs the same amount of time and materials to issue a boarding pass or provide an in-flight beverage to a passenger. Most companies have variable costs in their cost structure. Variable costs, therefore, make completing a number of calculations that are useful for management fairly straightforward because they stay the same on average regardless of the volume of work being done.

STEPPED COSTS AND THE RELEVANT RANGE

One of the most important assumptions we made in developing the cost information was that we were looking at only one person working in the bakery, which placed fairly strict limits on the number of loaves of bread that could be made. We defined the situation around an assumed level of activity and for a specific set of resources. Our cost formulas should be reasonably accurate as long as we do not violate these assumptions. We call the set of assumptions, or conditions, that we use to define our cost analysis the **relevant range,** *the assumed volume of activity within which estimates of costs are accurate*.

What if we were to expand our analysis, however, to include all of the costs Best Bread faces in an average month? We would now need to recognize that not all of our resource costs would change quite so logically with changes in the number of loaves made. For instance, Best Bread's phone bill would change with the number of minutes of long-distance calling Tim actually did in a month. In a similar fashion, Tim could change his electric bill by running his lights, ovens, and other electrical equipment longer or shorter periods of time. Accurately estimating our total costs, therefore, would require that we expand the number of factors considered in the analysis. We will see the results of this type of change in Chapter 4 when we learn about activity-based costing methods.

Other resources, however, offer quite a different challenge. There are some resources, such as people, who have to be bought in a specific **purchase package**, or *the minimum size or quantity of a purchased resource* (for example, one individual). If we only need one person, we would have one chunk of cost. As we add people, however, we also increase our total cost in "chunks" that correspond to the size of the purchase package. We call resources that behave in this manner **stepped costs,** *costs that change in "chunks" when volume changes*.

If the resource is both divisible and storable, it really does not matter if we have to buy it in larger quantities than we may need to meet current demand. Why? Because we can consume just what is needed, and keep the rest. When we do more or less work, we can use more or less of the resource with little or no waste of its value-creating ability.

Unfortunately, there are many other resources that have to be purchased in this "all or nothing" way that cannot be *both* subdivided into smaller units and stored. People normally fall into this category.[4] In this case, the second we exceed the capacity of a specific individual, whether it is hourly for part-time employees or monthly for full-time employees, we have to hire another person; in other words, we would

---

4 If Tim paid someone to work at a flat rate per loaf of bread made, the labor cost would become much closer to a true variable cost. The same holds if we charged out the useful life of the ovens based on number of hours used, converting a pure fixed cost into one that varies with the amount of work done. We will need to keep in mind that we can change the cost pattern of many resources based on how we structure the contract, how we do the estimating, or how we actually use the resource.

need to buy another whole package of the resource. Also, when we cannot store any of the residual value-creating ability, whatever we do not use will become waste.

While it is true that stepped costs create more challenges for us in developing and using cost estimates than fixed, variable, or mixed costs, they are actually a very common form of cost in every organization. Since organizations are made up of people, and people costs are usually stepped costs, every organization's **cost structure,** *the estimated combination of a firm's fixed, mixed, stepped, and variable costs*, has a large percentage of stepped costs.

To understand the nature of stepped costs a bit better, let us take an example from Easy Air: its passenger reservation activity. When we think about the resources we need to perform this activity, they would likely include:

- People
- Desks
- Computers
- Telephones
- Internet service
- Fax machines
- Copiers
- Space

If Easy Air only had one person doing the reservation activity, it would hire one person and buy that person a desk, computer, and telephone. Easy Air's management would also need to buy or lease a copier and set up the necessary telephone and internet services. At least some space would need to be set aside to house the reservation specialist and the related equipment and furniture.

One of the first questions we would have to address when we set up the passenger reservation process is the number of passenger requests a reservation specialist could handle effectively. If we assume one person works eight hours a day, and an average customer inquiry takes 15 minutes (or four customer calls per hour), one person would have the capacity to handle up to 32 customer inquiries per day (eight hours multiplied by four calls per hour). If the demand increases to 33 inquiries, more resources would have to be added. For now, let us assume the department actually has to handle 1,600 inquiries per day. This means we would need to have 50 people in this department (1,600 inquiries divided by 32 inquiries per employee per day equals 50 employees).

What would happen to our resource demands and costs if we had to add another 49 people? If they are all working on the day shift, we would clearly need to add 49 more desks, computers, and telephones. We would get 49 more *steps* of each of these resource costs. On the other hand, we would not want 49 more copiers. We will assume we need two more copiers. In other words, this "step" for copiers is larger than it is for the other resources. Finally, we would see increases in telephone, internet, and space costs, but it would be unlikely that these costs would multiply as fast as the desk and people costs would. The total increase, in fact, would depend on how we structured the department and the flexibility we have in how we buy these additional resources. Table 3.9 illustrates these changes for three levels of customer inquiry volume per day: 32, 800, and 1,600 inquiries.

TABLE 3.9 STEPPED COSTS FOR DIFFERENT CUSTOMER INQUIRY LEVELS

Easy Air			
Number of Customer Inquiries	**32**	**800**	**1,600**
		Number of Purchase Packages Needed	
People	1	25	50
Desks	1	25	50
Computers	1	25	50
Telephones	1	25	50
Telephone/internet services	Basic	Expanded	Premium
Copiers	1	2	3
Space	250 sq. ft.	2,200 sq. ft.	4,600 sq. ft.

Stepped cost patterns are clearly more complex to deal with in our cost estimating, but once we define our assumptions (for example, the relevant range), it becomes a simple matter of determining how many packages of each stepped resource we will need. Once this estimate has been made, we can treat the total stepped costs *for that level of activity* as if they were fixed *at that level.* This simplifies greatly our effort to develop a cost estimate, allowing us to use a number of valuable analytical tools, such as cost-volume-profit (CVP) analysis. Before we turn our attention to CVP, however, let us see what's happening at Easy Air.

IN CONTEXT ➤ Developing and Using Cost Estimates at Easy Air—Part 2

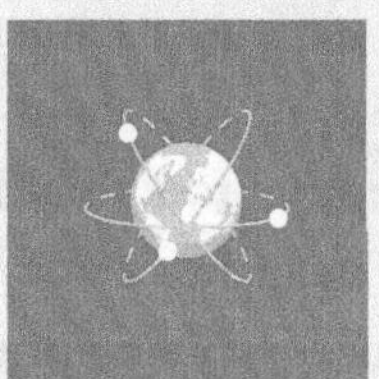

"Sanjiv, I'm not sure I understand why you've created all these reports. I wanted to know how much it costs to serve a passenger, but you've given me costs we incur not only when a passenger flies, but for booking flights, cleaning the plane, and scheduling a flight. Why have you included all of these costs?" asked Fran.

"I wanted to give you a 'fully loaded' cost estimate, Fran. If our ultimate goal is to make sure the company makes money, it seemed like the number we needed," Sanjiv said.

"Are you saying that if I add a passenger, it is going to immediately cost me another $43.35 in expenses?" Fran asked. "And a passenger doesn't have anything to do with our decisions here at corporate headquarters, so why are those costs included?"

"Actually, that's not what would happen," Sanjiv said. "In fact, the only costs that would change if we add one more passenger are the ones that vary, or change, on a passenger-by-passenger basis. That's roughly $4.88 of cost. As long as we still have a seat on the plane, that's all we'll have to spend to add a passenger."

"What about reservations? We'd need that, wouldn't we?" Fran asked.

"Well, yes, but you see, we pay the reservation agents whether or not one specific passenger flies with us. If you want only those costs a new passenger adds, it is $4.88," replied Sanjiv.

"But at the end of the day, I only make $1.98 per passenger if your numbers are right. Do our stepped and fixed costs really add that much? That's a very slim margin! If we make any mistakes, that will be gone, too!" Fran exclaimed.

"I agree," Sanjiv said. "I've told you before that these new pricing programs have caused some sleepless nights in Finance. There just isn't much that stands between us and losing money on every passenger mile flown."

"Something is troubling me, though," Fran replied. "You would think flying full makes good sense. Empty seats mean no revenue at all. What I really need to know is what the optimal number of passengers is for a flight. I always thought that we wanted every seat full, but when I talk to the flight and ground crew managers, they point out that as we near 'full flight' status, problems seem to snowball. We can't get all of the carry-on bags on board, boarding slows down, and, before you know it, we're running late. And if the hold fills up with baggage, we can't take on any cargo, which means we have to pay to ship it on another airline. Not good for the bottom line or my ego!"

Fran paused, giving Sanjiv a chance to think through her request. After a few moments, he responded.

"Fran, I think I see what you want; I'm sorry it's taking us so long to get your answers, but we really needed to get to this stage. Now that we have some estimates of the variable and fixed costs of a flight, and some estimates of the variable, fixed, and stepped costs of the rest of our operations, I think we can begin looking at these issues. If I've understood you correctly, you'd like us to look at the entire system—where do our costs seem in line, where are they too high, and what should we do about them. Right?"

"Yes, that's more in line with what I want. I know it's asking a lot, Sanjiv, but I can't seem to get my arms around our cost structure any more. What causes us to 'kick a step' in key areas, and how firm are those limits? You and your team clearly can't answer all of these questions, but I would really appreciate it if you could take these cost estimates and use them in different analyses and different settings so I can see how you think they will change, and what impact the change will have on our profitability. The work you've done so far is great; I look forward to our next meeting."

Cost-Volume-Profit Analysis

OBJECTIVE 3

Apply CVP to identify the impact of potential changes in price, costs, or volume on a firm's profitability.

Many different tools can be used to get a better understanding of the impact of change on a company's costs and profitability. One such tool, **cost-volume-profit (CVP) analysis,** *is used to understand how changes in costs, prices, or sales volume will impact a company's estimated profitability.* It is the focus of the remainder of this chapter. CVP helps us analyze the impact of changes in output volume on total costs and profitability. It is a useful tool for understanding some basic facts, such as the number of loaves of bread Best Bread needs to sell to just cover the actual costs of running the bakery. While there are limitations to the usefulness of CVP, it provides a good starting point for understanding a firm's current operations.

THE BASIC CVP FORMULA

CVP uses two basic concepts to develop a range of potential profit scenarios: cost variability and the **basic profit equation** *(revenues minus total costs equals profit) used to calculate the profit potential of different sales levels given costs*. Let us derive the basic CVP formula, focusing first on the formula to derive the breakeven volume of sales for a company.

Revenue - Total Costs = Income before Tax

or

$$R - TC = I_B$$

Where:

R = Price x Volume Sold, or PV

TC = (Variable Cost per Unit x Volume Sold) + Total Fixed Costs

I_B = Income before Tax

Total cost is equal to the variable cost per unit multiplied by the number of units we sell plus the total fixed costs for the specific relevant range of operations.

$$TC = (VC \times V) + TFC$$

We now substitute into the original formula:

$$PV - ((VC \times V) + TFC) = I_B$$

We want to solve for V, so we need to regroup our equations:

$$PV - (VC \times V) - TFC = I_B$$
$$(P - VC)V - TFC = I_B$$
$$(P - VC)V = I_B + TFC$$

and

$$V = \frac{I_B + TFC}{(P - VC)}$$

In other words, the volume we need to sell to cover our fixed costs and make a specific level of before-tax profit is desired income before tax plus total fixed cost divided by price minus variable cost. When we calculate price less variable cost, it is called the **contribution margin**, or *the constant amount of money available after paying for variable costs that contributes to covering fixed costs and making a profit*.

With this equation, we can now solve for the number of loaves of bread Tim needs to sell. When we **break even**, which is *the point at which the total contribution margin ((price minus variable cost) times units sold) earned equals total fixed costs, and the profit for the company is zero*, our formula becomes:

$$V = \frac{TFC}{(P - VC)}$$

In other words, when there is no profit, the volume we need to sell is exactly equal to the total fixed costs divided by the contribution margin, or price minus variable costs, on a per-unit basis.

To use this equation, let us now set Tim's price at \$2.75 per loaf and plug in the other numbers we derived earlier in the chapter.

$$P = \$2.75$$
$$VC = \$0.998$$
$$TFC = \$52{,}530$$

So the volume Tim needs to sell to break even is his fixed costs divided by his contribution margin for a loaf of bread, or:

$$V = \frac{52{,}530}{(\$2.75 - \$0.998)}$$

V = 29,983 **loaves**[5]

Since we determined earlier that by working a normal 2,000-hour year, Tim can make 72,000 loaves of bread (2,000 hours times 60 minutes per hour) divided by 1.67 minutes per loaf), he clearly has the potential to make a profit in his business. If Tim wants to increase this profit, however, or perhaps even expand his product line to include other types of bread, rolls, and perhaps even a cake or two, more analysis will

5 If you do the calculations, you will see that the number of loaves Tim needs to sell to just break even is 29,982.88. So why did we round up to 29,983? Because we want to at least break even. If he does not sell the additional loaf, Tim will actually lose a small amount of money.

need to be done. The breakeven volume of sales, therefore, is a very useful estimate for a firm to have. There will be no profit, nor any money to contribute toward the other business costs that Best Bread may incur to stay in business (such as advertising), but Tim will come out even. Tim may want to grow his business, however, so we may need to look at other solutions for him, such as hiring another baker.

As we have seen, the difference between price and variable cost per unit is called the contribution margin. After reaching breakeven sales, every dollar of additional contribution margin flows directly to profit. Why? Because all fixed costs have been covered by the contribution margin earned up to the breakeven point. The contribution margin, therefore, is a very useful estimate, making it much easier for us to calculate the impact of changing volumes on costs and profits. Let us look at some different volumes of sales just to see how the contribution margin can be used to help us understand business dynamics (see Table 3.10):

TABLE 3.10 SALES DYNAMICS

Best Bread Bakery						
Price per Unit (P) (1)	Variable Cost per Unit (VC) (2)	Contribution Margin per Unit (P-VC) (3) = (2) - (1)	Volume Sold (V) (4)	Total Contribution Margin (TCM) (5) = (3) x (4)	Total Fixed Costs (TF) (6)	Profit or (Loss) (I) (7) = (5) - (6)
$ 2.75	$ 0.998	$ 1.752	10,000	$ 17,520	$ 52,530	$ (35,010)
$ 2.75	$ 0.998	$ 1.752	20,000	$ 35,040	$ 52,530	$ (17,490)
$ 2.75	$ 0.998	$ 1.752	30,000	$ 52,560	$ 52,530	$ 30
$ 2.75	$ 0.998	$ 1.752	40,000	$ 70,080	$ 52,530	$ 17,550
$ 2.75	$ 0.998	$ 1.752	50,000	$ 87,600	$ 52,530	$ 35,070
$ 2.75	$ 0.998	$ 1.752	60,000	$ 105,120	$ 52,530	$ 52,590
$ 2.75	$ 0.998	$ 1.752	70,000	$ 122,640	$ 52,530	$ 70,110
$ 2.75	$ 0.998	$ 1.752	80,000	$ 140,160	$ 52,530	$ 87,630
$ 2.75	$ 0.998	$ 1.752	90,000	$ 157,680	$ 52,530	$ 105,150
$ 2.75	$ 0.998	$ 1.752	100,000	$ 175,200	$ 52,530	$ 122,670

The contribution margin is a very useful number for us, therefore, giving us a shorter way to calculate outcomes over a variety of conditions. To use the contribution margin in this way, we use the following equations:

Contribution Margin per Unit = Price - Variable Cost per Unit

CM = P - VC

Therefore, our formula for the volume we need to sell to break even becomes total fixed costs divided by the contribution margin, or:

$$V = \frac{TFC}{CM}$$

We can use these relationships to solve for any part of the equation, or to check on how changes in our assumptions impact profits and required breakeven sales. The difference between current sales and the breakeven volume is the organization's **margin of safety,** *the difference between the current or estimated sales of a company and the level of sales needed for it to break even*. Let us say Tim currently sells 60,000 loaves of bread; his margin of safety in units is:

Actual Sales – Breakeven Sales = Margin of Safety

60,000 – 29,983 = 30,017 **loaves**

If we want to express these results in dollars, we can take the margin of safety in units times the current contribution margin per loaf to get Tim's revenue dollars of safety margin, or 30,017 loaves at $1.752 per loaf, or $52,589.78. In formula terms, this is:

Margin of Safety in Units x Contribution Margin = Dollars of Safety Margin

Tim's profit if he sells 60,000 loaves of bread is $52,590 (rounded) per Table 3.10, the same number we just calculated. Hopefully, you now can see the power of CVP analysis for doing a first-pass analysis of business profit dynamics. While we know in reality there are a lot of stepped costs, CVP still provides a good first look at what is going on. We will use CVP as just one tool in our analytical tool kit, one that can be used to get a first-pass approximation of the viability of a business plan.

Whenever we do CVP analysis, we *round up the volume we need to sell to break even*. Why? Because we do not want to know how much business we need to lose just a little money, but instead want to know at what level we will start to make some profit. If we round a CVP answer down, we would get the former, correct? Therefore, always round your CVP answers up, even if the fraction of a whole unit sold is very small.

THE VARIABLE COST INCOME STATEMENT AND OPERATING LEVERAGE

When we separate an organization's variable and fixed costs, we are able to make some judgments about how a company is being operated and how responsive its profits will be to shifts in the volume of its activities. The analytical approach we use to capture this information requires us to use a unique form of an income statement, a **variable cost income statement,** *which recasts the presentation of costs in terms of fixed and variable categories* rather than the emphasis in financial accounting on operational costs vs. selling, general, and administrative costs.

When we develop a variable cost income statement, we present the information to management in the following way:

Revenues

Less: Total Variable Costs
Total Contribution Margin

Less: Total Fixed Costs
Net Operating Income

We can recast Best Bread's income in terms of fixed and variable components now by using this revised approach to the income statement for its current production volume of 60,000 loaves of bread, as shown in Table 3.11.

TABLE 3.11 A VARIABLE COST APPROACH

Best Bread Bakery Variable Cost Income Statement For the period ending December 31, 20XX	
Sales (60,000 loaves x $2.75 per loaf)	$ 165,000.00
Less: Variable Costs (60,000 loaves x $0.998 per loaf)	$ 59,880.00
Total Contribution Margin	$ 105,120.00
Less: Fixed Costs	$ 52,530.00
Operating Income	$ 52,590.00

Management is now able to see those costs that will change as the volume of production or sales goes up, and those costs that will remain the same even though volumes drop off. Often we will find it necessary to work from a variable cost income statement to derive the variable cost per unit. This is easy since we know that variable costs are constant on a per-unit basis. Divide the total variable costs by the number of units being sold, and you have the variable cost per unit. For Best Bread, we see that $59,880 divided by 60,000 loaves gives us the $0.998 variable cost per unit that we derived earlier. While financial accounting does not use this income statement approach, we will find it very useful for our purposes.

With this information, we can now see the dynamics of the cost model for any organization. We now can add another measurement or insight to our set of cost tools: **operating leverage,** *a measure of how sensitive profit is to a given percentage change in revenues*. It allows us to determine how much impact a change in revenue will have on the profitability of a company. We use it in financial analysis, for instance, to know whether an organization is highly constrained by its fixed costs or whether it has a more responsive cost structure that contains a large portion of variable costs. The measurement we use to capture operating leverage is the following:

$$\textbf{Operating Leverage} = \frac{\textbf{Total Contribution Margin}}{\textbf{Net Operating Income}}$$

Which for Best Bread would be:

$$2.0 = \frac{\$105{,}120.00}{\$52{,}590.00}$$

These results suggest that Best Bread's operating profits grow two times as fast as its sales growth.

To understand the impact of operating leverage, let us assume Tim is able to raise his sales by 10%. We now can use the operating leverage information to determine how much Tim's profits will increase using the following formula:

$$\textbf{Percentage Change in Net Operating Income} = \textbf{Degree of Operating Leverage} \times \textbf{Percentage Change in Sales}$$

For Best Bread, we see Tim will get a positive result in terms of improved profitability if he can boost sales. If Tim could get a 10% increase in sales, he would get a 20% increase in net operating income (2 times 10% equals 20%). This would mean net operating income would go up to $63,108 ($52,590 times (100% + 20%) equals $63,108). In other words, the degree of operating leverage allows us to see how a percentage change in sales volume will affect net operating income.

This is useful information to tell us how quickly Tim's operating profit will grow as he increases the revenue of the business. Given the degree of leverage he currently has, Tim can boost profitability significantly if he can find a way to increase sales. There is a catch, however: The further away from the breakeven point that Tim goes, the less his operating leverage becomes. Let us look at how operating leverage changes as sales change (Table 3.12) using our variable cost income statement (the current situation at Best Bread is in red).

TABLE 3.12 OPERATING LEVERAGE DYNAMICS

Best Bread Bakery					
Volume Sold	60,000	65,000	70,000	75,000	80,000
Price per Loaf	$ 2.75	$ 2.75	$ 2.75	$ 2.75	$ 2.75
Sales	$ 165,000.00	$ 178,750.00	$ 192,500.00	$ 206,250.00	$ 220,000.00
Variable Costs	$ 59,880.00	$ 64,870.00	$ 69,860.00	$ 74,850.00	$ 79,840.00
Contribution Margin	$ 105,120.00	$ 113,880.00	$ 122,640.00	$ 131,400.00	$ 140,160.00
Fixed Costs	$ 52,530.00	$ 52,530.00	$ 52,530.00	$ 52,530.00	$ 52,530.00
Operating Income	$ 52,590.00	$ 61,350.00	$ 70,110.00	$ 78,870.00	$ 87,630.00
Operating Leverage	2.00	1.86	1.75	1.67	1.60

How did we arrive at these numbers? Let us walk through the $192,500 sales revenue scenario. Variable costs are $0.998 per loaf. At $192,500, we sell 70,000 loaves. That means total variable costs are $69,860 (70,000 loaves times $0.998 per loaf). That leaves us with a contribution margin of $122,640. We remove the fixed costs of $52,530 to get the net operating income of $70,110. Now we divide the contribution margin by the net operating income to derive our degree of operating leverage, getting a result of 1.75 at this higher sales level ($122,640 divided by $70,110 equals 1.75). That means even at $192,500 in sales revenue, Tim can expect a 10% increase in sales to generate 17.5% improvement in net operating income. These results are the reasons why companies work very hard to improve their sales performance.

USING CVP TO IMPROVE PROFIT PERFORMANCE

With the information we have developed for Best Bread, we can now look at several different options for the company to improve its overall profitability. Specifically, we can use the data from our CVP analysis to look at such things as the impact of higher prices, higher volumes, lower costs, or even the hiring of a new employee on profits. Each of these options is open to Best Bread, but which will provide the most reliable and realistic options for profit improvement?

We have already looked at the impact of changing the volume of loaves sold by Tim in Table 3.10. Using our contribution margin per loaf sold and changing volumes, we see that Tim can increase his profitability if he can make and sell more bread. The constraint, however, is that Tim can only increase his production of bread to 72,000 loaves, his current maximum capacity if he wants to continue to work 2,000 hours per year. Therefore, adding volume alone is not going to provide much improvement in Tim's profits. Let us try some other options first, such as raising the price to \$3 a loaf. What is our breakeven volume now? Remember that volume sold is equal to total fixed costs divided by the contribution margin, which is price minus variable costs.

$$\mathbf{V} = \frac{\mathbf{TFC}}{\mathbf{(P - VC)}}$$

$$\mathbf{V} = \frac{\$52{,}530}{(\$3 - \$0.998)}$$

or

26,239 **loaves**

This is a drop of 3,744 loaves, or a 12.5% (3,744 divided by 29,983 loaves) reduction in the volume Tim needs to break even. To break even, therefore, Tim would only have to work 729 hours (26,239 loaves times 1.67 minutes per loaf divided by 60 minutes in an hour). That said, he would still work at least 2,000 hours per year as he is in business to make a profit, not simply break even. By increasing the price per loaf to \$3, Tim would increase his profits by \$15,000 (\$3 minus \$0.998 times 60,000 loaves minus \$52,530) to \$67,590, a 28.5% increase (\$67,590 minus \$52,590 divided by \$52,590).

There is one catch before we go too crazy recommending this price increase to Tim. If you remember from your economics class, for most commodities, if you raise the price, the volume you can sell will probably drop. We do not know what Tim's competition is doing, but it is always dangerous to suggest a price hike first. He is bound to lose customers if they have to pay \$0.25 more for a loaf of bread with no changes in quality or service. So let us see what other options he could explore.

Tim is currently paying retail prices for his ingredients because he does not have enough buying power to negotiate reductions in these costs. Recently, however, Tim was approached by a local representative of a buying cooperative that negotiates better prices for goods for a group of small businesses. Tim is skeptical at first, but now that he has the CVP analysis to help him out, he decides to give the cooperative a chance. He is amazed once he gets involved to find out it can shave 25% off of the costs of his raw materials. Since this is what makes up most of the cost of a loaf of bread, Tim decides to sign with the cooperative, which would add slightly to his fixed costs, bringing them up to $55,000. Now he needs your help in determining what it will save him. Let us start by recalculating the variable costs (see Table 3.13) with the reduction in ingredient costs.

TABLE 3.13 COSTS OF ONE LOAF OF BREAD WITH COOPERATIVE BUYING

Best Bread Bakery					
Ingredient	Amount Used	Current Cost per Unit	Current Total Cost	Cost per Unit if Use Co-Op Buying	Total Cost if Use Co-Op Buying
Water	7 1/2 cups	FREE	-	FREE	-
Lard	10 Tbsp	0.045	$ 0.446	$ 0.033	$ 0.334
Sugar	10 Tbsp	0.049	$ 0.492	$ 0.037	$ 0.369
Salt	3 Tbsp	0.025	$ 0.075	$ 0.019	$ 0.056
Yeast	6 packets	0.250	$ 1.500	$ 0.188	$ 1.125
Flour	20 cups	0.067	$ 1.333	$ 0.050	$ 1.000
Plastic bag	6 each	0.023	$ 0.138	$ 0.017	$ 0.104
Twist tie	6 each	0.001	$ 0.004	$ 0.000	$ 0.003
Baker	10 minutes	0.200	$ 2.000	$ 0.200	$ 2.000
Total Cost for Six-Loaf Batch			$ 5.988		$ 4.991
Cost per Loaf (Batch Cost / 6)			$ 0.998		$ 0.832

Note: Columns are rounded.

Tim's variable costs drop from $0.998 to $0.832 per loaf, or a 16.7% drop. It is not 25% because labor is unchanged in our analysis, correct? What does this do to Tim's breakeven sales? Once again, we are dividing total fixed costs by the price minus variable cost, or the contribution margin, to get the breakeven sales.

$$V = \frac{TFC}{(P - VC)}$$

$$V = \frac{\$55{,}000}{(\$2.75 - \$0.832)}$$

or

28,676 **loaves**

At this volume, what would Tim's margin of safety be? His total profits?

Margin of Safety = **Actual Sales** - **Breakeven Sales**

31,324 **loaves** = 60,000 - 28,676

and

Profitability = **Margin of Safety** × **Contribution Margin per Loaf**

\$60,079.43 = 31,324 **loaves** × (\$2.75 - \$0.832)

At his current 60,000-loaf sales level and current costs, Tim's profit is \$52,590 per Table 3.12. Joining the co-op will increase Tim's profits by \$7,489.43 or 14.24% (\$7,489.43 divided by \$52,590 equals 14.24%).

Clearly we will be recommending to Tim that he follow through on the cooperative so that he can improve profits without facing the risks that a price hike could create. We have Tim making bread 1,667 hours out of the 2,000 available, or 83% of the time. Realistically, he is probably working more than 2,000 hours since he is also serving customers throughout the day. While Tim's wife comes in for a few hours a day to lend a hand, Tim really is working hard with few options for improving profitability unless he changes how he manages his business.

To explore other options, we can look at what might happen if Tim decides to hire a baker so he can increase the amount of bread he can make per day. Right now since Tim also minds the counter, the time it takes to actually make a loaf of bread is greater than it would be if all he did was make and bake bread. Let us assume that if Tim were uninterrupted, the time spent on one loaf of bread would drop to one minute, or six minutes total for the batch of six loaves. Therefore, if Tim wanted to improve output and profits, hiring someone whose only job would be to make bread might make sense. A new baker will cost Tim $42,000 a year, or $0.35 per minute. With it now taking only one minute to make a loaf, labor would increase to $0.35 from the current $0.33 per loaf.

This might not sound like a good decision, but the new baker would be able to make 120,000 loaves vs. the 72,000 loaf capacity limit Tim currently faces. Tim would also still be able to make some bread besides running the retail operation. He estimates he could still make 30,000 loaves. With the added baker, Tim also believes he could expand the days and hours of operation from the current eight hours a day on Tuesday through Saturday to 10 hours a day, Tuesday through Sunday, with a little help from his wife. So, he would be able to sell bread for 3,120 hours, a 56% increase in the hours customers can be served ((3,120 minus 2,000) divided by 2,000). While Tim cannot be certain that simply being open more hours will help him sell all of his potential output, he could still reasonably hope to improve sales and profitability significantly.

To increase output and sales, Tim will need to add some more loaf pans and cooling racks to handle the new volume plus face an increase in electricity to run the oven a longer period of time. Tim estimates he will be looking at a $10,000 increase per year in his fixed costs in addition to the $2,470 increase caused by joining the buying cooperative, making his new total fixed costs $65,000. Variable costs per loaf using the baker will increase only two cents above the last amount we calculated in Table 3.13 to $0.85 per loaf. To see how these changes impact Tim's profitability, let us have a look at Table 3.14.

TABLE 3.14 CO-OP AND NEW BAKER

Best Bread Bakery						
Price per Loaf (1)	Revised Variable Cost per Loaf (2)	Revised Contribution Margin per Loaf (3) = (2) - (1)	Estimated Volume Sold (4)	Total Contribution Margin (5) = (3) x (4)	Total Fixed Costs (6)	Estimated Profit (7) = (5) - (6)
$ 2.75	$ 0.85	$ 1.90	60,000	$ 113,880	$ 65,000	$ 48,880
$ 2.75	$ 0.85	$ 1.90	70,000	$ 132,860	$ 65,000	$ 67,860
$ 2.75	$ 0.85	$ 1.90	80,000	$ 151,840	$ 65,000	$ 86,840
$ 2.75	$ 0.85	$ 1.90	90,000	$ 170,820	$ 65,000	$ 105,820
$ 2.75	$ 0.85	$ 1.90	100,000	$ 189,800	$ 65,000	$ 124,800
$ 2.75	$ 0.85	$ 1.90	110,000	$ 208,780	$ 65,000	$ 143,780
$ 2.75	$ 0.85	$ 1.90	120,000	$ 227,760	$ 65,000	$ 162,760
$ 2.75	$ 0.85	$ 1.90	130,000	$ 246,740	$ 65,000	$ 181,740
$ 2.75	$ 0.85	$ 1.90	140,000	$ 265,720	$ 65,000	$ 200,720
$ 2.75	$ 0.85	$ 1.90	150,000	$ 284,700	$ 65,000	$ 219,700

Note: Column 2 and Column 3 are rounded from $0.852 and $1.898, respectively.

If Tim can only sell the same number of loaves as he is currently selling (60,000 loaves), hiring the baker would actually reduce profits from the $60,079 we calculated from Table 3.13 to $48,880, an 18.6% drop (($60,079 minus $49,880) divided by $60,079). His breakeven sales level would increase from 28,676 loaves to 34,247 loaves, a 19.2% increase. Therefore, if Tim does not think he can sell more bread, he should go with the co-op option but not hire a baker.

What if, however, Tim could actually increase his sales by being open longer hours and having more bread to sell? As seen in Table 3.14, if he can only sell 10,000 more loaves, his profits will increase to $67,860, a 12.9% increase ($67,860 minus $60,079 divided by $60,079) over what would be earned if he goes with the co-op but does not hire a baker. This appears to be a pretty reasonable sales goal. The decision to hire the baker, therefore, is a fairly low-risk option for Tim, one with tremendous upside potential in terms of improved profits that could grow to $219,700 if he can sell the 150,000 loaves that represents his new capacity limits. To be able to sell his maximum output, Tim may need to make other changes, such as adding some features to his product line (such as different flavors or shapes of bread) or find a new, large customer. These are opportunities that can be examined independently as they arise. For now, it looks like Tim will be well-served in both joining the co-op and hiring someone to help in the kitchen.

Before we leave this setting, let us do one more thing with our breakeven formula. So far we have had to do a lot of calculating to get to some of our answers in terms of revenue dollars. Well, just in the way that we have found it useful to use the contribution margin to determine breakeven volumes, we can use the percentage of contribution margin (the contribution margin ratio) to calculate breakeven revenues themselves. The **contribution margin ratio** *is the contribution margin divided by revenues*, or:

$$\text{Contribution Margin Ratio (CMR)} = \frac{\text{Contribution Margin in Dollars}}{\text{Selling Price}}$$

This formula gives us a lot of flexibility when we do not have the information needed to use the basic CVP formulas because we can work off of percentage of variable costs to get our solutions. Let us calculate the contribution margin ratio for Best Bread using our last analysis in Table 3.14:

$$\text{CMR} = \frac{\$1.90}{\$2.75}$$

or 69%

This means that for every dollar of current sales, roughly 31% of the sales price, or $0.85, goes to pay for the variable costs of production (the variable cost ratio), leaving $1.90, or 69%, to cover fixed costs and generate a profit. Thus, the **variable cost ratio** *is the total of all variable costs divided by revenues.* Let us now assume Tim wants to ensure he gets $100,000 in profit under the new operating conditions. What sales revenue (in dollars) does he need?

$$\textbf{Revenue Needed} = \frac{\textbf{Fixed Costs} + \textbf{Desired Before-Tax Profit}}{\textbf{Contribution Margin Ratio}}$$

or

$$\textbf{Revenue Needed} = \frac{\$65{,}000 + \$100{,}000}{.69}$$

$$= \$239{,}130$$

At $2.75 per loaf, Tim needs to sell 86,956 loaves of bread. We can always use the contribution margin ratio in a variable income statement format to prove our answer, as we see in Table 3.15.

TABLE 3.15 VARIABLE COST INCOME STATEMENT IF WE SELL 86,956 LOAVES

Best Bread Bakery Variable Cost Income Statement For the period ending December 31, 20XX		
Sales (86,956 loaves x $2.75 per loaf)	$ 239,129	100%
Less: Variable Costs (86,956 loaves x $0.85 per loaf)	$ 73,912	31%
Total Contribution Margin	$ 165,217	69%
Less: Fixed Costs	$ 65,000	27%
Operating Income	$ 100,217	42%

Given that there is always a small rounding error when dealing with the CVP calculations, it appears our solution will meet Tim's goals. Now let us grow Tim's business a little bit more by adding other products to his product line and deal with the taxes that cannot be avoided.

EXPANDING THE BASIC CVP FORMULA

There are many different ways we can expand the simple CVP formula to increase the amount of information it provides or the number of questions we can use it to answer. We will briefly examine two such changes to conclude this discussion of CVP: (1) solving for the volumes needed to achieve desired before- and after-taxes profit levels, and (2) multiproduct CVP analysis.

Adding before-tax profits. One of the simplest changes we can make to the formulas we have been using is to shift away from the breakeven point, or zero profit focus to one that includes the potential for the firm to make a profit. We allowed for profit before tax in our original calculation of the CVP formula, specifically:

$$\textbf{Volume Sold} = \frac{\textbf{Income Before Tax} + \textbf{Total Fixed Costs}}{\textbf{(Price - Variable Cost)}}$$

We used this formula when we calculated how many loaves of bread Tim would need to sell if he wanted to make $100,000 in before-tax profit. It is a simple change to the analysis completed earlier, so no further time will be spent on a specific example.

Companies are often more concerned, however, with achieving desired after-tax profits than before-tax profits. It is after-tax dollars that the stock market uses in assessing a company's performance. Dividends are paid out of after-tax profits, which impacts shareholder satisfaction with a company and its management. While there are several different ways we could make this adjustment from before-tax to after-tax dollars, one of the simplest is to convert the desired after-tax profitability into its before-tax amount. We can then use the formulas we have derived for CVP without any further modifications. How is this transformation done? The formula is:

$$\textbf{Income After Tax} = \textbf{Income Before Tax} - \textbf{(Income Before Tax x Tax Rate)}$$

or

$$\textbf{Income After Tax} = \textbf{Income Before Tax} \times \textbf{(1 - Tax Rate)}$$

And solving for Income Before Tax, we get

$$\textbf{Income Before Tax} = \frac{\textbf{Income After Tax}}{\textbf{(1 - Tax Rate)}}$$

Best Bread is taxed at a rate of 30% on its pre-tax income. Therefore, if Tim now wanted to earn $100,000 in after-tax profits, how many loaves would it need to sell?

$$\$100{,}000 = \textbf{Income Before Tax} \times (1 - 0.3)$$

so

$$\textbf{Income Before Tax} = (\$100{,}000) \;/\; .7$$

so

$$= \$142{,}857$$

Using Tim's selling price of $2.75 per loaf, he would now need to cover $142,858 in before-tax profits plus the $65,000 in fixed costs, or $207,857. Dividing this revenue requirement by Best Bread's contribution margin, or $1.90 ($207,858 divided by $1.90 equals 109,398), that is 109,398 loaves of bread, or $300,846 (109,399 loaves times $2.75 per loaf) in revenue. When we convert the desired profits to after-tax dollars, Tim has to earn significantly more profit in before-tax dollars to reach his after-tax goals. Tim is going to need to rely on more than one product if he is going to achieve this goal.

MULTIPLE PRODUCT CVP

The last issue we will look at is one that most companies face: the need to incorporate a number of different products into the CVP analysis. In fact, there are very few companies that have only one product or dedicated facilities (and, hence, costs) for each of its product lines. This means we have to find some way to incorporate the information about the different products in our overall breakeven formulas.

There are many ways these additional products can vary—price, variable cost, fixed cost, and volume sold. As we saw when we did the after-tax profit calculations, it is often easier to find a way to modify our data to make it fit into the standard CVP formulas than it is to try to change the formulas to reflect the change in our conditions and assumptions. The same holds true for multiple product CVP analysis. Specifically, we need to find a way to develop an estimate of the contribution margin for the *combined* set of products. This is accomplished by weighting the contribution margin of each product by the current **sales mix,** *sales of a given product compared with the combined sales of all of a company's other products* or average sales volume for the different products reduced to its lowest common denominator. We call this revised contribution margin approach a **package contribution margin,** *the combined contribution of a group of products used to derive the breakeven point.*

In order to develop this information in a manner consistent with the examples we have used from Best Bread, we will need to add a small amount of data. Specifically, while Tim could continue to just offer white bread, he wants to expand his line to include wheat bread, white hoagie rolls, and wheat hoagie rolls. The variable costs for these different products are contained in Table 3.16. Given what we have learned, we can now derive the contribution margin for each product with ease. What we need to make this multiple product example work is to ask Tim how much he thinks he will sell in a year. He decides he is likely to sell 100,000 units of white bread to 60,000 units of wheat bread. Tim also thinks he will sell 30,000 six-packs of white hoagies and 10,000 six-packs of wheat hoagies.

Before we start calculating, we need to complete the picture. With these sales volumes and the costs and labor time noted in Table 3.16, we are able to calculate the contribution margin per product as well as the average contribution margin. The unit contribution based on the sales mix percentage is derived by taking the percentage sales of each type of product times the contribution margin each product provides. We end up with an average contribution margin of $2.015 and new total fixed costs (Tim has to buy more racks, run the oven longer, and so on) of $90,100.

TABLE 3.16 PRODUCT LINE EXPANSION

Best Bread Bakery											
Product	Price per Unit (1)	Units Sold (2)	% Sales Mix (3) = (2) / 200,000	Materials Cost (4)	Labor Time in Minutes (5)	Labor Cost per Unit at $0.35 per Minute (6)	Total Labor Time in Hrs. (7) = ((5) x (2)) / 60	Total Variable Costs per Unit (8) = (4) + (6)	Unit Contribution Margin (9) = (1) - (8)	Contribution Margin Based on Sales Mix % (10) = (3) x (9)	Fixed Costs by Product (11)
White Bread	$ 2.75	100,000	50.0%	$ 0.50	1	$ 0.35	1,666.7	$ 0.85	$ 1.90	$ 0.95	$ 65,000
Wheat Bread	$ 3.00	60,000	30.0%	$ 0.59	1	$ 0.35	1,000	$ 0.94	$ 2.06	$ 0.618	$ 10,100
White Hoagies	$ 3.50	30,000	15.0%	$ 0.62	2	$ 0.70	1,000	$ 1.32	$ 2.18	$ 0.327	$ 10,000
Wheat Hoagies	$ 3.75	10,000	5.0%	$ 0.65	2	$ 0.70	333.3	$ 1.35	$ 2.40	$ 0.12	$ 5,000
		200,000	100%				4,000			$ 2.015	$ 90,100
							2	Employees		Average CM	

We can now use the average contribution margin in place of the one product unit-based contribution margin to determine how many total units need to be sold for Best Bread to break even. Specifically:

$$\textbf{Breakeven Total Volume} = \frac{\textbf{Total Fixed Cost}}{\textbf{Package Contribution Margin}}$$

$$= \frac{\$90{,}100}{\$2.015}$$

$$= 44{,}715 \textbf{ Total Units}$$

Given this total, we now need to calculate the unit sales of each type of product. We do this by reapplying our information from Table 3.16 to generate Table 3.17.

TABLE 3.17 INDIVIDUAL UNIT SALES

Best Bread Bakery						
Product Line	Total Units to Sell	Sales Mix %	Units to Sell	Contribution Margin	Total Contribution Margin	Fixed Cost
White Bread	44,715	50.00%	22,357	$ 1.900	$ 42,478.91	$ 65,000
Wheat Bread	44,715	30.00%	13,414	$ 2.060	$ 27,633.65	$ 10,100
White Hoagies	44,715	15.00%	6,707	$ 2.180	$ 14,621.69	$ 10,000
Wheat Hoagies	44,715	5.00%	2,236	$ 2.400	$ 5,365.76	$ 5,000
				Total	$90,100.00	$ 90,100

We could now do a safety margin analysis. Looking at Table 3.18, we see that Tim has gained in terms of his safety margin. He now can expect to earn $312,900 before taxes with his current plan. This is, of course, assuming he can actually sell the quantities in his projection, but we can see that moving to multiple products is a good move for Tim.

TABLE 3.18 SAFETY MARGIN FOR PLANNED LEVEL OF SALES

Best Bread Bakery					
Product Line	Contribution Margin per Unit (1)	Units Planned to Sell (2)	Units to Break Even (3)	Safety Margin in Units (4) = (2) - (3)	Projected Profit (5) = (1) x (4)
White Bread	$ 1.900	100,000	22,357	77,643	$ 147,521.09
Wheat Bread	$ 2.060	60,000	13,414	46,586	$ 95,966.35
White Hoagies	$ 2.180	30,000	6,707	23,293	$ 50,778.31
Wheat Hoagies	$ 2.400	10,000	2,236	7,764	$ 18,634.24
Total Before Tax Dollars of Profit					$312,900.00

This last section may seem a bit more difficult, but, with practice, you will get very good at working with contribution margins, contribution margin ratios, and all sorts of product mixes. Remember, in the real world, there are multiple prices, multiple products, and multiple markets, so we are just touching the tip of the iceberg when we deal with a simple company like Best Bread. Perhaps the fact that our tool, CVP analysis, is so flexible and intuitive is the reason it continues to be popular among managers who are always looking for ways to estimate how changes in how they do business will affect company profits and its future. CVP analysis is only a starting point, however. If a major decision is being made, CVP analysis would be used as a first pass to see if the plan has merit. If the plan looks good using CVP analysis, the next step would be to develop a more in-depth analysis using the incremental cost approach (see Chapter 5).

Building an Effective Business Case

OBJECTIVE 4

Understand how to create an effective business case.

When we get close to an answer, we develop a business case that goes into more detail, properly picking up all of the stepped costs and other factors the business will face if it changes operating conditions. As you may remember from Chapter 2, a business case is a decision support and planning tool that projects the likely financial results and other business consequences of an action.[6] Focused on a specific problem or opportunity, a sound business case analyzes and summarizes the financial and nonfinancial implications of various alternatives open to an organization. A business case emphasizes the costs and benefits of these alternatives, presenting the issue and the potential solutions in a logical, and complete, manner.

6 Marty J. Schmidt, *The Business Case Guide*, Boston: Solution Matrix, Ltd., 2002: p. 1.

The components of an effective business case are presented in Table 3.19. As you can see, there are five major sections in the completed document:

- Introduction
- Methods and assumptions
- Business impacts
- Sensitivity, risks, and contingencies
- Conclusions and recommendations

In developing a business case, therefore, we are focused on detailing the issue or problem, and our suggested solution, in such a way that another individual can understand and assess both our methods and our conclusions.

TABLE 3.19 COMPONENTS OF AN EFFECTIVE BUSINESS CASE

1. **Introduction**
   - 1.1. Subject—What is being studied?
   - 1.2. Purpose—Why is it being studied?
   - 1.3. Situation and Motivation
     - 1.3.1. Objectives—What the project hopes to accomplish
     - 1.3.2. Opportunities—Major opportunities that can be exploited
     - 1.3.3. Threats—How will competition respond? Other threats?
     - 1.3.4. Problems—Issues that make the problem difficult to analyze
     - 1.3.5. Limitations—Things not considered

2. **Methods and Assumptions**
   - 2.1. Scope—Where the boundaries of the decision are set
   - 2.2. Metrics—How the decision is to be analyzed
   - 2.3. Major Assumptions—What is being assumed in the decision setting?
   - 2.4. Alternatives Considered—Full list of potential solutions
   - 2.5. Methods Used to Analyze Alternatives—CVP, for instance

3. **Business Impacts**
   - 3.1. Cash flow projections—The numbers we use to solve the problem
   - 3.2. Financial analysis and development of financial metrics—The results of analysis
   - 3.3. Rationale for including important nonfinancial metrics—Why certain nonfinancial metrics matter to the decision (such as quality)
   - 3.4. Recommended course of action

4. **Sensitivity, Risks, and Contingencies**
   - 4.1. Sensitivity of the model used to changes in assumptions—What is the safety margin, for instance

4.2. Risks that the decision will represent—What if sales do not reach their limits or other problems that might occur

4.3. Contingency plans for dealing with the business risks—How these problems will be dealt with if they occur, perhaps running a sale on hoagies

5. **Conclusions and Recommendations**

   5.1. Summary of the problem statement—What was analyzed

   5.2. Alternatives considered—Solutions considered

   5.3. Alternative chosen and why (briefly)—Best course of action

   5.4. Implementation recommendations—How to go about making it happen

Table 3.19, therefore, details the content of each of the five major sections. We may not need to deal with all of these elements of the business case every time we are faced with the need to make a decision, but we should try to understand the situation from multiple perspectives, laying out our assumptions, how we analyzed the problem, recommendations, and the risks the decision involves. In other words, a business case should include all of the parts noted above (introduction through conclusion) with as much detail as you can provide. You should also include graphics such as Figure 3.3 to bring your message to the reader in a visual way.

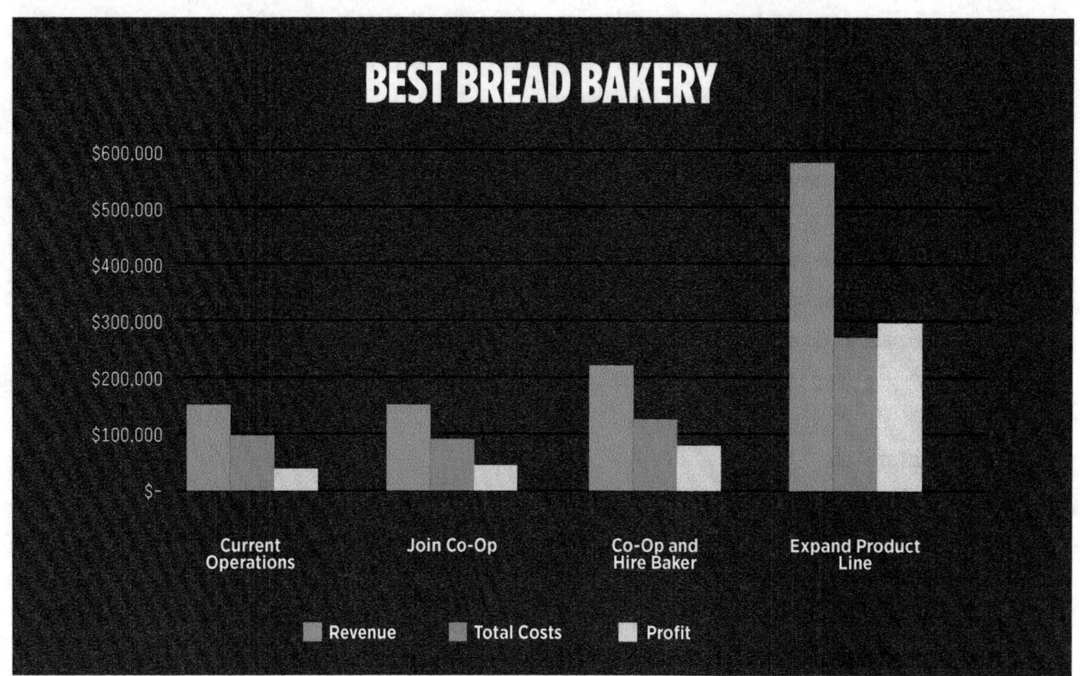

FIGURE 3.3 EXAMPLE OF GRAPHIC THAT MIGHT BE INCLUDED IN A BUSINESS CASE

How might a business case for the options Tim has considered to improve his profitability look? In order of presentation, we see:

1. **Introduction**
    - **Subject:** The profitability of Best Bread Bakery
    - **Purpose:** To find a way to boost profitability
    - **Situation and motivation:** Tim wants to find a way to increase profitability to more than $100,000 per year after taxes. The opportunities lie in offering a wider range of alternative products, joining the food cooperative, and hiring a new baker. The threats are that our competition may copy our plan; the new baker may not work out; or the projected sales cannot be reached. The problems are that the average work hours in a year are 2,000 per person. The limitations to the analysis are that we are looking only at the impact of adding three new products to the product line, all forms of bread rather than looking at expanding to new product lines, such as cakes. We are constrained by the available production time and the capacity of the oven and other equipment to handle any increase in demand.
2. **Methods and Assumptions**
    - **Scope:** We are looking only at existing capabilities of the bakery. Our expansion plans do not include new sites or more space.
    - **Metrics:** We are going to use cost projections to analyze the decision. The focus is on the most profitable combination of changes to Tim's business.
    - **Major assumptions:** That Tim can find a new baker; that if he raises prices, he can still sell enough loaves of bread to make a profit; that the buying cooperative is a stable enterprise; and that there is adequate demand for the hoagies and wheat bread to justify adding them to the product line.
    - **Alternatives considered:** Adding a new baker, raising the price of a loaf, joining the buying cooperative, expanding the bakery's product line to include wheat bread, and white and wheat hoagie rolls.
    - **Methods used in analysis:** CVP analysis.
3. **Business Impacts**
    - **Cash flow projections:** We analyzed each of these decisions using tables 3.13 through 3.18. (Note: If this was a real business case, we would actually insert these tables in this section along with our description of their underlying assumptions and limitations.)
    - **Nonfinancial metrics:** We considered the available working hours as well as the oven's capacity. Quality was assumed but would be an important consideration of hiring a new baker and ramping up output.

- **Recommended course of action:** Join the buying cooperative (much lower variable costs) and expand the product line, hiring four new bakers to handle the increased volume (much higher profits).

4. **Sensitivity, Risks, and Contingencies**
    - **Sensitivity of decisions:** We ran sensitivity analysis in the form of the safety margin for some of the decisions. We would expand this to all of the options for a final business case analysis.
    - **Risks of each alternative:** What if there is no demand for hoagie rolls? What if the new bakers do not make bread that is as good as Tim's? What if one or more of the new bakers quits when Tim has committed to more output for a key customer? What if the oven breaks down due to overuse? What if the buying cooperative ceases to exist? (Note: If this was a real business case, we would list the risks of each alternative separately.)
    - **Dealing with the risks:** Tim will ask his new hires to bake bread several times and check on the quality each time. Tim will continue to use his regular suppliers for some of his ingredients so he has a fallback position. Tim will keep a list of potential bakers in case he runs into problems. Tim will test the market for the hoagies and wheat bread using a sales promotion. Tim will institute regular maintenance of the oven to ensure it continues to function properly. (Note: We would explain methods to offset the risk for each alternative listed.)

5. **Conclusions**
    - We set out to find ways to improve Best Bread's profitability. We looked at a variety of options and determined that Tim should pursue three changes to his business—adding four bakers, joining the buying cooperative, and expanding his product line. Tim should advertise and network to find the new bakers, train them thoroughly on his methods and recipes, negotiate with the buying cooperative, and introduce his new products by launching a sales promotion to bring customers into the store.

This is an abbreviated approach to the business plan because we did not include all of the tables we ran to actually examine the impact of the various decisions on Tim's profitability and safety margin of projected sales. The entire section on CVP and Best Bread Bakery was actually a business case that explored the various options open to Tim to increase his profitability and how each option might affect the riskiness of his business model. You will be using business cases throughout the text to justify a position that you take when looking at alternatives a company can use to deal with competition and profit goals. The ultimate goal—serving customers better—lies behind all of the decisions a company makes. We will always want to make sure that the analysis and recommendations we make will ensure high levels of profitability and customer satisfaction.

Sanjiv and his team have been running the same types of analysis we just did for Best Bread Bakery in order to meet Fran's request for ways to better understand the current cost structure at Easy Air as well as to explore various options available to Easy Air that would improve current profits. You will do some of the same analysis that Sanjiv and his team did when you do the database problems at the end of the chapter. And as you will see in Chapters 4 and 5, there are many other tools and analyses that Easy Air can use to better understand, and leverage, its costs and assets. Let us rejoin Sanjiv and the team to finish out the chapter.

IN CONTEXT ➤ Developing and Using Cost Estimates at Easy Air—Part 3

"Sanjiv, these numbers are really interesting, and exactly what I had in mind when I put you to work on this project," said Fran.

"Thanks, Fran; without Fritz's help, and Rudy and Sherry's dedication and effort, we wouldn't have gotten this far. And, I really don't want you to use these numbers just yet. The team and I really feel that we should take the most promising scenario and develop a more comprehensive solution. CVP treats all the nonvariable resources as if they're fixed costs. We know that's not true—and I'm sure we'll eliminate some stepped costs if we add the additional passenger load Toni is projecting... Actually, we'd like to explore several different issues in greater depth, which will mean expanding our analysis from simple costs to activity-based costing and then shifting from CVP to incremental analysis. Our goal is to provide you with a complete business case for two or three of the most promising alternatives."

"That sounds good, Sanjiv. And I'd love you to get rolling right away, but I think it would be wise to allow you a bit more time to dig deeper and check your assumptions. I may share some of these insights with Bob Adams, but I'll make sure he understands that these are very preliminary figures. Do you think another week will do it?"

"We'll try, but it's more likely to be two weeks before we're finally done. If we finish earlier, you'll get the results and analysis earlier, okay?"

"Fair enough...and by the way, why don't the three of you go out for a nice dinner this weekend, on the company? You've earned it!"

"Thanks, Fran. I'm sure the team will appreciate it! And, we'll see you in two weeks."

Summary

Cost is a form of performance measurement that focuses on the resources consumed by a firm's output or activities. Each resource has its own unique set of characteristics, such as its **purchase price,** *the amount of money paid to obtain a resource*, and purchase package. These characteristics determine how much of a resource will have to be purchased. If a resource cannot be stored, or cannot be divided into and used in smaller amounts than the purchase package, there is a heightened potential for high costs and a lot of wasted resources.

The relationship between a change in the amount of resources used and a change in the amount of outputs or activities completed is called the behavior of cost. There are four primary behaviors, or cost patterns: variable costs, fixed costs, mixed costs, and stepped costs. The higher the percentage of variable costs in a firm's overall cost structure, the more responsive its costs of doing business will be to changes in customer demand. If, as we saw in Best Bread, fixed costs are also an important part of the firm's cost structure, then the more fixed costs there are as a percentage of total costs, the less responsive the firm's total costs will be to changes in demand.

Cost-volume-profit (CVP) analysis is one analytical tool that we can use to explore the firm's cost structure and estimated breakeven sales volumes. CVP is a relatively simple tool that emphasizes the impact of changes in price, costs, or volumes on a company's profitability. We can modify CVP analysis to incorporate desired before- or after-tax profits, to estimate breakeven sales in dollar terms, or to include a package or mix of products. The resulting estimates are useful to gain an understanding of approximate profitability of a firm under a range of conditions and operating assumptions. While simple in nature and focus, CVP provides a good starting point for a more detailed analysis of a firm's total costs and profits under a number of different situations and assumptions.

Key Terms

Actionable costs: costs that can be affected by management action or decisions.

Activity-based costing: used to assign the cost of nonmachine-based work to a firm's products, services, and customers.

Average fixed cost: the total fixed costs divided by the units sold or made.

Average total cost: the total fixed cost divided by the number of units produced.

Average variable: the total variable cost divided by the number of units produced.

Avoidable cost: a cost that can be eliminated from a firm's cost structure if its processes or products are changed in some way.

Breakeven: the point at which the total contribution earned equals total fixed costs.

Capacity: the amount of work a resource is capable of supporting before it must be replenished.

Contribution margin: *price – variable cost per unit = contribution margin*; the amount of money that each unit sold contributes to covering the firm's fixed costs and profits.

Contribution margin ratio: the contribution margin divided by revenues.

Conversion cost: the total of direct labor and overhead costs used to turn raw materials into finished goods.

Cost: the economic value of resources consumed in making a product or process, or completing an activity.

Cost estimate: the evaluation of the resources used in providing a product or service.

Cost structure: the estimated combination of a firm's fixed, mixed, stepped, and variable costs.

Cost variability: how costs change in response to changes in the volume of work.

Cost-volume-profit analysis: a tool used to understand how changes to costs, prices, or sales volume will impact a company's estimated profitability.

Direct cost: a cost that can be uniquely assigned to one specific activity or outcome.

Divisibility: the degree to which a resource can be subdivided into smaller consumption units.

Economies of scale: fixed cost per unit made or sold drops as a result of spreading fixed costs over more output units.

Fixed cost: a cost that does not change with changes in volume.

Indirect cost: a cost that is not traceable to a specific output unit or activity, but is shared by two or more outcomes or activities.

Labor costs: all of the labor expenses directly traceable to making product.

Marginal cost: the cost to make one more unit of a product.

Manufacturing cost: the cost incurred in manufacturing companies that can be directly tied to making the product they sell.

Margin of safety: the difference between the current or estimated sales of a company and the level of sales needed for it to break even.

Material costs: all of the physical resources used to make a product.

Mixed cost: a cost that has both fixed and variable components.

Nonmanufacturing cost: a cost in manufacturing companies that cannot be directly tied to making the product.

Operating leverage: a measure of how sensitive profit is to a given percentage change in revenues.

Overhead cost: the sum of all of the indirect costs of making a product.

Period cost: one that is incurred every period (normally per month) regardless of whether or not the company produces a product or provides a service.

Price: what a seller charges the customer.

Prime cost: the sum of the direct materials and direct labor used to make a product.

Product cost: one that can be directly tied to making a product.

Profit: when the price is greater than the cost.

Profit equation: *revenues – total costs = profit;* used to calculate the profit potential of different sales levels given costs.

Purchase package: the minimum size or quantity of a purchased resource.

Purchase price: the amount of money paid to obtain a resource.

Relevant range: the assumed volume of activity within which estimates of costs are accurate.

Sales mix: sales of a given product compared with the combined sales of all of a firm's other products.

Stepped cost: a cost that changes in "chunks" as volume changes.

Storability: the ability of a resource to be held for future use without a loss of its value-creating ability.

Total cost formula: *variable cost per unit x volume sold + fixed costs.*

Unavoidable costs: those that remain regardless of actions or decisions of management.

Value: the worth to the customer of the product or service.

Variable cost: a cost that changes a constant amount in direct response to changes in volume.

Variable cost ratio: the total of all variable costs divided by revenues.

Appendix to Chapter 3

There are many different aspects to costs, and many different issues we face when using them to estimate potential profitability. The main material in this chapter emphasized pure variable and pure fixed costs as the means to support the development and use of one of our first management accounting analytical tools, CVP analysis. The focus of this appendix is on one of the other types of cost—mixed cost. The information provided in this appendix, therefore, can be used in any setting where we are not able to look at the cost pattern of individual resources, but are instead faced with the need to separate fixed and variable costs from each other when all we have is a combined number.

VARIABILITY AND MIXED COSTS

In the chapter, we derived the variable cost and fixed costs for Best Bread Bakery by using our analytical skills and the simple formula for change, or:

$$\textbf{Cost Variability} = \frac{\textbf{Change in Cost}}{\textbf{Change in Volume}}$$

When we start to deal with more complex problems, it is important to be able to tell how much a specific resource cost varies across a range of volumes. While we are solving for the same thing—cost variability—we find out that it is much more complex to identify the variability pattern when we are dealing with mixed costs. Specifically, a mixed cost has some portion of variable cost and some portion of fixed cost. It can be very hard to separate out the fixed and variable portions of a mixed cost. To do so, we can use one of several methods. They all have strengths and weaknesses and will require you to calculate a few numbers to generate the final line (variable cost, or b) and intercept (fixed cost, or a). To do our calculations, we are going to use an example from an airline (not Easy Air) to see if we can estimate the cost of handling a number of checked bags on a flight. Table 3A.1 contains the data we will be working with:

TABLE 3A.1

Observation	Number of bags (x_i)	Baggage-Handling Cost (y_i)
1	10	$ 55.00
2	30	$ 65.00
3	40	$ 70.00
4	50	$ 75.00
5	80	$ 90.00
6	90	$ 95.00
7	100	$ 100.00
Sum	400	$ 550.00

HIGH-LOW METHOD

Let us look at the simplest method first, or the **high-low** method. Here we use our cost variability formula but focus on two specific points in our data set—the highest volume of bags (x) less the lowest level of bags, divided by the highest value of cost (y) less the lowest value of costs. In other words, we will use observations 1 and 7 in our variability formula, as follows:

$$\textbf{Cost Variability} = \frac{\textbf{Change in Cost}}{\textbf{Change in Baggage Volume}}$$

$$= \frac{\textbf{(Highest Cost - Lowest Cost)}}{\textbf{(Highest \# of Bags - Lowest \# of Bags)}}$$

or

$$= \frac{(\$100 - \$55)}{(100 - 10)}$$

$$= \$0.50$$

This number tells us how much more it will cost us—an additional $0.50 for each bag checked during a flight. We have to have someone in the baggage area all the time even if there are very few bags, so we need to estimate the fixed portion of this cost. Now it is easier to use a simple formula:

Total Cost of Baggage Handling = (Cost per Bag x Bags Handled) + TFC of Handling Bags

And let us set bags handled, or our (x) variable in this problem, equal to 10. We could use any number, but 10 is convenient. Our formula then becomes:

$$\$55 = (\$0.50)(10) + \textbf{TFC}$$
$$\$55 = \$5 + \textbf{TFC}$$
$$\$50 = \textbf{TFC}$$

We now have a complete cost formula for number of bags handled:

Total Cost of Baggage Handling = ($0.50 x Bags Handled) + $50.00

As long as our variable costs are a constant amount across all volumes, this formula works for us. Sometimes life is not quite this simple, as we will see when we do the exercises and problems in the chapter. But for now, we see that the high-low approach yields a usable formula.

There are strengths and weaknesses that go with any method of estimating. For the high-low method, we know we have taken in the extreme conditions in our estimates. The shortcoming, however, is that the average, or mean, number of occurrences may not correspond to the high and low metrics. If we are looking for average results, we may want to turn to scattergram diagrams.

SCATTERGRAM DIAGRAM

Another method that can be used is called the scattergram diagram approach (see Figure 3A.1). Here we plot the numbers we have on an *x* and *y* axis grid, then drop a line through what appears to be the middle. We then use the slope of the line to estimate the degree of change in the dependent variable, cost of baggage handling or *y*, vs. the change in the independent variable, total bags handled or *x*.

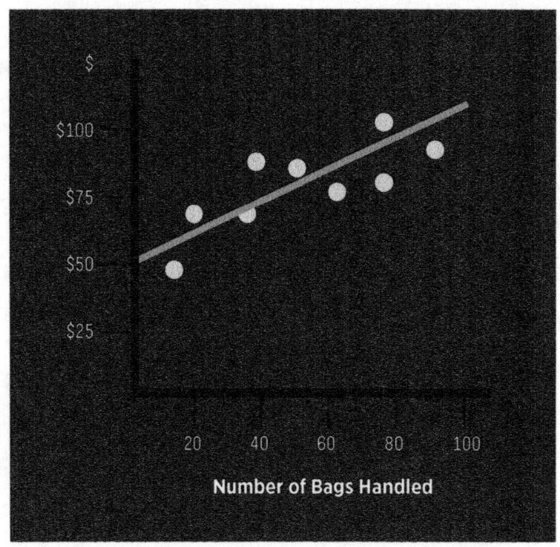

FIGURE 3A.1 SCATTERGRAM ANALYSIS

Here we once again see that $50 must be close to the fixed cost for handling bags because that is where our "best fit" line crosses the axis marking out dollars spent (the *y* axis). We would need to calculate the slope of the line, which would lead right back to the formula we just worked with, namely:

$$\textbf{Cost Variability} = \frac{\textbf{Change in Cost}}{\textbf{Change in Baggage Volume}}$$

We could work at using any two points, not simply the high and low points we used earlier. Let us compare the costs at 50 bags to that at 90 bags.

$$\textbf{Cost Variability} = \frac{(\$95.00 - \$75.00)}{(90 \textbf{ bags} - 50 \textbf{ bags})}$$

or $0.50

We can see how we would once again end up with the basic cost formula:

Total Cost of Baggage Handling = ($0.50 x Bags Handled) + $50.00

So both methods work, and for our simple example, with constant variability so easy to spot, it is easy to calculate and prove our work. Let us look at the last method, which can be a bit more challenging.

LEAST SQUARES REGRESSION

Our last method is the one most commonly used by organizations when simple analytics (the method used in the chapter) do not work because the numbers are too large or the relationships are not quite stable. It is called ordinary least squares regression analysis (LSR), and is a method you will use a lot in your college career. We now need to be clear on our x's and y's, so we can apply some formulas.

The LSR formula is used to explain changes in (y), the dependent variable, by changes in (x), the independent variable. In simple terms, (y), or our costs of handling baggage, is clearly dependent upon how many bags are checked (the (x) axis), correct? That is how we establish the (x) and (y) axis—what variable causes a change in the other one. Once we have (x) and (y) sorted out, we are solving for the following equation:

$$y = a + bx$$

where: y = **total cost to handle bags**
a = **fixed cost to handle bags**
b = **variable cost to handle bags**
x = **number of bags handled**

Where (a) is the intercept from our scattergram, now calculated, not derived. It is therefore the fixed costs of the activity, and (b) then becomes the variability estimate, or our variable cost per unit of work done. Now we need to add a bit of math to the analysis to solve for (a) and (b):

$$b = \Sigma[(x_i - \bar{x}) \text{ times } (y_i - \bar{y})] \;/\; \Sigma(x_i - \bar{x})^2$$

$$a = \bar{y} - b\bar{x}$$

where: x_i = **the observed value of the cost of handling bags**
$\bar{x}$ = **the mean of the observed costs for handling a bag**
y_i = **the observed number of bags handled**
$\bar{y}$ = **the mean of the observed number of bags handled**
a = **the fixed costs for handling baggage**
b = **the variable cost for handling baggage**

To use this formula, it is best if we now employ Excel to do the calculations, although the calculations can be done by hand. For this example, we used Excel to derive the results as shown in Table 3A.2.

TABLE 3A.2

Observation	Number of Bags (x_i)	Baggage-Handling Cost (y_i)	x_i - mean of x	y_i - mean of y	(x_i - mean of x) times (y_i - mean of y)	(x_i - mean of x)^2
1	10	$ 55.00	-47.14	-23.57	1,111.22	2222.45
2	30	$ 65.00	-27.14	-13.57	368.37	736.73
3	40	$ 70.00	-17.14	-8.57	146.94	293.88
4	50	$ 75.00	-7.14	-3.57	25.51	51.02
5	80	$ 90.00	22.86	11.43	261.22	522.45
6	90	$ 95.00	32.86	16.43	539.80	1079.59
7	100	$ 100.00	42.86	21.43	918.37	1836.73
Sum	400	$ 550.00	0.00	0.00	3371.43	6742.86
Mean	57.14	$ 78.57				
Therefore b equals:		$ 0.50				
		$ 50.00				
So the equation is: y = 50.00+.50x						

Once again our formula is $50 fixed cost plus $0.50 per bag handled. In most situations, these numbers would change when we use regression analysis because it is much more precise in calculating the intercept point (fixed costs) and slope of the line (variable costs) for the equation. No matter what approach we use, it is always critical to separate out as much of the cost due to the fixed costs that are there whether or not we do any work. This must be done using a reliable method based on the amount of work done with a resource (its variable component).

You can also use Excel to calculate the (a), (b), and r-squared value (goodness of fit of the regression line) for your regression. You enter the basic information for (y) and (x) in columns on your spreadsheet. Then enter the argument to calculate (a). Your Excel sheet will look as follows in Figure 3A.2.

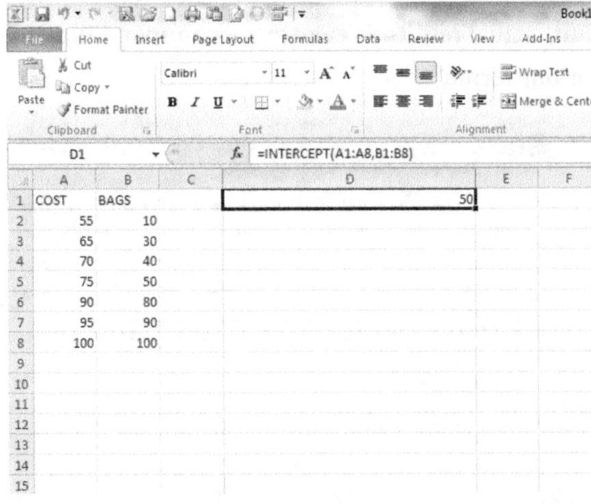

FIGURE 3A.2 EXCEL REGRESSION WORKSHEET

Next we want to calculate (b), or the slope of the line which represents our variable costs. When you do so, your dialogue box and results look like Figure 3A.3.

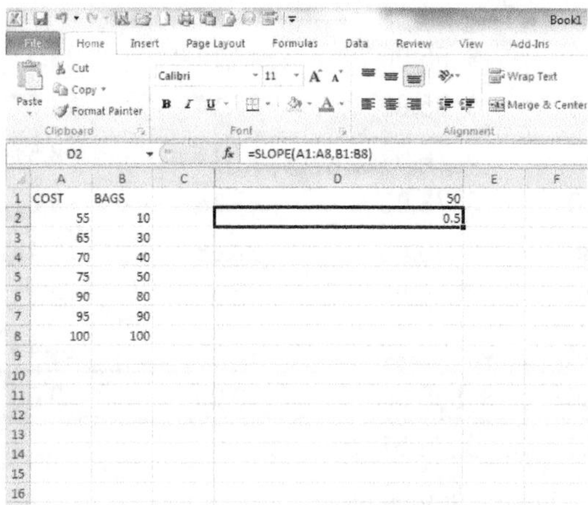

FIGURE 3A.3 EXCEL CALCULATION OF VARIABLE COST

What we can see from the results is that the (b) value is $0.50 per bag and the (a) value is $50. That leaves our formula at:

Total Cost of Baggage Handling = $50 + $0.50 per Bag Handled

This matches the analysis we did using the more laborious hand method. We can now ask ourselves how good the fit of the line is. We use the r-squared value to make this calculation. The closer this value is to "1," the better the line fits actual results. We enter the command illustrated in Figure 3A.4 in Excel to calculate the "r-squared" for our formula.

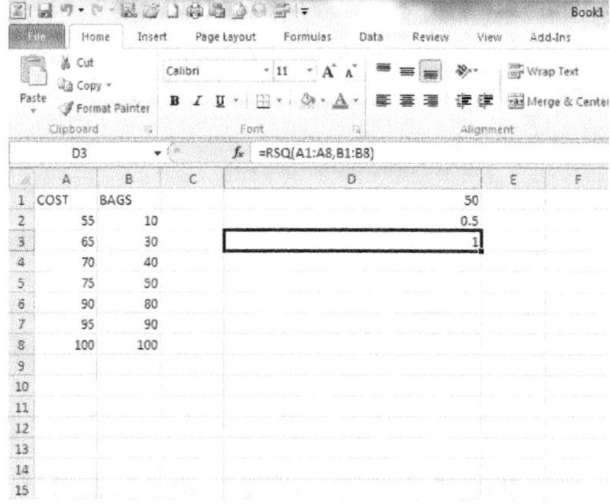

FIGURE 3A.4 SOLVING FOR "R SQUARE"

We see the line has a perfect fit. This reflects the structure of the problem. You should not expect such a high r-squared. It captures the percentage of explained variation divided by the total variation. R-squared values that are not as close to 1 do not necessarily mean the results of the regression are bad. It can be a signal that the ability to predict the relationship is lower than the norm. In costing exercises, however, we like to see the r-squared fairly close to 1 because we are using the information to predict future costs.

LSR is the most accurate of the methods, but it also makes the most assumptions about our relationships. These assumptions are the domain of your statistics class. Let it simply be said that there are a variety of ways to tease out variability, but our job is to always do so as accurately as we can with the data we have at hand. That is why we always need to do a business case, so we can separate the assumed cost patterns from what is currently being spent. We need to always be aware that the way in which we manage a resource can change its cost pattern, making it actually actionable vs. unavoidable in a cost formula. It is this latter set of relationships a manager is always concerned with in doing his daily work. It is why we need managers, to separate those actionable items from those that will take decisions at the top level to change.

Questions

1. What is the relationship between a cost and a price, if any? When do we need to know these relationships?
2. What is the difference between a direct and an indirect cost? When does knowing these differences lead to changes in decision making?
3. What is the basic cost estimate? How is it used in making decisions?
4. What are the different definitions of cost that are used in management accounting? Please briefly describe them.
5. What does "unavoidable" mean when we talk about a cost? Why is it important?
6. What is cost variability? How do we use this concept in analyzing a product's profitability?
7. What are the four basic types of cost variability? Please define each term. How does each type of variability impact our ability to develop accurate product costs?
8. Provide an example of each type of cost variability using your college as the baseline for your analysis.
9. What does the term "cost structure" mean? How does it affect the operations of the firm?
10. What is CVP analysis? Why do we use it?
11. What is the basic profit equation? Please state it in terms of fixed and variable costs. How can we use this equation to understand a business?
12. What does the term "breakeven" mean? What is the breakeven formula? When do we use these concepts?

13. What is the contribution margin? How can we use it in CVP analysis?
14. What is the margin of safety? Why do we care what the margin of safety is?
15. What is a contribution margin ratio? When do we use it?
16. What does the term "sales mix" mean? How does it affect our CVP analysis?
17. What is a package contribution margin? How do we use it?
18. What is a business case? When do we use it?

Exercises

1. **RESOURCE FEATURES.** Create a table that compares the seven basic features of a resource to the following resources: raw materials, labor, machines, and buildings. Basically, set up a table that looks like this:

	Materials	Labor	Machines	Buildings
Purchase Package				
Purchase price				
Resource Driver				
Divisibility				
Capacity				
Storability				
Useful life				

For purchase price, simply note small, medium, or large. For useful life, think through that type of resource and suggest a time frame for how long it would last. As an example, materials can be stored for medium periods of time. So use short, medium, or long for this answer.

2. **DIRECT VS. INDIRECT COSTS.** For the following list of resources, note whether they would be direct (D) or indirect (I) to making a cake:

a. Oven
b. Flour
c. Eggs
d. Cake pan
e. Sugar
f. Butter
g. Cooling rack
h. Vanilla
i. Plate

3. **DIRECT VS. INDIRECT COSTS.** For the following list of resources, note whether they would be direct (D) or indirect (I) to making a canoe:

a. Plastic
b. Machines
c. People
d. Nylon cord
e. Paddles
f. Building
g. Labor
h. Management
i. Shipping clerk

4. **VARIABLE COST ESTIMATING.** Using the information in the following table, please develop an activity-based variable cost estimate for each of the activities described.

Activity	Cost	Work Done (Driver)	Cost per Unit of Work Done	Driver
Bake cakes	$15	5 cakes		
Mow lawns	$60	4 lawns		
Write purchase orders	$200	20 purchase orders		
Develop x-rays	$500	25 x-rays		
Flour for cake	$5	5 cakes		
Building for bakery	$30,000	30,000 cakes		
Oven to make cakes	$5,000	60,000 cakes		
Lawn mowers	$500	1,000 lawns		
Desks	$1,000	60,000 purchase orders		

As a hint for the next two exercises, remember that a variable cost will change at the same rate with changes in volume, so your numbers for 500 units to 750 units, and 750 units to 1,000 units, will be the same. Stepped costs jump in varying quantities. Fixed costs do not change at all as we go from one level of work to another.

5. **BEHAVIOR OF COST.** For the following set of costs, determine whether it is a variable or fixed cost using your cost variability formula (change in cost divided by change in volume).

Sam's Kayak Manufacturing						
Resource	Cost at 500 Units of Output	Cost at 750 Units of Output	Cost at 1,000 Units of Output	Change in Cost, 500 to 750 Volume	Change in Cost, 750 to 1,000 Volume	(Variable, Fixed, or Stepped)
Labor	$12,500	$18,750	$25,000			
Materials	$400,000	$600,000	$800,000			
Drying racks	$2,500	$3,000	$3,000			
Machines	$50,000	$50,000	$75,000			
Building	$100,000	$100,000	$100,000			
Wrapping materials	$5,000	$7,500	$10,000			
Shipping clerks	$30,000	$30,000	$60,000			
Purchasing agents	$40,000	$50,000	$50,000			

6. **BEHAVIOR OF COST.** Johnson Hardware offers a range of merchandise for the maintenance of the home and cars. It is a small and simple business, with Pete Johnson doing most of the managerial and office work himself. He employs three clerks on an hourly basis who check out customers and help to stock the shelves. The following are his costs for various levels of business:

Johnson Hardware						
Resource	Cost at $10,000 Sales	Cost at $20,000 Sales	Cost at $30,000 Sales	Change in Cost, $10,000 to $20,000 Sales	Change in Cost, $20,000 to $30,000 Sales	Variability (Variable or Fixed)
Labor	$1,500	$2,500	$3,500			
Building	$40,000	$40,000	$40,000			
Bags	$500	$1,000	$1,500			
Cash register	$2,500	$2,500	$2,500			
Display shelves	$20,000	$20,000	$20,000			
				$-	Total Variable Costs	
Cost Formula:		Dollar Sales Plus				

REQUIRED:

a. Determine which costs are fixed and which are variable.
b. Develop a cost formula for Johnson Hardware.

7. **BASIC CVP ANALYSIS AND BEHAVIOR OF COST.** Nancy's Beauty Salon does mainly haircuts for men and small children. Each haircut is a unique job, but takes about the same amount of time to complete. Nancy charges $25 per haircut regardless of whether someone is going bald or has a full head of hair. Clearly, she gets very few bald customers! Below are Nancy's costs for running her business.

Nancy's Beauty Salon						
Resource	Cost for 100 Haircuts	Cost for 200 Haircuts	Cost for 300 Haircuts	Change in Cost, 100 to 200 Haircuts	Change in Cost, 200 to 300 Haircuts	Variability (Variable or Fixed)
Labor	$1,000	$2,000	$3,000			
Building	$25,000	$25,000	$25,000			
Beauty supplies	$100	$200	$300			
Cash register	$500	$500	$500			
				$ –	Total Variable Cost for 100 Haircuts	
Cost Formula		per Haircut	Plus			

REQUIRED:

a. Complete the above chart, noting which costs are fixed and which are variable.
b. Develop a cost formula for Nancy. Be careful here because you want the costs for one haircut, not 100, right?
c. Develop a breakeven analysis for Nancy's Beauty Salon in number of customers.
d. Develop a breakeven analysis for Nancy in dollars of revenue.
e. Nancy wants to make $5,000 per month before-tax profit. How many haircuts does she need to do now?

8. **BASIC CVP ANALYSIS AND BEHAVIOR OF COST.** Ruby's Buffet offers customers a choice of various dishes for a flat price of $10 per person. While people choose different items, it is remarkable that they all eat roughly the same amount (except for those football players!). Since it is a buffet, the only help Ruby needs is a cook. Ruby cleans the tables and handles the cash register on her own. She only draws a salary if there is a profit. Below is a table detailing Ruby's operating costs for two different volumes of customers.

Ruby's Buffet						
Resource	Cost for 50 Customers	Cost for 100 Customers	Cost for 150 Customers	Change in Cost, 100 to 150 Customers	Change in Cost, 50 to 100 Customers	Variability (Variable or Fixed)
Cook	$3,000	$3,000	$3,000			
Food	$200	$400	$600			
Beverages	$25	$50	$75			
Cash register	$150	$150	$150			
Tables	$1,500	$1,500	$1,500			
Plates and silverware	$750	$750	$750			
Building	$2,000	$2,000	$2,000			
					$-	Total Variable Costs for 50 Customers
Cost Formula:		per Customer	Plus			

REQUIRED:

a. Complete the above chart, noting which costs are fixed and which are variable.
b. Develop a cost formula for Ruby. Be careful here because you want the costs for one customer, not 50, right?
c. Develop a breakeven analysis for Ruby's Buffet in number of customers.
d. Develop a breakeven analysis for Ruby in dollars of revenue.
e. Ruby wants to make $4,000 per month before-tax profit. How many customers does she need to handle now?
f. Ruby has changed her mind and wants a guarantee of $4,000 after-tax profit. She pays 25% taxes on her salary. How many customers does Ruby need now?

Problems

1. **BEHAVIOR OF COSTS.** Nestor Travel Services books airline flights, cruises, and various package tours for its customers. These booking operations use the same resources, in roughly the same quantities.

Nestor Travel Services				
Resources	Cost for 500 Travelers	Cost for 1,000 Travelers	Variability, 500-1,000 Passengers	Fixed Portion for 500 Passengers
Booking agents	$70,000	$70,000		
Computers	$2,000	$2,000		
Accounting clerk	$25,000	$25,000		
Telephones	$1,060	$2,060		
Fax machines	$150	$150		
Telephone/fax service charge	$225	$350		
Desks	$800	$800		
Rent on building	$30,000	$30,000		
Tickets issued	$500	$1,000		
Management costs	$50,000	$50,000		
Totals			$-	$-

REQUIRED:

Using the above data, derive the cost formula for Nestor Travel Services. Make sure you run both sets of numbers and then use the second cost formula to determine if there are any mixed costs in this problem.

2. **BEHAVIOR OF COST.** Pete's Lawn Care is a medium-sized company with customers in three counties in northwestern Connecticut. Pete cuts grass and provides basic cleanup services for his customers, with each job taking approximately 30 minutes to complete. Pete's costs for doing business are in the following table:

Pete's Lawn Care Services				
Resource	Cost for 250 Customers	Cost for 500 Customers	Cost for 750 Customers	Cost Pattern (Variable, Fixed, Stepped, Mixed)
Labor	$1,875	$3,750	$5,625	
Mowers	$2,000	$2,500	$2,500	
Trucks	$15,000	$15,000	$20,000	
Telephones	$200	$250	$300	
Billing supplies	$25	$50	$75	
Desks	$400	$400	$400	
Rent on building	$2,500	$2,500	$2,500	
Gasoline	$1,000	$2,000	$3,000	
Totals				
Cost formula up to 500 Customers		Variable Cost per Customer	Plus	
Cost formula at 750 Customers		Variable Cost per Customer	Plus	

REQUIRED:

a. Complete the above table.
b. Derive a cost formula for Pete's if he has up to 500 customers.
c. Derive a cost formula for Pete's when he has 750 customers. Be careful here!
d. Why are these different?

3. **BEHAVIOR OF COST PLUS SIMPLE BREAKEVEN.** Rogers Manufacturing makes ball bearings that are used in several industries. The ball bearings are sold with lubricant so they are ready to install. It sells each set for $50. The following is Rogers' cost for making one unit of the ball bearings:

Rogers Manufacturing				
Resource	Cost for 5,000 Sets	Cost for 10,000 Sets	Variability, 5,000-10,000 Sets	Fixed Portion for 5,000 Sets
Labor	$25,000	$50,000		
Materials	$115,000	$230,000		
Packing	$7,500	$15,000		
Office workers	$4,000	$4,000		
Telephones	$300	$300		

Rogers Manufacturing				
Resource	Cost for 5,000 Sets	Cost for 10,000 Sets	Variability, 5,000-10,000 Sets	Fixed Portion for 5,000 Sets
Telephone/fax service charge	$150	$300		
Desks	$2,500	$2,500		
Rent on building	$5,000	$5,000		
Management costs	$8,000	$8,000		
Totals			$-	$-

REQUIRED:

a. Using the above data, derive the cost formula for Rogers Manufacturing. Be careful here to derive the formula for one set of ball bearings, not 5,000.

b. Do you question the pattern of any of the costs? Specifically, does anything look variable by number of sets that does not quite seem to make sense? Why?

c. What is Rogers' breakeven volume in sets of ball bearings?

d. What is Rogers' breakeven volume in dollar sales of ball bearings?

4. **BEHAVIOR OF COST AND SIMPLE BREAKEVEN.** Smith and Company manufactures pens in a variety of ink colors. Each pen sells for $0.75. While the colors vary, the costs of making a pen are pretty constant, as suggested by the table below.

Smith and Company				
Resource	Cost for 10,000 Pens	Cost for 50,000 Pens	Variability, 10,000-50,000 Pens	Fixed Portion for 50,000 Pens
Labor	$1,000	$5,000		
Materials	$2,500	$12,500		
Packaging	$500	$2,500		
Office workers	$2,500	$2,500		
Telephones	$200	$200		
Telephone/fax service charge	$250	$500		
Desks	$1,000	$1,000		
Rent on building	$2,500	$2,500		
Management costs	$4,000	$4,000		
Totals				
Cost Formula	$-	per Pen	Plus	$-

REQUIRED:

a. Using the above data, derive the cost formula for Smith and Company. Be careful here to derive the formula for one pen, not 10,000.
b. Do you question the pattern of any of the costs? Specifically, does anything look variable by number of sets that does not quite seem to make sense? Why?
c. What is Smith and Company's breakeven volume in number of pens?
d. What is Smith and Company's breakeven volume in dollar sales of pens?

---

5. **CVP ANALYSIS.** Angie's Cleaning Service does routine cleaning of houses. She charges $100 for a house taking four hours of cleaning, her standard product offering. Each time she cleans, she uses $5 in variable supplies such as cleaning fluids and paper towels. She has fixed costs of an accountant, a van, a vacuum cleaner, and sundry items amounting to $25,000 per year.

REQUIRED:

a. Develop Angie's cost formula for cleaning houses.
b. What is Angie's breakeven point in number of houses cleaned per year?
c. What is the revenue dollars for Angie's breakeven point?
d. Angie wants to make $50,000 a year in before-tax profits. How many houses does she have to clean now?
e. Angie wants to make $50,000 a year in after-tax profits. Now how many houses does she have to clean? She pays 25% in taxes on average.
f. Angie is considering adding a second person to her company. It would cost her $50 per house for labor, but she could increase the number of houses cleaned per week from her current 12 to 22. Should Angie hire this worker? Why or why not? Develop a brief business case to explain your conclusions.

---

6. **CVP ANALYSIS.** Scott Randall operates a small manufacturing company that makes basic sound pre-amplifiers. Scott buys the wafer from one company, then does the slicing and packaging himself. He has several employees that help with the tasks. Each pre-amp sells for $4.50. There is $1.50 in variable costs for labor and materials for each pre-amplifier sold. Fixed costs are significant because Scott needs to have very precise and expensive machinery to slice the wafers, test the resulting wafer, and then package it to customer specifications. His fixed costs of operations are $25,000 per year.

REQUIRED:

a. Develop Scott's cost formula per year of sales.
b. What is the breakeven formula in number of pre-amplifiers sold?
c. What is Scott's breakeven revenue?
d. Scott wants to make $60,000 per year in before-tax profits for running his business. Now how many units does he have to sell?
e. Scott wants this $60,000 in after-tax profit. Now how many units does he have to sell? He pays 30% on average in income tax.
f. Scott has been approached by a salesman for various high-tech machines. He claims he can replace two of Scott's current machines at an additional fixed cost of $25,000 per year but a reduction in variable costs of $0.25 per unit made. Should Scott buy the new machine? Why or why not? Develop a brief business case to explain your recommendations.

7. **CONTRIBUTION MARGIN RATIO.** James Manufacturing wants to estimate its breakeven revenue and level of profitability at different ranges of sales revenue. It provides you with the following table:

James Manufacturing	
Revenue	$300,000
Less: Variable Costs	180,000
Total Contribution Margin	120,000
Less: Fixed Costs	60,000
Profit Margin before Tax	60,000

REQUIRED:

a. Calculate the contribution margin ratio.
b. What is James Manufacturing's breakeven point in revenue dollars?
c. If the company wants to increase its profits to $100,000 before tax, what revenue will it need to make?
d. The company has been approached by a salesman from a national distributor of office products that says he can reduce James Manufacturing's variable costs by 10% if the company buys a machine that costs $10,000. Should the company buy this machine? Why or why not? Develop a brief business case to explain your conclusions.

8. **CONTRIBUTION MARGIN RATIO.** Hot Juices, Inc., makes hot sauce for use by various Mexican restaurants in the Northeast. It has asked you to help it do some analysis of its business using the following data:

Hot Juices, Inc.	
Revenue	$900,000
Less: Variable Costs	450,000
Total Contribution Margin	450,000
Less: Fixed Costs	400,000
Profit Margin before Tax	$50,000

REQUIRED:

a. Calculate the contribution margin ratio.
b. What is Hot Juices, Inc.'s breakeven point in revenue dollars?
c. If the company wants to increase its before-tax profits to $150,000, how much revenue will it need to make?
d. The company has been approached by a salesman from a national distributor of office products that says he can reduce Hot Juices, Inc.'s variable costs by 5% if the company buys a machine that costs $50,000. Should the company buy this machine? Why or why not? Develop a brief business case to explain your conclusions.

9. **MULTIPLE PRODUCT BREAKEVEN POINT.** Tandry Associates offers a variety of tax and accounting services for local small businesses. It is a simple operation, with high variable costs per job completed but low fixed costs. In fact, it only costs Roger Tandry $25,000 a month in fixed costs to run his business. The details on the various products Tandry offers are in the table below.

Tandry Associates			
Product	Price per Month	Variable Cost per Month	Jobs Sold
Basic Bookkeeping	$500	$400	100
Tax Preparation	$750	$600	50
Audit Services	$1,000	$900	25
Billing Services	$600	$500	50
Payroll Services	$500	$400	75

REQUIRED:

a. What is Tandry's product mix?
b. What is Tandry's package contribution margin? You may use either method to do this calculation.
c. Perform a multiproduct breakeven point for Tandry Associates. How many of each type of job does he need to sell in order to break even?
d. What is Tandry's current profit for the business?
e. What is Tandry's current margin of safety in terms of revenue dollars?
f. Tandry wants to make $10,000 per month before taxes. How many jobs of each type does he need to sell now? What is his required revenue dollars of sales?
g. Tandry wants this profit in after-tax dollars. He pays a 20% tax rate. How many jobs of each type does he need to sell now? What are his required revenue dollars of sales?

10. **MULTIPLE PRODUCT BREAKEVEN POINT.** Angus Manufacturing makes basic tools for sale in hardware stores across the country. It is a successful business, with the following unit sales in a month. It faces fixed costs of $225,000 per month. Angus wants you to help him understand how his product mix affects his business.

Angus Manufacturing			
Product	Price per Unit	Variable Cost per Unit	Units Sold
Hammers	$10	$7.50	25,000
Socket wrenches	$25	$15.00	10,000
Plain screwdriver	$8	$6.40	10,000
Phillips-head screwdriver	$8	$6.40	5,000
Pliers	$10	$7.50	25,000

REQUIRED:

a. What is Angus's product mix?
b. What is Angus's package contribution margin? You may use either method to do this calculation.
c. Perform a multiproduct breakeven for Angus Manufacturing. How many of each type of product does he need to sell in order to break even?
d. What is Angus's current profit for the business?
e. What is Angus's current margin of safety in terms of revenue dollars?

f. Angus wants to make $100,000 per month before taxes. How many units of each type of product does the company need to sell now? What is its required revenue dollars of sales?
g. Angus wants this profit in after-tax dollars. He pays a 20% tax rate. How many units of each type of product does the company need to sell now? What are its required revenue dollars of sales?

11. **APPENDIX 3A ESTIMATING VARIABILITY.** Peters Pots makes a large ceramic pot that it sells through a nationwide distribution channel. The following table details the sales and costs for the first seven months of this year.

Observation	Number of Units (x_i)	Manufacturing Cost (y_i)
January	1,000	$40,100.00
February	2,500	$100,100.00
March	500	$20,100.00
April	1,000	$40,100.00
May	1,500	$60,100.00
June	1,200	$48,100.00
July	800	$32,100.00
Sum	8,500	$340,700.00

REQUIRED:

a. Using the high-low method, calculate the variable and fixed costs of production for Peters Pots.
b. Using the scattergram method, estimate the variable and fixed costs of production for Peters Pots.
c. Using least squares regression, calculate the variable and fixed costs of production for Peters Pots.

12. **APPENDIX 3A ESTIMATING VARIABILITY.** Andrews Manufacturing makes folding chairs that are sold by various retailers across the country. The following table details the company's sales and costs for the first six months of this year.

Andrews Manufacturing		
Observation	Number of Units (x_i)	Manufacturing Cost (y_i)
January	500	$9,500.00
February	750	$11,000.00
March	600	$9,800.00
April	1,000	$13,000.00
May	900	$12,200.00
June	800	$11,400.00
Sum	4,550	$66,900.00

REQUIRED:

a. Using the high-low method, calculate the variable and fixed costs of production for Andrews Manufacturing.

b. Using the scattergram method, estimate the variable and fixed costs of production for Andrews Manufacturing.

c. Using least squares regression, calculate the variable and fixed costs of production for Andrews Manufacturing.

Database Problems

For database templates, worksheets, and workbooks, go to MAdownloads.imanet.org

DB 3.1 AVERAGE COSTS. Using the template in the chapter workbook that contains the direct costs of flying passengers for Easy Air, do the following computations on the worksheet for DB 3.1:

1. Calculate the average number of flights, passengers, and revenue miles flown for three years.
2. Calculate the average total revenue, costs, and profits for Easy Air.
3. Now get the revenue, cost, and profit by flight. You should end up with $ 368.56 as your average profit per flight.
4. Repeat these efforts to complete the template for average passengers flown and average revenue seat miles flown.

REQUIRED:

a. Turn in your completed worksheets.

b. Which set of numbers do you like the best? Why?

c. Do these results look better or worse than Easy Air's performance in 2012? To answer this question, you'll have to complete the template for DB 3-1g. Use the same types of analysis as above but only look at the 2012 results for revenue, costs, and the various drivers.

DB 3.2 BREAKEVEN ANALYSIS. You are now going to do a simple breakeven point for number of passengers on a flight.

Go to the worksheet that says "Template for DB 3-2a." Complete the breakeven analysis according to the provided template structure.

REQUIRED:

a. Turn in your completed worksheet.
b. What do the results tell you about Easy Air's performance trends? Please be specific.

DB 3.3 ANALYSIS OF PERFORMANCE USING BREAKEVEN. You are now going to do a bit of analysis of Easy Air's profitability performance, specifically complete a CVP analysis.

Go to the worksheet that says "Template for DB 3-3a." Using the structure of the provided template, analyze Easy Air's performance using CVP analysis.

REQUIRED:

a. Turn in your completed worksheet.
b. Looking at these various results, what trends do you see that explain what is happening at Easy Air? Specifically, where do you think the problems lie for this year's profitability decline?
c. Draft a one-paragraph memo to Sanjiv explaining your concerns. Focus your memo on making positive suggestions for his team to explore.

Cases

CASE 3.1 BEHAVIOR OF COST AND BREAKEVEN ANALYSIS. Adelle Watson owns a small manufacturing company, Easy Bake, which makes one product, a ceramic pie plate that features even heating that helps prevent pie shells from getting burnt in patches. It is one of the products carried by most high-end kitchen stores throughout the United States. Even though she sells everything she makes in a month, the product is not selling fast enough to generate a steady profit for Adelle. She has decided to hire you for $1,000 a month for three months to do a complete analysis of her business.

The first person you talk to is Joey Blake, the company accountant. He provides you with the following information for March:

- Sales: 5,000 units
- Total cost of production: $23,900
- Average cost of production: $4.78
- Average price: $5.00

When you ask Joey for more information on the costs of the company, you find out that all he has been doing is taking the total costs and dividing it by units made to get his cost numbers. You know there is a better way to do this, so you ask Joey to let you look at the books. He does so, providing you with the following information:

Easy Bake's Costs for Varying Volumes

Volume Sold	Materials	Direct Labor	Supplies	Indirect Labor	Electricity	Depreciation	Other Overhead	Rent
5,000	$6,250.00	$2,500.00	$750.00	$3,000.00	$1,500.00	$2,900.00	$3,500.00	$3,500.00
4,000	$5,000.00	$2,000.00	$600.00	$2,900.00	$1,300.00	$2,900.00	$3,200.00	$3,500.00
3,000	$3,750.00	$1,500.00	$450.00	$2,800.00	$1,100.00	$2,900.00	$2,900.00	$3,500.00

After completing some basic analysis, you suggest to Adelle that she drop her price by 10% to increase demand. You also make some suggestions about variable costs and fixed costs. Adelle is nervous, but she goes along with your suggestions. It takes a month to make all of the changes you recommend. Before your salary is added, Joey gives you the following results for April and May:

	Volume Sold	Materials	Direct Labor	Supplies	Indirect Labor	Electricity	Depreciation	Other Overhead	Rent	TOTALS
April	5,500	$5,500	$2,200	$550	$3,050	$1,600	$2,900	$3,100	$3,500	$22,400
May	6,000	$6,000	$2,400	$600	$3,100	$1,700	$2,900	$3,200	$3,500	$23,400

It seems like you have had an impact. The company is now selling its product at $4.50, which is resulting in a rapid rise in sales. You want to have some specifics for Adelle, however, so now you are going to do some analysis and then write a memo.

REQUIRED:

a. Analyze the data Joey originally gave you for March, coming up with the cost formula and breakeven sales in units and dollars.
b. Using the data from April and May, recalculate your cost formulas. Do not forget to add $1,000 to the fixed costs each month to cover your salary!
c. What is Adelle's breakeven point now?
d. You decide your job is done, so you give Adelle your notice. This makes her a bit worried, but you console her with the fact that her fixed costs will drop back to the previous $11,400. Recalculate Adelle's breakeven point without your salary.
e. What is Adelle's margin of safety in units and revenue dollars in April and May?
f. Draft a memo to Adelle with the results of your analysis, including percentage change figures where logical. Use a business case structure that details each of the alternatives and results you attained.

CASE 3.2 CONTRIBUTION MARGIN ANALYSIS. Judy Holmes, owner and primary manager of Holmes Industry, has recently completed a course in BPA. She has decided to try to take a look at her company, which makes a variety of sink faucets, from the perspective of its cost structure as well as the impact various ideas she has been having would have on profitability. The following is her income statement for last year restated in the variable costing format. This year looks like it will be similar to last year unless she makes some positive changes.

Holmes Industry Income Statement	
Revenue	$2,500,000
Less: Variable Costs	$1,225,000
Contribution Margin	$1,275,000
Less: Fixed Costs	$1,150,000
Income before Tax	$125,000
Less: Income Taxes (30%)	$37,500
Incomes after Tax	$87,500

Having pulled this basic information together with the help of her accountant, Larry Black, Judy decides to hold a meeting of top management to look at various options. The following discussions occur:

Judy: I've brought all of you together to see if we can find ways to improve the company's performance. We are currently only making 3.75% in after-tax profit on over $2,500,000 in sales. We're moving 100,000 units at $25 per unit, which isn't bad, but the profits aren't there. We've got a pretty small margin, especially since my entire salary is based on these results.

Martin, VP Marketing: Judy, you know my feeling. We need to lower the price of our faucets if we're going to get a sales bump. The big box stores need that price concession from us or it's no go for them. I think we should lower prices 10% across the board.

Judy: If all we do is lower prices, Martin, how will that help us? Basically, I'm not saying no, but I do want to figure out what that would do to our margins and breakeven sales. Have you calculated how lower prices would impact sales?

Martin: I've run a few projections. I think we could raise sales to 125,000 units if we reduce our average price to $22.50. That would increase our total revenues by $312,500 to $2,812,500. That's a 12.5% increase.

Larry: I'm not so sure that's so good, unless we can find a way to bring the costs per unit down. Right now they're 95% of the total sales dollar. The variable portion of that is 49%, or $12.25. That won't change unless we make some major shifts to how we make the faucets, which could be dangerous.

Sam, VP Manufacturing: I don't know, Larry. I think I could shave 5% off of the variable costs if Judy would let me buy the new machine I want. Sure, the machine would be an outlay of $1,000,000, but it has a 10-year useful life, so that would only ramp up fixed costs a bit.

Judy: These are two big changes we're talking about. I was hoping for something a little less risky than cutting prices or buying new machines. Aren't there any other ideas?

Martin: Well, I've gotten some inquiries from a small hardware chain. They would like to buy 10,000 units, one time, for $20. That wouldn't change our price to the rest of the market, but would just generate some additional sales. I could look for these types of opportunities.

Larry: You think you can drop prices that much to one small customer and not have the word get around? Sounds risky to me!

Judy: Tell you what. I'll analyze the impact of each of your suggestions and we can talk them over at next week's meeting.

REQUIRED:

a. Calculate the company's current variable cost ratio, contribution margin ratio, breakeven sales dollars, and margin of safety in dollars.
b. Analyze the three alternatives that have been suggested to Judy during the meeting.
c. Now combine alternatives one and two (new sales price and new machine) to see what the impact would be on profitability.
d. Based on your results, which option(s) seem the best idea? Why?
e. Draft a brief memo to Judy with your recommendations using a business case structure to explain your conclusions.

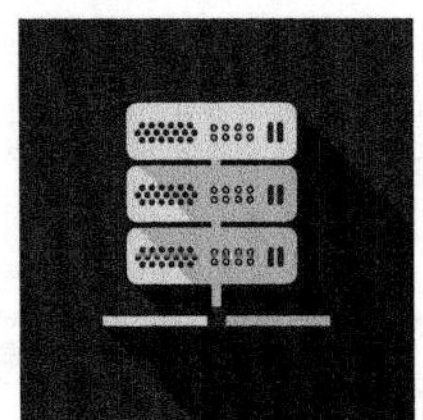

CHAPTER FOUR

Cost Pools, Capacity, and Activity-Based Costing

Perhaps the most valuable result of all education is the ability to make yourself do the thing you have to do, when it ought to be done, whether you like it or not.

WALTER BAGEHOT[1]

CHAPTER ROADMAP

1. **From Resources to Cost Pools**
   - ➤ *Resource Drivers: Combining Direct and Indirect Resources*
   - ➤ *Homogeneous vs. Heterogeneous Cost Pools*
2. **Capacity and Cost Pools**
   - ➤ *Capacity Costing Explored*
   - ➤ *Managed and Committed Costs*
   - ➤ *Productive, Nonproductive, and Idle Capacity*
3. **Activity-Based Costing**
   - ➤ *Using ABC to Estimate Costs*
   - ➤ *People-Paced vs. Machine-Paced Cost Pools*
4. **From Cost Pools to Cost Objects**

LEARNING OBJECTIVES

After studying this chapter, you should be able to:

1. **Define the key characteristics of a cost pool, and combine direct and indirect resources into cost pools using resource drivers.**
2. **Explain capacity and calculate: 1) managed and committed capacity costs using the avoidability criterion and 2) productive, nonproductive, and idle capacity costs for a machine-paced cost pool.**
3. **Define and know how to use activity drivers and identify key differences between machine- and people-paced cost pools.**
4. **Characterize a cost object and assign costs to individual units of output.**

1 Allen Klein, *The Wise and Witty Quote Book*, New York: Gramercy Press, 2005: p. 162.

IN CONTEXT ➤ Understanding Costs at Easy Air

It was one week since Fran, Sanjiv, and his teammates Rudy and Sherry had isolated the variable and fixed costs for a specific flight, which gave them a starting point, but only that. It was now very clear that a lot of money was being spent on activities that were only indirectly related to actually flying the airplane. The remaining costs were related to running the business. When Sherry pointed this out, Rudy initially did not understand. "Cost is cost, isn't it?" he said.

"Not really," Sherry explained. "When we consider the cost of flying an airplane, it all comes down to either seat miles flown, or, something even more promising, how well we're using the plane's capacity. We can define the *capacity* of a plane using time—minutes flown, idle time, maintenance time, and so on. We can also define capacity in terms of the load factor—the number of seats available every minute vs. those actually flown. These are big choices, but since everything can be defined in terms of time, we have an absolute baseline."

Sanjiv joined in: "Why do we care about that?" Sherry responded: "We care, because whenever we don't use capacity productively, Easy Air loses money. By doing these calculations, we can know precisely—right down to the minute—how much value we can create if we maximize capacity.

"On the other hand," Sherry continued, "when we look at the cost of running the business, it becomes clear that the driving force is personnel, who have a different capacity every day if not every hour. And, all employees aren't the same; not everyone is capable of working at the same pace."

"That's interesting," Sanjiv interjected. "It ties into something I recently learned about how to look at costing. It's called activity-based costing, and it looks at costs from more of a people perspective. It might be what we need to come up with the costs of running the business."

"I'm willing to learn new things," Rudy noted. "But we really need to speed things up if we're going to make our delivery date. So far we're just working the costs, not answering questions."

"True," Sanjiv agreed. "But if we can correctly define our costs, we should be able to use those numbers to effectively analyze the problems. Without good cost estimates, we'll end up starting from scratch every time there's a question. The next time we meet with Fran, we need to have a clear, defensible way to talk about our costs."

Sherry added, "I think we can use our understanding of the business for this first pass, but at some point we're going to have to go out to the departments and find out what they really do."

"I agree we need more detail if we're going to suggest using these new cost models to run the business, but for now estimates will get us to our next group of goals," responded Sanjiv.

"Sounds good, let's get rocking!" said Rudy and Sherry in unison. The team was back to work, adding high-level activity analysis to their to-do list.

IN THE LAST CHAPTER, WE SPENT A LOT OF TIME LOOKING AT VARIOUS RESOURCES and how they change as the amount of work being done changes. This is the most basic of the relationships that make up the costs and measurements in the management accounting database. In this chapter, we take this discussion a bit further and examine cost relationships that are not so clear-cut. We combine resources to generate cost pools that have their own unique capability to do work. Some of these cost pools focus on machine capability (capacity costing), while others center on the work people do in organizations (activity-based costing). Let us start by getting a better idea of what it means to make up a cost pool.

From Resources to Cost Pools

OBJECTIVE 1

Define the key characteristics of a cost pool, and combine direct and indirect resources into cost pools using resource drivers.

Although managers purchase resources one at a time, if they are to access their value-creating ability, they often have to combine them into groups, or **cost pools,** *a combination of resources that support a common goal*. In fact, it is the ability to group resources efficiently and effectively to create value that defines a profitable company. As we begin to group resources together, we focus on putting together those items that support the same type of work or that are integral to the completion of a specific activity or outcome. The grouping of resources is not random. Our goal is to put resources together that have something in common. The more accurately we are at cost pooling, the better our cost estimates will be. This is the lesson learned by companies today, such as Caterpillar, which uses activity-based costing (ABC) that emphasizes pools of cost that can be traced to specific causes.

Table 4.1 highlights the characteristics of a useful cost pool. The most important of these is **homogeneity**, which means *it contains only those resources from which the cost pool directly benefits*. We want to group resources to ensure that they support the same type of work. Of course, the other features of a cost pool also matter. First, we want to know if the resources can be clearly traced to a specific cost pool, because if they are shared, we will have to estimate their use. Our next concern is to what extent we can avoid the resource expenditure if the rest of the resources are idle. In other words, how avoidable are those resource expenditures? Finally, we want to know the nature of the output of the cost pool. Is it attachable directly to a specific output or work product or is it indirect in nature? Costs that are indirect to all of the company's cost pools are often called **overhead,** *the sum of indirect product costs that are not assigned to a specific capacity- or activity-based cost pool.*

TABLE 4.1 FEATURES OF ACCURATE COST POOLS

Feature	Definition
Homogeneity	All of the resources combine to support the same type of work or output; they have the same purpose. Thus, the pool contains only those resources from which it directly benefits.
Traceability	The costs can be easily assigned to one, and only one, cost pool. If the resources are shared, estimate the untraceable costs.
Avoidability	The ability to eliminate unneeded resource costs from the firm's cost structure, or cost pools, if its processes or products are changed in some way.
Capacity	The amount of work a cost pool is capable of supporting before major resources must be replenished.
Causality	Use of the resource can be unambiguously attached to one or more specific cost pools.
Commonality	The resources in the cost pool can be charged to output using a single driver, or performance measure.

RESOURCE DRIVERS: COMBINING DIRECT AND INDIRECT RESOURCES

One useful way to think about grouping resources is to look at the flow of work that they support. We call this flow a **process**, or *a linked sequence of activities that transforms some forms of input into outputs*. Not all inputs are physical resources or materials, nor are all forms of output physical products. For a software development company, such as Microsoft, intellectual capital is its major value-creating resource (a non-physical input), a resource that is used in a process to create software, which is an intangible, or nonphysical, output. We will focus on process issues in more depth in Chapters 8 and 9. In this chapter, we will simply use the concept of a process to help us organize our discussion.

To get a clearer understanding of how we trace resources to specific cost pools, let us look at a fictitious company, Standard Soap, which makes different types of bar soaps for hotels. Figure 4.1 illustrates the order-to-payment process of a single transaction that begins when the company receives an order from a hotel for 5,000 oval bars of white soap weighing 1.5 ounces each, each wrapped in pleated tissue fastened by a gold seal bearing the customer's logo. This is a unique job for Standard Soap, and the hotel is a new customer, so the company wants to make sure to price the bar right and make the product correctly the first time so it gets repeat business.

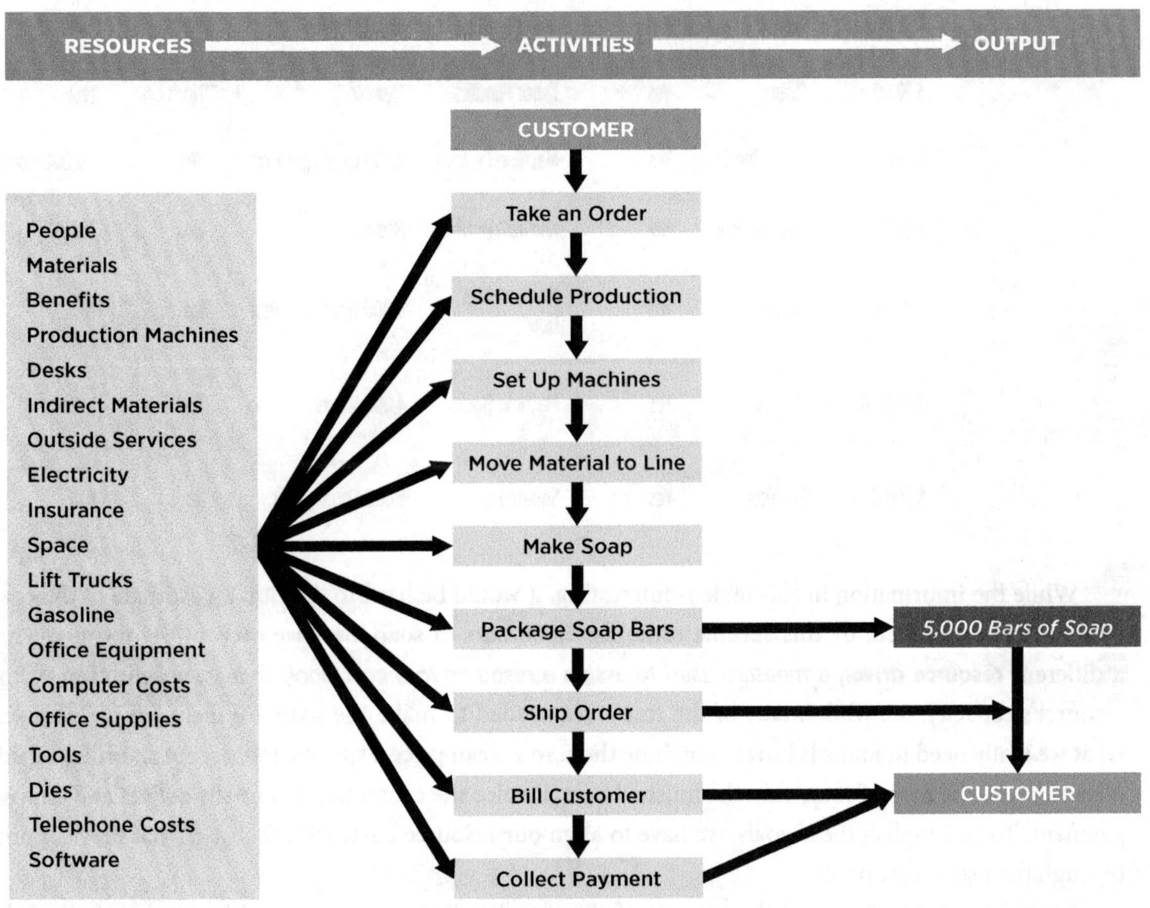

FIGURE 4.1 ORDER-TO-PAYMENT PROCESS

The receipt of a customer order starts the **order-to-payment process,** *the primary process, or linked set of activities, that begins with the receipt of a customer's order and ends with the customer's payment for the goods or services received.* Of all the processes that exist in a company, the order-to-payment process is the most important because it is how the company directly meets customer needs and earns its revenues. Standard Soap has many different resources at its command to enable the company to meet its customers' needs, including people, machines, buildings, materials, and electricity. Table 4.2 provides a summary of the basic features of Standard Soap's resources.

TABLE 4.2 SUMMARY OF RESOURCES

Standard Soap							
Resource	Purchase Price	Purchase Package	Divisible	Resource Driver	Capacity	Storable	Useful Life
Soap	$0.75	Pounds	Yes	Ounces	Flexible	Yes	3 months
Packaging	$0.03	Gross	Yes	Cost per Bar	Flexible	Yes	Unlimited
Line Workers	$10.00	Hours	Yes	Labor Minutes	Flexible	No	N/A
Soap Press	$250,000	1 Machine	Yes	Machine Cycles	2,500 Cycles per Hour	Yes	20,000 Hours
Electricity	$0.002	Kilowatt Hour	No	Kilowatt Hour	Flexible	No	N/A
Machine Maintenance	$200,000	Hours	Yes	Maintenance Hour	4,000 Hours per Year	No	N/A
Machine Supplies	$40,000	Various	Yes	Machine Hours	4,000 Hours	Yes	1 Year
Rent on Building	$300,000	Per Year	Yes	Square Feet	5,000 Square Feet	No	N/A

While the information in this table is interesting, it would be hard to develop an estimate of the cost, or resources consumed, by this specific order for 5,000 bars of soap, because each of the resources has a different **resource driver,** *a measure used to assign a resource to a cost pool*; that is, a definition of the resource's capacity. So, while many of the resources needed to make the soap are included in Table 4.2, what we really need to know is how to combine them so we can price a specific job, accept an order, schedule and make the bars of soap, ship the finished bars, invoice the customer, and finally collect and deposit payment. To accomplish these goals, we have to align our resource costs with the work that they support through the use of cost pools.

In Chapter 3, we discussed the concept of *direct* and *indirect* resources, and know that if all of the resources can be traced exclusively to one activity or output, then they clearly belong in that specific cost pool—they are direct costs of doing that type of work. However, far more of our resources are shared among many uses—they are indirect to any specific activity or outcome. In constructing a cost pool for a machine, as we see in Figure 4.2, space is a shared resource that we can assign based on a per-foot basis to the machine itself. Many other costs that go into making a machine cost pool are direct to the machine, such as the people who run it, the machine's depreciation, and its maintenance. When we make a cost pool, therefore, we are combining both indirect and direct charges to result in a total cost pool that reflects all of the resources consumed by running the machine. The more costs we can assign directly, the more accurate our cost pool becomes.

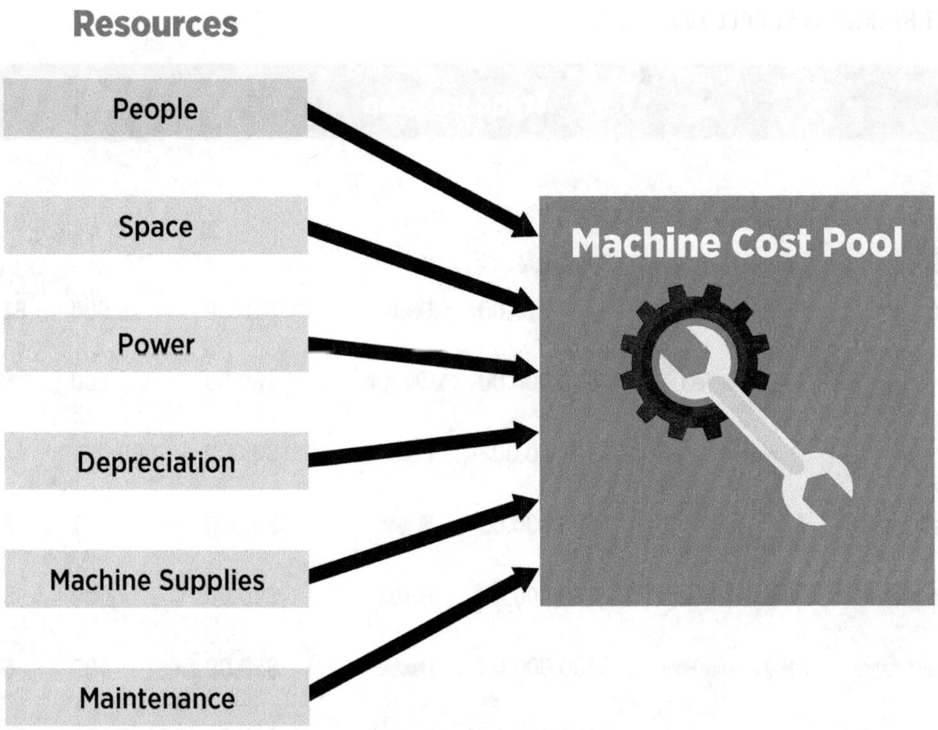

Resources

People

Space

Power

Depreciation

Machine Supplies

Maintenance

Machine Cost Pool

FIGURE 4.2 CONSTRUCTING A MACHINE COST POOL

To attach the indirect costs to the activities or outputs that benefit from their consumption, we need to use resource drivers, which most often are nonfinancial measurements, chosen because they reasonably proxy, or mirror, how the resource is used up. If you look back at the list of resource characteristics in Table 4.1, you will see for instance that the amount of time a person spends doing a specific activity is a reasonable resource driver for attaching labor costs. For machines, we might want to use the amount of time, or machine hours, that are available to be used in any specific year (8,760 hours if we use a 24-hour clock).

As we look at the soap-making machine, however, it becomes clear that we cannot really make the product if all we have is the machine. We would, in fact, need some space in the building to house the machine, some electricity to run it, insurance to protect our investment, maintenance to keep it in top running condition, and a person to operate it. We need all of these resources before the machine is ready to make a product; we must add them to the estimated cost of using the machine.

HOMOGENOUS VS. HETEROGENEOUS COST POOLS

If we are to accurately estimate the cost of a bar of soap, therefore, we will clearly want to include all of these resource costs in our analysis. We accomplish this by creating a cost pool for the soap-making machine that includes not only its own costs, but also some portion of the building costs, insurance, and the salaries paid to the people who operate it. Table 4.3 shows the cost pool for Standard Soap's machine.

TABLE 4.3 MACHINE COST POOL FOR A YEAR

Standard Soap						
Resources	Resource Driver	Purchase Price	Capacity	Cost per Resource Driver	Quantity Needed per Year	Estimated Cost
Line Workers - 4	Labor Hours	$10.00	Flexible	$10.00	16,000	$160,000.00
Space	Square Feet	$30,000.00	5,000 sq. ft.	$60.00	500	$30,000.00
Power	Kilowatt Hours	$0.002	Flexible	$0.002	500,000	$1,000.00
Soap Press Depreciation	Years	$500,000.00	10 Years	$50,000	1	$50,000.00
Machine Supplies	Machine Hours	$40,000.00	Flexible	$10.00	4,000	$40,000.00
Machine Maintenance	Maintenance Hours	$200,000.00	Flexible	$50.00	400	$20,000.00
Supervisor	Shifts	$50,000.00	2,000 Hours	$25.00	4,000	$100,000.00
Insurance	Total Hours per Year	$1,000.00	8,760 Hours	$0.114	8,760	$1,000.00
					Total	$402,000.00

When we group resources together around a common purpose, such as providing the capability to make a bar of soap, we say that the resource costs are homogeneous. If we mix costs that do not support the same type of work into the pool, we say that the costs are **heterogeneous**, or *a cost pool that contains a mix of resources that are the result of many different causes*. When we have a heterogeneous pool of costs, or overhead, we cannot be certain that the work that is being done *caused* the cost, which is something we try to keep foremost in our minds. **Causality,** *the reason for a specific outcome or activity; the thing that drives the cost*—is one of our primary criteria for claiming that our cost estimates are accurate. The less causality there is, the lower the probability that the costs will really respond to increases or decreases in the amount of work done within the cost pool.

Homogeneity is a very desirable feature of a cost pool because it increases the accuracy of our cost estimates. While we cannot always achieve it, we should always try to minimize the number of "mixed" or heterogeneous cost pools we create because these types of pools can create cost distortions that can bias management's judgment, decisions, and actions.

Capacity and Cost Pools

Capacity is one of the oldest concepts in management accounting, and it underlies the discipline of management accounting. It has its roots in the scientific management movement of the early 1900s and is a term most commonly associated with the amount of work a machine can do.

OBJECTIVE 2

Explain capacity and calculate: 1) managed and committed capacity costs using the avoidability criterion and 2) productive, nonproductive, and idle capacity costs for a machine-paced cost pool.

CAPACITY COSTING EXPLORED

Capacity refers to the value-creating ability of an organization and its resources.[2] Capacity is what an organization sells when it promises to do work for a customer. When a company acquires resources, it is their capacity that the firm wishes to harness to create more value (for example, revenue) than is consumed (for example, cost).

In even simpler terms, capacity is the *denominator in our cost equation*, the amount of work the resource or cost pool can be expected to complete before its value-creating ability is used up. Every cost estimate a company makes has an implicit definition of capacity built into it. When capacity is not used before it expires, it is called waste. In fact, we can look at our resources in terms of usability, storability, and waste. As we saw earlier, if we can store the capacity of a resource, we call it an asset. If we cannot store it and do not use it, it is waste. No customer will pay a company for the waste it creates as a result of its management practices.

MANAGED AND COMMITTED COSTS

When we begin to study capacity, we find that there are many new concepts added to our vocabulary for costs. One of the first of these is the concept of **managed** vs. **committed capacity cost**. These two terms reflect the **avoidability criterion**, which is a *measure of cost in relation to work; specifically concerned with whether costs go away when no work is being done*. Specifically, it deals with whether or not cost will go away if we do not do any work (or do less work) with a set of resources in a cost pool. A managed cost is one that is avoidable if, for instance, a machine is not doing any work. This would include the cost of the people required to operate the machine, the electricity needed to run the machine, and the cost of any supplies, such as the oil used to keep it lubricated. All of these **managed capacity costs,** *expenses that go away if a machine is idle (unstaffed)*, are avoidable if no work is done. As you can see, most of these managed costs are either variable or stepped costs where the steps are very small (labor is commonly purchased by the hour). When we charge these costs out, we want to charge them only to hours when the machine is staffed and ready to produce product.

---

2 Carol J. McNair and Richard Vangermeersch, *Total Capacity Management: Optimizing at the Operational, Tactical and Strategic Levels*, New York: St. Lucie Press, 1998.

Committed capacity costs are very different. They are *expenditures that do not go away even when a machine is not in use*. These costs are most commonly fixed or stepped costs with large steps, although there are times when a resource that might look variable responds in a committed way (for example, the cost of electricity if a computer is never shut down). These costs get charged to the machine 24 hours a day, seven days a week because they are always there, no matter what. There are 8,760 hours in an average year (8,784 in a leap year). This fact probably makes those hours playing video games more significant.

LOOKING BACK ➤ The Cost of Idleness

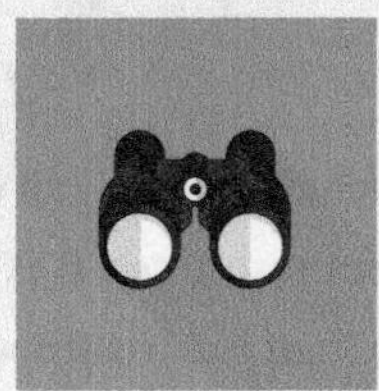

H.L. Gantt was a premier industrial engineer during the early 1900s. He was famous for supporting such work as Taylor's time and motion studies. He was also known for bringing idleness costs into the cost equation, which he saw as a form of waste that could not simply be passed on to customers.

> *"It has been common practice to make the product of a factory running at a portion of its capacity bear the whole expense of the factory. This has long been recognized by many to be illogical...the amount of expense to be borne by the product should bear the same ratio to the total normal operating expense as the product in question bears to the normal product. The expense of maintaining the idle portion of the plant ready to run...is really a deduction from profits, and shows that we may have a serious loss on account of having too much plant, as well as on account of not operating our plant economically."*

H.L. Gantt
"The Relation between Production and Costs"
American Machinist, June 17, 1915

Table 4.4 shows what happens to those Standard Soap costs in the machine cost pool when they are sorted into managed and committed categories and the cost per hour is recalculated. We are now able to attribute cost to actual machine usage—cost per staffed hour—instead of attributing all of the costs as if the machine were idle—committed cost per hour.

TABLE 4.4 MANAGED AND COMMITTED COSTS ON ONE SOAP-MAKING LINE

Standard Soap			
Resources	**Type of Cost**	**Managed Cost per Year**	**Committed Cost per Year**
Line Workers - 4	Managed	$160,000.00	$-
Space	Committed	$-	$30,000.00
Power	Managed	$1,000	$-
Soap Press Depreciation	Committed	$-	$50,000.00
Machine Supplies	Managed	$40,000.00	$-
Machine Maintenance	Managed	$20,000.00	$-
Supervisor	Managed	$100,000.00	$-
Insurance	Committed	$-	$1,000.00
TOTAL		$321,000.00	$81,000.00

Number of Hours of Manned Capacity	4,000
Number of Hours of Committed Capacity	8,760

Managed Cost per Hour	$80.00
Committed Cost per Hour	$9.25

Cost per Manned Hour	$89.25
Cost per Idle Hour	$9.25

PRODUCTIVE, NONPRODUCTIVE, AND IDLE CAPACITY

We have our cost pools; all that is left is to attach these costs to the bars of soap Standard Soap is producing for the hotel. As you might expect, not every usable minute of capacity is actually put to work. This brings us to four other concepts you need to know before we can generate a capacity report for our soap machine and cost out the capacity costs for this order for 5,000 bars of soap. Figure 4.3 shows how these concepts relate to one another and to the capacity costing structure.

The first of these concepts is **productive capacity,** *the amount of a cost pool's time*—the actual use of a cost pool—*that results in the completed product for the customer*. It is the only part of our capacity that generates revenue for the firm.

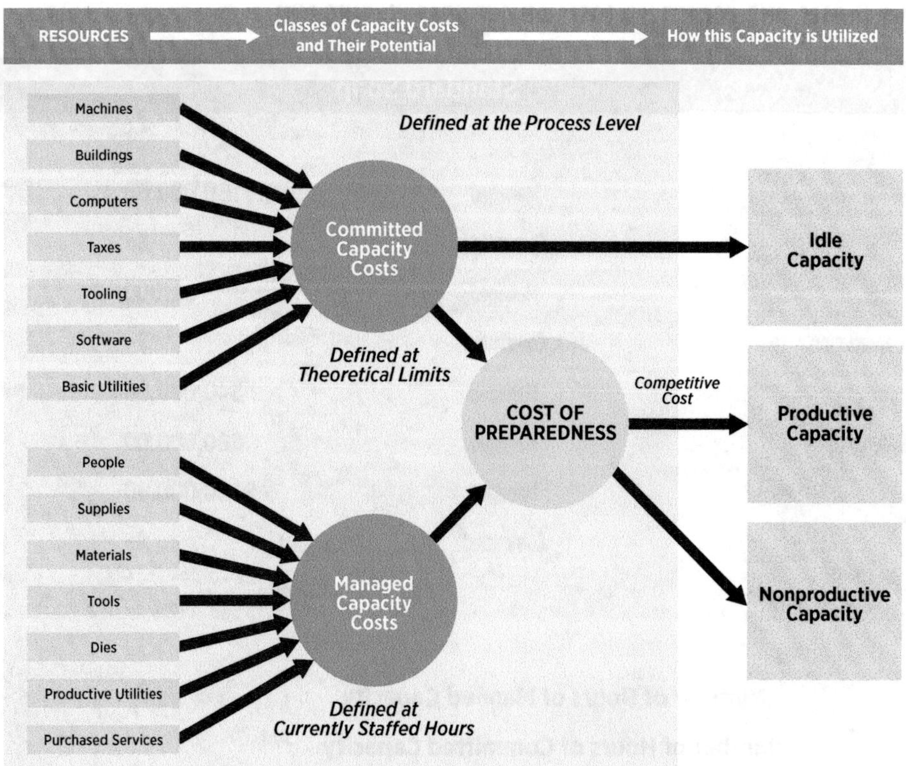

FIGURE 4.3 THE COMPLETE CAPACITY COSTING STRUCTURE

As Figure 4.3 illustrates, our cost pool can generate two other types of capacity: nonproductive capacity and idle capacity. **Nonproductive capacity** *is time wasted when a machine is fully staffed but no output is generated.* It is the largest form of waste in a company. Nonproductive capacity represents time when all of the resources a machine requires are in place to produce output, but there is no output. A good example is when a machine breaks down in the middle of a shift, and everyone assigned to that machine for the day is now idle while the repairs are made. No bars of soap come off the line during this period, but the machine is still on, using electricity and generating cost. There are, unfortunately, many different ways a company can experience nonproductive capacity in any one day or year, as we will see in a moment. Productive and nonproductive capacity make up the **cost of preparedness**, or *the sum of all the resources needed to make a machine ready to do work*, as is demonstrated in Figure 4.4.

The final way we deploy the total resources of a cost pool is to simply *not* deploy them, but to purposely leave them idle for a period of time. This is called **idle capacity,** *a period during which a company plans to not use a machine, which is unstaffed; therefore, only committed capacity costs are wasted.* Most companies do not operate 24 hours a day. In manufacturing settings, two shifts of 2,080 hours per year is the most common utilization pattern. That means we avoid the managed capacity cost for the remaining 6,680 hours that make up a year's worth of time (remember, there are 8,760 hours in a normal year). When we purposely leave machines idle, we waste only their committed capacity cost. These costs do not have to be charged to output, but can instead become part of general and administrative costs.

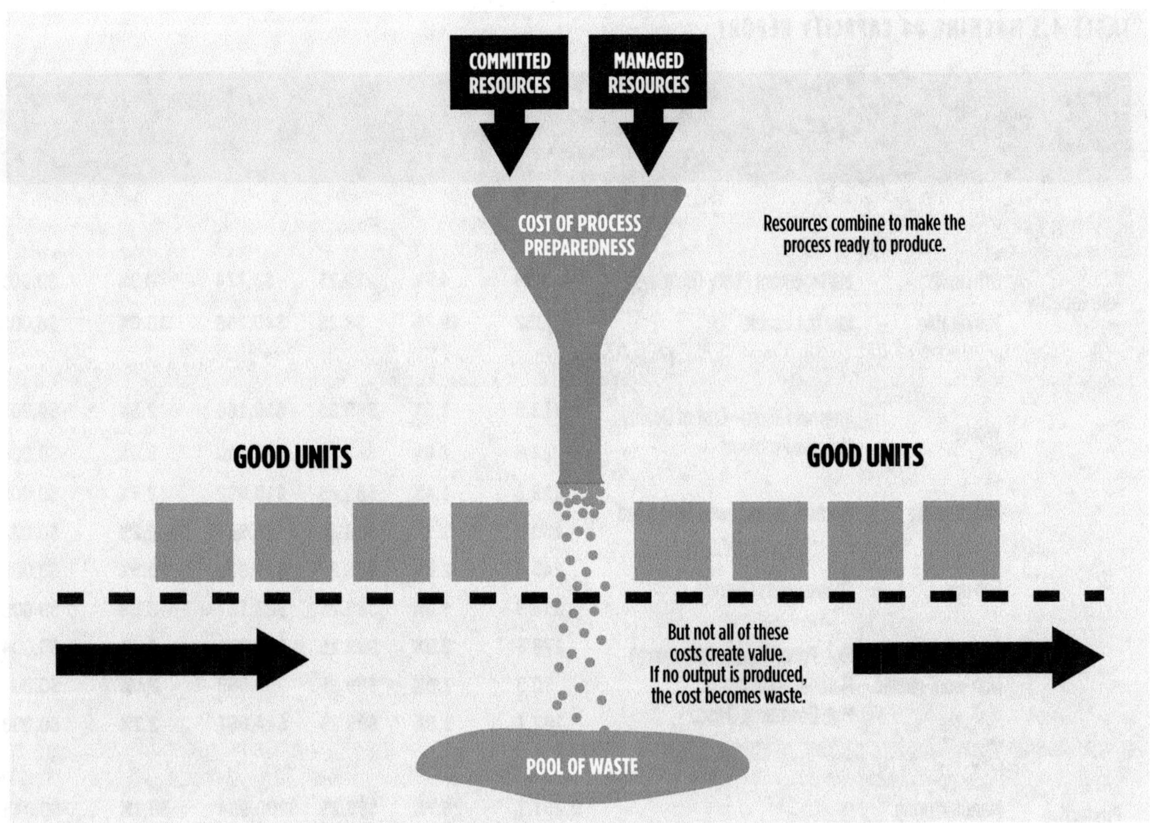

FIGURE 4.4 UTILIZING VS. WASTING THE COST OF PREPAREDNESS

The last concept we need to discuss before we have the basic language of capacity in place is **cycle time**—*the amount of time that elapses between units coming off of the end of a production line or process.* It also represents the amount of time a specific activity or output unit spends on the bottleneck. Cycle time approximates the total machine resources that one unit of output consumes.

Returning to Standard Soap, cycle time multiplied by the cost per second to run the machine gives us the cost we need to charge to one bar of soap. The cost of preparedness is stated in seconds so we can match our denominators, something we always have to be careful to do. At Standard Soap, there are two seconds between bars of soap coming off of Machine #4, the machine we are going to look at in more detail in Table 4.5. Before we do that, however, let us think through the cost of one bar. It costs Standard Soap $89.25 per staffed hour to run the machine. That translates to an average $0.0248 per second ($89.25 divided by 3,600 seconds in an hour). One bar of soap takes two seconds, so one bar costs $0.0496 in machining costs ($0.0248 per second times two seconds). The entire order, therefore, costs $248 in machining costs (5,000 bars at $0.0496 per bar).

The results for Standard Soap on Machine #4 for the entire year are detailed in Table 4.5. The company shuts down for two weeks in the summer (idle time), so it operates two shifts of 2,000 hours per shift year, or 4,000 total staffed hours per year. In actuality, however, it appears the company gets only 2,500 productive hours on the machine; 1,500 are nonproductive and 4,760 are idle.

TABLE 4.5 MACHINE #4 CAPACITY REPORT

Standard Soap Cost Center: Soap Machine #4 Year Ending: 12/31/20x6									
Summary Category	Type of Capacity Utilization	Reason for Utilization	Hours	% of Total Hours	Rate per Hour	Total Dollars	% of Total $'s	Cost per Good Bar
Idle Capacity	Off-Limits	Management Policy (Holidays)	408	4.7%	$9.25	$3,774	0.9%	$0.001
	Marketable	Idle but Usable	4,352	49.7%	$9.25	$40,256	10.0%	$0.009
Total Idle Capacity			4,760	54.4%		$44,030	11.0%	$0.010
	Waste	Internal Failure—Cost of Quality	113.9	1.3%	$89.25	$10,166	2.5%	$0.002
		Material Problems	224.6	2.6%	$89.25	$20,046	5.0%	$0.004
	Maintenance	Machine Breakdowns Scheduled	119.8	1.4%	$89.25	$10,692	2.7%	$0.002
			100.7	1.1%	$89.25	$8,987	2.2%	$0.002
	Set-ups	Changeovers Cleanup	245.6	2.8%	$89.25	$21,920	5.5%	$0.005
			258.9	3.0%	$89.25	$23,107	5.8%	$0.005
	Non-work-related	Mgt. Policy (Lunch, Allowance)	178.5	2.0%	$89.25	$15,931	4.0%	$0.004
		Material Handling	90.3	1.0%	$89.25	$8,059	2.0%	$0.002
		Mgt. Downtime (Misc.)	167.7	1.9%	$89.25	$14,967	3.7%	$0.003
Total Nonproductive Capacity			1,500	17.1%		$133,875	33.4%	$0.030
Productive Capcity	Manufacturing		2,251.7	25.7%	$89.25	$200,964	50.1%	$0.045
	Developmental	Process/Product	248.3	2.8%	$89.25	$22,161	5.5%	$0.005
Total Productive Capacity			2,500.0	28.5%		$223,125	55.6%	$0.050
Total Capacity Hours + Costs			8,760.0	100.0%		401,030	100.0%	$0.089

Cycle Time (Seconds per bar) 2

No. of Good Bars Produced	4,500,000
Competitive Cost per Good Bar	$0.045
Supplemental Unit Cost	$0.044
Total Cost per Unit	$0.089

Table 4.5 shows us that, when we think about the cost to produce a good bar of soap, we can either use the $0.045 estimate that results from considering the costs of production for the entire year—its **competitive cost,** *the amount of direct cost—without waste or idle time—incurred to make the product.* However, if we use an average of all of the costs for the year on soap Machine #4, our estimate jumps to $0.089, almost double the competitive amount. Which number should we use in costing? Since customers do not pay a company for waste, the lower competitive cost estimate is more in line with what the market expects. That does not mean the $0.0394 in waste does not matter. But this amount comes out of the profit the company earns; it is not part of the value it adds to a bar of soap. Companies need to keep their eyes on the waste embedded in their processes if they are to avoid financial trouble.

We also see from the capacity report in Table 4.5 that Machine #4 is idle 54.4% of the year, is nonproductive 17.1% of the time, and creates value for the firm's customers 28.5% of the time. In other words, the machine only earns revenue for the firm 28.5% of the time it is available. If Standard Soap wants to improve its profitability, it needs to concentrate its attention here. Specifically, it can improve profitability by using its machines more productively during the hours they are staffed.

Before we wrap up this discussion of capacity, let us take these key concepts and convert them into formulas that we will be able to use when we do the end-of-chapter problems. Table 4.6 contains the formulas a typical company might use.

TABLE 4.6 CAPACITY COST FORMULAS

Type of Cost	Definition	Calculation
Committed cost per hour	The current cost incurred for the "24/7" resources needed to operate the cost center.	Total Committed Cost / Total hours per year or $81,000 / 8,760 hours = $9.25 per hour
Managed cost per hour	The current shift/line incremental cost required to prepare it to produce good units.	Total Managed Cost / Staffed hours per year or $321,000 / 4,000 hours = $80 per hour
Cost per available hour	The current cost incurred when the line is ready to produce; includes both committed and managed hourly costs.	$9.25 per hour + $80 per hour = $89.25 per available hour and $89.25 per 3,600 seconds per hour = $0.0248 per second
Competitive cost per unit	The minimum cost of units currently made on the line.	Cycle time per unit x Cost per available hour or 2 seconds per unit x $0.0248 per second = $0.0496 per unit
Additional Calculations		
Productive capacity cost	The amount of resource cost that actually yields good product for customers; hence, revenues.	Good units produced x Competitive cost per unit or 4,500,000 good units x $0.0496 per unit = $223,200
Productive capacity cost—%	Capacity utilization can be examined in terms of percentage of time and/or percentage of cost.	Productive Capacity Cost / Total Costs for the Cost Center or $223,200 / $402,000 = 55.5%
Total productive capacity time	The amount of time the system was used to make products that were sold or inventoried for future sale.	(Good units produced x Cycle time per unit) / 3,600 seconds per hour or (4,500,000 good units x 2 seconds) / 3,600 seconds per hour = 2,500 hours
Percent productive utilization	Percentage of total time used to make good product—actual utilization.	Productive capacity time / Total time or 2,500 hours / 8,760 hours = 28.5%
Total nonproductive time	The total staffed time not traceable to good products; assignable to different categories of waste in the final reports.	Total staffed hours less total productive time or 4,000 hours - 2,500 hours = 1,500 hours

Type of Cost	Definition	Calculation
Percent nonproductive utilization	The total nonproductive time as a percentage of the total capacity available in the department.	Nonproductive time / Total time or 1,500 hours / 8,760 hours = 17.1%
Total nonproductive cost	The dollars of cost incurred due to nonproductive activities. If eliminated, this cost would become profit.	Nonproductive time x Cost per available hour or 1,500 x $89.25 = $133,875
Percent nonproductive cost	Measure of the percentage of total cost consumed in nonproductive efforts.	Nonproductive cost / Total cost or $133,875 / $401,000 = 33.4%
Total idle time	Time that capacity is not staffed for use. Before buying new assets, analyze this capacity.	Total time less staffed hours or 8,760 hours – 4,000 hour = 4,760 hours
Percent of idle time	Comparison of idle hours to total hours. This result ranges between 50% and 75% in the firms studied to date.	Idle time / Total time or 4,760 hour / 8,760 hours = 54.3%
Total idleness cost	The total cost of idle capacity, or waste, in the final reports.	Idle time x committed cost per hour or 4,760 hours x $9.25 = $44,030
Percent of idleness costs	The relative amount of idleness costs incurred by the firm. To use these resources, managed costs would also be incurred.	Idleness costs / Total costs or $44,030 / $401,000 = 11.0%

The capacity we have focused on here is that of Machine #4, but as you will see as we continue, every single cost pool requires that some definition of capacity be attached to it if we are going to be able to attribute that cost to some form of work or output of the firm. Machines are the easiest because we can use time as the denominator. There is a finite amount of time in a year, so there is a finite calculation we can do regarding productive, nonproductive, and idle time and cost. When we deal with pools paced by people, our estimates become much fuzzier. We can estimate roughly how much work is currently being done, perhaps even adjust that to some estimate of potential work, but since every output may be different, take different amounts of time, and be done by workers with different skill sets, our capacity numbers will be much less precise.

Having gone into depth on machine capacity costs, let us now turn our attention to the cost system we use in people-paced environments—the activity-based cost system.

IN CONTEXT ➤ Direct Costs and Overhead at Easy Air

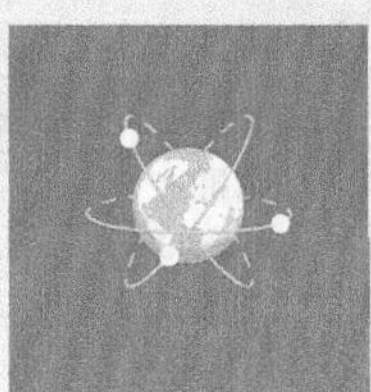

"Sanjiv, I think we're onto something here. While we can't charge every cost out to a plane, I think stepping away from the industry definition of capacity, which is revenue miles flown, and looking at some sort of measure of the time used to actually fly passengers gets us much closer to a decision-relevant piece of information," Sherry said.

"I know we're close. Think about it. We sell seats, not the whole plane, so we can't just focus on the plane. Setting the limits on the capacity of an airplane is much harder than simply looking at the capacity of a machine in a factory. Our machines can hold up to 130 passengers, and they move in space and time. We need to know our capacity by seat minutes, or something like that, to really crack these numbers," Sanjiv replied.

"We could calculate the number of seats per minute as our capacity, and then calculate how much of that capability we use," noted Rudy.

Sanjiv looked surprised. "We can? How?"

Rudy continued, "We currently keep track of every plane, and we also track the 'fill rates'—the load—on every flight. We know where the plane is and what it is doing, so we know whether the seats are producing revenue or not. It'll be simple once we combine the two databases we currently maintain in flight operations."

"I'd love to be able to present something this new and exciting to Fran next week," said Sanjiv. "We should all attend the meeting, because we're breaking new ground here, and I want everyone to get the credit.

"Rudy, I want you to focus on generating a new form of capacity measurement that evaluates whether our planes are earning any money. Sherry, I want you to work with me to focus on all of the company's other costs. No matter how good a job we do containing our direct costs, our profits seem to be eaten up by the indirect costs of running the business."

Having defined the focus of the costing project more concisely, they returned to work with new enthusiasm for the week ahead.

Activity-Based Costing

OBJECTIVE 3

Define and know how to use activity drivers, and identify key differences between machine- and people-paced cost pools.

As we examine the different types of activities that had to be completed to fill the order for 5,000 bars of soap, it is clear that each requires a unique set of resources. Table 4.7 lists all of the resources used and their total costs for each of the process steps in Standard Soap's order-to-payment process. For each cost pool, we have identified an **activity driver**, or *the event that causes us to use the cost pool's resources, as well as the total estimated amount of work the pool's capacity can support*. For example, when we discussed capacity, our activity driver was time.

As you can see from Table 4.7, not every resource a company has is needed, or used, by every activity. Also, each activity uses different amounts of the available resources. We use resource drivers to assign both direct and indirect costs to these cost pools. Remember, when we develop a cost pool, we have to make sure that we trace as many of the resources directly to that pool as we can. In most companies, this "tracing" takes place during the annual planning period when the firm develops its formal **budget,** *its financial plan for one or several years; used to establish capacity- and activity-cost estimates*. Once costs are assigned to a specific activity-based cost pool, we divide the total by the estimate of how much and what type of work will be done with those resources to get the activity-based cost estimate.

One of our major costing objectives is to find a logical way to assign specific resources to specific uses. We call this effort **cost tracing,** *attaching a cost to the specific activity, product, or service that uses it.* This tracing can be a one-to-one mapping (for example, *direct costs),* or a one-to-many assignment (for example, *indirect costs).* When we talk about the *traceability* of a resource cost, we are asking whether we can accurately and unambiguously attach that cost to a specific outcome. If we cannot directly trace a cost to one cost object, but we have a reasonably precise way to attach it to several different activities, products, or services, also known as cost objects, we use the term **cost assignment**—*the use of estimates to attach costs to specific activities, products, services, customers, or units of output that directly benefit from their consumption*—to describe this activity.

Finally, if we are simply "pushing the cost" somewhere (such as, full cost inventory valuation in financial accounting), we use the term **cost allocation,** *the arbitrary assignment of costs to an activity, product, customer, or unit of output*, to capture the fact that our costing methods are more arbitrary than accurate. When we use allocation, the cost estimates we produce become blurred. We can no longer say that the output of the firm causes the cost in quite the same way as when we trace or assign our resource costs to cost pools.

USING ABC TO ESTIMATE COSTS

The cost estimates in Table 4.7 comprise the activity-based costing (ABC) system for Standard Soap. We have already dealt with the costs to actually produce a bar of soap using capacity costing. Now the objective is to understand what it costs to complete the other activities that make up the "order-to-payment" process at Standard Soap. To arrive at each of these estimates, we follow several basic steps:

1. Trace and/or assign the resources the company uses to cost pools based on the type of work done with those resources. In other words, we use the homogeneity principle and *resource drivers* to develop cost pools.
2. Identify the *activity driver* for each pool. This should be some measure of the type of work the cost pool supports.
3. Estimate the quantity of work the pool can support before it needs major replenishment. This is your *capacity* estimate for the ABC pool.
4. Divide the costs in the cost pool by the estimated quantity of the activity driver to get the cost per activity.
5. Attach these activity costs to output using *cost drivers* that focus on how the capacity of the cost pool is consumed.

TABLE 4.7 MAPPING RESOURCES TO THE ORDER-TO-PAYMENT PROCESS

Standard Soap								
Resources	Take Order	Schedule Order	Set Up Machines	Move Materials	Package Order for Shipping	Ship Order	Bill Customer	Collect Payment
People	$160,000	$70,000	$240,000	$140,000	$204,000	$84,000	$120,000	$150,000
Benefits	$32,000	$14,000	$42,000	$28,000	$40,800	$16,800	$24,000	$30,000
Production Machines					$250,000			
Desks	$2,500	$500			$1,800	$500	$2,500	$4,000
Indirect Materials	$3,500	$600			$68,000	$750		
Outside Services			$10,000	$3,500	$12,000		$3,800	$2,500
Electricity	$2,400	$3,500		$20,000	$36,500	$3,000	$2,400	$2,400
Insurance	$1,500	$1,500	$7,500	$9,000	$10,500	$6,000	$1,500	$1,800
Space	$7,500	$1,800	$1,500	$45,000	$30,000	$9,000	$7,500	$9,500
Lift Trucks				$25,000		$10,000		
Propane				$8,400		$1,800		
Office Equipment	$7,500	$4,800	$2,250			$18,500	$30,000	$37,500
Computers	$16,000	$13,500	$3,000		$1,200	$2,800	$40,000	$50,000
Office Supplies	$13,500	$3,500	$1,500	$1,200	$12,500	$10,500	$25,800	$15,000
Tools			$15,000	$500	$3,500			
Soap Molds								
Telephone Service	$3,600	$400	$250	$250	$150	$1,250	$2,400	$3,600
Software	$7,500	$10,000			$2,600	$5,000	$10,800	$12,000
TOTAL RESOURCE COSTS	$257,500	$124,100	$323,000	$280,850	$673,550	$169,900	$270,700	$318,300
ACTIVITY DRIVER	Orders Taken	Schedules Run	Set-up Hours	Material Moves	Cases Packed	Shipments Made	Invoices Completed	Payments Received
ACTIVITY "CAPACITY"	25,000	200	8,000	200,000	180,000	40,000	50,000	75,000
COST PER ACTIVITY	$10.30	$620.50	$40.38	$1.40	$3.74	$4.25	$5.41	$4.24

What we see in this table is that each of our different drivers captures a different element of the costing puzzle. First, resource drivers capture the concepts of traceability and homogeneity. In Table 4.7, resource drivers were used to estimate the total amount of the various resources used by Standard Soap that each activity consumes. Once we have these costs in pools by activity, we need to understand what *causes* us to use up these resources. Activity drivers capture this *causality* effect, which is one of our key criteria for establishing sound cost estimates.

We then use capacity estimating to determine quantity of the driver each pool can support. These cost drivers capture the actual use of the resources in the pool. As work is done for individual customer orders, we can use these activity cost estimates to attach costs directly to them. While there may still be some untraceable overhead, such as the salary and support costs for the company president, if we carefully develop our activity cost pools, these types of costs can be minimized. In developing activity cost estimates, we do have flexibility when choosing how many, and how detailed, we want our cost pools to be and what specific drivers will provide the best proxy for how the capacity of the activity cost pool is consumed. Your goal is to make these relationships reflect reality as closely as possible within the bounds of the cost-benefit constraint—we should not spend more money doing costing than the benefits these estimates create in terms of improved decision making and performance.

IN THE NEWS ➤ Using ABC to Improve Costing in the Healthcare Industry

As has been well-publicized, U.S. healthcare costs per capita have been increasing significantly, growing to more than $10,000 per person, or roughly 17% of total gross domestic product. Clearly there is a need to gain control over these rising costs. The question that faced the University of Pittsburgh Medical Center (UPMC) was how this objective could be attained. With 20 hospitals and more than 500 clinics, it was a question that not only needed answering, but would have to be addressed using a well-designed, focused methodology. The approach chosen? Activity-based costing.

UPMC leaders recognized that the new costing system would have to incorporate the two major strategic goals of their hospital system: to improve care and to effectively compete in their healthcare market. To achieve these goals, UPMC needed to change its approach to providing healthcare: It needed to emphasize the patient perspective, not traditional facility or departmental approaches that resulted in costing and management silos. The traditional structure was replaced by four new service lines: Women's Health, Orthopedics, Heart and Vascular, and Neurology and Neurosurgery. These were added to the preexisting service lines: Pediatrics, Cancer, and Psychiatric Services. The resulting seven service lines were then organized across all of the clinical and hospital organizations, with all sites reporting to the management team dedicated to the service line.

This structural change, combined with a shift in management philosophy to the patient perspective, created a setting where activity-based costing (ABC) could now be deployed. Activities across sites could be standardized, which with proper management would result in an improved quality of care for UPMC's patients. The new costing information would also help management identify the relative efficiency and effectiveness of the services provided at the various sites. Measurable results of UPMC's service lines and ABC methodology include: $42 million in cost reduction opportunities, $5 million in realized supplies savings, ability to measure and compare the contribution margin for specific procedures, and a 97% reduction in the time needed to access information. Implementation of ABC continues, helping UPMC thrive in its highly competitive market.

Source: www.healthcatalyst.com/success_stories/activity-based-costing-in-healthcare-upmc, obtained on 11/28/2016.

PEOPLE-PACED VS. MACHINE-PACED COST POOLS

Once we have the activity-based costs in place, we use activity drivers to estimate the usable capacity of the people-paced pool to do work. Looking at Table 4.7, you can see that all of these drivers are quantifiable measures, but they are no longer time-defined. For instance, order-taking costs are divided by the number of orders taken to get an average cost per order taken. It is an average cost because we have not separated out the fixed and variable components. Since we used resource cost drivers to create the pools, variability is now a more difficult concept to implement because all of the costs do not move on a one-to-one basis with an increase in the driver frequency. That said, however, we can still use analytics or cost modeling approaches to gauge the degree of variability in each cost pool. As each cost pool is created, the characteristics of each resource can be estimated. The question we then face is how to best proxy the relationship between the resources in the cost pool and their consumption by the cost driver. At the least, we should try to identify the resources that have the largest purchase package as they will provide a reasonable estimate of the relevant range, or total potential work, the cost pool can support. Knowing which resources are divisible and can also be stored for future use is also very useful information for ongoing decision making.

The goal is to provide management not only with an average cost estimate for current operating conditions (the ABC estimates in Table 4.7), but also some understanding of how much these estimates will change if the amount of work being done increases or decreases significantly. As noted by a brewery manager at Labatt Brewing Company, what managers need to know is when they will "kick a step"—at what point will the cost estimates and assumptions they are using no longer be accurate enough for decision making.

Activity-based cost pools consist predominantly of traced and assigned costs. For those costs that cannot be assigned, a general overhead pool of allocated cost is created. Most companies charge this overhead to output using some form of cost driver, such as units produced or direct labor hours. Activity drivers cannot be used because there is no common activity that ties these costs together—overhead pools contain heterogeneous resource costs. Overhead charges distort the final cost number so you should use them with great care in decision making and analysis.

As you can see, there are some significant differences between machine (capacity-based) and people-paced (activity-based) cost pools. These differences are detailed in Table 4.8. What this table clearly shows is that activity-based cost pools are less precise because they use a greater number of estimates. More importantly, however, is the fact that we also cannot precisely define the capacity of a people-paced pool. The combination of these two estimates leaves us with significant margins of error. That said, it is far better to develop ABC estimates to aid ongoing costing requirements than to simply put all of the indirect resource costs into one pool, call it overhead, and spread it like peanut butter over all the goods and services an organization provides to its customers. Simply because we are using ABC, we are doing a better job of informing management about what is being spent in the organization, where it is being spent, why it is being spent, and finally, some key parameters that capture the underlying variability and controllability of these costs.

TABLE 4.8 KEY DIFFERENCES BETWEEN CAPACITY- AND ACTIVITY-BASED COSTING

Feature	Machine-Paced Cost Pools	People-Paced Cost Pools
Capacity	Can be defined precisely using time-based measures of capability and actual output.	Must be estimated because different people have different capabilities as does one person across time.
Activity drivers	Time-based.	Varies; defined by the dominant type of work done with the resources in the activity pool.
Precision	Extremely precise measurements because actual time is metered.	All costs and drivers are estimated; although the results can be reasonably accurate, they are never precise.
Variability	Some variability patterns are built in because two cost pools, managed and committed capacity, are used.	Variability is difficult to estimate, but analytics can be performed when the cost pool is created to gauge how the cost pool will respond to changes in the volume of activities performed.
Responsiveness	Costs respond directly to how the machine resources are used (productive, nonproductive, idle).	Costs are much less responsive to the occurrence of one more activity.

As you learn more about activity-based management, you will see that sometimes it is better to stop our analysis when we know why we spend the money and not try to attach the costs to a specific outcome. In other words, it is sometimes better to stop our costing based on *optimal accuracy* when choosing a driver that might lead management to believe a cost will vary if the activity is repeated. It is true that using an average cost may make the ABC estimate *look variable* to management. It is also true that because it is an average, not a variable, cost, we have to be very careful about the conclusions we draw when using the ABC estimate. The total costs in the pool probably will not change at all if one less activity is done; only the average cost of doing remaining activities will go up. This is a difficult concept to understand at first, but the more you learn about average costs in the chapters to come, the clearer this idea will become.

ABC contains all the components of capacity costing. Some people even present capacity costing as a subset of ABC, but when we do this, we ignore a lot of information that the more detailed and precise capacity costing estimates provide for us. Throughout this book, we will treat machine-based costs as capacity cost estimates and deal with people-paced work using activity-based cost estimates. As you will see, we can attach activity costs at any level of the firm, from the process domain up to the entity domain. On the other hand, capacity costs are of most use in the product domain. In the end, our goal is always the same—*to attach costs as accurately as we can to their causes.*

From Cost Pools to Cost Objects

OBJECTIVE 4

Characterize a cost object and assign costs to individual units of output.

Now that we know what it costs to perform each of the activities in the order-to-payment process at Standard Soap, we can determine what it costs to fill the order for the 5,000 bars of soap. Specifically, using the information in Table 4.2 for materials, plus the costs of running the soap press from Table 4.5, and the costs of completing the other activities in Table 4.7, we can total up the costs that Standard Soap will incur. These are compiled in Table 4.9, where we can see that completing the order will cost Standard Soap $944.30, or a little under $0.189 a bar.

We are next going to use **cost drivers,** *a measure used to attach a cost to its final use (activity drivers can often serve this purpose)*, to attach specific costs to the batch of soap. Cost drivers estimate the amount of a cost pool used by one **cost object,** *the activity or outcome that is the focus of the costing effort—the company's work product*. The number and type of cost objects we can examine is practically limitless. One house in a new development is a cost object for a construction firm. In banking, a customer account or a specific type of banking service, such as a safe deposit box, are examples of cost objects. In manufacturing, a bottle of shampoo, a personal computer, or the distribution of these products are all things we might want to estimate the cost of—they are all cost objects.

If we wanted to know, instead, the impact of a change in how we make a product or complete an activity, how we structured the new manufacturing process would also be a cost object. In fact, whenever we combine costs to analyze any opportunity, decision, or potential outcome, we are focusing our efforts on a cost object. Thus, the cost object in our Standard Soap example is the job they undertook to make 5,000 bars of hotel soap.

TABLE 4.9 ESTIMATING THE COST OF AN ORDER

Standard Soap				
Cost Item or Activity	Cost per Occurrence	Driver	Quantity Used by Order	Estimated Cost of Order
Materials	$0.047	Ounce	7,500	$352.50
Take order	$10.300	Orders taken	1	$10.30
Schedule production	$620.500	Schedules run*	0.008	$4.96
Set up machine	$40.375	Set-up hours	1	$40.38
Move materials	$1.404	Moves	12	$16.85
Make soap bars**	$0.089	per bar	5,000	$445.59
Packaging Order	$3.742	Cases packed	10	$37.42
Ship order	$4.248	Shipments made	2	$8.50
Bill customer	$5.414	Invoices mailed	2	$10.83
Collect payment	$4.244	Checks received	4	$16.98
Total Cost of Order				$944.30
Estimated Cost per Bar (Total cost divided by 5,000 bars)				$0.189

*Standard runs 200 schedules a year for its 25,000 orders, so each order uses 0.008 of a run.

**The cost to make soap bars is $0.089118.

At Standard Soap, the current cost object is the cost to produce an order of 5,000 bars of specialty hotel bar soap. We call such a cost object a **job,** *a discrete custom order from a specific customer*. We could just as easily make the cost object the cost for processing purchase orders, or, for that matter, any activity that takes place at Standard Soap or Easy Air. **Job-order costing,** *which traces actual materials, labor, and activity costs to a specific order*, is often used by companies that do unique jobs for each customer. In job-order costing, a company calculates the actual materials, labor, machining costs, and activity costs used by a specific customer order. They also often add an amount of overhead to the order to ensure that they keep their eyes on the total costs of running the business. Standard Soap does not use an overhead pool, but some of the companies we look at in the chapter exercises, problems, and cases will. The total of all of the costs assigned to a specific job is that job's cost.

If Standard Soap charged only $944.30 for the completed order, it would not make a profit on it. What Standard Soap's sales force now needs to know is whether this cost is above, or below, the normal **market price,** *the customer's assessment of the value of a product or service*. Of course, the company could also use a **cost-plus pricing method**, whereby *a percentage of profit is automatically added to the cost of making a product or providing a service*. This method is used in some industries to establish prices when each order is different, when market prices are not readily known, or a variety of bundled options are available that differ in terms of resources consumed. The calculation looks like this:

Cost of order	$ 944.30
Plus: 25% profit on cost	236.07
Sales price	$1,180.37

In this case, the price to the customer is 125% of the cost to produce the product. If we knew the price was $1,180.37 and that the company marked up its costs by 25% to get the sales price, we could divide the $1,180.37 by 1.25 and get the cost. This is an easy way to set a price and is sometimes the best that a company can do if there is no ready market for the product or it is a custom job, such as the run of hotel bar soap at Standard Soap.

In a competitive market, however, what matters is what the firm's competitors would charge for the order. While we clearly cannot know this fact for sure, over time a company builds up knowledge about current competitors' prices and products. It is no coincidence that prices for comparable products are very close. Companies constantly collect intelligence on the features and prices of products offered by their competitors to ensure they keep not only their prices in line, but are able to set limits on cost. This is why it is always important to remember that prices for most goods are set by the market. A company that is a price taker has to factor these market prices into its decision-making process to ensure that it continues to be able to make products or provide services within the constraints of the market price.

We use the cost estimate to understand if the company can make a profit on this order, *given its current market price.* If the answer to this question is "no," the company should not abandon the opportunity to bid for the order. Instead, it should look at how it plans to meet the customer's demands. The cost estimate provides the information needed to decide on a price for the order, or, if the product is freely available, to change how we plan to meet the customer's demands to ensure we make a reasonable profit. For example, perhaps Standard Soap could reduce the cost of this order by using less expensive packaging material, a different ingredient for the soap itself, or it could move the materials twice instead of 10 times. A cost estimate is one of the key pieces of information used in this type of management decision making.

Unless a specific cost object is defined, the costing activity has little or no value. Cost estimates exist to provide information about cost objects, and for no other reason. And, as we shall see, as we change the cost object, we change the type of costs we want to include and how we calculate them. This fact gives rise to the oldest saying in costing, first coined by J.M. Clark in 1935, namely that we use *"different costs for different purposes."* When we look at the cost of making a unit of product, we are going to consider a much different set of resources than when we ask ourselves how best to manage our supply chain to bring down the cost of raw materials and support services. Each new cost object, each new decision, requires that we step back and, using our databases and knowledge of resource costs and uses, develop an estimate of the cost of that particular cost object. It is a skill set you will be refining for years to come, one that will often spell the difference between the success and failure of a firm.

IN CONTEXT ➤ Assigning People Costs at Easy Air

By the end of the week, Sanjiv was deeply engaged in pulling data from the company databases to populate a new capacity reporting scorecard while Sherry and Rudy continued to work on the activity side of the cost picture. They had one more week before they were to present their conclusions to Fran and the management team. They were going to put in some long hours before they would be ready for that meeting.

"Sanjiv, I think we're going to have to put together a quick survey to be more precise about our activity-based cost estimates," Sherry said. "For now, it's useful to know how many dollars we spend completing reservations, but I know that reservation agents do other things, like working with customers who run into problems using our website to book tickets or who want to change their tickets. They are our reservation experts, but they often are the first line of defense in providing quality customer care."

Sanjiv agreed, and added, "We also have a customer service department that fields a lot of these same questions and undertakes a wide range of activities. Everyone goes to meetings, which consumes time. We do ongoing computer and service training. The list is endless. And we only have a week. If we had the time, I'd bet we'd discover that our staff spends about 35 to 50% of their time doing actual productive work just as our physical assets do. And for jobs like our direct customer service people perform at the airports, there is a lot of downtime between flights. None of this is easy to assign costs to unless we accept the use of average cost estimates and ignore the underlying reality."

"I hope we don't have to take one path or the other. Can't we define our activities more broadly so that people across the company can 'clock in' against them?" asked Sherry.

"I think we can do it, but I'm just not sure we can do it in a week," Sanjiv replied. "I think we should use average costs for now so we get a usable data set, then ask Fran if we can expand the study to do what my professor called activity-based management. If we take this final step, we can link resources across departments to get a more accurate estimate of what it takes to do certain types of work, and who contributes to getting that work done. For now, let's be a bit less ambitious. It'll be enough if Rudy has some ballpark numbers on our capacity utilization and we split the rest of the management costs into logical pools."

"Sounds good. I guess I'm getting ahead of myself, but it is so exciting to think we may actually be innovating in our industry by using the tools and techniques that companies and experts in other industries have developed. I just want to make sure we're as accurate as we can be."

"We will be before we're done, Sherry. For now, let's take one logical step at a time," said Sanjiv.

Summary

In this chapter, we examined how to put our resources into cost pools so that we can get work done in organizations. Very seldom does one resource provide all of the capability that is needed to get something done. A machine needs people, space, electricity, and maintenance, for instance, before it can be relied on to do any work. People often need space, desks, telephones, and computers before a company can tap their potential. Line workers in a factory are part of the machine-paced process, while workers in an office set the pace for the work done there.

Once we learned how to assign resources to specific cost pools, we considered the question of accuracy. When a cost can be unambiguously assigned to one cost pool, we call it a direct cost. Most costs, however, are shared by two or more cost pools. In that case, we have to use a resource driver to assign a portion of the resource cost to every activity and output that uses it. We use resource drivers to assign indirect costs to their uses.

Finally, there are times when we cannot logically assign a specific resource cost to any cost pool. At that point, we have several options, which include simply leaving these costs in the larger general and administrative category or creating an overhead pool that contains the untraceable indirect costs of running the business. If a company decides to assign these overhead costs to output, we call the process "allocation." When we allocate, we are being arbitrary in our assignment of cost, with all of the inaccuracy such an approach suggests. Our goal, therefore, is to assign as much cost as possible, leaving as small a pool of "leftover" costs, or overhead, as possible. To help us achieve this goal, we use two different costing approaches.

Capacity-based cost analysis traces costs to a machine that can be used for a finite period of time. In capacity-based systems, we can use managed and committed cost as the cost pools. We use a product's cycle time to attach the machine pool's costs to a specific unit of output. Capacity costing is very accurate because we can measure, with precision, exactly how much of the machine pool's capacity is being used productively. A machine that is ready to make product but sits idle for some reason is expensive. We call this unused staffed time "nonproductive time." It should be minimized. Finally, we sometimes decide to only use a machine one or two shifts. When it lies purposely idle, we only incur the committed (fixed or large stepped) costs. While still a form of waste, the cost of idle time is usually smaller than that of nonproductive time. This assumption clearly changes as the machine becomes larger and more expensive to run. That is why some companies, such as paper mills, run the plant 24/7, 365 days a year.

Organizations, however, have many more people than those who are only needed to run the machines. We need some way to estimate the costs, and benefits received, from these individuals. To accomplish this goal, we use activity-based costing (ABC). In ABC, we trace resources to cost pools based on a common type of work, such as processing purchase orders or issuing invoices to customers. ABC helps us understand the costs of running the business much better, and the more time we put into identifying the major activities and accurately costing them out, the more benefit we receive from the ABC system. While ABC is not as precise as capacity costing, it is still much better than simply putting all of the costs of the business into one large overhead pool and allocating. We will do a bit of allocation so you can see the impact it has on costing accuracy in the exercises and problems we will do to lock in our learning.

In the final part of the chapter, we turned our attention to assigning the costs from the cost pools to specific cost objects. While we used a common cost object, a job requiring 5,000 bars of soap, we noted that cost objects can be found anywhere a decision needs to be made. The term "cost object," in fact, simply refers to the reason for doing the cost estimating. It can range from one unit of output to a decision to add an entirely new product line to a business. As long as a cost is employed to answer a question, a cost object exists.

Throughout the development of the cost side of our management accounting database, therefore, we are making estimates. Sometimes our estimates are quite precise, but normally there is going to be some degree of error. Our goal is to learn how to estimate a cost object with the least amount of error possible. It is a continuous journey, one that never ends in any organization. Decisions need to be made with the information available, but there is always the potential to add to our database so we can answer more questions, more accurately, and more rapidly. Making the decision about how large and complex the management accounting database should be is in itself a cost object, one that varies by company and industry.

Key Terms

Activity driver: the thing that depletes the cost pool's resources, as well as the total estimated amount of work the pool's capacity can support.

Avoidability criterion: measure of cost in relation to work; specifically concerned with whether costs go away when no work is being done.

Budget: a company's financial plan for one or several years; used to establish capacity- and activity-based cost estimates.

Causality: the reason for a specific outcome or activity; the thing that drives the cost.

Committed capacity costs: expenditures that do not go away even if a machine is not in use.

Competitive cost: the amount of direct cost—without waste or idle time—incurred to make the product.

Cost allocation: the arbitrary assignment of costs to an activity, product, customer, or unit of output.

Cost assignment: the use of estimates to attach costs to specific activities, products, services, customers, or units of output that directly benefited from their consumption.

Cost driver: a measure used to attach a cost to its final use; activity drivers can often serve this purpose.

Cost object: the activity or outcome that is the focus of the costing effort—the company's work product.

Cost-plus pricing: a percentage of profit is automatically added to the cost of making a product or providing a service.

Cost pool: a combination of resources that support a common goal.

Cost of preparedness: the sum of all of the resources needed to make a machine ready to do work.

Cost tracing: attaching a cost to the specific activity, product, or service that uses it.

Cycle time: the amount of time that elapses between units coming off of a production line or process; also the amount of time a specific activity or output unit spends on the bottleneck.

Heterogeneous: a cost pool that contains a mix of resources that are the result of many different causes.

Homogeneity: a cost pool that contains only those resources from which it directly benefits.

Idle capacity: a period during which a company plans to not use a machine, which is unmanned; therefore, only committed capacity costs are wasted.

Job: a discrete custom order from a specific customer.

Job-order costing: traces actual materials, labor, and activity costs to a specific order.

Managed capacity costs: expenditures that go away if a machine is idle (unmanned).

Market price: the customer's assessment of the value of a product or service.

Nonproductive capacity: time wasted when a machine is fully manned but no output is generated.

Order-to-payment process: the primary process, or linked set of activities, that begins with the receipt of a customer's order and ends with the customer's payment for the goods or services received.

Overhead: the sum of indirect product costs that are not assigned to a specific capacity- or activity-based cost pool.

Process: a linked sequence of activities that transforms input into output.

Productive capacity: the amount of a cost pool's time that results in completed product for the customer.

Resource driver: measure used to assign a resource to a cost pool.

Questions

1. What is a cost pool? Give an example of one.
2. What does the term homogeneous mean? Heterogeneous? How do they impact the nature of cost pools?
3. List and explain the features of accurate cost pools.
4. Define overhead. What problems does it create in cost analysis? Use the features of an accurate cost pool as the basis for your analysis.
5. Define a resource driver and give an example of one that could be used to create a machine-based cost pool.
6. What does the term capacity mean? How do we use it in developing a cost estimate?
7. Define managed and committed capacity costs. What are their primary differences? Specifically, how does their activity driver change?
8. What is productive capacity? Nonproductive? Idle capacity? Why are these different types of capacity utilization important?
9. What does the term cost of preparedness mean? Which type of capacity cost (managed or committed) does it include?
10. What is the cost driver in capacity-based costing? How does it differ from the activity driver(s)?
11. Define a firm's competitive cost. How is it related to market price?
12. What is the difference between tracing and assigning a cost? Between assigning and allocating a cost? Why is this important?
13. List the steps needed to develop an activity-based cost.
14. What are the key differences between capacity- and activity-based costing? When should each be used?
15. Define the term cost object and give at least one example of a cost object.
16. Define cost-plus pricing. When is it the preferred way to price a job? When is it not a good way to price a job?

Exercises

1. **COST POOLS.** Redwood Grills makes a custom line of outdoor grills. It has a broad network of retail stores that distributes its products across the country. It has compiled the following information about its invoicing operations.

Resource	Resource Driver	Cost	Capacity	Quantity Used
People	Labor hours	$25	2,000 hours	6,000 hours
Desks	Units	$500	10 years each	3
Computers	Units	$1,200	4 years each	3
Copiers	Units	$2,500	5 years each	1
Telephones	Units	$100	5 years each	2
Invoices	Units	$0.20	1 invoice	2,500

REQUIRED:

a. Using the above list of costs and resource drivers, which resources and quantities should be used to determine the cost of processing the company's invoices?
b. Estimate the cost per invoice using 25,000 invoices per year as your activity driver.

2. **COST POOLS.** Franklin and Sons handles investment portfolios for a variety of customers. One unit of the company deals specifically with small investors. It has compiled the following information about its small investors branch, which has 5,000 customers.

Resource	Resource Driver	Cost	Capacity	Quantity Used
Investment Advisors	Months	$5,000	50 investors	10
Desks	Units	$600	10 years each	10
Computers	Units	$1,200	4 years each	10
Copiers	Units	$2,400	4 years each	1
Telephones	Units	$144	6 years each	10
Internet	Monthly	$250	10 users	100%

REQUIRED:

a. Using the above list of costs and resource drivers, please combine the correct amounts to put together into the cost of managing small investor portfolios in the company on a monthly basis.
b. Estimate the cost per customer using 5,000 small customers per month as your activity driver.

3. **CLASSIFICATION OF COSTS.** Hightower Enterprises manages apartment buildings for various small investors. It spends a significant amount of time on two activities: maintenance and rent collection. Sort the following costs into maintenance and rent collection using M for maintenance and R for rent collection. If the resource seems shared, use an S. Finally, if you are unsure, use an O for overhead.

Lawn mowers	Desks
Computers	Rakes
Rent collectors	Telephones
Trucks	Building
Maintenance supervisor	Office manager
Electricity	Leaf blowers
Invoices	Deposit slips
Maintenance crew	Company president

4. **CLASSIFICATION OF COSTS.** Puff 'n Stuff makes various small toys for dogs and cats using a large machine that cuts the fabric and machine-stitches the seams. The toys are then hand-stuffed and packaged. Sort the following costs into direct, machine-based, and people-based costs using D for direct to product, M for machine, and P for people. If the resource seems shared, use an S. Finally, if you are unsure, use an O for overhead.

Depreciation	Insurance
Salaries	Thread
Machine maintenance	Stuffing
Packaging materials	Worktables
Electricity	Materials
Building	Machine oil
Supervisor	Payroll service

5. **CAPACITY COSTING.** BabyCare makes "Binkies," a specialty line of pacifiers using one large machine that both makes and packages the pacifier. The machine's managed capacity cost is $250,000 per year to run one shift of 2,000 hours. Its committed costs are $150,000 per year.

REQUIRED:

a. Calculate the managed cost per hour.
b. Calculate the committed cost per hour.
c. It takes four seconds to make one Binkie (its cycle time). Using competitive cost, what does it cost to make one Binkie?

6. **CAPACITY COSTING.** SureSeed Company makes a lawn repair mixture that is sold in five-pound bags. One machine mixes the seed, soil, fertilizer, and special ingredients to make the lawn repair mix. The machine runs two shifts, or 4,000 hours per year. The committed costs of running the machine are $1,200,000 per year. Managed costs are $800,000 per year.

REQUIRED:

a. Calculate the managed cost per hour.
b. Calculate the committed cost per hour.
c. It takes two seconds to fill and seal one bag (its cycle time). Using competitive cost, what does it cost to make one bag of lawn repair mixture?

7. **CAPACITY COSTING.** Clip-A-Long makes binder clips of various sizes. The clips are made on one machine that takes precut strips of metal, bends them, adds the flange that helps hold the papers, and then boxes them in groups of 10. Materials cost $0.05 per clip. The items sell for $1.25 per box. The machine usually has $1,800,000 in committed costs and $600,000 in managed costs for a year and runs three shifts of 2,000 hours each.

REQUIRED:

a. Calculate the managed cost per hour.
b. Calculate the committed cost per hour.
c. It takes two seconds to make and package one box (its cycle time). Using competitive cost, what does it cost to make one box of clips?
d. Using your cost estimate, what is the profit per box? Make sure to include materials in your calculations.

8. **ACTIVITY-BASED COSTING.** CalcOne makes small, solar-charged, 10-key handheld calculators from purchased parts. It is a manual operation consisting of three stages. Materials cost $1.25. Several back office employees handle the orders and invoices. Finally, the company has a sales force that sells the product. The following are the cost pools and driver information for each of these departments.

Activity	Driver	Driver Frequency	Cost
Assembly	Units made	750,000	$562,500
Order processing	Orders taken	10,000	$200,000
Invoicing	Invoices mailed	25,000	$150,000
Accounting	Checks received	50,000	$250,000
Sales	Orders taken	10,000	$300,000

REQUIRED:

a. Calculate the activity cost rates for each of the cost pools.
b. One customer buys 5,000 units on one order. It takes two invoices to get payment, which comes in three checks that are processed by Accounting. What is the total cost of this customer's order?

9. **ACTIVITY-BASED COSTING.** Muldoon's Window Washing Company handles basic window washing, power washing, and light window maintenance. It divides its company into the following activities and cost pools.

Activity	Driver	Driver Frequency	Cost
Window washing	Number of windows washed	250,000	$312,500
Power washing	Hours of washing	2,000	$25,000
Small repairs	Hours of repair	2,000	$30,000
Accounting	Customer invoices	10,000	$60,000
Sales	Orders taken	5,000	$75,000

REQUIRED:

a. Calculate the activity cost rates for each of the cost pools.
b. One customer has 20 windows washed, two hours of power washing, and one hour of minor repair. It took two invoices before the customer paid with one check, which was processed in Accounting. What is the total cost of servicing this customer?

10. **ACTIVITY-BASED COSTING.** Sullivan's Auto Repair does small repair jobs on automobiles, including oil changes, brake jobs, and tire repair. It divides its company into the following activities and cost pools.

Activity	Driver	Driver Frequency	Cost
Oil changes	Number of oil changes done	10,000	$100,000
Brake repairs	Hours of repair	2,000	$50,000
Tire repairs	Tires repaired	5,000	$40,000
Radiator repairs	Hours of repair	1,000	$25,000
Customer service	Number of customers	5,000	$30,000

REQUIRED:

a. Calculate the activity cost rates for each of the cost pools.
b. One customer needs an oil change, one tire repaired, radiator fluid, which takes five minutes to add to the car, and new brake shoes, which take half an hour to put on. What is the total cost of servicing this customer?

11. **JOB-ORDER COSTING.** Tony's Pizza makes a variety of pizzas and grinders for local customers. He needs to set the price of a regular pizza, which has two ingredients. Tony's costs for making a pizza are as follows.

Resource	Amount Used	Cost
Crust	1 crust	$0.25 per crust
Meat toppings	2 oz.	$1 per oz.
Vegetable toppings	2 oz.	$0.50 per oz.
Cheese	4 oz.	$0.30 per oz.
Pizza chef	3 minutes	$15 per hour
Brick oven	3 minutes	$30 per hour

REQUIRED:

a. Calculate the cost for one sausage and mushroom pizza.
b. Tony wants to make 30% profit on each pizza. What price should he charge?

12. **JOB-ORDER COSTING.** Speedy Print is a small copy shop that has both black and white and color printers. It also offers a range of binding choices. The cost for running the shop are:

Resource	Cost per Unit
Paper	$0.01 per sheet
Black and white copier	$0.03 per sheet
Color copier	$0.06 per sheet
Binding machine	$0.25 per unit bound
Labor	$12 per hour

REQUIRED:

a. Speedy Print takes a job that requires 25 black and white sheets and 10 color sheets per booklet for a total of 25 booklets. The customer wants them bound. It will take four minutes to make each booklet. What is the direct cost of this order?

b. Speedy marks up every order by 40% to cover overhead and generate a profit. What price will Speedy need to charge for this order?

Problems

1. **COST POOLS.** Certainty Seedlings is a medium-sized nursery located in Western Pennsylvania. Recently, Joel Beale, the company's owner, completed a course in business planning and analysis. He decided he would like to try to put the costs his company incurs into cost pools to see if he can get a better idea of where he makes his profit and to see where he might need to change the way he thinks about the business. Joel decided to split his costs into five pools: lawn installations, garden installations, lawn maintenance, garden maintenance, and general overhead. Joel pays his workforce $20 per hour regardless of what job they do. The buildings used by the business cost $150,000 per year. Electricity costs $24,000 per year, and general office costs are $200,000 per year. The following table details by resource what part of the business is supported by each pool and how much each contributes.

Certainty Seedlings					
Resource	Lawn Installations	Garden Installations	Lawn Maintenance	Garden Maintenance	General Business Costs
Labor hours	6,000	4,000	10,000	4,000	
Lawn mowers	$500.00		$4,000.00		
Hoes, rakes, etc.	$1,500.00	$1,000.00	$1,200.00	$800.00	
Sprinkler units	$25,000.00	$10,000.00			
Seeds	$2,500.00	$5,000.00	$500.00		
Plants		$25,000.00		$10,000.00	
Bushes	$5,000.00	$15,000.00		$5,000.00	
Trucks	$20,000.00	$10,000.00	$50,000.00	$30,000.00	
Building	20%	30%	30%	20%	$150,000.00
Electricity	30%	40%	15%	15%	$24,000.00
Back office costs	25%	25%	25%	25%	$200,000.00
General Overhead on DLH	??	??	??	??	$50,000.00

Driver	Lawns Installed	Gardens Installed	Lawns Mowed	Gardens Maintained	Direct Labor
Driver Frequency	250	100	10,000	1,000	24,000

REQUIRED:

a. Complete the grid above by transforming all of the percentages and hours into actual costs by cost pool. It will be easier if you enter the table into Excel.

b. Assign the overhead to the four main cost pools using direct labor hours as your driver.

c. Calculate the cost per driver using the drivers given.

d. Certainty Seedlings marks up its costs by 20% to provide profit for Joel. What would Joel have to charge by product line to make his 20% profit per year?

2. **COST POOLS.** Chewy Treats, Inc., makes several lines of caramel-based candies and treats. Each product runs on its own set of machines. The lines Chewy makes are Wrapped Caramels, Chocolate-Covered Caramels, Caramel Cookie Bars, and Caramel Nut Bars. Direct labor on the assembly lines is paid $15 per hour. Lift trucks cost $120,000 per year. The building that Chewy occupies costs $300,000 per year, and electricity is $120,000 per year. Back office costs are $400,000 per year. Details about Chewy's costs for the various product lines for the year are contained in the following table.

Chewy Treats, Inc.					
Resource	Wrapped Caramels	Chocolate-Covered Caramels	Caramel Cookie Bars	Caramel Nut Bars	General Business Costs
Direct labor hours	12,000	8,000	12,000	12,000	None
Machine hours	6,000	4,000	4,000	4,000	None
Direct materials	$200,000.00	$250,000.00	$400,000.00	$500,000.00	None
Machine costs	$120,000.00	$160,000.00	$200,000.00	$200,000.00	None
Machine maintenance	$30,000.00	$30,000.00	$40,000.00	$50,000.00	None
Supplies	$75,000.00	$60,000.00	$120,000.00	$100,000.00	None
Lift trucks	20%	30%	30%	20%	$120,000.00
Building	30%	40%	15%	15%	$300,000.00
Electricity	25%	25%	25%	25%	$120,000.00
Back office costs on MH	??	??	??	??	$400,000.00
Driver	Pieces Made	Pieces Made	Bars Made	Bars Made	Machine Hours
Driver Frequency	20,000,000	16,000,000	5,000,000	4,000,000	18,000

REQUIRED:

a. Complete the grid above by transforming all of the percentages and hours into actual costs by cost pool. It will be easier if you enter the table into Excel.

b. Assign the overhead to the four main cost pools using machine labor hours as your driver.

c. Calculate the cost per unit made using the driver information given.

d. Chewy marks up its costs by 25% to provide profit. What would Chewy have to charge by unit of product made to generate its 25% profit per year?

3. **CAPACITY COSTS.** Energetic Treadmills is a medium-sized company that makes three models of treadmills on one large machine. The products share this machine. The machine is run 4,000 hours per year. Other information about the costs for the machine and the products made by Energetic Treadmills are shown in the following table.

Energetic Treadmills	
Cost Information about the Machine	
Depreciation	$500,000.00
People	$600,000.00
Supplies	$250,000.00

Energetic Treadmills	
Cost Information about the Machine	
Maintenance	$400,000.00
Electricity	$250,000.00
Building space	$350,000.00

Treadmill Model	Units Made	Cycle Time in Minutes
Model 1000	1,000	20
Model 1200	1,500	30
Model 1500	2,500	50

REQUIRED:

a. Using the total time used to make the three products, calculate what percentage of the productive time the machine is used to make each product.
b. Cost out the three products using their respective percentage of the total productive time.
c. Now put the costs of running the machines into one of the two cost pools, managed or committed capacity.
d. Calculate the cost per managed hour, per committed hour, and total cost per staffed hour.
e. Calculate the competitive cost of the three products using the staffed hourly rate you calculated in (d).
f. Explain as precisely as possible the differences in the estimated costs of the products.

4. **CAPACITY COSTS.** Majestic Toys makes three different types of stuffed animals for various arcades across the country. The information on the work done on the factory's machines is contained in the following table.

Majestic Toys	
Cost Information about the Machine	
Depreciation	$50,000.00
People	$100,000.00
Supplies	$25,000.00
Maintenance	$75,000.00
Electricity	$20,000.00

Majestic Toys	
Cost Information about the Machine	
Building space	$30,000.00

Stuffed Animal	Units Made	Cycle Time in Minutes
Bunnies	10,000	2
Chickadees	15,000	3
Panda bears	25,000	4

REQUIRED:

a. Using the total time used to make products, calculate what percentage of the productive time the machine is used to make each product.

b. Cost out the three products using their respective percentage of the total productive time.

c. Now put the costs for running the machines into one of the two cost pools, managed or committed capacity.

d. Calculate the cost per managed hour, per committed hour, and per total cost staffed hour.

e. Calculate the competitive cost of the three products using the staffed hourly rate you calculated in (d).

f. Explain as precisely as possible the differences in the estimated costs of the products.

5. **ACTIVITY-BASED COSTING.** Daisy Bakeries is a medium-sized bakery producing four lines of products: bread, cakes, pies, and cookies. It is currently charging its $750,000 of overhead to the product lines based on the number of direct labor hours. Its owner, Rhonda Daisy, recently went to a Small Business Association meeting where she attended a presentation on ABC. Rhonda wants to see if ABC makes any sense for her business. She has done a basic study to identify her key activities and their costs. She has also identified how much of each cost goes to each product line. This information is contained in the following two tables.

Daisy Bakeries			
Activity	Number	Driver	Dollars
Blend batter	4,400	Machine hours	$132,000
Bake	8,050	Baking hours	$362,250

Daisy Bakeries			
Activity	Number	Driver	Dollars
Cleanup	2,750	Batches	$33,000
Frosting	5,000	Units frosted	$90,000
Packaging	17,750	Packages	$88,750
Miscellaneous	10,000	Direct labor hours	$44,000
TOTAL			$750,000

Daisy Bakeries					
Driver	Bread	Cakes	Pies	Cookies	Total
Units Made	450,000	225,000	325,000	3,600,000	N/A
Direct labor hours	3,500	1,500	2,000	3,000	10,000
Machine hours	2,500	750	400	750	4,400
Baking hours	3,000	750	1,600	2,700	8,050
Batches made	1,000	500	1,000	250	2,750
Units frosted	-	2,000	-	3,000	5,000
Packages	10,000	2,500	4,000	1,250	17,750

REQUIRED:

a. Using direct labor hours as your driver, calculate how much overhead is currently being charged to each of the product lines.
b. Calculate the amount of overhead per unit for each of the product lines.
c. Calculate the activity rates for each of the ABC drivers noted.
d. Charge out overhead using the ABC rates.
e. Calculate total overhead by product line.
f. Calculate overhead by unit made for each of the product lines.
g. What does this information tell you? What specific recommendations would you make to Rhonda regarding Daisy Bakeries?

6. **ACTIVITY-BASED COSTING.** Get Up 'n Go Fitness Club is an exercise club that offers four basic products: weight training, supervised fitness routines, aerobics, and swimming. It currently charges the firm's $1,500,000 labor and overhead combined out on hours of operation. Sam Gentry, the firm's owner, has recently been approached by a student team from a local university to do an activity-based cost analysis of the operation. Sam agrees, figuring anything he can do to settle some ongoing struggles between his operating managers is worth a try. The students compile the following information for you.

Get Up 'n Go Fitness Club			
Activity	Number	Driver	Dollars
Personal training	2,000	Trainer hours	$80,000
Weight training	20,000	Bench hours	$100,000
Circuit training	40,000	Machine hours	$1,000,000
Aerobics	1,000	Classes taught	$50,000
Swimming	6,000	Hours of operation	$120,000
Miscellaneous	8,000	Direct labor hours	$150,000
TOTAL			$1,500,000

Get Up 'n Go Fitness Club					
Driver	Weight Training	Supervised Fitness	Aerobics	Swimming	Total
Hours of operation	6,000	6,000	1,000	6,000	19,000
Direct labor hours	1,000	5,000	2,000	-	8,000
Personal training	500	1,500	-	-	2,000
Weight training	15,000	5,000	-	-	20,000
Circuit training	10,000	24,000	6,000	-	40,000
Aerobics	50	100	700	150	1,000
Swimming	500	1,500	-	4,000	6,000

REQUIRED:

a. Calculate Sam's current overhead rate per hour of operation.
b. Using hours of operation as your driver, calculate how much overhead is currently being charged to each of the product lines.
c. Calculate your activity rates for each of the ABC drivers noted.
d. Charge out overhead to product lines, using the ABC rates.
e. Calculate total overhead by product line.
f. Calculate overhead by hours of operation for each of the product lines.
g. What does this information tell you? What specific recommendations would you make to Sam regarding Get Up 'n Go Fitness Club?

---

7. **ACTIVITY-BASED COSTING AND JOB-ORDER COSTS.** Bernelli Machining operates as a job shop making various metal parts for tractors. It has several large customers across the country who order parts when their own facilities run out of capacity. Each

job is unique, requiring its own labor, materials, and support activities. Bernelli currently charges $5,000,000 of plant and back office overhead out on 80,000 machine hours. Its customers, however, are starting to ask Bernelli to justify what he charges them, so Joe Bernelli is thinking about instituting an activity-based cost system. All labor is included in one of the activity pools. The following table contains the information Joe has accumulated on his company's operations:

Bernelli Machining			
Activity	Driver	Driver Frequency	Cost of Activity
Machining	Machine hours	80,000	$2,800,000
Set-up	Set-up hours	6,000	$300,000
Inspection	Inspection hours	10,000	$350,000
Shipping	Shipments made	15,000	$630,000
Customer service	Orders taken	10,000	$360,000
Invoicing	Invoices mailed	20,000	$560,000
Total			$5,000,000

Bernelli has just completed three jobs. The details for these jobs are contained in the table below.

Bernelli Machining			
Activity	Job 101	Job 102	Job 103
Materials	$150,000	$50,000	$100,000
Machine Hours	500	250	100
Set-up hours	10	25	30
Inspection hours	25	40	100
Shipments	1	2	5
Orders	1	1	2
Invoices	1	2	5

REQUIRED:

a. Calculate the current overhead rate per machine hour.
b. Calculate the cost of each of the jobs using machine hours as the rate.
c. Joe targets a 25% margin on each job he does. How much would he charge for each of these jobs?
d. Calculate the ABC charging rates.
e. Recalculate the costs for each job using these new rates.

f. Once again calculate the price Joe would charge for each of these jobs.
g. What does a comparison of the results suggest? Be specific.

8. **ACTIVITY-BASED COSTING AND JOB-ORDER COSTS.** Ajax Pool Services does a wide range of pool maintenance and repair jobs over the course of a swimming season in New England. The company has five vans and five work crews. Some crews consist of one repair person, while others contain five workers for such things as opening and closing pools, which is very labor-intensive. There are also various machines and support work that is needed for the different kinds of jobs. Right now, Ajax charges materials directly to a job, and then adds a charge based on direct labor hours to account for the rest of the costs of running the business. Ajax adds 35% profit onto every job because the season is short, so the work that is done has to support the company during the lean winter months. Recently, Ajax has been losing customers to a new competitor in town, Swim Lanes. Tom Aaron, the owner of Ajax, has asked you to help him complete an activity-based analysis of his company to see if he can figure out why he is losing most of his repair business. The nonmaterial costs for running the business are $1,650,000 per year. There are 50,000 direct labor hours expended each season. Tom wants you to look at three specific jobs to help him figure out what is happening. You work for a week and develop the following information on Tom's operations and three recent jobs.

Ajax Pool Care			
Activity	Driver	Driver Frequency	Cost of Activity
Direct labor	Direct labor hours	50,000	$1,250,000
Vacuuming	Machine hours	2,000	$62,000
Set-up	Jobs	5,000	$200,000
Testing	Tests made	5,000	$60,000
Customer service	Orders taken	1,200	$30,000
Invoicing	Invoices mailed	2,400	$48,000
Total			$1,650,000

Ajax Pool Care			
Activity	Pool Opening	Pump Repair	Pool Cleaning
Materials	$350	$1,000	$50
Direct labor hours	15	40	2

Ajax Pool Care			
Activity	Pool Opening	Pump Repair	Pool Cleaning
Vacuuming	3	0	2
Set-up	1	1	1
Testing	3	0	2
Orders taken	1	1	1
Invoices	2	2	1

REQUIRED:

a. Calculate the current overhead rate per direct labor hour.
b. Calculate the cost of each of the jobs using direct labor hour as the rate.
c. Calculate the price charged for the job.
d. Calculate the ABC charging rates.
e. Recalculate the costs for each job using these new rates.
f. Once again calculate the price Tom would charge for each of these jobs.
g. What does a comparison of the results suggest? Be specific.

Database Problems

For database templates, worksheets, and workbooks, go to MAdownloads.imanet.org

DB 4.1 CAPACITY COSTING. Easy Air wants to get a handle on how effectively it is using its available capacity. Rudy has done a basic study, resulting in the information contained in the DB 4.1a and DB 4.1c templates in your database.

REQUIRED:

a. Using template DB 4.1a, calculate the percentage of time Easy Air's planes spend in each type of capacity utilization.
b. Based solely on time utilized, where is the largest problem at Easy Air? Be specific.
c. Now go to the DB 4.1c template. Rudy tells you that the committed capacity cost for the month under study is $112, while the managed capacity cost is $760. Using these cost estimates, calculate the cost for each category of capacity utilization.
d. Using your answer to (c), calculate the percentages of cost in each category of capacity utilization.

e. Where do the biggest problems now appear to be? How does this differ from what the time-based percentages suggested? Be specific.
f. Turn in your answers to the questions and worksheets to your instructor.

DB 4.2 ACTIVITY-BASED COSTING. Sherry has also made progress tackling many of Easy Air's activity-based costs. The information contained in the DB 4.2a and DB 4.2c templates in your database is the result of her work. In addition to these templates, you will also need the worksheet ABC Driver Information to answer these questions.

a. Using the information in template DB 4.2a, calculate the average cost per passenger for each of the activities identified by Sherry.
b. Using the results from (a) calculate the percentage of the total cost per passenger for each category of cost.
c. You need to repeat these calculations for years 20x5 and 20x4.
d. Where do the problems seem to be? Specifically, where does most of the money from a passenger fare (remember, this is approximately $40 per ticket) go?
e. Next, move on to template 4.2d, where you will need to start applying activity-based logic. First, using the information in the ABC Driver Information worksheet, choose a driver for each of the cost pools in your datasheet. It is okay to use the same driver multiple times, so choose the most logical driver given the category and type of cost. For each choice, fill in the information in columns D, H, and L. You should use the same driver across the three years. If you cannot find a logical driver, default to number of passengers.
f. Using the driver you chose in (d) divide each of your costs by that driver for the year you are looking at in template 4.2d.
g. Now where does the problem appear to be? There may be more than one trouble spot, so be specific.
h. You may have noticed in template 4.2d that you are not asked for either percentages or totals. Why do you think this was done? Hint: The answer is not to make this problem shorter for you!
i. ***Advanced.*** Using the cost per driver occurrence, generate a percentage change analysis to help you better understand Easy Air's cost issues. Use 20x4 as your baseline. Hint: When you fill in the template correctly, every number in 20x4 should read 100%. Every year after that should be less than 100%. What are the trends now?
j. ***Advanced.*** Using the cost per driver occurrence (for example, columns C, D, and G) generate a percentage change analysis from one year to the next. In this case, we will look at 20x4 vs. 20x5, followed by 20x5 vs. 20x6. Use the

lower-numbered year as your baseline year. Do not bother to do the analysis in 20x2 as there is no other baseline year to compare it to. What do you see now?

k. Turn in the answers to the questions above and the associated worksheets to your instructor.

Cases

CASE 4.1 LANDRY ASSOCIATES CAPACITY ANALYSIS. Landry Associates produces a broad range of components for stereos and similar electronic products. It has been having problems with profitability over the past few years. It runs a number of machines that make most of the components, but the machines sit idle a good percentage of the time. Since they are fairly expensive machines, Bruce Landry knows that this is the heart of his problem, but even when the lines are staffed, it seems like the factory is down more often than it is working.

Landry Associates began as a small machine shop back in the 1970s. It has always believed in treating its workforce well, so it provides employees with paid breaks and lunches. The company loses 816 hours a year for holidays and vacations, which is part of the total idle time. Management tries to get the most out of its machines, however, so it changes them over often to run a new type of component. The orders themselves can be fairly small, ranging anywhere from 5,000 to 100,000 units of one component. Each time a new order is run, the machines have to be set up. In addition, they often run into material problems as the parts that go into making a component can be very small and hard to handle. Consequently, just starting up a run can lead to significant material problems.

The company recently implemented capacity cost management for tracking its plant floor costs. The following table summarizes the information that was gathered for the last 12 months of operation for one of its cost centers, circuit board assembly.

Summary of Nonproduction Hours	
Developmental	153.4
Internal Failure—Cost of Quality	113.9
Material Problems	224.6
Machine Breakdowns	65.8
Scheduled (Preventive Maint.)	13.9
Changeovers	953.2
Cleanup	357.8
Mgt. Policy (Lunch, Allowance)	928.6
Material Handling	46.4
Mgt. Downtime (Misc.)	167.7
	3,025.3

Operational Assumptions		
Number of lines	2	
Total Capacity	17,520	Hours per year
Cycle time	3.8	Seconds per Unit
Good units	4,949,000	

Financial Assumptions	
Committed $'s	$848,371
Managed $'s	$1,635,658

Capacity Distribution	
Manned hours	8,249.2
Idle hours	9,270.8
Total hours	17,520.0

REQUIRED:

Using the information in this table, help management answer the following questions. Suggestion: Generate a capacity report; it will help you answer these questions in an organized fashion.

a. What is the managed capacity cost per hour? Committed capacity cost per hour?

b. What is the estimated competitive capacity cost for a good unit?

c. What is the total cost of each of the nonproductive activities? What amount of the total costs is chargeable to idle capacity?

d. What are these costs on a per-unit basis?

e. What is the total average cost for making a good unit?

f. What recommendations would you make to management to improve profitability?

CASE 4.2 SUTLAND PET FOODS—CAPACITY AND ABC ANALYSIS. It was Monday morning at 8 a.m. John was pacing the front of the room, waiting for each of his key managers to make their way to a seat. As he glanced around, he saw a lot of weary and anxious faces—not a good sign. By 8:10, everyone was seated, and the meeting got under way.

John: You all know why we're here. As you can see from Exhibit 1, the results for 20x6 are dismal, and the board wants to know why. Simply saying that the new plant is taking longer to get up to speed than we thought it would isn't going to cut it. The board wants details.

Sue, Marketing VP: All I know is we hit our sales projections right on the nose. There was some resistance to the price increases, but we were able to hit our sales goals and keep the majority of our customers. We did our job, that's all I can say.

Adam, Production VP: Guess that depends on what you call "sales goals." As far as I can see, total shipments for both product lines are down. We have a lot of fixed costs around here, so when the volumes drop like they have, we're in trouble.

John: Let's save the finger-pointing for later. Right now we need teamwork, not arguments. I agree that marketing hit its dollar goals, and also, that volumes are down. These are obvious facts. The issue is...what are we going to do about them?

Adam: You're right, John; sorry, Sue. Anyway, on a more positive note, we did a study of the plant's capacity utilization for last year, Exhibit 2 in today's materials. My thanks to Wendy for Finance's help in sorting the costs into committed and managed capacity costs for each sub-plant (cat and dog food production), so we could get a general idea of what was going on.

Wendy, CFO: I'm glad you found the information useful, Adam. I wanted you to know, Sue, that we also used the two weeks to do a first pass at developing a better understanding of the back office using activity-based costing. I've wanted to look at the business that way for a while, and thought there was no better time than the present. The information is Exhibit 3—the page I handed out when you walked in.

Adam: Interesting stuff, but the new look at the factory you gave me combined with this one of the back office still leaves me a bit confused. I'd like to see these developed further so I can see where I need to focus.

John: I agree with you, Adam. In fact, I think I'd like to set the data aside for now and return to it at our next meeting. In the meantime, Wendy, can you tell me what the minimum costs of production are right now? And, if we were to take your ABCM data, what would the profitability of the two product lines look like?

Wendy: We'll give it a shot.

John: Okay, Wendy. In the meantime, Adam, I'd like you to help me understand how we are using our hours in production. What is this "cycle time" number? And, Wendy, I need to know how we're going to get volumes back up. Let's brainstorm for the next few hours and see what we can come up with.

EXHIBIT 1 SUTLAND'S INCOME STATEMENT RESULTS FOR 20x6

Sutland Pet Foods, Inc.			
Year ending 12/31/20x6			
	Dog Food	Cat Food	Company Total
Total Pounds Sold	862,836,117	398,232,054	1,261,068,171
Revenue	$776,552,506	$517,701,670	$1,294,254,176
Less: Materials	215,709,029	129,373,647	384,393,490
Direct Labor	25,237,956	13,201,393	38,439,349
Indirect Labor	17,666,570	9,240,975	26,907,544
Plant space (Mfg)	53,668,406	25,082,646	65,346,893
Electricity	35,333,139	18,481,950	53,815,089
Insurance	5,047,591	2,640,279	7,687,870
Machine Depreciation	101,620,524	39,604,178	115,318,047
Supplies	12,618,978	6,600,696	19,219,675
Maintenance	37,856,935	19,802,089	57,659,024
Total Cost of Goods Sold	504,759,129	264,027,852	$768,786,981
Gross Margin	$271,793,377	$253,673,818	$525,467,195
Advertising	$46,127,219	$30,751,479	$76,878,698
Purchasing	30,443,964	27,399,568	$57,843,532
Sales	24,575,557	10,532,382	$35,107,939
Customer Service	34,334,027	22,889,351	$57,223,378
Accounting	31,636,097	36,155,539	$67,791,636
Personnel	10,495,480	8,746,233	$19,241,713
Scheduling	15,953,867	10,635,912	$26,589,779
General Management	19,569,473	19,569,473	$39,138,945
Segment Margins	$58,657,693	$86,993,882	$145,651,575
	7.55%	16.80%	11.25%
Common Fixed Costs			$132,709,034
Income before Tax			$12,942,542

EXHIBIT 2 CAPACITY DATA FOR 20x6

Cat Food Lines #1 and #2		
Data that is linked to the capacity reports		
Summary of Hours		
1	Developmental	175.2
2	Internal Failure—Cost of Quality	403.0
3	Material Problems	87.6
4	Machine Breakdowns	438.0
5	Scheduled (Preventive Maint.)	17.5
6	Changeovers	350.4
7	Cleanup	315.4
8	Mgt. Policy (Lunch, Allowance)	350.4
9	Mgt. Downtime (Misc)	75.3
		2,212.8

Operational Assumptions		
Number of lines	2	
Capacity	17,520	Hours per year
Cycle time	0.14	Seconds per Bag
Good units	79,646,411	Bags

Financial Assumptions	
Committed $'s	$67,327,102
Managed $'s	$67,327,102
Ttl Non-mat'l $'s	$134,654,204

Capacity Distribution	
Manned hours	7,523
Idle hours	9,997
Total hours	17,520

Dog Food Lines #1 and #2		
Data that is linked to the capacity reports		
Summary of Hours		
1	Developmental	438.0
2	Internal Failure—Cost of Quality	578.2
3	Material Problems	70.1
4	Machine Breakdowns	613.2
5	Scheduled (Preventive Maint.)	35.0
6	Changeovers	175.2
7	Cleanup	350.4
8	Mgt. Policy (Lunch, Allowance)	403.0
9	Mgt. Downtime (Misc.)	77.1
		2,740.0

Operational Assumptions		
Number of lines	2	
Capacity	17,520	Hours per year
Cycle time	0.10	Seconds per Bag
Good units	86,283,612	Bags

Financial Assumptions	
Committed $'s	$160,336,521
Managed $'s	$128,713,578
Ttl Non-mat'l $'s	$289,050,099

Capacity Distribution	
Manned hours	7,877
Idle hours	9,643
Total hours	17,520

EXHIBIT 3 RESULTS OF THE ABC ANALYSIS

Sutland Pet Foods

Results of ABM Study for 20x6

Cost Category	Reported Costs	Percent Assigned to Purchasing	Percent Assigned to Sales	Percent Assigned to Customer Service	Percent Assigned to Accounting	Percent Assigned to Personnel	Percent Assigned to Scheduling	Percent Assigned to Gen'l Mgt.	Total
Office Space	$61,502,958	$9,225,444	$6,457,811	$14,453,195	$9,717,467	$8,487,408	$2,214,107	$10,947,527	$61,502,958
Salaries	$184,508,875	$17,528,343	$23,063,609	$21,218,521	$24,908,698	$17,528,343	$10,147,988	$70,113,373	$184,508,875
Advertising	$76,878,698			To product lines: 60% Dog Food; 40% Cat Food					$76,878,698
Computer costs	$112,755,424	18,604,645	2,818,886	14,094,428	39,464,398	4,510,217	11,275,542	21,987,308	$112,755,424
Dep'n on office equipment	$30,751,479	4,151,450	307,515	4,305,207	8,610,414	1,845,089	2,490,870	9,040,935	$30,751,479
Professional services	$38,439,349	10,763,018	1,921,967	3,075,148	7,303,476	1,921,967	384,393	13,069,379	$38,439,349
Fees and licenses	$7,687,870	615,030	538,151	76,879	384,393	691,908	76,879	5,304,630	$7,687,870
Total SG&A	$512,524,654	$60,887,929	$35,107,939	$57,223,378	$90,388,848	$34,984,933	$26,589,779	$130,463,151	$512,524,654

	Purchasing	Sales	Customer Service	Accounting	Personnel	Scheduling	Gen'l Mgt.
Driver	Purchase Orders	Sales Orders	# of Customers	Accounting Transactions	# of Employees	# of Scheduled Runs	# of Bags
Estimated Frequency in 2016	2,500,000	600,000	125,000	9,000,000	10,000	1,000	165,930,023
% Assignable to Dog Food	50%	70%	60%	35%	30%	60%	15%
% Assignable to Cat Food	45%	30%	40%	40%	25%	40%	15%
% Common to Business	5%	0%	0%	25%	45%	0%	70%

REQUIRED:

Using the information provided in these exhibits, including the financial statements for the last year, answer the following:

a. Capacity analysis: What are SPFI's committed and managed costs per hour for the two lines in 20x6? Using this information, and the cycle time estimates, what is the competitive (that is, "good") cost for a bag of cat food? Dog food?

b. Capacity analysis: What is the total percentage and dollars for productive, nonproductive, and idle capacity for the two product lines for 20x6? How do they compare?

c. Activity-based cost management analysis: Using the information that is presented in Exhibit 3, calculate the activity costs for each of the activities Wendy's staff identified. Assign these costs to cat food or dog food using the percentages given.

d. ABCM analysis. Using the results of (c), how do you feel about the accuracy of this information? What would you like to know to better understand these results?

e. What should John do to correct the problems facing his firm? Please back up your recommendations with relevant case facts.

CHAPTER FIVE

Understanding the Management Process

Understanding: n. A cerebral secretion that enables one having it to know a house from a horse by the roof on the house. Its nature and laws have been exhaustively expounded by Locke, who rode a house, and Kant, who lived in a horse.

AMBROSE BIERCE[1]

CHAPTER ROADMAP

1. **Planning for Performance**
   - *Creating Plans for Action*
   - *Planning and the Role of Information*
   - *Benchmarking the Plan*
   - *Standard Setting*
2. **Comparing Actual Results with Plan**
   - *Gap Analysis*
   - *Trend Analysis*
   - *RADAR Chart Analysis*
   - *Variance Analysis*
3. **Applying Analytical Tools to Solve Problems**
   - *Pareto Analysis*
   - *Cause-and-Effect Analysis*
4. **Making Adjustments**
   - *Assessing the Impact of Change: Incremental Analysis*
   - *Balancing Objective and Subjective Information*
   - *Using Incremental Analysis to Build an Effective Business Case*

LEARNING OBJECTIVES

After studying this chapter, you should be able to:

1. **Summarize the issues and tools used during the planning stage of the management process.**
2. **Complete gap, trend, RADAR, and variance analyses.**
3. **Develop and use Pareto and cause-and-effect diagrams.**
4. **Use incremental analysis to assess potential options for change.**

1 Ambrose Bierce, *The Devil's Dictionary*, New York: The Neale Publishing Company, 1911.

IN CONTEXT ➤ Creating a Business Case at Easy Air

It was a busy Monday. After a brief meeting and responding to a series of requests for information, the team turned to the key task at hand: converting their preliminary analyses into a more comprehensive business case that Fran could use with confidence. The issues had not changed, but the focus definitely had.

"Sanjiv, where should we start? We made a ton of assumptions to get the first-pass analysis done, and we promised we would revisit them when we had time. Guess that's now. Should we look at the revenue side first, the costs, or the nonfinancial data?" Sherry, as was so often the case, was the first to get back to business.

"Good question; let's see. Logically, I think we should look at the nonfinancial information first because that drives our financial estimates. Rudy, can you pull up that file we were working on? The one with various levels of passenger volumes, load factors by market, and so on?" asked Sanjiv.

"Can do...here it is. So where should we look? There are quite a few tabs in the workbook. I'd suggest we start with tab number one and work forward," replied Rudy.

"Sounds like a logical first step," Sanjiv replied. "We'll see what we have right now to work with, then identify what is missing in terms of nonfinancial information before we turn to the financial information."

Planning for Performance

OBJECTIVE 1

Summarize the issues and tools used during the planning stage of the management process.

THE ONGOING CYCLE OF ACTIVITY THAT DEFINES business begins with the establishment of goals and the plans that will make them a reality. How these goals are defined, where responsibility for outcomes and actions is assigned, when and how performance is measured against established objectives, and how the actions that should be taken when a performance shortfall are defined are all factors that must be considered when plans are first put in place. In this chapter, we will do a brief overview of planning and the ways in which we obtain data to define and create plans and their related performance measurements. Attention will then turn to the other elements of the management process—comparison of actual performance to plan and the development of a business case to modify or improve outcomes. Let us now look at the area of planning and the tools we use to complete this activity.

CREATING PLANS FOR ACTION

Planning *is the basis for action. It is the development of goals and objectives for performance.* It guides management's decisions and actions—it is the basis for creating an effective organization. In Chapter 1, we defined planning as decision making in advance, or the setting of objectives followed by the determination of what needs to be done to reach them. There are five basic problems that the planning process attempts to resolve:[2]

1. What should we be doing?
2. How do we get it done?
3. When do we want/need things done?
4. How well do we need them done?
5. Who should be given responsibility for achieving the desired results?

These questions are applied on an ongoing basis at many different levels of the organization. Planning is not solely a top management task. It can and should be undertaken by line workers, supervisors, middle managers, and executives. Planning can also be done for a short time period, or it can span from one to many years into the future.

One of the key factors defining effective planning is the identification of an acceptable end result. While it may seem counterintuitive to start planning with defining the ultimate objective, if you think about it, only when the ends are identified can the most effective means (or ways to reach these ends) be determined. In other words, an effective plan begins at the end point, and then moves backward in time, one step at a time, until the plan arrives in time and state at the present moment.

The resulting **plan,** *an estimate or projection of future outcomes,* is comprised of a set of physical documents that explain the intended sequence of actions and results. It includes a number of estimates and assumptions that the planner believes will yield the desired results. Dynamic in nature, a good plan is still just an estimate or projection of the future—not a sure thing. In fact, if you think about times when you have planned for a future event, such as hosting a party for your friends, you may remember having to estimate how many people would come, what they might enjoy eating and drinking, what time would be best to start the party, what type of music everyone would enjoy, and so on. Even with the best of plans, however, you may have found yourself short on food because everyone you invited did come (you planned on about 75% of your friends being available), and many brought one or more other friends with them. Your plans were well thought through, but your plan did not give you control over the future—it simply reduced the uncertainty you faced. In other words, good business plans can reduce the risk and uncertainty faced by the business, but they cannot determine the future. No management tool can do that.

For this reason, business planning is a process that is dynamic in nature, revisited often, and revised when necessary. An effective business plan looks at the problem from several perspectives using the input of many different individuals to ensure that key factors and concerns are addressed. As a result, a business plan will often be presented as a series of scenarios, or potential paths the organization can

2 D. Scott Sink and Thomas C. Tuttle, *Planning and Measurement in Your Organization of the Future*, Norcross, Va.: Industrial Engineering and Management Press, 1989: pp. 82-83.

take in the future. Each path brings with it unique benefits and costs, risks and rewards. The essential point to remember is that a plan is a logical method of analyzing and then pursuing specific goals or objectives that is based on assumptions, and is flexible and responsive to changing conditions.

PLANNING AND THE ROLE OF INFORMATION

Planning is an information-dependent, analytical process that should draw from all available sources of data and individual insights. The sources of information for planning are limited only by one's imagination and the time available to do the information search. That said, there are several forms and sources of information that should always be incorporated into the planning process, including summaries of prior performance; competitive information; customer satisfaction, loyalty, and preferences; data on macroeconomic trends; and cost data for key activities or processes.

In addition to this basic information, it is also important to include a summary of current practices and to gather input about current challenges or opportunities from managers who will either affect, or be affected by, the actions and objectives contained in the final plan. Finally, the current vision, mission, and strategic objectives developed by top management should be incorporated into the planning process. Even plans that are focused on daily activities should reflect the overarching objectives of the firm.

Each of these sources of information has value for shaping some aspect of the planning process, whether in the establishment of the initial goals or the development of the steps that will be used to reach the desired ends. While much of this information is available in a company's archives, there are times when the questions the plan is trying to address need answers that may require going outside of the firm to find new practices or new insights. One of the primary tools we use to gather external information is benchmarking.

BENCHMARKING THE PLAN

Benchmarking *is an external focus on internal activities, functions, or operations in order to achieve continuous improvement.*[3] The objective is to gather new insights and new information to address current performance problems, develop business plans at various levels of the organization, and provide the basis for organizational learning. The key element of benchmarking is that it takes an external perspective, looking for answers that lie outside of the firm's, or the business unit's, current practices and knowledge.

Figure 5.1 shows the three basic steps that make up the benchmarking process: measurement, analysis, and change. Before any activity is undertaken, it is important to understand what the focus and scope of the benchmarking study is going to be. For instance, if Easy Air wants to improve the performance of its customer service group, it would need to identify specific aspects of customer service to study. It might decide that it should focus on the reservations system where customers initially come in contact with the company. The scope of this benchmarking study, therefore, would be limited to gathering information to improve the reservations process.

---

3 The sources for this discussion on benchmarking are Carol J. McNair and Kathleen H. J. Leibfried, *Benchmarking: Tool for Continuous Improvement,* New York: John Wiley & Sons, 1993, and Robert C. Camp, *Benchmarking: The Search for Industry Best Practices that Lead to Superior Performance*, Milwaukee, Wis.: ASQC Press, 1989.

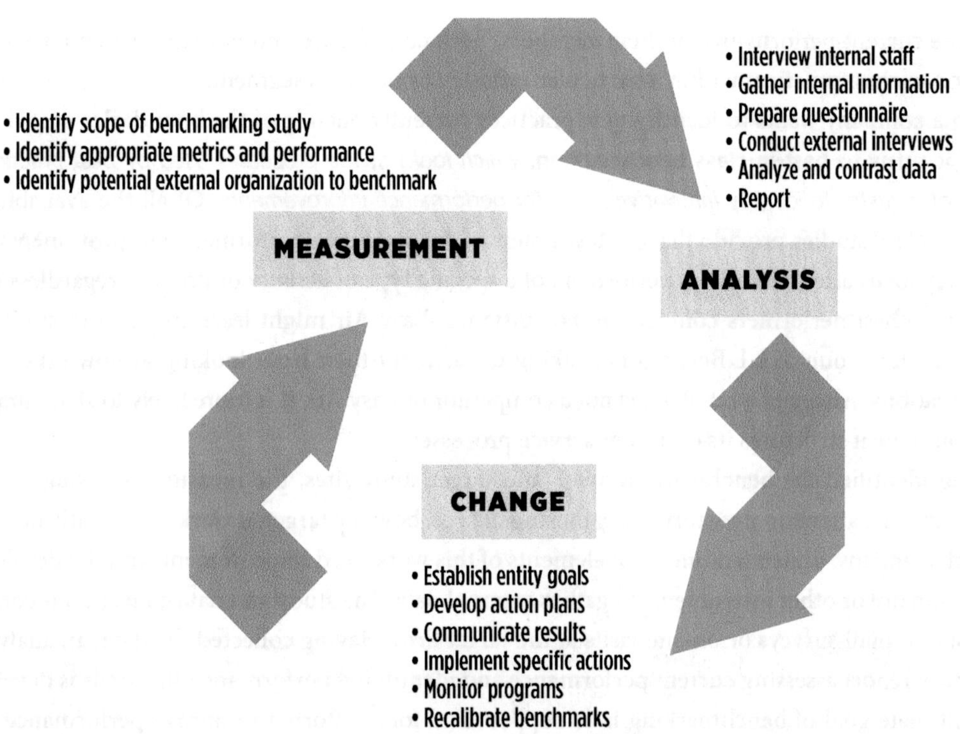
• Identify scope of benchmarking study
• Identify appropriate metrics and performance
• Identify potential external organization to benchmark
MEASUREMENT
• Interview internal staff
• Gather internal information
• Prepare questionnaire
• Conduct external interviews
• Analyze and contrast data
• Report
ANALYSIS
CHANGE
• Establish entity goals
• Develop action plans
• Communicate results
• Implement specific actions
• Monitor programs
• Recalibrate benchmarks

FIGURE 5.1 THE BENCHMARKING PROCESS

Having chosen one element of customer service, the benchmarking team would need to find ways to measure and define performance for reservations, such as the length of time it takes to complete a transaction with a customer, the length of time a customer is queued up waiting for an available customer service agent, or the number of reservations errors made. These measures will be very important during the data-gathering stage of the benchmarking study, helping to focus attention on key elements of the reservations process.

A second major element of the benchmarking study's scope involves choosing the target for external data gathering. There are four basic targets, or approaches, that can be used: internal, competitive, industry, or best-in-class benchmarking. **Internal benchmarking,** *the use of data from multiple internal locations to establish current best practice in the organization,* is useful when a company has many different locations where the same type of work is performed; for example, the branch offices of a bank. Data is collected and analyzed in order to identify the current best practices from across the entire range of internal locations. A "straw man" model that incorporates the best practices into a hybrid ideal process is then constructed.

Internal benchmarking can precede the external collection of information for the competitive, industry, or best-in-class approaches. **Competitive benchmarking** *emphasizes data on the performance of the firm's key competitors and its implications on the firm's performance.* It focuses attention on one or two key competitors in an attempt to determine how they are providing key services or products. **Industry benchmarking** *looks at key performance areas for the sector at large.* These studies are often conducted by trade associations to assess the current performance of their members. Both competitive and industry benchmarking focus attention on current practices within a particular industry or business segment.

When a company wants to identify new practices currently outside of the boundaries of its industry practices, it turns to **best-in-class benchmarking,** *which looks at the processes used by best practice firms regardless of industry to identify innovative paths for performance improvements*. Of all the available methods, best-in-class studies provide the greatest potential for quantum performance improvements. Why? Because they focus attention on top performers of a specific type of activity or process, regardless of what industry these best performers compete in. For instance, Easy Air might learn more from studying the customer service group at L.L.Bean's order-taking department than from looking at how other airlines book reservations. Also, since L.L.Bean is not a competitor of Easy Air, it is more likely to share important details about how it structures its customer service processes.

Having identified the benchmarking issue and target study sites, the measurement stage is undertaken. Specifically, attention now turns to gathering data on how the targeted work is currently done in the benchmark company, understanding what elements of this work need improvement, and the development of a questionnaire or other instruments to gather external data. The study and data collection is completed using phone or mail surveys or on-site visits at the target firm. Having collected the data, an analysis and a preliminary report assessing current performance and identifying performance shortfalls is developed.

The ultimate goal of benchmarking is to support and focus efforts to improve performance. In the last stage of the study, therefore, attention turns to establishing the entity goals for the improvement process, developing action plans to achieve these goals, and to implement changes, measure results, report progress, and, if necessary, make adjustments to the plan as new challenges or issues emerge. Part of a dynamic, ongoing process of organizational learning, benchmarking provides the focus and knowledge required to transform plans into reality.

Having established the plan using the best internal and external information available, attention now turns to establishing performance standards and embedding these standards in the structure of the firm.

STANDARD SETTING

Once a specific approach or solution to a problem or opportunity is chosen, the plan becomes a guide to action and the basis for measuring and assessing performance. At this point, our performance measures are used to define **standards,** *or predefined—usually in quantitative terms—performance expectations.* Standards create a basis for action, the means to measure and track progress against goals, and serve as information sources for subsequent decisions, estimates, and analyses.

There are many different methods available for establishing standards. Engineering or management studies of the processes that should take place, reviews of the levels of performance that have been achieved in the past, and the levels of performance that have been achieved by peers (benchmarking) are three of the most common approaches. Engineering studies are most useful for setting the initial cost or performance expectations for a product, service, or activity. For many years, engineering studies were used to set most of the standards used by companies because they were seen as being objective and unbiased. Unfortunately, while the engineering studies may be both of these things, whenever we set out to study the behavior of people, we by definition alter that behavior. So, when engineers study a process, the people in it will often act differently than they would if no one was watching, which can create a bias in the resulting standards.

Historical results provide a different challenge for the standard setter. In this situation, future expectations are set based on levels of past performance. How the historical information is used now becomes the key factor. For instance, if a rolling average of actual results is used as the standard, performance improvements are captured. If a company pursues **continuous improvement,** *a philosophy that advocates constant positive changes in a firm's performance as new goals are achieved*, performance trends captured by standards derived from rolling averages are an effective means to communicate both expectations and accomplishments. Unless an engineering study is used to identify the upper limits, or ideal standard, however, it is hard to objectively evaluate this progress. That is why many companies use a combination of historical and engineering study-based standards in their systems.

The final method for establishing standards is through benchmarking. As described previously, benchmarking looks to external information sources to identify and define performance expectations. Benchmarking can be used in place of either engineered or historical standards, or in combination with them. Because the information gathered by benchmarking is obtained from outside sources, it can help establish both short- and long-term capabilities and goals for a company.

TABLE 5.1 DIFFERENT APPROACHES TO STANDARD SETTING

Standard	Approach	Sample Calculation
Engineered	Identify theoretical maximum for the process, then adjust to 80% to calculate practical standard	Theoretical: 500 units per day x 80% Practical std. 400 units per day
Historical	Rolling average of prior output used to set standard for next period; as each new period ends, the standard is adjusted by adding the newest output and dropping the oldest.	Period 1: 375 units per day Period 2: 425 units per day Period 3: 400 units per day Period 4 standard: (375 + 425 + 400) / 3, or 400 units per day Period 4 actual: 455 units per day Period 5 standard: (425 + 400 + 455) / 3, or 427 units per day
Benchmarked	Identify other organizations with relatively the same process, determine their average output per period, identify best practice firm (highest output), and use average output for current standard and best practice output for continuous improvement goal.	Co. A: 400 units per day Co. B: 500 units per day Co. C: 450 units per day Co. D: 600 units per day—best practice firm; future goal Current average standard: (400 + 500 + 450 + 600) / 4, or 487 units per day

Looking at the information presented in Table 5.1, we can see the key differences in how these three ways of arriving at standards are defined and calculated.

The benchmark information leads to an interesting question. If Company D can make 600 units per year, why does our engineer feel our maximum or ideal is only 500 units? What does Company D do that we are not doing? Is an output of 600 units really possible, and if so, what needs to be changed in our product, process, or equipment to help us reach this goal? No matter what the product being made is, a 50% increase (600 minus 400 divided by 400 is 50%) in output using approximately the same equipment and people will mean more profit for the company. While we would need to do a complete study of the differences in how Company D organizes and manages its operations before we can determine if its methods would work for us, without the benchmarked information, we would not even attempt to produce 600 units. In other words, different types of standards lead to different human and organizational actions and results.

LOOKING BACK ➤ Recognizing the Need for Standards

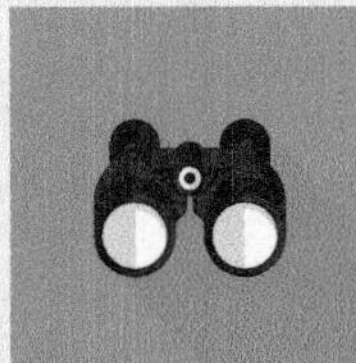

There has long been a controversy about which is the "*best*" cost for an organization to use. The question was often discussed in the practitioner literature of the mid-1940s when standard costs were steadily being adopted as "the one best way" for an organization to calculate costs. About this controversy, the National Association of Cost Accountants (NACA) editorial department commented:

"Cost accounting is a means to an end, and not an end in itself. Accordingly, any study of the field of cost accounting should start with a study of the ends to be served—the uses to be made of cost data. Only by clearly describing and relating the various purposes for which costs are to be used is it possible to determine the types of cost data needed for each purpose and the principles and techniques which should govern their development."

So while there was recognition that there were many different methods, and objectives, in calculating a cost, emphasis remained on the use of a standard costing system with engineered standards.

As knowledge about the uses, impact, and ramifications of engineered standards began to be questioned in the late 1980s, attention turned toward developing alternative standard setting approaches that would more clearly reflect management intent and organizational goals. Today, improvements continue to be made in how standard rates are defined, measured, applied, and revised. However, standard costing came into its heyday in the 1940s.

* *N.A.C.A. Bulletin*, Vol. XXVII, No. 18, Section II, May 15, 1946, p. 940.

No matter what method we use to identify and define our performance standards, once in place they provide the basis for guiding and evaluating actions and results in organizations. Without specific plans, measurements, and standards, the cycle that defines the management process cannot be completed. Finally, while it is clear that not every important goal or plan can be captured in specific measurements, it is always important to establish a clear logic and relationship between goals and downstream evaluation methods, measures, and criteria. Since we get what we measure and reward in organizations (and life), if an organization does a good job specifying standards, measures, and expectations, it should stand a good chance of achieving its goals.

IN CONTEXT ➤ Setting Standards at Easy Air

Sherry hung up just as Rudy and Sanjiv came through the door after meeting with Jen Alhouser, head of flight operations. They were all intent on getting the same information—a basis for developing a set of standards to help focus the team's profit and performance improvement recommendations.

"Hi, guys! How did it go?" Sherry asked.

"Okay," Sanjiv replied. "I think we've uncovered some opportunities for change in the way we buy and use resources in flight operations, and Jen had some reports that will help us put some numbers to current and potential performance. How about you?"

"I just got off the phone with my friend at *Aviation Week.* Seems like they've been putting together some benchmark data for the industry that may be just what we need. They've also published some books with articles by various experts on different aspects of the business, from economics to marketing and operations," replied Sherry.

"Hey, I've heard about those manuals; I think that's a great idea! I don't know why I didn't think about them before," Rudy joined in the conversation. "I think they'll help us write up the business case."

"Sounds good!" said Sanjiv. "But getting back to benchmarking, Sherry, what did you find out?"

"My friend is going to send the entire report, but just to give you an idea of what we can expect, I found out that the industry average for passenger-driven costs, such as our passenger supplies, is $10.50. On that end, we look pretty good. But our station costs are awfully high. The average from the benchmark study is $1.68. Since ours are $1.82, it looks like that's going to be one area we'll need to examine closely. We already know we have some baggage-handling issues." Sherry paged through her notes, looking for other gems.

"That's good stuff, but it doesn't help me know how we'll get there. Maybe those manuals will point us in the right direction. Maybe there will be some obvious things we're not doing, or vice versa." Sanjiv began jotting notes for the burgeoning report file.

"Oh, one more thing, Sanjiv," said Sherry. "My friend said that we should look at our reservation costs. He used to work for Consolidated Express Small Business Services—they take orders and reservations for various shipping options for small companies. He said that, clearly, a package isn't a passenger, but on the other hand, he thought there might be a lot of similarities in the activities done by Consolidated and our reservations group. It seems a bit far-fetched, I know, but he said that Consolidated is known as a 'best practice' firm in this area, and it only costs them $1.85 to make a reservation. We're spending $2.04 on average per reservation. Maybe we could learn something there? We can get a company tour if you want!"

"Let's plan on it for the end of the week," replied Sanjiv. "For now, why don't we see what type of standards we can put together so we can begin analyzing our performance against them, okay?"

Comparing Actual Results with Plan

OBJECTIVE 2
Complete gap, trend, RADAR, and variance analyses.

Once standards are in place, managers have a basis for evaluating performance and for determining what types of changes to plans or actions are needed. Plans are not needed for actions to occur—only for the actions to be focused and controlled. If actions were allowed to continue without checking their accompanying results against the plan, however, there is a high probability that the organization will not reach its goals.

There are a number of tools that we use in management accounting to compare actual results to the plans that have been established. Figure 5.2 summarizes the various types of charts and analyses that can be done to explore results and identify problem areas. Each of these tools helps us understand how current results compare to plans, and, when problems have occurred, identify potential causes for these performance shortfalls. The charts and analyses are used under different conditions and provide a range of information to management. We will be using six of these tools throughout the text to focus attention on problems and potential solutions in the various decision domains—to complete the "do-check" activities in the management process. Specifically, we will use gap analysis, trend analysis, and RADAR or "spider" charts to identify problem areas, while variance analysis, Pareto analysis, and cause-and-effect analysis will be used to explore patterns in results and to identify potential causes for performance shortfalls.

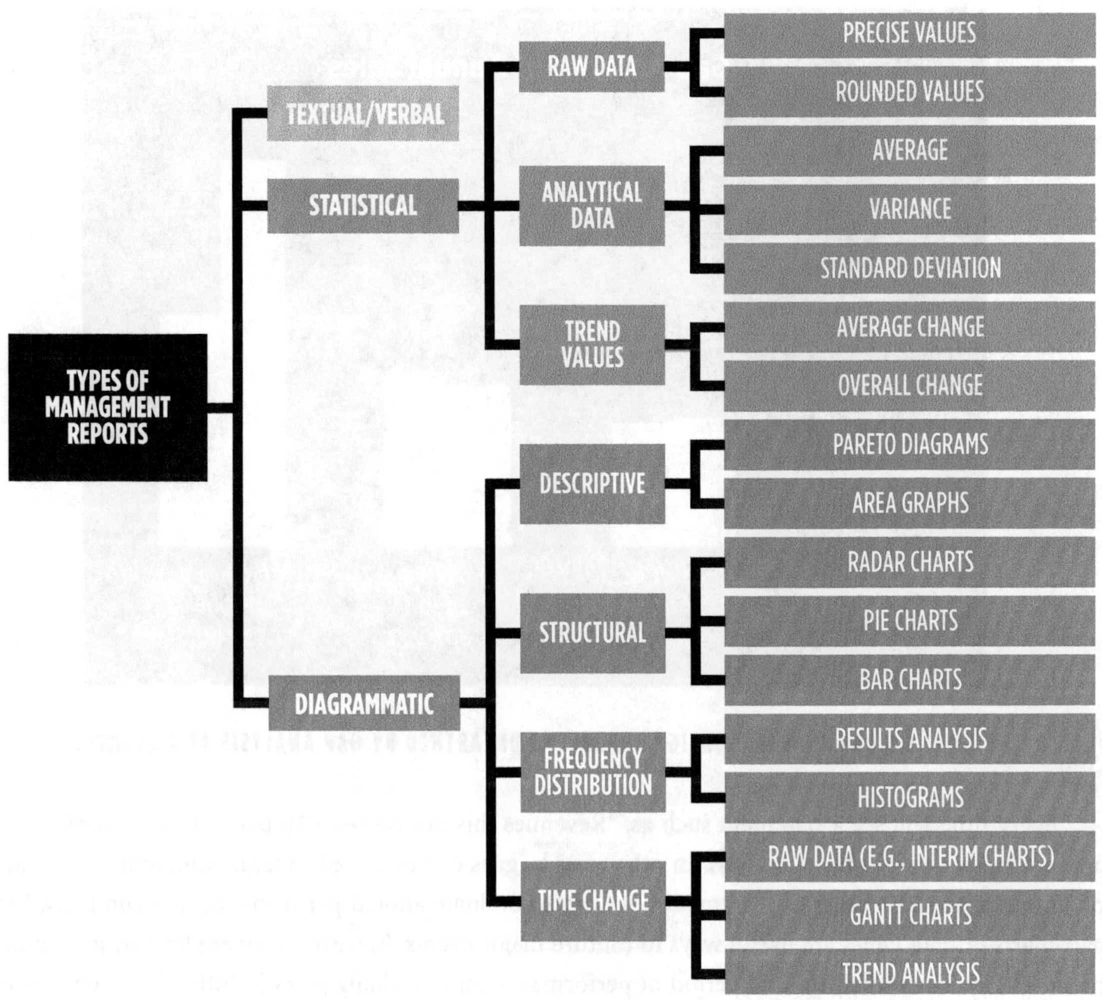

FIGURE 5.2 MANAGEMENT REPORTS TAKE MANY FORMS.

GAP ANALYSIS

Gap analysis is the simplest of the analytical tools we can use to understand and evaluate performance. As the name suggests, **gap analysis** *visually or numerically identifies the difference between targeted results and actual results*. Gap analysis focuses on one observation of results against the goal that was set for that result. For instance, if a company planned to sell 5,000 units of its product in May but actually only sold 4,800 units, it would have a 200-unit output gap, or shortfall.

We can present the results of gap analysis to management in many different ways. One of the common graphical approaches is a bar chart (see Figure 5.3) that compares the actual sales of the company's three main products (A, B, and C) to planned sales. Specifically, we see that only product B sold more units than planned, and while product A posted a small shortfall, we have a major problem brewing with respect to product C. This visual representation makes it easy for management to review and assess the results, highlighting major problems at a glance.

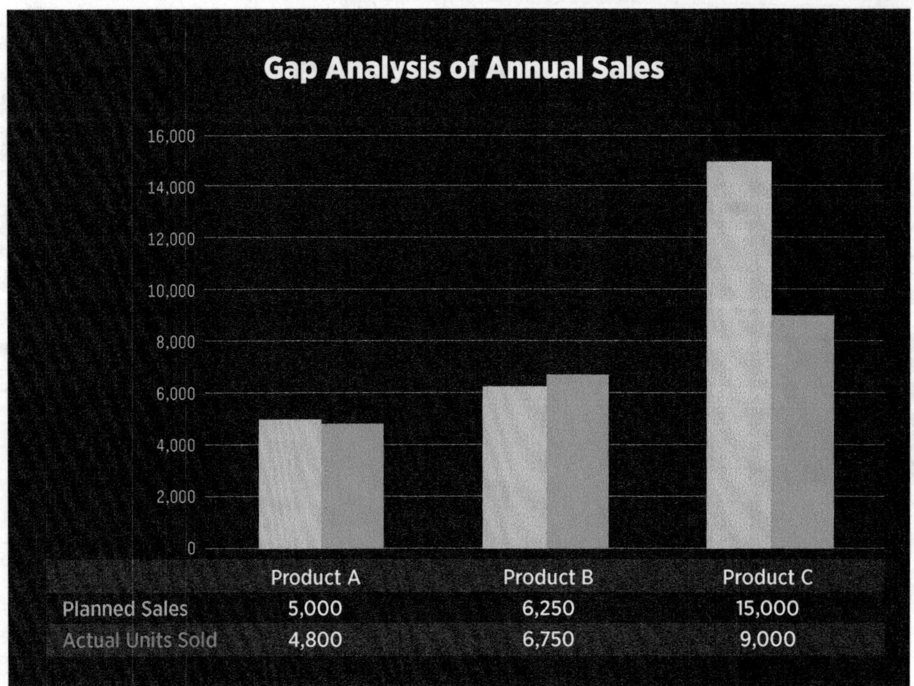

FIGURE 5.3 BAR CHARTS HIGHLIGHT PROBLEMS UNEARTHED BY GAP ANALYSIS AT A GLANCE.

Every time you see a statement such as, "Revenues this period were 10 percent below forecast," you are looking at a form of gap analysis. In other words, gaps can be stated in many different ways, and are often one of the key pieces of information we use to evaluate annual performance of a company. While gap charts or data tables are useful ways to capture major events, however, they are limited in usefulness because they focus solely on one period of performance and normally provide little, if any, guidance on how to remedy the problem. The first of these shortcomings is addressed by trend analysis.

TREND ANALYSIS

Looking at just one point in time, or one result, does not provide a solid basis for evaluating the performance of an organization or any of the individuals who populate it. This would be similar to taking a class that had only one basis for your grade—a final exam. You might have worked hard all semester, kept up with the readings, and participated in class. On the day of the exam, however, you woke up with a terrible headache. You would probably still have to take the exam, but would it be a fair way to evaluate your total effort in the class? It is doubtful because it would not capture trends in your performance.

As we first saw in Chapter 2, trend analysis allows us to sort out onetime events, such as your headache, from overall performance patterns. Specifically, **trend analysis** *analyzes performance over multiple time periods, or observations, focusing on how results change during the period being studied.* In looking at performance changes over time, we can spot improvements, assess the impact of changes to how the work is done, or identify other factors, such as seasonal sales patterns, that may be affecting the organization's or individual's performance.

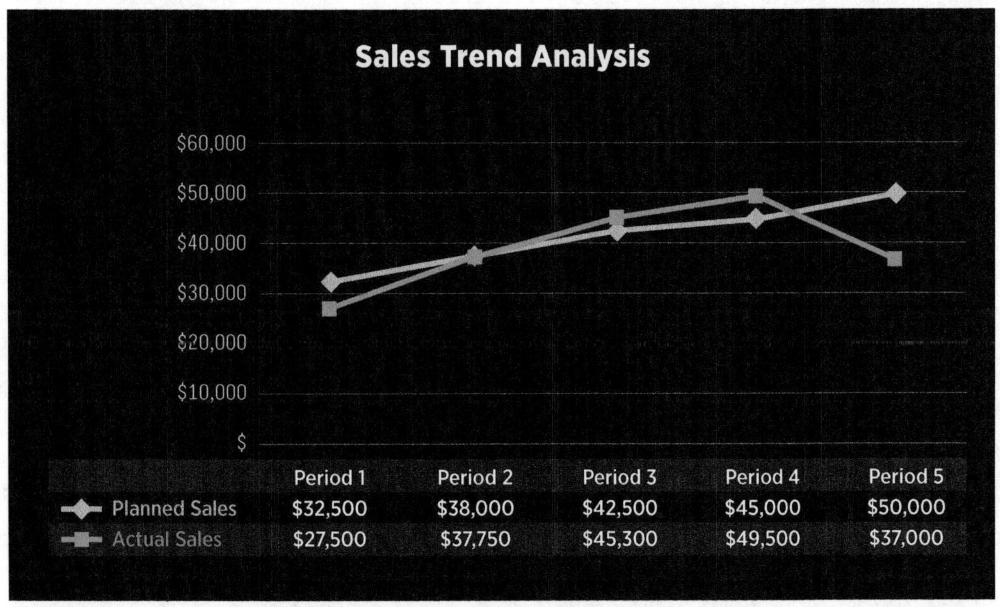

FIGURE 5.4 A LINE CHART HIGHLIGHTS PERFORMANCE UPS AND DOWNS OVER TIME REVEALED BY TREND ANALYSIS.

One of the most common ways to portray trend analysis is through a line chart, such as that presented in Figure 5.4. Focusing attention on the relationship between planned sales and actual sales, this chart quickly pinpoints the performance shortfall in Period 5. It also provides us with another piece of information—sales had been steadily climbing every period up to Period 5. The question that would now need answering is whether the sales decline in Period 5 is a temporary phenomenon, or if it is a signal that the firm's products are no longer as attractive to its customers.

RADAR CHART ANALYSIS

RADAR, *or "spider," charts look at performance on multiple dimensions simultaneously.* They assess the performance of a process or organization on multiple dimensions. For instance, the diagrams in Figure 5.5 detail the relative performance of two fire departments in terms of productivity, prevention, suppression of fires, and levels of effort put out by the departments. By comparing the performance of the two fire departments through RADAR charts, the difference in how the two are managed is clearly visible. Which department is performing better? That would depend on the expectations of the county and city managers and citizens. The circle drawn around the diagrams reflects what a balanced approach would look like. That said, clearly, a fire department centrally located in a city would not have to travel as far to a fire or deal with challenges such as locating a source of water, such as a fire hydrant. It would also appear from the diagrams that the city fire department is much more focused on conducting prevention activities and forums than is the county department. RADAR charts can be much more detailed, but, regardless of the detail, the goal is the same: to present a visual picture of performance on multiple dimensions.

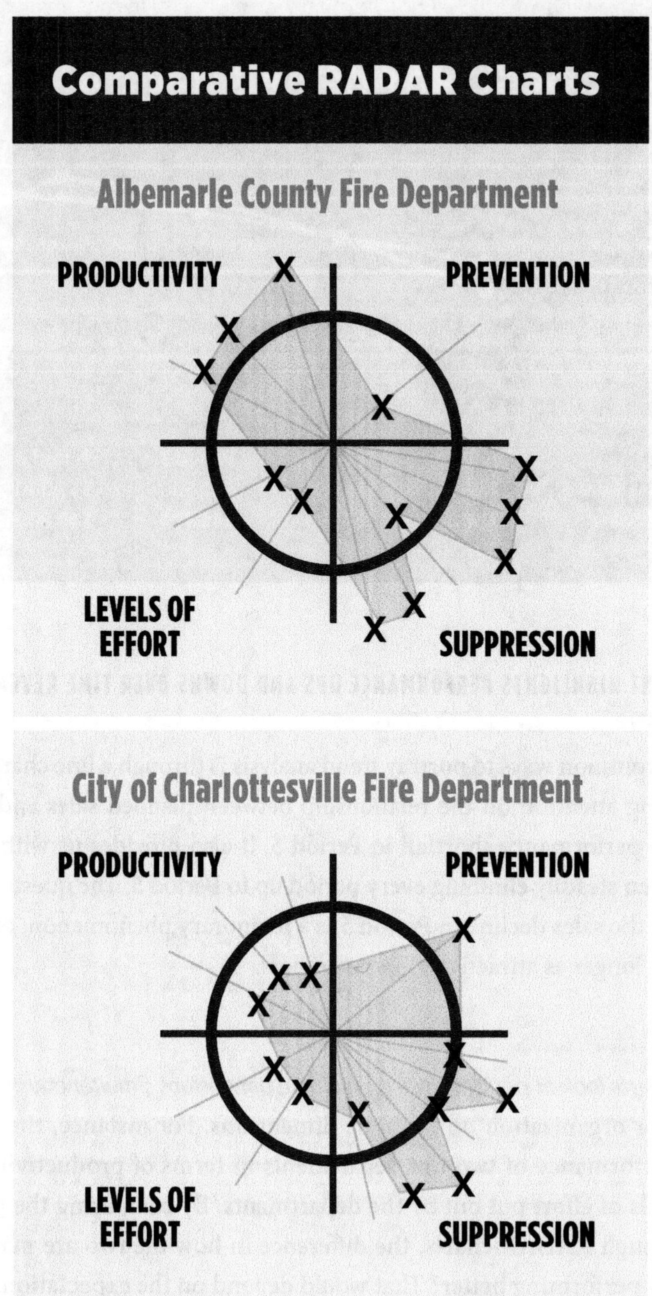

FIGURE 5.5 BY LOOKING ACROSS MANY DIMENSIONS, RADAR CHARTS HELP MANAGEMENT IDENTIFY PERFORMANCE STRENGTHS AND WEAKNESSES.

Some common uses of RADAR charts include sales or production efficiency analysis; performance evaluation of an individual, group, or organization; comparative performance of business units or organizations; and any type of analysis of fluctuations in performance over time. The RADAR chart can also be adapted to have as many dimensions as necessary to accommodate the issue under study. Specifically, the charts can be used to evaluate performance over time, against other companies or processes using benchmark information, or with respect to a preestablished standard or planned level of performance.

VARIANCE ANALYSIS

The first three tools we have looked at provide information for comparing actual performance to plan. Specifically, gap analysis looks at one aspect of performance against plan for one time period, trend analysis focuses on one or a small number of actual-to-planned results over time, and RADAR charts display multiple performance measures or multiple time period results. This is valuable information, but it does not provide us with the basis for explaining any differences in actual vs. planned performance. To address this issue, we need to apply several other tools: variance analysis, Pareto analysis, and cause-and-effect analysis. Variance analysis is the most common tool used in management accounting, so we will start our exploration here.

Variance analysis *explores differences between a preset standard and actual performance by isolating one causal factor at a time.* The most common use of this tool is the examination of actual costs against standard or expected costs for making a product or providing a service. Other applications, however, include capacity utilization analysis and profitability analysis. In fact, any time we are trying to understand results that are impacted by many different events or variables, variance analysis can prove quite useful.

Let us take a simple example to gain a deeper understanding of this valuable tool. Specifically, Smith Industries, Inc. (SIS), makes a variety of toys for children. Its best-selling toy is a rubber ball that is made in batches of 1,000 units using the resources listed in Table 5.2.

TABLE 5.2 VARIANCE ANALYSIS: ESTIMATED COSTS

Smith Industries, Inc.			
Resource	Standard Price of Resource	Standard Amount Needed to Make 1,000 Units	Total for 1,000 Rubber Balls
Materials (rubber)	$15.00 per pound	6 pounds	$ 90.00
Labor	$20.00 per hour	4 hours	80.00
Machinery	$100.00 per hour	1 hour	100.00
Total			$ 270.00

During May, SIS made a batch of rubber balls. While it should have cost the company $270 for the batch, or $0.27 per ball made ($270 divided by 1,000 units per batch), the actual costs were just over $334, broken down in Table 5.3.

TABLE 5.3 VARIANCE ANALYSIS: ACTUAL COSTS

Smith Industries, Inc.			
Resource	Actual Price of Resource	Actual Amount Needed to Make 1,000 Units	Total for 1,000 Rubber Balls
Materials (rubber)	$14.00 per pound	7 pounds	$ 98.00
Labor	$24.00 per hour	3.8 hours	91.20
Machinery	$90.00 per hour	1.5 hours	135.00
Total			$ 324.20

The actual cost of the batch was $324.20, or 16.7% more than the expected, or standard, cost ($324.20 minus $270 equals $54.20 divided by $270 equals 16.7%). Since the market for rubber balls is very competitive, SIS cannot raise its price to recoup these excess costs. That means it has to find out what went wrong, why it went wrong, and how to fix the problem before it makes the product again. In this case, the variance is unfavorable because actual results are worse than planned, or standard, results. Clearly there can also be cases where actual results are better than the standard, in which case the variance would be favorable.

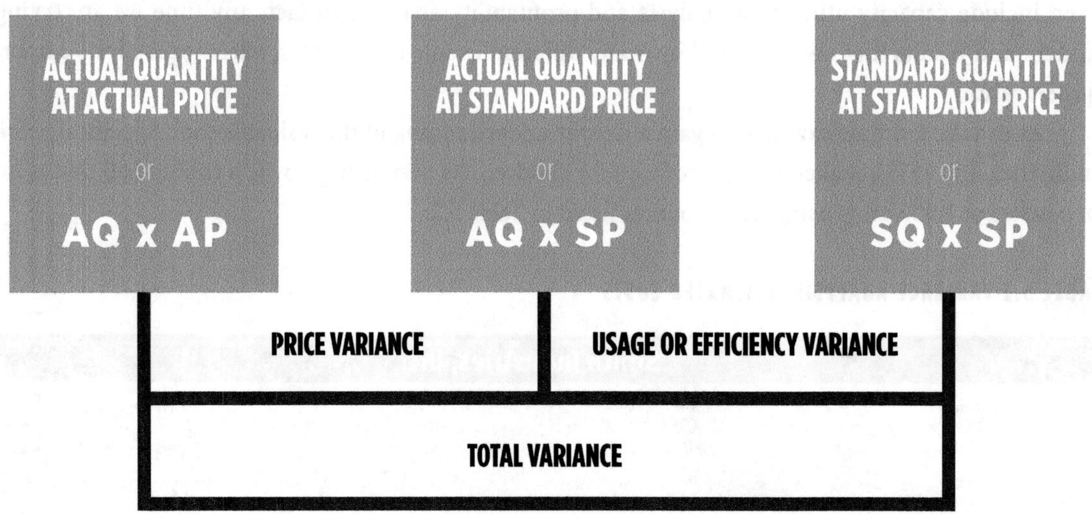

FIGURE 5.6 VARIANCE ANALYSIS HELPS COMPANIES ASSESS THE DIFFERENCE BETWEEN ESTIMATED AND ACTUAL COSTS.

As we look at the actual vs. standard cost estimates in Figure 5.6, we can see that both the cost and the amount of each resource differ from standard. How can we tell, therefore, what amount of the cost overrun is due to paying more or less for a resource vs. using more or less of the resource than was planned? If we look carefully at the diagram, we see that we change one variable at a time. We get this information by applying variance analysis, which allows us to separate one cause of a cost difference from another, as captured in Figure 5.7. Let us now apply this logic to the rubber that was used to make a batch of the product.

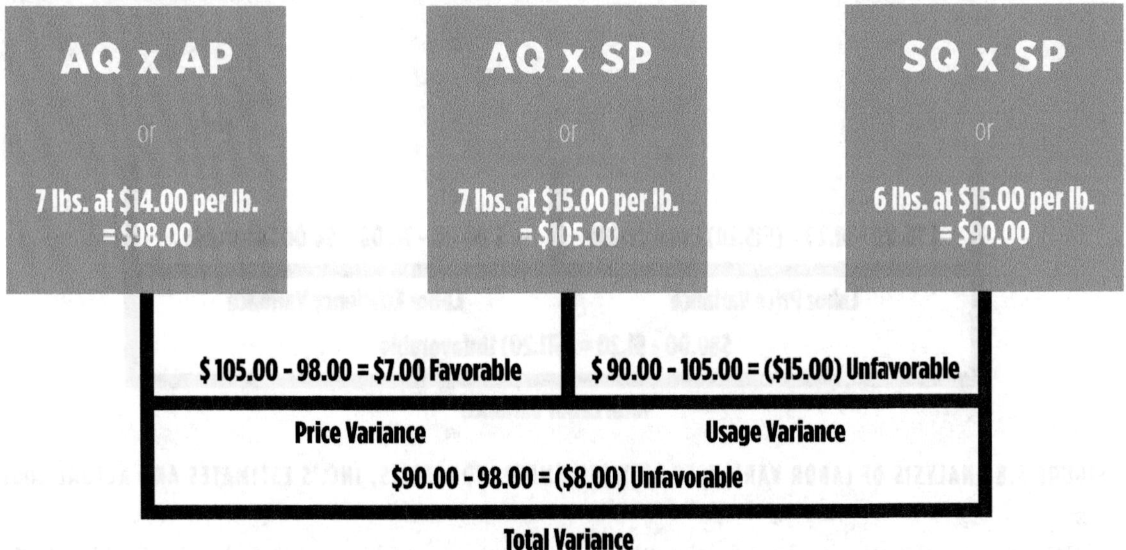

FIGURE 5.7 ANALYSIS OF MATERIAL VARIANCES BETWEEN SMITH INDUSTRIES, INC.'S ESTIMATES AND ACTUAL COSTS

As you can see, if we want to focus solely on the difference in total cost due to variations in the price we paid for the rubber, we hold the quantity purchased "constant" (for example, we do not change it) and change our price from actual amount paid to the standard or expected prices. When we do this, we see that the total cost for the rubber in the batch of balls would have been $105, or $7 more than was spent. This is called an **unfavorable variance**, and *occurs when more is spent or used on a resource than planned.* On the other hand, a **favorable variance** *occurs when less is spent or used on a resource than is planned.* Smith had a $7 *favorable* price variance for this batch of balls. A **price variance** *occurs when we spend more or less than planned on a resource.*

On the other hand, when we look at the amount of rubber used, we see that one more pound was used than was expected. This variance is isolated by slightly changing the information in the center box (AQ x SP). Specifically, actual quantity (AQ) is changed to the standard quantity (SQ) of rubber used in making a batch of balls. In making this change, we have isolated the amount of cost difference resulting from the quantity used, which results in a $15 **efficiency, or usage, variance,** *the result of using more or less of a resource than planned.* Common practice is to use the term usage variance for materials, and efficiency variance for labor and overhead; the calculation itself does not change. For SIS, its material usage variance is unfavorable by a total of $15. Now let us expand our analysis. Figure 5.8 deconstructs SIS's labor variance, which in this instance is unfavorable. Specifically, the total $11.20 of unfavorable labor variance is decomposed into its two main components: a $15.20 unfavorable labor price variance (Smith paid $4 more an hour than it had planned to do) and a $4 favorable labor usage variance (Smith used 0.2 fewer hours than the standard given).

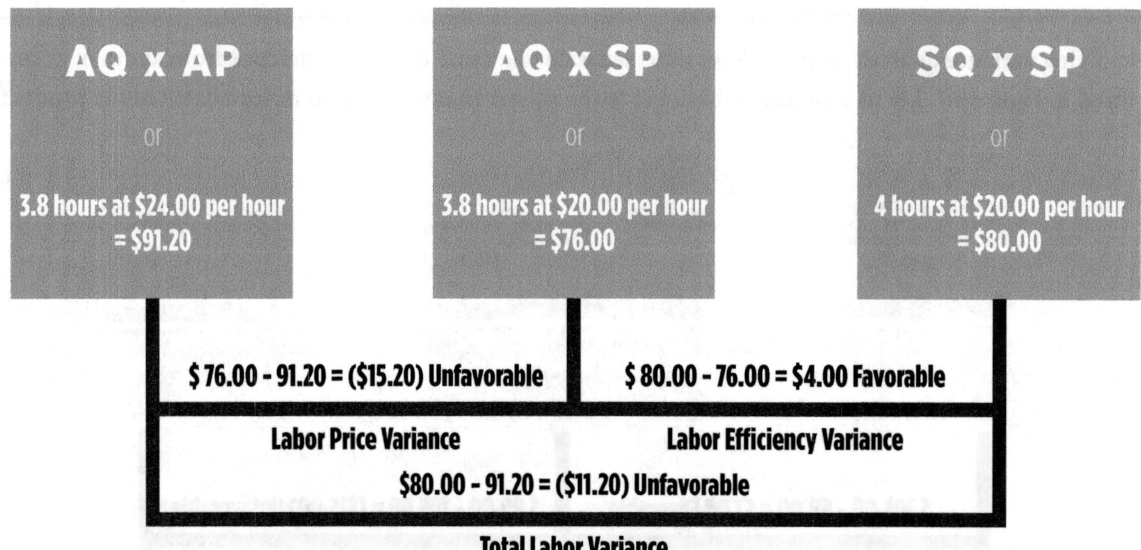

FIGURE 5.8 ANALYSIS OF LABOR VARIANCES BETWEEN SMITH INDUSTRIES, INC.'S ESTIMATES AND ACTUAL COSTS

We can complete this analysis for the other direct resource used in making a batch of rubber balls at Smith Industries, Inc.—machining—as summarized in Figure 5.9. In a similar way, we see that while Smith paid $10 less an hour for its machining activities ($90 actual hourly costs vs. $100 at standard, or a $10 favorable price variance), the company ended up having to use 1.5 hours instead of the normal one hour of machining time, which generated a $50 unfavorable machining efficiency variance. In total, therefore, Smith's machining activity cost us $35 more than it should have—the overall variance was unfavorable.

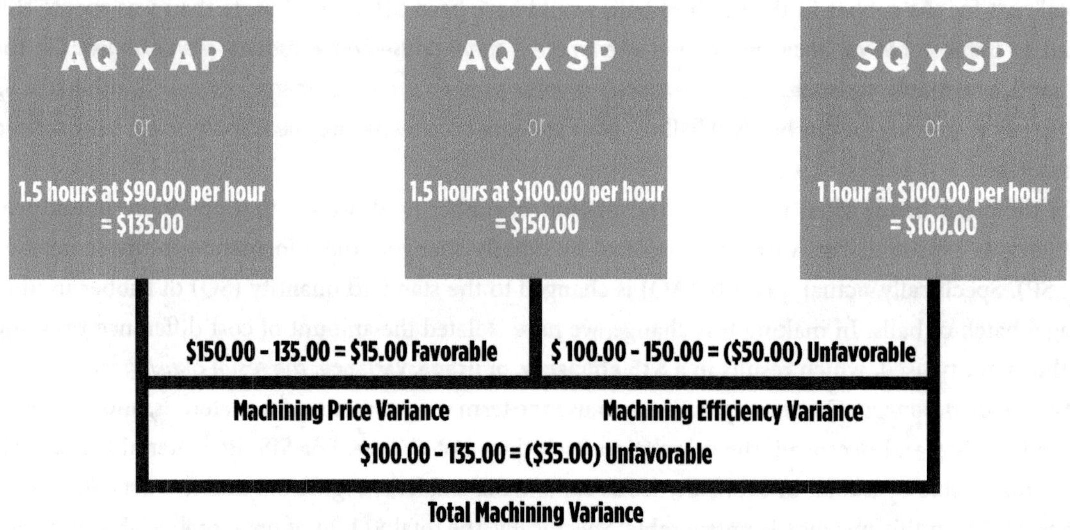

FIGURE 5.9 ANALYSIS OF MACHINING VARIANCE BETWEEN SMITH INDUSTRIES, INC.'S ESTIMATES AND ACTUAL COSTS

Variance analysis is used in many different ways in companies, but its overall focus is always the same. Specifically, we use the tool *to develop explanations for differences between actual vs. planned cost or performance by isolating one effect or cause at a time, such as the actual vs. planned price paid for a resource.* By changing only one factor at a time, we can identify more precisely where the performance problems are. This information allows us to create more effective action plans to eliminate or address the problem, to assign responsibility for managing and improving performance, and to increase the probability that a firm will achieve its performance objectives.

Applying Analytical Tools to Solve Problems

Having learned several new tools, let us see how we can use each of these "check" tools to help out our friends at Easy Air. To get us started, Table 5.4 restates key Easy Air information that was presented in Chapter 1 and the database.

TABLE 5.4 PERFORMANCE DATA 20x4-20x6

Summary of Easy Air's Performance 20x4-20x6			
Performance Indicator	**20x6**	**20x5**	**20x4**
Total flights flown	3,575,240	3,489,434	3,297,515
Total passengers flown	373,369,464	363,557,175	342,354,639
Total revenue seat miles flown (in thousands)	54,405,612	53,796,413	48,215,413
Available seat miles (in thousands)	63,557,958	62,993,458	56,657,360
Average miles per passenger flight	265	260	233
Number of stations	120	112	106
Total operating revenue (in thousands)	$9,303,359.7	$9,521,965.1	$9,112,713.1
Total operating expenses (in thousands)	$8,899,038.1	$8,536,503.9	$7,430,858.9
Operating profit (in thousands)	$404,321.6	$985,461.2	$1,681.854.1
Average revenue per revenue seat mile flown	$0.171	$0.177	$0.189
Average expense per revenue seat mile flown	$0.164	$0.159	$0.154
Average profit per revenue seat mile flown	$0.007	$0.018	$0.035

As noted above, gap analysis can be performed for any type of measured feature of a product or process. In doing a gap analysis, we are looking at the cumulative impact of events and outcomes to determine if any significant problems exist. For instance, profit is a measure of the cumulative gap between revenues and costs for a reporting period. As suggested in Figure 5.10, we could look at this gap in a slightly different way—as a comparison of actual average profitability per seat mile flown vs. the revenue and cost.

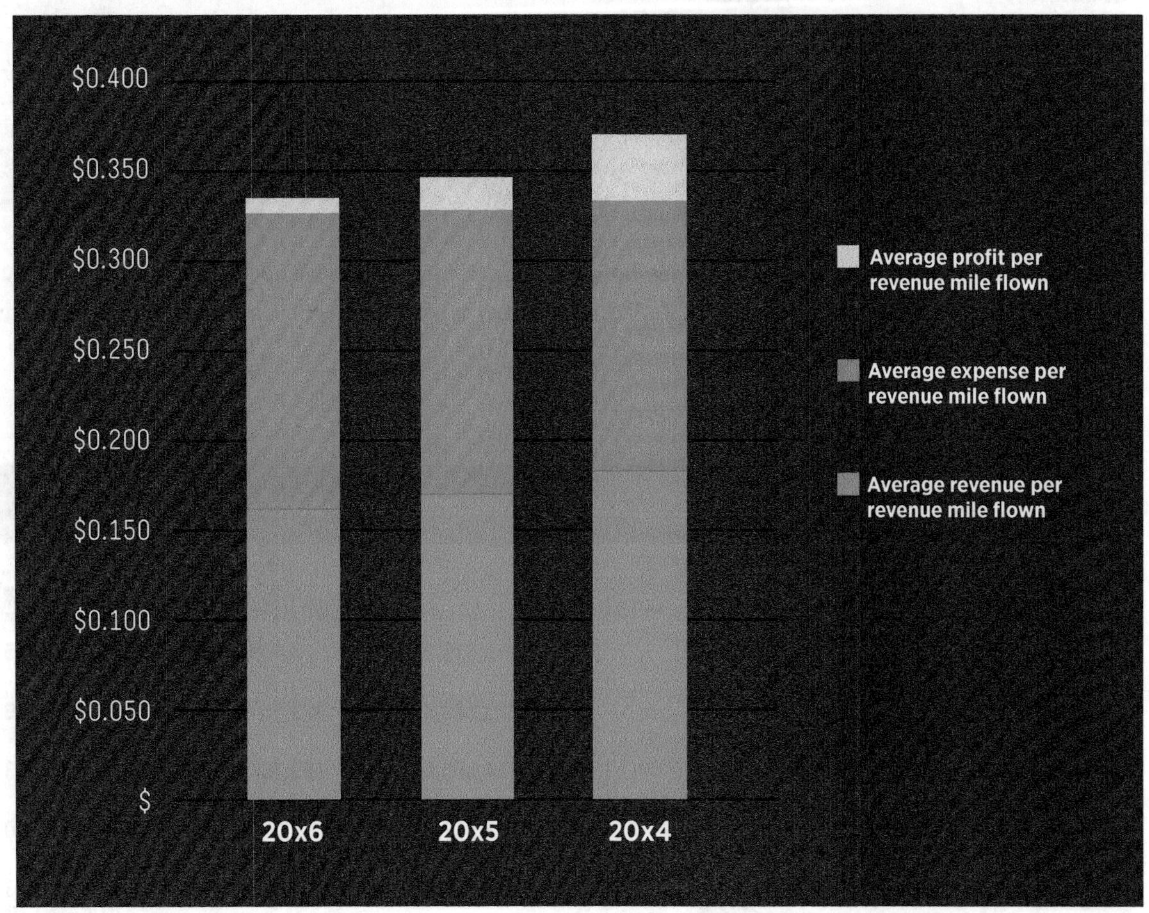

FIGURE 5.10 GAP ANALYSIS OF EASY AIR'S PROFITABILITY

To look at the trends over the three-year period from 20x4 to 20x6, we might want to develop a chart like the one presented in Figure 5.11. Here we can clearly see the issues that are bothering Fran—while revenues have gone up dramatically since 20x4, profits have plummeted over the same two-year period. While in the case of Easy Air we can probably see these effects as easily from the numerical table as we can from the trend analysis, in many cases the trended data provides new insights that might not have been spotted using a different form of analysis.

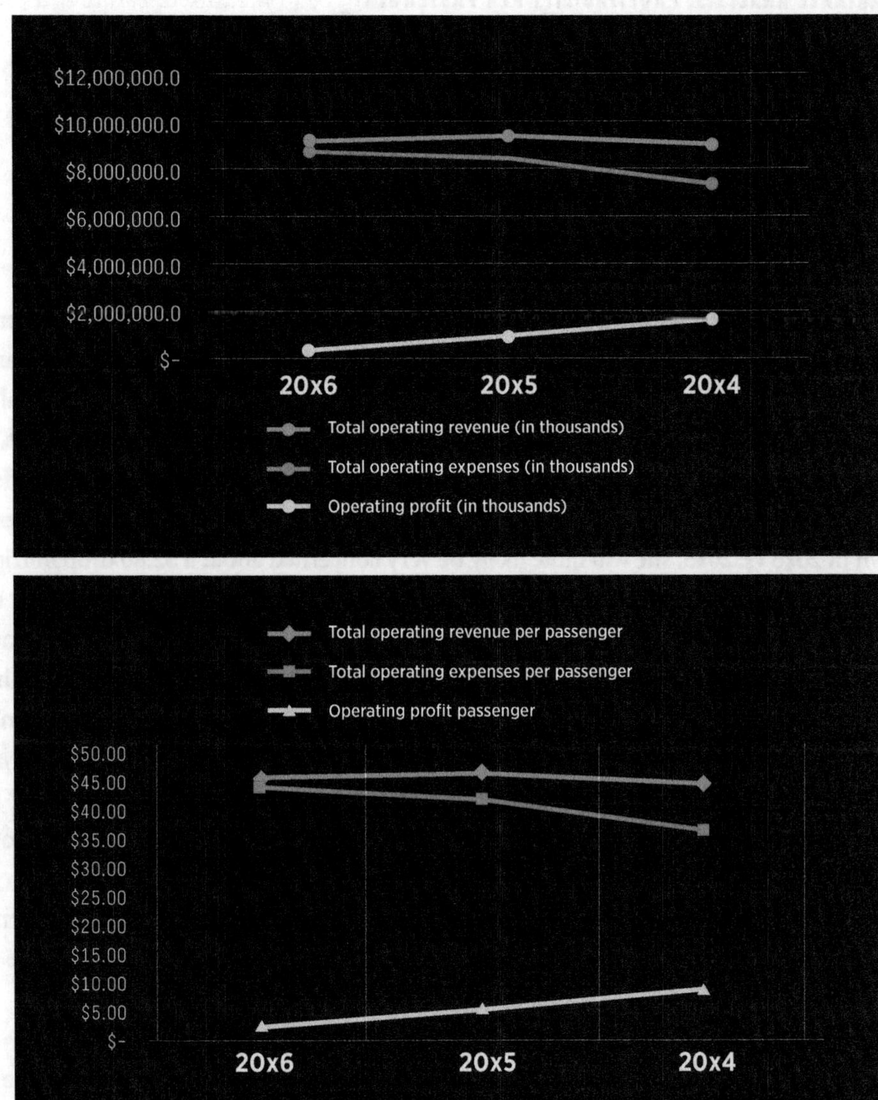

FIGURE 5.11 TREND ANALYSIS FOR EASY AIR 20x4-20x6

If we wanted an even more full explanation of the difference in profitability between 20x5 and 20x6 for Easy Air, we might want to look at the cost, revenue, and profit effects at the same time. Table 5.5 breaks out these factors, allowing us to separate out the positive events from the less than positive. Specifically, while revenues and profits per passenger have dropped, cost per passenger has increased. The biggest difference is clearly due to an increase in costs per passenger. The $0.71 drop in revenue per passenger is the price variance, while the $2.09 is a loss in efficiency. These combine for a $2.80 drop in profits. (Remember, costs and revenues move in different ways with regard to favorable and unfavorable variances. Every variance in the table is unfavorable.)

TABLE 5.5 VARIANCE ANALYSIS: PROFITABILITY PER PASSENGER

Easy Air			
Per Mile Results	**20x6**	**20x5**	**Difference**
Revenue per passenger	$45.33	$46.04	($0.71)
Cost per passenger	$43.35	$41.26	$2.09
Profit per passenger	$1.98	$4.78	($2.80)

Variance analysis is a useful way for us to check on the progress of a company, department, or process. By isolating the difference one variable at a time, we are able to gain a much better understanding of Easy Air's performance in 20x6. We can make this comparison using a preset standard or the actual performance of the company in a prior period, as we did here for Easy Air. In completing a variance analysis, our goal is to dig below the summary data on an item-by-item basis to get a better understanding of the offsetting causes of the shift in performance. While Fran may only be slightly concerned about earning $0.71 less per passenger trip flown in 20x6 vs. 20x5, she will quite likely be very concerned about a $2.80 drop in trip profits.

To summarize these issues, during the "check" phase of the management process, we use measures in various ways to analyze the differences between our plans and actual results, both by general size (gap analysis) and cause (variance analysis) as well as trends in performance. While we have emphasized financial results in this example, we could just as easily focus our attention on the on-time performance metrics, ground operations, or the baggage-handling area. In other words, we can use variance analysis to explore a range of performance problems. But we cannot stop once the numbers are analyzed. Why? Because once we know where the problems are, we want to find ways to fix them. Regardless of the type of measure, or its focus, our goal during the "check" phase remains the same—to determine if we need to make adjustments to get the organization back on track toward its goals. For this information, we turn to two final tools: Pareto analysis and cause-and-effect analysis.

PARETO ANALYSIS

OBJECTIVE 3

Develop and use Pareto and cause-and-effect diagrams.

One of the first questions we ask when we attempt to improve the performance of a process or organization is, "What are the primary problems facing it?" **Pareto analysis** *visually examines the various causes of missed targets or shortfalls in performance by comparing the total quantities or occurrences of one error or cause against others* to better understand where a company should focus.

Let us continue with our Easy Air example to help us learn about this simple, but powerful, tool. One of the problems that Sanjiv and his team have uncovered during the course of their analysis is a troubling increase in the number of flights that are posting late departures. Unless this lost time can be made up during the flight, the delays ripple through the entire system, creating excess cost and customer dissatisfaction.

To gain a better understanding of the issue surrounding the flight delays, Sanjiv and his team decide to collect information on the problems that appear to be causing the delays. In exploring this question, they compiled the data presented in Table 5.6.

TABLE 5.6 PARETO ANALYSIS: CAUSES OF FLIGHT DELAYS

Easy Air				
Event Causing Flight Delay	Number of Times Noted	Cumulative Total	Percent of Total	Cumulative Percent
Delay in loading baggage	125	125	25%	25%
Excessive customer carry-on baggage	100	225	20%	45%
Air traffic delays or holds	75	300	15%	60%
Excessive cleaning time	60	360	12%	72%
Delays in restocking galley	50	410	10%	82%
Other causes	90	500	18%	100%
TOTAL	500	–	100%	–

A Pareto chart, illustrated by Figure 5.12, can be developed to visually depict this information. As we can see, 45 percent of the problems are due in one way or another to baggage issues. While both of these causes for delays (delay in loading baggage and excessive customer carry-on baggage) need to be addressed, it is probably going to be easier to identify internal problems with baggage-handling procedures than it is to change how many or what size bags the customers bring onto the plane.

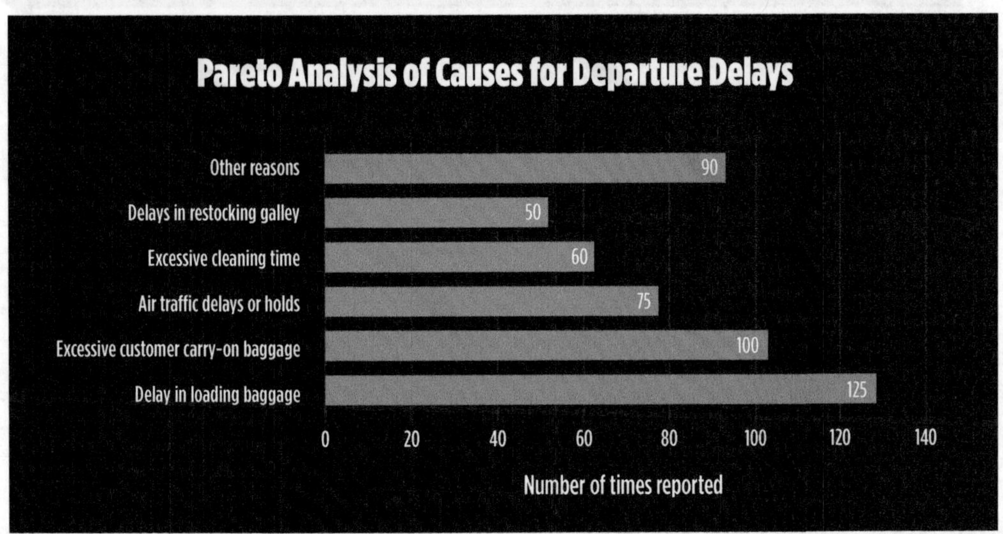

FIGURE 5.12 RESULTS OF A PARETO ANALYSIS OF EASY AIR'S FLIGHT DELAYS

Knowing where the problems are centered, Sanjiv and his team can now focus their attention on finding solutions to one issue at a time. For this they turn to the final of our analytical tools: cause-and-effect analysis.

CAUSE-AND-EFFECT ANALYSIS

Cause-and-effect analysis is a graphical tool that focuses on identifying the **root cause**, or *primary reason for a performance shortfall*, such as Easy Air's baggage-handling problems. Using brainstorming and related group problem-solving approaches, **cause-and-effect analysis** *visually analyzes the various factors creating a performance shortfall*. The result is a diagram of the problem focused on four primary dimensions: human or labor-based, machine or equipment-based, process-based, and customer-based problems (see Figure 5.13). Another common name for this diagram is "Ishikawa fishbone diagram," which reflects its shape and credits its originator.

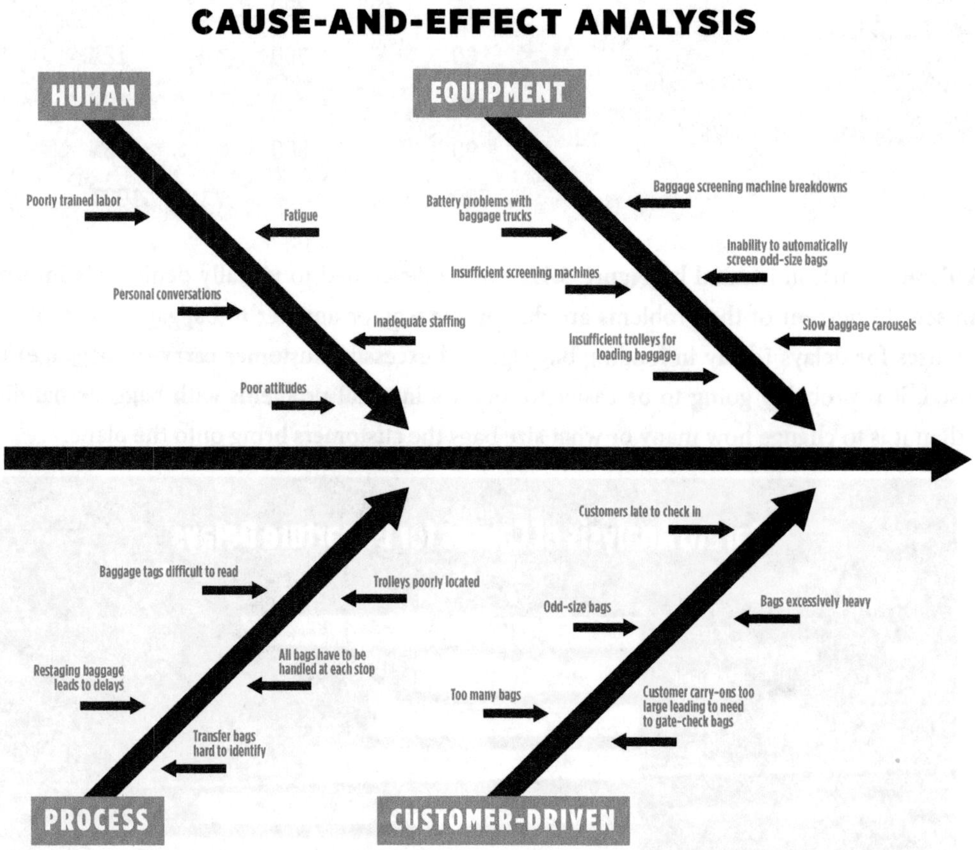

CAUSE-AND-EFFECT ANALYSIS

HUMAN
Poorly trained labor
Fatigue
Personal conversations
Inadequate staffing
Poor attitudes

EQUIPMENT
Baggage screening machine breakdowns
Battery problems with baggage trucks
Inability to automatically screen odd-size bags
Insufficient screening machines
Slow baggage carousels
Insufficient trolleys for loading baggage

PROCESS
Baggage tags difficult to read
Trolleys poorly located
All bags have to be handled at each stop
Restaging baggage leads to delays
Transfer bags hard to identify

CUSTOMER-DRIVEN
Customers late to check in
Odd-size bags
Bags excessively heavy
Too many bags
Customer carry-ons too large leading to need to gate-check bags

FIGURE 5.13 CAUSES OF EASY AIR'S FLIGHT DELAYS USING A CAUSE-AND-EFFECT DIAGRAM

As we review Figure 5.13, we see that there are a number of process and equipment problems resulting in baggage-handling delays. To expand on this analysis, we can now combine the cause-and-effect results with a Pareto analysis to see which of these problems is the most important so that we can focus on it (see Figure 5.14). The major problems are now evident. While there are many different causes that might explain these trends in performance, it appears that two pieces of baggage equipment are having the biggest effect. Specifically, the baggage screening machines are breaking down, creating 28 percent of the delays (35 occurrences in the total 125 times that baggage handling has caused flight delays, or 28 percent). The second major "culprit" is the failure to have enough trolleys to load the luggage on, which accounts for 20.8 percent of this class of problem. If Easy Air is going to make a significant improvement in this area, it needs to address these equipment problems.

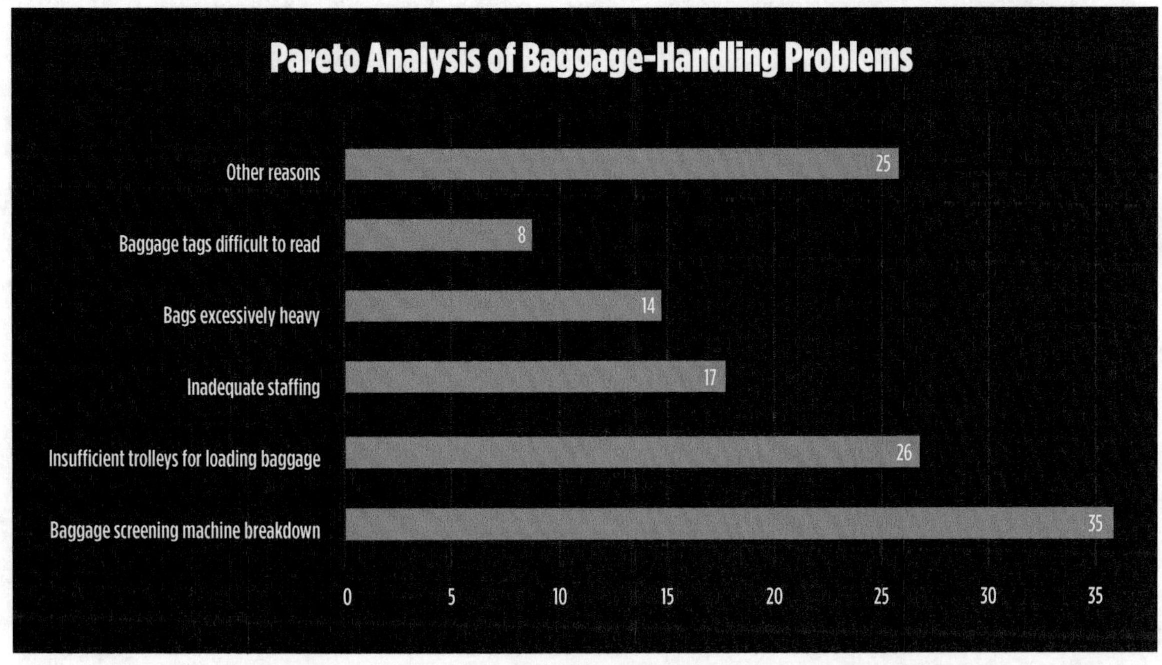

FIGURE 5.14 CAUSES OF EASY AIR'S BAGGAGE-HANDLING PROBLEMS BY COMBINING CAUSE-AND-EFFECT ANALYSIS AND PARETO ANALYSIS

In developing a complete analysis of operational or business problems, we will often use several different tools or even one tool more than once. Each tool has specific strengths and weaknesses, or helps us capture certain types of information. Table 5.7 summarizes this information for the six primary tools we have discussed in depth.

TABLE 5.7 USES, STRENGTHS, AND WEAKNESSES OF SIX PRIMARY ANALYTICAL TOOLS

Tool	Primary Focus	Primary Strengths	Primary Weakness(es)
Gap analysis	Measures difference between actual and planned results	- Quickly identifies problem areas - Emphasizes magnitude of difference between actual and plan	- One-period focus - Causes not identified
Trend analysis	Analyzes changes in actual results over time	- Makes shifts in performance visible - Identifies whether a specific outcome is an outlier or part of an overall change in results	- Only small number of variables handled easily - Causes not identified

Tool	Primary Focus	Primary Strengths	Primary Weakness(es)
RADAR chart analysis	Provides a multidimensional analysis of measured results	- Supports analysis of more than one variable at a time - Isolates areas where performance is better or worse than planned	- Can become complex - Causes not identified
Variance analysis	Analyzes performance gap data one variable or dimension at a time	- Isolates causes for performance shortfalls - Separates problems into distinct categories	- One-period focus - Interrelationships hard to identify
Pareto analysis	Identifies the relative frequency of various types of problems	- Makes key problems in current performance visible - Very visible means to communicate problems within the organization	- One-period focus - Causes not identified
Cause-and-effect analysis	Details the causes of performance problems	- Highlights problems across the process - Separates causes by categories that can then be assigned to individual managers for remediation	- Frequency/magnitude of problem not identified

Making Adjustments

Identifying problems and isolating their causes provides the basis for the final step in the management process—making adjustments to current processes, activities, or products to improve performance and profitability. To accomplish this final goal, we need to identify potential solutions to our problems and then compare these alternative solutions based on their overall impact on profit and performance. Once the alternatives are assessed, a solid business case or proposal for change can be developed. We now turn to the final activities in the management process.

IN CONTEXT ➤ Identifying Problems and Their Causes at Easy Air

"These are really interesting. Are you planning to create more charts for the report?" Sanjiv asked as he looked over the series of charts and analyses Sherry had completed over the last few days.

"I can if you'd like me to. What I did was take a run at one of our major headaches—the recent increase in flight delays—to see how the results looked when analyzed in different ways. I'm a big fan of RADAR and Pareto diagrams, but each of these graphs can be useful in certain settings. Do you have a preference, or do you think Fran would prefer any of them easier to use?" Sherry, as always, had her eye on the goal—meeting Fran's request for information on ways to improve Easy Air's performance.

"I think we should use different charts for different issues. For instance, I really like your 'one-two' punch on the baggage handling—cause-and-effect and Pareto charts. That really shows how we can burrow down into the information and find answers to those troubling 'why' questions."

"Okay, Sanjiv, a mix it is. Now what should we analyze first? We've got the data, now we need to give it some structure," Sherry replied.

"Why don't we start with the biggest issues—our cost creep and key performance shortfall, such as the delayed flights problem. If we can identify the issues that are creating most of the cost and performance problems, we'll be ready to meet with Fran, and to help get us back on the road to improved profitability!"

ASSESSING THE IMPACT OF CHANGE: INCREMENTAL ANALYSIS

OBJECTIVE 4
Use incremental analysis to assess potential options for change.

When changes are made to the way that work is done, there is normally a direct and identifiable impact on a firm's revenues and costs. Clearly, we want to capture these impacts in such a way that management can determine whether the changes are desirable or not. Also, if there is more than one alternative available to a company for making these changes, we need to find a way to compare the potential solutions and select the one that will yield the greatest benefits overall. **Incremental analysis** *is the tool used to compare the current method of doing work and the changes that may occur if alternative courses of action are adopted.* The emphasis is on the increment, or change, in performance. Incremental analysis allows a company to isolate, assess, and choose among the alternative courses of action that may be taken in the future.

The series of steps that are used to complete an incremental analysis of a problem and its potential solutions is as follows:

1. Define the problem and its primary causes.
2. Identify the objective(s) of the performance improvement effort.
3. Generate one or more alternative solutions for the problem.
4. Develop metrics that capture the financial and nonfinancial impact of each alternative, paying special attention to overall business risk and other qualitative issues.
5. Compare each of the alternatives and their impact to the original, or "as is" situation.
6. Choose the solution that will have the greatest potential to achieve the goals driving the improvement effort.

Returning to Easy Air, we originally began with a simple problem—declining profitability. While the problem is easily stated in those terms, identifying some of the underlying causes of this problem has taken considerable time and effort. Using a combination of benchmarking information and experience, however, Sanjiv's team has been able to identify two primary areas of concern—the costs and performance of its stations and its customer reservations system.

To focus their efforts, the team has decided to explore the performance of its stations first. The benchmark study revealed that while Easy Air is spending $1.82 per passenger for its station operations (gate fees, baggage handling, ticket counter, and gate activities), the industry average is $1.68.

As detailed in Table 5.8, if Easy Air could reduce its costs to the industry average, it would save $0.14 per passenger, or $52.27 million dollars. This is a cost reduction that would drop directly to the bottom line. In other words, Easy Air would be able to improve its profits from the current $404.3 million to more than $456.59 million, a 13% improvement. Even small improvements can have a radical impact on the bottom line.

TABLE 5.8 INCREMENTAL ANALYSIS OF STATION COSTS

Easy Air		
Variables and Analysis	If Reduce Station Costs to Industry Average	If Reduce Station Costs to Best-in-Class
Current station costs per passenger	$1.82	$1.82
Benchmarked station costs	$1.68	$1.49
Potential Cost Reduction	$0.14	$0.33
Times: Number of passengers in 20x6	$373,369,464	$373,369,464
Total Estimated Cost Reduction (1)	$52,271,725	$123,211,923
Profit reported by Easy Air in 20x6 (2)	$404,321,562	$404,321,562
Revised Profits if Cost Improvements Made	$456,593,287	$527,533,485
Improvement percentage (1) / (2)	13%	30%

As we have seen, one of the key activities performed by the station is the handling of passenger baggage. In exploring the station costs, Sherry comes across a troubling fact: The baggage handling is not only a costly activity per passenger flown, it also appears to be one of the root causes for a sharp increase in the number of delayed flights over the last year. If Easy Air can make improvements in this area, it can reduce costs in the short run and potentially improve revenues downstream as its "on-time" and baggage-handling performances get better.

Through a combination of RADAR and Pareto analysis, Sherry has uncovered several major equipment issues that seem to be creating a majority of the baggage-handling problems. According to the list of steps previously described, we now need to develop several solutions to these problems and assess their relative costs and benefits. In thinking through the issues at Easy Air, three potential alternative approaches should be explored: (1) outsourcing the baggage handling to an outside firm; (2) purchasing new baggage-handling equipment (tractors, trolleys, and screening machines); or (3) doing nothing. Option three is, in reality, our "as is" scenario, and it is the baseline that we will use to judge the other two alternatives.

Baggage-handling problems are high on the list of issues to be addressed. Sherry identifies four options for handling the baggage problems. Remember that, currently, there are a lot of lost or damaged bags that, for now, we have not put a cost on. These options are:

1. Buy new baggage-handling equipment.
2. Outsource baggage handling.
3. Charge passengers $10 per checked bag.
4. Do nothing.

Looking first at the outsourcing option, we see that the cost to Easy Air for lost or damaged luggage is eliminated—the outsource firm will be responsible for these costs. And, if baggage handling is outsourced, there is no need for Easy Air to have its own equipment, a $124,500,000 savings. Sherry also determines that the baggage-handling activity can be outsourced for a cost of $3 per checked bag. This cost would be incurred on average for each and every passenger—it would become a variable cost that would be driven by the number of bags flown. Sherry knows from prior experience that, on average, each passenger checks 1.25 bags (five bags checked for every four passengers), resulting in an average cost of $3.75 per passenger if baggage handling is outsourced ($3 per bag checked times 1.25 bags per passenger).

In a related way, we see that if Easy Air buys new equipment, increasing its annual depreciation to $250,000,000, it is estimated that it will reduce the number and cost of lost and damaged bags by 75% and the total nonmachine costs for baggage handling by 25% overall. The total estimated cost of this option is $390,596,886, which is more than $109 million less than the estimated costs of outsourcing baggage handling. In addition, if Easy Air improves its baggage handling, it will see an 8% increase in passenger load and revenues as more passengers choose Easy Air.

Now let us look at the results if Easy Air decides to charge $10 per checked bag. Sherry estimates that adding this charge will result in a 10% reduction in the number of passengers that choose to fly Easy Air, resulting in incremental revenue of $3,360,325,170 for baggage-handling fees that has to be offset by the $2,240,216,801 loss of passenger revenues. The net result is only a $0.63 incremental increase in revenues, compared to a $3.48 per passenger increase if Easy Air purchases new baggage-handling equipment.

Therefore, it would seem that Easy Air would need to improve its operations, incurring the new equipment costs, if it is going to start charging a baggage fee. Right now, lost baggage activities cost the company $126,433,230 plus 20% of its station-driven capacity costs, or $181,781,230. Doing both of these things would result in a net loss of 2% of its current passenger load (8% improvement for better baggage handling less the 10% loss in passenger load due to the new fee). So while the result is better than just charging a fee, the net incremental impact is still less than Easy Air will experience if it simply improves its baggage-handling operation. The impact of each of these changes on the revenues and costs for the baggage-handling activity are summarized in Table 5.9.

TABLE 5.9 BAGGAGE-HANDLING ANALYSIS

Easy Air					
	Current situation (the "as is" alternative)	Outsource baggage handling	Buy new equipment	Charge for baggage handling	Charge for baggage handing and get new equipment
Estimated number of passengers flying	373,369,464	373,369,464	403,239,021	336,032,517	365,902,074
Incremental Revenue					
New baggage fees				$3,360,325,170	$3,659,020,744
New revenue from better service			$1,792,173,439		
Lost revenue from charging for baggage				$(2,240,216,801)	$(2,240,216,796)
Total incremental revenue	$-	$-	$1,792,173,439	$1,120,108,369	$1,418,803,948
Per passenger incremental revenue	$-	$-	$4.44	$3.33	$3.88
Incremental Costs					
Outsourcing costs	$-	$606,725,378	$-	$-	$-
Depreciation of new equipment	$-	$-	$100,000,000	$-	$100,000,000
Cost of lost/damaged luggage	$181,781,230	$-	$36,356,246	$181,781,230	$36,356,246
Baggage-handling costs—as is	$317,800,800	$-	$254,240,640	$317,800,800	$254,240,640
Total incremental cost	$499,582,030	$606,725,378	$390,596,886	$499,582,030	$390,596,886
Per passenger incremental cost	$1.34	$1.63	$0.97	$1.49	$1.07
Total Net Estimated Baggage-Handling Revenue (Cost)	$(499,582,030)	$(606,725,378)	$1,401,576,553	$620,526,339	$1,028,207,062
Per passenger	$(1.34)	$(1.63)	$3.48	$1.85	$2.81

If we did not do this complete analysis, it would seem logical that charging $10 per checked bag is the best alternative open to Easy Air. But, let us think about the issue from a different perspective—the total costs per passenger if Easy Air is able to achieve the 8% increase in passengers flown if it solves its baggage-handling problems and thereby improves its on-time performance. So, if we factor in the competitive risk of adding baggage fees, we see that charging for checked bags looks much less desirable. Buying new equipment and keeping our competitive profile as it is appears to be the least risky solution, getting us down below best-in-class costs, a real advantage for the company. In other words, we have to consider business risk whenever we use incremental analysis to examine alternatives. While many airlines do charge for checked bags, Easy Air will actually have the greatest improvement in its profitability if it continues to allow passengers to check up to two bags for free and focuses on improving its baggage-handling performance.

If we are only concerned about the numbers, then we have enough information to make a recommendation to Easy Air. Specifically, if Easy Air is able to increase the number of passengers flown by 8% due to improvements in its baggage-handling and on-time performance levels, it should buy new equipment. On the other hand, if it is unlikely that this increase in number of passengers will occur, then Easy Air should consider adding a baggage-handling fee even though ridership will drop off. It is a risky decision, but one that leaves it making more than $620.5 million more a year in profits without incurring any new costs for equipment.

Before completing an incremental analysis, therefore, we should test some of the assumptions that have been made to determine their impact on the final decision. This type of examination is called **sensitivity analysis,** *which looks at how small changes in assumptions change the outcomes predicted by incremental analysis*. In Table 5.10, we have changed the increased passenger load from 8% to 5% to see what happens to our preferred solution. Charging for baggage and buying the new equipment now looks like the best option open to Easy Air. If it is likely that the increased passenger load will be 8%, Easy Air should simply buy new equipment. If the increased load is more likely to be 5%, then both charging for checked bags and buying the new equipment looks like a better solution.

TABLE 5.10 SENSITIVITY ANALYSIS ASSUMING 5% INCREASED PASSENGER LOAD

Easy Air					
	Current situation (the "as is" alternative)	Outsource baggage handling	Buy new equipment	Charge for baggage handling	Charge for baggage handing and get new equipment
Estimated number of passengers flying	373,369,464	373,369,464	392,037,937	336,032,517	380,276,799
Incremental Revenue					
New baggage fees				$3,360,325,170	$3,802,767,988
New revenue from better service			$1,120,108,391		
Lost revenue from charging for baggage				$(2,240,216,801)	$(705,668,286)
Total incremental revenue	$-	$-	$1,120,108,391	$1,120,108,369	$3,097,099,701
Per passenger incremental revenue	$-	$-	$2.86	$3.33	$8.14

Easy Air					
	Current situation (the "as is" alternative)	Outsource baggage handling	Buy new equipment	Charge for baggage handling	Charge for baggage handing and get new equipment
Incremental Costs					
Outsourcing costs	$-	$606,725,378	$-	$-	$-
Depreciation of new equipment	$-	$-	$100,000,000	$-	$100,000,000
Cost of lost/damaged luggage	$181,781,230	$-	$36,356,246	$181,781,230	$36,356,246
Baggage-handling costs—as is	$317,800,800	$-	$254,240,640	$317,800,800	$254,240,640
Total incremental cost	$499,582,030	$606,725,378	$390,596,886	$499,582,030	$390,596,886
Per passenger incremental cost	$1.34	$1.63	$1.00	$1.49	$1.03
Total Net Estimated Baggage-Handling Revenue (Cost)	$(499,582,030)	$(606,725,378)	$729,511,505	$620,526,339	$2,706,502,815
Per passenger	$(1.34)	$(1.63)	$1.86	$1.85	$7.12

BALANCING OBJECTIVE AND SUBJECTIVE INFORMATION

Other nonfinancial considerations might also help Easy Air's management make this important decision. For instance, if Easy Air decides to outsource its baggage-handling activity, it will lose control over this activity and its costs. The company doing the outsourcing could raise its prices down the road, making outsourcing much less attractive financially. Since Easy Air would have sold off its equipment and eliminated the trained labor currently doing this work, it would be very costly for it to reverse the outsourcing decision. And the simple fact that Easy Air ends up letting go of some of its labor force in and of itself can create unexpected problems, affecting the morale and behavior of remaining employees. Add to this fact the likelihood that the outsource vendor may in reality be unable to effectively and efficiently do this activity for Easy Air, it could even potentially reduce the number of passengers that fly the airline or increase other costs in the company. In other words, we need to always consider the nonfinancial implications of an alternative before making a final decision. While the numbers are important, so is the level of business risk, control over performance, and other key nonquantitative issues. It seems that upgrading its equipment and retaining control over baggage handling is Easy Air's best long-term option.

Having completed the incremental analysis, let us formalize these conclusions for presentation to Fran by developing a business case.

USING INCREMENTAL ANALYSIS TO BUILD AN EFFECTIVE BUSINESS CASE

If you remember from Chapter 3, a business case is a decision support and planning tool that projects the likely financial results and other business consequences of an action.

How would this look for Easy Air's decision to change its baggage-handling approach? To find out, see Figure 5.15.

EASY AIR

Business Case for Changing Baggage-Handling Procedures

1. **Introduction**
    - *Subject:* Changes to baggage-handling procedures at Easy Air
    - *Purpose:* To improve financial and nonfinancial performance
    - *Situation and motivation:*
        - » *Objective*: To reduce the number of flights delayed due to baggage-handling problems, which will reduce the costs and increase the on-time performance metrics for the firm
        - » *Opportunities*: Improved baggage handling will both reduce station costs and lead to increases in the number of passengers who choose to fly Easy Air
        - » *Threats:* If Easy Air does not make these changes, it stands to lose passengers and/or face increased costs, which may push the company into bankruptcy. Also, current problems with on-time performance and mishandled baggage may provide competitors with an opening to convince passengers to switch to their airline.
        - » *Problems*: Making improvements will lead either to the need to increase the firm's asset base, further increasing its debt load and cash flow strain, or result in loss of control over this vital function.
        - » *Limitations*: The analysis focused on companywide issues rather than completing a station-by-station analysis. Also, financing impacts have not been factored into the numbers presented.
        - » *Constraints*: Time available to analyze problem, need to implement in short time period, limited access to competitive information.
2. **Methods and Assumptions**
    - The scope of the analysis is limited to current baggage-handling operations and methods at the existing stations in the Easy Air system.
    - Several metrics have been used, including incremental revenues and costs as well as the current on-time performance metrics.
    - The major assumptions are:
        - » That the current baggage-handling problem is one of the primary causes of current performance problems (as established during our Pareto analysis);
        - » That the primary causes of these problems are due to equipment shortages and failures;
        - » That the results of the analysis during the study period are representative of ongoing operational characteristics, and are not a onetime or isolated sequence of events;

    - » The linkage of improved baggage handling and on-time performance to financial results and the potential for increased numbers of passengers are correctly stated;
    - » That the options can be implemented in a brief period of time with minimal other costs or repercussions to the company.
- Five primary options were evaluated: buy new equipment, outsource baggage handling, charge for checked baggage, buy equipment and charge for checked baggage, and "do nothing," or the status quo.
- The case analysis and final recommendations utilize incremental revenues, costs, and analysis.
- The cost impact model uses benchmark and industry data to establish boundaries and assess the potential costs and benefits of the alternatives. The analysis uses economic results rather than solely emphasizing cash flow impacts.
- The benefits model estimates the impact of the proposed changes on current costs and potential passenger loads in the short and long term, using an economic rather than purely cash flow focus. The rationale for these benefits lies in the belief that as Easy Air improves its baggage-handling procedure, it will reduce the costs of delayed flights in the short term and in the long term become a more attractive travel option to the flying public.

3. **Business Impacts**
   - The results suggest that improvements in baggage handling due to buying new equipment will lead to a cost reduction of $109 million in one year of operations.
   - The dynamic analysis suggests that profits could be increased up to $2.71 million if the new equipment and baggage handling solution is taken and passenger load actually increases 5%.
   - Financial analysis: See Tables 5.9 and 5.10.
   - Inclusion of nonfinancial impacts: Several nonfinancial issues were deemed to be important, including the firm's control over one of its core activities, the potential for reliable long-term support from the proposed vendor, potential for price increases, passenger satisfaction and loyalty estimates, and the impact of the decision on employee morale and behavior. Each of these nonfinancial issues increases the risks and concerns associated with outsourcing the baggage-handling procedures and should be factored into all analyses of the issue.
4. **Sensitivity, Risks, and Contingencies**
   - Several critical assumptions drove the conclusions. First, we assumed that the increases in passenger loads will be between 5% and 8% of existing

loads if baggage handling is improved. Under a 5% increase, the solution to add baggage fees and buy new equipment becomes attractive. Second, we assumed that current average fare and average cost structures will remain fairly static in the short run. Third, we assumed that all of these changes will have a onetime impact that will be experienced within the first 12 to 18 months of the proposed change. Fourth, we assumed that the estimates and quotes received for the equipment upgrades and purchases are accurate.

- Risk analysis: The core team believes that the results presented here are highly likely to occur. Whether examined in terms of current loads (worst-case scenario; 10% chance of occurrence), a 5% increase (the most likely outcome, with a 50% chance of occurring), or 8% load increase (the optimistic projection, with a 40% likelihood), the results all point to the same conclusion: Baggage-handling procedures must be changed. The recommendation to purchase equipment is recommended under all of the scenarios, especially when nonfinancial issues are considered.
- Contingencies: While these changes will address current problems, it is important that the baggage-handling process be monitored more carefully, that additions to the amount of equipment available for baggage handling be evaluated periodically to ensure that problems are not recurring, and that these changes will improve on-time performance. In addition, the progress toward "best-in-class" baggage-handling costs should be monitored and further process changes instituted as appropriate.

5. **Conclusions and Recommendations**
   - The purpose of this analysis was to identify ways in which Easy Air can rapidly improve its financial performance. In light of this goal, and after a review of overall operations and a benchmarking study, it was determined that station costs had to be reduced. Through cause-and-effect and Pareto analysis, these objectives were linked to baggage-handling problems that were negatively impacting both on-time performance and station costs.
   - The business team recommends that Easy Air purchase additional baggage-handling equipment and screening devices immediately. This solution is the most likely to achieve the objective of increasing company profitability in the short and long term through cost reductions and revenue enhancements. It is also recommended that a comprehensive benchmarking study be conducted to identify other ways in which the baggage-handling process can be improved.
   - Optimizing the results of this suggestion requires a careful study of each station to determine its exact equipment needs, negotiations with the

baggage-screening equipment suppliers to find economical and efficient ways to upgrade or replace existing machines, and training to aid baggage handlers in operating the new equipment. In addition, new processes need to be designed to reduce bottlenecks and problems due to equipment placement, baggage-handling area design, and passenger baggage monitoring for size, shape, weight, and number.

FIGURE 5.15 BUSINESS CASE FOR CHANGE IN PROCEDURE

To develop the logic and structure of this business case, we apply the entire range of the management process "check and adjust" tools, from simple gap and trend analysis, through variance analysis, Pareto analysis, and cause-and-effect diagrams. Each tool helped us understand the problem in a slightly different way, ultimately helping us pinpoint a key problem area.

Having identified what we felt was the core problem, or major factor causing the performance shortfall at Easy Air, we then used incremental analysis to develop and analyze several alternative solutions to the baggage problem. With the development of recommendations for improvement and the completion of a business case that Fran can use to implement the changes in baggage handling, we completed the management process cycle at Easy Air. These changes will now become part of the ongoing structure and operations of the firm, providing the basis for future plans and future results.

Summary

The management process is the "Plan-Do-Check-Adjust" cycle that lies at the heart of organizational actions and results. During the planning stage, tools such as benchmarking, and strategic and historical analysis are used to develop a set of objectives for the organization or one of its primary processes or activities. Once defined, measures have to be developed for each of the major objectives. Measures, whether financial or nonfinancial in nature, help management communicate its objectives to the rest of the organization, as well as creating the basis for downstream evaluation and improvement of outcomes.

As action takes place, attention turns toward monitoring actual outcomes against the plan. Many tools can be used to complete this "check" activity, including gap analysis, trend analysis, RADAR charts, variance analysis, Pareto analysis, and cause-and-effect analysis. Each tool has different strengths and weaknesses. That means we should use more than one tool to explore results and identify trends and potential problems. Combining tools helps ensure that we fully understand, and document, current results vs. planned outcomes. There are many situations where we may want to use the tools in an iterative manner, looking deeper and deeper into performance opportunities or problems.

Seeking to avoid "analysis paralysis," we never want to lose sight of the fact that all of the analysis completed during the "check" activity in the management process has one primary goal—to trigger adjustments that will improve performance. In this last stage of the management process, we employ incremental analysis to gain a richer understanding of the subjective and objective issues involved, to identify alternative future courses of action, and to analyze and compare potential options so that a choice can be made among them. Once completed, the entire management process can be encapsulated in a formal business case, which then starts the cycle all over again.

Throughout this text, you will be using these tools and the logic of the management process to learn about the different issues, and challenges, facing modern organizations. Mastering these skills and tools will provide a solid basis for your own career and for planning, measuring, managing, and improving the performance of the organizations you come in contact with over time. We now turn our attention to applying our new knowledge within each of the primary decision domains.

Key Terms

Benchmarking: an external focus on internal activities, functions, or operations in order to achieve continuous improvement.

Best-in-class benchmarking: looks at the processes used by best practice firms regardless of industry to identify innovative paths for performance improvements.

Cause-and-effect analysis: visually analyzes the factors creating a performance shortfall.

Competitive benchmarking: emphasizes data on the performance of key firm competitors and the implications on the firm's performance.

Continuous improvement: a philosophy that advocates constant positive changes in a firm's performance as new goals are achieved.

Efficiency variance: the result of using more or less of a resource than planned.

Favorable variance: occurs when less is spent or used on a resource than is planned.

Gap analysis: visually or numerically identifies the differences between targeted and actual results.

Incremental analysis: the tool used to compare the current method of doing work and the changes that may occur if alternative courses of action are adopted.

Industry benchmarking: looks at key performance areas for the sector at large.

Internal benchmarking: the use of data from multiple internal locations to establish current best practice in the organization.

Pareto analysis: visually examines the various causes of missed targets or shortfalls in performance by comparing the total quantities or occurrences of one error or cause against others.

Plan: an estimate or projection of future outcomes.

Planning: the basis for action; it is the development of goals and objectives for performance.

Price variance: occurs when we spend more or less than planned on a resource or activity.

RADAR, or spider, charts: look at performance on multiple dimensions simultaneously.

Root cause: the primary reason for a performance shortfall.

Sensitivity analysis: looks at how small changes in assumptions change the outcomes predicted by incremental analysis.

Standard: a predefined, usually in quantitative terms, performance expectation.

Trend analysis: analyzes performance over multiple time periods, or observations, focusing on how results change during the period being studied.

Unfavorable variance: occurs when more is spent or used on a resource than planned.

Variance analysis: explores differences between a preset standard and actual performance by isolating one causal factor at a time.

Questions

1. What are the five basic problems the planning activity attempts to resolve?
2. What is a plan?
3. What does the term benchmarking mean and why is it used?
4. List the four different types of benchmarking and explain their differences.
5. Define a performance standard. What are the ways it can be established?
6. What is the continuous improvement philosophy?
7. Identify five tools that can be used to compare actual results to plan. What are the strengths and weaknesses of each?
8. In performing a variance analysis, what are the common dimensions used to isolate the causes for performance shortfalls?
9. What are the primary differences between a Pareto and a gap analysis?
10. What is the key difference between a favorable and unfavorable cost variance? Revenue variance?
11. What is incremental analysis and when do we use it?
12. What are the primary steps in doing an incremental analysis?
13. What role does subjective, or nonquantitative, information play in incremental analysis?
14. What is sensitivity analysis, and why is it used?
15. What are the primary features of a sound business case?

Exercises

1. **PARETO AND RADAR CHART ANALYSIS.** Westerly Cable offers a series of products such as cable television, telephone service, internet service, and an entire range of business products. Recently the company has been receiving a lot of complaints about its business service. Ron Harriman, the company's CEO, has asked his business analysis team to look at the reasons for the complaints. The following is the data it has collected.

Problem	# of Complaints
Slow download speed	125
Service drops	75
Slow customer service response	200
Telephone outages	100

REQUIRED:

a. Draw a Pareto chart of these problems.
b. Draw a RADAR chart of these problems.
c. Which chart is more informative?

2. **PARETO AND RADAR CHARTS.** William Blake runs a local taxi service. Lately his phone has been flooded with customer complaints. He gives you the following list of complaints.

Problem	# of Complaints
Late pickups	100
Dirty taxi	150
Poor attitude of driver	250
Driver took a roundabout route	125

REQUIRED:

a. Draw a Pareto chart of these problems.
b. Draw a RADAR chart of these problems.
c. Which chart is more informative?

3. **TREND ANALYSIS AND GAP ANALYSIS.** Susie Grace runs Grace Deli. She has set monthly sales goals for this year and is now trying to understand how well she is doing. The following table lists the goals by month and actual results.

	Goal	Actual
January	5,000	4,500
February	6,000	6,500
March	7,000	6,500
April	7,500	6,500

REQUIRED:

a. Do a gap analysis for each month.
b. Draw a trend analysis chart of these results.
c. Which approach to the data is more informative?

4. **TREND ANALYSIS AND GAP ANALYSIS.** Robert Treadwell runs a medium-sized machine shop. He sets monthly sales goals for his salespeople, who get bonuses for exceeding their sales goals. Robert uses these goals to help him manage his workforce and order materials. The results for the first four months of the year are contained in the following table.

Month	Sales Goal	Actual
September	$25,000	$28,000
October	$30,000	$32,000
November	$32,500	$35,000
December	$30,000	$33,000

REQUIRED:

a. Do a gap analysis for each month.
b. Draw a trend analysis chart of these results.
c. Which approach to the data is more informative?

5. **MATERIAL VARIANCE ANALYSIS.** Using the numbers in the following table for materials used in manufacturing, develop a variance analysis of price vs. efficiency (usage) variances for the two main materials in the product.

Material	Standard Quantity	Standard Price	Actual Quantity	Actual Price
Cotton	5,000 pounds	$0.25 per pound	4,800 pounds	$0.26 per pound
Thread	1,000 yards	$0.10 per yard	1,200 yards	$0.09 per yard

6. **MATERIAL VARIANCE ANALYSIS.** Using the numbers in the following table for materials used in manufacturing soap, develop a variance analysis of price vs. efficiency (usage) variances for the two main materials in the product.

Material	Standard Quantity	Standard Price	Actual Quantity	Actual Price
Soap base	10,000 pounds	$0.05 per pound	10,500 pounds	$0.045 per pound
Scent	50 pounds	$25.00 per pound	55 pounds	$26.00 per pound

7. **DIRECT LABOR VARIANCE ANALYSIS.** There are two labor departments in the following business. Their results for January are in the following table. Please develop a price vs. efficiency variance for each of these two departments.

Department	Standard Quantity	Standard Price	Actual Quantity	Actual Price
Grinding	6,000 hours	$15.00 per hour	6,500 hours	$14.00 per hour
Polishing	4,500 hours	$14.00 per hour	4,200 hours	$14.50 per hour

8. **DIRECT LABOR VARIANCE ANALYSIS.** There are two labor departments in the following business. Their results for September are in the following table. Please develop a price vs. efficiency variance for each of these two departments.

Department	Standard Quantity	Standard Price	Actual Quantity	Actual Price
Baking	5,000 hours	$18.00 per hour	4,750 hours	$19.00 per hour
Frosting	2,000 hours	$15.00 per hour	2,200 hours	$14.00 per hour

9. **MAKE VS. BUY INCREMENTAL ANALYSIS.** Tudor Associates currently makes its own parts for the microwaves it sells. It has recently been approached by a local machine shop that has offered to make the outer casing of the microwaves. The current cost to make the casing is $20, which consists of $12 in materials, $4 in labor, and $4 in overhead. The price offered by the local machine shop is $15. If Tudor takes the offer, it can eliminate its current materials and labor but only $1 of the overhead.

REQUIRED:

a. Analyze the current situation ("as is" is to make) vs. the offer from the local machine shop.
b. What should Tudor do? Why?

10. **MAKE VS. BUY INCREMENTAL ANALYSIS.** Excell Corporation makes thumb drives for use by consumers and businesses. Right now, Excell performs all of the operations for making the thumb drives. It has recently been approached by a memory manufacturer to supply the memory chips for the thumb drives. Current cost to make the memory chips is $1 per unit for a four-megabyte drive. Fifty percent of this cost is labor, and 50% machining cost (which includes labor and overhead). The offered price is $0.80 per chip. If the change is made, the machine currently used will be idled 75% of the current utilized time.

REQUIRED:

a. Analyze the current situation ("as is" is to make) vs. the offer from the memory chip manufacturer.
b. What should Excell do? Why?

11. **SELL "AS IS" OR PROCESS FURTHER INCREMENTAL ANALYSIS.** Yellowtail Manufacturing makes a product that is currently sold to health food stores. It recently has discovered it could sell its product, Real Yellow, at an earlier stage in its production to another manufacturer. Current costs to complete the Real Yellow product are $5 per pound. It sells for $6 per pound. It could sell Yellow Only when it is only 75% complete as to total costs for $4.25 per pound.

REQUIRED:

a. Should Yellowtail continue to make the product Real Yellow or sell it as Yellow Only?
b. Why or why not?

Problems

1. **PARETO, TREND, AND RADAR CHARTS.** Troyhill Manufacturing makes a variety of lawn products. It keeps track of problems that occur during the manufacturing process. The results of the tracking of number of occurrences for the company for the last three months are contained in the following table.

Problem	January	February	March
Paint chipping	100 units	125 units	110 units
Dented metalwork	50 units	40 units	75 units
Missing screws	150 units	160 units	180 units
Fabric tears	40 units	50 units	30 units

REQUIRED:

a. Perform a Pareto analysis for each of the three months of operation. Use only one graph and put all three months on this graph.
b. Perform a trend analysis for the list of problems noted here. Use only one graph and put all three months on this graph.
c. Develop a RADAR chart for each of the three months of operations. Use only one graph and put all three months on this graph.
d. Which approach is most helpful? Why?

2. **PARETO, TREND, AND RADAR CHARTS.** Magic, Inc., makes a number of magic tricks. Recently it has been experiencing problems in its manufacturing process, as the table below suggests:

Problem	April	May	June
Missing parts	500 units	450 units	400 units
Bad packaging	400 units	500 units	600 units
Duplicate parts	250 units	200 units	250 units
Missing instructions	300 units	350 units	500 units

REQUIRED:

a. Perform a Pareto analysis for each of the three months of operation. Use only one graph and put all three months on this graph.
b. Perform a trend analysis for the list of problems noted here. Use only one graph and put all three months on this graph.
c. Develop a RADAR chart for each of the three months of operations. Use only one graph and put all three months on this graph.
d. Which approach is most helpful? Why?

3. **CAUSE-AND-EFFECT DIAGRAMS.** Samson, Inc., is trying to understand the causes behind some ongoing problems it is having in making good kitchen cabinets for its customers. It decides to do a cause-and-effect diagram using four dimensions: man, machine, methods, and materials. It holds a brainstorming session with its line workers and gets the following set of problems identified.

Problems	Problems
Lack of training	Poor attitudes
Unclear instructions	Sloppy workplace
Machine out of specification	Scratched wood
Screws stripped	Machine breakdowns
Lack of skill at job	Wood splinters
No gloves available	Line moves too fast
Lack of supervision	Andon lights do not work
Glue too thin	Take too long on breaks
Machine scratches surface	Poor machine maintenance
Material delayed getting to line	Assembly sequence wrong
Too many small parts	Not enough screwdrivers
Paint too thick	Saw blade on machine dull

REQUIRED:

a. Sort all of these problems into which dimension of the diagram they affect (man, machine, methods, or materials).

b. Make a cause-and-effect diagram using your answer to part (a).
c. Where do the major problems appear to be?

4. **CAUSE-AND-EFFECT DIAGRAMS.** Hard Earth does plant maintenance for large industrial companies. It recently has faced a significant increase in customer complaints regarding the quality of its work. The company decides to pull its workforce together to identify where the problems are coming from. It decides to arrange the problems into one of four categories: man, methods, materials, and customer. Even though the customer is never wrong, they can make the job more complex. The following is the list of problems it identifies.

Problems	Problems
Cleansers are clumped	Workforce on the floor
Workers are lazy	No set procedures for tasks
Customers leave materials on floor	Run out of cleaning product
Lack of supervision	Poor attitudes
Too many jobs for one person	Not enough brooms
Cleansers leave stains	Lack of training
Customers leave parts in lavatory	Too much space to clean
No vacuums	Dusting spray is oily
Run out of toilet paper	Customers leave oil spills
No instructions for specific jobs	Lack of customer input
Too many smoking breaks	Not enough time to get work done
Poor scheduling	Cleansers have bad odor

REQUIRED:

a. Sort all of these problems into which dimension of the diagram they affect (man, methods, materials, or customer).
b. Make a cause-and-effect diagram using your answer to part (a).
c. Where do the major problems appear to be?

5. **VARIANCE ANALYSIS.** Blue Spruce Small Appliance Repair has well-defined time and material specifications for every type of job that comes into the shop. During April, while there was a lot of business, profitability was off. Gordon Andrews, manager of Blue Spruce, decides to do a variance analysis of the month's activities to determine what happened. The following table details the results of this study.

Measure	Materials	Labor
Actual quantity	2,150 parts	188 hours
Standard quantity	2,000 parts	168 hours
Actual price	$5.75	$20.00 per hour
Standard price	$5.00	$18.00 per hour

a. Complete a price and efficiency variance for the materials used by Blue Spruce.
b. Complete a price and efficiency variance for the labor used by Blue Spruce.
c. Where is the biggest problem? Why?

6. **VARIANCE ANALYSIS.** Hang Ten is a small manufacturer of fasteners used in the manufacturing of hang gliders. It is a competitive business, with only a few major customers and a lot of machine shops like Hang Ten competing for this specialized business. The company has improved its materials to improve it product offerings. In order to stay on top of things, management at Hang Ten runs a variance analysis every month to make sure it stays on target. The following table contains its results for September.

Measure	Materials	Labor
Actual quantity	1,500 pounds	4,000 hours
Standard quantity	1,600 pounds	3,600 hours
Actual price	$1.50 per pound	$15.00 per hour
Standard price	$1.45 per pound	$16.00 per hour

a. Complete a price and efficiency variance for the materials used by Hang Ten.
b. Complete a price and efficiency variance for the labor used by Hang Ten.
c. How well did Hang Ten perform? Why?

7. **MAKE VS. BUY INCREMENTAL ANALYSIS.** Bangor Industries makes staplers. It currently buys the parts that make up the casing of the stapler, only producing the internal mechanicals. It makes and sells 5,000,000 staplers per year. Recently, Tom Burns, manufacturing vice president, has been looking into the potential to make all of the parts that would go into the product. It currently pays $1.25 for the outer parts. The company could buy a used machine to make these parts for $24,000. The machine would have a four-year life. It would require four workers, paid $15 per hour to operate it for 2,000 hours per year. Materials would cost $1. Overhead would be 25% of labor.

REQUIRED:

a. Perform an incremental analysis of this opportunity for Bangor. Do the analysis in total dollars for the year under each alternative.
b. Should it make or continue to buy this part? Why?

---

8. **SELL "AS IS" OR PROCESS FURTHER INCREMENTAL ANALYSIS.** Gypsum Powders makes four compounds for dogs off of one raw material, Just Gyp—tick powder, flea powder, itch powder, and talcum powder. The company makes 200,000 pounds of Just Gyp per year. It has recently been approached by an outside customer who would like to buy the talcum powder before it has been fully processed. The company could also sell the other powders at an earlier stage of production. The volumes and prices for the various products if sold at the split-off point (when we go from raw material to four different products) vs. if processed further are included in the table below. If processed further, the company needs to add one half-pound of filler for every pound of product at a cost of $0.30 per pound. It also needs to package the product, which costs $0.20 in materials per quarter pound of Just Gyp material and $0.10 in labor per unit of finished product (one quarter-pound of the product with its filler). Hint: We add the filler so there is more final product in total pounds. One pound of Just Gyp makes 1.5 pounds of final product.

Product	Pounds Made	Cost per Pound at Split-Off Point	Price per Pound at Split-Off Point	Price per Pound if Processed Further
Tick Powder	100,000	$1.50	$2.00	$3.50
Flea Powder	50,000	$1.75	$2.50	$4.00
Itch Powder	40,000	$1.00	$1.50	$2.25
Talcum Powder	10,000	$0.50	$1.00	$2.00

REQUIRED:

a. Perform an incremental analysis of this opportunity for Gypsum Powders. Do the analysis in total dollars for the year under each alternative.
b. Should it make or continue to buy these products? Why?

---

9. **KEEP OR DROP A PRODUCT LINE INCREMENTAL ANALYSIS.** Hard Rock Company currently offers several lines of decorative stone. It takes the larger rocks and splits them down into smaller pieces that it then sells by the pound in both bags and in

bulk quantities. Recently, there has been a 25% increase in the cost of granite as more people put in granite countertops. Bob Neely, owner of Hard Rock, is considering dropping the granite line. Most people who buy bags of the rock only buy one type, so there should be no problem with this element of the product line. But bulk purchasers often need multiple types of stone and will go where they can get all of their stone in one stop. Bob estimates he will lose 20% of bulk sales if he drops the granite line.

If Hard Rock stops making granite stones, it will save the raw materials cost, packaging for bags, and the labor used for the bags. It will not get rid of any machines, however, as it still needs its productive capacity for other products. Any unused capacity of the machine will have to be added to overhead. It also will not be able to get rid of any overhead. The total prices and costs for the various products currently sold by Hard Rock are in the table below.

Hard Rock Company					
	Granite	Flint	Limestone	Blue Rock	Pea Gravel
Bag Sales Information per Pound					
Pounds Sold	50,000	25,000	40,000	60,000	30,000
Price per Pound	$5.00	$3.50	$4.00	$6.00	$4.50
Less Cost per Pound:					
Stone	$3.00	$2.00	$2.25	$3.25	$2.50
Bags	$0.05	$0.05	$0.05	$0.05	$0.05
Labor	$0.25	$0.20	$0.15	$0.25	$0.15
Machining	$0.75	$0.75	$0.75	$0.75	$0.75
Overhead	$0.50	$0.40	$0.30	$0.50	$0.30
Bulk Sales Information Per Pound					
Pounds Sold	100,000	50,000	80,000	150,000	75,000
Price per Pound	$4.50	$3.00	$3.50	$5.25	$4.00
Less Cost per Pound:					
Stone	$3.00	$2.00	$2.25	$3.25	$2.75
Labor	$0.15	$0.15	$0.15	$0.15	$0.15
Machining	$0.50	$0.50	$0.50	$0.50	$0.50
Overhead	$0.30	$0.30	$0.30	$0.30	$0.30

REQUIRED:

a. Calculate the total revenues, costs, and profits under the current operating conditions. How much money does the company currently make in total?

b. Now drop the granite line and recalculate all of your revenues, costs, and profits. What is total profit now? Be careful here. Remember bulk sales of other products will drop by 20%, but bag sales will be unaffected.

c. **Finally, calculate all of the revenues, costs, and profits if you keep the granite line and absorb the cost increases.**
d. **Which alternative looks the best to Hard Rock? Why?**

---

10. **BUY A NEW MACHINE OR REPAIR AN OLD ONE INCREMENTAL ANALYSIS.** Cedar Shakes, Inc., makes a variety of cedar siding materials for houses. It is facing a major problem with one of its key machines. Specifically, it will either have to overhaul the machine, at a cost of $1,000,000, which will give it five more years of life and reduce maintenance costs by 15%, or buy a new machine, which will cost $2,500,000 and operate for 10 years. The new machine would be more efficient, using two less labor workers at $30,000 per year. It would take up less space in the factory, although there is no use for this space right now. Finally, it would use 10% less electricity (currently $20,000 per year) and need 25% less maintenance (currently $50,000 per year). There will be no salvage for the old machine.

REQUIRED:

a. **Calculate the total costs per year to run the existing machine if it is overhauled.**
b. **Calculate the total costs per year faced if the existing machine is replaced.**
c. **What would you recommend to management? Why? Would there be any qualitative concerns you would have?**

Database Problems

For database templates, worksheets, and workbooks, go to MAdownloads.imanet.org

---

DB 5.1 INCREMENTAL ANALYSIS. Easy Air has decided to look at a couple of options for dealing with its late flight problem. While the number of solutions could be endless, it has narrowed it down to two: increase the turn time for flights or invest more money in flight operations.

If it increases the turn time, it will see a reduction of 3% in passenger load, so revenues will be down. At the same time, however, canceled flight costs will drop 30% and turn time costs will increase 25%, while new tickets issued will drop 5% and reservations costs will drop 3%.

If, instead, it decides to invest more in flight operations, it will see a 3% increase in passenger load, so revenues will go up as problems diminish. Flight operation costs, however, would go up 25%, while canceled flights will drop 25%. Turn times will drop by 5%, while new tickets issued costs will increase 3% and reservations will increase 4%.

You will need two data sheets to complete the incremental analysis on Template DB 5.1: Basic Driver Information for revenues and your solution to DB 4.2d for the activity information for the remainder of the problem. "New tickets issued" should include ticket counter and gate charges.

REQUIRED:

a. Using the two supporting worksheets, fill in the "as is" scenario column (column B) in your DB 5.1a-c template. The "as is" data is for 20x6. Note that the "profit" is actually just the difference between current revenues and the itemized costs that are affected by this problem.
b. Now, using the changes in assumptions noted above, fill in column C for the increased turn time. Since you have filled in the "as is" column, you can do the rest of your calculations directly on the worksheet.
c. Finally, using the assumptions for the flight operations alternative, fill in column D. Once again, use your "as is" column B as the basis for your calculations.
d. Turn in your completed worksheet.
e. What should Easy Air do? Why?

DB 5.2 PARETO AND SPIDER DIAGRAMS. The worksheet in workbook DB 5.2 named Basic Driver Information provides all of the raw data you will need for this exercise.

REQUIRED:

a. Do a three-year trend analysis of the four basic problems plaguing Easy Air: To complete this, first go to the template for Problem DB 5.2a and fill in the data for the four problems: number of canceled flights, number of ground/gate delays, number of customer complaints, and number of baggage claims. Having filled in the data grid, now select cells B2 through D6. With these cells highlighted, now go to the Insert tab. You will see a variety of charts you can choose from. Pick the chart you feel is most informative and insert it in your worksheet.
b. Now go to the template for DB 5.2b. Here we are going to do a spider diagram. Follow the same instructions for populating your data fields. Now click on Insert. You will see an option for more graphs. At the bottom of that list is RADAR charts. Choose one of the three options for your RADAR chart and insert it into your worksheet.
c. Now let us do a percentage change analysis of the four problems. Specifically, use 20x4 as our baseline year. Note that you go directly to the cells on your solution to (b) for this data. Fill in the same information in cell C3 using 20x5 less 20x4 as your calculation basis. Beware! You cannot click and drag these solution formulas because the cells are locked with $, so please fill each of

the eight cells separately. Once you have these percentages done, please make a bar chart of the results using the same instructions you used in (a) of this problem.

d. Turn in your worksheets, charts, and answers to the following two questions: Which chart is most useful? What do the results of your analysis suggest?

Cases

CASE 5.1 INCREMENTAL ANALYSIS. Bright Views is a window manufacturer. It produces high-quality windows in a variety of sizes, shapes, and colors. One of the leaders in its industry, Bright Views offers a lifetime warranty on its products. Recently, however, it has started to face increased competition for lower-end windows for the replacement business. Consumers, faced with having to replace all of their windows when problems occur, often choose a lower-quality window to save money on the job. While Bright Views does very well in the new building segment, which is 40% of the industry, it is losing share in the replacement window segment. This is a very negative situation for Bright Views because a downturn in the economy has new housing down while replacement window demand has been increasing.

The statistics for Bright Views' sales over the last three years are in the table below.

Category	20x6	20x5	20x4
New Housing Windows	27,800,000	20,600,000	13,400,000
Bright Views Market Share	60%	55%	50%
Replacement Window Sales	35,000,000	32,200,000	29,700,000
Bright Views Market Share	20%	25%	28%

The current average price of Bright Views per window is $500. Current manufacturing costs are 60% of the price. The average price in the marketplace for new windows ranges between $590 and $440. The replacement window market is much less expensive, with average price per window sitting at approximately $295 per window. Since Bright Views currently only offers one line of windows, its premium collection, its price in the replacement market is 69% above the average price for replacement windows offered by other firms. The toehold Bright Views has in the replacement market is it is known for high quality and a lifetime warranty. When faced with the higher price, however, customers often opt for less quality and a less robust warranty as they do not see themselves in the same home for more than five years.

Dan Swaim, the vice president of marketing, has pulled together a team of people to see if they can develop a lower-end product that will help the company gain share in the replacement window market. They do not want to lower the price on their premium windows as that might signal a reduction in quality. The following is the discussion that takes place at a team meeting.

Dan: Thank you all for being here. We have a tough job ahead of us. We need to design a new line of windows for Bright Views that continues to keep our reputation for quality in place but enables us to drop our prices by 25% to $375 per window. We don't need to compete with the lowest-priced windows, but we do need to get our prices down if we aren't going to be squeezed out of the replacement window business. That means we have to get costs down to $225 or less if we are to continue to hit our profit goals.

Pete Wilson, Manufacturing: With our existing workforce and plant, I simply don't see how we can make these goals. We'd need to start from scratch. That would mean $8,500,000 depreciation per year for a new factory, $20,000,000 in annual depreciation for new machines, and then we could hire workers for $15 per hour rather than the current $25 per hour. The new machines would also use less labor than our labor-intensive lines now, so we could make 10,000 windows per line worker vs. the current 5,000 windows per line worker. That means our labor costs would drop by 50% from the current 30% of total costs for the new windows. Overhead would increase, though, from 20% of cost to 35%. Big expense up front, though, one we can't avoid. And remember, we need to consider materials, which are normally 50% of the window.

Dan: Great information, Pete, but I need to see all of these numbers put together to make any sense of your details. If we can make these new windows well enough, we should be able to increase our market share in replacement windows by 50% in the first year. But we have to have quality or it could cause problems with our other sales.

Fran Daley, Personnel: I see it as more difficult to open up the new plant with new labor than Pete apparently does. I have another concern, too. What if someone decides to use the lower-quality replacement window for a new house? Couldn't that hurt the company's reputation?

Dan: I have to hope we could manage with Pete's recommendations, Fran. But the reputation issue is one that keeps popping up. The only other option I see is to lower our prices by 10% across the board. That will up our new housing market share by 10% and increase our replacement market share by 15%, but our costs won't change so we're directly hitting profit here.

Wendy Silvers, Finance: Dan, why don't I take all of these assumptions and put together an analysis of the differences if we do nothing, open a new plant, or simply lower prices? That should help us wade through the financial details so we can then focus attention on things like reputation effects and other qualitative concerns, like the impact on our workforce.

Dan: Sounds good, Wendy. Thanks. And would you do me a favor and add one more assumption to the new plant option? Let's assume that Fran has a point about the impact on new unit sales if we offer lower-priced windows. For now, assume we'll lose 10% of existing market sales of our premium line if we begin to offer lower-end products. Let's break for now and meet again in a week. In the meantime, put your thinking caps on to both look for other options and think through the qualitative concerns we need to keep in mind.

REQUIRED:

a. Using the information contained in the discussion, do an analysis of the "as is" situation, the differences that will occur if you open a new plant, and finally the impact of lowering prices. Be careful to include both new construction and replacement windows in all of your calculations as both markets are affected.
b. What should Bright Views do? Why?
c. What are the qualitative concerns you would voice to Bright Views' management team?

CASE 5.2 TREND, PARETO, AND RADAR CHARTS. Big Top Toys makes a variety of badminton and volleyball sets for people's home use. The company sells 100,000 badminton sets and 75,000 volleyball sets per year. The company just hired a new quality control manager, George Burns, who has decided to make a study of current performance and provide this information to top management. The data he has collected is in the following table.

Big Top Toys			
	20x6	20x5	20x4
Bent stakes	2,500	2,000	1,800
Missing stakes	2,000	2,500	3,000

Big Top Toys			
	20x6	20x5	20x4
Holes in net	4,000	3,000	2,200
Missing rackets	1,000	1,200	1,100
Missing balls	1,200	1,000	1,100
Missing shuttle cocks	2,000	2,500	2,700
Bent poles	3,000	3,500	3,800
Missing instructions	2,500	1,800	1,700

George decides to hold his first quality control team meeting. He arrives with the table above and starts the discussion.

George: Welcome, team. Time for us to get to work!

Frank, line supervisor: We aren't exactly working. We're sitting in a meeting, missing our production goals. This had better be important!

George: Just look at that table in front of you. Isn't that saying we need to start paying more attention to quality around here?

Julie, Finance: I see a lot of numbers here, but it's awfully hard to see any trends. It does look like we need to pay attention to the net production line, but outside of that, the rest is hard to understand from just the numbers.

George: Well, we could look at this in several different ways, I guess. I just thought this would do for a first pass, but I'm not getting that feeling from the faces in this room. Why don't we call this meeting earlier, and I'll take another look at the data and see if there is a better way for us to understand what is happening.

Frank: Good idea. I'll get back to making badminton sets.

REQUIRED:

a. Using the data in the chart, develop a Pareto, trend, and RADAR chart for the data.

b. What do the charts suggest? Is the message more or less clear than that contained in the numbers alone?
c. Now, using percent change in each error area, redo your Pareto, trend, and RADAR chart analysis. Use 20x4 as your base year.
d. Which chart is most informative now? Why?
e. What would be your recommendation to Big Top Toys? Why?

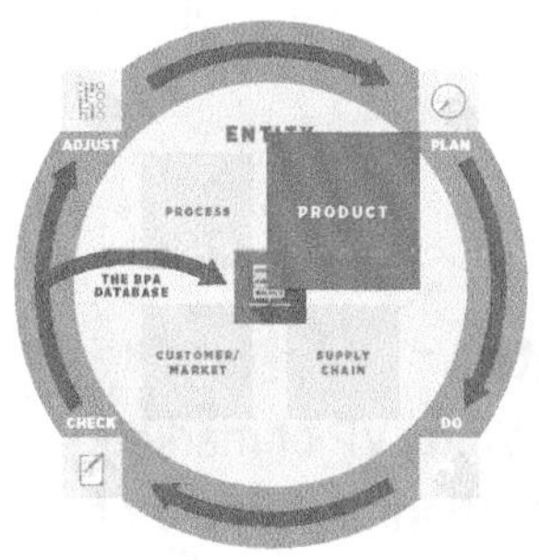

Planning in the Product Domain

Thinking always ahead, thinking always of trying to do more, brings a state of mind in which nothing seems impossible.

HENRY FORD

CHAPTER ROADMAP

1. **Target Costing: Planning in the Product Domain**
   - *Understanding and Using Target Costing*
   - *Achieving the Target Cost*
   - *Applying Target Costing*
   - *Committed vs. Incurred Product Costs*
2. **Organizing for Production**
   - *Job Shop*
   - *Process Manufacturing*
   - *Large Batch*
   - *Assembly Line*
   - *Cellular Manufacturing*
3. **Estimating Product Costs**
   - *What Is a Product Cost?*
4. **Estimating Overhead and Job Order Costs**
   - *Plant-Wide vs. Departmental Overhead Rates*
   - *Developing and Using Departmental Overhead Rates*
5. **Product Costing in Complex Settings**
   - *Conversion Costs in Machine-Paced Settings*
   - *Activity-Based Cost and Product Cost Estimates*

LEARNING OBJECTIVES

After studying this chapter, you should be able to:

1. **Describe target costing and how it is used in organizations.**
2. **Explain the major differences among job, process, large batch, manufacturing cell, and assembly line production.**
3. **Define the three components of a product cost estimate and identify the resource costs that make up the overhead pool of manufacturing and service companies.**
4. **Estimate product costs using a job order costing system and then develop and apply plant-wide vs. departmental overhead rates.**
5. **Calculate and compare product cost estimates in a complex setting.**

IN CONTEXT ➤ A New Product Idea at Kinkaid Cabinets

The week started off normally enough for Shelley White, VP of marketing at Kinkaid Cabinets. There had been a few meetings, a couple of calls from customers, then more meetings—the usual. All of that changed when Sam Perkins, the CEO, called her into his office. That was an hour ago.

Sam had decided that it was time for the company to "spread its wings." He wanted to expand the product line to include a full line of office furniture. His logic was simple—office furniture was just another type of cabinet. Since Kinkaid made great kitchen cabinets, it could make great office furniture. Currently, not all of Kinkaid's machines and processes were being utilized at 100% capacity. To Sam, adding a new line seemed a win-win solution.

Shelley did not disagree with Sam's logic, but she believed it was not going to be as easy to do as Sam seemed to think. Kinkaid had lots of data on what customers wanted in their kitchen cabinets, but she doubted someone buying a desk or modular office furniture would want the same features. Kinkaid made great kitchen cabinets, but would it really be possible to make office furniture along the same lines and with the same equipment? By the end of their meeting, Shelley's head was spinning as she considered the implications of this "simple" change.

Brad Andres was Kinkaid's resident "absent-minded professor"—always thinking through some engineering problem or product design challenge. He was so absorbed in his thoughts that he paid little attention to anything else, including where he was walking. When he collided with Shelley, he braced himself for the expected tongue-lashing. You can imagine his surprise when instead Shelley gave him a big smile and said, "You're just the person I was looking for!" Normally, Shelley was only glad to see him when she had something for him to do. So it was not a surprise when she said, "Brad, I'm so glad to see you. I just got out of a meeting with Sam. Your name came up more than once, I might add. He's really a big fan of yours! Do you have time to talk about one of Sam's ideas? In fact, let's go to lunch right now and talk it over. My treat! I won't take 'no' for an answer."

AN ORGANIZATION IS DEFINED AROUND THE PORTFOLIO OF PRODUCTS and/or services it provides to customers. These products and services are both the primary source of the firm's revenues and the primary driver of its costs. When you hear the name Nike, you probably think of athletic shoes. Hilton brings to mind fine hotels, while the name McDonald's creates images of cheeseburgers and french fries. Purdue is synonymous with chicken, and the name Morton is associated with salt. The list goes on and on.

The product domain, which includes both the physical products and the services offered by a company, is of critical importance to an organization. Successful management of the firm's product and service portfolio can mean economic prosperity. Mismanagement or poor decision making in the product domain can damage a firm's short- and long-term performance. Even large companies can teeter on the brink of disaster when problems occur in their core products. The Toyota automobile recalls of 2009 and 2010 for sudden unanticipated acceleration problems provide a vivid example of how product performance affects a firm. In this case, both the maker of the automobiles, Toyota, and the manufacturer of the company's floor mats, which sometimes caused the problem, experienced a major corporate fine: $1.2 billion. These financial problems fade in comparison with the toll taken in human terms, including multiple fatalities, by such product failures, and the damage done to Toyota's reputation.

Issues affecting the product domain make up the heart of management accounting practice. Whether the firm is focused on designing new products or services, or bringing the resulting products and services to market, management needs to have information on the affected resources and activities. Examples of this information include:

- The estimated cost, or resources, consumed in manufacturing one unit of the product.
- The performance requirements the product must meet (for example, sales volume, quality, and profitability).
- The costs and benefits of internal vs. external sourcing of key components and services.

Whether the decision is about today's products, or tomorrow's, the challenge is the same—how to meet customer requirements profitably.

In this chapter, we will examine the questions faced by a company that plans for and then produces specific products and services. Key topics include target cost management and the basics of developing a product cost estimate. Kinkaid Cabinets will play a major role in our discussion to help us understand key concepts and anchor your learning. We start by getting a better feel for the issues and challenges facing a firm in the product domain.

Target Costing: Planning in the Product Domain

OBJECTIVE 1

Describe target costing and how it is used in organizations.

One of the major challenges facing any organization is the need to understand what product or service features will create the most value for the maximum number of customers. When Apple creates a new model of its popular iPad, for instance, it starts by asking its customers, and potential customers, what features they would like in a new model, and why. For example, customers might value improvements to the iPad's ability to absorb "shocks" without causing damage to the hard drive or graphics card.

As Apple and other companies have learned, in the unending quest for customers' loyalty, and dollars, the value provided to customers sets an upper bound on the price that can be charged for the product. Clearly, the price the company earns from these efforts has to exceed the costs of producing and delivering the product or service if the firm is to be profitable. The ongoing trade-offs that are made between customer value creation and the need to make a profit are the focus of a key management accounting tool—target costing.

UNDERSTANDING AND USING TARGET COSTING

Target costing *is a market-driven management system in which cost targets, or objectives, are set based on defined customer requirements and an assessment of competitive offerings.*[1] It is used in the product domain during the strategic planning and development cycle. As Figure 6.1 illustrates, target costing is an iterative process that is linked to the firm's competitive strategy.

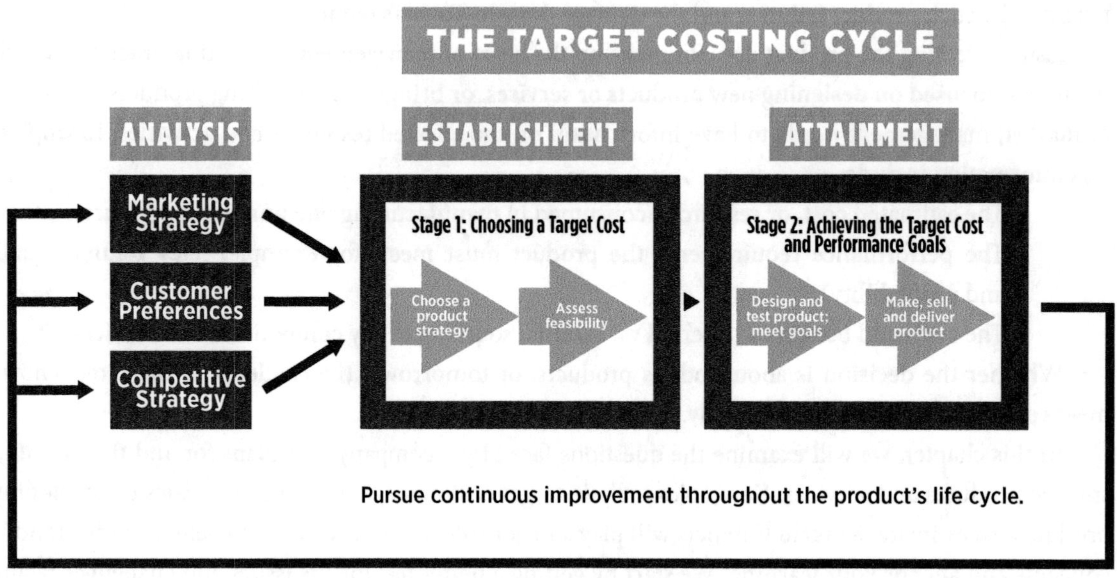

FIGURE 6.1 THE PHASES OF TARGET COSTING ARE REPEATED UNTIL KEY FEATURES ARE IDENTIFIED AND A MARKET PRICE FOR THE PRODUCT IS DETERMINED.

Setting the **target cost,** *the predefined maximum market price for a new product or service given customer preferences, the optimal price, and desired profit*, is the focus of the **establishment phase,** *the period in which the target cost and product features are set*, of target costing. Building upon market research that includes the analysis of competitors' products, examination of existing customer segments and their unique requirements, and identification of key product features, the company sets a market price for the product or service. Figure 6.2 illustrates the interrelationship among the target price, the company's desired profit, the target cost, and the factors that influence the analysis. As you will see, price is not based solely on the cost of the product. The market price is based, instead, on a combination of the customer's perception of the product's value, market competition, and the relative importance of the product to the customer.

---

1 Shahid L. Ansari, Jan E. Bell, and the CAM-I Target Cost Core Group, *Target Costing: The Next Frontier in Strategic Cost Management*, Chicago: Irwin Professional Publishing, 1997: p. 238.

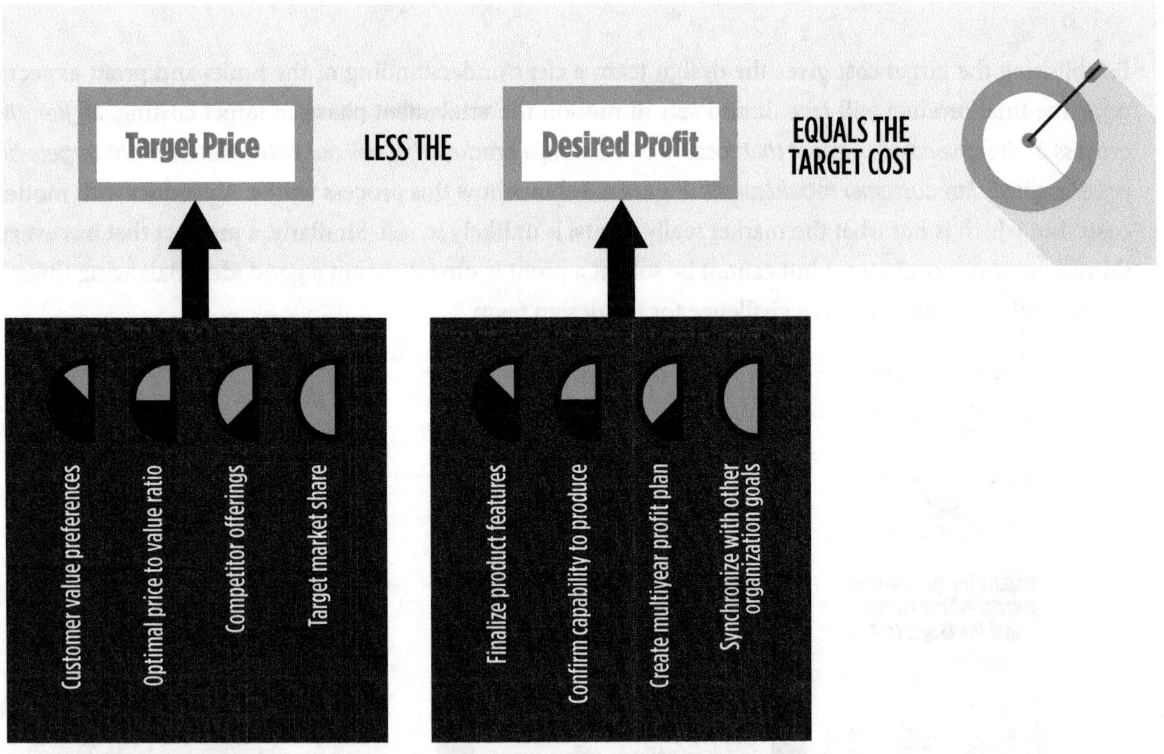

FIGURE 6.2 IN ESTABLISHING THE TARGET COST, A COMPANY MUST CONSIDER THE TARGET PRICE AND ITS DESIRED PROFIT, AS WELL AS THE FACTORS THAT GO INTO EACH.

There are no hard or set rules that you can use to identify the "right" price for a product. If there are similar products already on the market, choosing an optimal price can be relatively straightforward—set the price to match or better the market price of those products. If there really are not any comparable products, setting the price can be quite a challenge. Often a company will use customer focus groups to try to understand the price-to-value product features relationships.

At the end of the day, the goal of target costing's pricing analysis is simple: to set a price for the product that will maximize its profit potential. Once a price is established, attention turns to establishing a required profit level for the product. The profit target has to provide sufficient funds over the entire life of the product to ensure that the development and production costs are recouped and that the firm earns a reasonable return on its investment in the product.

Subtracting the desired profit from the chosen market price gives us the product's target cost. As we go through the design and development of the product, we constantly compare our current product cost estimate to the target cost to determine the amount of excess cost that we still need to remove through product or process simplification, material changes, or some other means. The driving objective is to reduce product costs by eliminating waste.

ACHIEVING THE TARGET COST

Establishing the target cost gives the design team a clear understanding of the limits and profit expectations the final product will face. It also sets in motion the **attainment phase** of target costing, *an iterative process of design and adjustment that focuses on creating a product that will not only meet its profit targets but will also satisfy key customer requirements*. Figure 6.3 shows how this process works. A product with modest costs, but which is not what the market really wants, is unlikely to sell. Similarly, a product that has everything a customer could want but cannot be sold at a profit is obviously not a good idea. Balancing these at times conflicting objectives is a challenge for the design team.

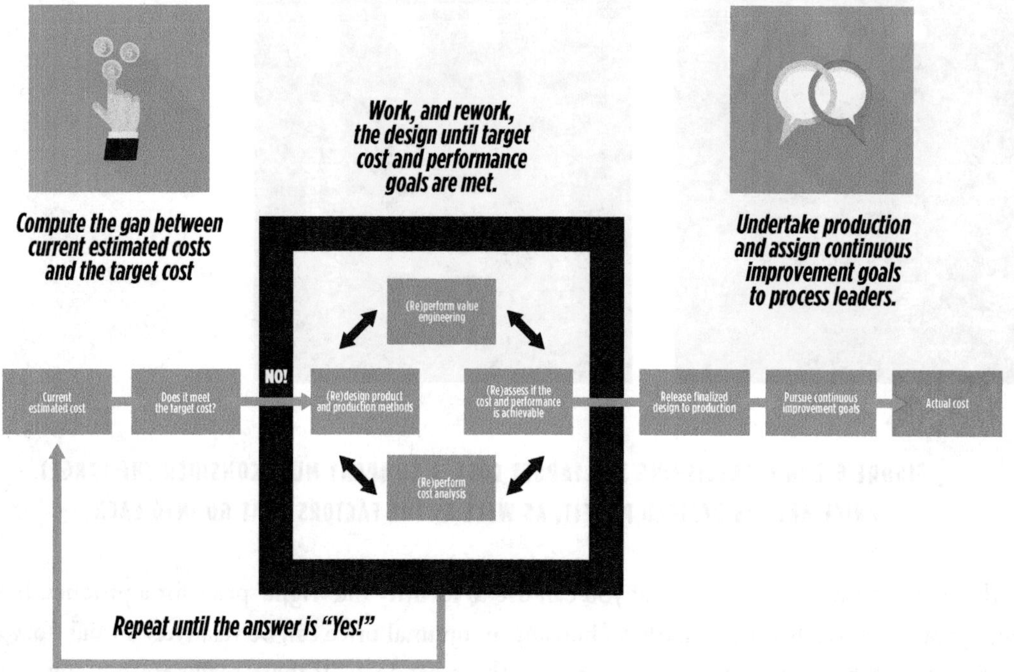

Work, and rework, the design until target cost and performance goals are met.
Compute the gap between current estimated costs and the target cost
Undertake production and assign continuous improvement goals to process leaders.
(Re)perform value engineering
NO!
Current estimated cost
Does it meet the target cost?
(Re)design product and production methods
(Re)assess if the cost and performance is achievable
Release finalized design to production
Pursue continuous improvement goals
Actual cost
(Re)perform cost analysis
Repeat until the answer is "Yes!"

FIGURE 6.3 THE GOAL OF THE ATTAINMENT PHASE OF TARGET COSTING IS TO GET THE DIFFERENCE BETWEEN ESTIMATED COST AND TARGET COST DOWN TO ZERO WHILE INCLUDING THE FEATURES THAT THE CUSTOMER WANTS.

As you can see from the figure, the attainment phase is comprised of three primary stages: 1) computing the cost gap; 2) designing the excess costs out; and 3) production. The **cost gap** *is the difference between the current estimated cost and the target cost of a product or service*. The goal is to drive this gap as close to zero as possible without compromising on the features that the customer wants. This objective is achieved through **value engineering,** *the technique used to analyze the various parts of a product to determine how to provide their function at the lowest possible cost*. Equally important during value engineering is the need to ensure that these cost targets are met with no reduction in basic product performance, reliability, maintainability, quality, safety, or usability of the product.

We will visit most of the issues faced during the attainment phase of target costing in Chapter 7. In this chapter, we will emphasize the establishment phase.

APPLYING TARGET COSTING

To see how we apply the target costing technique, let us take a simple example. The company Green Acres offers a full line of residential lawn equipment. It has decided to add a new product to its lawn care line, Perfect Trim, a lawn edging and trimming device. A review of the market yields the competitive information described in Table 6.1.

TABLE 6.1 COMPETITIVE ANALYSIS

Green Acres			
Company	Competing Product	Price	Estimated Units Sold in 20x6
Randall Lawn Products	Mighty Trim	$250.00	200,000
Best Corporation	Best Trimmer	$225.00	350,000
LawnMasters	Trim and Go	$175.00	175,000

Obviously, there is an upper limit to how much Green Acres can charge for its new product. Looking at sheer volume, it seems that Best Corporation offers a good product at a price that appeals to many customers. The mid-price trimmer market, currently dominated by Best Corporation, fits well with Green Acres' existing corporate price and product strategies. To take sales away from Best Corporation, the proposed new product will have to match or exceed Best Trimmer's features and have a retail price between $175 and $250. Since the average retail markup is 100%, Green Acres must be able to sell the product for between $87.50 and $125 to hit the targeted retail market price. Green Acres management decides on a wholesale target price of $100 for Perfect Trim.

Green Acres management wants to earn a 25% profit on the product in order to recoup its development costs and meet its corporate profit goals. The resulting target cost for Perfect Trim under these assumptions is:

Target price	$ 100.00
Less desired 25% profit	25.00
Target cost	$ 75.00

The design team has to find a way to bring the unit product costs in under $75 before top management will allow the product launch to proceed.

TABLE 6.2 ESTIMATED MANUFACTURED COST—CURRENT

Green Acres			
Part	Quantity Used	Manufactured Cost per Part	Total Cost
Motor	1	$ 35.00	$ 35.00
Motor housing	1	$ 10.00	$ 10.00
Trimming heads	2	$ 12.50	$ 25.00
Starter	1	$ 17.50	$ 17.50
Handles	2	$ 4.25	$ 8.50
Total Estimated Cost			$ 96.00

Table 6.2 summarizes the design team's initial estimate of the costs to make a Perfect Trim unit using its existing technology, suppliers, and design methods. As you can see, the initial design exceeds the target cost by $21. This is the current cost gap.

Current cost	$ 96.00
Less target cost	75.00
Excess cost (cost gap)	$ 21.00

In other words, for the Perfect Trim product to go forward, the design team has to find a way to eliminate $21 of excess cost. If it does not, the profit per unit sold will be only $4, far below the required profit goal set by top management.

The first decision the design team makes is to limit the trimming heads to one per unit, which removes $12.50 of cost. That still leaves $8.50 ($21 excess cost less $12.50) of excess cost. Purchasing pitches in some ideas, identifying a different supplier for the starter. This supplier will provide a comparable unit for $15 or a $2.50 cost reduction.

Progress is being made, but the design team still has $6 to eliminate. The team decides to redesign the handle and motor housing, substituting an advanced polymer that is both stronger and lighter than the original metal parts. The polymer is also available in a range of colors and textures, which is a plus. The new polymer also improves the product's value to customers, who complain about Best Trimmer's weight and the tendency for its paint to peel after several years of use. Had it not been for the need to hit the target cost, it is likely that the Green Acres design team might never have tried the new polymer. One of the major benefits of the discipline of target costing is that it forces a company to find new solutions to old problems. This final change reduces the combined costs of these two components by $6. Table 6.3 summarizes the results of these changes.

TABLE 6.3 COST ESTIMATES—REVISED

Green Acres			
Part	Original Cost	Revised Cost	Net Change
Motor	$ 35.00	$ 35.00	$ - 0 -
Motor housing	$ 10.00	$ 6.00	($ 4.00)
Trimming heads	$ 25.00	$ 12.50	($ 12.50)
Starter	$ 17.50	$ 15.00	($ 2.50)
Handles	$ 8.50	$ 6.50	($ 2.00)
Total Estimated Cost	$ 96.00	$ 75.00	$ (21.00)

Clearly, it may not always be this easy to hit the target cost, but the goal is to close the cost gap as much as possible without impairing the value of the product in the customer's eyes.

COMMITTED VS. INCURRED PRODUCT COSTS

The decisions that are made during the design process affect the product over the entire period of time it is sold, or its **life cycle,** *the entire period that a product exists, from its inception to final disposal*. In the traditional marketing literature, this life cycle is defined around changes in the product's sales pattern as it goes from introduction to growth, then on to maturity and eventual decline. The longer a product is available in the market, the greater the chance that competitors will offer a similar, maybe even better, product. More competition forces prices downward. At a certain point, the market becomes saturated—most potential customers already have the product. Demand drops off, sales volumes decrease, and the product begins its slow descent into obscurity.

While the sales of a product follow this general pattern, **committed product costs,** *expenditures driven by the constraints of the product design and the processes used to produce it*, are incurred before any production of the item takes place. In other words, the features, materials, and production methods the design team chooses lock in the downstream costs and the performance of the product. For instance, when the design team at Kinkaid chooses the materials, methods, and overall look of the new office furniture line, they will be defining the minimum total and per-unit costs for the products in the line. While few of these are **incurred costs,** *actual expenditures on resources used during the design or production of a product or service*, almost all of these downstream costs are committed to once the design is chosen. How committed and incurred costs compare with one another is illustrated in Figure 6.4. The two costs meet at the point where the product is fully developed.

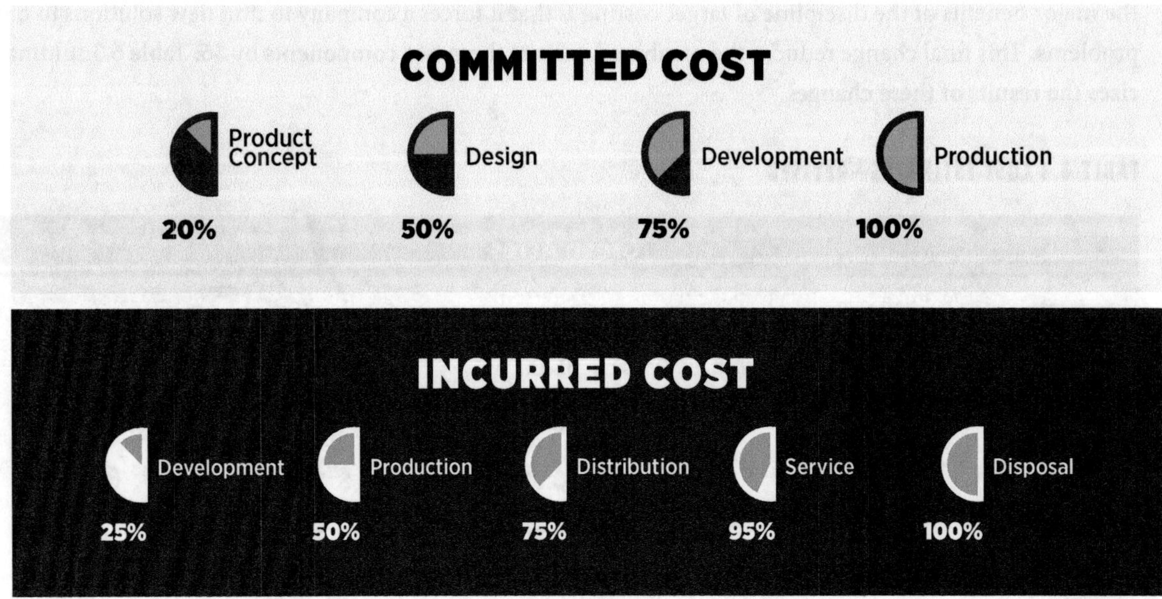

FIGURE 6.4 COMMITTED COSTS BUILD FROM PRODUCT CONCEPT THROUGH PRODUCTION, WHILE INCURRED COSTS BUILD FROM DEVELOPMENT TO DISPOSAL.

For example, had the original Perfect Trim design with a metal motor housing and handles gone through, and the equipment and processes needed to make these parts been purchased, changing to the new polymer material would have been very expensive. But it was relatively easy to make the change since the design team made the decision early in the design process, long before any manufacturing equipment was purchased. The moral of the story is simply this: If a company wants to make sure it makes a profit on a product, it has to build this profit in, not try to recoup it after the product has been put into production.

When we think about creating a cost estimate for a product or service, we have to make sure that all of the costs that the product causes are included in our estimates, from the moment the product is conceived until it is abandoned. This is known as a product's **life cycle costs**, *the total costs incurred to support a product or product line from its initial conceptualization and research through production and downstream maintenance once it is in the customer's hands*. We also need to understand how our production processes affect our ability to estimate these costs, a topic we take up next.

As you can see, the challenges in the product domain begin the moment a product or service is envisioned by an individual or company. They continue on through the entire **product life cycle,** *the entire period that a product exists, from its inception to its final disposal*. It begins with product development, to production, and on to the final abandonment of the product by the firm.

Target costing is an essential element of planning in the product domain. It is used to establish performance goals for a new product or service (the establishment phase) as well as to create the action plans required to attain these objectives (the attainment phase). Driven by a keen knowledge of customer expectations and requirements, effective target costing creates the discipline needed to meet these needs profitably.

Organizing for Production

When we organize work, we are trying to find the most efficient and cost-effective way to arrange and use available activities and resources. Manufacturing and service firms organize production flows in five main ways: 1) as a job shop; 2) as process, or constant flow; 3) in large batches; 4) as a manufacturing cell, or cellular; or 5) as an assembly line. The main differences among these five settings are summarized in Table 6.4.

OBJECTIVE 2

Explain the major differences among job, process, large batch, manufacturing cell, and assembly line production.

TABLE 6.4 TYPES OF MANUFACTURING SETTINGS

	Job Shop	Process/ Constant Flow	Large Batch	Assembly Line	Manufacturing Cell
Nature of product	Discrete units	Hard to distinguish units	Discrete units	Discrete units	Discrete units
Size of run	One unit or a small batch	Large batch or continuous flow	Large batch	"Batches of one"	"Batches of one"
Frequency of manufacture	Once or infrequently	Continuously	Repetitively	Continuously	Regularly
Key organizing feature	Job	Time period	Batch	Unit made	Level-loaded demand
Main costing elements	Materials, labor, and a "fair share" of overhead	Materials and conversion	Materials conversion activities	Materials conversion activities	Materials conversion activities

JOB SHOP

A couple of examples may help put these settings in perspective. We use the term **job shop** to describe *a manufacturing setting where every order is uniquely made for a specific customer*. You have seen how jobs are costed in earlier chapters. Many of the products and services you use are made in a "job shop" manner, including professional services (for example, lawyers and accountants), construction projects (such as your family home), and personal services (for instance, your hairstylist). When you call and order a pizza, personnel in the pizza shop make it specifically for you, with your choice of toppings. To the pizza shop, your pizza is a "job" to be done.

PROCESS MANUFACTURING

Process manufacturing *is a setting where a continuous flow of a consistent (indistinguishable) output makes it difficult to attach resource costs to specific units or batches.* It covers a range of products, from oil to steel to paper to various chemicals, that are produced in continuous flows. Normally operating 24 hours a day, seven days a week, these industries are defined by high fixed asset costs, including large, complex machines and buildings. Another common feature of many process settings is that they use one raw material that is then broken down into multiple unique end products. For instance, one barrel of crude oil will yield a blend of final products, including fuel oil, kerosene, gasoline, and diesel fuel. When we have both shared materials and shared processes, estimating costs becomes very difficult.

Process production settings can be quite complex. Even estimating the number of units made by a process can be difficult at times. Because of these challenges, we will not spend any more time on product costing for process manufacturing in the main part of this chapter. We will leave process costing to the chapter's appendix.

LARGE BATCH

When you purchase a frozen pizza at the supermarket, you must choose from a limited number of options. If you like anchovies on your pizza, for example, you will probably be out of luck. A company that makes frozen pizzas makes them in large batches, in the same way, using the same common set of ingredients, over and over again. A **large batch** *is a manufacturing setting, where a group of like products are made at the same time*. It is quite likely that this entire pizza-making process is done automatically, using one or more large machines. The company schedules a new production run of pepperoni, supreme, or cheese pizzas, for instance, whenever they are needed to fill specific orders from its customers—food distributors and grocery stores. Frozen pizza is made in a large batch manufacturing setting. Most of the products that we purchase in retail stores are made in large batches.

ASSEMBLY LINE

To understand the next setting, we have to move beyond the simple world of pizza. Let us think instead about automobiles. Henry Ford invented the **assembly line method**—*a manufacturing setting that links production activities into an uninterrupted flow*—in the early 1900s. The Ford Motor Company grew out of this invention. Ford wanted to create a car that every family could own. His first automobile, the Model T, was available in one style and only one color—black. By making all of the cars exactly the same, using interchangeable parts, Ford was able to develop a standard sequence of steps to assemble the automobile. He then devised a means of moving the automobile down a fixed line, with workers every few feet performing the next task required to assemble the automobile. Ford's innovations combined to create a highly efficient, effective manufacturing system that is still in use today.

LOOKING BACK ➤ Streamlining the Manufacturing Process

"Take just one idea—a little idea in itself—an idea that any one might have had, but which fell to me to develop—that of making a small, strong, simple automobile, to make it cheaply, and to pay high wages in its making. On October 1, 1908, we made the first of our present type of small cars. On June 4, 1924, we made the ten millionth. Now, in 1926, we are in our thirteenth million....

Henry Ford, *Today and Tomorrow*, 1926

Henry Ford was an eccentric but brilliant engineer who built a company (Ford Motor Company) and an industry. Demanding of himself and others, he constantly sought new ways to decrease cost and time from the manufacturing process. By the early 1920s, he was able to produce a car in three days—starting with raw metal ore, raw rubber, leather, flax (for linen), and sand (for glass). No modern automobile manufacturer has ever been able to match Ford's efficiency or speed of manufacture.

Despite these accomplishments, Ford was known to say that he had made a major mistake when building the River Rouge facility in Michigan by putting it on the wrong side of Lake Erie. Iron ore, one of his major raw materials, had to be mined and then shipped across the lake, which created delays and uncertainty, which, in turn, led to waste and reduced the number of cars he could produce. Despite this error, the River Rouge facility is still in production today. Ford did not make the same mistake when he built his second plant in the Twin Cities area of Minnesota.

To quote Ford, "It is not possible to repeat too often that waste is not something which comes after the fact...Progress is not marked by a definite boundary across which we step, but by an attitude and an atmosphere."

Ford would have been the last person to think that the systems he developed in 1908 would be the right ones to use in the 21st Century. In the early 1950s, Eiji Toyoda, of Toyota Motor Company, used Ford's own logic to create a new approach to manufacturing that would allow an automobile plant to achieve the efficiency and effectiveness of Ford's River Rouge plant with one major difference—customers could have the variety they wanted at a price they were willing to pay. Standardization of the product had made it possible for Ford to design a highly effective, efficient manufacturing system. The problem was, consumers wanted to be able to make choices about their cars—they wanted variety as well as low prices.

Toyota determined that the primary waste that variety created was the cost of changing over from manufacturing one product to another. If the time, effort, and cost of changing over could be minimized, a production process could accommodate a large variety of colors and options with minimal cost. Toyota has used this logic to design its manufacturing plants since the early 1970s[2]. Toyota's major U.S. plant in Kentucky completes a Camry every 30 seconds—that is how long it takes a paint gun to flush and get ready to paint a new color. That fact by itself might not be overly impressive, until we factor in that a two-door model in white could be followed by a four-door model in green, and so on. The plant can absorb significant variety in terms of model, options, and colors with no loss of productivity or quality. That would likely impress even Henry Ford.

CELLULAR MANUFACTURING

Not every company needs to have a large assembly line to benefit from the methods developed by Ford and refined by Toyota. In fact, companies such as Motorola, Hewlett-Packard, and Dell have used these methods and logic to create an alternative to traditional repetitive production methods—**cellular manufacturing,** *a setting that uses commonality of parts and methods to support efficient and effective production of assembled products in a "virtual" batch size of one*. In cellular manufacturing, the machines and activities needed to complete a product, such as a computer, are arranged in sequence. This reflects Ford's assembly line methods. The cells, however, are small, self-contained systems able to make any product that uses approximately the same sequence of steps, regardless of its size (within limits), color, model, or advanced features.

Variety is absorbed in cellular manufacturing by designing products around modular parts that have the same relative shape and connections, and require the same production methods, but that have different levels of capability—Ford's interchangeable parts concept. Making changeovers from one model to another takes mere seconds. The production flow is not interrupted—one of the workers in the cell simply rolls out the cart with the materials from the product currently being made and rolls in the components for the new model. Interchangeability, redefined around shape, fit, assembly methods, and flow, is exploited to reduce the cost of design, production, service, and support. Each of these manufacturing approaches brings with it costing challenges. Since the job shop setting is the simplest of all these manufacturing settings, it is a good place to learn about the basics of product cost estimating.

Estimating Product Costs

OBJECTIVE 3

Define the three components of a product cost estimate and identify the resource costs that make up the overhead pool of manufacturing and service companies.

An integral part of target costing and of product management in general is the development of cost estimates. Organizations use these cost estimates in many different ways, including as a means to place a value on inventory, estimate product line and company profits, assess the desirability of new or special customer orders, and develop estimates of future company performance.

2 H. Thomas Johnson and Anders Broms, *Profit Beyond Measure*, New York: The Free Press, 2000: p. 16.

As we found out in Chapter 3, there are many different ways to develop cost estimates. To develop an accurate product cost estimate, we need to concern ourselves with several issues. For instance, how the company organizes its work impacts the resources it needs, specifically the nature of the consumption of these resources during the production of a product or service. The organization of work, in fact, creates many of the long-term committed costs for a product. It is a fact we need to keep constantly in mind as we learn about the various ways that costs can be estimated and changed.

WHAT IS A PRODUCT COST?

Developing an estimate of the resources used, or cost, of a product or service is one of an organization's major management accounting activities. When we estimate a product cost, we are trying to assign the use of specific resources to one unit of output. As we learned in Chapter 3, many of these resources are actually shared by a number of different cost objects. That means that we can never come up with the exactly right, or "true," cost—only better or worse cost estimates. If that is the case, how do we build these estimates?

Material, labor, and overhead are the three main components of a traditional product costing system. These are the costs that must be included in the product cost estimate that we use for valuing inventory and estimating the cost of goods sold by a company, no matter how it organizes its work. As we saw previously, in a job shop, each specific job is unique. That makes it relatively straightforward to estimate the materials and labor that a job uses—they can be directly assigned to it. **Job order costing** *is the method we use to assign specific resource costs—material, labor, and overhead—to a specific job.*

Many different resources, however, are shared by all of the jobs done by the company. For instance, every job made in the building that the company occupies benefits from this resource—its capability is shared by many jobs. The challenges we face in creating cost estimates in job shop settings stem from the wide variety of shared resources, which we call **overhead,** *the sum of all of a company's shared and indirect costs of production.*

To help you understand these concepts, let us look to a pizza shop—Giovanni's Pizza Pie Shop. You have just called up and ordered a large pie with sausage, mushrooms, and green peppers. Table 6.5 summarizes the materials your order uses.

TABLE 6.5 CALCULATING DIRECT PRODUCT COSTS

Giovanni's Pizza Pie Shop			
Resource	**Amount Used**	**Cost per Unit**	**Cost to Customer**
Pizza dough	4 oz.	$2.00 per pound	$ 0.50
Tomato sauce	½ cup	$0.50 per cup	$ 0.25
Sausage	4 oz.	$6.00 per pound	$ 1.50
Mushrooms	3 oz.	$2.40 per pound	$ 0.45
Green peppers	3 oz.	$0.80 per pound	$ 0.15
Pizza box	1	$0.15 per box	$ 0.15
Total Materials			$ 3.00

Labor is another key part of a product cost. Giovanni pays his pizza maker $15 per hour. It takes five minutes to put your pizza together, so the labor cost that can be directly traced to your pizza is:

Labor cost per hour **$ 15.00**

So,

Labor cost for your pizza: 5 minutes x ($15.00 / 60 minutes), or $1.25

This makes the total direct costs of making your pizza $4.25: $3 cost of materials and $1.25 cost of labor. These are called **direct product costs** because *the economic value of a resource can be traced to one specific unit or batch of a product*—your pizza.

These are not the only resources your pizza benefits from, however. For instance, the ingredients for your pizza were ordered by Giovanni, who used a phone and paid for them with a check that was processed by a local bank that charges Giovanni for its services. The pizza was made on a counter, and then cooked in an oven, which sits in the building that Giovanni rents from Ben Sayers. The total of the cost of these various resources for an average year are shown in Table 6.6.

TABLE 6.6 INDIRECT COSTS—OVERHEAD

Giovanni's Pizza Pie Shop	
Resource	**Cost**
Pizza oven depreciation	$8,500.00
Counter depreciation	$3,250.00
Kitchen staff	$18,400.00
Delivery boy	$3,600.00
Pizza pans and supplies	$4,500.00
Taxes and insurance	$3,100.00
Electricity	$5,700.00
Telephone	$2,400.00
Other utilities	$2,800.00
Office equipment depreciation	$1,600.00
Rent	$18,000.00
Bank fees	$150.00
Total annual overhead costs	$72,000

These are all **indirect costs** that go into making your specific pizza. They are part of the overhead, the general costs, of being in the pizza business. Table 6.7 summarizes the various types of overhead costs in job shop settings.

TABLE 6.7 TYPICAL OVERHEAD COSTS

Production-based overhead	Selling, general, and administrative overhead
Building depreciation	Management and clerical salaries
Supervisors	Information systems
Material handling	Desks and equipment
Electricity and other utilities	Office space
Indirect materials	Utilities
Indirect labor	Memberships and fees
Insurance	Legal expenses
Security guards	Accounting costs, such as audits
Cleaning crews	Travel
Taxes paid on the building	Human resources

Estimating Overhead and Job Order Costs

OBJECTIVE 4

Estimate product costs using a job order costing system and then develop and apply plant-wide vs. departmental overhead rates.

If Giovanni does not include some portion of the indirect costs of doing business in his estimate of what it costs him to make your pizza, he may not make enough money to stay in business, let alone pay the mortgage on his own house. Therefore, these costs have to in some way be factored into the price Giovanni charges you. The question is: How?

To associate these costs with a specific pizza, Giovanni has to find a **cost driver,** *the thing that causes the cost*. In other words, he needs to find a measurable, identifiable event that happens with every pizza made, one that can be easily tracked and calculated. What driver options are open to Giovanni? Clearly, the chosen driver should be easy to measure and logically tied to making a pizza. Table 6.8 summarizes these options, which include the number of pizzas made, direct labor hours, direct labor dollars, total material dollars, and **prime cost,** *the total materials and direct labor expenditures traceable to a specific job or batch*. Since prime cost remains the same for a product regardless of volume made, it is a useful number to use in cost estimating. When we look at various overhead charging approaches, prime cost plus the resulting overhead charge is the total cost.

TABLE 6.8 CREATING DIFFERENT OVERHEAD RATES

Giovanni's Pizza Pie Shop		
(1) Cost Driver	(2) Average Annual Amount	(3) Overhead Cost Estimate ($72,000 / by column 2)
Pizzas made	50,000	$1.44 per pizza
Direct labor hours	4,000	$18.00 per direct labor hour
Direct labor dollars	$ 60,000	$1.20 per direct labor dollar
Direct material dollars	$ 180,000	$0.40 per material dollar
Total prime costs	$ 240,000	$0.30 per dollar of prime cost

To understand how we use these rates to attach costs to a specific pizza ordered from Giovanni, let us choose one option: labor hours. To calculate the amount of overhead to charge to the sausage, mushroom, and green pepper pizza using the direct labor driver, take:

Overhead rate (cost per direct labor hour)	**$18.00**
Direct labor time needed to make pizza	**5 minutes**

We can use this information to figure out how much overhead to charge to a single pizza:

Overhead charged to pizza:		
($18.00 / 60 minutes)	**x 5 minutes**	**or $ 1.50**

Using this overhead charging rate and the direct costs calculated above, we can now calculate the total estimated cost of our sample pizza:

Direct materials	$3.00
Direct labor	1.25
Overhead	1.50
Total estimated cost	$5.75

Therefore, if Giovanni charges more than $5.75 for the pizza, he should make a profit.

Whichever overhead rate you use, you will accomplish the same goal—attaching some fair share of the overhead costs to the pizzas Giovanni makes. However, the results derived would result in different costs for our pizza. To better understand this concept, we will now estimate the overhead charged to our pizza using each of the overhead options available to us. These overhead costs are listed in Table 6.9. As you can see, the amount of overhead charged to the pizza varies depending on which option you choose.

TABLE 6.9 CHARGING OVERHEAD TO A PRODUCT USING DIFFERENT OVERHEAD RATES

Giovanni's Pizza Pie Shop			
Overhead Charging Option	(1) Overhead Rate	(2) Amount Used by One Pizza	(1) x (2) = (3) Overhead Charged to Pizza
Pizzas made	$1.44 per pizza	1	$1.44
Direct labor hours	$0.30 per direct labor minute	5 minutes	$1.50
Direct labor dollars	$1.20 per direct labor dollar	$1.25	$1.50
Material dollars	$0.40 per material dollar	$3.00	$1.20
Total prime costs	$0.30 per prime cost dollar	$4.25	$1.275

As you can see from Table 6.10, each overhead rate gives us a slightly different product cost estimate for each pizza. This shift in cost occurs because producing the pizza requires varying amounts of each unique driver. For example, it uses $3 in material costs, but only $1.25 in labor costs. Table 6.10 summarizes the product costs using each method.

TABLE 6.10 PRODUCT COSTS USING DIFFERENT OVERHEAD DRIVERS

Giovanni's Pizza Pie Shop				
Overhead Charging Option	(1) Estimated Overhead Cost per Pizza	(2) Material Costs for the Pizza	(3) Labor Costs for the Pizza	(1) + (2) + (3) Total Estimated Cost of the Pizza
Pizzas made	$1.44	$3.00	$1.25	$5.69
Direct labor hours	$1.50	$3.00	$1.25	$5.75
Direct labor dollars	$1.50	$3.00	$1.25	$5.75
Material dollars	$1.20	$3.00	$1.25	$5.45
Total prime costs	$1.275	$3.00	$1.25	$5.525

Which cost is "right"? All of these overhead options charge the overhead to the pizzas that Giovanni makes, but they result in different cost estimates. Since our goal is to choose a cost driver that is most closely related to the *cause* of the cost, we must ask ourselves if, for example, we used more labor or more materials, would we expect the amount of overhead to increase. If the answer is "yes" for a specific overhead cost driver, then that is the driver we should use. Unfortunately, many of the overhead costs Giovanni faces are more related to how he runs the business than to how many pizzas he makes. To capture these effects accurately, it is often important to break out overhead into smaller buckets or **cost pools,** *a group containing two or more resource costs.*

PLANT-WIDE VS. DEPARTMENTAL OVERHEAD RATES

Developing an accurate cost estimate requires more than simply doing the "math" correctly. Accuracy entails the creation of cost pools around a common purpose—that all of the resources support the same type of work; in other words, we need to create **homogeneous cost pools,** *groups of resources that support the same type of work.* This is an aspect of the costing principle, discussed earlier, called ***homogeneity.*** Our goal in applying homogeneity is to make sure that we understand the work that is being done, and how different types of activities and outputs use different resources. To achieve this goal, it is often necessary to create more than one overhead pool.

In the pizza example, Giovanni was charging all of his business overhead out on one driver—direct labor hours. It is a measure that is usually easy to calculate, and for a service business, it is often a reasonably good indicator of the relative amount of effort and resources used by one job vs. another. If we were thinking about a copy center, such as FedEx Office, we might select machine time as the cost driver. While any cost driver will allow us to charge out the overhead, we always want to choose the one that provides the least amount of distortion to our estimated product costs. When a business uses only one cost pool and one cost driver, it is called a **plant-wide overhead rate,** *all of the overhead is combined and charged to a product using one cost driver.*

If the work a company does is fairly uniform, or if there is only one main product, using a plant-wide overhead rate is adequate for much of management's decision making. As we begin to add more products or activities to the situation, the simple plant-wide method for assigning overhead results in inaccurate cost estimates. Why? Because producing each of the different products and services the company offers to its customers may require more or less work, or may use more of one type of machine, activity, or resource than another. If these differences are significant, we need to capture them in our cost estimate.

To increase the accuracy of our cost estimate, we use cost pools to improve our ability to assign the indirect resource costs only to the products and services that benefit from them. We also need to use different cost drivers—for example, machine hours for machine-driven costs and inspection hours for inspection activities—for each of these overhead pools. The addition of more cost pools, each charged on the most relevant driver, greatly improves the accuracy of our product cost estimates.

We can split the total overhead costs of a company into smaller, more focused cost pools in many different ways. Many companies use **departmental overhead rates**—*where costs are first assigned to departments and then to the products or services that use that department's capacity*—to improve the accuracy of their overhead costing systems. Indirect costs are traced to the departments that use the resources, creating an overhead cost pool for each department. An appropriate driver is then chosen for each department's overhead pool.

The drivers chosen should capture the *cause* of the overhead costs in the different departments. For instance, in a department that does a lot of machine-based work, the departmental overhead might be charged out on machine hours. In another department, labor hours might be the best choice for driving out the overhead costs. In yet a third case, in a support activity such as final product inspection, inspection hours or units inspected might be good overhead drivers. Whether we focus on machines, people, or activities, our goal in developing and using multiple overhead pools and drivers remains the same—to improve the accuracy of our cost estimates.

DEVELOPING AND USING DEPARTMENTAL OVERHEAD RATES

Let us return to Giovanni's pizza shop to see how, and why, we develop and use departmental overhead rates. For this example, let us assume that Giovanni has decided to add indoor dining and pizza delivery to the services he provides and that he has also expanded his menu to include sandwiches, pasta, main courses, and salads. These changes have added costs to Giovanni's business, which have increased his total overhead from $72,000 to $150,000 per year.

To manage this new level of complexity, Giovanni has hired a person on each shift who is responsible for "order processing"—taking orders, preparing orders for pickup and delivery, and handling cash and credit card payments. There are now several "production" departments: food preparation (activities such as cutting and slicing raw ingredients), assembly, and baking and cooking; each uses different resources and performs different activities.

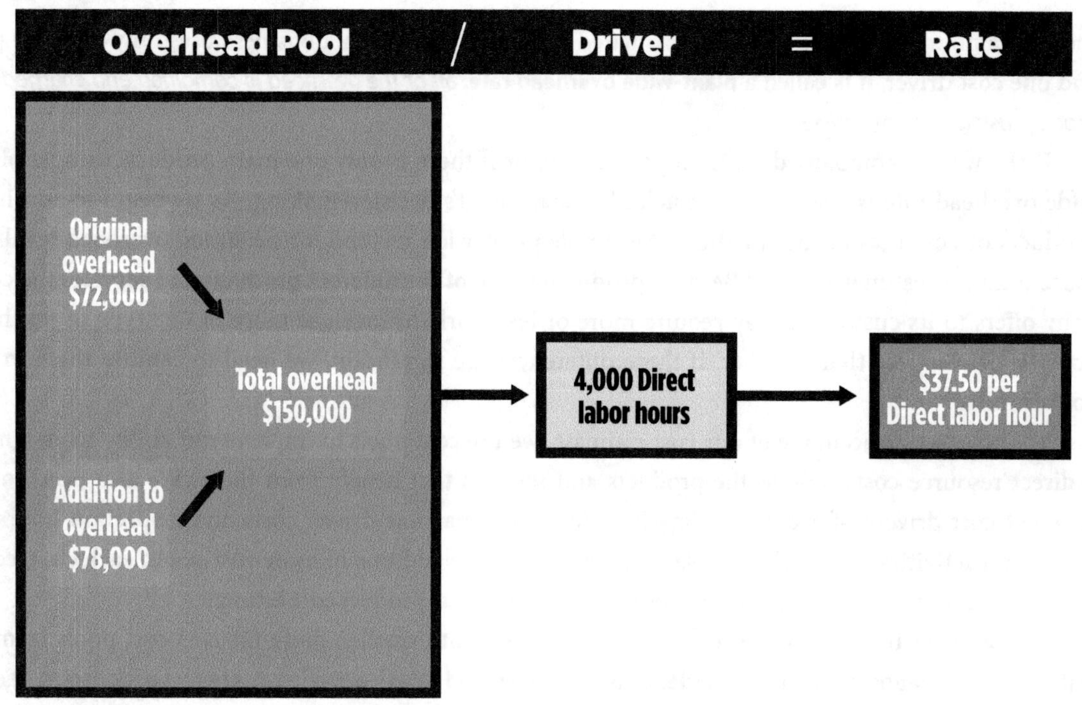

FIGURE 6.5 FORMULA FOR DETERMINING PLANT-WIDE OVERHEAD RATE (GIOVANNI'S PIZZA PIE SHOP)

Giovanni could continue with his traditional method of charging overhead, using the direct labor that each "job" represents. As Figure 6.5 suggests, we would now have an overhead rate of $37.50 per direct labor hour, or more than double the prior rate of $18. Giovanni's indirect costs, or overhead, have gone up, driving up his overhead rates. How does this affect the estimated cost of the pizza we looked at earlier?

Overhead rate (cost per direct labor hour)			**$37.50**
Direct labor time needed to make pizza			**5 minutes**
Overhead charged to pizza:			
($37.50 / 60 minutes)	**x 5 minutes**	**or**	**$ 3.125**

Now our estimated cost of the pizza is:

Direct materials	$3.000
Direct labor	1.250
Overhead	3.125
Total estimated cost	$7.375

This is $1.625 more than it cost to make a pizza when we first estimated it. It would be pretty difficult for Giovanni to explain to a customer who ordered this same pizza two weeks in a row that his costs escalated more than 28% in such a short period of time. Unless Giovanni changes the way he estimates his costs, this is exactly what would happen.

As the complexity of Giovanni's business increases, it becomes more important than ever to ensure that he attaches costs to the products and customers that benefit most directly from these resources. In other words, he needs to make sure that pizza delivery costs are not assigned to customers who pick up their pizza. Similarly, we want to ensure that customers who have their pizza delivered do not end up paying for the cost of the inside dining room service.

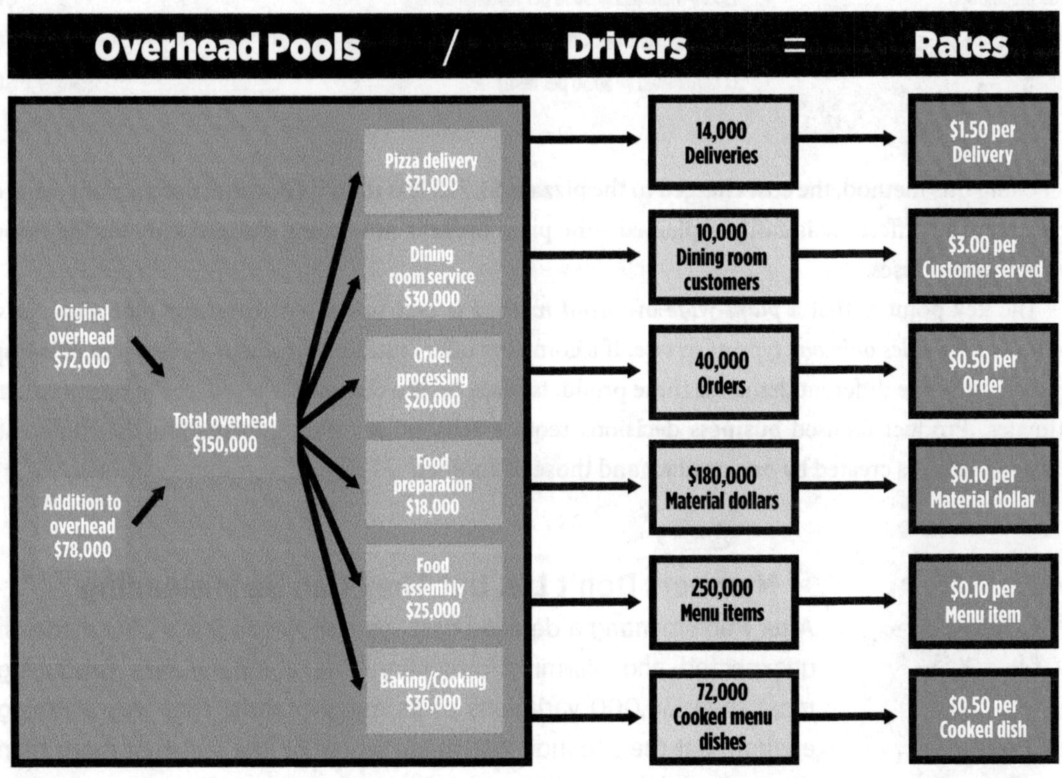

FIGURE 6.6 FORMULA FOR DETERMINING DEPARTMENTAL OVERHEAD RATE (GIOVANNI'S PIZZA PIE SHOP)

Figure 6.6 breaks down the $150,000 of overhead costs into six separate cost pools, one for each department. Each department performs a different service or activity, so the resource costs of each department are charged out on a different cost driver. For instance, pizza delivery costs are $21,000 of the total $150,000 of overhead. There are 14,000 deliveries in a normal year. Therefore, every delivery costs Giovanni $1.50.

Let us look one more time at the cost of the pizza we examined above. Now let us assume that the customer is picking up the pizza, so there are no delivery or dining room charges. The pizza does benefit from the services provided by the other four indirect departments, so it will have to be charged for their use. We can now re-cost the pizza using the new costing system as is illustrated in Table 6.11.

TABLE 6.11 ADJUSTING COSTS TO REFLECT CHANGES IN DEPARTMENTAL OVERHEADS

Giovanni's Pizza Pie Shop		
Resource	**Amount Used**	**Cost for Pizza**
Direct materials	Direct cost	$3.00
Direct labor	Direct cost	$1.25
Order processing	(1 order @ $0.50 per order)	$0.50
Food preparation	($3.00 materials @ $0.10 per material dollar)	$0.30
Food assembly	(1 item @ $0.10 per item)	$0.10
Baking	(1 item baked @ $0.50 per item)	$0.50
Total estimated cost		$5.65

Using this method, the cost charged to the pizza is $1.725 less than if Giovanni used a plant-wide overhead rate. The difference is easily explained—the pizza order is now being charged only for the resources and activities it uses.

The key point is that a *plant-wide overhead method is best suited to a company that makes a single product or provides only one type of service.* If a company offers multiple products or services, it is important to capture the different demands these products place on the company's resources in our product cost estimates. Product-focused business decisions require reliable, accurate information that differentiates between the costs created by one product and those of another.

IN THE NEWS ➤ Numbers Don't Lie, but They Can Be Misleading

After implementing a detailed cost system, Nestlé S.A.'s CEO made an unexpected and alarming discovery: The company was producing more than 130,000 variations of its many brands. That was alarming enough, but the situation was made worse by the fact that more than 30 percent of the products sold were losing money for the company. In fact, production cost for these products, before considering administrative and marketing costs, was greater than their current market price.

An excessive focus on variable costs and spare capacity by Nestlé's operating managers had led them to believe that many of the new products were "profitable" and long-term winners because they were leading to higher utilization rates on the company's machines. Nestlé's margins on these products were lower than their competitors', however, which strongly suggested that these seemingly "profitable" products were actually decreasing the firm's overall profit. By focusing solely on one aspect of the business—machine utilization—new products were added that would never be profitable. As Nestlé's CEO discovered, identifying the best product costing system for new product decisions is challenging, but it is a choice that is essential in guiding a firm's product strategy. Using a system that focuses on the wrong driver(s) can lead to faulty strategic decisions that can have alarming results.

Adapted from Joseph G. Fisher and Kip Krumwiede, "Product Costing Systems: Finding the Right Approach," *Journal of Corporate Accounting and Finance*, Vol. 23, Issue 3, March-April, 2012, pg. 43..

Before leaving this topic, we need to recognize that in many companies a single department may perform many different activities for many different products and customers. When this situation arises, we have to break down the departmental cost pools even further into activity-based cost pools to capture these differences. As you will see in Chapters 8 and 9, it is quite likely that several departments may work together to provide a service or complete an activity. This is a **process,** *a horizontal linkage of activities and resources that occur in different parts of an organization*. In complex, modern organizations, process structures are very common. For now, we will focus on a simpler world in which each department does one major type of work, independent of other departments.

These are just a few of the issues we face when we set out to estimate a product cost. To reinforce these points, let us return to the more complex world of Kinkaid Cabinets and its search for a cost estimate for the potential decision to launch the new product line.

Product Costing in Complex Settings

OBJECTIVE 5
Calculate and compare product cost estimates in a complex setting.

Some companies use a variety of manufacturing processes, which complicates how we estimate product costs. Kinkaid Cabinets is such a company. Kinkaid makes cabinets using a combination of repetitive, assembly line, and cellular manufacturing methods, which are illustrated in Figure 6.7. The cutting department (the red square) takes the large pieces of wood the company receives and cuts them to a number of preset sizes. The cutting department's work is scheduled using a *kanban* inventory management system where a simple "card" signals that the next step in production needs a certain part. The card is pulled whenever inventory of the part drops below a predefined, or buffer, level. Although some of these parts are purchased, the cutting department at Kinkaid fills all cut wood needs. Therefore, when the inventory of wood or particle board parts needed to make doors, frames, or any other wood component runs low, the cutting department makes just enough of these parts to fill the preset kanban level.

While cutting works in a *repetitive* fashion—doing the same work over and over in small batches—the pantry units, special cabinets (such as corner units with spinning shelves), and drawers are "made to order" using a *cellular* manufacturing approach. Finally, for the completion of higher-volume products, Kinkaid uses *assembly lines*. While the work flows differently in these three types of manufacturing settings, they are all machine-paced. That means while we need to use departmental overhead rates, we use a machine-based overhead rate to assign each department's costs to specific products.

The royal blue squares in Figure 6.7 represent manufacturing support activities. Some of these activities are driven by a batch of products (such as shipping and receiving), while others are done for each unit made (such as quality control inspection and packaging). We need to make sure that we choose *cost drivers* for these activities and departments that most accurately capture how different products and customers use these services.

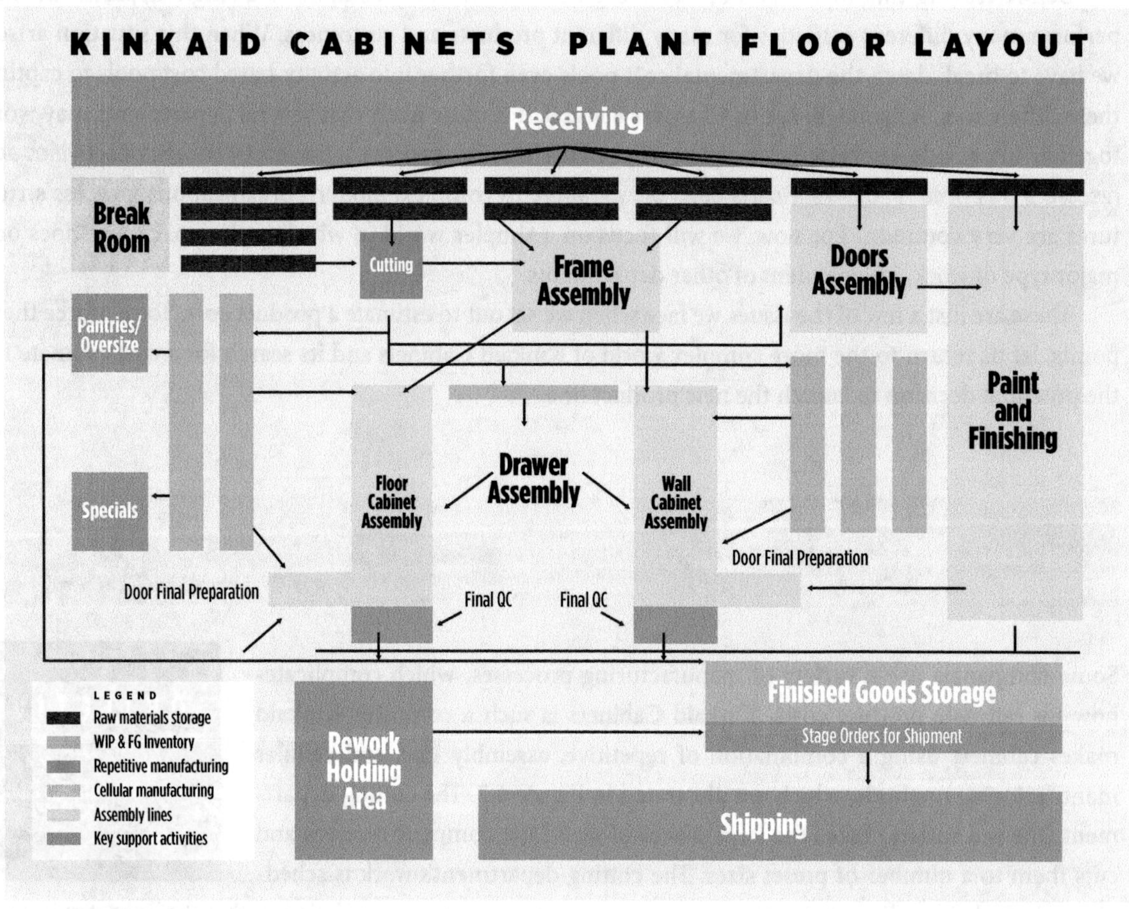

FIGURE 6.7 MANUFACTURING PROCESSES AFFECT PRODUCT COST ESTIMATES (KINKAID CABINETS).

The only way that Kinkaid can ship its products is if all of these production and support areas work together. Each department contributes in some way to the productive process. That means that the product cost estimates we develop will need to include not only the cost of materials used in making a specific cabinet, but also the costs it causes in each of the productive and support departments. Let us see how we actually develop these estimates at Kinkaid.

IN CONTEXT ➤ Competitive Cost Analysis at Kinkaid Cabinets

Back at Kinkaid, progress has been made in defining the new product line. Shelley has researched the office furniture market to determine its overall size, major competitors, and key customer market segments. Brad looked at the existing products and processes to better understand how the new products might fit in with the production processes currently in use at Kinkaid.

Shelley is convinced that Kinkaid should focus on modular office furniture rather than the more traditional products that have the look and feel of fine furniture. Her reasoning is quite straightforward: Kinkaid does not have any expertise in making fine furniture. Modular office furniture, on the other hand, has the look and feel of a kitchen—simple cabinet and countertop combinations. Equally compelling is the fact that the modular market is currently posting sales of $1.2 billion. Modular furniture sales are growing at 15% a year, while other office furniture segments have been losing volume.

To get a better feel for the market, Shelley did some comparison "shopping." The four top-selling product lines in the modular office furniture market were similar in both the options offered and prices charged. Looking at the competition, Shelley determined that a wall cabinet system in black lacquer (two cabinets joined by a shelf) costs between $250 and $325.

Company	Estimated Units Sold	Average Price
Hargrove Office Products	200,000	$ 280
Littleton Cabinet Makers	175,000	$ 300
Kraft Made Cabinets	325,000	$ 250
Tanner Corporation	100,000	$ 325

This was a much higher price than Kinkaid could charge for a similar kitchen wall cabinet. Sam might be onto something in choosing this market, she thought. Based on her market analysis of the competition, Shelley decided that charging a $250 price was Kinkaid's best option. Its reputation depended on providing a quality product at a fair price. The $250 price level would fit the company's pricing strategy and should provide sufficient market share.

With price settled, at least in theory, Shelley turned her attention to creating a project team to look at profitability. While the kitchen products were earning 10%, the office furniture line would need to do better. Kinkaid's initial investment in designing and tooling up to make kitchen cabinets was recouped long ago. The 10% profit was just that. The office furniture line would require new investments in capital assets and marketing, not to mention the costs to design the products. Using a conservative estimate of these costs, Shelley's initial opinion was that the office furniture line would need to earn 20% over the first five years. That meant her target cost would need to be $200 for the delivered product ($250 price less 20% desired profit, or $200).

Using this target price and her knowledge of the industry, Shelley estimated that the product line would sell 50,000 units in Year 1, 150,000 units in Year 2, and 200,000 units for the next three years, for a total of 800,000 units in the first five years of production.

Armed with this information, Shelley headed off to a meeting with Brad and his design team. It was time to see what it would cost Kinkaid to make the required products using Brad's latest design concepts and production plans. She was dedicated to creating a project team that would make the redesign work—the first time!—and she knew that John Adkins and Barb Boreen could help support her project analysis. They were top-notch analysts who could make or break the team result.

As we have seen, a product cost is a combination of material and conversion (for example, labor and overhead) costs caused by making the item. What would these different cost items be for the proposed wall cabinet unit? We get some of this information from the product's unique **bill of materials,** *a list of the direct components used to make a unit of product*, including their size, color, shape, and total number used in the production process. Table 6.12 shows what goes into the bill of materials for the proposed cabinet.

TABLE 6.12 BILL OF MATERIALS

Kinkaid Cabinets—Proposed Wall Cabinet Unit			
	(1)	(2)	(1) x (2)
Material	Purchase Package	Amount Used	Cost per Cabinet
Solid wood for doors	$12.00 per square foot	4 square feet	$48.00
Particle board for sides and shelf joiner	$1.50 per square foot	14 square feet	$21.00
Wood for frame parts	$1.00 per linear foot	28 linear feet	$28.00
Paint	$0.50 per ounce	8 ounces	$4.00
Glue	$0.25 per ounce	4 ounces	$1.00
Screws	$0.60 per dozen	2 dozen	$1.20
Hinges	$1.00 each	4	$4.00
Door handles	$2.00 each	2	$4.00
Packaging materials	$0.40 per cubic foot	18 cubic feet	$7.20
Total Materials			$118.40

To make the wall unit, we will need two standard one-door, no-shelf wall cabinets and a "joiner" shelf unit that spans the distance between the two cabinets. The wall cabinets will be 15 inches wide by 15 inches long and 12 inches deep, and the shelf unit joiner will be 18 inches wide, making the entire wall unit 48 inches wide. We can now use this information to develop a reasonable estimate of the material costs for the proposed wall cabinet using existing processes.

To accurately attach the remaining costs caused by the new wall unit, we have to follow the cabinet through the factory to determine what activities and processes it uses. As things are currently organized at Kinkaid, there are many different steps that the product has to go through to be completed. We call this list **product routing,** *the steps a product has to go through to be made*. Figure 6.8 demonstrates the steps required to create Kinkaid's wall cabinet.

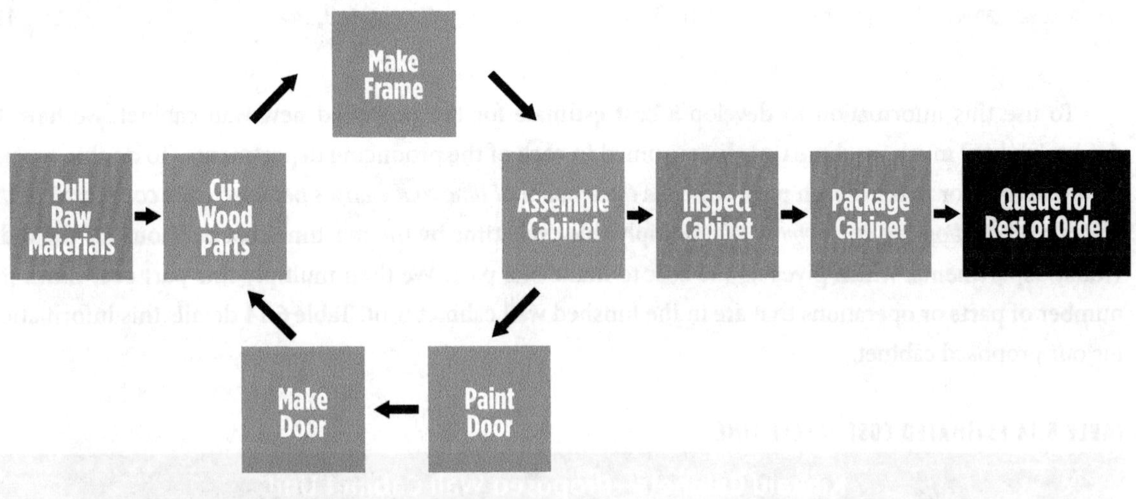

FIGURE 6.8 THE PRODUCTION SEQUENCE WILL AFFECT HOW COSTS ARE ASSIGNED TO A PRODUCT (KINKAID CABINETS' OFFICE CABINETS).

The blue squares in Figure 6.8 represent machine-paced work (cut wood, make frame, make door, paint door, and assemble cabinet), while the three red squares are all activities (pull raw materials, inspect, and package the final cabinet). In developing a product cost estimate for the new wall cabinet, we will need to include the costs of each of these efforts. Let us begin with the machine-based costs.

CONVERSION COSTS IN MACHINE-PACED SETTINGS

While the main production processes used at Kinkaid are a blend of repetitive, cellular, and assembly line structures, they are all paced by machines. This makes estimating cost much easier because we can focus our costing effort on the time required to make one specific unit of output. The machine-paced production processes that the new wall cabinet specifically uses are: cut wood, assemble frame, assemble door, paint door, and assemble the final cabinet. The costs and driver information for these departments is contained in Table 6.13.

TABLE 6.13 CONVERSION COST DATA

Kinkaid Cabinets—Machine-Paced Departments			
Department	Department Conversion Costs	Machine Hours Worked	Overhead Rate per Machine Hour
Cut flat wood parts	$5,620,590	7,493	$750.11
Make frames	$2,120,190	26,679	$79.47
Make doors	$1,966,589	38,386	$51.23
Paint parts	$10,446,780	4,486	$2,328.75
Assemble wall cabinet	$10,758,740	9,344	$1,151.41

To use this information to develop a cost estimate for the proposed new wall cabinet, we have to determine how much machine time is consumed in each of the producing departments. To do this, we use the **cycle time** for making each part, which is *the amount of time that elapses between units coming off of the end of a production line or machine*. We multiply this cycle time by the machine cost per hour for the individual departments, which gives us the cost to make one part. We then multiply this part cost times the number of parts or operations that are in the finished wall cabinet unit. Table 6.14 details this information for our proposed cabinet.

TABLE 6.14 ESTIMATED COST—CYCLE TIME

Kinkaid Cabinets—Proposed Wall Cabinet Unit					
Department	(1) Overhead Rate per Machine Hour	(2) Cycle Time per Part Made	(1) x (2) = (3) Conversion Cost per Part	(4) Number of Parts in Cabinet	(3) x (4) = (5) Conversion Cost per Cabinet
Cut flat wood parts	$750.11	0.0002	$0.15	37	$5.55
Make frames	$79.47	0.0311	$2.47	2	$4.94
Make doors	$51.23	0.0887	$4.54	2	$9.08
Paint parts	$2,328.75	0.0005	$1.16	3	$3.48
Assemble	$1,151.41	0.0144	$16.58	2	$33.16
Total Conversion Cost per Unit					$56.21

The manufacturing costs of the unit are $56.21. Added to the material costs of $118.40 (see Table 6.12), gives us a total cost of $174.61 to make the new wall cabinet, which is only $25.39 less than our target cost of $200. Let us see if we can complete the remaining activities necessary to make the new unit and still stay under our target cost.

ACTIVITY-BASED COSTS AND PRODUCT COST ESTIMATES

You will recall that when we develop an activity-based cost, we take the total resource costs that the activity causes and then divide these costs by the number of times we do it. This is known as the **activity cost driver,** *the cause of an action; it is used to attach a cost to the product, service, or customers who benefit from it*. For the proposed wall unit, Kinkaid plans to pull materials into kits, or groups, three times: once for the doors, once for the frame, and once for the flat stock that will be used for the joiner shelf as well as the back, sides, and bottom of the two cabinets. In addition, Brad estimates it will take four minutes to inspect the unit on the line. Finally, the unit will be packed into three separate boxes for shipment. The total estimated activity costs for our proposed wall cabinet unit are summarized in Table 6.15.

TABLE 6.15 ESTIMATED ACTIVITY COSTS

Kinkaid Cabinets—Proposed Wall Cabinet						
Activity	(1) Total Annual Cost of Activity	Activity Driver	(2) Number of Times Activity Done per Year	(1) / (2) = (3) Cost per Activity	(4) Driver Frequency per Unit Made	(3) x (4) = (5) Activity Cost per Unit
Kit materials	$7,150,030	Number of kits made	1,000,000	$7.15 per kit	3 kits	$ 21.45
Inspection	$6,969,850	Inspection time	1,200,000	$5.81 per minute	4 minutes	$23.24
Packaging	$4,762,490	Number of units made	4,173,320	$1.14 per unit	3 units	$3.42
Total Cost per Unit						$ 48.11

Having calculated these costs, one area of concern remains—the treatment of the costs for designing, piloting, and launching the new product line. These are part of the product's life cycle costs and they should be looked at before the final production decision is made. While accounting rules do not permit us to attach these costs to a unit placed into inventory, they are very relevant to Kinkaid's management in its analysis of the potential new product line. When we calculate a cost estimate, we want to include these costs to ensure that the decisions that are going to be made use the best estimate of the total costs the decision will cause.

Kinkaid normally charges off these types of costs over a five-year period. Traditionally, design changes either are made at the five-year point or the product line is dropped. In either case, the benefits of these preproduction costs are charged off to units made within the first 60 months of a product's life. Shelley has estimated that a total of 800,000 units will be sold over the first five years.

Based on this information, Kinkaid's management estimates that it will take $8.8 million to develop and launch the new product line. Dividing this by the estimated 800,000 units the company expects to sell during this five-year period results in a per-unit charge of $11 per unit of preproduction cost, as detailed in Table 6.16.

TABLE 6.16 ESTIMATED RESEARCH AND DEVELOPMENT COSTS

Kinkaid Cabinets—New Office Product Line	
Preproduction Activity	**Estimated Cost (Five Years)**
Product design	$ 2,500,000
Pilot tests	$ 500,000
Tooling and production equipment	$ 3,800,000
Market samples	$ 500,000
Market launch campaign	$ 1,500,000
TOTAL	$ 8,800,000
Projected five-year unit sales	800,000
Estimated Preproduction Cost per Unit ($8,800,000 / 800,000 units)	$11.00

Table 6.17 summarizes the estimated product cost for the proposed cabinet unit by combining the estimated material, conversion, activity, and development costs. The total estimated cost is $233.56.

TABLE 6.17 TOTAL ESTIMATED UNIT COSTS

Kinkaid Cabinets—Proposed Wall Cabinet	
Cost Element	**Estimated Unit Cost**
Material	$118.40
Conversion Costs	56.05
Activity Costs	48.11
Preproduction Costs	11.00
Total Estimated Cost	$ 233.56

How does this compare to our target cost?

Estimated Current Cost	$233.56
Target Cost	200.00
Current Excess Cost	$ 33.56

As currently designed and manufactured, the wall unit is too costly. As we saw earlier in the Green Acres example, the excess cost has to be removed if Kinkaid is to proceed. Brad's design team now moves from the establishment to the attainment phase of target costing to find a way to eliminate the excess cost. There are many different options the team can pursue; for example, changing the materials and changing the methods used to make the product. Let us rejoin Shelley and Brad to see what they feel is the best thing to do.

IN CONTEXT ➤ Attaining Target Cost at Kinkaid Cabinets

"And that's the unit and estimated costs. What do you think, Shelley? Looks great, doesn't it? We pulled out all of the stops on this one!" Brad's enthusiasm was almost contagious, but Shelley did not wait long before bursting Brad's bubble. Where Brad saw beauty, Shelley saw major problems. That is why she wanted John and Barb on the team.

"Brad, the unit looks great, but it costs way too much! If we want to sell the unit for $250, it sure can't cost $233.56. And, even though it was his idea, if we want Sam to approve the project, it had better cost less than $200!"

"Why not just raise the price? If you charge $300 for the unit, we'll make Sam's profit targets. Isn't that all that counts?" Brad was visibly upset. He saw three months of hard work going down the drain.

"There's making profit on the unit, and making profit on the product line. If we price these units too high, we're not going to sell enough units to hit the product line targets Sam set. The customer sets our limits, Brad, not me. And the customers want a reasonably-priced unit, not an expensive one."

"Okay, Shelley, I get the point. But what would you like me to take out? Should we get rid of the shelf? The doors? The hinges? We put together a high-quality product using our existing processes. I don't relish the idea of telling my team that they've got to go back to the drawing board."

"I know, but we've got to get as close to the original target cost as we can. Tell you what, Brad, let's talk about it over lunch—my treat. I'm sure there's something we can do. We need to apply more of John and Barb's costing focus to the problem."

"Sounds good to me. How does Giovanni's sound?"

Summary

In this chapter, we have focused on planning in the product domain. We began with target costing, which is a market-driven costing system that is used to guide decision making during the design and development phase of a product. During the establishment phase of target costing, customer input and competitive analysis are used to set a target price, profit, and allowable cost for the product. As we saw, the initial design of a product usually meets customer needs but can cost too much to produce. When this happens, a company moves to the attainment phase of target costing. The goal of these efforts is to remove excess costs, not value, from the product. To achieve this objective, we have to be able to estimate the current as well as potential future cost of the product or service.

The production processes in a company, whether intended to deliver a service or make a product, can be organized in many different ways. In a job shop, the work is organized around a specific order that is unique to a specific customer. Process settings, on the other hand, continuously make a common set of products that often use a common raw material. Finally, there are three different ways to organize work that are repetitive in nature—large batch, assembly line, and cellular manufacturing.

Differences in how work is done are reflected in differences in our product cost estimates. For instance, whether a job shop makes a pizza or a customized set of golf clubs, it will probably use job order costing. In job order costing, we directly trace materials and labor to the specific job. Indirect costs, or overhead, are attached to the job using an overhead rate that is tied to a key driver, such as direct labor or machine hours. It is potentially possible to use a more complex costing method, such as activity-based costing (ABC), in a job shop. However, it is important to remember that we want to make sure that the benefits we would gain from this additional effort exceed the expense of maintaining the more complex system.

In repetitive production settings, we estimate product costs using conversion and ABC for all nonmaterial costs. Whether the company makes automobiles or processes checks, as long as its products or services are produced over and over again in the same way, we can estimate its nonmaterial costs using ABC for its people-paced work and conversion costs wherever machines set the pace.

In simple settings, such as job shops, it is difficult to justify the complexity and cost of using both conversion- and activity-based costing for overhead. As we increase the number of products, processes, and challenges management has to deal with, the ability to trace specific costs to specific outcomes becomes increasingly important. While it is uneconomical to use complex costing methods in simple production settings, it is risky to use simple methods in complex settings. Why? Because a simple overhead costing method, such as one plant- or company-wide rate applied on direct labor hours, can make it difficult for management to see, understand, and predict the impact of their decisions on the company's costs and performance. In the end, our goal is to match the complexity of the costing system to the complexity of the organization.

In the next chapter, we turn our attention to the ongoing management of existing products and product lines; that is, the "check and adjust" elements of the management process in the product domain. As we evaluate current performance and look for ways to improve outcomes, we will be able to better evaluate the efficiency and effectiveness of the various product cost methods.

Key Terms

Activity cost driver: the cause of a cost; it is used to attach a nonmachine-based cost to the products, services, or customers that benefit from its use.

Assembly line: a manufacturing setting that links production activities into an uninterrupted flow.

Attainment phase: an iterative process of design and adjustment that focuses on creating a product that will not only meet its profit targets but will also satisfy key customer requirements.

Average cost method: puts all of the beginning and new costs into one pool to determine the value of output.

Batch: a group of like products that are made at the same time.

Bill of materials: a list of the direct components used to make a unit of product.

Cellular manufacturing: a setting that uses commonality of parts and methods to support the efficient and effective production of assembled products in a "virtual" batch size of one.

Committed product costs: expenditures driven by the constraints of the product design and the processes used to produce it.

Conversion costs: the combination of labor and overhead spent to make a unit of output.

Cost driver: the thing that creates the expense.

Cost gap: the difference between the current estimated cost and the target cost of that product or service.

Cost pool: a group containing two or more resource costs.

Cycle time: the amount of time that elapses between units coming off of a production line or machine.

Departmental overhead rates: costs are first assigned to departments and then to the products or services that use that department's capacity.

Direct product cost: the economic value of a resource that can be traced to one specific unit or batch of product.

Establishment phase: the period in which the target cost and product features are set.

Equivalent unit: an estimate of the nearest number of completed, or whole, units that would have been made during a given period of time.

Homogeneous cost pool: a group of resources that support the same type of work.

Incurred costs: actual expenditures on resources used during the design or production of a product or service.

Job order costing: the method used to assign specific resource costs—material, labor, and overhead—to a specific job.

Job shop: a manufacturing setting where every order is uniquely made for a specific customer.

Large batch: a manufacturing setting where a group of like products are made at the same time.

Life cycle: the entire period that a product exists, from its inception to final disposal.

Life cycle costs: the total costs incurred to support a product or product line from its initial conceptualization and research through production and downstream maintenance once the product is in the customer's hands.

Overhead: the sum of all of a company's shared and indirect costs of production.

Plant-wide overhead rates: all of the overhead is combined and charged to a product using one cost driver.

Prime cost: the total materials and direct labor expenditures traceable to a specific job or batch.

Process: the horizontal linkage of activities and resources that occur in different parts of an organization.

Process manufacturing: a setting where the continuous flow of consistent (indistinguishable) output makes it difficult to attach resource costs to specific units or batches.

Product life cycle: the entire period that a product exists, from its inception to its final disposal.

Product routing: the steps a product has to go through to be made.

Target cost: the predefined maximum market price of a new product or service given optimal price and desired profit.

Target costing: a market-driven management system in which cost targets, or objectives, are set based on defined customer requirements and an assessment of competitive offerings.

Value engineering: the technique used to analyze the various parts of a product to determine how to provide their function at the lowest possible cost.

Appendix: Process Costing

Process costing is a challenge because we need to estimate how much work was done in a specific time period. In a process manufacturing setting, the work never stops. Therefore, when we arbitrarily conclude an accounting period at the end of a month or week, there always is some work still going on—it is *in process*. As a result, we must estimate how much work to give the department credit for during the period we are analyzing. This estimate of production output is called an **equivalent unit,** *an estimate of the nearest number of completed, or whole, units that would have been made during a given period of time.*

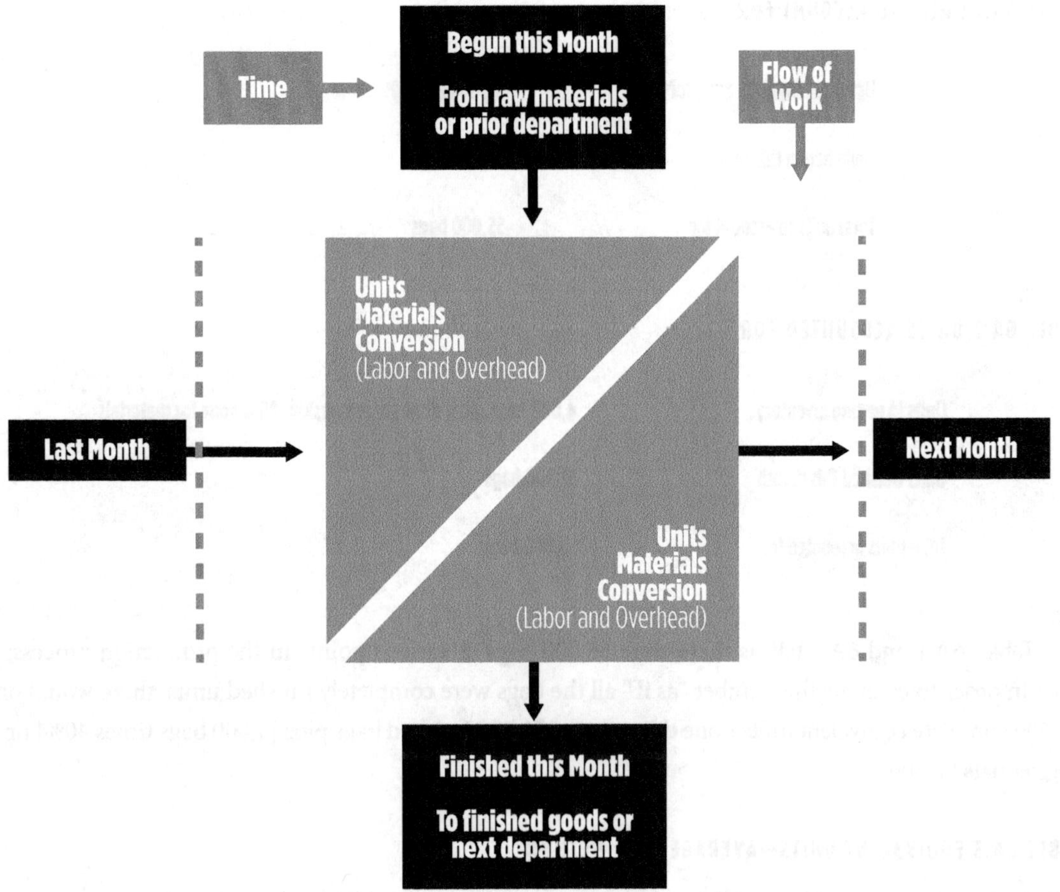

FIGURE 6A.1 THE PROCESS COSTING STRUCTURE

To start our discussion of process costing, let us begin with Figure 6A.1, a diagram of the problem that illustrates a specific point frozen in time. In this case, it is the period between when end-of-the-month production was completed—at midnight of the last day of the month—and when it recommenced—one second later on the first day of the new month. Throughout this time, the production of fresh units begins and the production of other units finishes. Completed units are either sent to finished goods or moved on to the next stop in the production sequence. In process costing, we need to reconcile the physical flow of units over the given time period and then estimate the amount of cost earned as a result. For the sake of simplicity, we are going to assume what is called the **average cost method**—*which puts all of the beginning and new costs into one pool to determine the value of output*—for process costing.

Since it is a given that work never stops, the first step in process costing is to determine the physical flow of units vs. the equivalent unit of work we will be using to estimate cost. Tables 6A.1 through 6A.3 do this for Lucky Foods, which manufactures 25-pound bags of dog food around the clock. The beginning, ending, physical, and equivalent units calculations are contained in these following tables.

TABLE 6A.1 UNITS TO ACCOUNT FOR

Units in beginning inventory	**5,000 bags, 50% done**
Units begun this month	**50,000 bags**
Total units to account for	**55,000 bags**

TABLE 6A.2 UNITS ACCOUNTED FOR

Units in ending inventory	**4,000 bags, 40% done for conversion, 80% done for materials**
Units finished this month	**51,000 bags**
Total units accounted for	**55,000 bags**

Tables 6A.1 and 6A.2 tell us there were 55,000 bags at various points in the production process; however, in order to estimate the number "as if" all the bags were completely finished units, there would only be 52,600 complete equivalent units done this month (51,000 finished bags plus [4,000 bags times 40%] or 1,600 bags equals 52,600).

TABLE 6A.3 EQUIVALENT UNITS—AVERAGE COST METHOD

Category	Status	Equivalent Units—Materials	Equivalent Units—Conversion
Units in ending inventory	4,000 bags, 80% done materials, 40% done conversion	3,200	1,600
Units finished this month	51,000 bags	51,000	51,000
Total equivalent units	55,000 actual bags	54,200	52,600

Similarly, 54,200 equivalent bags of materials were completed in the month (51,000 finished bags plus [4,000 times 80%] or 3,200 bags equals 54,200). Notice we ignore the partially done units at the beginning of the month. This is the basic assumption of the average cost method—we include all physical units and dollars from beginning inventory in our average calculations for the month *as if* all the work had been done during the month.

Once we sort out the units, we need to deal with dollars. We know how much money was spent on the process, so we need to determine how to assign the costs to the work that was done—its output or work-in-process. This is the entire purpose of process costing.

The costs we have to deal with are shown in Table 6A.4. They are split between materials and **conversion costs,** *the combination of labor and overhead spent to make a unit of output* for this problem.

TABLE 6A.4 INPUT COSTS FOR LUCKY FOODS

Cost Element	$ in Beginning Inventory	$ Spent this Month	Total Cost to Account for
Materials	$ 22,000	$ 285,600	$ 307,600
Conversion	$ 3,125	$ 65,000	$ 68,125

We can now complete the problem. We know how much cost must be accounted for: $307,600 in materials and $68,125 in conversion. We now must decide how much to charge to each output unit. To do this, we use the equivalent units. The calculation is shown in Table 6A.5.

TABLE 6A.5 COST PER EQUIVALENT UNIT

Cost Element	Total Cost (1)	Equivalent Units (2)	Cost per Equivalent Unit (3) = (1) / (2)
Materials	$307,600	54,200	$ 5.6753
Conversion	$ 68,125	52,600	$ 1.2952

Now, all that is left is to assign the costs to the finished goods and work-in-process. These calculations appear in Table 6A.6. Note that there is a small rounding error that we will add to the cost of finished goods. In other words, if we use the estimate of $5.6753 per good unit multiplied by the 51,000 units, the resulting total materials cost would be $289,440. When we add the rounding error, we get $307,600 less the $18,161 in ending work-in-process, or $289,439. The same logic applies to conversion; again the amount of the rounding error is applied to finished goods.

TABLE 6A.6 ASSIGNMENT OF COST PER EQUIVALENT UNIT

Cost Element	Cost per Equivalent Unit (1)	Units in Finished Goods (2)	Cost to Finished Goods (3) = (1) x (2)	Equivalent Units in Ending Work-in-Process (4)	Cost to Ending Work-in-Process (5) = (1) x (4)
Materials	$5.675	51,000	$ 289,439	3,200	$18,161
Conversion	$1.295	51,000	$ 66,053	1,600	$2,072

Our last step is to make sure we assigned all of the costs we had to account for to either work-in-process or finished goods. Table 6A.7 shows this calculation.

TABLE 6A.7 TOTAL COSTS ACCOUNTED FOR

Cost Element	To Finished Goods	To Ending Work-in-Process	Total Costs Accounted for
Materials	$289,439	$18,161	$307,600
Conversion	$66,053	$2,072	$68,125

These are the basic steps needed in order to complete a process costing exercise. If we decided to do FIFO costing, we would also have to deal with the partial units in the opening materials and conversion work-in-process. In average costing, however, we throw the opening units into both the unit count and the dollar amounts as if they were whole units and then take the average of beginning plus this month's costs to get our equivalent unit costs.

Actually, many companies, even outside of the process industries, have to deal with partial units completed at the beginning and end of a month, so they have to make these estimates. Once you get the procedures down, they will be easy. We simply need to make sure we account for all of the dollars and units coming in, and make sure when we are done we have accounted for the same units and dollars in our calculations. What comes in must go out somewhere!

Questions

1. What is the product domain and why is it so important to companies?
2. What does the term target costing mean?
3. During the establishment phase of target costing, what main activities take place?
4. How is a target price established in a competitive market with similar offerings? If it is a new market, how is price established?
5. What is a firm's target cost? How is it used during the new product development stage?
6. Describe the attainment phase of target costing. What are its primary objectives?
7. What is the difference between a committed and an incurred cost? Which is more actionable before a product is designed? After a product is designed?
8. What are the five ways work can be organized in manufacturing or service firms?
9. Describe a situation that would be best served by using job order costing. Why did you choose this setting?
10. What is the defining feature of an assembly line? How does cellular manufacturing incorporate the strengths of an assembly line at the same time as it allows for different features in output units?
11. Identify and define the three main components of a product cost.
12. What does the term prime cost mean? Conversion cost? How do we use them in costing products?
13. Define the key differences between plant-wide and departmental overhead rates.
14. How does activity costing differ from departmental costing methods?
15. What does the term life cycle costing mean? When do we use life cycle costs?

Exercises

1. **TARGET COSTING.** Sam's Sports makes several lines of tennis racquets. Recently, Sam decided to carry an entire line of graphite racquets. He has done his competitive analysis and found that his competitors' products sell for between $65 and $129 per racquet. He wants to manufacture a racquet that will sell for $100. Current materials estimates are $50, labor $28, and overhead $25 for a similar high-performance racquet in Sam's line.

REQUIRED:

a. If Sam wants to make a 20% profit on the racquet, what is his target cost?
b. Given existing estimates, what is Sam's current cost gap?

2. **TARGET COSTING.** Green Hills makes coffee pods for one-cup coffee machines. It was recently approached by Tracy's Coffees, a high-end coffee shop, to see if it can make pods for its special blends of coffees. Current pod prices are $13.99 for a box of 24. Normal pods yield a 50% profit margin (shared by the manufacturer and retailer). For a normal box of 24 pods, $2.50 is the cost of the coffee (one-third of a pound); $0.50, the cost of the pod and top sealer; $0.50 for the box; and $3.49 for the manufacturer's machining and overhead costs. These costs are for 24 pods. Tracy's coffees sell for $12 per pound.

REQUIRED:

a. If Green Hills wants to make a 50% profit on the coffee pods, what is its target cost for Tracy's coffee pods?
b. Given existing estimates, what is Green Hill's current cost gap if it decides to make Tracy's coffee pods?

3. **JOB ORDER COSTING—PLANT-WIDE RATE.** Josie's Copy Shop performs a variety of copy jobs for its customers. Job 123 takes 500 sheets of paper at $0.01 per sheet and 10 bindings at $0.25 per binding. It takes 10 minutes of labor and 15 minutes of machine time on the black and white copier, 15 minutes of labor and 20 minutes of machine time on the color copier, and 10 minutes of labor and 15 minutes of machine time on the binding machines. The following table contains the operating costs and overhead for the various machines.

Josie's Copy Shop			
	Black and White Copier	Color Copier	Binding Machine
Machine costs	$60,000	$120,000	$24,000
Overhead	$60,000	$75,000	$36,000
Direct labor hours	4,000	2,500	1,500
Machine hours	6,000	6,000	3,000

REQUIRED:

a. Use direct labor hours to develop the rate for the machining time the job requires.
b. Using one plant-wide rate based on direct labor hours, develop a cost for Job 123.

4. **JOB ORDER COSTING—ONE PLANT-WIDE RATE.** Using the information in Exercise 3, recalculate the cost of Job 123 using machine hours for both the machine costs and the overhead costs. How much does Job 123 cost now?

5. **JOB ORDER COSTING—DEPARTMENTAL RATES.** Using the information in Exercise 3, recalculate the cost of Job 123 using machine hours for the overhead on the black and white printer and the color printer, and direct labor hours for the binding machine. What does Job 123 cost now?

6. **LARGE BATCH MANUFACTURING—ONE PLANT-WIDE RATE.** Wholesome Oats makes several lines of breakfast cereals using large batch manufacturing. It takes three departments—Prepping, Blending, and Boxing—to make the products. It also has a general plant overhead pool for scheduling, inspection, and related activities, as suggested by the following table. Currently all of the overhead is charged out based on direct labor hours.

Wholesome Oats				
	Prepping	Blending	Boxing	General Overhead
Overhead	$250,000	$600,000	$400,000	$750,000
Direct labor hours	10,000	4,000	6,000	N/A
Machine hours	4,000	20,000	10,000	N/A
Batches made	800	800	N/A	N/A
Boxes packed	N/A	N/A	20,000,000	N/A

REQUIRED:

a. Calculate the plant-wide overhead rate for Wholesome Oats using direct labor hours as the driver.

b. How much overhead gets charged to each department?

7. **LARGE BATCH MANUFACTURING—ONE PLANT-WIDE RATE.** Using the information in Exercise 6, recalculate your plant-wide overhead rate using machine hours as the driver. How much overhead gets charged to each department now?

8. **LARGE BATCH MANUFACTURING—MULTIPLE RATES.** Using the information in Exercise 6, charge general overhead on direct labor hours first; then re-total your overhead by department. Next, charge out the total overhead in a department using the following drivers: Prepping on batches made, Blending on machine hours used, and Boxing on number of boxes produced. What four rates do you get now? How much total overhead gets charged out in each department?

9. **CELLULAR MANUFACTURING.** BestMade Electronics makes a variety of cellular telephone units. It uses cellular manufacturing. All of the costs incurred in the cell get charged to good units produced. It also pays its share of general overhead costs of $2,500,000 based on the driver chosen by the company. The general statistics for the cell are:

BestMade Electronics		
	Cell Performance	General Plant
Total direct costs	$10,000,000	2,500,000
Direct labor hours	10,000	50,000
Machine hours	2,000	20,000
Units made	500,000	N/A

REQUIRED:

a. Assume general plant overhead is charged out using direct labor hours. How much total cost is there in the cell including this overhead?

b. How much does it cost per good unit to produce the cell phone?

10. **CELLULAR MANUFACTURING.** Using the information in Exercise 9, charge out the general overhead using machine hours.

REQUIRED:

a. **How much total cost is there in the cell including this overhead?**
b. **How much does it cost per good unit to produce the cell phone?**

11. **PROCESS COSTING: EQUIVALENT UNITS.** Stuart's Oil Refinery runs on a 24/7 clock. For the month of January, it had 20,000 gallons in process at the beginning of the month, added 400,000 gallons to the process, and had 30,000 gallons in process at the end, 50% completed.

REQUIRED:

a. **What are the equivalent units of production for Stuart's Oil Refinery in January?**
b. **If materials cost $104.16 per barrel, and there are 42 gallons in each barrel, what is the materials cost per gallon? Round your answer to the nearest penny.**
c. **If conversion costs are $31.50 a barrel, and there are 42 gallons in each barrel, what is the conversion cost per gallon? Round your answer to the nearest penny.**

Problems

1. **TARGET COSTING: VALUE ENGINEERING.** Sparrows Specialty Products makes a wide variety of specialty home products. Joey Sparrow, the owner, has recently decided to add a special type of wine opener—one with a granite base that can be etched with the owner's initials—to his line. It will also have a long metal "neck" with an elaborate cork-pulling mechanism. While his will be a novelty item, there are competitive corkscrews ranging anywhere from the $2.50 simple plastic model to very elaborate one-touch devices that can sell for $250 or more. He decides he wants to keep his price below $200. He and his engineering team gather the following information for the first part of the establishment phase:

- Target price: $200
- Target profit: 25%
- Granite base: $20

- Etching: $5 labor, $10 overhead
- Metal neck: $15 plus $2 labor and $4 overhead to mount it
- Cork-pulling mechanism: $75 materials, $25 labor, $50 overhead

The cost after the first round of analysis is simply too high. Joey puts his design team to work looking for alternatives. They come up with the following suggestions:

- Buy the cork-pulling mechanism from an Italian manufacturer for $80. It will still cost $10 labor and $20 in overhead to mount the device.
- Substitute a high-level polymer for the granite base. The polymer could still be etched. It would cost $8. It would need to be weighted to hold the cork-pulling head. The weighting would cost an additional $4. The labor and overhead costs would remain.
- Charge for the etching to recover cost. Fewer people would choose etching, so labor would be idled. This might make the product less desirable overall.
- Buy a new etching machine. Labor would drop to $1 with only $2 in overhead. The machine costs $5,000 and could be used on other products. Machine cost is $1 for each etching.

REQUIRED:

a. Develop the target cost for the product.
b. Compute the current cost gap.
c. Choose among the options the design team has identified to close the cost gap.
d. Do you have any concerns about the value proposition of any of these options? In other words, could they turn customers off?

---

2. **TARGET COSTING: VALUE ENGINEERING.** Drip-No-More, Inc., makes various faucets for home use. It has a patented design feature that practically ensures there will be no dripping from the faucet in the first 10 years of use. This patented pressure washer drives up the cost of the faucet, but is a great marketing tool.

Sara Jones, marketing vice president, wants to launch a new line of moderately priced faucets that retain the no-drip feature. The company currently does not have any other products in this market, which is growing as people turn to remodeling their existing home rather than buying a new home. Always on a budget, the home remodeler wants top-of-the-line features at a moderate price. That is the sweet spot in the market Sara wants to hit.

Working with the product design team, Sara gets the first set of estimates for making the faucet using existing methods and materials:

- Target price: $150
- Target profit: 30%
- Faucet housing: $50 plus $10 in labor and $15 in overhead
- Drip-No-More pressure washer: $20 plus $5 in labor and $7.50 in overhead
- Nozzle sprayer: $25 plus $8 in labor and $12 in overhead
- Assembly: $10 in labor and $15 in overhead

The cost as currently designed is simply too high. Sara begins working with Pete, supervisor in Design, to identify ways to eliminate cost. They come up with the following ideas:

- Outsource the production of the faucet housing. The company has a supplier that can provide a similar part, though not quite as high in quality as Drip-No-More's high-quality line. The part would cost $40. There would be no internal labor or overhead charged to the part.
- Use lesser-quality materials in the pressure washer. This would save $10 in materials.
- Outsource the nozzle sprayer to a company in Canada. It could get the sprayer for $15 and avoid the labor and overhead costs. Once again, the nozzle sprayer would not be as high in quality as the company's existing line.
- Find new ways to do the assembly to cut down labor time for all steps across the board by 50%. Overhead would also go down by 50% if these new methods are adopted.
- Buy a new machine to make the pressure washer. The new machine would drop labor to $1 and overhead to $1.50. It could be used for all of the company's other products. Machining costs would be $1.

REQUIRED:

a. Develop the target cost for the product.
b. Compute the current cost gap.
c. Choose among the options the design team has identified to close the cost gap.
d. Do you have any concerns about the value proposition of any of these options? In other words, could they turn customers off?

3. JOB ORDER COSTING: PLANT-WIDE VS. DEPARTMENTAL OVERHEAD RATES. Dan's Custom Cabinets makes stereo cabinets for new homes and remodeling jobs. Dan crafts each cabinet to fit special places and uses solid wood throughout, making his cabinets of much higher quality than can be bought in the normal cabinet market. The labor, machine hours, and assembly hours for the three departments as well as the overhead incurred in each department used to make the cabinets are in the table below.

Dan's Custom Cabinets				
	Cutting Dept.	Stain and Paint	Assembly	General Plant
Overhead	$24,000	$100,000	$60,000	$36,000
Direct labor hours	4,000	8,000	6,000	N/A
Machine hours	6,000	2,000	2,000	N/A
Assembly hours	2,000	4,000	10,000	N/A

Each cabinet requires a different amount of work in each department. For three cabinet orders, the following are the details:

	Job 408	Job 409	Job 410
Materials	$300	$500	$750
Direct labor	$120	$250	$375
Direct labor hours—Cutting	2	4	5
Direct labor hours—Stain and Paint	3	4	6
Direct labot hours—Assembly	1	3	5
Machine hours—Cutting	3	2	4
Machine hours—Stain and Paint	1	2	3
Machine hours—Assembly	1	3	2
Assembly hours—Cutting	1	2	1
Assembly hours—Stain and Paint	2	2	1
Assembly hours—Assembly	3	6	8

REQUIRED:

a. Using direct labor hours as the driver, develop an overhead rate for the entire factory. Make sure to include general overhead in your calculations.

b. What does each job cost using the plant-wide rate on direct labor hours? Do not forget to charge out the actual labor to each job.

c. Using machine hours as the driver, develop an overhead rate for the entire factory. Make sure to include general overhead in your calculations.

d. What does it cost to make each product? Continue to charge your direct labor cost to the product. These calculations only affect overhead. Machine hours are used for overhead allocation.
e. Next, do the following: Charge general overhead on direct labor hours, Cutting's overhead on machine hours, Stain and Paint's overhead on direct labor hours, and Assembly's overhead on assembly hours. Be careful here. You want to choose only one driver for each department. Direct labor costs continue to be charged out on direct labor hours.
f. Recompute your job order costs using these new departmental rates.
g. Compare the costs you have computed. Which method appears to be best? Why?

4. JOB ORDER COSTING: PLANT-WIDE VS. DEPARTMENTAL OVERHEAD RATES.

Jenny's Painting Company paints and power-washes for industrial and residential customers. The company currently charges all overhead out on direct labor hours but is considering making changes because it has not been as competitive on painting jobs as it would like. The following is the information for the company.

Jenny's Painting Company			
	Painting	Power Washing	General Overhead
Overhead	$40,000	$150,000	$50,000
Direct labor hours	24,000	6,000	N/A
Machine hours	2,000	10,000	N/A

Jenny has recently been asked to bid on the following three jobs:

	Job 141	Job 142	Job 143
Materials	$12,000	$2,000	$5,000
Direct labor	$10,000	$1,000	$2,000
Direct labor hours	400	50	100
Machine hours	20	75	150

REQUIRED:

a. Develop a plant-wide overhead rate using direct labor hours. Do not forget to include the general overhead in your calculations.
b. Using this direct labor-based overhead rate, complete the bid for the three jobs Jenny is considering by adding in overhead.
c. Now develop a plant-wide rate using machine hours as the driver.

d. Use this machine hour-based overhead rate to attach overhead costs to the three jobs.
e. Next, develop three charging rates: General Overhead on direct labor hours, Painting on its own direct labor hours, and Power Washing on machine hours.
f. Use these three rates to re-cost the jobs. What is their new cost?
g. Which approach is better? Why?

5. **LARGE BATCH COSTING: PLANT-WIDE VS. DEPARTMENTAL OVERHEAD RATES.** Brewer's Magic makes the basic yeast and flavoring packets for the home beer-brewing industry. It makes these products in large batches on a repetitive basis, so it has gotten to know quite a bit about the costs of the various ingredients and the costs to run the primary departments: Blending, Cubing, and Packaging. The following table details the costs of the three departments and other key data.

Brewer's Magic				
	Blending	Cubing	Packaging	General Overhead
Overhead	$500,000	$300,000	$800,000	$400,000
Direct labor hours	6,000	2,000	12,000	N/A
Machine hours	12,000	6,000	8,000	N/A
Pounds made	1,000,000	N/A	N/A	N/A
Packages produced	N/A	N/A	8,000,000	N/A

The vice president of manufacturing, Jane Sneed, wants to look at her current overhead rates. Direct labor currently makes $15 per hour. She provides you with the following details for three large batches the company currently makes monthly.

	Magic Brew	Magic	Best Flavor Packet
Materials	$24,000.00	$36,000.00	$50,000.00
Direct labor hours—Blending	40	20	50
Direct labor hours—Cubing	10	8	16
Direct labor hours—Packaging	30	40	50
Machine hours—Blending	100	80	150
Machine hours—Cubing	60	-	50
Machine hours—Packaging	40	30	100

	Magic Brew	Magic	Best Flavor Packet
Pounds made	1,200	2,400	5,000
Packages produced	2,400	9,600	15,000

REQUIRED:

a. Using machine hours as the driver, develop an overhead rate and use it to charge overhead to the three batches. Do not forget to charge labor costs to each batch.
b. What is the cost per package made for each of the three batches?
c. Now develop four overhead rates, specifically use direct labor hours for general overhead, pounds made for blending, machine hours for cubing, and packages produced for packaging.
d. Re-cost the three batches using your four overhead rates. What does it now cost per package of output for each of the three products?
e. Which approach do you prefer? Why?

6. **LARGE BATCH COSTING: PLANT-WIDE VS. DEPARTMENTAL OVERHEAD RATES.** Made-Rite Foods makes several lines of sauces, including barbecue sauce and hot sauces, on a large batch basis. The products use different departments at the company, including Batch Preparation, Blending, and Bottling. The estimated costs and activity levels in each of the departments are included in the chart below.

Made-Rite Foods				
	Preparation	Blending	Bottling	General Overhead
Overhead	$400,000	$600,000	$1,200,000	$800,000
Direct labor hours	20,000	12,000	8,000	N/A
Machine hours	4,000	24,000	36,000	N/A
Ounces made	50,000,000	N/A	N/A	N/A
Bottles produced	N/A	N/A	20,000,000	N/A

The president, Julie Atkins, wants to look at the impact her overhead charging rates are having on product profitability. Direct labor is paid $20 per hour. To help do the analysis, she pulls together recent production information on the following products:

	Yankee BBQ Sauce	Hot Mama Hot Sauce	Yangtze Duck Sauce
Materials	$120,000	$90,000	$150,000

	Yankee BBQ Sauce	Hot Mama Hot Sauce	Yangtze Duck Sauce
Direct labor hours—Preparation	100	40	40
Direct labor hours—Blending	75	20	30
Direct labor hours—Bottling	50	40	40
Machine hours—Preparation	40	60	100
Machine hours—Blending	100	50	240
Machine hours—Bottling	100	250	150
Ounces made	240,000	80,000	800,000
Bottles produced	20,000	20,000	100,000

REQUIRED:

a. Using direct labor dollars as the driver, develop an overhead rate and then use it to charge overhead to the three batches. Do not forget to charge labor costs to each batch.
b. What is the cost per bottle made for each of the three batches?
c. Now develop four overhead rates, specifically use direct labor dollars for general overhead, ounces made for batch preparation, machine hours for blending, and bottles produced for bottling.
d. Re-cost the three batches using your four overhead rates. What does it now cost per bottle of output for each of the three products?
e. Which approach do you prefer? Why?

7. **LARGE BATCH COSTING: PLANT-WIDE VS. ABC OVERHEAD RATES.** Zippy Bags manufactures plastic bags with zippers for the consumer market. It makes the product in three sizes: one pint, one quart, and one gallon. It produces the product in large batches using the following production sequence: Molding, where the bags are produced; Assembly, where the zippers are added; and Packaging, where the bags are boxed for sale to customers. One-pint sandwich bags do not have zippers but have a simple flap that folds over to hold the contents. Overhead in the plant is currently charged out on direct labor dollars. Labor is paid $15 per hour. The information for the four departments and for a batch of each of the three bag types is in the following tables.

Zippy Bags						
	Molding	Assembly	Packaging	Set-Up	Inspection	General Overhead
Overhead	$1,000,000	$3,000,000	$2,400,000	$120,000	$800,000	$1,600,000
Direct labor hours	100,000	240,000	60,000	N/A	N/A	N/A
Machine hours	10,000	4,000	12,000	N/A	N/A	N/A
Bags made	5,000,000,000	N/A	N/A	N/A	N/A	N/A
Zippers attached	N/A	2,500,000,000	N/A	N/A	N/A	N/A
Boxes packaged	N/A	N/A	125,000,000	N/A	N/A	N/A
Set-up hours	N/A	N/A	N/A	2,400	N/A	N/A
Inspection hours	N/A	N/A	N/A	N/A	32,000	N/A

	Pint bags	Quart Bags	Gallon Bags
Materials	$45,000.00	$50,000.00	$52,000.00
Labor hours—Molding	500	400	300
Labor hours—Assembly	0	500	300
Labor hours—Packaging	80	80	60
Machine hours—Molding	100	200	300
Machine hours—Assembly	0	500	400
Machine hours—Packaging	200	300	250
Bags made	1,500,000	1,000,000	800,000
Zippers attached	-	1,000,000	800,000
Boxes packed	25,000	20,000	15,000
Set-up hours	10	40	50
Inspection hours	10	60	50

REQUIRED:

a. Calculate the current overhead rate using direct labor hours as your driver for Zippy Bags. Be sure to include all forms of overhead, no matter where the money is spent.

b. How much does it cost per box of bags of each type using direct labor dollars as the overhead rate?

c. Now develop six rates for your plant. Molding will be charged on machine hours, Assembly on direct labor hours, Packaging on boxes packaged, Set-Up on set-up hours, Inspection on inspection hours, and General Overhead on direct labor dollars.

d. How much does it cost now to make a box of each type of bag?
e. Which method for calculating overhead is better? Why?

8. **LARGE BATCH COSTING: PLANT-WIDE VS. ABC OVERHEAD RATES.** New Dawn Cleaning Supplies makes a variety of cleaning products, including powder cleansers, window-washing fluid, and dishwashing soap. The company currently has $12,000,000 in overhead, which it charges out on its 100,000 direct labor hours. Sam Houston, manufacturing supervisor, has asked Joey Burns to look at changing over to ABC for the various batches of product made. He believes he will get much greater accuracy if it switches methods, giving him better control over the plant. Direct labor is paid $15 per hour on average.

Information about the different departments and information on the latest batches of products made are in the tables below.

New Dawn Cleaning Supplies						
	Molding	Blending	Filling	Set-Up	Material Handling	General Overhead
Overhead	$1,500,000	$3,400,000	$2,600,000	$250,000	$600,000	$1,650,000
Direct labor hours	30,000	20,000	50,000	N/A	N/A	N/A
Bottles made	40,000,000	N/A	N/A	N/A	N/A	N/A
Batches blended	N/A	400	N/A	N/A	N/A	N/A
Containers filled	N/A	N/A	75,000,000	N/A	N/A	N/A
Set-up hours	N/A	N/A	N/A	2,500	N/A	N/A
Moves made	N/A	N/A	N/A	N/A	20,000	N/A

	Cleanser	Window-Washing Fluid	Dishwashing Detergent
Materials	$300,000	$625,000	$1,500,000
Labor hours—Molding	0	500	750
Labor hours—Blending	500	400	300
Labor hours—Filling	800	600	1,000
Bottles made	0	2,500,000	5,000,000
Batches blended	1	1	2

	Cleanser	Window-Washing Fluid	Dishwashing Detergent
Containers filled	2,000,000	2,500,000	5,000,000
Set-up hours	5	10	15
Material moves	20	10	5

REQUIRED:

a. Calculate the current overhead rate using direct labor hours as your driver. Be sure to include all forms of overhead, no matter where the money is spent.
b. How much does it cost per container of each type of product using direct labor dollars as the overhead rate?
c. Now develop six rates for your plant. Molding will be charged on bottles made, Blending on batches made, containers filled in Filling, Set-Up on set-up hours, Material Handling on moves made, and General Overhead on direct labor hours.
d. How much does it cost now to make a box of each of the types of cleaning supplies?
e. Which method of calculating overhead is better? Why?

9. **CELLULAR MANUFACTURING: GOOD UNITS VS. ABC COSTING RATES, TARGET COSTING.** Best Brew Coffee, Inc., makes single-serve coffee pots that use coffee pods. It has become very popular. Even though the cost per cup is greater than for brewed coffee, the freshness and variety continue to appeal to customers. It makes four different models of coffee pots on a cellular manufacturing line. Current costs are charged as direct materials to each type of pot, and then the rest of the manufacturing costs are charged evenly to good units produced. Total labor and overhead for the cell is currently $3,010,000. The data on the four models of coffee pots made this last year are:

Best Brew Coffee, Inc.				
	Model 100	Model 150	Model 200	Model 500
Materials costs	$75.00	$90.00	$120.00	$150.00
Good units made	25,000	40,000	60,000	15,000

Recently, there have been many discussions between the product line managers about these units. While right now they are all being charged the same manufacturing cost, the products use very different amounts of support activities. Of the $3,010,000 in labor and overhead, $1,610,000 is overhead for support activities that are done while the cell is producing output. The activities performed, their costs, and how each product uses these services is contained in the table below.

	Total Driver Frequency by Model						
	Total Dollars	Driver	Model 100	Model 150	Model 200	Model 500	Total
Labor	$1,400,000	Good units	25,000	40,000	60,000	15,000	140,000
Material handling	$400,000	Moves	400	600	800	700	2,500
Kitting	$250,000	Kits made	30,000	50,000	80,000	40,000	200,000
Inspection	$350,000	Inspection Hrs.	500	750	2,250	1,500	5,000
Purchase orders	$360,000	Purchase orders	300	600	1,100	1,600	3,600
Invoices	$250,000	Invoices mailed	100	500	1,000	900	2,500
Total	$3,010,000						

REQUIRED:

a. Determine the cost per good unit produced for labor and overhead.

b. Using the normal cellular costing approach, determine the cost per good unit produced. Specifically, charge materials directly to unit; then charge each output unit the same amount of labor and overhead based on your answer to (a).

c. Develop activity-based rates for all of the activities listed here. Also develop a rate for labor in the cell, which is still charged out on good units produced as noted in the table.

d. Now create a cost per total amount of each type of coffee pot made using your ABC information.

e. What does it cost per unit of coffee pot now? In other words, divide the solution to (d) by the total units of each type made.

f. If the target costs for the various products are those described in the following table, what is the cost gap for the original vs. revised estimate for each coffee pot?

	Model 100	Model 150	Model 200	Model 500
Target Cost	$95.00	$105.00	$140.00	$160.00

g. What recommendations would you make to Best Brew's management?

10. **APPENDIX: PROCESS COSTING.** Time Tells makes children's storybooks in a continuous run. It changes plates while the large machines are running, losing roughly 100 copies in the changeover process. This has long ago been determined to be the cheapest way to run the large-scale presses. All children's books are 32 pages with end matter bringing the page count to 40 pages per book. They are bound with a hard cover. The entire process is automated, with finished good books coming out at the end of the line. The plant runs 24 hours a day, seven days a week.

Because the plant operates continuously, there are always books in process at the end of the month. For July, the company incurred $6,573,000 in materials costs and $4,861,800 in conversion costs. There were 2,000 units in beginning inventory, and 2,628,000 new units were started during the month. Ending inventory consisted of 4,000 units, materials 80% done, and conversion 50% done.

REQUIRED:

a. Calculate the physical units for materials and conversion for the month.
b. Calculate the equivalent units for materials and conversion for the month.
c. Develop a cost per equivalent unit for materials and conversion.
d. Charge materials and conversion costs to finished goods and work-in-process using equivalent units as the basis.
e. Verify that all of the costs you had to account for have been accounted for.
f. What is the cost per good unit produced?

11. **APPENDIX: PROCESS COSTING.** NewsCorp prints and sells a variety of news magazines and newspapers on presses that run on the company's presses 24 hours a day, seven days a week. This has always been the cheapest way to produce newsprint.

Since the plant is always in operation, there are always papers in process at the beginning and end of any month. For September, the company incurred $2,691,000 in materials costs and $3,227,280 in conversion costs. Beginning inventory was 10,000 units, and 5,380,000 units were begun this month. At the end of the month, 16,000 units were in production, 50% done for materials, and 30% done for conversion.

REQUIRED:

a. Calculate the physical units for materials and conversion for the month.
b. Calculate the equivalent units for materials and conversion for the month.
c. Develop a cost per equivalent units for materials and conversion.
d. Charge materials and conversion costs to finished goods and work-in-process using equivalent units as the basis.
e. Verify that all of the costs you had to account for have been accounted for.
f. What is the cost per good unit produced?

Database Problems

For database templates, worksheets, and workbooks, go to MAdownloads.imanet.org

DB 6.1 ONE PLANT-WIDE RATE PRODUCT COST ESTIMATE FOR 20X6. To get started, you'll need the workbook DB 6-1. Using the overhead driver "Material Dollars," you are to develop an overhead rate using this driver, and then apply it to the individual units made. There are two steps in this process:

Develop the rate. To develop the overhead rate, the calculation is:

$$\frac{\textbf{Total Overhead Cost}}{\textbf{Total Material Dollars}}$$

This calculation tells us the amount of overhead we will charge to the product for every dollar of materials it uses. It does not eliminate the need to charge material cost—it is the overhead per dollar of material—a separate charge. You do this calculation on the worksheet DB 6.1 O-H Mat'l $ Template using information from the worksheet Product Cost Summaries—20x6.

Apply the rate to a unit made. You will now calculate the overhead cost for the various units made at Kinkaid using the rate you just developed and then for the company in total. There are four worksheets in the DB 6.1 workbook for this part of the exercise: DB 6.1 KitcCr-OH Mat $ Template, DB 6.1 CustCr-OH Mat $ Template, DB 6.1 KitcCr-OH Mat $ Ttl Tmpl, and DB 6.1 CustCr-OH Mat $ Ttl Tmpl. You will use two worksheets for these calculations: your solution to Part 1 above (the material dollar overhead rate) and the Product Cost Summaries—20x6 worksheet.

REQUIRED:

Turn in your completed product costing worksheets to your instructor along with the answer to the following questions: Which products are the most profitable? Least profitable?

DB 6.2 DEPARTMENTAL OVERHEAD RATES. The emphasis in this exercise is on first assigning overhead to departments with different drivers, and then looking at the impact of using direct labor hours at the departmental level as the overhead driver. There are four worksheets that you will need to complete for this exercise: DB 6.2 Overhead Rate Template, DB 6.2 OH to Part-DLH Template, DB 6.2 KitcCr-OH Dept DLH Templ, and DB 6.2 CustCr-OHK Dept DLH Templ. You will also see that there are three worksheets with data that will be useful: Product Cost Summaries-20x6, Mfg CC An'ls for 20x6, and Labor and Line Hour Data 20x6. The steps you will follow are:

DB 6.2 Overhead Rate Template: Begin by entering the total overhead for the company using the Product Summaries-20x6 worksheet in cell B3. Next, fill in cells B6 to D6 with the data from the Labor and Line Hour Data 20x6 worksheet and then calculate the overhead rate by driver (for example, B3/B6 for direct labor hours). Now, fill in rows 12 to 15 using the information from the Labor and Line Hour Data 20x6 worksheet. Next, calculate the amount of overhead charged to each department for rows 18 to 20 using the three different overhead rates and the driver quantity by department. Finally, given your results, answer the following question: Does the driver chosen impact how much overhead is charged to a department?

DB 6.2 OH to Part-DLH Template: Here you are going to determine how much overhead would be charged to a part, by department, first using the plant-wide DLH rate and then developing and using rates that charge the actual overhead costs by department to the parts made in that department. For each column, you will complete the calculation for rows 5 to 13. Using your results, answer the following question: Does the driver chosen impact how much overhead is charged to individual parts?

DB 6.2 KitcCr-OH Dept DLH Templ: Here you are going to calculate the overhead per unit using your departmental overhead cost per part using direct labor hours from Part 2. Begin by entering the cost per part, by department, from the DB 6.2 OH to Part-DLH Template in column D, rows 4-12. Next, enter the selling price, materials, and labor cost per unit using the Product Cost Summaries-20x6 data worksheet. Complete the rest of the calculations and then answer the following question: Which products appear to be the most profitable?

DB 6.2 CustCr-OH Dept DLH Templ: You will repeat the commands that were used in part 3 for the Kitchen Craft line for the Custom Craft product line. When you are done, answer the following question: Which products appear to be the most profitable?

REQUIRED:

Turn in your completed product costing worksheets and your answers to the four questions in parts 1 through 4 in to your instructor.

Cases

CASE 6.1 TARGET COSTING AND VALUE ENGINEERING. Easy Sweep makes vacuum cleaners for both residential and commercial customers. It has been making vacuum cleaners for more than 50 years, starting with one small model that was sold door-to-door. It is now a multi-billion-dollar producer of high-end vacuum cleaners using an international distribution network of retail outlets and specialty shops.

Easy Sweep's management has recently decided to enter the market for bagless vacuum cleaners and has designed a product that meets the company's high-quality image. They plan to produce two models, the ES 600 and the ES 800. The ES 600 will retail at $240, while the commercial-grade ES 800 will retail at $290. The company sells its vacuums to the distribution channel at roughly 60% of the retail price, making the target price for the ES 600 model $144, while the target price for the ES 800 model is $174. The company likes to make a 25% profit on all of its models. The resulting target cost and current estimated costs for producing the two vacuum models are in the table below.

Easy Sweep		
	ES 600	ES 800
Target price	$144.00	$174.00
Less: Desired profit	$36.00	$43.50
Target cost	$108.00	$130.50
Current Cost Estimates:		
Materials	$54.00	$65.25
Labor	$27.00	$32.50
Overhead	$33.75	$40.50
Selling costs	$10.00	$15.00
General and administrative costs	$15.00	$20.00
Total Current Cost	$139.75	$173.25

Easy Sweep		
	ES 600	ES 800
Cost Gap	$31.75	$42.75

Seeing that the current costs consume almost all of the company's selling price, Lisa Adams, VP of manufacturing, calls together the design team. Some of the comments made at the meeting are:

Lisa: We've got a real problem with these first-pass estimates. We would barely make a profit with these costs the way they are. We've got to cut somewhere. The question is where.

Paul Gable, design engineer: Lisa, I don't know how we can take much out of the cost unless we outsource the making of the drive engine. That's the most expensive part and it uses components that are unique to these vacuums. I got a quote, and we could reduce the cost of materials by $10 per model if we outsource it. That would also reduce labor by $5 and overhead by the 125% of labor that we use for our plant-wide rate. I don't know what we can do with the other overhead here, which is where an awful lot of the cost is going.

Lisa: If I get your numbers right, we could eliminate $15 in direct cost and $6.25 in manufacturing overhead if we outsource the drive engine. That gets us $21.25 closer to our target cost, closing the gap to $10.50 for the ES 600 and $21.50 for the ES 600. I still don't think management will be happy with these results.

Mark Eaton, marketing VP: I'm not happy with the thought of outsourcing a key part of the vacuum. Won't we lose control of quality and open ourselves up to potential problems in the market? We're known for our quality. How can we guarantee this?

Paul: We have done a lot of work in the past with this supplier. We would clearly need to do more inspection, which would drive costs back up by $3 per unit, so our cost gaps would likely be $12.50 and $23.50 respectively. With more inspections, we can guarantee quality. Also, our design team will spend significant time working with the supplier.

Lisa: Wait a minute. We already have a missing charge for development in cost estimate, don't we? And you want to add the amount of time and effort that goes into design to outsource the unit. Why can't that time be spent making internal design changes to get us in line with the outsourced unit? We try not to outsource here at Easy Sweep. I'd hate to see us start down that path because no matter how well we inspect, we lose control over the component if it isn't made here. And who's to say that once we outsource the drive engine, the supplier won't raise prices?

Paul: We can estimate that design work will cost on average $5 per unit if we outsource the drive engine and $6 a unit if we do it internally. That cost would apply to the first 100,000 units of each product made if you want to recoup the development cost in the unit cost. I agree we could get the cost of the drive engine down by $15 in materials and $5 in labor, with a reduction of 125% of labor in our overhead charge if we really work the design. Where does that leave us now?

Lisa: Hmmm....Down $20 but back up $6, so we'd be closing the cost gap by $14 if we make the part internally, in keeping with company policy. That would make our new cost gap for the ES 600 $14.75 and $28.75 for the ES 800. I can't do that overhead calculation in my head, but that's got to be another $6 or so in savings, right? Even so, the cost gap is still too big.

Mark: I think we could cut the marketing costs by 30% if that would help. We have the distribution channel in place. My question is why is general company overhead so high? What is the back office really adding to their workload when we're using existing customers and channels? They may have to do a few more purchase orders and invoices, but not to the tune of $15 and $20 per unit. That's a lot of money on the projected 100,000 unit sales planned for this year. Can't we reduce these by 40%?

Lisa: Both the general overhead and the manufacturing overhead were estimates based on current charges for other models. I bet we could get some money out there as we're going to be using cellular manufacturing, which is much more efficient. We could probably cut manufacturing overhead by 25%. Tell you what, I'll put all of these suggestions together and see how close we get. We may have to find a few more savings, but we're making progress.

REQUIRED:

a. **Use the final changes in estimates suggested by Mark and Lisa to develop a new estimate of the cost gap. How much further do they need to go to make the product hit its profit goals?**
b. **Does it seem reasonable to use new costing assumptions for the new models or do you think the entire system of overhead charges should be examined to determine exactly how much of the overhead costs for manufacturing and general overhead should be charged to the new vs. existing units?**

c. How do you feel about the outsourcing option? Do you feel Mark is right to worry about the quality risk; or do you think that outsourcing might be a better option? Why or why not?

CASE 6.2 PLANT-WIDE VS. DEPARTMENTAL OVERHEAD RATES. Better Yet Dishware produces dishes and drinking mugs for a large domestic market. It uses both traditional retail outlets and its own company stores where slightly flawed product is sold. Decorating the dishes is done by hand, while the entire production process for drinking mugs is automated.

John Kluny, president of Better Yet, has recently been concerned with the costs of making dishware vs. coffee mugs. The cost of the products used to be roughly comparable until the huge mug-making machine was put in place last year. The mug-making machine cost the company $2,500,000 and is supposed to last five years with two shift-a-day operations. Other costs caused by running the machine add up to $250,000 per year, including the space, power, and insurance it requires. Only one direct labor worker is needed to run the machine. In the past, it took 15 people to make the mugs. Dishware is a larger department, but it only uses machines to form the dishes. This machine is old and fully depreciated. The rest of the cost in the department is related to labor. More than 50 people work in the dishware department, hand-painting each set as it comes down the production line.

The following table summarizes the material, labor and overhead costs, and activity drivers for the two departments before and after the new machine was put in place.

Better Yet Dishware					
Before Purchasing the New Machine			After Purchasing the New Machine		
	4 Place Serving Set of Dishware	Box of 8 Mugs		4 Place Serving Set of Dishware	Box of 8 Mugs
Materials	$30,000,000	$10,800,000	Materials	$30,000,000	$10,800,000
Labor ($15 per Hour)	$1,500,000	$450,000	Labor ($15 per Hour)	$1,500,000	$60,000
Overhead (600% Labor)	$9,000,000	$2,700,000	Overhead	??	??
Total Cost	$40,500,000	$13,950,000	Total Cost	??	??
Divided by quantity made	2,500,000	1,200,000	Divided by quantity made	2,500,000	1,200,000
Cost per Unit Sale	$16.20	$11.63	Cost per Unit Sale	??	??
Drivers per Year			Drivers per Year		
Labor Dollars	$1,500,000	$450,000	Labor Dollars	$1,500,000	$60,000
Machine Hours	4,000	2,000	Machine Hours	4,000	6,000

The new overhead rate had yet to be determined. Overhead costs in total, however, have gone up by the cost of the new machine. John has asked you to help him better understand his costs. You have gladly volunteered and decide to follow the steps below.

REQUIRED:

a. Develop an estimate of the new total amount of Better Yet's overhead.
b. Using direct labor dollars and a plant-wide rate, recalculate the overhead charged to each product and the cost per sales unit for each of the products.
c. Now develop two overhead rates. Specifically, assume that the overhead that was charged to the dishware department before the new mug-making machine was purchased was about right. Take the rest of the newly calculated overhead from (a) and charge it to mug-making. Continue to charge overhead out in dishware by using direct labor dollars. Create a new rate for mug-making using machine hours as your driver.
d. What are your product costs now? Which approach is better? Why?
e. Do you think it was a good idea to purchase the new machine? Why or why not?

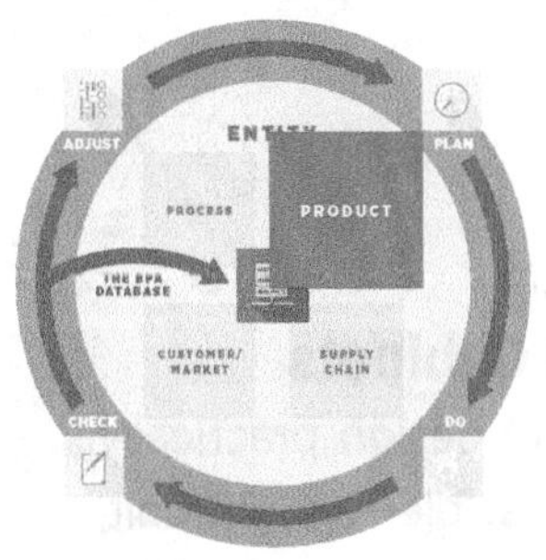

CHAPTER SEVEN

Assessing and Improving Product Profitability

Take nothing on its looks; take everything on evidence. There is no better rule.
CHARLES DICKENS
GREAT EXPECTATIONS

CHAPTER ROADMAP

1. **Moving Beyond Target Costing: Attainment Phase**
   - *Attaining the Target Cost*
   - *Setting and Meeting Standards*
   - *Creating and Supporting Continuous Improvement*
2. **Analyzing Product Profitability**
   - *Financial Measures of Product Performance*
   - *Evaluating Product Cost Variances*
3. **Analyzing Product Performance**
   - *Product-Focused RADAR Analysis*
   - *Product-Focused Pareto Analysis*
   - *Product-Focused Cause-and-Effect Analysis*
4. **Developing the Case for Change**
   - *Leveraging Existing Processes: Cost-Volume-Profit Analysis*
   - *Assessing Structural Changes: Incremental Analysis*
5. **Developing a Product-Focused Business Case: Behavioral, Strategic, and Operational Considerations**

LEARNING OBJECTIVES

After studying this chapter, you should be able to:

1. **Explain how a company identifies cost improvement targets and establishes standards and methods to achieve these targets.**
2. **Develop a comprehensive set of financial and nonfinancial measures to assess product performance and complete a cost variance analysis.**
3. **Develop a comprehensive set of nonfinancial measures to assess product line performance and use this information to evaluate it.**
4. **Apply cost-volume-profit and incremental analysis to improve product line performance.**
5. **Develop a business case for improving product line profitability; include the behavioral, strategic, and operational issues.**

IN CONTEXT ➤ Cutting Costs, Not Corners, at Kinkaid Cabinets

The need to reduce the cost of the initial product design practically brought Brad to his knees. "Shelley wants the impossible—a $200 unit, but with all of the bells and whistles. Not possible!" he muttered to himself. He considered asking her to find someone else for the project, but his pride—or stubbornness—would not let him. He told himself there was no challenge he could not meet.

Tensions were still running high when Brad dialed Shelley's extension. For more than a week, Brad had doggedly tried various options in his attempt to meet Shelley's demand. Finally, convinced it was impossible, he blurted out, "I know you want a $200 cabinet, Shelley, but using our usual methods and materials, I can't find a way to get us there," Brad said.

"Jeez, Brad, you did your best; you can't do the impossible? If we can't use our existing materials and methods, I'm giving you carte blanche to get creative with materials, processes, and anything else you think you need to meet the target—*except* sacrificing the attributes our customers care about!"

"I'll try again, Shelley; you've opened up a whole new way of thinking about it. How much longer can I have?"

Shelley was convinced the problem was solved. "How about talking at the beginning of next week, once you've had a chance to think about it? Then let's put our heads together, okay?" Brad shook his head. It was going to be a long week.

His first step was to meet with his team and fill them in. To Brad's surprise, they took the news calmly. "I think we can put together something to show Shelley when you meet," John said.

"That's great!" Brad responded. "The past couple of weeks have been difficult; we explored existing options and they didn't pan out. Now I think we're going to make progress!"

ONE OF THE MOST DIFFICULT THINGS FOR MANAGERS TO DO WHEN DEVELoping a new product is to find the best blend of price and features to convince potential customers that they will be getting superior value for their money. Unless a company operates as a monopoly, it must take the market into account. If one competitor does a better job at providing a product with a higher **value proposition**—*the perceived worth of a product or service compared to its price*—customers will buy the competitor's products. It is as simple as that. In a competitive global market, the company that best finds the balance between price and value will optimize its market share.

In the last chapter, we learned about target costing and how managers use it to define and attain desired product attributes during the product development cycle. We also learned some of the basics of estimating product costs, such as how to develop and apply various overhead allocation methods. Having examined the planning tasks that management accounting supports in the product domain, it is now time to turn our attention to assessing actual performance and improving these results.

Moving Beyond Target Costing: Attainment Phase

OBJECTIVE 1
Explain how a company identifies cost improvement targets and establishes standards and methods to achieve these targets.

When managers know how much it costs to produce products and how much customers value those products, the organization is in a better position to control costs and increase profits. Target costing increases the likelihood that a company will gain the knowledge and control that lead to the long-term profits so essential for fueling both future growth and providing returns to stockholders. Serving as the basis for defining these goals during the establishment phase, the attainment phase of target costing ensures that the product's performance and profitability goals are met. As Figure 7.1 illustrates, the attainment phase focuses on eliminating the cost gap: the amount of excess cost in a new product or service, or, the difference between the target cost and the estimated cost.

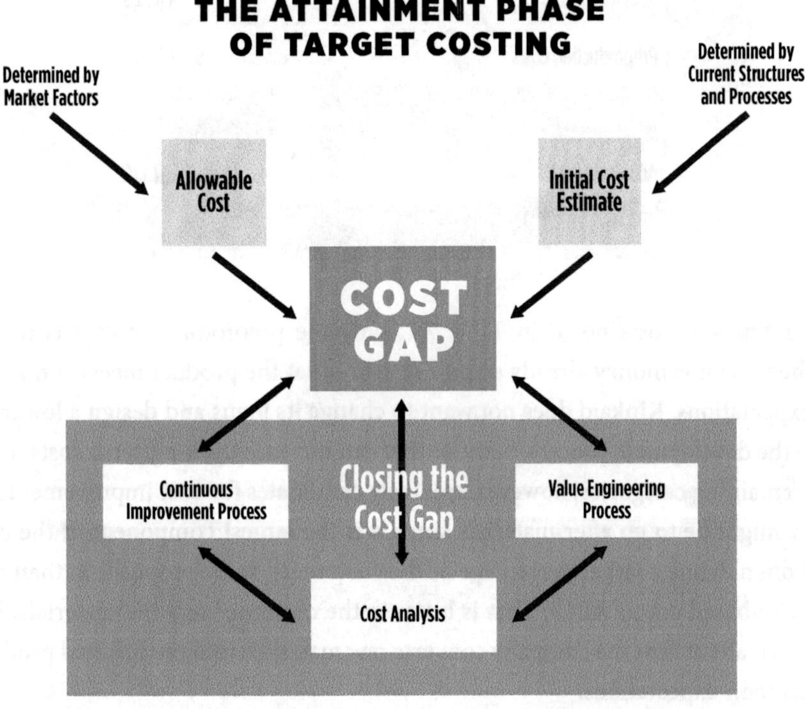

FIGURE 7.1 THE GOAL OF THE ATTAINMENT PHASE IS THE ELIMINATION OF ANY EXISTING GAP BETWEEN THE ESTIMATED AND TARGET COST.

ATTAINING THE TARGET COST

Target costing is a disciplined, focused approach for managing a company's product lines. In Chapter 6, we saw how managers establish these costs and performance features. In the Green Acres example, using value engineering, we actually changed the Easy Trimmer's materials and the firm's design methods to help Green Acres achieve its target cost goals.

To further clarify the process of setting and achieving target costs, let us see if we can accomplish the same objective with Kinkaid's new line of office furniture by analyzing the current product design and help Brad determine how to eliminate $33.56, the excess cost projected for the wall cabinet unit. Table 7.1 outlines these costs.

TABLE 7.1 TARGET COST ANALYSIS

Kinkaid Cabinets—Proposed Wall Cabinet	
Cost Element	**Estimated Unit Cost**
Material	$ 118.40
Conversion Costs	$ 56.05
Activity Costs	$ 48.11
Preproduction Costs	$ 11.00
Total Estimated Cost	$ 233.56
Allowable Cost	$ 200.00
Excess Cost	$ 33.56

Of the four types of costs noted in Table 7.1, only the preproduction cost is not a candidate for improvement because it is money already spent to ensure that the product meets company and customer performance expectations. Kinkaid does not want to change its focus and design a lower-quality product, or shortchange the development process, because that can increase the long-term costs of the product line.

The three remaining categories, however, are likely candidates for cost improvements. But, while your first inclination might be to go after materials since it is the largest component of the cabinet's cost, the materials used often define a larger percentage of the customers' value proposition than a company's conversion or activity-based costs (ABC). That is because the customer *sees* the materials, but probably has little or no concern about how the company converts raw materials into the finished product as long as the end result meets their expectations.

Therefore, let us first consider the activity and conversion cost categories. Table 7.2a and b summarize the information we compiled in Chapter 6.

TABLE 7.2A INITIAL CONVERSION COSTS SUMMARY

Kinkaid Cabinets—Proposed Wall Cabinet Unit					
Department	(1) Overhead Rate per Machine Hour	(2) Cycle Time per Part Made	(1) x (2) = (3) Conversion Cost per Part	(4) Number of Parts in Cabinet	(3) x (4) = (5) Conversion Cost per Cabinet
Cut flat wood parts	$750.11	0.0002	$0.15	37	5.55
Make frames	$79.47	0.0311	$2.47	2	$4.94
Make doors	$51.23	0.0887	$4.54	2	$9.08
Paint parts	$2,328.75	0.0005	$1.16	3	$3.48
Assemble	$1,151.41	0.0144	$16.58	2	$33.16
	Total Conversion Cost per Unit				$56.21

TABLE 7.2B ACTIVITY-BASED COSTS

Kinkaid Cabinets—Proposed Wall Unit						
Activity	(1) Total Annual Cost of Activity	Activity Driver	(2) Number of Times Activity Done per Year	(1) / (2) = (3) Cost per Activity	(4) Driver Frequency per Unit Made	(3) x (4) = (5) Activity Cost per Unit
Kit materials	$7,150,030	Kits made	1,000,000	$7.15 per kit	3 kits	$21.45
Inspection	$6,969,850	Inspection minutes	1,200,000	$5.81 per minute	4 minutes	$23.24
Packaging	$4,762,490	Units made	4,173,320	$1.14 per unit made	3 units	$3.42
Unit total						$48.11

Looking at the information in Table 7.2a and 7.2b, we can identify three activity areas we would probably want to look at first: assembly, **kit materials**—*an internal process that focuses on bringing together all the parts needed to produce the product*, and inspection. Together, their total cost is $77.85, more than double the amount we need to eliminate to make the target cost of $200 per unit. While this may simplify production, there probably are other ways to accomplish this objective.

Let us start with a simple goal: to reduce the number of kit materials activities from three (once for the doors, once for the frame, and once for the flat stock that is used for the joiner shelf, and the back, sides, and bottom of the two cabinets) to one (containing all of the required items), which will generate $14.30 in savings on this product. We will have to check downstream to make sure this is an attainable goal, but, for now, we will make the assumption that we can and will attain it.

The second activity that looks too expensive for the work being done is inspection. While Kinkaid wants to maintain its high standards and would not want to send out a defective product, Brad feels that this cost could be cut in half to $11.62 once production gets under way. Again, assuming that Kinkaid can make this change, we estimate that these two process changes alone will generate $25.92 of the needed $33.56 in cost reductions, leaving $7.64 left in excess cost. Remember, our goal is to minimize the impact of process changes on the perceived value of the product in the customer's eyes.

Having taken steps to reap the "low-hanging fruit," it is now more difficult for Brad and the design team to remove cost. The assembly process is not one that is easily adjusted—they are already using modern manufacturing methods for that activity. In one respect, if they could entirely do away with the kit materials activity, they would be within a few cents of the required cost target. Going this last step may be unrealistic using existing production methods. But what if an outside vendor quoted $24.75 per door delivered? Doors are a major cost component, and each wall unit has two doors. Table 7.3 looks at the costs associated with making the doors.

TABLE 7.3 CALCULATING MANUFACTURING COST PER COMPONENT

Kinkaid Cabinets—Proposed Wall Unit			
Cost Item	(1) Cost rate	(2) Amount needed	(1) x (2) = (3) Estimated cost
Wood for doors	$12.00 per square foot	4 square feet	$48.00
Cut wood parts	$0.147 per part	12 parts	$1.76
Make two doors	$51.23 per hour	0.1774 hours	$9.09
Paint doors	$2,328.75 per hour	0.001 hours	$2.33
Total to manufacture doors			$61.18

The decision to outsource would remove $11.68 [$61.18 less ($24.75 times 2)] from the cost of the proposed product, bringing us to $195.96, or $4.04 below the allowable cost. The cost savings, of course, would have to be considered against the reduced flexibility and control Kinkaid would have over the total production process, along with the potential for vendor-based delays or future price increases once Kinkaid outsourced manufacturing the doors.

Finally, there is something else to consider: Although this change would remove the cost of the doors from this product line, it would not remove the cost of door-making from Kinkaid's books—the department would still be there to manufacture doors for other products. Therefore, if this product was using otherwise idle time in the door-making department, the company as a whole might not be better off after outsourcing—its idle cost would increase. On the other hand, if the company could run the door-making facility at full capacity without these cabinet doors, the decision would be simple—outsource the doors. In the case of Kinkaid, the decision is made to outsource the doors as the rest of the plant will see only minor impact—other manufacturing areas would return to the steady state they had been in before the decision was made to develop the modular line.

These observations also raise another question that we might want to pursue at Kinkaid, which is, would it be better if all of the doors for all of Kinkaid's products were purchased from an outside vendor? Clearly, we could analyze the impact of this decision and generate a business case if the numbers suggest that it is a viable option. Uncovering issues such as this is an unanticipated benefit of target costing. In the quest to bring a new product within or under its target cost, a company is often driven to reexamine the existing practices and assumptions for the business as a whole.

At this point, you may be wondering how we move beyond identifying potential areas for removing excess cost to ensuring that the proposed changes are both feasible and desirable. With respect to the kit materials activity, if we do not pull all of the parts together into a kit, we will have to find another way to get materials where they are needed to make a specific cabinet. And, if we make these changes in the layout and flow on the plant floor for the new product line, it may create the need to make further changes to the processes used to make other products at Kinkaid. In other words, no change is made in isolation in a company—one decision will likely lead to another in the continuous pursuit of improved performance and profits. Let us now move into the next phase of product development: pilot testing and standard setting.

SETTING AND MEETING STANDARDS

After a firm completes the design phase of product development, it is important to pilot the production of an item before attempting to establish its final production and cost parameters. If a firm skips this step, it may launch a product that is either impossible to produce or impossible to produce within the defined standards. For instance, in the mid-1980s, in order to comply with new environmental laws, Revlon Corporation was exploring different types of propellants for its line of fragrances, such as Charlie. But, faced with the challenge of finding a new propellant, the company decided to improve its products at the same time.

The initial search for a new propellant was undertaken by the research and development group, which located a very good alternative that actually reduced total costs over time. It performed the standard battery of tests on the new material, and then released it to the production line without direct testing on the machines actually used to make the product. Almost immediately, problems became evident, as the costs skyrocketed past the established standards and the amount of scrap, or bad units, produced rose precipitously.

In reexamining the issue, the management team uncovered the problem—the new propellant was quite caustic, eroding the gaskets used to hold a seal while the propellant was added to a bottle of fragrance. A simple process change corrected the problem—instead of changing the gasket monthly, Revlon now replaced it once every hour of operation. While this increased the number of gaskets needed, they cost less than $0.05 each, a trivial cost compared to the cost of the propellant and scrap. While management found the right solution, it would have been less costly had it detected this problem during a pilot run on the plant floor.

Returning to Kinkaid, let us assume the test run of the new office wall unit on the production line resulted in only minor changes to Brad's original projections. The cabinet can be made as planned, and within the stated process and quality parameters; therefore, Kinkaid can now establish standards that will provide the basis for managing, evaluating, and improving the production of the wall unit. Managers should establish these standards for every key element of the product and process. Specifically, managers should establish material standards for the product and time or frequency standards for the activities required to convert these materials into the finished product. Because this is an initial launch, Brad and his design engineers will need to develop the first set of standards. These will be engineered standards as illustrated in Table 7.4. As time goes on and Kinkaid gains experience in making this product, managers can adjust these engineering estimates based on actual manufacturing conditions.

TABLE 7.4 ESTIMATING ENGINEERING STANDARDS

Kinkaid Cabinets—Proposed Wall Unit			
Materials	(1) Rate	(2) Amount needed	(1) x (2) = (3) Estimated cost
Purchased door	$24.75 per door	2 doors	$49.50
Particle board	$1.50 per square foot	14 square feet	$21.00
Wood for frame	$1.00 per linear foot	28 linear feet	$28.00
Paint	$0.50 per ounce	4 ounces	$2.00
Glue	$0.25 per ounce	4 ounces	$1.00
Screws	$0.60 per dozen	2 dozen	$1.20
Hinges	$1.00 per hinge	4 hinges	$4.00
Door handles	$2.00 per handle	2 handles	$4.00
Packaging material	$0.40 per cubic foot	18 cubic feet	$7.20
	Total materials		$117.90
Conversion and other activities			
Cut flat wood parts	$0.147 per part	25 parts	$3.68
Make frames	$2.469 per frame	2 frames	$4.94
Paint parts	$1.116 per part	3 parts	$3.35
Assemble cabinet	$16.627 per cabinet	2 cabinets	$33.25
Kit materials	$7.15 per kit	2 kits	$14.30
Inspection	$5.81 per minute	2 minutes	$11.62
Package unit	$1.14 per unit	3 units	$3.42
	Total conversion		$74.56
Total standard cost			$192.46

Note: The cost of the items highlighted in yellow were decreased based on the target costing effort.

Outsourcing the door helped reduce inspection time from four minutes to the targeted two minutes, because, in the past, inspecting the door had taken more time due to unavoidable manufacturing and painting problems. On the other hand, the pilot production proved that Kinkaid still needed two kits of materials—one for each of the two current wall cabinets that make up the new office wall unit. Without piloting the production of the new product under actual operating conditions, Brad might have missed this fact.

LOOKING BACK ➤ Anticipation vs. Reality

Frank Brugger was a leading industrialist during the scientific management era (approximately 1880 to 1930). He was a major proponent of the need to use standards to control operations when developing a product.

In developing his standards, Brugger's primary emphasis was on the need to understand the potential demand for the product. This established the basis for estimating the cost of manufacturing, the cost of distribution, the amount of fixed investment and working capital needed, and the net income required to make the endeavor a successful one. These estimates served as the basis for setting a market price. After revisiting the estimate of demand based on the calculated price, the decision to pursue the new product could be made. Estimated costs played a major role in this exercise.

Once the estimates were made, Brugger had the company's cost accountant begin tracking actual costs against the standards in order to provide a means of control to management. Only by having a system in place that compared actual performance to expected performance could management understand the reason for shortfalls or overages. Representing a strong argument for standard costs, Brugger's articles remain a timeless reminder of the role sound cost estimates play in managing the launch of a new product.

Frank Brugger
"Standard Costs—Their Development and Use"
N.A.C.A. Bulletin, March 2, 1925

In developing a set of standards for production, the goal is to establish *"tight but attainable" standards.* If the standards are too tight, they either will not be met or they may lead to dysfunctional behavior as line workers take shortcuts or find other ways to meet the standards. If they are too loose, they can build waste into the organization, and the cost of waste cannot be passed on to customers. Kinkaid will know when the standard is approximately correct after it gains experience in making the product and sees the actual costs and effort it requires, and managers see in the production process a repeatable pattern that has minimal variance from one month to the next.

CREATING AND SUPPORTING CONTINUOUS IMPROVEMENT

The initial standards set during target costing represent the best of what managers currently know and what the company can attain. As the product moves into actual production, many opportunities arise for improving the process and product. Recognizing and implementing the changes needed to turn opportunities into reality is the focus of a **continuous improvement program,** *a process where every aspect of making a product or providing a service is constantly reviewed in order to make it better*. It incrementally improves yields, eliminates waste, reduces response time, simplifies design, and improves quality. This is an ongoing process in successful firms in which employees continuously improve every stage in the production of goods and services in order to improve quality, increase quantity, eliminate waste, and reduce response time to customer requests.

There are many different management methods and tools used to deploy the continuous improvement concept in modern organizations, from self-managed work teams and quality circles empowered to identify and implement improvements, to just-in-time models, total quality management (TQM), and various forms of value and process engineering initiatives.

Continuous improvement objectives underlie the ongoing cycle of "Plan-Do-Check-Adjust" activities that make up the management process. In fact, many of the tools and techniques that we developed in Chapters 4 and 5, such as spider diagrams and Ishikawa fishbone (cause-and-effect) diagrams, originated in the continuous improvement philosophy. Whenever we focus on identifying and implementing incremental changes to existing processes and products, we are engaged in the process of continuous improvement.

We will discuss the details of identifying opportunities for improvement in a bit more depth in Chapters 8 and 9 as we explore issues within the process domain.

IN CONTEXT ➤ Taking Stock at Kinkaid Cabinets

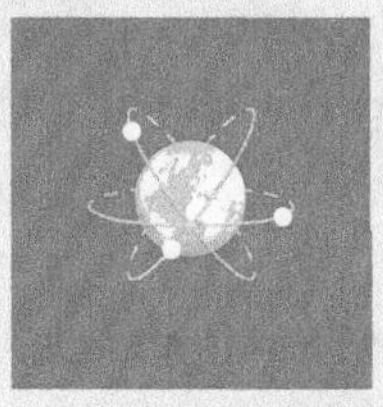

It has been a year since we looked at Kinkaid's new product launch initiative. In that time, it designed the line and marketed the units, and sales of the modular furniture met or exceeded all expectations. From the original wall cabinet unit, Kinkaid expanded the line to include several types of desks, credenzas, and computer workstations, as well as a broad range of modular wall units and dividers.

While the picture is rosy in terms of units sold, the line's profitability is not quite what Kinkaid hoped. At management's request, Brad's team initiated a study to determine how to make improvements and attain or exceed the original profit and performance targets for the line. Let us join Brad and his team during their weekly management briefing session to see what their plans and concerns are.

Brad wasted no time in getting to the point. "Sam, as you can see, we're making our production quotas, with only minimal quality problems. But, we often ship incomplete orders because we haven't received the doors from the outside vendor that are needed to finish one or more of the units. If I were on the receiving end, I wouldn't be happy—and Shelley says—neither are our customers."

"You're right, Brad. There were a few complaints and we did lose some sales because of delivery problems, which resulted in lost revenues, which dropped the overall profit number. What are your plans to fix the issue?" asked Sam.

"We need to find a different vendor or go back to making them ourselves. I won't know which makes the most sense until we complete our study, but this is one area we need to focus on. Also, we need to study the production line to see why it's taking longer than we thought it would to assemble and inspect the units. Originally, we assumed these costs and time requirements would drop over time, but they haven't. Barb's group is helping us there. We should have some idea of the issues and potential solutions in time for next week's meeting."

"Okay. I can see you're making progress, and I know that we'll get this issue resolved. If your team needs anything, make sure you let me know; I'll do what I can to help." As always, Sam ended the meeting on a positive note. Keeping the team motivated was essential—and he was not going to let anything get in their way.

Analyzing Product Profitability

OBJECTIVE 2

Develop a comprehensive set of financial and nonfinancial measures to assess product performance and complete a cost variance analysis.

It is not uncommon for a new product line, no matter how well-designed and tested it is, to need some adjustments and improvements to achieve its prelaunch objectives. Even if prelaunch goals are met from the beginning, the quest to reduce costs and enhance performance continues. In fact, whether old or new, established or under design, there is always room for product-based profit and performance improvements. To find, measure, analyze, and then implement these opportunities, we rely on many of the tools and techniques we learned in Chapters 4 and 5.

FINANCIAL MEASURES OF PRODUCT PERFORMANCE

In the opening pages of the chapter, we developed a series of standard cost measures for Kinkaid's new wall unit. These are important metrics, but they are not the only measures we use to track and improve a product's profitability and performance. For example, we might want to know the overall scrap or return rate for the product, the number of units sold, and overall customer satisfaction with them. Some of the measures we use to track and evaluate a product include:

- Units sold
- Average price per unit
- Market share

- Average cost per unit
- Standard cost per unit
- Value-added cost per unit
- Average profit per unit
- Cycle time (speed at which units are made)
- First-pass quality rates
- Units scrapped
- Units reworked
- Total quality costs
- Return rates
- Warranty costs
- On-time delivery rates
- Degree of customer satisfaction

This might seem like a large list of items to keep track of, but most companies maintain this information about their products. Since a company's products and services are the source of its revenues and its future, keeping a close watch on how well a product or service performs is critical.

As you look at this list of measures, you can see that some of them are financial (for example, standard cost) and others are nonfinancial in nature (market share). In developing a set of performance metrics for a product, we try to create a **management dashboard,** *a one-page summary of performance on key measures of quality, delivery, productivity, and cost*. In fact, no matter what decision domain we are in, or what type of organization we are discussing, the basic measurement concepts we learned in the first five chapters of this book apply. Table 7.5 summarizes the most recent performance of three different products from the new modular office furniture line at Kinkaid using each of the measures in our list.

TABLE 7.5 MANAGEMENT DASHBOARD

Kinkaid Modular Furniture Performance Results for the Year Ending 12/31/20x8			
Measurement	Wall Unit	Executive Desk	Computer Workstation
Forecasted unit sales	10,000	2,500	7,500
Actual units sold	15,000	2,000	15,000
Average price	$240.00	$650.00	$350.00
Market share	4%	2%	5%
Average cost per unit	$209.39	$515.35	$256.00
Standard cost per unit	$192.46	$506.50	$275.00
Value-added cost per unit	$123.65	$329.25	$201.50
Average actual profit per unit	$30.61	$154.65	$94.00

Kinkaid Modular Furniture Performance Results for the Year Ending 12/31/20x8			
Measurement	Wall Unit	Executive Desk	Computer Workstation
Cycle time	0.025 hours	0.06 hours	0.015 hours
First-pass quality rates	70%	60%	99%
Units scrapped	250	100	50
Units reworked	1,000	250	100
Return rates	10%	15%	5%
Scrap and rework costs	$65,400	$52,500	$18,000
Warranty costs	$3,500	$5,000	$500
On-time delivery rates	75%	65%	98%
Customer satisfaction	Medium	Medium/Low	High

As we examine these results, we see that wall units and computer workstations are selling more units than forecasted, while executive desks are selling 20 percent fewer units than expected. Quality problems are evident in at least two of the lines (wall units and executive desks), which, combined with on-time delivery problems, are creating lukewarm reception in the market (medium-to-low customer satisfaction). Only computer workstations are exceeding projections and meeting high satisfaction in the marketplace. The performance problems are also affecting the cost side, with the actual average cost per unit for wall units and executive desks being higher than standard cost projections.

These results lead to some obvious questions, such as what is causing the quality and delivery problems for wall units and executive desks? What is being done during the manufacture of computer workstations that is not being done for executive desks or wall units? What are the underlying differences in materials or methods that would explain the marked differences in performance results? Finally, why are computer workstations and wall unit sales so high and executive desk sales so low? While sales greater than forecast is "good news" for Kinkaid, unless the team knows what is driving these results, it may not properly adjust its production plans in the future. Let us take a closer look at the computer workstation and wall unit results to see if we can pinpoint the source of the differences in overall performance, starting with cost variance analysis.

EVALUATING PRODUCT COST VARIANCES

One of the primary tools we use to understand the performance of a product is variance analysis. The primary focus of variance analysis is the comparison of actual costs to standard or estimated costs for a period of time. As Table 7.6 details, during the first year of operation, the average actual cost of production for the wall unit exceeded the amount estimated during the attainment phase of target costing by $25.42 or 13.2%.

TABLE 7.6 VARIANCE ANALYSIS

Kinkaid Cabinets						
Standard vs. Actual Cost Estimates for New Wall Unit in the First Year of Production						
Standard Cost Estimate				Actual Results		
Materials	(1) Rate	(2) Amount needed	(1) x (2) = (3) Estimated cost	(4) Rate	(5) Amount needed	(4) x (5) = (6) Actual cost
Purchased door	$24.75 per door	2 doors	$49.50	$27.05 per door	2 doors	$54.10
Particle board	$1.50 per square foot	14 square feet	$21.00	$1.58 per square foot	16 square feet	$25.28
Wood for frame	$1.00 per linear foot	28 linear feet	$28.00	$1.00 per linear foot	30 linear feet	$30.00
Paint	$0.50 per ounce	4 ounces	$2.00	$0.50 per ounce	5 ounces	$2.50
Glue	$0.25 per ounce	4 ounces	$1.00	$0.25 per ounce	4 ounces	$1.00
Screws	$0.60 per dozen	2 dozen	$1.20	$0.60 per dozen	2 dozen	$1.20
Hinges	$1.00 per hinge	4 hinges	$4.00	$1.00 per hinge	4 hinges	$4.00
Door handles	$2.00 per handle	2 handles	$4.00	$1.90 per handle	2 handles	$3.80
Packaging material	$0.40 per cubic foot	18 cubic feet	$7.20	$0.40 per cubic foot	18 cubic feet	$7.20
	Total materials		$117.90	Total materials		$129.08
Conversion and other activities						
Cut flat wood parts	$0.147 per part	25 parts	$3.68	$0.15 per part	28 parts	$4.20
Make frames	$2.469 per frame	2 frames	$4.94	$2.55 per frame	2 frames	$5.10
Paint parts	$1.116 per part	3 parts	$3.35	$1.116 per part	3 parts	$3.35
Assemble cabinet	$16.627 per cabinet	2 cabinets	$33.25	$20.50 per cabinet	2 cabinets	$41.00
Kit materials	$7.15 per kit	2 kits	$14.30	$7.15 per kit	2 kits	$14.30
Inspection	$5.81 per minute	2 minutes	$11.62	$5.81 per minute	3 minutes	$17.43
Package unit	$1.14 per unit	3 units	$3.42	$1.14 per unit	3 units	$3.42
	Total conversion		$74.56	Total conversion		$88.80
Total standard cost			$192.46	Total actual cost		$217.88

Conversion costs, or the labor and overhead, for the new product line came in very close to the original estimate, but some of the work is taking much longer than originally anticipated, driving production costs up by $14.24. Material costs were also significantly over the numbers Brad used in his analysis. Doors were a major culprit, accounting for $4.60, or roughly half, of the cost overrun for materials. There have been ongoing discussions with the door supplier, who maintains that the quantities actually ordered are less than those on which they based the original prices. The higher price reflects these reduced quantities. The remaining material cost overruns are due to a combination of price variances (particle board and door handles) and usage variances (particle board, wood for the frames, and paint).

Table 7.7 summarizes the variances between the original standard cost estimates developed by Brad and his team, and the average actual costs incurred during production. Problems occurred in several areas; however, the price of the doors and inspection time represent two of the most significant problems. In actuality, 28, not 25, wood parts had to be cut and used to make the product, which suggests that there might have been an error in the original design specifications. Regardless, once having identified the areas where performance has not met the specifications set during target costing, the managers' next step is to try to isolate the causes for the performance problems and remedy them.

TABLE 7.7 SUMMARY OF VARIANCES

Kinkaid Cabinets										
Variance Analysis for the new Wall Unit in the First Year of Production										
	Analysis of price variances					Analysis of usage variances				
Materials	(1) Actual price	(2) Standard price	(2) - (1) = (3) Unit price variance	(4) Actual quantity	(3) x (4) = (5) Price variance	(6) Actual quantity	(7) Standard quantity	(7) - (6) = (8) Unit usage variance	(9) Standard price	(8) x (9) = (10) Usage variance
Purchased door	$27.05 per door	$24.75 per door	$(2.30)	2	$(4.60)	2 doors	2 doors	0	$24.75	$-
Particle board	$1.58 per square foot	$1.50 per square foot	$(0.08)	16	$(1.28)	16 square feet	14 square feet	2 square feet	$(1.50)	$(3.00)
Wood for frame	$1.00 per linear foot	$1.00 per linear foot	$-	30	$-	30 linear feet	28 linear feet	2 linear feet	$(1.00)	$(2.00)
Paint	$0.50 per ounce	$0.50 per ounce	$-	5	$-	5 ounces	4 ounces	1 ounce	$(0.50)	$(0.50)
Glue	$0.25 per ounce	$0.25 per ounce	$-	4	$-	4 ounces	4 ounces	0	$0.25	$-
Screws	$0.60 per dozen	$0.60 per dozen	$-	24	$-	2 dozen	2 dozen	0	$0.60	$-
Hinges	$1.00 per hinge	$1.00 per hinge	$-	4	$-	4 hinges	4 hinges	0	$1.00	$-
Door handles	$1.90 per handle	$2.00 per handle	$0.10	2	$0.20	2 door handles	2 door handles	0	$2.00	$-
Packaging material	$0.40 per cubic foot	$0.40 per cubic foot	$-	18	$-	18 cubic feet	18 cubic feet	0	$0.40	$-
	Total materials price variance (Unfavorable)				$(5.68)	Total materials usage variance (Unfavorable)				$(5.50)

Kinkaid Cabinets										
Variance Analysis for the new Wall Unit in the First Year of Production										
Analysis of price variances						Analysis of usage variances				
Materials	(1) Actual price	(2) Standard price	(2) - (1) = (3) Unit price variance	(4) Actual quantity	(3) x (4) = (5) Price variance	(6) Actual quantity	(7) Standard quantity	(7) - (6) = (8) Unit usage variance	(9) Standard price	(8) x (9) = (10) Usage variance
Conversion activities										
Cut flat wood parts	$0.15 per part	$0.147 per part	$(0.003)	28	$(0.084)	28 parts	25 parts	(3 parts)	$0.147	$(0.441)
Make frames	$2.55 per frame	$2.469 per frame	$(5.019)	2	$(10.038)	2 frames	2 frames	0	$2.469	$-
Paint parts	$1.116 per part	$1.116 per part	$-	3	$-	3 parts	3 parts	0	$1.116	$-
Assemble cabinet	$20.50 per cabinet	$16.627 per cabinet	$(3.873)	2	$(7.746)	2 cabinets	2 cabinets	0	$16.627	$-
Kit materials	$7.15 per kit	$7.15 per kit	$-	2	$-	2 kits	2 kits	0	$7.150	$-
Inspection	$5.81 per minute	$5.81 per minute	$-	3	$-	3 minutes	2 minutes	(1 minute)	$5.810	$(5.810)
Package unit	$1.14 per unit	$1.14 per unit	$-	3	$-	3 units	3 units	0	$1.114	$-
	Total conversion price variance (Unfavorable)				$(17.868)	Total conversion usage variance (Unfavorable)				$(6.251)
	Total price variance				$(23.55)	Total usage variance (Unfavorable)				$(11.75)
Total variance=$13.67 plus $11.75, or $25.42 (Unfavorable)										

Reaching the original target cost is important if the product line is to achieve its profit goals. To close the gap between current actual costs and their related targets, Kinkaid will need to pursue continuous improvement.

Analyzing Product Performance

OBJECTIVE 3

Develop a comprehensive set of nonfinancial measures to assess product line performance and use this information to evaluate it.

Kinkaid can use many different management accounting tools and techniques to gain control of its production process and achieve the target costs and performance for its new product line. As we have just seen, variance analysis provides some insight into performance problems, isolating differences in price vs. usage for the key resources and processes. However, the review of the complete set of performance measures suggests that these may not be the only problems facing the company. In fact, there are prevalent quality and delivery problems over the first year of production, quite likely leading to the high return rates and moderate-to-low levels of customer satisfaction with the wall unit and executive desk.

PRODUCT-FOCUSED RADAR ANALYSIS

As suggested by Figure 7.2, using RADAR charts, we can compare the performance of the three new products against Kinkaid's traditional levels of performance with its other products. The multidimensional nature of the RADAR chart helps us spot inconsistencies, patterns, and outliers much more rapidly than we could using a simple list of these metrics.

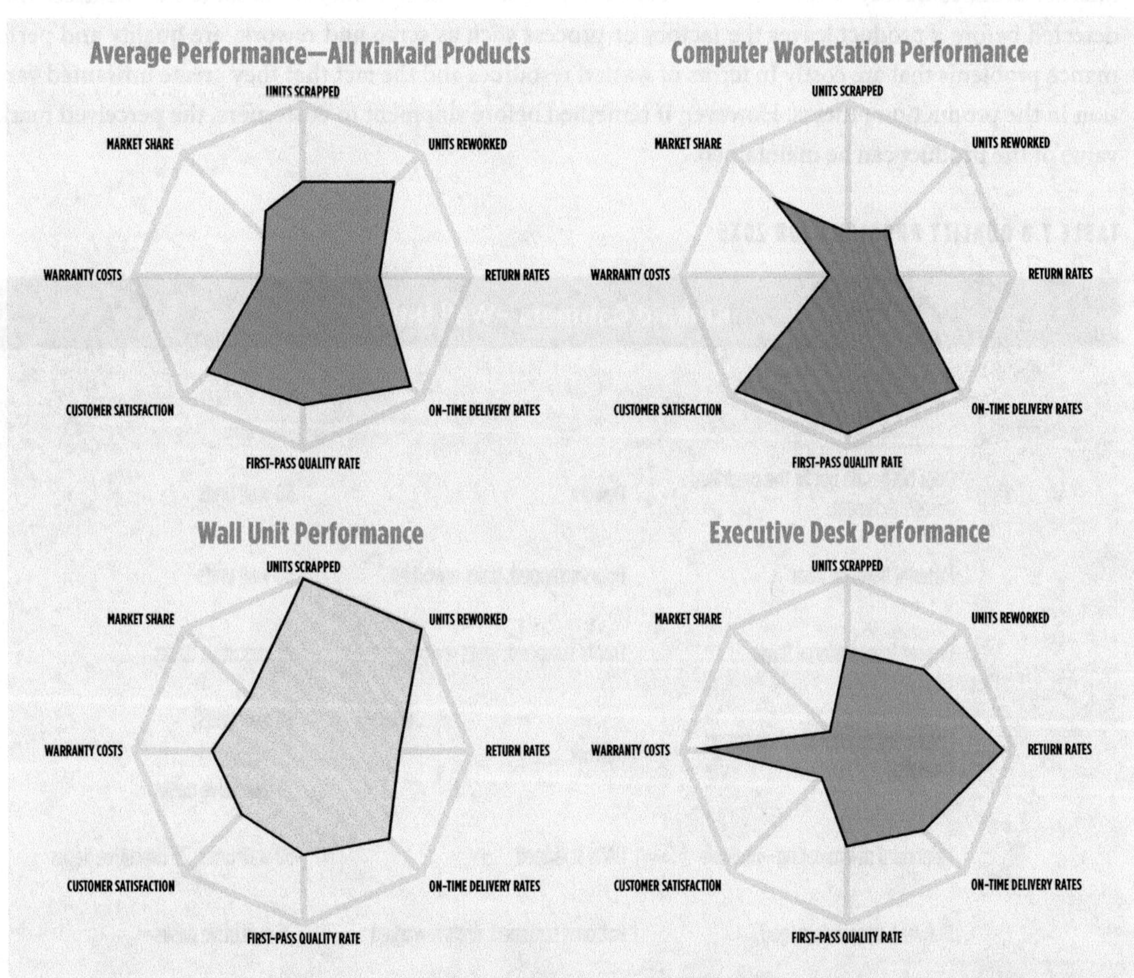

FIGURE 7.2 RADAR ANALYSIS FACILITATES COMPARISON AND MAKES SPOTTING ANOMALIES EASIER AND QUICKER.

What do we see when we look at these diagrams? First, on all of the core measurements except market share, it appears that the new computer workstation actually outperforms the standard Kinkaid product. Specifically, on the measures where a low score is a good thing (for example, scrap rates and return rates), the computer workstation scores below Kinkaid's normal level. Similarly, in situations (such as customer satisfaction and first-pass quality rates) where high ratings are a good thing, the computer workstation scores above the norm. These patterns do not hold for the other two new product lines—in fact, both score below the normal level of performance for Kinkaid's products.

Visually, we see that the primary problem for the wall units is high scrap and rework rates, while high return rates and warranty problems are the key issues for the executive desk. Of the two, the latter is more troubling because it directly affects Kinkaid's customers. Quality and performance problems that make it out the door, known as **external product quality**—*customer experience with a purchased product*—failures can significantly impair the long-term viability of a product because of its low perceived value. **Internal product quality**—*manufacturer experience with its product during its production*—failures, those detected before a product leaves the factory or process such as scrap and rework, are quality and performance problems that are costly in terms of wasted resources and the fact that they create unwanted variation in the production process. However, if remedied before shipment to customers, the perceived market value of the product can be maintained.

TABLE 7.8 QUALITY PROBLEMS FOR 20X6

Kinkaid Cabinets—Wall Units			
Date	**Problems**	**Action Taken**	**Number of Units Affected**
1/15	Door hinges do not fit the predrilled holes/placement.	Rework	50 wall units
2/3	Material flaws on door	Doors scrapped; units reworked	50 wall units
2/8	Drawer front material flaws	Fronts scrapped; units reworked	25 executive desks
3/14	Chipboard splintered when screws inserted	Rework	50 wall units; 25 executive desks
3/21	Chipboard delaminating—multiple	Units scrapped	50 wall units; 25 executive desks
4/5	Drawer bottoms damaged	Bottoms scrapped; units reworked	25 executive desks
4/8	Door hinges do not fit the predrilled holes/placement	Rework	25 wall units
5/1	Joints glued improperly	Rework	75 wall units
5/9	Chipboard splintered when screws inserted	Rework	50 wall units; 25 executive desks
6/10	Parts did not match up for assembly	Units scrapped	50 wall units; 25 executive desks
6/25	Joints glued improperly	Rework	200 wall units; 50 executive desks

Kinkaid Cabinets—Wall Units			
Date	**Problems**	**Action Taken**	**Number of Units Affected**
7/8	Material flaws on door	Doors scrapped, units reworked	100 wall units
7/30	Chipboard delaminating—multiple	Units scrapped	50 wall units; 25 executive desks
8/15	Door hinges do not fit the predrilled holes/placement	Rework	25 wall units
9/3	Parts did not match up for assembly	Units scrapped	50 wall units; 25 executive desks
9/28	Joints glued improperly	Rework	100 wall units; 25 executive desks
10/7	Joints glued improperly	Rework	25 wall units
10/20	Chipboard splintered when screws inserted	Rework	50 wall units; 25 executive desks
11/3	Door hinges do not fit the predrilled holes/placement	Rework	100 wall units; 25 executive desks
11/30	Parts did not match up for assembly	Units scrapped	50 wall units
12/15	Joints glued improperly	Rework	50 wall units; 25 executive desks
12/20	Joints glued improperly	Rework	50 wall units

IN THE NEWS ➤ Continuous Improvement in Action

In multiple customer interviews about a continuous improvement event, interviewees were asked to rate six variables as they related to the process. For example, if training was the best it could be, the interviewee would rate training as a 5. A rating of 1 would mean it was completely ineffective or absent.

The six variables examined included:

- Safety
- Training
- 5S—Orderly workplace
- Leadership

- Standard operating procedures (SOP)
- Metrics

The figure below shows the results plotted on a RADAR chart. With a score of 2, training presented the largest opportunity for improvement. The 5S system, which emphasizes an orderly workplace with specific placement of tools and materials to reduce lost time looking for a part or a tool, was rated the best component of the process with a score of 5 (needing no improvement).

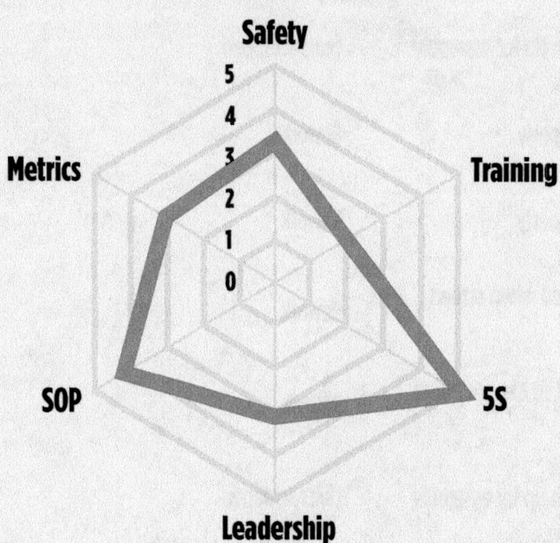

Source: ASQ 22nd Annual Service Quality Conference.

ASQ NewsSource ASQ Weekly http://asq.org/copyright/index.htmlS

PRODUCT-FOCUSED PARETO ANALYSIS

To overcome these problems, Kinkaid's managers need to gain a better understanding of what aspects of the new product and its supporting processes are creating the failures and cost overruns. While we might focus on any number of things, including the assembly process, raw material quality, or labor training issues, it is best if we first take the time to understand the pattern of failures. Pareto analysis provides us with this type of information. Quality failures played a major part in the performance problems of the new modular furniture line. Table 7.8 summarizes the comments pertaining to these quality problems as recorded by the various work teams and engineers over the last year.

We can convert this information into a Pareto chart, as illustrated in Figure 7.3. Looking at the results, it is clear that the most significant problem overall is the joint-gluing failures. Almost half (600 of the total 1,250 units needing rework) are traceable to this problem. Looking at the scrap data, two primary factors account for the losses: delamination of the chipboard (150 units scrapped) and an inability to assemble the unit due to misalignment of parts and connectors (200 units scrapped).

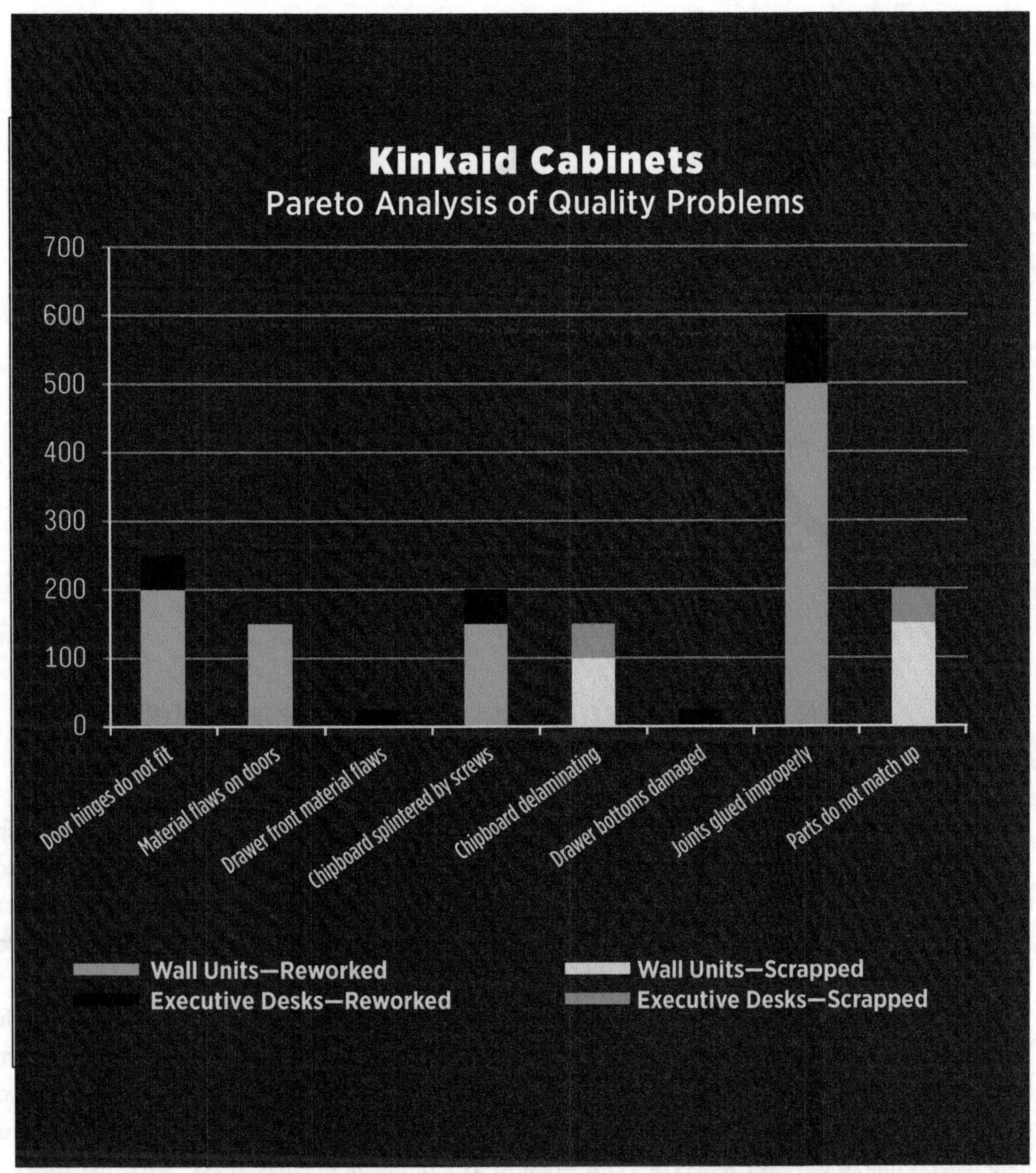

FIGURE 7.3 PARETO ANALYSIS HELPS CLARIFY THE MAGNITUDE OF EACH PROBLEM.

PRODUCT-FOCUSED CAUSE-AND-EFFECT ANALYSIS

The second largest reason for rework is a misfit between the door hinges and their predrilled holes (250 reworked units, or 20%). This problem is quite likely related to the larger issue of scrapping 200 units resulting from assembly problems, which is a very costly event. Both the gluing problem and the misalignment issues are worthy of further investigation. For now, let us look at Figure 7.4, which analyzes the misalignment problems more closely using a cause-and-effect diagram.

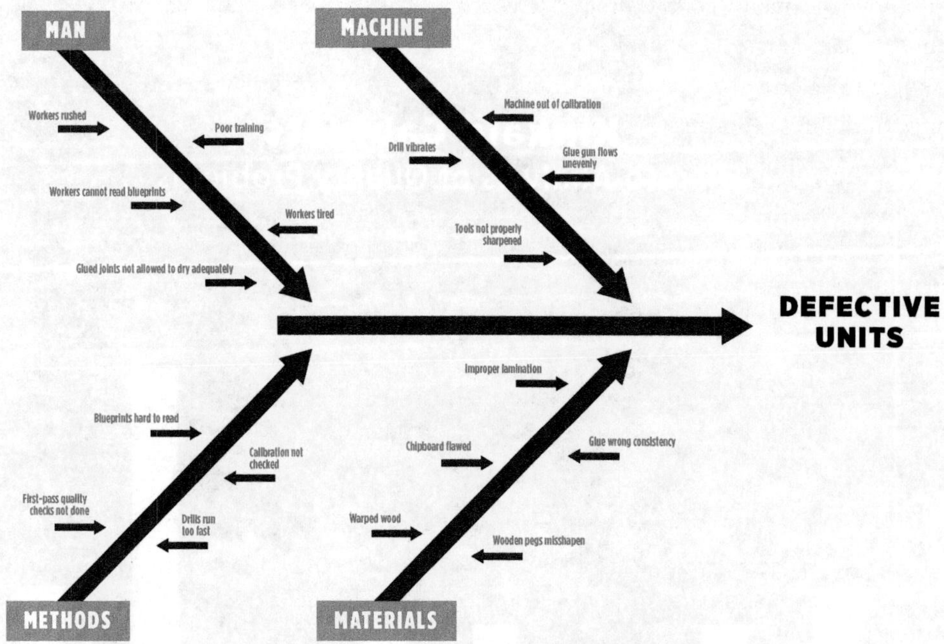

FIGURE 7.4 CAUSE-AND-EFFECT ANALYSIS OF PART MISALIGNMENT PROBLEMS IS A COMPONENT OF AN ONGOING PROCESS TO IMPROVE QUALITY.

By examining the reasons for misalignment of final parts during assembly, we see something interesting—three of the causes for misalignment identified by the modular furniture work team relate to some aspect of the gluing process. If we had looked at the gluing process first, we might have missed the fact that these two quality problems are related. On the other hand, had we improved the gluing process, we would have, by definition, improved part alignment.

The causes of the overall quality problem are identified and understood by the line workers and first-level managers as part of an ongoing process of troubleshooting and process improvement known as **total quality management (TQM),** *a series of processes and techniques used to build quality into a product or service from the point of design through production*. The iterative approach to problem-solving that we used here reflects one of the basic tenets of TQM—that to fix a problem, one has to ask "why" five times. The goal is to identify the root cause of the problem—not its symptoms—in order to find solutions that fix the problem. Given these results, Brad's quality team decides that it is going to tackle the problems on five different fronts:

1. Change suppliers for the chipboard to improve the overall strength and quality of lamination.
2. Replace the supplier of glue guns and glue to improve consistency.
3. Increase the time allowed for glued joints to set before any further operation is performed on them.
4. Improve the calibration sequence and frequency for the drill press operation.

5. Improve the quality control process to check part performance and increase frequency of quality sampling.

These five solutions address materials and methods problems that were major contributors to the entire range of quality problems for the modular furniture line. While some additional training may be warranted, it appears that the workforce is not causing the quality problems. It is, rather, weaknesses in the processes used to acquire and convert materials. Before these changes can be put in place, however, Brad has to develop a business case that will convince Sam Perkins to provide additional funding to the modular furniture project.

IN CONTEXT ➤ Making Changes at Kinkaid Cabinets

"Shelley, do you think that Sam is going to approve these changes or not? My team has convinced me that one simple change won't do it—we have to hit the problems head-on with a multiphased solution."

"I don't see why not, Brad. They look like reasonable changes and shouldn't be expensive to implement. But, before you see Sam, make sure that you're not overlooking something big. If you do, Sam will spot it. Have Barb and John run the numbers on these proposals."

"Good idea. Do you see anything that I may have overlooked? Marketing people have a different perspective than production folk," Brad could not resist the slight jab.

"Let's not go there," Shelley said. "If I were Sam, I might want to know what happens to the total costs and profits if we don't change anything and our volume goes up. That's a good starting point for comparing results."

"A cost-volume-profit type of thing, focusing solely on the profits we'd see if we ramp up volume and make no changes to how we manage the business. I can see that," Brad responded. "That sets up a nice baseline for understanding the improvement potential of our proposed changes."

"Right, Brad," Shelley answered enthusiastically. "Then you can add in the various changes and estimate their impact on current costs and profits, as well as how they change as volume picks up—which it will, if we can get these problems under control. That should ease the impact of any new machines or other cost increases we may have to accept to get past the quality problems."

"Good ideas, Shelley. May I ask for one more favor? Could you estimate the market impact of the quality problems—in other words, what might happen if we fix them and what we can expect in terms of volume and share if we don't? That will help me put my numbers together, and will help Sam see that we're all in agreement on the need for improvement."

"Sure, Brad. It will only take me a few hours to get the information together; I can have it for you on Monday."

"See you Monday. And thanks in advance!"

Developing the Case for Change

OBJECTIVE 4
Apply cost-volume-profit and incremental analysis to improve product line performance.

Whenever changes need to be made to the way work is done in a company, or the amount of output that it plans to produce with its assets, it is important that management takes some time to assess the economic and operational impacts of these changes on the business. At Kinkaid, management asked Brad to develop these analyses for the proposed changes to the modular furniture line.

One of the most important elements in developing an effective business case is to establish a sound "as is" analysis of current operations. The performance reports and analyses developed earlier in this chapter provide this baseline for Brad for the current products. With the information provided by Shelley, Brad can build on these cost and performance reports as he explores the impact of volume and process changes on the quality and profitability of the modular furniture line. Combined with the RADAR, Pareto, and cause-and-effect analysis developed by the production team, Brad should be able to support his case for improvement to Sam. To begin the development of the business case, let us first look at the basic cost and profit impacts of the "change" and "no change" scenarios.

LEVERAGING EXISTING PROCESSES: COST-VOLUME-PROFIT ANALYSIS

As we saw in Chapter 3, we can use cost-volume-profit (CVP) analysis to explore the effect of changes in cost, price, or volume sold of a product or bundle of products on a firm's profitability. While CVP only allows us to do a simple sort on costs, segregating them into "fixed" and "variable" categories, it does help narrow down potential options by identifying those products that have high breakeven volumes or high business risks (for instance, low margins of safety, or a small gap between profitable and unprofitable operations).

To begin the CVP analysis, we summarized the key information on the modular furniture line for the year 20x6 in Table 7.9.

TABLE 7.9 BASIC CVP DATA SUMMARY: NO CHANGES

Kinkaid Cabinets—Modular Furniture Line			
Data Type	Wall Units	Executive Desks	Computer Workstations
Price	$240.00	$650.00	$350.00
Variable cost*	$129.08	$317.45	$158.72
Contribution margin (price less variable cost)	$110.92	$332.55	$191.28
Total fixed costs	$1,200,000	$400,000	$1,400,000
Volume sold–20x6	15,000 units	2,000 units	15,000 units
Breakeven point by product	10,819 units	1,203 units	7,320 units
Margin of safety	4,181 units	797 units	7,680 units

*Only materials are considered purely variable for purposes of this analysis.

Looking at the information in this way, it seems that the product line is doing reasonably well overall. To run the analysis one product at a time, Brad split the fixed costs for the product line into three parts, roughly corresponding to the current cost and volume performance levels of the three products. We will use this simplified version of the information here. Once we understand the cost and profit dynamics of the proposed changes, we will expand it to the actual multiproduct solution.

In developing a preliminary analysis, Brad needed some estimates of the impact of the proposed changes to the processes and materials used on the key elements of the CVP formula (such as price, volume sold, variable cost, and fixed costs):

- Estimated sales volumes under two specific conditions: Leave the process and materials in their current state (the "as is" option) and forecasted sales if quality improvements are made (the "to be" option).
- Estimated impact of the proposed changes on the fixed and variable costs of each of the products in the modular line.

There is no reason to believe that the price of the products will be directly affected by the proposed changes.

The first piece of information is generally obtained from the marketing department. Table 7.10 summarizes the numbers that Shelley gave Brad for this analysis. As you can see, Shelley estimates that sales will fall next year if the problems are not fixed, and that there will be greater reductions in sales volume with each subsequent year as the defects become more common knowledge among office furniture buyers. Shelley also believes that although computer workstations have not experienced the same level of quality problems, sales of **complementary products,** *those whose sales are linked in a defined ratio or relationship to another product or service offered by the company*, will also fall. She reasons that because a customer who buys a desk from a company is likely to buy matching wall units and executive desks, any quality problems with one product will likely impact the entire line's sales.

TABLE 7.10 CVP ANALYSIS: ESTIMATED SALES VOLUME

Kinkaid Cabinets—Modular Furniture Line			
Situation	Estimated Wall Unit Sales	Estimated Executive Desk Sales	Estimated Computer Workstation Sales
Scenario 1: No change			
Year 20x7 Sales	12,000	1,800	15,000
Year 20x8 Sales	10,000	1,500	12,000
Year 20x9 Sales	7,500	1,200	10,000
Scenario 2: Improve Quality			
Year 20x7 Sales	15,000	2,000	15,000
Year 20x8 Sales	20,000	2,500	20,000
Year 20x9 Sales	25,000	3,000	25,000

Looking at Table 7.11, we see that if Kinkaid makes no change to the methods used, wall unit sales will drop below its breakeven volume of 10,819 units by year 20x8, and sales of executive desks will fall below their breakeven volume of 1,203 units by year 20x9. Only computer workstations will remain profitable, with an estimated total contribution margin, or total revenue less total variable costs, of $512,630.40.

TABLE 7.11 CVP ANALYSIS: ESTIMATED PROFITABILITY BY PRODUCT LINE—"AS IS" CASE

Kinkaid Cabinets—Modular Furniture Line					
	(1)**	(2)*	(1) - (2) = (3)	(4)*	(3) x (4) = (5)
Product by year	Estimated Sales	Breakeven Sales	Margin of Safety (Units)	Contribution Margin per Unit	Total Contribution for Product
Year 20x7:					
Wall units	12,000	10,819	1,181	$110.92	$130,996.52
Executive desks	1,800	1,203	597	$332.55	$198,532.35
Computer workstations	15,000	7,320	7,680	$191.28	$1,469,030.40
		Product Line Total			$1,798,559.27
Year 20x8					
Wall units	10,000	10,819	-819	$110.92	$(90,843.48)
Executive desks	1,500	1,203	297	$332.55	$98,767.35
Computer workstations	12,000	7,320	4,680	$191.28	$895,190.40
		Product Line Total			$903,114.27
Year 20x9					
Wall units	7,500	10,819	-3,319	$110.92	$(368,143.48)
Executive desks	1,200	1,203	-3	$332.55	$(997.65)
Computer workstations	10,000	7,320	2,680	$191.28	$512,630.40
		Product Line Total			$143,489.27

* From Table 7.9 **From Table 7.10

Table 7.11 clearly depicts that as the volumes drop on the various products in the modular line, the total contribution made by the line to company profits plummets from almost $1.8 million in Year 20x7 to less than $150,000 in Year 20x9, or a 91.7% decrease over the three-year period. These numbers alone suggest that improvements should be made.

Brad, with the help of John and Barb, also developed some rough estimates of the impact of the proposed changes on the materials and other resources used for modular furniture production. To keep the analysis simple, the team continued to assume that only materials will act as purely variable costs, meaning that they will change directly in proportion to changes in methods and volumes. They treated all other resource costs as fixed for the three-year horizon of the analysis. Table 7.12 summarizes the information compiled by Brad's team.

TABLE 7.12 CVP ANALYSIS: ESTIMATED IMPACT OF QUALITY IMPROVEMENTS

Kinkaid Cabinets—Modular Furniture Line			
Cost per Proposed Change	Impact on Wall Units	Impact on Executive Desks	Impact on Computer Desks
1. Change chipboard supplier			
Estimated increase in variable costs	$6.45	$15.90	$7.95
2. Replace supplier of glue and glue gun technology			
Increase in variable costs—negligible			
Estimated increase in fixed costs per year	$250,000	$62,500	$362,500
3. Increase time allowed for glued joints to set before continuing assembly	N/A	N/A	N/A
Increase in holding costs—negligible			
4. Improve calibration methods and frequency for drill press			
Increase in fixed costs per year	$50,000	$12,500	$87,500
5. Improve quality control process			
Increase in inspection costs per year	$40,000	$10,000	$50,000

These estimates do not include the impact on the rest of the process, on cycle times, or other aspects of performance. As is typical with CVP, these are rough-cut cost estimates that will give Brad's team some idea about how the options will affect breakeven volumes and business risks. Also, although computer workstations are currently of higher quality than the other two products, they are more complicated to make than wall units. Therefore, manufacturing them will require more effort than a similar number of wall units should the changes be undertaken. With these limitations noted, we need to know the impact on breakeven points for the products in the modular line. The figures presented in Table 7.13 assume estimated 20x7 volumes.

TABLE 7.13 BASIC CVP DATA SUMMARY: AFTER IMPROVEMENTS

Kinkaid Cabinets—Modular Furniture Line			
Data Type	Wall Units	Executive Desks	Computer Workstations
Price	$240.00	$650.00	$350.00
Variable cost*	$135.53	$333.35	$166.67
Contribution margin (Price less variable cost)	$104.47	$316.65	$183.33
Total fixed costs	$1,540,000	$485,000	$1,900,000
Volume sold—20x7	15,000 units	2,000 units	15,000 units
Breakeven point by product	14,742 units	1,532 units	10,364 units
Margin of safety	258 units	468 units	4,636 units

*Only materials are considered purely variable for purposes of this analysis.

As Table 7.13 illustrates, breakeven volumes go up significantly with these changes, resulting in greatly reduced margins in Year 20x7 of the overall product launch. But as Table 7.14 details, these changes have a positive long-term impact because they result in increased sales volumes from Year 20x8 onward. Specifically, by Year 20x9, the product line's total contribution to Kinkaid's gross companywide margin increases to more than $4.2 million. There is little doubt that Kinkaid should make these changes if the product line is to continue.

TABLE 7.14 CVP ANALYSIS: ESTIMATED PROFITABILITY BY PRODUCT LINE—"TO BE" CASE

Kinkaid Cabinets—Modular Furniture Line					
	(1)**	(2)*	(1) - (2) = (3)	(4)*	(3) x (4) = (5)
Product by Year	Estimated Sales	Breakeven Sales	Margin of Safety (Units)	Contribution Margin per Unit	Total Contribution for Product
Year 20x7:					
Wall units	15,000	14,742	258	$104.47	$26,953.26
Executive desks	2,000	1,532	468	$316.65	$148,192.20
Computer workstations	15,000	10,364	4,636	$183.33	$849,917.88
		Product Line Total			$1,025,063.34
Year 20x8					
Wall units	20,000	14,742	5,258	$104.47	$549,303.26
Executive desks	2,500	1,532	968	$316.65	$306,517.20
Computer workstations	20,000	10,364	9,636	$183.33	$1,766,567.88
		Product Line Total			$2,622,388.34
Year 20x9					
Wall units	25,000	14,742	10,258	$104.47	$1,071,653.26
Executive desks	3,000	1,532	1,468	$316.65	$464,842.20
Computer workstations	25,000	10,364	14,636	$183.33	$2,683,217.88
		Product Line Total			$4,219,713.34

* From Table 7.13 **From Table 7.10

Brad's team now has a reasonably good feeling about the impact these changes will have on the company's performance. However, before sitting down with Sam, Brad knows that he will need to develop the analysis in greater depth, looking not only at costs in a more detailed manner but also at the potential impact of the proposed changes on other product line measures and costs.

ASSESSING STRUCTURAL CHANGES: INCREMENTAL ANALYSIS

CVP analysis is a good starting point for understanding the potential impacts of a change on how the company does business, but it is limited in usefulness because it uses simplified assumptions, such as assuming all costs are purely fixed or variable, which they are not. It is also unable to adequately incorporate nonfinancial issues into its calculations. Before Kinkaid can move ahead with Brad's team's recommendations, we need to do a more detailed study of the incremental impact of these changes. For this we need our more powerful tool—incremental analysis, which allows us to compare the impact of changes to the way work is done to see which yields the best results.

When we use incremental analysis, the focus shifts from the product to the total impact producing and supporting the product has on the company's profits and overall performance. Unlike CVP analysis, when we use incremental analysis, we no longer treat costs as purely fixed or purely variable; instead, we attempt to understand which costs will really change, and by how much. For example, if the demand for labor is reduced by a decision, but in reality the demand for labor is merely shifted to another part of the company, we will not recognize a cost savings. Using incremental analysis, we shift our attention to the entity level, thereby gaining a much better understanding of the underlying economics of the decision. At the entity level, in this example, the total costs of labor would remain unchanged.

Brad's team's proposed changes to the modular line's materials and methods raise a number of cost and performance issues, including:

- *Units scrapped* will decline radically. The team believes that after the changes, there will be 25 or fewer wall units scrapped, five or fewer executive desks, and 10 or fewer computer workstations. While the ultimate goal is to drive these numbers as close as possible to zero, these goals are probably realistic for the near term.
- *Rework units* will also drop from current levels of 1,000 for wall units, 250 for executive desks, and 100 computer workstations to roughly 5% of these amounts (for example, 50 wall units).
- *Return rates* should drop to under 1% for all products in the line, which will reduce shipping and handling costs, and customer service and accounting transactions, and increase customer satisfaction.
- *Scrap and rework costs* should drop to $15,000 in total for the entire modular line. A major part of this reduction will come from the elimination of two employees.
- *Warranty costs* will drop to 5% of their current level as the number of problems customers experience approaches zero.
- *Inspection* costs will go up by 10%. This increase was estimated in the CVP analysis and is based on the cost of retraining the two individuals who were freed up from rework and scrap activities.
- *First-pass quality rates* will increase to 95% overall. This will reduce other problems, allowing on-time delivery rates to approach 98% for all of the products (under the current system, a lot of time was lost replacing parts or units and doing rework, making on-time delivery for the wall units to be 75% and the executive desks 65%).
- *Customer satisfaction* should increase to the "high" range for all of the products.
- *Average actual costs* will change, as we will see when we complete the incremental analysis.

The changes to materials and methods will also bleed across to other lines, as the improved gluing capabilities and machine calibration methods reduce rework, scrap, and related problems in the existing lines. These additional cross-product line improvements that Brad's team estimates will result in $150,000 of additional savings to Kinkaid. Finally, because there will be fewer quality-based claims that slow down the payment process, these changes should improve the firm's cash flow, reducing the length of time between receipt of order and receipt of final payment on invoices for goods accepted by the customer. Brad's team conservatively estimates that in the first year alone, this should generate $25,000 in cost of capital savings.

This information is combined into the analysis presented in Tables 7.15 (the "as is" scenario) and 7.16 (the "to be" scenario). As you can see, we have shifted attention away from the product level to include entity-level changes. This is one of the major benefits of incremental analysis. With the modifications in analysis, we see that even though standard costs go up a small amount using the new assumptions (for instance, from $190.23 for wall units to $197.84), entity-level profits show a marked increase after the change. Specifically, entity profits practically double, going from $445,640 after considering the affected costs to $889,834 if the proposed changes are made, a 99.7% increase.

TABLE 7.15 INCREMENTAL ANALYSIS: QUALITY IMPROVEMENT EFFORTS "AS IS"

Kinkaid Cabinets—Modular Furniture Line For the year ending 12/31/20x7				
Cost element/Issue	Wall Unit	Executive Desk	Computer Workstation	Entity
Price per unit sold	$240.00	$650.00	$350.00	N/A
Units sold	12,000	1,800	15,000	28,800
Estimated revenue	$2,880,000	$1,170,000	$5,250,000	$9,300,000
Product level costs:				
Material	$129.08	$317.45	$158.72	N/A
Conversion (without inspection)	49.53	164.47	81.70	N/A
Shipping and handling	12.00	20.50	21.15	N/A
Inspection	11.62	24.58	34.58	N/A
Total product level costs	$202.23	$527.00	$296.15	
Multiply by unit sold = Total product costs	$2,426,760	$948,600	$4,442,250	$7,817,610
Margin after product costs	$453,240	$221,400	$807,750	$1,482,390
Product line level costs				
Scrap and rework	$65,400	$52,500	$18,000	$135,900
Warranty costs	$3,500	$5,000	$500	$9,000
	$68,900	$57,500	$18,500	$144,900
Product line margins	$384,340	$163,900	$789,250	$1,337,490
Entity level costs				
Customer service costs—returns	N/A	N/A	N/A	$300,000
Accounts receivable transactions—returns	N/A	N/A	N/A	$250,000
Rework and scrap due to glue gun problems	N/A	N/A	N/A	$115,000
Rework and scrap due to calibration problems	N/A	N/A	N/A	$75,000
Cost of capital traceable to product failures/rework	N/A	N/A	N/A	$75,000
Total Entity Affected Costs				$815,000
Entity margin after affected costs				$522,490

TABLE 7.16 INCREMENTAL ANALYSIS: QUALITY IMPROVEMENT EFFORTS "TO BE"

Kinkaid Cabinets—Modular Furniture Line				
For the year ending 12/31/20x7				
Cost element/Issue	Wall Unit	Executive Desk	Computer Workstation	Entity
Price per unit sold	$240.00	$650.00	$350.00	N/A
Units sold	15,000	2,000	15,000	32,000
Estimated revenue	$3,600,000	$1,300,000	$5,250,000	$10,150,000
Product level costs:				
Material	$135.53	$333.35	$166.67	N/A
Conversion (without inspection)	49.53	164.47	81.70	N/A
Shipping and handling	12.00	20.50	21.15	N/A
Inspection	12.78	27.04	38.04	N/A
Total product level costs	$209.84	$545.36	$307.56	
Multiply by unit sold = Total product costs	$3,147,630	$1,090,716	$4,613,370	$8,851,716
Margin after product costs	$452,370	$209,284	$636,630	$1,298,284
Product line level costs				
Scrap and rework	$7,218.54	$5,794.70	$1,986.75	$15,000
Warranty costs	$175.00	$250.00	$25.00	$450
	$7,393.54	$6,044.70	$2,011.75	$15,450
Product line margins	$444,976	$203,239	$634,618	$1,282,834
Entity level costs				
Customer service costs—returns	N/A	N/A	N/A	$210,000
Accounts receivable transactions—returns	N/A	N/A	N/A	$200,000
Rework and scrap due to glue gun problems	N/A	N/A	N/A	$20,000
Rework and scrap due to calibration problems	N/A	N/A	N/A	$20,000
Cost of capital traceable to product failures/rework	N/A	N/A	N/A	$50,000
Total Entity Affected Costs				$500,000
Entity margin after affected costs				$782,834

It will be much easier to convince Sam to accept the recommended changes with the results of the incremental analysis than it might have been using only the CVP approach. If these analyses are carried out to subsequent years, the cost and profit improvements would be even more noticeable as the gap in the forecasted sales volumes between the two options widens. We will not develop these analyses in depth here, but we will present their summary implications when Brad's team completes the development of the business case before he meets with Sam. However, before turning to this last issue, we need to examine the strategic and operational considerations of the proposed changes.

Developing a Product-Focused Business Case: Behavioral, Strategic and Operational Considerations

OBJECTIVE 5

Develop a business case for improving product line profitability; include the behavioral, strategic, and operational issues.

No decision of any magnitude should ever be undertaken without a careful evaluation of the potential behavioral, strategic, and operational impacts of the proposed changes. Brad's team considered some of the operational issues in its analysis when it included entity-level impacts of the proposed changes in customer service, accounting, gluing, and quality control. Similarly, Shelley's sales forecast for the two conditions—change and no change to current policies—provides some strategic information. Coupled with the anticipated change in customer satisfaction and on-time delivery, the details compiled by Brad and Shelley will be a good starting point for Sam's deliberations.

As president of Kinkaid, Sam must look beyond the issues of the modular line to anticipate overall impacts on the company's market reputation, customer loyalty, supplier relationships, labor relationships, and long-term financial strength. What is clear in the case of the modular furniture line is that the "do nothing" route is not an option because the ongoing quality problems will undoubtedly damage Kinkaid's reputation not only in the office furniture industry, but also in its other areas of operation. A customer who gets a faulty desk, whether that purchase is made for work or home use, will be less inclined to trust the quality of Kinkaid's kitchen cabinets. While difficult to measure, the external (customer-related) costs of quality failures are quite significant for any company. At Kinkaid, this is certainly true, as quality problems will both directly and indirectly impact its reputation in the market.

Moving beyond customer issues, Sam also needs to think carefully about his competitors' responses to Kinkaid's entry into the modular office furniture market. Specifically, will competitors now enter the modular office furniture segment, taking away sales volume from Kinkaid? Will competitors lower prices to take away sales volume from Kinkaid? Questions like these were faced by Apple, Inc., when it entered the tablet market. Other questions Sam should consider include:

- Will Kinkaid be able to reach Shelley's sales forecasts without having to adjust price?
- Will a higher-quality product improve Kinkaid's chances to become a significant player in the office furniture industry?
- Will the new supplier of materials be reliable, and, if so, should Kinkaid consider switching more of its material purchases to the new supplier?
- Will the improvements in gluing and calibration improve the quality and reputation of Kinkaid's low- and high-end kitchen cabinets? If so, what impact will this have on its future sales and profits?

Every decision made at the product level in some manner ultimately affects entity performance. It is important to always look beyond the current situation or question to examine the repercussions of a decision on other parts of the business, on the company's strategic and competitive position, and on the relationship of the organization with its key stakeholders. A decision that might save $1 per unit made, for instance, is not a good one if it ends up damaging the quality and long-term viability of a product. Similarly, a "onetime" price reduction for a special purchase by a customer may ultimately result in the permanent reduction of the perceived value of a product—*its market price*—in the eyes of the customer.

On the behavioral front, the proposed changes should be positive. Contrary to popular belief, people who manufacture products really dislike poor quality. They feel they are wasting their time, and it robs them of pride in a job well done. In the case of Kinkaid, the retraining that needs to take place should prove to be a positive, providing the two workers who were doing the unrewarding job of rework with the ability to learn new skills they can apply throughout their working careers.

As Brad completes his business case, each of these points needs to be developed and assessed. Only then will Sam be able to analyze and interpret Brad's recommendations from an entity perspective. Let us now turn to this last major activity in the management process within the product domain.

In Chapter 5, the elements of a well-designed business case were summarized. No matter what decision is being made or what option is being explored, its impact should be examined against those criteria. While it may seem like "overkill" in some situations, the logic embedded in any form of disciplined problem-solving reduces the risk of overlooking key issues that may damage an organization's long-term performance and viability.

Figure 7.5 presents the executive summary for the modular office furniture business case. As you can see, Brad's team has carefully defined its assumptions to incorporate overall issues that have entity-level implications and to suggest a path forward that will optimize Kinkaid's short- and long-term financial and nonfinancial performance, respectively illustrated in Table ES 1.1 and Table ES 1.2. While the team may not have access to all of the information Sam will need to consider before making a decision, it has, at least in some fashion, dealt with many of them.

Executive Summary

1. Introduction

Subject: Analysis of Quality Improvement Proposal for Modular Office Furniture

Purpose: The modular office furniture line experienced significant quality and performance problems in its first year of production. The analysis contained in this report details these problems, explores their cost and performance implications for the short- and long-term viability of the new product line, and details specific plans for addressing these problems.

Situation and motivation:

- The objective is to improve the quality and profitability of the modular furniture line.
- Recommendations provide an opportunity to improve the performance of Kinkaid's entire product portfolio.
- The threats to the business if changes are not made to this line are significant. They include the impairment of Kinkaid's reputation that will affect all

aspects of the business, financial losses as sales volumes drop, and the loss of competitive position within the office furniture industry.

- The problems Kinkaid will face in making these changes are minimal, with labor redeployed to new responsibilities. Additional training and capital expenditures totaling $925,000 will be required to implement the recommended course of action. Small increases in material and inspection costs are also anticipated.
- These analyses are limited to a three-year period and are constrained by current contracts, equipment commitments, and operating conditions.

2. Methods and Assumptions

Scope: The analysis focuses on the modular furniture line and related impacts on several key support activities and costs at the entity level.

Financial metrics and criteria: The analyses were completed using both cost-volume-profit analysis to assess business risk at the product line level and a more comprehensive incremental analysis to explore both product line and entity-level impacts of the "as is" and "make improvements" options. The decision rule was that the option that provided the maximum three-year sales volume and entity profitability was to be the recommended course of action.

Major assumptions: Marketing estimated potential impacts on sales volumes. Prices for the products were assumed to be constant over the three-year period of analysis. Only material and activity costs were considered; conversion costs were not recalculated. Rapid acquisition and deployment of new assets were assumed to be possible, along with the cross-training of employees to new responsibilities. Other business impacts were considered only as directly impacted by the proposed changes.

Scenario design: Two options were developed—leaving things as they are (the "as is" scenario) and implementing a five-prong improvement initiative (the "to be" scenario) with the following characteristics:

1. Change suppliers for the chipboard to improve overall strength and quality of lamination.
2. Replace the supplier of glue guns and glue to improve consistency.
3. Increase the time allowed for glued joints to set before performing any further operation on them.
4. Improve the calibration sequence and frequency for the drill press operation.
5. Improve the quality control process to check first part performance and increase frequency of quality sampling.

Further analysis of portions of the five-prong alternative can be made if desired to separate the effects of individual changes beyond those summarized in the report (see Tables ES 1.1 and ES 1.2).

Case structure: While incremental analysis is the focus of the financial details, these numbers appear in total at the entity level (full value).

Cost impact model: An activity-based method was used, with direct tracing of material, conversion, shipping and handling, and inspection costs; product line assignment of rework, scrap, and warranty costs, and entity-level assignment of transaction costs due to returns (accounting, customer service); rework and scrap costs for other product lines currently traced to gluing or calibration problems; and an overall cost of capital charge for work-in-process inventory levels.

Benefits model: A basic cost-benefit analysis comparing projected product line revenues and their direct and entity-affected costs were used to develop pro forma profitability analyses. CVP analysis was used to assess relative business risk. In both cases, a benefit is defined as an improvement in a key performance variable (such as increase in profitability, sales volume, and decrease in business risk).

3. Business Impacts

Cash flow projections: Table ES 1.1 summarizes the results of the financial analysis of cash flow effects:

TABLE ES 1.1 BUSINESS CASE FINANCIAL ANALYSIS SUMMARY

Kinkaid Modular Furniture Line						
Summary of Three-Year Analysis of Proposed Changes						
	CVP Results			Incremental Analysis		
"As is" profitability	Year 2	Year 3	Year 4	Year 2	Year 3	Year 4
Product line profitability	$823,500	$425,300	$143,489	$522,490	$311,572	$142,146
Entity total	$1,324,000	$910,800	$588,989	$1,022,690	$797,072	$587,646
"To be" profitability	CVP Results			Incremental Analysis		
Product line profitability	$835,600	$2,125,300	$3,575,000	$782,834	$2,056,912	$3,372,681
Entity total	$1,336,100	$2,610,800	$4,020,500	$1,283,334	$2,542,412	$3,818,181

Dynamic financial model: Incremental analysis and CVP applied over a three-year period with changes in volumes and costs to reflect changed conditions.

Development of financial metrics: Both the breakeven and margin of safety measures are done individually for each product. In addition, the incremental analysis results were not adjusted to their economic present value.

Rationale for including nonfinancial impacts: Kinkaid has long recognized that a balanced set of metrics provides the best basis for assessing performance. As such, these scenarios have been analyzed with attention to the core set of metrics in the Kinkaid integrated performance measurement model. These are presented in Table ES 1.2.

TABLE ES 1.2 "AS IS" SCENARIO

Kinkaid Modular Furniture Line			
For the Year Ending 12/31/20x6			
Measurement	Wall Unit	Executive Desk	Computer Workstation
Forecasted unit sales	12,000	1,800	15,000
Average price	$240.00	$650.00	$350.00
Market share	5%	1.8%	6%
Average cost per unit	$209.39	$515.35	$256.00
Average profit per unit	$38.50	$154.65	$94.00
First-pass quality rates	70%	60%	99%
Units scrapped	250	100	50
Units reworked	1,000	250	100
Return rates	10%	15%	5%
Scrap and rework costs	$65,400	$52,500	$18,000
Warranty costs	$3,500	$5,000	$500
On-time delivery rates	75%	65%	98%
Customer satisfaction	Medium	Medium/Low	High

"TO BE" SCENARIO

Kinkaid Modular Furniture Line			
Measurement	Wall Unit	Executive Desk	Computer Workstation
Forecasted unit sales	15,000	2,000	15,000
Average price	$240.00	$650.00	$350.00
Market share	6%	2%	6%
Average cost per unit	$197.84	$524.86	$286.41
Average profit per unit	$42.16	$125.14	$63.59
First-pass quality rates	95%	95%	95%
Units scrapped	25	5	10
Units reworked	50	12	5
Return rates	1%	1%	1%
Scrap and rework costs	$7,219	$5,795	$1,987
Warranty costs	$175	$250	$25
On-time delivery rates	98%	98%	98%
Customer satisfaction	High	High	High

4. Sensitivity, Risks and Contingencies

Sensitivity analysis: The key assumptions affecting these results are the market forecast of sales volume effects of the "as is" and "to be" scenarios. The results are very robust with respect to these assumptions.

Risk analysis: There is little doubt that a failure to address these quality problems will result in reduced sales volumes for the modular furniture line. The exact magnitude of these effects cannot be precisely stated, but the overall trend line is quite negative. These results could also put the main product lines at risk.

Contingency analysis: There should be ongoing monitoring of quality problems, customer complaints and returns, and related factors. If the recommended changes do not result in forecasted improvements in these areas, there should be further analysis of product line viability.

5. Conclusions and Recommendations

Results rationale: The goal of this analysis was to examine the impact of a proposed five-prong quality improvement initiative for the modular office furniture product line to identify the potential for profitability and performance gains. The results suggest that such a move will result in significant profit and performance improvements over the "as is," or no action, scenario.

Recommendation: That the five-prong improvement initiative be undertaken immediately.

Choice of scenarios: Two scenarios were chosen as the most likely paths for Kinkaid. Further sensitivity analysis can be conducted upon request.

Strategy for optimizing results:

- Begin retraining of workforce immediately.
- Undertake supplier negotiations within next two weeks.
- Perform line tests of new materials under existing conditions.
- Fully explore glue gun technology and supplies with a target purchase and implementation within six weeks.
- Evaluate and improve calibration methods on all tolerance-sensitive machines and methods immediately.
- Process time delay for additional joint gluing should be immediately put into practice to limit the rework and scrap problems due to failure to allow parts to set adequately.
- Develop and institute new quality control procedures within the next 30 days.

The aggressiveness of these recommendations is based on their perceived low cost and high-value impact on Kinkaid's overall performance.

FIGURE 7.5 THE EXECUTIVE SUMMARY PRESENTS THE BUSINESS CASE FOR KINKAID CABINETS' MODULAR FURNITURE LINE.

This business case for Kinkaid's modular furniture line completes one complete cycle of the management process within the product domain. Not every cycle results in such significant suggestions for change, but most companies look for ways to improve their performance all the time. Some changes are simple process improvements, as we will see in Chapters 8 and 9. In either case, there is only one absolute to keep in mind: A company that stands still—that fails to make ongoing changes to its products and processes—will ultimately find itself far behind its competitors in the race for profitability and customer loyalty.

Summary

The focus of this chapter has been on the "check and adjust" aspects of the management process in the product domain. Focusing first on the activities comprising the attainment phase of target costing, such as setting standards and establishing performance metrics for the product line, we then turned our attention to results for Kinkaid's modular office furniture line in the first year of its production. Specifically, we examined various methods for analyzing performance against plans and assessing the causes for performance shortfalls, including product cost variance analysis—RADAR analysis, Pareto analysis, and cause-and-effect analysis.

Once we identified problems and a set of potential action items to address these issues, we developed the analysis of the financial and nonfinancial impact of the proposed changes. Both CVP (cost-volume-profit) analysis and incremental analysis were used to explore the potential impact of making the recommended changes (the "to be" scenario) vs. not making them (the "as is" scenario). The results suggest that making the change is highly desired due to its favorable impact on profits and performance across the entire range of Kinkaid products.

In using both CVP and incremental approaches, we began to see when and how these two complementary tools can be used in business planning and analysis. We determined, for example, that CVP provides a useful "first cut" analysis of the desirability and impact of a proposed change. But, because of its heavy reliance on assumptions that seldom hold true in the real world, we also saw how and why CVP needs to give way to a more fully developed incremental analysis. Next, we looked at nonfinancial issues and the behavioral, operational, and strategic implications of change within organizations. Finally, we developed a complete business case that summarized what we learned from the Kinkaid experience.

These tools and techniques are applicable to a broad range of companies with many different goals, structures, and situations. As long as we understand the scenarios being analyzed, develop reasonably comprehensive estimates of their economic and noneconomic impacts, and apply the logic embedded in the tools and techniques properly, the resulting analysis can be used as the basis for decision making. Knowing the strengths and weaknesses of the various methods used to analyze results and potential improvement projects is the first step in applying them properly and achieving reliable results. Now that we have explored the product domain, we will turn our attention to the processes we use to support and deliver these products and services to customers.

Key Terms

Complementary products: those whose sales are linked in a defined ratio or relationship to another product or service offered by the company.

Continuous improvement program: the process in which every aspect of making a product or providing a service is constantly reviewed to make it better.

Cost gap: the amount of excess cost in a new product or service; the difference between the target cost and the estimated cost.

External product quality: customer experience with a purchased product.

Internal product quality: manufacturer experience with its product during production.

Kit materials: an internal process that focuses on bringing together all of the parts needed to produce the product.

Management dashboard: a one-page summary of performance on the key measures of quality, quality, delivery, productivity, and cost.

Product cost variance analysis: a study to determine why a product is not meeting its performance goals.

Total quality management (TQM): a series of processes and techniques used to build quality into a product or service from the point of design through production.

Value proposition: the perceived worth of a product or service compared to its price.

Questions

1. What is a product or service value proposition? How does it affect customer purchase decisions?
2. What are the key factors considered during the attainment phase of target costing?
3. What role does the cost gap play in the attainment phase of target costing?
4. Name the primary activities to focus on for cost reduction during the attainment phase.
5. How are standards developed and used during the production of products?
6. What does the term "tight but attainable" goal mean in the context of setting standards?
7. How does the continuous improvement philosophy affect the attainment phase of target costing?
8. Develop a list of potential measures of a product's performance. Identify each as financial (F) or nonfinancial (N).
9. How are balanced scorecards used in the product domain?
10. Identify the key types of variances looked at in the product domain. How are they calculated?

11. What are the key differences between RADAR and Pareto charts? Which are more useful in analyzing multidimensional problems? Why?
12. Describe the key differences between external and internal product quality problems.
13. What is total quality management (TQM) and how is it used?
14. Define the key differences between CVP analysis and incremental analysis.
15. What are the primary steps needed to develop a business case?

Exercises

1. **COST VS. PERFORMANCE GAPS.** Blue Goose Kitchenware produces a wide variety of kitchen tools. It has just developed the Handy Opener, which automatically opens jars of various sizes. The target price is $8.95, and Blue Goose plans to make it available in white or black. The company uses customer panels to test its designs and cost parameters prior to going into main production. Here are the results from the eight customer panels it ran for the Handy Opener:

Customer #	Best Cost	Ease of Use	Color	Quality Feel
1	$5.95	Medium	Okay	Medium
2	$9.95	High	More colors	High
3	$6.95	Medium	Okay	High
4	$6.95	Medium	More colors	Medium
5	$5.95	Low	More colors	Low
6	$7.95	High	No black	High
7	$6.95	Medium	Okay	Medium
8	$5.95	Low	More colors	Medium

REQUIRED:

a. What is the average price customers are willing to pay?
b. Compared to the target price, what is the price gap?
c. Looking at the responses to performance questions, does Blue Goose have a problem with its design? How many customers appear happy with the cost and performance features of the product?

2. **COST VS. PERFORMANCE GAPS.** Hercules Fitness makes a line of fitness machines. It recently decided to enter the elliptical trainer market. The company designed a trainer that would cost the customer $995. Hercules's target customer is the moderately fit, so

the trainer has reasonable resistance and multiple settings. Another goal was to make it of moderate size so it could fit into most rooms. Below are the results of the customer panels Hercules ran to evaluate its design:

Customer #	Best Price	Ease of Use	Size	Program Variety
1	$695.00	Low	Too large	Too few
2	$750.00	Moderate	Okay	Okay
3	$695.00	Low	Too large	Too few
4	$800.00	High	Okay	Too few
5	$750.00	Moderate	Too large	Okay
6	$650.00	Low	Too large	Too few
7	$850.00	High	Okay	Okay
8	$695.00	Low	Too large	Too few

REQUIRED:

a. What is the average price customers are willing to pay?
b. Compared to the target price, what is the price gap?
c. Looking at the responses to performance questions, does Hercules Fitness have a problem with its design? How many customers appear happy with the cost and performance features of the product?

3. **RADAR CHARTS.** Best Ever Jams makes strawberry, raspberry, and blueberry jams. The following scores reflect the results of a consumer panel that evaluated its jams. Ten is the highest, and zero is the lowest rating. Each response was based on an average of ratings from zero (0) to 10 points.

Feature	Strawberry	Raspberry	Blueberry
Spreadability	3	5	10
Taste	5	10	8
Consistency	4	6	10
Texture	3	5	8
Color	10	8	6
Smell	8	10	5
Bottle size	6	8	10
Label attractiveness	8	6	4

REQUIRED:

a. Create a RADAR chart for each of these jams.
b. How do the various jams compare?

4. **PARETO CHARTS.** Using the data in the table for Exercise 3, create a Pareto chart for each of the jams. How do they compare now? Which chart is easier to use? Why?

5. **RADAR CHARTS.** Big Top Pops makes a variety of popcorn products. It recently conducted a customer focus group and obtained the following results for three of its more popular products.

Feature	Caramel Corn	Cheddar Corn	Buttered Corn
Freshness	6	8	5
Taste	10	8	4
Consistency	8	4	10
Texture	8	4	10
Color	6	4	10
Smell	10	10	4
Container size	8	6	2
Labeling	6	8	10

REQUIRED:

a. Create a RADAR chart for each of these popcorn products.
b. How do the various popcorn products compare? Ten is the highest and zero is the lowest score.

6. **PARETO CHARTS.** Using the data from the table in Exercise 5, create a Pareto chart for each of the popcorn products. How do they compare now? Which chart is easier to use? Why?

7. **QUALITY PROBLEMS.** For the following list of quality problems, note whether it is an internal quality failure (I) or an external quality failure (E).

Quality Problem	Category	Quality Problem	Category
Warranty repairs		Inspection	
Scrap		Customer gets scratched unit	
Rework		Internal detection of warping	
Box disintegrates in store		Screws missing on line	
Broken product returned		Parts missing in box	

8. **QUALITY PROBLEMS.** For the following list of quality problems for a lawn mower, note whether it is an internal quality failure (I) or an external quality failure (E).

Quality Problem	Category	Quality Problem	Category
Engine will not start on first pull		Rework of motor housing	
Chassis arrives scratched		Screws for handle assembly missing	
Blades too dull to cut		Controls do not respond	
Warranty repairs		Broken product returned	
Internal inspection		Box disintegrates at factory	

9. **BALANCED SCORECARD.** For the following list of measures, please note whether they are cost-related (C), productivity-related (P), quality-related (Q), or delivery-related (D).

Measurement	Category	Measurement	Category
First-pass good units		Rework hours	
Gets to customer on time		Output per shift	
Meets cost target		Parts arrive on time to line	
Units produced per hour		Reduction in price of parts	
Defects		Piece parts made per day	

10. **BALANCED SCORECARD.** For the following list of measures, please note whether they are cost-related (C), productivity-related (P), quality-related (Q), or delivery-related (D).

Measurement	Category	Measurement	Category
Good units produced		Scratched units	
Returned goods		Capacity utilization	
Cycle time		Cost gap	
Raw materials on time to plant		Units produced per worker	
Next day delivery		Rework hours	

Problems

1. **CLOSING THE TARGET COST GAP.** Sunshine Products makes lawn furniture in various styles. Recently, it decided to launch a new line of reclining lawn chairs for poolside use. The design team put together the following information.

Component	Units Needed	Cost per Unit Used
Decking material	4 yards	$10.00 per yard
Steel tubing	20 feet	$0.25 per foot
Armrests	2	$0.75 each
Reclining ratchet mechanism	2	$1.50 each
Screws	20	$0.05 each
Grommets	20	$0.03 each
Labor	15 minutes	$16.00 per hour

The company wants to sell the units at $65 and wants a 40% margin to cover overhead and other company costs.

The design could be altered by using cheaper decking material ($6 per yard instead of $10) and cheaper steel tubing ($0.15 per foot), and redesigning the chair to eliminate half of the screws and grommets. This would reduce assembly time by half. It would also make the chair lighter to carry but would reduce its overall durability from the industry standard of five years to three years of reliable service.

REQUIRED:

a. What is the company's target cost?
b. What is the current estimated cost to make the recliner?
c. What is the cost gap?

d. Using the design team's suggestions for bringing down the cost, can the chair now meet its target cost?
e. How do you feel about the changes being made to the design? Think about them from the customer's perspective; that is, the attributes they care most about.

2. **CLOSING THE TARGET COST GAP.** Silver Spoons makes silverware and stainless steel eating utensils. It is considering adding a new line, a silver-clad stainless steel line that would give the look and feel of silver but cost considerably less and have a heavier gauge, something customers desire. The design team has put together the following information for you about a four-place setting service.

Cost Element	Amount Needed	Cost per Unit Used
Stainless steel	3 pounds	$1.25 per pound
Silver	6 ounces	$28.00 per ounce
Plastic wrappings	16	$0.01 each
Inner packaging	1	$0.25 each
Outer box	1	$0.30 each
Labor	20 minutes	$15.00 per hour
Machine time	10 minutes	$60.00 per hour

Since this is such a high-quality product, Silver Spoons believes it can command the premium price of $240 for four place settings (16 pieces). The company wants its costs to be 40% less than the price to cover profits and overhead.

The design team notes it can cut very little of the cost. It could reduce the weight of the product by one pound by using less stainless steel. It could also reduce the thickness of the silver coating, eliminating one ounce of silver. If it eliminated the plastic wraps, it could cut labor time in half. Machining time cannot be changed without physically damaging the product.

REQUIRED:

a. What is the company's target cost?
b. What is the current estimated cost to make the four place settings?
c. What is the cost gap?
d. Using the design team's suggestions for bringing down the cost, can the setting now meet its target cost?
e. How do you feel about the changes being made to the design? Think about it from the customer's perspective; that is, the attributes they care most about.

3. **MULTIPLE ITEM VARIANCE ANALYSIS.** Built Rite produces suitcases. The following are the results of last month's production.

Built Rite Products—Suitcase Results						
Standard cost estimates				Actual results		
Materials	Standard rate	Amount allowed	Standard cost	Actual rate	Amount used	Actual cost
Plastic	$1.50 per pound	4 pounds	$6.00	$1.40 per pound	4.2 pounds	$5.88
Hinges	$0.50 per hinge	2	$1.00	$0.60 per hinge	2 each	$1.20
Cloth lining	$3.00 per yard	2 yards	$6.00	$2.75 per yard	2.4 yards	$6.60
Elastic	$1.50 per yard	1 yard	$1.50	$1.75 per yard	1 yard	$1.75
Straps	$2.00 per yard	2 yards	$4.00	$2.25 per yard	2 yards	$4.50
Wheels	$2.50 per set	2 sets	$5.00	$2.25 per set	2 sets	$4.50
Handles	$0.50 per handle	2 each	$1.00	$0.60 per handle	2 each	$1.20
Rolling handle mechanism	$5.00 per mechanism	1 each	$5.00	$4.50 per mechanism	1 each	$4.50
Total materials at standard			$29.50	Actual materials		$30.13
Conversion and other activities						
Activity	Standard rate	Standard amount	Standard cost	Actual rate	Amount used	Actual cost
Mold plastic	$30.00 per hour	2 minutes	$1.00	$27.00 per hour	3 minutes	$1.35
Assemble suitcase	$15.00 per hour	5 minutes	$1.25	$18.00 per hour	4 minutes	$1.20
Set up	$48.00 per hour	10 minutes	$8.00	$45.00 per hour	12 minutes	$9.00
Kit materials	$5.00 per kit	2 kits	$10.00	$5.50 per kit	2 kits	$11.00
Inspection	$18.00 per hour	3 minutes	$0.90	$15.00 per hour	4 minutes	$1.00
Packaging	$15.00 per hour	2 minutes	$0.50	$16.00 per hour	3 minutes	$0.80
Standard conversion and activities			$21.65	Actual materials		$24.35
Total standard cost			$51.15	Total actual cost		$54.48

REQUIRED:

a. Using the table-based approach pictured in Table 7.7, decompose the variances for the month into price and usage variances. Do this for every cost element in the table.

b. How does performance for the month look? Explain your reasoning.

4. **MULTIPLE ITEM VARIANCE ANALYSIS.** WearWell Products makes a line of countertop grills for making hamburgers and related grilled products like panini. The following table contains information about the production of its countertop grill for last month.

WearWell Products—Countertop Grill Results						
	Standard Cost Estimates			Actual Results		
Materials	Standard Rate	Amount Allowed	Standard Cost	Actual Rate	Amount Used	Actual Cost
Metal casing	$2.00 per pound	3 pounds	$6.00	$2.10 per pound	3.2 pounds	$6.72
Hinges	$0.50 each	2	$1.00	$0.55 each	2	$1.10
Heating elements	$5.00 each	2	$10.00	$4.75 each	2	$9.50
Ridged grill panels	$0.75 each	2	$1.50	$0.80 each	2	$1.60
Flat grill panels	$0.75 each	2	$1.50	$0.80 each	2	$1.60
Electric cord	$1.25 each	1	$1.25	$1.15 each	1	$1.15
Dials	$0.40 each	3	$1.20	$0.45 each	3	$1.35
Screws and grommets	$0.05 each	10	$0.50	$0.04 each	12	$0.48
Total Materials at Standard			$22.95	Actual Materials		$23.50
Conversion and Other Activities						
Activity	Standard Rate	Standard Amount	Standard Cost	Actual Rate	Amount Used	Actual Cost
Stamp metal casing	$60.00 per hour	2 minutes	$2.00	$54.00 per hour	3 minutes	$2.70
Assemble grill	$18.00 per hour	5 minutes	$1.50	$15.00 per hour	6 minutes	$1.50
Set up machines	$48.00 per hour	8 minutes	$6.40	$45.00 per hour	10 minutes	$7.50
Kit materials	$4.00 per kit	3 kits	$12.00	$3.75 per kit	3 kits	$11.25
Inspection	$18.00 per hour	3 minutes	$0.90	$15.00 per hour	4 minutes	$1.00
Packaging	$15.00 per hour	2 minutes	$0.50	$16.00 per hour	3 minutes	$0.80
Standard Conversion and Activities			$23.30	Actual Activities		$24.75
Total Standard Cost			$46.25	Total Actual Cost		$48.25

REQUIRED:

a. Using the table-based approach pictured in Table 7.7, decompose the variances for the month into price and usage variances. Do this for every cost element in the table.

b. How does performance for the month look? Explain your reasoning.

5. **CVP AND INCREMENTAL ANALYSIS. TAKE A SPECIAL ORDER.** BlueJay Products makes one main product, Ever Blue, which is used to fertilize hydrangeas and keep their blossoms blue. The company usually sells through a distribution network for $15 per five-pound bag. Normal volumes are 5,000 bags per year. The costs for normal production are in the table below.

Ever Blue	$15.00	$8.50	$25,000.00

REQUIRED:

a. **Calculate the current breakeven volume in bags.**
b. **Calculate the margin of safety.**
c. **QRC Productions approaches BlueJay with an offer to buy 2,500 bags but at a reduced price of $10.50. QRC would be selling to many of the same markets BlueJay now serves. Using incremental analysis, does it make sense for BlueJay to take this special order? Why or why not?**

6. **INCREMENTAL ANALYSIS. MAKE VS. BUY.** Clear Skin, Inc., makes pump liquid soap dispensers that various manufacturers use. It currently makes all of the components that go into the pump dispenser on its high-end extrusion machines. Recently, a competitor offered to supply the pressure valve that controls the soap flow for 25% less than it costs Clear Skin to make it. Outsourcing would add to assembly time, driving those costs from the current $325,000 of labor to $375,000. Machining costs would go down 10%. The total cost picture for the product for a year in which the company makes 25,000,000 units internally (without outsourcing) is in the table below.

Clear Skin, Inc.	
Costs for 25,000,000 Bottles	
Plastic for bottle	$375,000
Pump materials	$500,000
Flow control valve	$125,000
Feeder tube	$250,000
Labor	$325,000
Machine costs	$375,000
Other overhead	$250,000
Total Costs per Batch	$2,200,000
Cost per Bottle Made	$0.088

REQUIRED:

a. Should Clear Skin make or buy this part?

b. What business risks should the company consider? Remember, the flow control valve is a critical component of the final product.

7. **LAUNCH A NEW PRODUCT. CAPACITY AND ABC COSTING.** Hop-a-Long Company makes rocking horses for the children's market. Recently it has been thinking of making a larger horse that would be suspended on springs; the current models sit on the floor and simply rock back and forth on wooden rockers. All of the products are brightly painted and are quite popular among grandparents who dote on their grandchildren! The new model would be targeted to a slightly older child, which would expand the company's product line.

   Jim Rangely, VP of product development, has pulled together some information but needs a lot of help in making sense of it for the new spring-suspended horse. Today's market price for the type of product Hop-a-Long is considering is $250. The horse will also need an audio component, which means more new technology for Hop-a-Long. The following table contains all of the information Jim has gathered.

Hop-a-Long Company

Production Item	Quantity	Price
Plush horse hair material	6 yds	$2.25 yd
Fringe	1 yds	$1.75 yd
Eyes	2 ea	$0.50 ea
Nose	1 ea	$0.75 ea
Springs	4 ea	$1.25 ea
Metal tubing	20 ft	$0.75 ft
Screw and grommets	30 ea	$0.05 ea
Machining—sewing	4 min	$540.00 hr
Machining—metal frame	3 min	$480.00 hr
Kitting	2 kits	$10.00 kit
Assembly	5 min	$24.00 hr
Inspection	5 min	$48.00 hr
Packaging	8 min	$18.00 hr
Shipping	1 pkg	$15.00 pkg

REQUIRED:

a. Using the information above, calculate the current cost of the new product.
b. The company needs to make a 50% profit to cover overhead, marketing, and other product- and company-based charges. What is the target cost?
c. What is the current cost gap?
d. Hop-a-Long has been approached by a Chinese company that is willing to manufacture the spring horse for Hop-a-Long for $140 delivered. Should Hop-a-Long outsource this product? Why or why not?

8. **LAUNCH A NEW PRODUCT. CAPACITY AND ABC COSTING.** Ache-No-More Company makes specialty chairs designed to take stress off of the lower back, reducing the tendency to get backaches from sitting too long. The chairs are very high-end, ranging from $1,395 for its least expensive product to $2,595 for its most expensive product. The company is thinking about entering the desk chair market. This is a highly competitive market, but Ache-No-More feels its reputation for stressless comfort will allow it to enter the market at the high end successfully.

Alice Green, VP of market development, is tasked with putting together the information for the new product. Ache-No-More plans to launch the product at a price of $1,400, well above the cost for the typical chair. Offered in one of three basic leather colors, the chair would feature high-end ergonomically designed seating for the busy executive. The company is used to making a 60% margin on its sales to cover the massive marketing and distribution costs it faces (Ache-No-More has its own stores). The new product will be sold in the company's own stores, but would also be sold through other channels. The information that Alice pulled together is in the table below.

Ache-No-More Company		
Production Item	**Quantity**	**Price**
Leather for chair	10 yards	$14.00 per yard
Armrests	2 each	$20.00 each
Ergonomic support mechanism	1 each	$90.00 each
Padded headrest	1 each	$12.00 each
Height-adjustable cylinder	1 each	$25.00 each
Wooden base	8 feet	$4.00 per foot
Wheel assemblies	4 each	$5.00 each

Ache-No-More Company		
Production Item	**Quantity**	**Price**
Screw and grommets	40 each	$0.05 each
Machining—sewing	6 minutes	$600.00 per hour
Machining—wooden Base	8 minutes	$540.00 per hour
Kitting	4 kits	$15.00 per kit
Assembly	15 minutes	$30.00 per hour
Inspection	10 minutes	$60.00 per hour
Packaging	10 minutes	$24.00 per hour
Shipping	1 package	$30.00 per package

REQUIRED:

a. Using the information above, calculate the current cost of the new product.
b. What is the target cost?
c. What is the current cost gap?
d. Ache-No-More has been approached by an Indian company that is willing to manufacture the desk chair for $590 delivered. Should Ache-No-More outsource this product? Why or why not?

Database Problems

For database templates, worksheets, and workbooks, go to MAdownloads.imanet.org

DB 7.1 CAPACITY COST ANALYSIS. Develop capacity cost reports for each of the direct manufacturing departments, then copy your results onto the worksheet DB 7.1 Est. Part Cost Template. Use the Mfg CC An'ls-Capacity $'s-20X6 and Summary Part Counts by Department worksheets.

DB 7.1 Cutting Data Template: You will need to fill in the blank data cells, doing a few calculations as you go along. Begin by filling cell F9 with the corresponding data from the Summary Part Counts by Department data worksheet. Next, cell F17 will be cells F8 times F9, divided by 3,600 to convert seconds to hours. Cell F18 is the total nonproductive from cell C20. Cell F10 then becomes cells F17 plus F18. Cell F19 is cell F7 – (cell F17 plus F18), with cell F21 then being the sum of F17 to F19. Next, do the percentage hour calculations in column G, rows 17 thru 21 by dividing each cell by the total in cell F21 (for example, G17 = F17/F21). Next, you are going to calculate the hourly rates by type of capacity, rows 27 through 30. Cell F27 comes from the data worksheet Mfg

CC An'ls-Capacity $'s-20x6, cell C40. Cell F28 is found on the same data worksheet, cell C42. Cell F30 then becomes F27 plus F28. Finally, the percentages in column G come from dividing cells F27, F28, and F30 by F30. You are now ready to do your capacity report for the department.

DB 7.1 Cutting Report Template: You have been given comments to help you with the calculations. For instance, Cell D6=17 x 24 x # of lines from the data sheet F6. For column E, you will use two rates from the data template: For cells F6 to F8, use the rate you calculated in cell G27 on the data sheet. For the remaining cells in column F, use the rate from cell G30 on the data template worksheet. Complete the worksheet. I25 is cell F9 from the data sheet. Use it to complete the boxed cells in column I. Repeat the first two parts for the remaining manufacturing departments.

DB 7.1 Est. Part Cost Template: Populating this final worksheet is a simple link command to each of the capacity report results cells I25 to I35.

DB 7.1 Est % Part Cost Templt: For all of Column H, divide the totals by category in column G by the total capacity cost in Cell G22. Make sure the results format as a percentage.

REQUIRED:

Turn in the worksheets DB 7.1 Est. Part Cost Template and DB 7.1 Est % Part Cost Templt to your instructor along with your answers to the following questions: Which department seems to have the highest level of productive cost? Nonproductive cost? Idle cost? Which summary data sheet was more informative? Why?

DB 7.2 ABC COSTS. The goal of this exercise is to use ABC to estimate the profitability of Kinkaid's current cabinet line. The data worksheets are Income Statement, Product Cost Summaries-20x6, Indirect Mfg Cost Centers, and ABC Driver Info-Mfg-20x6.

DB 7.2 ABC Ind Mfg Cost Template: Row 8 is from ABC Driver Info-Mfg-20x6, row 10. Columns D thru L, rows 11 thru 19 will be calculated by multiplying the rate for each column in row 8 times the driver frequencies in the ABC Driver Info-Mfg-20x6 worksheet, Columns D thru L, rows 12 thru 20. Row 21 is the sum of rows 11 through 19, by column. Column N is the sum, by row, for columns D through L.

DB 7.2 ABC Mfg CC 20x6 Template: Copy the data from Column N in the Ind Mfg Cost Template to Row 32.

DB 7.2 Part Calcs-ABC Template: Now you use the data from the ABC Mfg CC 20x6 Template to fill in Column G, rows 5 to 9, and Column I, rows 14-17 and then complete the calculations for the rest of the worksheet.

DB 7.2 Upstream $ to FG Templt: Now transfer the cost from the departments that produce parts to the finished goods units that use them moving row by row.

DB 7.2 FG Cost ABC Template: Rows 6 and 7 are found on the Product Summaries 20x6 data worksheet. Row 8 comes from Part Calcs-ABC Template, cells J14 to J17. Row 13 is from Upstream $ to FG Templt, Row 36. You will calculate all other rows.

DB 7.2 SG&A ABC $ Rate Template: You only need to complete two columns here: S and T.

DB 7.2 SG&A ABC Cost Template: The ABC rates by department should fill automatically. For Columns F thru S, Rows 6 thru 13, multiply the ABC rate for that row (department) times the driver frequencies in SG&A ABC $ Rate Template).

DB 7.2 Product Profit Template: Starting with the Kitchen Craft line: Row 7 is from the data worksheet Product Cost Summaries 20x6, Row 17. Row 9 is the total in Row 15 of the FG Cost ABC Template by column. Row 13 is from the SG&A ABC Cost Template, Row 15. Do the same for the Custom Craft line, then fill in the remaining rows.

REQUIRED:

Turn in the final worksheet, DB 7.2 Product Profit Template, along with the answer to the following question: Which products and product lines are responsible for most of Kinkaid's current profits?

Cases

CASE 7.1 CVP AND INCREMENTAL ANALYSIS. Sarah Drogo, president of Storage, Inc., a company that makes a wide variety of storage boxes for home and office use, is thinking about adding a new line of small plastic storage boxes. This would require a new technology. The company currently uses predominantly cardboard of various weights that are used in its other products. Since this is a big move for the company, Sarah wants to make sure that all of the financial and nonfinancial implications are understood before she gets under way. She thinks she can sell 3 million units.

Working with Jarrod White, her business analyst, Sarah puts together the following first-pass information on the new boxes. They would retail for $1.99. The company sells to the distribution channel at 50% of retail, so the product would net the company approximately $1 per box. Jarrod estimates that the boxes would cost $0.15 in direct materials, $0.10 in direct labor, $0.05 in packaging materials, and $0.20 in variable machining costs. The cost of the new equipment, insurance, space (new space would be needed for the operation), support activities, and so on are estimated at $500,000 per year. In addition to these simple estimates, Jarrod determines that manufacturing the new box will require an additional person in manufacturing, quality control, and purchasing. Their salaries would be $30,000, $35,000, and $45,000, respectively.

Adding the new line would also stress the packaging area. Jarrod believes there will be a one-time cost of $175,000 to retrofit the packing and shipping area to accommodate the new smaller boxes, which will be packed in boxes of 12 for shipment to customers. The company currently bundle-packs its products with a simple strap device. The new containers will require their own cardboard box, which means there will be many new activities in the packaging area. It is likely that to handle the increased workload, the company will need either a new person at a salary of $25,000 a year, or to pay overtime at $12.50 per hour for 10 hours a week to four existing workers.

The new machine's space requirements and noise level will be a challenge. Storage, Inc.'s existing machines are relatively quiet, but the high-pressure extrusion process needed for plastic is much noisier. It is also a bit more dangerous because of the high pressure required. Boxes can be damaged during the process, resulting in very sharp edges. Workers staffing the line will need to wear protective clothing and heavy gloves. Since the plant is not air-conditioned, the combination of the heat from the machine and the heavy protective gear could make the job very uncomfortable. Sarah is considering air-conditioning the part of the plant housing the new machine. This would drive the annual costs up from $500,000 to $650,000 a year, with a one-time cost of $75,000 for the air-conditioning units. Since it would be the only air-conditioned part of the plant, Sarah is concerned this will disgruntle the rest of the workforce.

Full of questions, Sarah is looking for help to sort out the quantitative and qualitative issues involved in this potential expansion.

REQUIRED:

a. Using as much of the information as possible, do a CVP analysis of the ongoing costs of running the new production line. How much does Sarah need to sell to break even? To make a $250,000 profit before tax? A $250,000 profit after tax with a tax rate of 25%? Do the analysis in two stages—Year 1 results with the nonrecurring expenditures and an ongoing production analysis for Year 2 that is believed to be the steady state for the line.
b. Sarah could buy the new box from an outside vendor in China for $0.80 per box. She would need new storage space to house the 250,000-unit minimum order required. This space would cost $30,000 a year. She would still need the new inspector to maintain quality control and the new shipping and packing capabilities as the order will be shipped in very large quantities bulk-packed. Review the numbers and do an incremental analysis of the make-vs.-buy option Sarah faces.
c. What should Sarah do? Use the numbers to justify your answer.
d. What qualitative issues should concern Sarah? How much impact do you feel these should have on her decision? Why?

CASE 7.2 COST GAP AND VARIANCE ANALYSIS. Rubens Company makes a number of special-edition glass perfume bottles. Each year, the company comes out with a new set of 12 bottles, which customers can buy either one at a time or as a set. The company uses target costing to set the price for the items, which are directly distributed to customers if purchased as a set, or sold through retail outlets as single bottles. The retail price of the individual bottles is $25. There is a 40% markup in the industry, so Rubens gets $15 per bottle. It sells the set of 12 for $240, or $20 per bottle. For practical purposes, the target price is set at $15 per bottle.

The target profit for each annual run of 250,000 sets of 12 is 50%. This has to cover development, marketing, internal operations costs, management salaries, and profit for the company.

Since this is a highly competitive industry, one where customers can easily be lost if quality is not perfect, significant time is spent on developing attractive, highly protective packaging. The packaging accounts for 10% of the total manufacturing cost.

Based on current production, it appears that Rubens is not going to make its target cost. Quality problems have added to the problem. The actual vs. standard information for production is presented in the following table.

Rubens Company Analysis of Results

Cost Component	Actual Quantity		Standard Quantity		Actual Price		Standard Price	
Decorative Glass	0.3	Pound	0.25	Pound	$18.00	per Pound	$15.00	per Pound
Stoppers	1.2	Each	1	Each	$0.40	Each	$0.35	Each
Packaging material	1	Box	1	Box	$0.80	per Box	$0.75	per Box
Glass blower	6	Minutes	5	Minutes	$18.00	per Hour	$15.00	per Hour
Packing labor	4	Minutes	3	Minutes	$14.00	per Hour	$12.00	per Hour
Quality control	5	minutes	3	Minutes	$15.00	per Hour	$16.00	per Hour

REQUIRED:

a. Compute the target cost.
b. Compute the current actual cost.
c. Compute the cost gap.
d. Compute the variances for all of the cost elements.
e. Where should Rubens focus its attention in getting its costs under control?

presented in the following table:

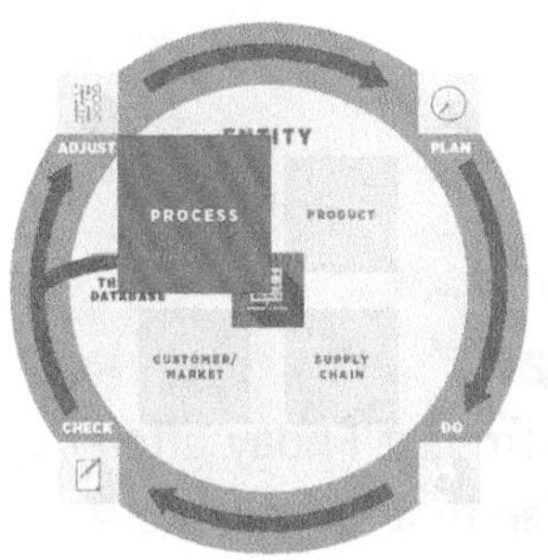

CHAPTER EIGHT

Setting Process Expectations

It is not enough to be busy...the question is: what are we busy about?

HENRY DAVID THOREAU[1]

CHAPTER ROADMAP

1. **Key Issues in the Process Domain**
   - *Process vs. Functional Organizations*
   - *Understanding the Process Flow*
2. **Going Lean**
   - *Lean Accounting*
   - *Applying Lean Accounting*
3. **Activity-Based Approaches to Process Management**
   - *Activity-Based Management*
   - *Activity-Based Budgeting*
4. **The Theory of Constraints, Just-in-Time Management, and Capacity**
   - *The Theory of Constraints*
   - *Just-in-Time Management and Cellular Process Flows*
   - *A Role for Capacity Analysis*
   - *Applying JIT and Capacity Analysis in Nonmachine Settings*

LEARNING OBJECTIVES

After studying this chapter, you should be able to:

1. **Define process management and identify its unique features.**
2. **Explain and illustrate lean accounting methods, objectives, and benefits.**
3. **Develop and apply activity-based management and activity-based budgeting.**
4. **Describe the key elements of the Theory of Constraints, just-in-time, and capacity management.**

---

1 *The Forbes Scrapbook of Thoughts on the Business of Life*, Chicago: Triumph Books, 1992: p. 384.

IN CONTEXT ➤ Process-Based Planning: Going Cellular

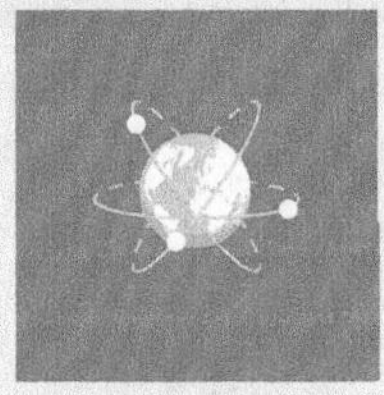

It was Monday morning, and the meeting with Sam last Friday afternoon had gone reasonably well. Brad had suggested that Kinkaid move away from its assembly line approach to cabinet-making to a cellular configuration. In a cell, the workers would not only be responsible for cost and quality, but also would have the right to make changes to the production process if they thought of a way to improve it. In addition, workers would be cross-trained, which would make the production process more flexible.

Brad's team was charged with coming up with a cellular approach in two weeks when the next meeting would take place. It was a major responsibility. He was determined to make a great presentation so that Sam would agree to implement his plan.

Shelley had some concerns. In cellular manufacturing, management gave up a lot of its control and placed it in the hands of the workforce. She was not sure if their plant workers could take on that responsibility. Shelley knew that some of the quality problems they were experiencing were caused by line workers who had not waited for joints to dry before pushing the product along to the next station because they were intent on meeting their own production goals. Now, Brad was suggesting that these same individuals accept a team structure and take on responsibility for quality as well as productivity.

"We're going to need a lot of training in the various quality control methods if we're going to go cellular," Shelley stressed over coffee with Brad on Monday. "I'm worried that we'd be asking an awful lot of the line workers. I'm also concerned about changing the role of our quality control experts from inspecting to teaching others to do their job."

"I understand your concerns, Shelley, but Sam is really intent on letting the workforce take on more responsibility. He's seen other companies reap the improved flexibility and productivity of cellular manufacturing. Our own experience in the specials kitchen cabinet area has shown that teams can take on the responsibility for output quality and quantity. Our specials line does some pretty amazing things in terms of output and quality. That's where I'm going to start my investigation. I want to see how our culture adapts to new roles."

"Good luck, Brad, and keep me posted. We're in this together."

"Will do. I know I'll need your help again."

ORGANIZATIONS BRING MANY PEOPLE AND RESOURCES WITH DIFFERENT capabilities together to meet a common objective. No individual can do everything. Work and ideas flow between individuals, making the final "product" of the group effort greater than what any one person could achieve on his or her own. Whether the ultimate goal is to produce and distribute a physical product, such as a bottle of shampoo, or develop a series of free summer concerts for a community, the requirements for success are the same—consistent, coordinated, and focused collaboration. **Process management** *is a system of tools and techniques used to manage activities across the organization.*

As you will see, managing the horizontal dimension of an organization forces managers to focus on *how* work is done. The goal of process management is to establish a clear, unambiguous system of handoffs from one individual or group to another. These efforts are driven by one overarching goal—to find better, faster, and cheaper ways to meet customer expectations. One management expert, Richard Schonberger,[2] defines process management as "building a chain of customers." But, as you will see, this chain is only as strong as its weakest link. In this chapter, your goal is to understand, and be able to apply the tools and techniques used to design and develop effective processes. We will begin this journey by exploring the key issues in the process domain.

Key Issues in the Process Domain

OBJECTIVE 1

Define process management and identify its unique features.

Shifting from a functional approach to a process perspective begins with understanding that a **process** *is a system of interdependent, sequential activities that produces a specific output*. This means that the "slice-in-time"[3] of responsibilities and reporting relationships that we see in hierarchical, functional organizations shifts in process management to a focus on how work is done. Where many measures are needed to guide behavior in hierarchical settings, process management relies upon cost, time, output quality, and customer satisfaction to unite action across the process. When cost is reduced or customer satisfaction improves, we know the process is enhanced.

When we think about a process, we have to take a holistic approach that emphasizes linkages and the handoff (passing) of a work product from one individual or group to another. Improving process performance requires an ongoing effort to remove problems from the system of activities—which means improving the interfaces between functional and product units. It is a cross-functional, cross-organizational endeavor that begins with defining the "white spaces," or what fills in the spaces between the boxes, in the organizational chart.[4]

For instance, at the U.S. Coast Guard Financial Center, accounts payable transactions were handled by a number of independent groups. One group would receive the invoices and date-stamp them, collecting them into a large pile that they would at some point "throw over the wall" to the accounts payable clerks, who worked independently on their batch of invoices. As batches were completed, they were released to the individuals who were responsible for issuing checks. Each of these groups operated as an island. The result was lost discounts for prompt payment. When these individuals were linked into payment process teams, the time it took to handle an invoice dropped from three weeks to three days. In the first month alone of these changes, the U.S. Coast Guard Financial Center was able to take more than $1 million in

---

2 Richard Schonberger, *Building a Chain of Customers*, New York: The Free Press, 1990.
3 Thomas H. Davenport, *Process Innovation: Reengineering Work through Information Technology*, Boston: Harvard Business School Press, 1993: p. 6.
4 This term was originally coined by Geary A. Rummler and Alan P. Brache in their book *Improving Performance: How to Manage the White Space on the Organization Chart*, San Francisco: Jossey-Bass Publishers, 1995.

early payment discounts—money that could be used to fuel the ships that the Coast Guard uses in its daily activities. Figure 8.1 illustrates one of the process flow diagrams that was used to analyze the accounts payable process and gain these improvements.

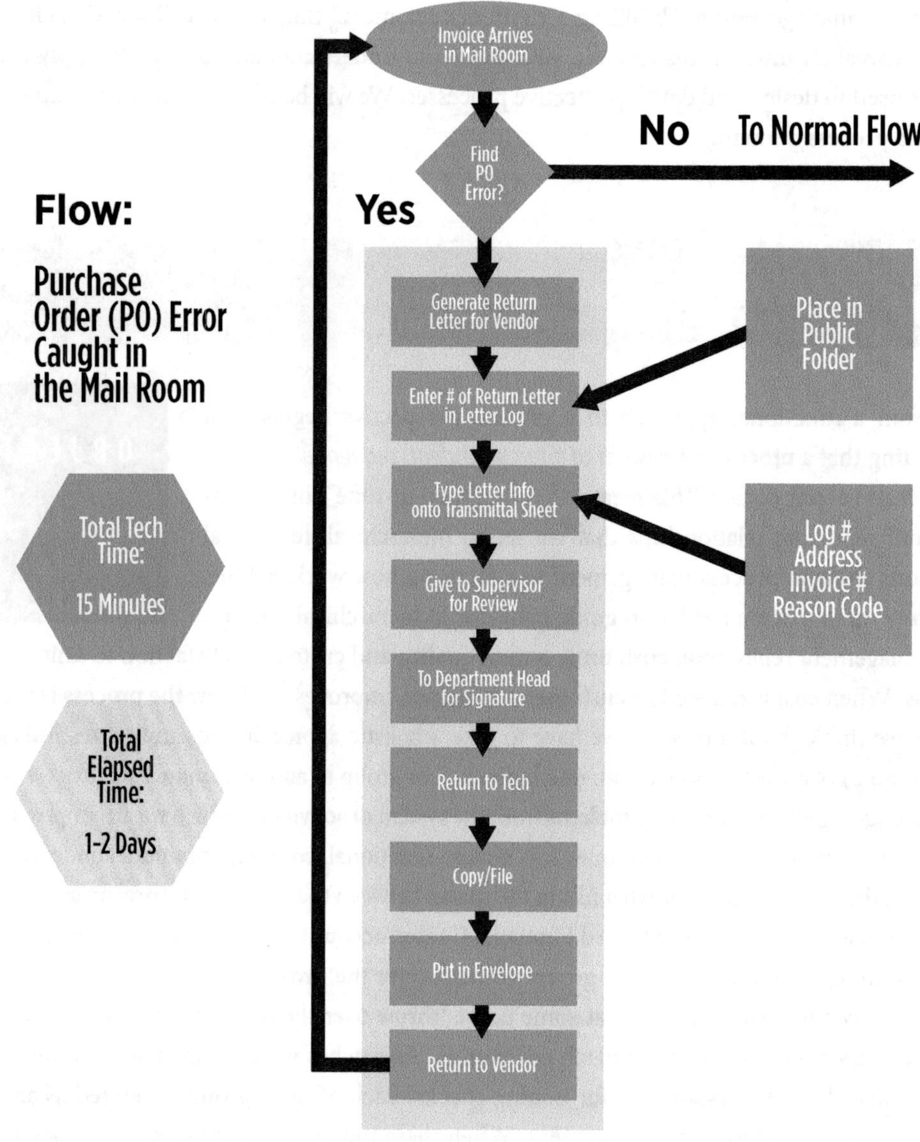

FIGURE 8.1 THE FINANCE DIVISION OF THE U.S. COAST GUARD USES PROCESS MAPPING AND PROCESS IMPROVEMENT METHODS TO CUT COSTS AND ELIMINATE PROBLEMS.

In other words, when we talk about managing a process, we are not solely concerned with a manufacturing setting. In fact, processes exist everywhere in an organization—an organization is actually a compilation of key processes that focus on different aspects of total performance—and in every sector of the economy. Some processes are at the core of servicing customers, such as the order-to-payment process. Others are focused on managing the organization, such as the process that focuses on developing and managing human resources.

PROCESS VS. FUNCTIONAL ORGANIZATIONS

Everyone in an organization has a customer—the next individual who handles the transaction, product, or activity. In the Coast Guard example, we saw the value that comes from linking the activities done in the mail room to those done in the accounts payable department into a flow of work: Problems can be isolated and solutions developed to eliminate them. Individuals complete tasks, but, unless the output of their effort is successfully and effectively conveyed to the next person in line, the ultimate customer's expectations will not be met. In other words, when we focus on a process, we are highlighting the activities performed by linked groups of people.

The underlying goal of process management is to combat the communication and response problems common in a functionally defined organization by identifying and managing the linkages between functions so that work flows smoothly and problems are identified and resolved more rapidly and effectively. Table 8.1 summarizes the key differences between a functional organization, one that is dominated by silos, and organizations that are process-oriented.[5]

TABLE 8.1 FUNCTIONAL AND PROCESS-ORIENTED ORGANIZATIONS COMPARED

Feature	Functional Organization	Process-Oriented Organization
Business focus	Internal functions	Customer
Customer contact	Divided into specialists	Single point, backed by computer technology
Organizational structure	Functional and hierarchical	Multiskilled teams
Managerial role	Control	Process planning, measurement, and management; facilitation and leadership
Material handling	Buffer stocks	Just-in-time production
Performance measures	Functional performance	Process output measures of customer satisfaction, timeliness, and value
Information and systems	Functional and technical requirements	Multidimensional; focused on customer satisfaction and internal communications

5 Source: "Implementing Process Management: A Framework for Action," Management Accounting Guideline #47, The Society of Management Accountants of Canada, Hamilton, Ontario, 1998: p. 6.

As this brief comparison suggests, traditional functional management and process-oriented management approaches have very little in common. When a company decides to implement process management, it not only has to make changes to how it defines, measures, and manages its work flows, it has to help its employees shift their mind-set away from the suboptimizing "us vs. them" model of traditional structures to one in which cooperation and collaboration are definers of individual and functional success. We will now explore these issues in greater depth.

UNDERSTANDING THE PROCESS FLOW

Process management provides a method of analyzing an operation by directly addressing the organization, its nature of work, and how it is conducted.[6] Documentation plays a key role in process management; its importance cannot be overemphasized. While it may be hard to believe, many managers do not have a complete picture of how work on a product or service proceeds through the organization. They likely know the route a product takes through the factory, but they seldom have as much understanding of how key customer transactions, either paper or electronic, get completed in the back office.

Standard flowcharting methods have been developed by the American Society of Mechanical Engineers (ASME) for the documentation of the activities and flow of work through a process. The core symbols and their meaning are summarized in Table 8.2.

TABLE 8.2 ASME ACTIVITY SYMBOLS

ASME Symbol	Name	Activity Represented
●	Basic process operation	Work that is done by machines and/or labor; it does not necessarily add value to the product.
➡	Move	Change in location of product from one workplace or workstation to another.
D	Delay/temporary storage/queue	Work-in-process temporarily held up, or queued.
■	Verification	Comparison of product with a standard of quantity or quality.
◆	Inspection	A control point established by management action.
▼	Storage	Storage of raw, work-in-process, or finished material.

6 Eugene H. Melan, *Process Management: Methods for Improving Products and Services*, New York: McGraw-Hill, Inc., 1993: p. 11.

These basic activities can occur multiple times within a single work process. As is clear from this list, not every activity in a process is necessarily desirable or adds value. For instance, move and delay are two activities that a customer is unlikely to value, and, therefore, they will not be willing to pay for them. In fact, in process management, move and storage, or queue, are considered waste. Since process management seeks to streamline work flows and improve an organization's ability to create value for customers, any activity that is marked by the delay or move symbols is immediately analyzed and eliminated if possible.

Linking these symbols together as demonstrated in Figure 8.2 captures the work flow for Grant Plumbing Supply. It is a typical **order-to-payment process,** *the linked steps that span from the time an order is received until it is filled, invoiced, and the payment is received*; it is the heart of the revenue- and profit-generating flow. As you can see, many different activities are completed in many different areas of the company before the customer's order can be filled. This process includes many moves (up to 12 per order), and a significant amount of delay (up to 15 days) is embedded in it, even if we do not consider the time consumed between sending an invoice and receiving payment. While the figure looks complex, in reality it is a fairly straightforward flow from receipt of an order until final payment is received. What makes it complex is the situation in which an order is taken out of the desired flow if it is flagged as a credit risk.

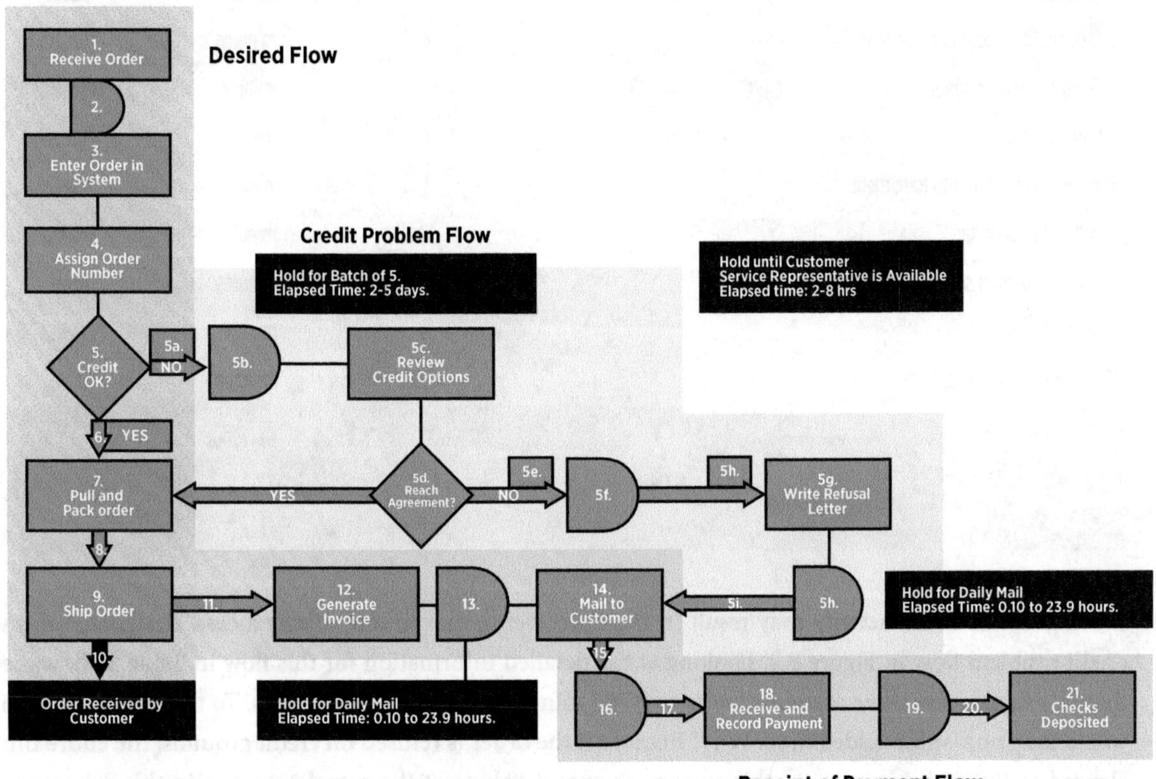

FIGURE 8.2 THE ORDER-TO-PAYMENT PROCESS FLOWCHART FOR GRANT PLUMBING SUPPLY

As seen in Table 8.3a, the time required by Grant Plumbing Supply to actually fill the customer's order and ship it following the desired flow's processing time is quite small (estimated at 36 minutes). The elapsed time from when the order is received, credit is granted, and until the customer gets the order, however, is estimated as 4,377 minutes when move and queue are incorporated. Given these estimates, *only 0.82% of the total elapsed time from the receipt of the order with no credit issue is actually used to work on activities the customer would value.* This result is not uncommon; process time in most work flows is usually just a small fraction of elapsed time. Of course, the customer experiences the elapsed time, suggesting that reducing the elapsed time could improve customer satisfaction. Careful analysis of the existing flow can help an organization make major improvements on this dimension of performance.

TABLE 8.3A DESIRED PROCESS FLOW

Grant Plumbing Supply			
Activity	Maximum Time to Complete		Type of Activity
1. Order request is received	1	minute	Process
2. Order queued for next available clerk	5	minutes	Queue
3. Order detail entered into system	8	minutes	Process
4. Order number assigned	1	minute	Process
5. Credit analyzed	6	minutes	Process
6. Accepted order sent to fulfillment	1	minute	Move
7. Pull and pack order	10	minutes	Process
8. Completed order sent to shipping	15	minutes	Move
9. Order shipped	10	minutes	Process
10. Order in transit to customer	4,320	minutes	Move
Elapsed Time	4,377	minutes	
Process Time	36	minutes	
Process % of Elapsed Time	0.82%		

The credit check activity may result in the order being moved into a subprocess, designated as the credit problem flow in Figure 8.2. Looking at the detailed information for this flow in Table 8.3b, we see that this subprocess alone accounts for up to 8,706 minutes, or more than six days. To the customer, this is worse than non-value-added time. Why? Because if the order is refused on credit grounds, the entire time elapsed to this point is waste in this customer's eyes. Looking at the actual activities in this subprocess, we see that only 41 minutes are actually spent completing the process activities, or only 0.47% of the total elapsed time. It is quite likely any customer who experiences the delays caused by credit issues may likely seek out a competitor for its plumbing supplies in the future.

TABLE 8.3B CREDIT PROBLEM FLOW

Grant Plumbing Supply			
Activity	Maximum Time to Complete		Type of Activity
5a. Rejected item sent to credit	10	minutes	Move
5b. Rejected order batched	1,440	minutes	Queue
5c. Credit analyst reviews account	15	minutes	Process
5d. Negotiation with customer	15	minutes	Process
5e. Order sent to be filled or back to customer service for refusal letter	15	minutes	Move
5f. Rejected order batched	1,440	minutes	Queue
5g. Refusal letter written	10	minutes	Process
5h. Refusal letter queued for daily mail	1,440	minutes	Queue
5i. Refusal letter mailed to customer	1	minutes	Process
Elapsed Time	4,386	minutes	
Process Time	41	minutes	
Process % of Elapsed Time	0.47%		

Looking back again at Figure 8.2, we see that the entire order-to-payment flow also includes a subprocess for processing the receipt of a payment from a customer. This subprocess is initiated when the order is shipped and terminates when the payment for the order is finally deposited in the bank. The activities involved in the receipt of payment subprocess are detailed in Table 8.3c. The process time is estimated at 22 minutes, or 0.09%, out of the total 25,002 minutes (17.4 days) of elapsed time due to significant move and queue times. If the customer decides to forego the prompt payment discount, the elapsed time for this final subprocess could expand to 53,802 minutes of elapsed time if the customer pays within the stated 30-day net terms, or just under 37.4 days. This increase in elapsed time would impact Grant's cash flow significantly, requiring that it keep at least 20 more days of average daily cash requirements on hand in order to pay its own bills. In this situation, however, there is very little Grant can do to change these results. It could reduce internal move and queue times, but outside of trying to entice the customer into prompt payment with a 3% reduction in the payment required for the invoice, Grant's management has few options for improvement.

TABLE 8.3C RECEIPT OF PAYMENT FLOW

Grant Plumbing Supply			
Activity	Maximum Time to Complete		Type of Activity
12. Generate invoice	10	minutes	Process
13. Invoice held for daily mail pickup	1,440	minutes	Queue
14. Invoice mailed to customer	2	minutes	Process
15. Invoice in transit to customer	4,320	minutes	Move
16. Invoice queued for payment by customer for 10-day prompt payment period	14,400	minutes	Queue
17. Check mailed by customer	4,320	minutes	Move
18. Payment received and recorded	5	minutes	Process
19. Checks batched for daily deposit	480	minutes	Queue
20. Deposit taken to bank	20	minutes	Move
21. Checks deposited	5	minutes	Process
Elapsed Time	25,002	minutes	
Process Time	22	minutes	
Process % of Elapsed Time	0.09%		

One thing that many companies are doing today to address the lengthy elapsed time for this process is to use electronic invoicing and payment options. While the delay at the customer's location based on its payment approach is not affected by this change, automating the rest of the subprocess could help eliminate almost 10,200 minutes of elapsed time, or more than 42% of the total time for the completion of this work flow. Making this change requires investment in software and computer hardware, but it will result in Grant freeing up more than seven days of operating cash. There will also be other potential savings in terms of labor, space, a company car, and other equipment as internal activities are eliminated or minimized.

Repeated analyses of processes such as the order-to-payment process in a variety of situations have, unfortunately, yielded very similar results in companies that were not actively focused on managing their process performance. Does that mean that these companies had poor managers? Not necessarily. The more likely explanation is that these managers were operating under a traditional set of assumptions and measurements. Gaining process improvements requires a shift in focus and objectives. Flowcharts and process analysis are valuable tools that aid in making these changes possible and making visible current performance problems and shortfalls. When used as a positive tool promoting continuous improvement, a process chart and accompanying analysis can help an organization make major gains in its responsiveness and ability to meet customer requirements. Finally, as you may have noticed, people were not the focus of the process analysis. Process management is built on the belief that people are the source of solutions, not problems.

Going Lean

OBJECTIVE 2

Explain and illustrate lean accounting methods, objectives, and benefits.

There is a specialized area of process management called **lean management,** *a set of techniques that emphasizes eliminating waste that is embedded in current work processes.* Process analysis makes all of the steps visible to management, which leads to desirable changes in both actions and results. Lean management provides the philosophy, or core set of objectives, pursued by process management. One of the primary issues driving lean management is the need to identify and eliminate all sources of waste in an organization. Waste is a profit bandit; it reduces profits in the short run and permanently removes the value-creating potential of the firm in the long run. Figure 8.3 provides a list of many of the common forms of waste that can be found in an organization.

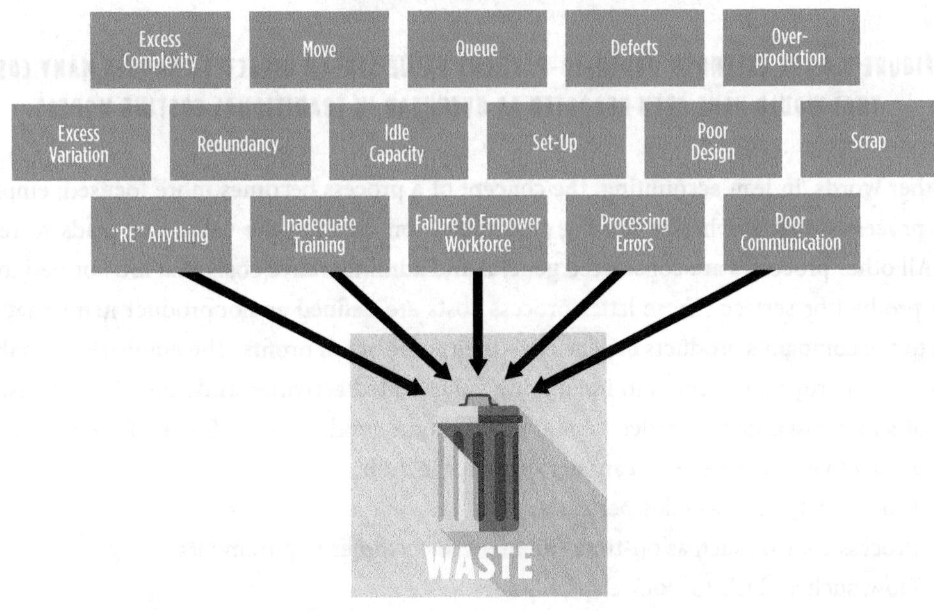

FIGURE 8.3 THERE ARE MANY FORMS OF WASTE IN ORGANIZATIONS THAT REDUCE PROFITS AND THE POTENTIAL FOR FUTURE GROWTH.

LEAN ACCOUNTING

Management accounting professionals have developed a number of methods and measures that complement lean management. One of these new approaches is lean accounting, which has been developed to more accurately report the financial performance of a company that has implemented lean manufacturing processes. **Lean accounting** *focuses on organizing costs by value stream and modifying financial statements to* *include nonfinancial information*. A **value stream** *is the complete set of linked activity centers that are required to deliver a specific outcome*, from initial receipt of an order from a customer to collecting payment for a specific product or service. Figure 8.4 illustrates the total value stream for a typical manufacturing company. As you can see, there are many supporting processes that are not directly traced to the order-to-payment value stream. In more traditional settings, the cost of these supporting processes would have either been charged as manufacturing overhead (for example, scheduling and facilities) or as part of general and administrative costs (such as order entry).

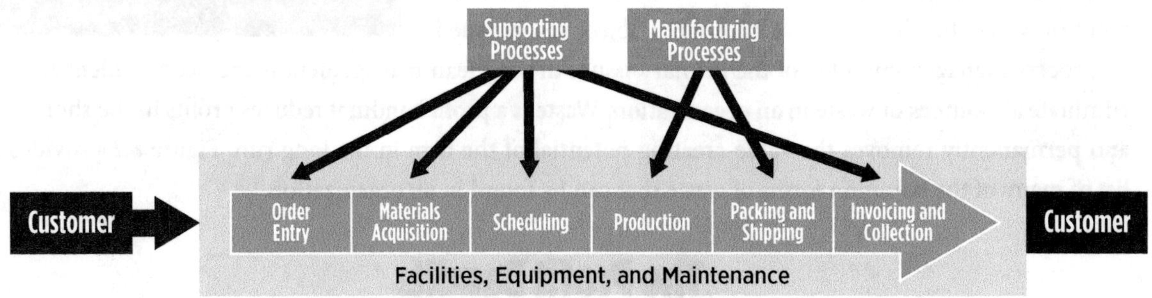

FIGURE 8.4 THE EXTENDED ORDER-TO-PAYMENT VALUE STREAM DIRECTLY CHARGES MANY COSTS THAT WOULD HAVE BEEN REPORTED AS OVERHEAD IN TRADITIONAL COSTING MODELS.

In other words, in lean accounting, the concept of a process becomes more focused; emphasis shifts to those processes that emphasize serving customers—on creating the value that leads to revenue and growth. All other processes are considered general and administrative costs that are not tied to the actual cost of a product or service. These latter process costs are defined as nonproduct items that do not get assigned to the company's products or services—they come out of profits. The emphasis in analyzing costs and measuring performance shifts to identifying value-added activities as defined by the customer. This means that some costs, such as order-taking, now become product costs. Some of the measures used by lean accounting to evaluate value stream performance include:

- Productivity, such as sales/person
- Process control, such as on-time shipment to customer requirements
- Flow, such as dock-to-dock elapsed hours
- Quality, such as the first-pass, no-defects rate
- Linearity and overall improvement, such as current cost vs. prior costs and target cost
- Number of people involved in continuous improvement efforts
- Safety record, such as trends in accident incidents
- Value stream performance, such as Pareto analysis of process errors

The emphasis in costing activities and outcomes in lean accounting is on *direct cost*, or the costs traceable to a specific value stream. As noted, however, direct or product cost in lean accounting includes many of the costs that were treated as overhead in traditional costing models. Overhead, or indirect cost, is any expenditure that cannot be tied directly to a value stream. It is isolated and managed separately by the individuals who control the different types of non-value stream expenditures. The logic is simple—do not spread costs across the products or value streams if they are not directly linked to the activities and outcomes of the value stream.

If costs are spread without an underlying linkage to the successful performance of work in a value stream, any effort to control and reduce these costs will be destroyed. In other words, the only way a cost is actionable is if it is visible, along with an understanding of who is responsible for a specific indirect cost. This is the only way that indirect cost creep can be minimized. In addition, in lean accounting, the goal is to understand the profitability of products, order by order. Traditional standard costs are not used to define cost and profits. Finally, in lean accounting, the core principle is that *price is based on the embedded value in a product or service in the customer's eyes*; price is not defined by cost—profit is. In other words, customer preferences define the market price of a specific good or service. Cost plays little or no role in this price-setting. Instead, a company that has good control over its costs will be able to make a profit at the current market price. Profit is not guaranteed to a company.

LOOKING BACK ➤ **FDR and NIRA**

A brief reading of any of the writings and positions taken on price, cost, and waste by any of the early giants of industry and management practice in the early 1900s leaves one puzzled. Why? Because individuals such as Henry Gantt and Alexander Hamilton Church made it clear that a customer would not pay a company for its wasted resources. This was such an embedded belief that pioneers like Henry Ford built entire production systems with one goal in mind: to minimize waste.

So the troubling question that arises from reading this early management literature is: Why did companies stop focusing on waste? When did standard costing, which builds a "normal" or "practical" level of waste into its calculations, begin to be used? The answer to this question may come as a surprise. This shift in practice is tied directly to President Franklin D. Roosevelt and one of his first New Deal initiatives: the National Industrial Recovery Act (NIRA).

NIRA was one of the first acts passed by Roosevelt in 1933. The goal of NIRA was simple—to develop policies and laws that would move the U.S. away from pure capitalism to social capitalism. The difference? Using trade associations, NIRA author Hugh Johnson imposed industry costing practices that emphasized the costs of the least productive association members. This high cost number clearly included waste that more efficient producers avoided. Given this mandated cost basis, market prices were set and enforced for each major industry. More efficient firms had no reason to argue—their profits were increased. In response, cost practices were simplified to reflect the new reality. Materials, labor, and overhead became the only metrics used; little or no attempt was made to understand or control costs.

In 1935, NIRA was struck down as unconstitutional by the Supreme Court, but that did not stop companies, such as U.S. Steel, from continuing to follow its practices. And, in 1941, as the U.S. entered World War II, NIRA policies were reinstituted as the Office of Price Administration (OPA), which continued until 1947. In 1951, as the Korean War dragged on,

President Harry Truman instituted price controls through the Office of Price Stabilization (OPS), which continued until the end of the war in 1953. The last president to enforce price controls was Richard Nixon in 1971. He issued a 90-day freeze on prices to combat rampant inflation.

So, how did early beliefs about the very different roles played by cost and price disappear? In more than 20 years of mandated pricing, managers and accountants got used to setting prices based on a cost they could justify to the bureaucrats who controlled their markets. This relationship between cost and price became embedded in practice, built into the organization through such things as standard costing techniques. Lean accounting and lean management are, therefore, a very real case of *Back to the Future.*

In a manufacturing setting, lean accounting only uses two accounting transactions: one for the receipt of raw materials, the second when the finished product ships. For both manufacturing and service organizations, the focus of pricing activities is on the embedded value as defined by customers. In this respect, lean accounting reflects the stance taken in target costing—that companies cannot pass on waste to their customers. And, by emphasizing customer-defined value over internal views of cost, lean accounting incorporates the logic of many of the activity-based cost management techniques. Taken in total, therefore, lean accounting is an integrated approach to management accounting that incorporates the key aspects of target costing, activity-based cost management, process management, lean management, and customer-defined, value-based cost management as captured in Figure 8.5.

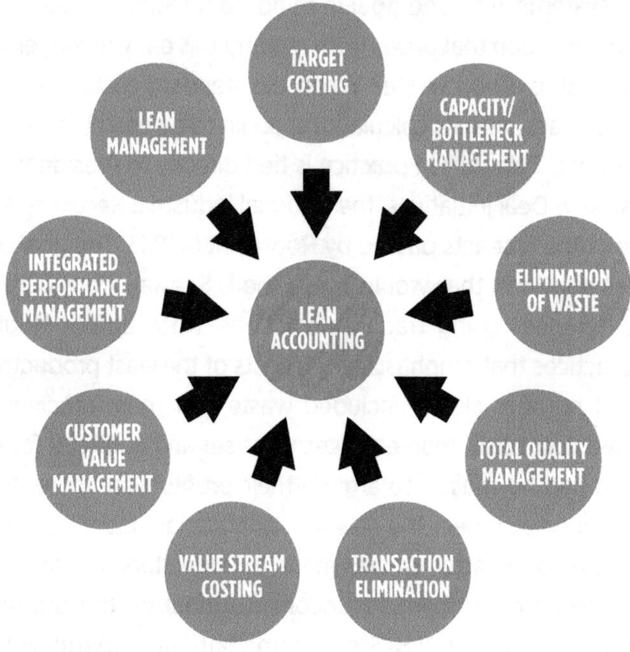

FIGURE 8.5 LEAN ACCOUNTING INTEGRATES THE CORE PRACTICES OF LEAN MANAGEMENT.

APPLYING LEAN ACCOUNTING

OBJECTIVE 3

Develop and apply activity-based management and activity-based budgeting.

To put lean accounting into perspective, let us take another look at the order-to-payment value stream and see how lean thinking can be applied at Adams Industries, a company that only produces one product: computer printers.[7] The company currently sells 500,000 printers per year at a wholesale price of $100 each. The bottleneck in the value stream is the soldering of the printer's circuit boards. This activity currently takes 6.84 seconds per circuit board. The company currently works two shifts a day, for a total of approximately 4,000 staffed hours per year. It is difficult to find qualified employees, so there is no plan to expand beyond two staffed shifts in the foreseeable future. Key lean accounting measurements for Adams Industries' printer value stream are detailed in Table 8.4.

TABLE 8.4 LEAN ACCOUNTING MEASUREMENTS

Adams Industries			
	Last Year	This Year	Target Performance
Units produced	500,000	525,000	800,000
Units sold	450,000	500,000	800,000
On-time shipments	85%	90%	98%
Elapsed days: dock-to-dock	12	9	5
First-pass acceptance rate	55%	70%	98%
Average product cost	$83.25	$79.50	$60.00
Bottleneck output rate	7.03 seconds	6.84 seconds	6.0 seconds
Units returned	28,000	19,800	1,000
Productive capacity	9.80%	10.8%	15.2%
Nonproductive capacity	24.80%	25.6%	18.7%
Unused marketable capacity	11.40%	10.3%	9.5%
Idle capacity	54.00%	53.3%	56.6%
Revenue	$47,250,000	$50,000,000	$76,000,000
Material cost	$25,042,500	$25,500,000	$35,720,000
Conversion cost	$13,230,000	$11,500,000	$15,200,000
Value stream gross profit	$13,140,000	$14,987,500	$25,080,000

7 If Adams Industries offered multiple products and services, it would have multiple value streams.

As can be seen from the range of measurements used by Adams Industries' lean accounting system, the four primary dimensions of performance detailed earlier in Chapter 2 are tracked: productivity, delivery, quality, and cost. In addition, the measures used are both financial and nonfinancial in nature. Lean accounting, therefore, emphasizes an integrated performance measurement approach, or balanced scorecard.

Management at Adams Industries has decided to separate material costs (which would include purchasing and related acquisition costs) from conversion costs, which include all of the other activities and resource costs that can be directly traced to the order-to-payment value stream for the printer line. The primary capacity measurements are also tracked, reflecting the recognition that wasting physical capacity, especially if staffed (for example, nonproductive capacity), significantly impacts value stream gross profit. So, why is the target for idle higher than the current level? Because, as you remember, intentionally idled capacity is only charged for committed capacity costs. If the value stream is not staffed, the wasted resource costs are minimized given the current production line design and bottleneck activity.

It might seem disconcerting to see an average used for the product cost, but the underlying calculation is actually quite explicit. Specifically, every order that goes through the system is charged based on the resources it actually uses. That means it is quite possible for two orders for the same number of printers to have different value stream costs based on how well the value stream performed. Were there production problems? Then the order might cost more to complete. The average presented here is based on actual costs, directly charged to each order based on value stream performance. Since the report is annualized, the cost number is an average of actual results over the year. If we were to compare these results on an order-by-order basis, only actual, traced costs would be detailed.

This leads to an important issue in lean accounting: Standards and variances are *not* used at any point in the costing or performance management cycle. Lean accounting strives to eliminate terminology and metrics, such as efficiency variances, replacing them instead with measures that have common sense meanings that reflect the controllability criterion. Costs are either deemed traceable to a specific value stream, or budgeted and reported separately. There are no overhead costs maintained by the lean accounting system. If a resource cost cannot be traced to a value stream, it is not charged out to the company's products and services. These untraceable costs are reported below value stream profit, reflecting the fact that they reduce profitability but do not add anything to the value created by the value stream.

Table 8.5 illustrates a typical income statement under a lean accounting approach at Adams Industries. Notice that changes in inventory (materials and finished goods) are actually included in the calculations. Why? Because the targeted performance for any value stream is to only acquire the materials it needs and only produces products and services that are purchased by a customer. In other words, a perfect lean management system would not carry any inventory that is not immediately used up either through production or sales. Inventory is not considered an asset, therefore, but rather something that causes costs that are waste (for example, space, carrying cost, and obsolescence) because a customer will not pay for them.

TABLE 8.5 LEAN ACCOUNTING INCOME STATEMENT

Adams Industries			
	Last Year	This Year	Target Performance
Price per unit	$105.00	$100.00	$95.00
Units sold	450,000	500,000	800,000
Net sales	$47,250,000	$50,000,000	$76,000,000
Cost of sales:			
Purchases	$31,303,125	$28,560,000	$35,720,000
Material inventory (increase)/decrease	$(6,260,625)	$(3,060,000)	$-
Total material costs	$25,042,500	$25,500,000	$35,720,000
Conversion costs:			
Direct labor costs	$4,222,800	$4,275,000	$3,438,400
Indirect labor costs	$1,490,400	$1,425,000	$1,105,200
Factory benefits	$993,600	$1,282,500	$1,473,600
Services and supplies	$869,400	$1,140,000	$1,228,000
Equipment and depreciation	$993,600	$1,282,500	$1,228,000
Scrap	$1,614,600	$1,425,000	$245,600
Building depreciation	$993,600	$1,425,000	$1,350,800
Building services	$869,400	$1,425,000	$1,473,600
Taxes and insurance on building	$372,600	$570,000	$736,800
Total conversion costs	$12,420,000	$14,250,000	$12,280,000
Total value stream costs	$37,462,500	$39,750,000	$48,000,000
Value stream gross profit	$9,787,500	$10,250,000	$28,000,000
Value stream gross profit percentage	20.7%	20.5%	36.8%
Value stream gross profit adjusted for finished goods inventory (increase)/decrease	$(4,162,500)	$(1,987,500)	$-
Total cost of sales	$5,625,000	$8,262,500	$28,000,000
General and administrative costs	$4,800,000	$5,100,000	$7,500,000
Income before tax	$825,000	$3,162,500	$20,500,000
Income before tax percentage of revenue	1.7%	6.3%	27.0%

As can be seen, if Adams Industries can make its improvement targets, it will experience a significant increase in profitability. Striving toward goals such as the elimination of inventory, the company is able to reduce non-value-added cost and waste, drive down average cost per unit made, and increase volumes because it can now offer its printers at a lower market price. General and administrative costs currently include research and development and other non-value stream costs. If a life cycle analysis were done for the printer, these costs would become relevant to the analysis of performance. Other administrative costs, such as general management and public relations, would probably never be justifiably charged as value stream costs.

As this example illustrates, lean accounting relies upon actual, traceable costs and reports the performance of a value stream using both financial and nonfinancial measures. The overriding objective is to provide organizations with the information they need to continuously improve their value streams by eliminating waste and improving productivity through active management and optimization of bottleneck activities. Having gained an understanding of lean accounting, let us now add one final piece to our costing puzzle: tying customer value preferences to the work done throughout the organization.

IN CONTEXT ➤ Benchmarking Process Performance

Brad's team was learning fast that Kinkaid needed to benchmark its processes to truly understand how to make the substantial improvements Sam wanted. The goal was to turn the modular line from an underachiever to a star performer.

The biggest question the team faced was how to identify a best practice firm for cellular production. Kinkaid had a few competitors in its industry, but they were unlikely to let Kinkaid's management come in and study their processes. However, many other companies manufactured products using a cellular design. For example, companies that made computer printers used cellular designs in order to create parts that could be connected to make a variety of products. Specials used common parts to make its products.

Another question concerned the way in which Kinkaid's modular team assembled the product. It occupied a large floor where it was physically moving from station to station in a sort of zigzag pattern. In studying other companies, Brad's team learned that a clean linear or U-shaped flow was the most efficient for this type of production. If it was going to have a more efficient work flow, design would be critical.

Brad decided to chart the existing production flow for the line. He knew this was a necessary first step in benchmarking, but it was also an overwhelming task. On Thursday afternoon, Shelley stopped by.

"Brad, what's with all the charts on the walls? What do these arrows and strange-looking 'D's mean, and what do all these scribbled times represent?"

"I'm analyzing our existing work flow for modular furniture. Then I'm going to do the same for specials. Once I complete these diagrams, I can begin a benchmarking study to figure out how to improve our flows."

"I'll leave you to it, but be careful not to tape yourself to one of your charts!" Shelley laughed, and rapidly left Brad to his work.

Activity-Based Approaches to Process Management

Activities are the key building blocks of processes. Process improvements are made by better management of each of its activities and the linkages between those activities. **Activity-based management (ABM)** *is a discipline that focuses on controlling activities to achieve performance goals, enhance customer value, and improve profitability.* It is an approach that focuses on the management of activities to achieve performance goals. ABM includes cost driver analysis, activity analysis, and performance measurement, drawing on activity-based costing (ABC) as its major source of data.

ACTIVITY-BASED MANAGEMENT

ABM encompasses an entire set of methods all focused on improving process performance by providing actionable information about the cost, efficiency, and effectiveness of the underlying activities. It bundles value analysis, cost driver assessment, and performance measurement together into one consistent data set. The resulting information is forward-looking, incorporating not only traditional cost information but also opportunity costs and risk analyses.

Nevertheless, we can categorize how ABM is used by the nature of the competitive challenges facing a firm, as Figure 8.6 illustrates.[8] When a business is growing, its primary focus is on improving its processes to gain more productivity and to find the funds for growth and improvement by removing waste from nonessential activities, such as order processing and order fulfillment.

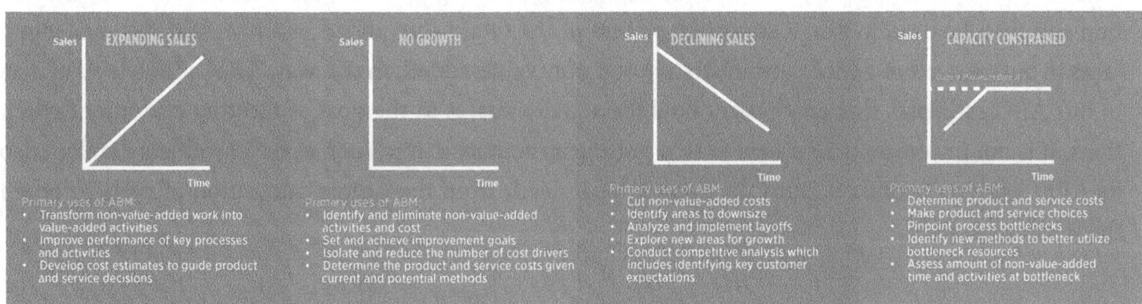

FIGURE 8.6 ABM INFORMATION CAN BE USED IN DIFFERENT WAYS DEPENDING UPON THE COMPANY'S SITUATION.

8 John A. Miller, *Implementing Activity-based Management in Daily Operations*, New York: John Wiley & Sons, 1996, is one source for a more detailed discussion of these issues.

In capacity-constrained settings, on the other hand, the emphasis shifts to managing bottlenecks and optimizing revenue based on the resources available to manufacture the product or provide the services. As growth diminishes, ABM is primarily used as an operational support tool, serving to identify non-value-added costs, to estimate product costs, and to find ways to improve operations to enhance profitability. Finally, as the business starts to decline, ABM provides information to support downsizing and cost-cutting decisions.

Table 8.6 illustrates how a company can use Excel spreadsheets to capture ABM information. In Table 8.6a, the top part of the Excel sheet—the data activity matrix—represents an estimate of the time spent by individuals to complete various tasks. The total time assigned must equal the total **full-time equivalents (FTEs)**—*the total hours worked by everyone divided by 40 to get the number of full-time people needed to do a job*—the department has under its command.

In the lower part of the spreadsheet—the activity-value assignment—the activity is spread across one of five subcategories: value-added (directly adds benefit to customers; for example, filling their orders) and business value-added: current (does not directly touch the customer, but does impact satisfaction; it includes such activities as processing an invoice).

The next two categories of cost—business value-added: future and business value-added: administrative—relate to the firm's own operations. Business value-added: future incorporates all of the costs and efforts spent to ensure the continuity of the firm, such as developing new products. Business value-added: administrative is the cost of doing such things as processing paperwork and holding meetings. Finally, things are done that add no value to the firm—they are non-value-added. The move and queue activities we saw earlier fit into this category. As you can see, each activity can have some portion of each of these categories embedded within it.

Table 8.6b takes the budget for the department and spreads it out across the activities based on the degree of value they add. The formula for this is simple multiplication of the percentage of the activity that goes to business value-added: current by the total cost for that activity (40% of the G&A Customer/Contact activity multiplied by the $1,729,672, the cost of doing that activity, or $691,869). This information can then be used to gain a summary picture of the total value-added in a firm and the challenges it faces in business value-added: administrative and non-value-added. In this way, ABM adds a level of detail to our ABC estimates that emphasizes how the activity relates to the goal of meeting customer expectations. It is not uncommon for a firm to skip putting an activity driver, such as new products developed, on its ABM analysis because it gains the knowledge it needs from the simple calculation of costs by type in the ABM analysis.[9]

---

9 The numbers listed under the process code column of Table 8.6 are based on the American Productivity and Quality Center (APQC) Process Classification Framework, which is considered a best practice guideline for classifying and organizing process activities. It allows an organization to identify and integrate costs and activities from many different areas and departments into one comprehensive process-based list. The complete framework is presented in the appendix to this chapter.

TABLE 8.6A ACTIVITY-BASED MANAGEMENT ACTIVITY ANALYSIS

1. Activity Data Matrix

Please identify key activities performed by this cost center, the number of employees engaged in this effort, and the percentage of their time (on average) dedicated to completing the activity.

Process Code	Activity Description	Number of Employees Doing Activity	Time Spent on Activity	"People" Equivalent Time	Cumulative People Time
1.1	Customer contact	8	25%	2	2
3.1.1	Document development process	2	50%	1	3
9.4.2	Engineering database maintenance	2	100%	2	5
3.2	Engineering conversion/process engineering	4	25%	1	6
2.1.4	Mechanical design/build	2	50%	1	7
3.2.5	Develop prototypes	1	100%	1	8
3.5	Detail production requirements	2	50%	1	9
				0	
	Totals	N/A	N/A	9	9
				TRUE	

2. Activity-Value Assignment

For each activity from step (1), please estimate the percentage of this effort that would be considered customer value-added (a customer would pay for it), business value-added (C, F, or A), or non-value-added.

Process Code	Activity Description	Customer Value-Added	Business Value-Added: CURRENT	Business Value-Added: FUTURE	Business Value-Added: ADMIN.	Non-Value-Added	Total (Must equal 100%)
1.1	Customer contact	50%	20%	20%	5%	5%	100%
3.1.1	Document development process		35%	50%	10%	5%	100%
9.4.2	Engineering database maintenance		35%	50%	10%	5%	100%
3.2	Engineering conversion/process engineering		35%	50%	10%	5%	100%
2.1.4	Mechanical design/build		35%	50%	10%	5%	100%
3.2.5	Develop prototypes		45%	35%	15%	5%	100%
3.5	Detail production requirements		55%	30%	10%	5%	100%

TABLE 8.6B ACTIVITY-BASED MANAGEMENT COST ANALYSIS

Activity Cost Estimates								
	Calculation Section	Budget	$7,783,524					
Process Code	Activity Description	Activity Costs	$'s Customer Value-Added	$'s Business Value-Added: CURRENT	$'s Business Value-Added: FUTURE	$'s Business Value-Added: Administration	$'s Non Value-Added
1.1	Customer contact	$1,729,672	$864,836	$345,934	$345,934	$86,484	$86,484
3.11	Document development process	$864,836	$-	$302,693	$432,418	$86,484	$43,242
9.4.2	Engineering database maintenance	$1,729,672	$-	$605,385	$864,836	$172,967	$86,484
3.2	Engineering conversion/ process engineering	$864,836	$-	$302,693	$432,418	$86,484	$43,242
2.1.4	Mechanical design/build	$864,836	$-	$302,693	$432,418	$86,484	$43,242
3.2.5	Develop prototypes	$864,836	$-	$389,176	$302,693	$129,725	$43,242
3.5	Detail production requirements	$864,836	$-	$475,660	$259,451	$86,484	$43,242
	TOTALS	$7,783,524	$864,836	$2,724,233	$3,070,168	$735,111	$389,176

ABM uses the same generic data collection and cost assignment logic that we explored in Chapter 4. The primary differences are that ABM:

- Uses less detail than ABC in the data collected;
- Emphasizes activity analysis rather than activity costing—drivers are not always assigned to every cost pool;
- Takes a forward (for example, planning and decision analysis) vs. historical (for example, product costing) approach;
- Emphasizes segregating value-added activities from non-value-added or nonessential work;
- Takes a process (horizontal) perspective rather than a product-focused one;
- Is dynamic rather than static in nature (activity weighting can change daily);
- Is more sensitive to the behavioral impact of cost drivers on other aspects of entity or individual performance; and,

- Tends to be incorporated as part of the firm's strategic and operational budgeting and planning processes rather than as an extension of its standard costing system.

Both the ABM and ABC approaches recognize the need to trace resources to the work they support, effectively creating multiple indirect cost pools, such as developing prototypes. As you can see, the ABM data collection emphasizes major activities, not tasks, and incorporates activity codes from the American Productivity and Quality Center (APQC) Process Classification Framework. In the case of Kinkaid, Brad provided the information for his entire department. The combination of this information across the entire organization provides the basis for both cost analysis and activity-based budgeting.

IN THE NEWS ➤ Caterpillar and ABM

Caterpillar has been using activity-based costing in its factories for more than 50 years. Recently, however, it became increasingly clear that it also needed to apply advanced cost management principles to its back office operations. Its Marketing and Product Support Department (MPSD) did just that, turning to activity-based management (ABM) and lean Six Sigma (discussed in Chapter 9) initiatives to drive the cost out of its operations. As their managers noted:

ABM helps a growing business identify key individuals who can be shifted away from handling existing processes to meeting the needs of new or expanding business opportunities. Developing and enhancing the ABM system while we are enjoying good economic times and strong growth helps us ensure that our processes are as lean as possible. This prepares us for whenever the next economic downturn occurs. ABM helps us identify areas where we can free up resources and reduce costs without giving up value-added services. This is what MPSD did. It helped us free up resources by using ABM while keeping employees engaged in the process to look for, and eliminate, further waste.

Based on David G. DeFreitas, John W. Gillet, Ross L. Fink, and Whitney Cox, "Getting Lean and Mean at Caterpillar with ABM," *Strategic Finance*, January 2013, pp. 24-33.

For example, it is likely that both customer service and marketing do work that would qualify for process code 7.3.1: Respond to customer information requests. To understand how many dollars of cost are being incurred to support this activity, you would add all of the estimated activity costs from every individual or cost center that uses this code for one or more of its activities. The output of this effort at Kinkaid is summarized in Table 8.7, where you can see how flexible ABM information is.[10] Because it is easily sorted and compiled, it is able to serve many different purposes within the organization. Let us now look at another major use of ABM information—activity-based budgeting.

---

10 In Table 8.7, you see how the activities performed in various cost centers have now been compiled into the process framework. In other words, the ABM information gathered across the organization can now be easily recast in process terms using the APQC framework to organize and classify the information.

TABLE 8.7 ACTIVITY-BASED MANAGEMENT COST ANALYSIS FOR PROCESS 7.3.1

Kinkaid Cabinets									
Cost Center	Cost Center Name	Activity Description	Activity Costs	Customer Value-Added	Business Value-Added: CURRENT	Business Value-Added: FUTURE	Business Value-Added: ADMIN.	Non-Value-Added
231	Doors—Administration	Resolve inquiries	$142,418	$-	$142,418	$-	$-	$-
719	Order Department	Quote/price products	$123,868	$12,387	$99,094	$-	$-	$12,387
721	Special Products	Processing customer glass quotes	$64,067	$19,220	$38,440	$-	$-	$6,407
755	Commercial Sales	Proposal development	$134,464	$13,446	$73,955	$40,339	$-	$6,723
830	Channel Services	Fulfill field administration requests	$372,201	$-	$-	$-	$372,201	
872	Promotions and Events	Quote and order custom displays	$67,651	$-	$-	$33,825	$-	$33,825
873	International	Quote/price products	$613,455	$306,728	$245,382	$-	$-	$61,346
		Total costs assigned	$1,518,124	$351,781	$599,289	$74,164	$372,201	$120,688

Activity-Based Budgeting

OBJECTIVE 4

Describe the key elements of the Theory of Constraints, just-in-time management, and capacity management.

While activity-based budgeting (ABB) can be considered an entity-level tool, it more often emanates from the issues and methods that define the process domain. Specifically, ABB is used to control and direct future spending on specific types of activities. For instance, a company may decide that it only wants to spend $500,000 in the coming year on developing prototypes for new products.

When traditional forms of budgets are developed, they focus on the different types of expenses a cost center or company might face in the coming year, such as salaries, supplies, and utilities. Managers seldom question what consuming these resources will accomplish. Rather, they focus on the level of funding a cost center will receive.

As with all forms of activity-based analysis and modeling, ABB shifts the emphasis away from resources to the work these resources will accomplish for the company and its primary stakeholders. This change allows management to see what processes and activities are the greatest users of resources, to balance current and future business needs, and to gain a better understanding of its level of waste and non-value-added work.

External benchmarking is often used to establish baseline expectations for ABB. For example, Kinkaid might want to know if it is spending too much or too little to process its invoices. After completing an ABM activity analysis, Sam is given the information presented in Table 8.8.

TABLE 8.8 ACTIVITY-BASED ANALYSIS SUMMARY FOR PROCESS 7: INVOICE AND SERVICE CUSTOMERS

Kinkaid Cabinets			
Process Stop	(1) Current ABM Cost	(2) Benchmark Cost	(2) - (1) = (3) Improvement Target
7.1.1 Develop and maintain customer billing	$296,913	$190,000	$(106,913)
7.1.2 Invoice the customer	$526,209	$325,000	$(201,209)
7.1.3 Respond to billing inquiries	$19,035	$45,000	$25,965
7.2.1 Provide post-sales service	$2,163,312	$2,600,000	$436,688
7.2.2 Handle warranties and claims	$1,515,373	$800,000	$(715,373)
7.3.1 Respond to information requests	$2,942,058	$1,475,000	$(1,467,058)
7.3.2 Manage customer complaints	$667,412	$900,000	$232,588
TOTALS	$8,130,312	$6,335,000	$(1,795,312)

For a business of its size and complexity, Kinkaid is spending more than it should on invoicing and supporting basic customer needs. Some of this is understandable—the nature of Kinkaid's products means that customers are going to have more questions than they would if they were buying a commodity like shampoo. A kitchen cabinet for a new or remodeled kitchen is a relatively large purchase, generating a large number of technical and product-based questions. In other areas, however, it is clear that Kinkaid should try to trim costs. For instance, it spends more than $201,209 more on its invoicing systems, activity 7.1.2, than the best-in-class benchmark firm as demonstrated in Table 8.8. If process improvements can be identified in invoicing that will not create confusion or other problems for customers, they should be implemented.

The ABB limits that Sam develops for the invoice and service customer process is summarized in Table 8.9. Sam is looking to decrease the total cost for this process over the next three years by $1.35 million, or 16.5%. Even with these changes, Kinkaid will spend $450,000 more on this process than the benchmark firms. However, Sam believes that it is an attainable goal that will free up considerable resources for more valued work.

TABLE 8.9 THREE-YEAR ACTIVITY-BASED BUDGET FOR PROCESS 7: INVOICE AND SERVICE CUSTOMER PROCESS

Kinkaid Cabinets					
	Process Step	Current ABM Cost	Budget 20x7	Budget 20x8	Budget 20x9
7.1.1	Develop and maintain customer billing	$296,913	$265,000	$225,000	$190,000
7.1.2	Invoice the customer	$526,209	$450,000	$382,500	$325,000
7.1.3	Respond to billing inquiries	$19,036	$20,000	$20,000	$20,000
7.2.1	Provide post-sales service	$2,163,312	$2,050,000	$1,947,500	$1,850,000
7.2.2	Handle warranties and claims	$1,515,373	$1,200,000	$960,000	$800,000
7.3.1	Respond to information requests	$2,942,058	$3,000,000	$3,000,000	$3,000,000
7.3.2	Manage customer complaints	$667,412	$650,000	$625,000	$600,000

Kinkaid should perform the same type of analysis for every major process. Once completed, Sam would be able to help direct the attention of his managers to the areas needing the greatest attention. Implicit in Sam's budgeting analysis is a setting of priorities that will also help his management team make better strategic and operating decisions. To achieve these goals, however, Kinkaid will need to use the entire range of process improvement tools and techniques. In the last part of this chapter, we will introduce some of these basic operational tools.

One phrase basically captures the essence of management in the process domain—focusing on the flow. Emphasizing how work is completed through a linked sequence of activities performed by many people in many different positions, process management is shaped by the knowledge that an organization is only as good as its ability to execute its work—the quality and effectiveness of its processes. To complete our discussion of planning within the process domain, we will now turn our attention to several day-to-day management models and techniques used to manage and improve process performance.

IN CONTEXT ➤ Making Improvements at Kinkaid Cabinets

Shelley decided to stop in to see how Brad and his team were doing. They had been awfully quiet for the past week and a half. The next meeting with Sam was right around the corner. She popped her head into Brad's office, half expecting him to look disheveled and nervous, but instead she saw a look of accomplishment on his face and the roomed buzzed with energy.

"What have you been up to, Brad? You look like you just swallowed a canary and can finally sing an aria!"

"I think we're getting somewhere. Once I got into the literature, I found out there is so much more that we can do in addition to cellular manufacturing to improve how we do things around here. Just for starters, I think I'm going to recommend that we adopt process management and activity-based budgeting!"

"Whoa, slow down, Brad. Those are great buzzwords, but what do we have that is concrete for Sam?"

"Lots, Shelley. I know we can make the process improvements on the floor, and, while moving to a cell is going to take time for training and re-equipping the process, once it's done, we'll really be more efficient and effective. But we shouldn't stop there. We can actually look at the back office operations to support getting orders out the door and trim costs there. At the end of the day, customers are less willing to pay us for back office activities that they can't see than they are to pay for activities on the plant floor that result in great product."

"So, you're shifting costs around?" asked Shelley.

"I guess you could think of it that way, but I'd rather think of it as starting to manage the flow of work rather than departments. By getting everyone working together, we can trim lots of time and money off activities that customers don't value. I think we've got the ticket this time. I can hardly wait to show what I've pulled together to Sam!"

"Well, you'll have your chance tomorrow. Is there anything I can read before we meet to get me up to speed?"

"Sure, take these slides. I'm going to use them tomorrow. Buzz me if you have questions."

"Okay! I'm off to try to learn some new ways to think about work!"

The Theory of Constraints, Just-in-Time Management, and Capacity

There have been numerous innovations in how work is organized and what elements of a process are emphasized over the past 50 years. Some of these innovations, such as just-in-time management, which employs a cellular work flow design, have their roots deeply embedded in the methods developed by pioneers like Henry Ford. Others, such as the Theory of Constraints, highlight the resources that define current limits on the output of goods and services. Let us now look at these innovations in more depth.

THE THEORY OF CONSTRAINTS

In 1987, Eli Goldratt, along with Jeff Cox, published what remains one of the top-selling books in management literature—*The Goal*. Using a simple example, a Boy Scout hike through the woods, it explains the complex notion of the impact of bottlenecks on a system's performance. One Boy Scout, named Herbie, seems to constantly lag behind the rest of the troop. If placed at the end of the line, he falls hopelessly behind. If placed in the middle, he holds up the back half of the troop while the front half races ahead. Only when Herbie is placed in the front of the line—as the **bottleneck**, the pacing or *slowest resource in a process*—does the troop stay together on the trail. The point is that regardless of the capability of the other scouts, the entire troop—the system—is only as strong as its weakest link.

By analyzing a series of similar situations, Goldratt develops the following set of principles that define the Theory of Constraints (TOC):[11]

- Identify the weakest link; that is the bottleneck.
- Do not try to subject the system to too great a load. The weakest link should set the pace for the entire system.
- Concentrate improvement efforts on the weakest link.
- If the improvement efforts are successful, eventually the weakest link will no longer be the constraint—bottlenecks will change as process performance improves.

One of the key things to keep in mind when thinking about TOC is that it does not try to change the organization of work in a process. Machines and activities are not moved around at all—the current layout of work is taken as a given and not addressed by TOC.

One of the primary messages of TOC is that a company only makes money when it receives payment for its goods or services from its customers. In TOC terms, this payment minus variable costs expended to earn it is called **throughput,** *the payment received for completed work in excess of traceable variable costs.* This is very close in definition to our concept of a contribution margin. **Operating expenses** *are defined as all of the internal resources and energy expended to produce final goods that are not variable.* Throughput less operating expenses is net operating profit, similar to what we have seen with our variable cost income statement. Finally, **inventory** *is a company's primary asset base—its investment in the business.* It is not its store of raw materials, work-in-process, and finished goods. As you can see, TOC uses many of the terms common to management accounting, but redefines them significantly. This makes it very difficult to compare the results of a TOC approach to that attained through other modern management techniques such as lean accounting.

Because TOC is concerned with ensuring that the bottleneck is kept busy, excess capacity is often retained in nonbottleneck areas. The result is that TOC is not always the least expensive way to operate. That said, many companies have benefited from applying TOC logic. The ultimate choice of management accounting techniques, therefore, will depend on the philosophy of management and its choice of an approach that provides the greatest amount of information at an acceptable cost.

The need to manage a process as a system rather than as a sequence of individual steps is not unique to TOC. In fact, it is the unifying principle for most of the tools and techniques used within the process domain. However, when the nature of the flow of work changes, we can adjust the way we manage process resources. Let us now turn to a different approach to organizing the flow of work in a process: just-in-time management and its utilization of cellular process flows.

JUST-IN-TIME MANAGEMENT AND CELLULAR PROCESS FLOWS

Just-in-time (JIT) management, *which emphasizes the elimination of excess inventory from a flow in order to have the right amount at the right time in the right place*, and **cellular flow management,** *a technique that focuses on how work is organized*, were originally developed by Toyota in the 1960s as it searched for ways

---

11 Eric W. Noreen, Debra A. Smith, and James T. (Cor) MacKey, *The Theory of Constraints and Its Implications for Management Accounting*, Great Barrington, Mass.: North River Press, 1995, p. xx.

to improve the performance of its products and to reduce the cost of providing this added value to customers. The underlying focus of JIT methods is on the sequencing of machines or people to match the sequence of steps used to make a product or provide a service. Once the resources have been physically arranged in the proper order, their output capacity is balanced. Specifically, a "drumbeat" is set up based on the optimal pace of the bottleneck resource. The result is a balanced, smooth flow of materials or transactions through the process.

The term just-in-time is the best descriptor of this balanced flow design. Materials are brought into the company only as needed, and units are made only when an order exists for them. By removing "queue" and "move" activities from the work flow, total **throughput time**—*the amount of time it takes for one unit of product to be completed*—drops drastically. It is not unusual for a company that moves to JIT methods to reduce throughput time from three months to less than an hour. This is possible because once the unit is put into production, each activity required to transform the raw material into finished goods takes place as soon as the unit reaches the workstation.

Looking at Figure 8.7, you can see the difference in the work flow for a JIT vs. a traditional factory setup. The "spaghetti" appearance of the traditional flow reflects the fact that the process is optimized around a different assumption—that every machine or activity should be performing at its maximum efficiency even if all of its output is not needed at the current time. In a JIT, or cellular, design, a small number of buffer inventories (kanbans) knit disparate steps together, allowing goods or services to flow smoothly through the cell. As can also be seen, the machines and people needed to support the production process are placed alongside each other based on the production sequence. The kanbans, therefore, are used to balance a line where machines or activities have different output capabilities. When the allowable (and minimal) number of units is in the kanban, the sourcing machine or person is idled. Why? Because there is no reason to continue to produce output that is not needed.

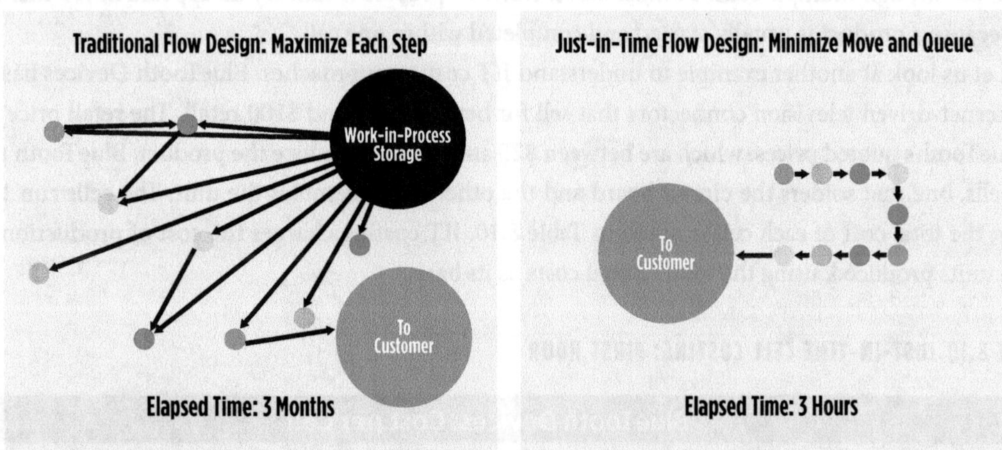

FIGURE 8.7 WHEN YOU COMPARE TRADITIONAL VS. JUST-IN-TIME FLOWS, IT IS CLEAR WHY JUST-IN-TIME REDUCES TIME SPENT ON EACH STEP IN THE MANUFACTURING PROCESS.

For instance, Machine A may only be able to work on one piece of in-process material at a time, while Machine B, the next in line, can work on three pieces at a time. Clearly, we need to get three pieces through Machine A to keep Machine B going. We do this by storing up the output on Machine A in three-piece kanbans. Kanbans can also be used when there are breaks in the flow due to required "rest" times for the products. In a traditional factory, this balancing inventory would be a large batch that had been made at one time to maximize efficiency on an individual machine. Large batches of in-process inventory would be found on the factory floor.

When, in Chapter 7, Brad decided to extend the amount of time required for the glued joints to set, he created the need for a kanban in the work flow. This balancing of inventory flows is the focus of JIT inventory methods, which emphasize the elimination of excess inventory from production flows. This is in contrast to traditional, scientific management approaches that emphasize output at one station over the needs of the entire process.

As you look at Figure 8.7, you can also see that much less space is needed for JIT processes than for traditional flows. The trade-off, of course, is that the **just-in-time cells,** *the linked sequence of activities required to complete a unit of output*, are dedicated to a specific series of steps. Any product that uses this sequence can be made in the cell. If a product requires a different set of steps, then a new cell is needed. Clearly, the more repetitive the work, the more likely it will be to benefit from JIT methods.

In both TOC and JIT models, the pace of production is driven by the bottleneck's capability, but in the JIT approach, all accounting transactions are entered when the product leaves a cell, not when it crosses the bottleneck. This is called **backflush costing,** *the practice of only charging cost to a unit when it leaves the cell*. All in-process work is valued at zero until the work is completed.

The accounting model for JIT systems varies from traditional TOC or capacity costing—cost is attached based on the number of good units produced per shift, day, or hour. The costs are accumulated in JIT settings in traditional ways, using labor, materials, and overhead. And the term inventory is reserved for finished goods or raw materials. The only time work-in-process inventory exists in JIT is if a product has to go through multiple cells. In most cases, work-in-process inventory disappears in JIT manufacturing because a product is usually started and completed within one cell.

Let us look at another example to understand JIT costing approaches. BlueTooth Devices has a range of internet-driven television connectors that sell for between $50 and $100 retail. The retail price is 200% of BlueTooth's quoted prices, which are between $25 and $50. To produce the product, BlueTooth uses two JIT cells, one that solders the circuit board and the other that assembles the unit. The cells run 16 hours a day; the total cost of each cell is noted in Table 8.10. JIT costing charges the cost of production only to good units produced, using the total annual costs as its basis.

TABLE 8.10 JUST-IN-TIME CELL COSTING: FIRST HOUR

BlueTooth Devices: Cost per Cell		
	Soldering Cell	Assembly Cell
Total costs for year	$2,400,000	$3,600,000
Hours in work year	16 x 200 or 3,200	16 x 200 or 3,200
Hourly cost for the cell	$ 750.00	$1,125.00

BlueTooth Devices: Cost per Cell		
	Soldering Cell	Assembly Cell
Good units produced in soldering the last hour of day	100	N/A
Good units produced in hour one of shift one in the assembly cell on day two	N/A	100
Cost per good unit finished in the assembly cell in hour one	$7.50	$11.25

What do we learn from this table? First, of the 100 units produced using the last hour of output in day one from soldering and the first hour of output on day two for assembly, the average cost of production was $18.75 ($7.50 plus $11.25). In the first hour, the assembly cell was working from units that had been produced in the soldering cell the previous day at the normal pace of 100 good units per hour. You can extend the example, as we have done in Table 8.11 for the second hour of production, where assembly uses the output from the 100 units of the soldering cell's first hour of operation on day two, resulting in only 85 good units produced by assembly. The 85 units bear the cost of $7.50 for the soldering cell costs and $13.24 for a total of $20.74. The difference in the costs reflected the waste resulting from not completing good units in assembly at the normal pace. Clearly, we could track the cells over the entire day, and get changing total cost numbers as the production day continued.

TABLE 8.11 JUST-IN-TIME CELL COSTING: SECOND HOUR

BlueTooth Devices: Cost per Cell		
	Soldering Cell	Assembly Cell
Total costs for year	$2,400,000	$3,600,000
Hours in work year	16 x 200 or 3,200	16 x 200 or 3,200
Hourly cost for the cell	$750.00	$1,125.00
Good units produced in soldering the first hour of day two	100	N/A
Good units produced in hour two of shift one in the assembly cell on day two	N/A	85
Cost per good unit finished in the assembly cell in hour two	$7.50	$13.24

We can also see that the assembly cell was more productive in the first hour of the day than the second. Good units produced fell off, driving up the average cost per unit over the two-hour shift. In JIT settings, these hourly cost estimates are tracked along with good units produced to create a visible measurement system that is maintained by the cell manager. In this way, costing information is transformed into a performance measurement that helps keep everyone's eyes on the need to control the throughput of the cell.

A ROLE FOR CAPACITY ANALYSIS

The capacity of a cost pool was defined in Chapter 6 as the amount of work its resources can support. In looking at a process, **capacity** *is the value-creating ability of a system*. Both definitions reflect the overall capability of the resources. The latter emphasizes the linkage of resource use to customer demand, reflecting the process perspective—that this is the only justifiable reason for consuming resource capability.

Three key issues need to be understood when thinking about analyzing the capacity of a process and its underlying activities:

- The goal is to define capacity using some form of "bounded" or finite scale. For instance, time is often used as the measure of capacity because there are always 24 hours in a day. A good boundary will give the resulting cost and operational analysis stability across many different situations.
- The entire cost of the process or activity is attached to one unit of work (for example, a product or service) based on the time it consumes at the bottleneck. This is a common assumption that defines the entire set of tools bundled under the concept of process management.
- The focus is on understanding and separating "good" uses of capacity (value-added efforts) from "bad" uses (nonproductive activities or waste). For instance, if a machine is allowed to process bad material, even if this activity would normally be value-adding, it is waste because the output would be scrapped.

Figure 8.8 illustrates a balanced production line making paper. These lines have to be balanced because there is no place to put a kanban buffer in the flow of paper across the series of machines leading from wood pulp to the finished product: a large roll of paper. Other machines could be added to the end that would immediately convert the paper into reams that you buy at the store. This would require significant balancing of production machines, however, so the conversion of the large rolls of paper into usable products is usually done in a separate operation.

FIGURE 8.8 A BALANCED PAPER-MAKING PRODUCTION LINE COMPRISED OF A SERIES OF MACHINES

In designing a process, it is important both to understand the capacity of each major step or machine and to balance the total capability of these machines as closely as possible. While unbalanced lines still accomplish their designated work, extra cost—waste—is embedded in their structures. Avoiding this waste is the primary objective of a JIT cellular design.

Capacity analysis can be used in many ways in TOC and JIT, but one of its most important applications takes place during the planning stages of process design and process deployment. As we saw when discussing ABM, capacity-constrained processes have very different features and information needs than nonconstrained processes. If a constraint cannot be broken, then it must be carefully managed to ensure that the productive capacity of the process is not wasted doing nonessential work. Capacity analysis reflects the basic goal of all process-based tools and techniques—continuous improvement through the elimination of waste. The forms of waste that are emphasized during capacity analysis are (1) excess capacity and (2) unnecessary or non-value-added work that erodes the amount of productive time available for meeting customer needs.

We will spend much more time revisiting the mechanics of capacity analysis and reporting in Chapter 9. The thing to remember is that capacity analysis is the tool we use first to balance a process and to establish its capability during the design and planning stages of the management process. Before we leave this chapter, let us look briefly at one more issue—the application of process concepts to nonmachine settings.

APPLYING JIT AND CAPACITY ANALYSIS IN NONMACHINE SETTINGS

A common misunderstanding in business is that service companies are radically different from manufacturing companies and need an entirely different set of tools, techniques, and measurements. While it is true that service companies present unique measurement challenges in some situations, in reality, service and manufacturing have quite a bit in common. Some service companies, such as copy shops and banks, have fairly significant material consumption issues. What is different is the nature of their final products—a service tends to be far less tangible than a bar of soap or kitchen cabinet made in a factory.

Figure 8.9 illustrates how JIT and capacity analysis is used in the service sector; in this case, a banking system. Clearly, the flow of the transaction through the system reflects the flow of product through a JIT cell. There are defined steps and relationships between these steps. Both people and machines (mainly computers) are involved in this process. Each step has a capacity; the step with the lowest capacity for check-clearing output paces the entire process flow.

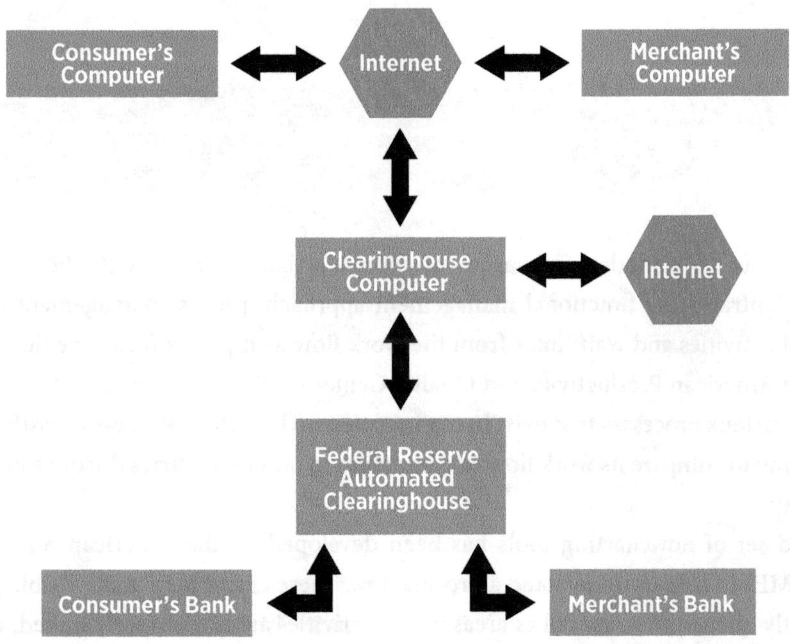

FIGURE 8.9 JIT AND CAPACITY ANALYSIS AS APPLIED TO CHECK-CLEARING

Having said this, JIT and capacity analysis can be used in nonmachine settings such as that depicted in Figure 8.9. In fact, many banks have reorganized their back offices into balanced process flows with defined sequences of work and minimal move and queue activities. If you think about it, the steps required to process checks are as repetitive and measurable as the ones used by Kinkaid to make a wall cabinet unit. Each of the activities has a capacity to do work. Some of these activities are machine-paced, however, and others are people-paced. In the manufacturing setting, all of the tools and models we have looked at can be applied directly. With respect to the service setting, however, we need to employ benchmarking or another form of "external" metric to evaluate the efficiency and capacity of an activity. ABM is very useful for this purpose.

This text contains multiple examples of service industry issues and the management accounting tools and techniques that are intended to address them. While JIT and capacity analyses are not always the first tools of choice for analyzing service-based processes, they are used whenever conditions support their application. In fact, this is a useful rule of thumb for all of the tools and techniques contained in this book.

Thus, if a company operates more like a job shop than a repetitive manufacturer, it is quite likely that TOC will be more applicable than JIT flow management. Conversely, TOC can result in a suboptimal solution if the work done is repetitive, as in clearing checks, because it fails to balance the entire flow that can result in excess cost. Knowing the nature of the process you are trying to manage is the essential first step in choosing the right management accounting tool or technique.

In the next chapter, we will spend more time developing specific cost and performance estimates for Kinkaid's processes as we move from the planning to the "check" and "adjust" aspects of the management process.

Summary

Process management is a modern management approach that emphasizes the flow of work across the organization. Contrary to a functional management approach, process management emphasizes eliminating wasteful activities and wait times from the work flow as it passes from one department or person to another. The American Productivity and Quality Center (APQC) has developed a standard set of definitions for the various processes that exist in organizations. The APQC Process Classification Framework allows a company to compare its work flow to companies in other industries during a best-in-class benchmarking activity.

A standard set of flowcharting tools has been developed by the American Society of Mechanical Engineers (ASME) to help us understand a process flow. These charts help make visible process waste and potentially costly queue times, as well as areas where activities are not properly linked, which greatly aids management in improving process flows and overall performance of the firm. In a process, it is the flow of work that matters, not the activity of individuals.

Lean accounting integrates the major improvement techniques and measurement methods available to organizations today. Emphasizing the profitability of a value stream, product costs include only materials and conversion costs. Overhead is not charged to output. That being said, conversion cost under lean accounting includes many costs that would normally be charged as overhead. The goal in lean accounting is to assign as much cost directly to a value stream, or linked set of processes and activities, as possible. The result is a simplified costing system that by nature includes a comprehensive set of performance metrics that are both financial and nonfinancial in nature. Driven by the continuous improvement philosophy, lean accounting supports lean management and process improvement.

Activity-based management (ABM) and activity-based budgeting (ABB) are two management tools that help to focus attention on the activities in a flow. In ABM, attention turns away from results, or the "what" a process does, to the "how" work is accomplished. Activities are linked together, and the costs of each step are noted. These steps can happen in disparate parts of the organization, but with ABM, we can link them to get a unified picture of the financial implications of the existing work flow. In ABB, we take the information from ABM and use it to develop a series of process improvement goals that directly target the cost to completion for the steps in a process flow. Both of these accounting-based tools provide direct support for process management.

The Theory of Constraints (TOC) is a very specific type of model developed around the concept of a bottleneck resource. In TOC, all of the attention is focused on the bottleneck resource, because it paces the amount of work the rest of the organization can do. All costing is simplified because all of the costs are dropped onto the bottleneck resource. Throughput is then defined as the completion of revenue-generating work, while operating expenses cover all of the consumed time, energy, and resources needed to generate throughput. Finally, inventory is redefined as the company's entire asset base. Physical inventory in the traditional sense still exists, but is considered a form of waste.

Just-in-time (JIT) and cellular manufacturing approaches physically redesign the plant floor to match the flow of production. Inside one cell, all of the machines and people needed to complete a product are arranged in order to provide a balanced flow that is paced by the cell's bottleneck. Kanbans are used to balance the flow of product or service through the cell to minimize the impact of the bottleneck on total output of the cell. Costing in JIT settings often emphasizes the cost of good units produced and uses backflush costing to generate an accounting transaction only when a unit is completed. This all but eliminates work-in-process inventory. In cellular designs, the goal is to eliminate as much as possible the move and queue activities that consume so much of a factory's productive capacity. This speeds up the output of the factory, often cutting weeks or months of throughput time down to mere hours. As long as an organization, either manufacturing or service, has a fairly repetitive process flow, it can use cellular designs to optimize performance.

Throughout the process domain, capacity analysis, management, and logic are applied to process flows. Focused on identifying bottleneck resources and optimizing their utilization, capacity analysis augments the use of tools such as lean accounting and ABM. Taken in total, therefore, the entire set of process management tools and techniques can be used by any organization, whether manufacturing or service in nature, to improve performance against customer expectations, eliminate waste, and improve financial performance.

Key Terms

Activity-based budgeting: a form of financial planning based on understanding activities and processes, and their relationship to achieving the organization's strategic goals.

Activity-based management: a discipline that focuses on controlling activities to achieve performance goals.

Backflush costing: the practice of only charging cost to a unit when it leaves the cell.

Best-in-class benchmarking: compares the process performance of organizations in different industries to identify best process practices.

Bottleneck: the primary constraint in a process flow.

Capacity: the value-creating ability of a system.

Flow management: a technique that focuses on how work is done.

Full-time equivalents: the total hours worked by everyone divided by 40 to get the number of full-time people needed to do a job.

Inventory: a company's primary asset; it is stored to create future value.

Just-in-time cells: the linked sequence of activities required to complete a unit of output.

Just-in-time inventory methods: emphasize the elimination of excess inventory from a flow, in order to have the right amount at the right time in the right place.

Lean accounting: focuses on organizing costs by value stream and modifying financial statements to include nonfinancial measurements.

Lean management: a set of techniques that emphasizes eliminating waste that is embedded in current work processes.

Operating expenses: all of the internal resources and energy expended to produce completed goods or services.

Order-to-payment process: the linked steps that span from the time an order is received until it is filled, invoiced, and the payment is received; the heart of the revenue- and profit-generating flow of activities.

Pacing resource: the slowest resource in a process; usually the bottleneck.

Process: a system of interdependent, sequential activities that produces a specific output.

Process management: a system of tools and techniques used to manage activities across the organization.

Throughput: the payment received for completed work in excess of variable expenses.

Throughput time: the amount of time it takes for one unit of product to be completed.

Value stream: the complete set of linked activity centers that are required to deliver a specific product or service to a customer.

Appendix

PROCESS CLASSIFICATION FRAMEWORK

Developed by APQC's International Benchmarking Clearinghouse
In Partnership with Arthur Andersen & Co., SC

PROCESS CLASSIFICATION FRAMEWORK: OVERVIEW

The Process Classification Framework was developed by the APQC International Benchmarking Clearinghouse, with the assistance of several major international corporations, and in close partnership with Arthur Andersen & Co. The goal is to create a high-level, generic enterprise model that will encourage businesses and other organizations to see their activities from a cross-industry process viewpoint instead of a narrow functional viewpoint.

The Process Classification Framework seeks to represent major processes and subprocesses, not functions, through its structure and vocabulary. The framework does not list all processes within any specific organization. Likewise, not every process listed in the framework is present in every organization.

RIGHTS AND PERMISSIONS

Please direct your comments, suggestions, and questions to:
APQC International Benchmarking Clearinghouse
Information Services Dept.
123 North Post Oak Lane, 3rd Floor
Houston, Texas 77024-7797
713-681-4020 (phone)
713-681-8578 (fax)
Internet: apqcinfo@apqc.org
For updates, visit our Web site at http://www.apqc.org

PROCESS CLASSIFICATION FRAMEWORK

1. UNDERSTAND MARKETS AND CUSTOMERS

1.1 Determine customer needs and wants

1.1.1 Conduct qualitative assessments

1.1.1.1 Conduct customer interviews

1.1.1.2 Conduct focus groups

1.1.2 Conduct quantitative assessments

1.1.2.1 Develop and implement surveys

1.1.3 Predict customer purchasing behavior

1.2 Measure customer satisfaction

1.2.1 Monitor satisfaction with products and services

1.2.2 Monitor satisfaction with complaint resolution

1.2.3 Monitor satisfaction with communication

1.3 Monitor changes in market or customer expectations

1.3.1 Determine weaknesses of product/service offerings

1.3.2 Identify new innovations that meet customer needs

1.3.3 Determine customer reactions to competitive offerings

2. DEVELOP VISION AND STRATEGY

2.1 Monitor the external environment

2.1.1 Analyze and understand competition

2.1.2 Identify economic trends

2.1.3 Identify political and regulatory issues

2.1.4 Assess new technology innovations

2.1.5 Understand demographics

2.1.6 Identify social and cultural changes

2.1.7 Understand ecological concerns

2.2 Define the business concept and organizational strategy

2.2.1 Select relevant markets

2.2.2 Develop long-term vision

2.2.3 Formulate business unit strategy

2.2.4 Develop overall mission statement

2.3 Design the organizational structure and relationships between organizational units

2.4 Develop and set organizational goals

3. DESIGN PRODUCTS AND SERVICES

3.1 Develop new product/service concept and plans

3.1.1 Translate customer wants and needs into product and/or service requirements

3.1.2 Plan and deploy quality targets

3.1.3 Plan and deploy cost targets

3.1.4 Develop product life cycle and development timing targets

3.1.5 Develop and integrate leading technology into product/service concept

3.2 Design, build, and evaluate prototype products and services

3.2.1 Develop product/service specifications

3.2.2 Conduct concurrent engineering

3.2.3 Implement value engineering

3.2.4 Document design specifications

3.2.5 Develop prototypes

3.2.6 Apply for patents

3.3 Refine existing products/services

3.3.1 Develop product/service enhancements

3.3.2 Eliminate quality/reliability problems

3.3.3 Eliminate outdated products/services

3.4 Test effectiveness of new or revised products or services

3.5 Prepare for production

3.5.1 Develop and test prototype production process

3.5.2 Design and obtain necessary materials and equipment

3.5.3 Install and verify process or methodology

3.6 Manage the product/service development process

4. MARKET AND SELL

4.1 Market products or services to relevant customer segments

4.1.1 Develop pricing strategy

4.1.2 Develop advertising strategy

4.1.3 Develop marketing messages to communicate benefits

4.1.4 Estimate advertising resource and capital requirements

4.1.5 Identify specific target customers and their needs

4.1.6 Develop sales forecast

4.1.7 Sell products and services

4.1.8 Negotiate terms

4.2 Process customer orders

4.2.1 Accept orders from customers

4.2.2 Enter orders into production and delivery process

5. PRODUCE AND DELIVER FOR MANUFACTURING-ORIENTED ORGANIZATIONS

5.1 Plan for and acquire necessary resources

5.1.1 Select and certify suppliers

5.1.2 Purchase capital goods

5.1.3 Purchase materials and supplies

5.1.4 Acquire appropriate technology

5.2 Convert resources or inputs into products

5.2.1 Develop and adjust production delivery process (for existing process)

5.2.2 Schedule production
- 5.2.3 Move materials and resources
- 5.2.4 Make product
- 5.2.5 Package product
- 5.2.6 Warehouse or store product
- 5.2.7 Stage products for delivery

5.3 Deliver products
- 5.3.1 Arrange product shipment
- 5.3.2 Deliver products to customers
- 5.3.3 Install product
- 5.3.4 Confirm specific service requirements for individual customers
- 5.3.5 Identify and schedule resources to meet service requirements
- 5.3.6 Provide the service to specific customers

5.4 Manage production and delivery process
- 5.4.1 Document and monitor order status
- 5.4.2 Manage inventories
- 5.4.3 Ensure product quality
- 5.4.4 Schedule and perform maintenance
- 5.4.5 Monitor environmental constraints

6. PRODUCE AND DELIVER FOR SERVICE-ORIENTED ORGANIZATIONS

6.1 Plan for and acquire necessary resources
- 6.1.1 Select and certify suppliers
- 6.1.2 Purchase materials and supplies
- 6.1.3 Acquire appropriate technology

6.2 Develop human resource skills
- 6.2.1 Define skill requirements
- 6.2.2 Identify and implement training
- 6.2.3 Monitor and manage skill development

6.3 Deliver service to the customer
- 6.3.1 Confirm specific service requirements for individual customer
- 6.3.2 Identify and schedule resources to meet service requirements
- 6.3.3 Provide the service to specific customers

6.4 Ensure quality of service

7. INVOICE AND SERVICE CUSTOMERS

7.1 Bill the customer
- 7.1.1 Develop, deliver, and maintain customer billing
- 7.1.2 Invoice the customer
- 7.1.3 Respond to billing inquiries

7.2 Provide after-sales service
- 7.2.1 Provide post-sales service
- 7.2.2 Handle warranties and claims

7.3 Respond to customer Inquiries
- 7.3.1 Respond to information requests
- 7.3.2 Manage customer complaints

8. DEVELOP AND MANAGE HUMAN RESOURCES

8.1 Create and manage human resource strategies
- 8.1.1 Identify organizational strategic demands
- 8.1.2 Determine human resource costs
- 8.1.3 Define human resource requirements
- 8.1.4 Define human resource's organizational role

8.2 Cascade strategy to work level
- 8.2.1 Analyze, design, or redesign work
- 8.2.2 Define and align work outputs and metrics
- 8.2.3 Define work competencies

8.3 Manage deployment of personnel
- 8.3.1 Plan and forecast workforce requirements
- 8.3.2 Develop succession and career plans
- 8.3.3 Recruit, select, and hire employees
- 8.3.4 Create and deploy teams
- 8.3.5 Relocate employees
- 8.3.6 Restructure and rightsize workforce
- 8.3.7 Manage employee retirement
- 8.3.8 Provide outplacement support

8.4 Develop and train employees
- 8.4.1 Align employee and organization development needs
- 8.4.2 Develop and manage training programs
- 8.4.3 Develop and manage employee orientation programs
- 8.4.4 Develop functional/process competencies
- 8.4.5 Develop management/leadership competencies
- 8.4.6 Develop team competencies

8.5 Manage employee performance, reward, and recognition

8.5.1 Define performance measures

8.5.2 Develop performance management approaches/feedback

8.5.3 Manage team performance

8.5.4 Evaluate work for market value and internal equity

8.5.5 Develop and manage base and variable compensation

8.5.6 Manage reward and recognition programs

8.6 Ensure employee well-being and satisfaction

8.6.1 Manage employee satisfaction

8.6.2 Develop work and family support systems

8.6.3 Manage and administer employee benefits

8.6.4 Manage workplace health and safety

8.6.5 Manage internal communications

8.6.6 Manage and support workforce diversity

8.7 Ensure employee involvement

8.8 Manage labor-management relationships

8.8.1 Manage collective bargaining process

8.8.2 Manage labor-management partnerships

8.9 Develop Human Resource Information Systems (HRIS)

9. MANAGE INFORMATION RESOURCES

9.1 Plan for information resource management

9.1.1 Derive requirements from business strategies

9.1.2 Define enterprise system architectures

9.1.3 Plan and forecast information technologies/ methodologies

9.1.4 Establish enterprise data standards

9.1.5 Establish quality standards and controls

9.2 Develop and deploy enterprise support systems

9.2.1 Conduct specific needs assessments

9.2.2 Select information technologies

9.2.3 Define data life cycles

9.2.4 Develop enterprise support systems

9.2.5 Test, evaluate, and deploy enterprise support systems

9.3 Implement systems security and controls

9.3.1 Establish systems security strategies and levels

9.3.2 Test, evaluate, and deploy systems security and controls

9.4 Manage information storage and retrieval

9.4.1 Establish information repositories (data bases)

9.4.2 Acquire and collect information

9.4.3 Store information.

9.4.4 Modify and update information

9.4.5 Enable retrieval of information

9.4.6 Delete information

9.5 Manage facilities and network operations

9.5.1 Manage centralized facilities

9.5.2 Manage distributed facilities

9.5.3 Manage network operations

9.6 Manage information services

9.6.1 Manage libraries and information centers

9.6.2 Manage business records and documents

9.7 Facilitate information sharing and communication

9.7.1 Manage external communications systems

9.7.2 Manage internal communications systems

9.7.3 Prepare and distribute publications

9.8 Evaluate and audit information quality

10. MANAGE FINANCIAL AND PHYSICAL RESOURCES

10.1 Manage financial resources

10.1.1 Develop budgets

10.1.2 Manage resource allocation

10.1.3 Design capital structure

10.1.4 Manage cash flow

10.1.5 Manage financial risk

10.2 Process finance and accounting transactions

10.2.1 Process accounts payable

10.2.2 Process payroll

10.2.3 Process accounts receivable, credit, and collections

10.2.4 Close the books

10.2.5 Process benefits and retiree information

10.2.6 Manage travel and entertainment expenses

10.3 Report information

10.3.1 Provide external financial information

10.3.2 Provide internal financial information

10.4 Conduct internal audits

10.5 Manage the tax function

10.5.1 Ensure tax compliance

10.5.2 Plan tax strategy

10.5.3 Employ effective technology

10.5.4 Manage tax controversies

10.5.5 Communicate tax issues to management
10.5.6 Manage tax administration

10.6 Manage physical resources

10.6.1 Manage capital planning
10.6.2 Acquire and redeploy fixed assets
10.6.3 Manage facilities
10.6.4 Manage physical risk

11. EXECUTE ENVIRONMENTAL MANAGEMENT PROGRAM

11.1 Formulate environmental management strategy
11.2 Ensure compliance with regulations
11.3 Train and educate employees
11.4 Implement pollution prevention program
11.5 Manage remediation efforts
11.6 Implement emergency response programs
11.7 Manage government agency and public relations
11.8 Manage acquisition/divestiture environmental issues
11.9 Develop and manage environmental information system
11.10 Monitor environmental management program

12. MANAGE EXTERNAL RELATIONSHIPS

12.1 Communicate with shareholders
12.2 Manage government relationships
12.3 Build lender relationships
12.4 Develop public relations program
12.5 Interface with board of directors
12.6 Develop community relations
12.7 Manage legal and ethical issues

13. MANAGE IMPROVEMENT AND CHANGE

13.1 Measure organizational performance

13.1.1 Create measurement systems
13.1.2 Measure product and service quality
13.1.3 Measure cost of quality
13.1.4 Measure costs
13.1.5 Measure cycle time
13.1.6 Measure productivity

13.2 Conduct quality assessments

13.2.1 Conduct quality assessments based on external criteria
13.2.2 Conduct quality assessments based on internal criteria

13.3 Benchmark performance

13.3.1 Develop benchmarking capabilities
13.3.2 Conduct process benchmarking
13.3.3 Conduct competitive benchmarking

13.4 Improve processes and systems

13.4.1 Create commitment for improvement
13.4.2 Implement continuous process improvement
13.4.3 Reengineer business processes and systems
13.4.4 Manage transition to change

13.5 Implement TQM

13.5.1 Create commitment for TQM
13.5.2 Design and implement TQM systems
13.5.3 Manage TQM life cycle

Questions

1. What does the term process management mean? What are the six key concepts that define a process management approach? How does the definition of a process impact how management approaches its work?
2. What is a process? Can you think of several processes that take place in your university?
3. What are the primary differences between functional and process-based organizations? How do these differences impact how the organization is managed?

4. What are the six primary activity symbols used by the ASME charting approach? What do they mean? How are they used to detail the steps in a process?
5. Give some examples of wasteful activities in a process flow that lean management might target for elimination.
6. What are the key features of lean accounting performance metrics? How do these features impact the value of the resulting measurements for decision making?
7. What is ABM? How does it differ from ABC? Which one is simpler to use? Why?
8. Define and give an example of how a company can use ABB.
9. What is the primary focus of TOC? How does this focus shape how managers approach work?
10. What do the terms throughput, operating expense, and inventory mean under TOC? How do these definitions line up with traditional accounting terminology? How do they differ from traditional accounting terms?
11. How would you describe JIT management methods? How do these relate to lean management?
12. The term kanban has special meaning inside JIT management. Exactly what does this term mean? How do kanbans help manage a process?
13. The term backflush costing is unique to JIT inventory management methods. What exactly does the term mean? How does backflush costing differ from other accounting approaches to product costing?
14. Can JIT or cellular approaches be used in service settings? Why or why not?
15. Looking at the material in the appendix, what are the primary differences you see between Process 5 (Produce and deliver for manufacturing-oriented organizations) and Process 6 (Produce and deliver for service-oriented organizations)? Do you think one company could end up using both sets of activities? Why or why not?

Exercises

1. **ASME FLOWCHARTING.** Bruce Calloway of BuyRite Shopping Service has decided it may be time to improve the flow of his back office. He collects the following list of activities that take place during the customer invoicing process.

- Order taken online
- Order batched with others to wait processing
- Orders distributed to invoice specialists
- Order sits in specialists' in-boxes
- Order processed
- Invoice generated
- Invoice waits for review
- Invoice redone if errors found

- Invoices batched
- Invoices moved to mail clerk
- Invoices sit in mail clerk's in-box
- Invoices stuffed in envelopes
- Invoices batched to be taken to mail room
- Invoices taken to mail room
- Invoices mailed

REQUIRED:

Using the ASME flowcharting symbols, draw the flow for this process.

2. **ASME FLOWCHARTING.** Nancy Godden is the owner of a small florist shop. Orders are taken via electronic sources for three national services that contract with local flower shops to make and deliver the actual flower arrangements. Nancy recently took a class in process management and decided to study the flow for these orders. The steps she found were:

- Order received online
- Order placed in "to-do" box
- Order waits for available arranger
- Arranger takes order to her desk
- Order placed in in-box
- Order waits until arranger has time to make arrangement
- Arranger obtains flowers
- Arranger makes arrangement
- Arrangement put in refrigerator awaiting delivery
- Arrangement waits in refrigerator for delivery van
- Arrangements are loaded in delivery van
- Arrangements are driven to customers' homes
- Arrangements delivered
- Delivery receipt brought back to shop
- Delivery receipts batched in Nancy's in-box
- Invoices generated from delivery receipts

REQUIRED:

Using the ASME flowcharting symbols, draw the flow for this process.

3. **CLASSIFYING ACTIVITIES AND ASSESSING ELAPSED VS. PROCESS TIME.** Munson's Machine Shop makes a variety of small metal parts on its machines. They are inventoried for later sale.

Activity	Time Required
Write up request for materials	10 minutes
Take request to parts bin	5 minutes
Wait for parts to be retrieved by storekeeper	20 minutes
Receive parts	5 minutes
Calibrate machine	30 minutes

Activity	Time Required
Run parts	30 minutes
Run QC tests on parts	15 minutes
Move parts to in-process inventory	10 minutes
Wait for parts to be received by storekeeper	20 minutes
Put parts in storage bin	10 minutes
Write up paperwork for inventory transaction	5 minutes
Part sits in storage waiting for order	10 days
Parts packed for shipment	15 minutes

REQUIRED:

a. Categorize the activities above using the ASME categories.
b. Add up all the time these activities take. What is the elapsed time?
c. How much of that time is used for process activities? In other words, what amount of the time would a customer be willing to pay for?

4. **CLASSIFYING ACTIVITIES AND ASSESSING ELAPSED VS. VALUE-ADDED TIME.** Taylor's Rental rents a variety of products to customers for home use. The following is the flow associated with one of the products offered by Taylor's.

Activity	Time Required
Customer order taken for rental	10 minutes
Customer waits	15 minutes
Item retrieved from inventory	5 minutes
Paperwork filled out	15 minutes
Credit card transaction run	5 minutes
Customer takes unit to car	3 minutes
Customer drives unit to home	25 minutes
Customer unloads unit	3 minutes
Customer has lunch	75 minutes
Unit put to work in garden	30 minutes
Unit moved back to car	3 minutes
Unit sits waiting for return trip to store	12 hours
Customer drives unit to store	25 minutes
Customer takes unit back into store	3 minutes
Customer waits for service	15 minutes
Paperwork completed	10 minutes

Activity	Time Required
Final credit card transaction run	5 minutes
Unit returned to inventory	20 minutes

REQUIRED:

a. Categorize the activities above using the ASME categories.
b. Add up all the time these activities take. What is the elapsed time?
c. How much of that time is used for process activities? In other words, what amount of the time would a customer be willing to pay for?

5. **LEAN ACCOUNTING.** Sitwell Services cleans offices. It runs several cleaning crews that are given standard times for cleaning certain spaces. Given the experience of the crew, these standards can allow for more or less time. Crew B has just begun work for the company. It is evaluated using a rolling average standard that reflects the amount of improvement in its productivity. The following are the elapsed times for cleaning Joe's Plumbing Supplies for six weeks.

Week 1	120 minutes
Week 2	115 minutes
Week 3	110 minutes
Week 4	105 minutes
Week 5	100 minutes
Week 6	95 minutes

REQUIRED:

Using three weeks as the basis for your lean accounting elapsed time metric, calculate the average time Crew B takes to complete the Joe's Plumbing Supplies job over time. Specifically, use the first three weeks as your baseline, then add one new observation and delete one to get the Week 4 average, and so forth through Week 6.

6. **LEAN ACCOUNTING.** Blue Moon Limousine Service runs an hourly shuttle from the local airport to the waterfront district in downtown. Its drivers are expected to learn their route and then be able to meet the company's standard time of one hour for the round trip. They are monitored during the training period. Below is the record of times for Joe Black, a new driver for Blue Moon.

Trip 1	100 minutes
Trip 2	95 minutes
Trip 3	90 minutes
Trip 4	85 minutes
Trip 5	80 minutes
Trip 6	70 minutes

REQUIRED:

Using three weeks as the basis for your lean accounting elapsed time metric, calculate the average time Joe Black takes to complete a round trip to downtown. Specifically, use the first three trips as your baseline, then add one new observation and delete one to get the Trip 4 average, and so forth through Trip 6.

7. **ACTIVITY-BASED BUDGETING.** Dunn's Manufacturing uses ABB. A recent study was done of the activities of the company's one purchasing manager who is paid $75,000 per year for her efforts. The following is the list of activities and how much time (in percentage terms) she reported spending on each activity.

Activity	% of Time
Review purchase requests	5%
Place orders	10%
Expedite orders	20%
Verify shipment records	5%
Validate invoices	10%
Go to meetings	20%
Manage purchasing clerks	30%

REQUIRED:

Using the information in the above table, develop an activity-based budget for the purchasing manager. Specifically, use the data and the manager's salary to generate a list of activities and their costs.

8. **ACTIVITY-BASED BUDGETING.** Shallwell Diaper Service uses ABB. A recent study of the activities of the company's one call center representative who makes $45,000 a

year for his efforts produced the following list of activities and how much time (in percentage terms) he has reported spending on each activity.

Activity	% of Time
Take customer calls	45%
Transfer customers	5%
Handle paperwork	10%
Issue work orders	15%
Type memos	5%
Prepare reports	10%
Go to meetings	10%

REQUIRED:

Using the information in the above table, develop an activity-based budget for the call service representative. Specifically, use the data and the representative's salary to generate a list of activities and their costs.

9. **PROCESS VARIATION: SHEWHART CHARTS.** Using the Shewhart charting methods described in Figure 2.4 in Chapter 2, analyze the performance of a check-clearing process. The standard time to clear a check is six seconds. The allowed variation is two seconds more or less than this time (your control limits).

Check #	Time to Process
1	6 seconds
2	7 seconds
3	3 seconds
4	8 seconds
5	10 seconds
6	5 seconds
7	6 seconds
8	10 seconds

REQUIRED:

a. Complete a Shewhart control chart for this activity.
b. Would you say the activity is under control? Why or why not?

10. **PROCESS VARIATION: SHEWHART CHARTS.** Using the Shewhart charting methods described in Figure 2.4 in Chapter 2, analyze the performance of the following invoice processing activity. The standard time to validate an invoice for payment is five minutes. Allowed variation by the company's management is three minutes more or less than this time (your control limits). Below are the times for Beth, a relatively new employee.

Invoice #	Time to Process
1	5 minutes
2	15 minutes
3	10 minutes
4	12 minutes
5	8 minutes
6	6 minutes
7	20 minutes
8	10 minutes

REQUIRED:

a. Complete a Shewhart control chart for this worker.

b. Would you say she is meeting company expectations? Why or why not?

11. **APQC CLASSIFICATION: APPENDIX.** For the following list of activities, find the APQC category that most closely matches the activity and put its number alongside the activity. Use a table like the one provided below.

Activity	Classification Code
Prepare purchase order	
Take customer order	
Retrieve materials from storeroom	
Develop strategic plan	
Hold continuous improvement meeting	
Evaluate employees	
Ensure quality service	
Measure customer satisfaction	

12. **APQC CLASSIFICATION: APPENDIX.** For the following list of activities, find the APQC category that most closely matches the activity and put its number alongside the activity. Use a table like the one provided below.

Activity	Classification Code
Develop sales forecast	
Make product	
Manage inventories	
Apply for patents	
Create teams	
Establish security protocols for mainframe	
Manage customer complaints	
Measure cycle time	

Problems

1. **THE COST OF WASTE.** DC Watts, Inc., makes power cords for a variety of electronic products. Lately, it has been having significant problems with the quality of its output. It also appears that making a batch of power cords takes longer and longer. Donald Wright, the head of manufacturing, has just completed a study of one of the main power cord lines. The following is the list of activities, times, and costs estimates for the various activities.

Activity	Time	Cost
Retrieve materials from stores	15 minutes	$60.00
Write up paperwork	10 minutes	$40.00
Produce	20 minutes	$120.00
Recalibrate machine	15 minutes	$80.00
Sort out scrap units	30 minutes	$100.00
Produce	60 minutes	$360.00
Repair machine	60 minutes	$240.00
Sort out scrap units	30 minutes	$100.00
Recalibrate machine	15 minutes	$80.00
Produce	30 minutes	$180.00

It takes 0.5 minutes on the machine to make one power cord. The power cords normally sell for $8. After sorting out good from bad units, 80% were good units and 20% were bad.

REQUIRED:

a. Calculate the total elapsed time in this cycle.
b. Calculate the process time in this cycle. What percentage of time is used to complete process activities?
c. Determine how many power cords were successfully made during the morning shift.
d. Calculate the total cost of the operations.
e. Calculate the average cost of a good power cord.
f. Calculate the total process costs of operations. What percentage of cost is used for process activities?
g. Develop a rough profit analysis for the morning's operations. Specifically, using the times and prices noted, determine how much revenue was generated by the morning's production vs. how much cost was incurred. Set up your analysis as follows:

Revenue
Less: Process costs
Potential profit
Less: Nonprocess costs
Profit (loss) for morning shift

h. What would you say to Donald about his operations? Why?

2. **THE COST OF WASTE.** Miles Industries makes a number of different molds used by other manufacturing companies to produce plastic products. The molds are made using special numerically controlled equipment that can be very sensitive to vibration and run speeds. The following is a list of the activities undertaken to produce a set of molds for one customer.

Activity	Time	Cost
Retrieve materials from stores	20 minutes	$120.00
Input numerical codes	40 minutes	$360.00
Calibrate machine	15 minutes	$120.00
Produce	30 minutes	$240.00
Recalibrate machine	15 minutes	$120.00

Activity	Time	Cost
Produce	30 minutes	$240.00
Inspect units	20 minutes	$160.00
Sort out scrap units	30 minutes	$240.00
Recalibrate machine	15 minutes	$120.00
Produce	30 minutes	$240.00

It takes three minutes on the machine to make one good mold. The molds normally sell for $75. In sorting out good from bad units, 80% were good units and 20% were bad.

REQUIRED:

a. Calculate the total elapsed time in this cycle.
b. Calculate the process time in this cycle. What percentage of time is used for process activities?
c. Determine how many molds were successfully made during the afternoon shift.
d. Calculate the total cost of the operations.
e. Calculate the average cost of a good mold.
f. Calculate the total process costs of operations. What percentage of cost is used by process activities?
g. Develop a rough profit analysis for the afternoon's operations. Specifically, using the times and prices noted, determine how much revenue was generated by the afternoon's production vs. how much cost was incurred. Set up your analysis as follows:

Revenue
Less: Process costs
    Potential profit
Less: Nonprocess costs
    Profit (loss) for morning shift

h. What would you say to Miles Industries about its operations? Why?

3. **CLASSIFYING MEASUREMENTS.** Hi-Value Secretarial Services provides a broad range of secretarial support services, including temporary office workers, to businesses in the tristate area. In order to monitor the effectiveness of its support processes, such as placement of the right worker in the right job, Hi-Value uses a broad number of measurements that are listed below.

- Customer wait time
- Number of customer complaints
- Number of invoices processed per day
- Cost per hour for secretarial services

- Cost of invoicing customers
- New customers per month
- Return customers per year
- Compliments received from customers
- Time required to fill customer request
- Number of placements per week
- Customer calls answered on the first ring
- Number of new employees placed on jobs
- Number of interviews conducted for new employees
- Cost to hire a new worker

REQUIRED:

a. Classify each of the above measures as one of the following four types of measurements: cost, time, output quantity, or customer satisfaction.

b. Do you think this is a good set of measurements? Why or why not?

4. **CLASSIFYING MEASUREMENT.** Samuelson's Car Repair is very focused on customer service. Over the last few years, it has developed a range of performance measurements it uses for various parts of the organization. These measurements are listed below.

- Number of customer complaints
- Number of repeat customers
- Cost to invoice customers
- Service costs per hour
- Customer wait time
- Number of customers who get appointments when wanted
- Number of customer problems fixed the first time
- Number of tires sold
- Back office costs per month
- Number of customer calls answered by the third ring
- Customers served by a service representative
- Number of oil changes done per shift
- Time required to do a tire rotation
- Number of customers answering "very pleased" on service questionnaire
- Number of new customers referred by another customer
- Cleanliness of shop floor
- Number of technicians that are cross-trained

REQUIRED:

a. Classify each of the above measures as one of the following four types: cost, time, output quantity, or customer satisfaction.

b. Do you think this is a good set of measurements? Why or why not?

5. **LEAN ACCOUNTING.** John Wells is vice president of manufacturing for White Goods, Inc., a maker of household appliances. John has been studying the performance of one of his order fulfillment departments for the small parts used in repairing the company's appliances. He has benchmarked the performance against L.L.Bean and found his department

sadly lacking in terms of performance. The key performance metrics and his company's comparable performance are listed in the table below.

Performance Measure	L.L.Bean	White Goods
Time to fill order	90 minutes	2 days
Orders filled correctly	99%	85%
Number of items missing from order	None	3
Labor time to fill order	10 minutes	30 minutes
Cost to fill order	$5.00	$20.00

Based on this information, John decides to monitor performance focusing on continuous improvement on a rolling average basis. He chooses two metrics, labor time to fill order and cost to fill order, to establish his first round of goals. Below is his 12-month performance record. John is going to use a three-month rolling average as his standard. His goal for the first year is to shave 20% off of the *time* required to fill the orders, and 25% off of the *cost* to fill the orders.

Performance Metrics	Periods											
	1	2	3	4	5	6	7	8	9	10	11	12
Labor fill time	30	29	31	30	28	26	27	28	26	24	23	25
Cost to fill order	$20.00	$19.50	$19.00	$19.50	$20.00	$18.50	$18.00	$18.50	$18.00	$17.50	$17.00	$16.00

REQUIRED:

a. Do a trend analysis chart for the two measures.

b. Calculate the rolling average performance level for each of the 12 months of this year. Use the first three observations as your starting benchmark, and then update your average each month by adding one month of observations on and dropping the oldest month off. You will have 10 observations.

c. Does it appear that John's fulfillment operations are improving? Specifically, did the operation meet John's goals? Why or why not?

6. **LEAN ACCOUNTING.** Happy Days Greeting Card Company recently completed a best-in-class benchmarking activity for its accounts payable operations. It benchmarked against Johnson & Johnson, a leader in this activity. The results were distressing. Jason Wright, the company change manager, has been tasked with taking the results of the study and seeing if improvements can be made in operations at Happy Days. The results of the study are in the table below.

Performance Metric	Johnson & Johnson	Happy Days
Time to process an invoice	5 minutes	20 minutes
Percentage of discounts taken	99%	60%
Number of payments paid on first pass	99%	80%
Percentage of errors in payments	0.5%	10%
Cost to process an invoice	$8.00	$25.00

Looking at these results, Jason decides to put in place a continuous improvement program. He decides to monitor only two of the performance metrics for the first year: time to process an invoice and cost to process an invoice. He decides to use a rolling average approach, using three months as the baseline. That leaves him with 10 observations for the continuous improvement study. The results of the yearlong effort are in the table below. He has set the goal of taking 25% off of the processing time and 30% off of the processing cost.

	Periods											
Performance Metrics	1	2	3	4	5	6	7	8	9	10	11	12
Time to process invoice	20	19	19.5	18	18.5	19	18	17	17.5	17	16.5	16
Cost to process invoice	$25.00	$24.00	$23.00	$22.00	$23.00	$24.00	$23.00	$22.00	$21.00	$22.00	$22.50	$21.50

REQUIRED:

a. Do a trend analysis chart for the two measures.

b. Calculate the rolling average performance level for each of the 12 months of the first year. Use the first three observations as your starting benchmark, then update your average each month by adding on one month of observations and dropping off the oldest month. You will have 10 observations.

c. Does it appear that Jason's fulfillment operations are improving? Specifically, did the operation meet Jason's goals? Why or why not?

7. **ACTIVITY-BASED BUDGETING.** Janice Dewey is the head of the accounts receivable department for a home nursing service called Helping Hands. The process can become quite complex as many of the payments the company receives come from insurance companies that often make it very difficult to collect on a claim. Janice has recently been told that she has to get a better handle on what her people are doing so the company can begin to meet some of its benchmark goals. She decides to ask two of her workers to fill out an activity-based budget analysis questionnaire to give her an understanding of where their time is being used. She chooses Babs Boreen, who makes $50,000 a year due to her seniority, and Joan Kolemay, who makes $40,000 a year as a new hire. The results of the study are:

Babs Boreen		Salary	Joan Kolemay		Salary
Activity	% of Time	$50,000.00	Activity	% of Time	$40,000.00
Process receivables	50%	$25,000.00	Process receivables	40%	$16,000.00
Prepare reports	5%	$2,500.00	Prepare reports	20%	$8,000.00
Work with auditor	10%	$5,000.00	Organize desk	5%	$2,000.00
Attend quality team meetings	5%	$2,500.00	Work with marketing	10%	$4,000.00
Organize desk	15%	$7,500.00	Answer telephone	5%	$2,000.00
Answer telephone	10%	$5,000.00	Answer letters	10%	$4,000.00
Attend other meetings	5%	$2,500.00	Attend meetings	10%	$4,000.00
	100%	$50,000.00		100%	$40,000.00

REQUIRED:

a. Babs processes 10,000 receivables while Joan processes only 7,000 receivables. What is the activity cost for processing invoices for each individual?
b. Which employee do you think should be made the model for the department? Why? Use a business case structure to underscore your argument.

---

8. **ACTIVITY-BASED BUDGETING.** Blue Ray is a local cable company that installs cable television, internet, and telephone systems for customers in a three-county area. Jack Ryder, the head of operations, has recently learned about ABB and wants to use it to study the work done by his technicians in the field. He asks two of his technicians, Joel and Andy, to prepare the standard ABB report. Both technicians make $45,000 per year. The results of this study are given in the following two tables.

Joel Coward		Salary	Andy Remains		Salary
Activity	% of Time	$45,000.00	Activity	% of Time	$45,000.00
Install cable systems	40%	$18,000.00	Install cable systems	50.0%	$22,500.00
Repair cable systems	20%	$9,000.00	Repair cable systems	25.0%	$11,250.00
Drive to work site	10%	$4,500.00	Drive to work site	10.0%	$4,500.00
Attend quality team meetings	5%	$2,250.00	Answer customer calls	5.0%	$2,250.00
Answer customer calls	10%	$4,500.00	Work with marketing	2.5%	$1,125.00
Work with scheduling	10%	$4,500.00	Organize truck	2.5%	$1,125.00
Attend other meetings	5%	$2,250.00	Attend meetings	5.0%	$2,250.00
	100%	$45,000.00		100%	$45,000.00

REQUIRED:

a. Joel processes 1,500 new installations and 500 repairs, while Andy processes 1,600 new installations and 600 repairs. What is the activity cost for each individual for these two tasks?
b. Which employee do you think should be made the model for the company? Why? Can you build a business case to make your argument clearer? Please do so.

9. **ACTIVITY ANALYSIS AND ASME ACTIVITIES.** Johnny Roberts, owner of Bunson Marine, has his workforce keep time sheets so he knows where their time is going and also to help guide his billing. A recent graduate of the local MBA extension program, Johnny learned to attach the ASME symbols to his work to help him organize his thoughts. He has pulled together all of the work tickets for Jonah Whales, one of his employees. Jonah's record for the year is shown in the table below. Jonah makes $60,000 per year as a senior repair master for the boats.

Bunson Marine			
Activity	% of Time	Cost	ASME Type
Fix engines	10.0%		
Retrieve paperwork	2.5%		
Put orders in to-do boxes	2.5%		
Wait for parts	7.5%		
Inspect work	7.5%		
Move boats	2.5%		
Wait for engineer	10.0%		
Repair hulls	15.0%		
Inspect hulls	5.0%		
Carry parts to boat	10.0%		
Repair fittings	10.0%		
Test engines	5.0%		
Wait for bridge to open	7.5%		
Place finished work orders in out-box	5.0%		
	100.0%		

REQUIRED:

a. Calculate the total cost for each of the activities Jonah completed over the last year.
b. Place the correct ASME symbol in the box to the left of your costs.
c. Total up all of the costs by ASME symbol.
d. How would you describe Jonah's productivity for the year? In other words, do you think that Johnny should give Jonah a raise? Why or why not?

10. **ACTIVITY ANALYSIS AND ASME ACTIVITIES.** Sally Wields has been asked to do an assessment of how the time of her scheduling department is being used and to assign costs to each. She has been asked to do an activity analysis for the department, assign relative percentages of time to each task, and then categorize the tasks using the ASME flowcharting logic. The department costs $575,000 per year to run. The following chart contains Sally's results.

Scheduling Department

Activity	% of Time	Cost	ASME Type
Write schedule	20.0%		
Verify schedule	10.0%		
Attend meetings	2.5%		
Reschedule	5.0%		
Answer phone calls	5.0%		
Wait for orders	2.5%		
Walk schedule to plant departments	10.0%		
Wait for marketing	10.0%		
Inspect work orders	5.0%		
Wait for accounting	5.0%		
Expedite parts	7.5%		
Develop reports	5.0%		
Distribute work orders to desk	7.5%		
Place orders in in-box	5.0%		
	100.0%		

REQUIRED:

a. Calculate the total cost for each of the activities Sally's department performed.
b. Place the correct ASME symbol in the box to the left of these costs.

c. Total up all of the costs by ASME symbol.
d. How would you describe the department's productivity for the year?

Database Problems

For database templates, worksheets, and workbooks, go to MAdownloads.imanet.org

DB 8.1 ACTIVITY-BASED BUDGETING. The objective of this exercise is to attach costs for the Marketing, General, and Administrative Departments to specific activities performed by these departments. The two data worksheets are: Income Statement and Mktg, Gen & Admin Dept. The instructions for eight of the templated worksheets are identical. These are summarized on the final template.

Purchasing Template: First, you will fill in Cell D75. Left click on Cell D75, enter = then go to the Mktg, Gen & Admin Dept worksheet and left click on Cell C7 and multiply this amount by 1,000 to convert it to actual dollars. Use this information to do the calculations of cost for rows 78–97, Columns C thru G. Repeat this process for the remaining seven Mktg, Gen and Admin departments. NOTE: You can copy and then paste the commands for Columns C to H, rows 78 to 97, from one worksheet to another.

Summary Sheet Template: This is a simple worksheet. For Columns C thru H and Rows 5 to 12, you are simply going to insert the amounts on line 99 for each of the departmental worksheets.

REQUIRED:

Turn in the Summary Sheet Template to your instructor with the answer to the following question: Looking at the results of the analysis, what would you say about Kinkaid's management? Be precise; use the results of your analysis to support your recommendations in a business case framework.

DB 8.2 ABB AND THE APQC CLASSIFICATION APPROACH. In this problem, you are simply going to add process codes from the APQC Framework to the activities performed in each of the Mktg, Gen & Admin Dept worksheets. You can use the same code more than once. Note: If the answer is "attend meeting," default to code 8.1, and if the response is "manage workforce" in some manner, use code 8.3. If you cannot identify a three-digit code, it is okay to use a two-digit code. Try not to use only the major code; although, if you really cannot decide, it will do for the exercise.

The data worksheets are the same as for DB 8-1: Income Statement and Mktg, Gen & Admin Dept. The templates for each department are altered slightly, incorporating the room for your Process codes in Column B.

DB 8.2 Purchasing Template: This uses the results of DB 8.1. Simply copy the results from Cell E75 to E75 then highlight the entire solution in Columns C thru H, Rows 78 to 99, right click, and choose Copy from the table. Now go to Cell D78 in the Purchasing Template in the DB 8.2 workbook, right click, then choose "Paste Special—Values" and hit Enter. Do this for the other seven departments. Now enter the process codes, starting on Row 15 through 34 in Column B. You only have to do this for Rows 15 thru 34; they will automatically copy to the rest of the worksheet.

DB 8.2 Cst-Value Det'l Template: Highlight the information in Columns A through I and from Row 78 to the last row populated for the department on its Template. For Purchasing, this would be Row 87. Right click, select Copy, and then move to the Cst-Value Det'l Template and select the next open cell in Column A. For Purchasing, this would be Row 8. Right click and select Paste Values (the rows will differ from the original template so if you don't do this, you'll get entire rows of...well...garbage!). Do this for the remaining seven departments. When you are done, summarize each column and then copy that sum to Row 3 and calculate Row 4.

REQUIRED:

Turn in the Cst-Value Det'l Template solution to your instructor along with your answers to the following questions: Which department had the least amount of diversity in process codes? Second, did you find that you had to use codes from multiple processes for single departments? What does this tell you about how organizations are managed?

Cases

CASE 8.1 ACTIVITY-BASED ANALYSIS AND BUDGETING. Doubtfire Press produces children's books for national distribution through mainstream distributors such as Baker and Taylor. It has recently decided to implement activity-based analysis and ABB to help it gain control over its publication costs.

There are a number of activities and professionals involved in publishing a children's book, as summarized in the table below.

Individual	Activity
Writer	Writes the 32 pages of story line
Illustrator	Creates the art for the book
Designer	Combines the word and art to make a digital file
Printer	Takes the digital file and prints books
Publisher	Organizes the publication process
Distributor	Offers the book to the distribution network
Retailer	Sells the book to the market

This list of people make up the value chain for the children's book industry. Doubtfire has its own set of writers, illustrators, and designers. It is also the printer and publisher of the books. Kay Doubtfire, the company's owner, describes the process:

> *We first need a good story line. This can come from one of our current authors or may be a new acquisition. Once the story line is set, the designer lays out the page so the illustrator knows what spaces need to be filled in. The project then goes into the art stage, which normally takes about a month for a standard 32-page book. The artist and designer are working in tandem during this period. Once the artwork is done, it has to be digitized. The designer does this using special equipment to scan the work into high-resolution files. The designer then combines the text and the artwork into one, ready-to-print file.*
>
> *The digital file is sent off to the printer, who puts the book in the printing queue. Before the book can be printed, color proofs are generated. These are gone over in detail by the writer, illustrator, and designer to look for any final errors, color matching, and any flaws that may have crept in. Once the proofs are approved, the printing process begins. This requires printing the pages in large, multipage sheets, then folding the "signature" into pages, cutting and binding the pages into a book. Once the book is done, the publisher, who has managed the entire process, negotiates with the distributor, setting price and promotion guidelines.*

The activities, time line, and costs for these activities are in the table below.

Activity	Duration	Cost
Write book	2 months	$15,000
Design book	30 hours	$50.00 per hour
Illustrate book	1 month	$10,000
Negotiate art and design	40 hours	$75.00 per hour
Create digital files	20 hours	$50.00 per hour

Activity	Duration	Cost
Send digital files to printer	15 minutes	$50.00 per hour
Create color proofs	2 weeks	$2,500
Approve color proofs	1 hour	$100.00 per hour
Rescan and correct proofs	1 week	$1,000
Create plates for printing	1 day	$1,500
Print pages for 5,000 books	4 hours	$5,000
Bind pages into 5,000 books	8 hours	$3,000
Negotiate terms with distributor	1 week	$1,200
Ship book to distribution warehouse	2 days	$500
Market book	1 month	$12,000

Kay wants to develop a standard budget for a book using these average figures. But, given the high competition in the children's book publishing industry, she wants to carve off 15% of the total time and costs of production. Some areas she cannot touch are the artist and writer. These are standard industry fees and really are not open for negotiation. In fact, the cost and time reductions will need to come out of the production process itself, which includes design work.

REQUIRED:

a. Using the data provided in the table, develop a total elapsed time and total cost for producing 5,000 units of a children's book.
b. What is the cost of one book in this 5,000-unit run?
c. Calculate what 15% of the time and cost for the process is. Can Kay reasonably expect to remove 15% of the time and cost from this process if she cannot change her terms with her writers and illustrators?
d. Of the time that is spent, what do you feel is truly value-adding, in other words, something the customer would willingly pay for? Is there enough non-value-added time and activities to meet Kay's 15% goal? Why or why not? Use a business case structure to present your argument.

CASE 8.2 ELAPSED VS. VALUE-ADDED TIME. Betsy Homemaker makes and distributes a line of aprons for both commercial and residential use. The standard products consist of white full-length aprons used for restaurants and multipatterned bib aprons for home use. Sadie Burns, the owner of the company, is trying to see which product line offers the best opportunity for profitable growth in the future. The plain white standard commercial apron sells for $4.50, while the patterned bib apron for home use sells for $7.50. The commercial aprons are sold to linen supply companies that handle the needs of restaurants, while home use aprons are distributed through a variety of kitchen stores and retail outlets. The process flow for making a batch of 50 units of the two products, along with the relative costs per step, is presented in the tables below. The company only has six employees who do all of the work noted in these steps. Each worker could theoretically complete one apron (cut and sew) every four minutes at a cost of $20 per hour if they did not have to do other work.

Commercial Aprons		
Process Step	**Time**	**Cost**
Purchase fabric	120 minutes	$ 25.00
Store fabric	2 weeks	$ 30.00
Retrieve fabric from stores	5 minutes	$ 1.66
Cut apron	1 minute each	$ 0.33
Put cut pieces in work-in-process inventory	2 minutes	$ 0.67
Retrieve cut pieces from inventory	5 minutes	$ 1.66
Sew apron	2 minutes each	$ 0.67
Put aprons in work-in-process inventory	2 minutes	$ 0.67
Retrieve aprons from inventory	3 minutes	$ 1.00
Package aprons for shipment	1 minute each	$ 0.33
Ship aprons	10 minutes	$ 3.33

The materials for the commercial apron cost $1, while those for the residential market cost $2. Marketing for the commercial apron is $25,000 per year. The company sells 100,000 commercial aprons per year. Marketing and distribution for the residential aprons is $50,000 per year. The company sells 50,000 units per year into this market.

If Betsy Homemaker could find a way to produce more commercial aprons, it could sell them as it has a very good reputation in the marketplace. The residential market does not hold as much promise, so if Sadie wants to expand her business, it has to come in the commercial lines.

REQUIRED:

a. Calculate the total elapsed time for making an apron.
b. What is the value-added time in this process? State it both in terms of hours and a percentage of total time.
c. What is the total production cost of the two products?
d. Including marketing, what is the total cost for the two lines for a year?
e. What is the total profit per line per year? Unit profit per product?
f. Which product is the most profitable?
g. If Sadie wants to expand output, what activities does she need to focus on to free up time for production?
h. Should Sadie consider having her workforce specialize; that is, to do specific tasks to maximize output? Why or why not? Use a business case structure to make your points.

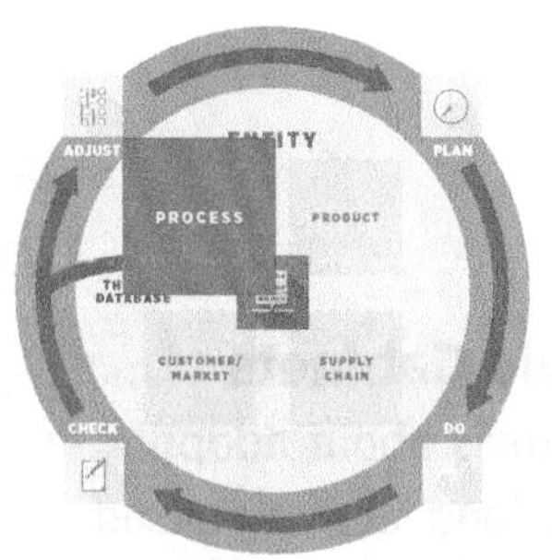

CHAPTER NINE

Evaluating and Improving Process Performance

The most powerful thing you can do to change the world is to change your own beliefs about the nature of life, people, reality, to something more positive.

SHAKTI GAWAIN[1]

CHAPTER ROADMAP

1. The Continuous Improvement Philosophy
   - *East Meets West: Kaizen*
   - *Identifying and Eliminating Waste: Muda*
2. Total Quality Management and the Cost of Quality
   - *Cost of Quality Reporting*
   - *The Taguchi Loss Function*
   - *The Malcolm Baldrige Award*
3. Capacity Analysis and Reporting
   - *Capacity Variance Analysis*
4. Measuring Delivery Performance
5. Incentives and Behavior: A Process Perspective
   - *Using Incentives to Foster Improvement*
   - *Building a Portfolio of Incentives*
   - *Behavioral Issues or, Who's in Charge?*

LEARNING OBJECTIVES

After studying this chapter, you should be able to:

1. **Summarize the basic elements of the continuous improvement philosophy and explain how it is used in process settings.**
2. **Describe the basic features of total quality management and how they are captured in a cost of quality report.**
3. **Develop a capacity variance analysis.**
4. **Explain the four basic delivery metrics used to evaluate process performance.**
5. **Assess the various ways incentives are used to generate and sustain continuous improvement.**

---

1 Allen Klein, *The Wise and Witty Quote Book*, New York: Gramercy Books, 2005: p. 165.

IN CONTEXT ➤ Letting Go and Building Trust at Kinkaid Cabinets

During a recent meeting, Sam accepted Brad's ideas about adopting continuous improvement, process management, and activity-based budgeting at Kinkaid Cabinets. Ever the manager, however, Sam now wanted to know how he would be able to tell that the workforce was achieving its objectives.

"You need to come up with concrete, measurable examples," Shelley told Brad. "There must be variances we can run off of the activity-based budgets. There must be some way to have control over the cells."

"The cells are self-managed: That's the concept behind them. Sam has to learn to trust his workforce if the change process is going to work. We use measurements, such as Shewhart control charts, at the point of action so the workers know when they need to make adjustments. With continuous improvement, the workers are the first line of defense against process problems. Managers are the cheerleaders and facilitators; they make sure that the workers get whatever they need. Management doesn't direct anymore; it listens."

"That may take some getting used to, Brad. Letting go of the reins and having the workers tell management what to do is a bit frightening. Do you really think they can accept this and learn how to do it?"

"They have to, Shelley. That's the only way these new approaches work. All of us must rely on the workers, who will be trained to monitor the process, to let us know when they need help. We need to trust them or the whole system falls apart."

"You've convinced me, Brad. I like being in front of a curve, not catching up to it. I'd love to learn to work with our workforce instead of in spite of them! But I'm not sure others, especially Sam, are ready for it."

WHEN YOU ARE TRYING TO FIND THE WAY TO THE NEAREST RESTAURANT, you assume that you can pull up the category "Restaurants" on your smartphone and then get the driving directions to the restaurant you choose. You are assuming the information on the smartphone is correct and actionable. The assumptions you make about how the world operates, what you pay attention to, and how you apply measurements and ideas to solve problems and manage change allow you to function in highly complex settings. Without assumptions and simplifying notions about "how things work," you would spend so much time analyzing a situation that you would be unable to respond quickly and effectively to shifting conditions. You have to trust your smartphone with these requirements.

However, making the wrong assumptions about the world and how it operates can blind us. For example, we may see only what we are looking for, and gather only the information needed to meet the demands of our "world model." We may choose "Restaurants" and blind ourselves to music venues. While assumptions can provide an efficient way to operate, what we do not notice often matters most. What is not measured is ignored, and what is assumed away in our initial framing of a problem seldom emerges during decision making. It is sometimes said that important solutions are "hidden in plain sight." The technical term for this type of response to data input is **cognitive bias,** *a pattern of deviation in judgment where projections about other people and situations may be drawn in an incomplete or illogical fashion.*

In this chapter, we look at the measurements used to control outcomes in the process domain using the **balanced scorecard,** *a set of measurements that captures the key dimensions of performance in a decision domain*. Consistent with the *continuous improvement philosophy*, we will include quality, productivity, cost, and delivery metrics. Developed in Japan as a means for Japanese corporations to gain a competitive foothold after World War II, the continuous improvement philosophy has transformed modern business—not only in Japan, but around the world—because it changes the key assumptions about what defines and drives profits and performance. Combined with its defined bundles of incentives and measures, the continuous improvement philosophy transforms a culture and an organization from a traditional to a process perspective by applying a distinctive set of assumptions to the business process in order to draw attention to a different set of activities.

The Continuous Improvement Philosophy

OBJECTIVE 1:
Summarize the basic elements of the continuous improvement philosophy and explain how it is used in process settings.

Process management takes a **systems perspective,** *a way of looking at an organization as a whole, not a set of parts.* Everything is interrelated, not a set of independent events and activities, but rather a comprehensive, integrated structure working toward a desired end. Emphasis is shifted from the parts to the whole—from individual actions to bottlenecks and interdependent effects. Small changes in one part of the system directly and immediately impact all other areas, as the linked set of people and processes constantly respond and adapt to changing conditions.

Process management is built on the assumption that every process can be made better in some way—that continuous improvement is always possible whether in terms of cost, quality, delivery, or productivity. To fully understand process management, you have to start at its roots, which lie in the continuous improvement philosophy and the Japanese school of management.

EAST MEETS WEST: KAIZEN

In the mid-1970s, the economy in the United States was shaken to its core by the onslaught of Japanese competition in the steel and auto industries. Japan had slowly regained its productive capability in the aftermath of World War II, but had faced ongoing quality problems that made it very difficult for Japanese companies to compete effectively with products from established Western companies. Recognizing that it would have to provide a superior product to gain a foothold in the West, Japan embarked on a national drive to improve the quality and performance of its products and processes.

Japan faced unique constraints, but had unique strengths that shaped the ways in which it strived to improve its competitive position. Japan is an island nation—both space and natural resources are in scarce supply. Any solution to its competitive challenges had to be shaped around these unavoidable facts of economic life. Its strength, however, arose from the unique combination of Eastern philosophies and cultural norms that defined its social structure. As it made improvements to its management philosophy and methods, Japan moved beyond the lessons of the quality experts, such as Deming and Juran. Reflecting a basic tenet of the Japanese culture—to identify and eliminate waste wherever it occurs—the companies that formed the backbone of the Japanese economy developed and implemented *kaizen* management methods (see Figure 9.1).

FIGURE 9.1 KAIZEN MANAGEMENT HAS BEEN APPLIED WITH GREAT SUCCESS TO JAPANESE MANUFACTURING.

Kaizen—*the philosophy of continuous improvement that starts with recognizing problems and then looks to everyone in the organization to solve them*—is the embodiment of the Japanese approach to management and business structures, which is often called *lean management*. As described by Dr. Masaaki Imai, a noted expert on Japanese management systems:

> *Kaizen means improvement...ongoing improvement involving everyone—top management, managers, and workers. Kaizen is everybody's business.*[2]

2 Masaaki Imai, Kaizen: *The Key to Japan's Competitive Success*, New York: Random House, 1986: p. ix.

If you were asked to name the most important difference between Japanese and Western management concepts, the answer would be simple: Japanese kaizen and its process-oriented way of thinking vs. the West's innovation and results-oriented thinking. Kaizen starts with recognizing that every corporation has problems. Kaizen solves these problems by establishing a corporate culture in which these problems can be openly discussed. Kaizen uses a customer-driven strategy to drive improvement efforts. In kaizen, all activities are assumed to lead to increased customer satisfaction.

Reflecting the Japanese view that change is an ongoing, constant event, kaizen is deeply ingrained in Japanese thinking. It reflects the ancient Japanese proverb, "If a man has not been seen for three days, his friends should take a good look at him to see what changes have befallen him."[3]

Kaizen improvement is focused on small changes to the status quo made as a result of ongoing efforts. On the other hand, **innovation** *is a far-reaching change to the status quo that often is the result of a large investment in new technology and/or equipment and/or process improvements*. Both of these changes are in stark contrast to **maintenance,** *upkeep that reinforces existing practices and assumptions*. The relationships among the three and their impact on performance over a period of time are illustrated in Figure 9.2.

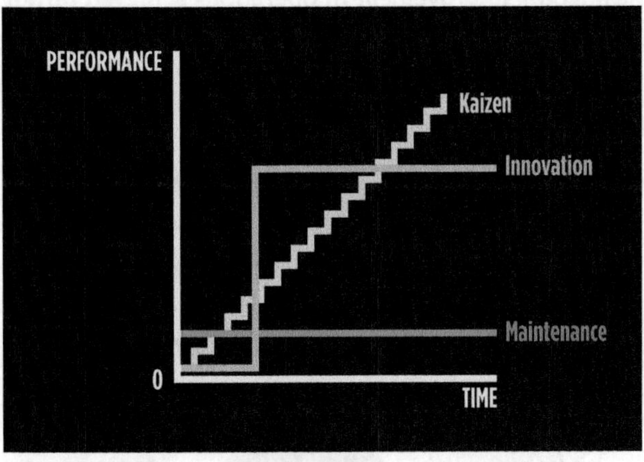

FIGURE 9.2 IMPACT OF CHANGE AS COMPARED WITH MAINTENANCE ON PERFORMANCE IS SIGNIFICANT; NOTICE HOW BOTH KAIZEN AND INNOVATION RISE OVER TIME WHILE MAINTENANCE REMAINS FLAT AFTER A SMALL INITIAL RISE.

Kaizen leads to process-oriented thinking, because, to improve results, the processes themselves must be improved. In Japan, kaizen is everybody's business. Managers do not make the decisions—they facilitate learning on the part of self-directed work teams and individuals working within the overall production system. People improve the process; management supports and stimulates these efforts. Clearly, part of this improvement can be created by the **learning curve,** *the ability of people to become better at a task through frequent repetition*. The intrinsic and extrinsic rewards that come with kaizen management,

3 ibid, p. 5.

however, move improvement beyond those that could be obtained solely by the learning curve because of the constant changing of standards to reflect the view that performance can always improve. Kaizen does not look solely to individual learning, but seeks to identify process changes that can lead to an overall improvement for all individuals in the process.

As you can see, these beliefs are quite contrary to scientific management. Where scientific management looks to remove decision making and control from line workers, kaizen gives it back. In fact, on every major assumption shaping management's actions and responsibilities, traditional Western and kaizen approaches differ markedly. While both can pursue continuous improvement, they do it in very different ways. They are opposite, not complementary or comparable, models. Gaining the improvements pursued in kaizen requires eliminating waste from processes; whereas, gaining the improvements using the Western approach focuses more on trying to make labor more productive.

IDENTIFYING AND ELIMINATING WASTE: MUDA

If we were to ask five managers to define the continuous improvement philosophy, it is likely more than one would talk about the ongoing improvement in operations achieved through the elimination of waste. **Muda (the Japanese term for waste)** *is the continuous process of eliminating waste from operations*, which, as we have seen, can be found in every process and every activity. Some of the various forms muda can take are detailed in Figure 9.3.

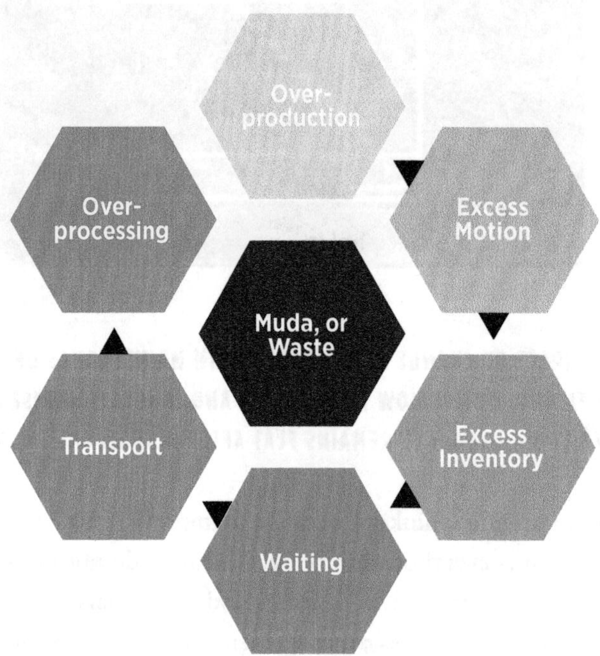

FIGURE 9.3 WASTE IS FOUND IN ALL PROCESSES AND ACTIVITIES. WITH CONTINUOUS IMPROVEMENT, IT IS ELIMINATED BEFORE IT BECOMES EXTREME AND DETRIMENTAL TO THE PROCESS OR ACTIVITY.

As you can see, kaizen and muda are complementary terms. When we use the word kaizen, we are focusing on ways to improve the throughput of a process or operation. Muda is the means by which improvement is attained—through the elimination of wasteful activities and operations. For instance, overproduction refers to situations where there may not be an order for a specific product, but it is made anyway in order to keep machines and people busy. The problem is, the unneeded production can eliminate flexibility—if a new order comes in, the required machines and people may be tied up working on the unnecessary output. When we use the term muda, therefore, we are trying to find areas where the organization is actually trying to do too much—it is doing work that either has no value to customers or is not required right now, if ever. Driving out waste and looking for every opportunity to improve performance are two of the guiding principles of Japanese management.

In the world of kaizen, all of the sources of waste have to be managed to ensure that the organization as a whole functions smoothly for customers and other stakeholders. Eliminating waste becomes a form of organizational religion, where everyone is given the right, and responsibility, to find better ways to do the work. While eliminating waste can be a top-down activity, it works best when the workforce is closely involved.

Total Quality Management and the Cost of Quality

OBJECTIVE 2

Describe the basic features of total quality management and how they are captured in a cost of quality report.

Improving *process* performance begins by finding and fixing the "hot spot"—the activity in this linked chain of customers that is constraining the efforts of everyone involved in the process. Total quality management (TQM) is not simply a tool, but a number of interrelated concepts and models that emphasize quality in terms of all of the processes and activities that occur in an organization. It is premised on the belief that the successful organization constantly seeks out ways to improve its products, processes, and services—in order to achieve continuous improvement. With an ever-watchful eye on ensuring that customer expectations are met, TQM provides the basis for sustainable growth.

Xerox Corporation opened a research center to implement TQM. Xerox focuses on benchmarking, a reduced supplier base, and leadership teams in its pursuit of TQM. Benchmarking is widely used by improvement teams. It provides a standard or point of reference for measuring performance of a process or operation. When a company uses benchmarking to guide its improvement efforts, it looks at what the competition is doing and sets a level of quality and value against which it compares all of its products. Once the standard that has been set is met, then a new and higher standard is set so that the company is continually striving to do better and have a higher-quality product.

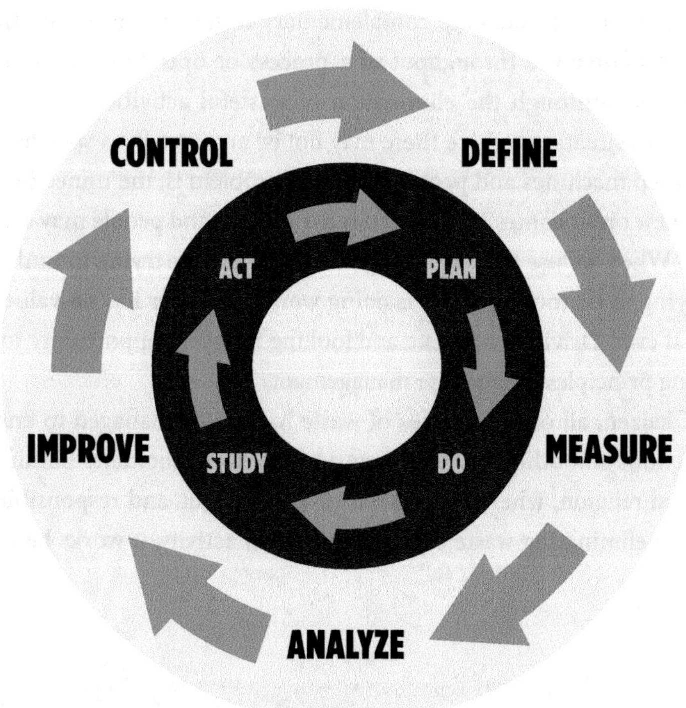

FIGURE 9.4 THE TQM CYCLE AT XEROX EMBEDS THE MANAGEMENT PROCESS WITHIN A CYCLE OF CONTINUOUS IMPROVEMENT.

What exactly does the term "quality" mean? Dictionaries offer many definitions, but two are the most applicable to the TQM movement. The first defines quality in terms of *product features*. In other words, in the customer's eyes, the product with the most attributes has the highest quality. This definition emphasizes customer satisfaction and competitive concerns. A high-quality product should support a price premium in the market or achieve a higher market share, both of which boost revenues. Thus, a product-defined view of quality looks at quality solely in terms of its competitive effects.

The second definition of quality emphasizes *reliability*. Specifically, it defines quality in terms of *freedom from deficiencies*—the fewer the problems or deficiencies of a product, the better.[4] Higher quality means lower operating costs for the consumer as well as lower error rates, scrap, and rework for the producer. The result is a reduction in field failures, warranty costs, and customer dissatisfaction and improved capacity utilization and material yields. **Quality**, therefore, has two definitions: (1) *a product or process that contains the most desired characteristics*, and (2) *the lack of flaws in a product or process*.

4 Joseph M. Juran, *Juran on Quality by Design*, New York: The Free Press, 1992: p. 9.

One of the most popular books in the TQM movement, *Quality Is Free*, was written in the late 1970s by Philip Crosby.[5] Although almost 50 years have passed since its publication, this book provides a good starting point for understanding TQM by identifying the four "absolutes" of effective quality management[6]:

- Quality is ***defined*** as conformance to requirements, not "goodness."
- Prevention, not detection, is the best ***system*** for achieving quality.
- The performance ***standard*** is zero defects, not "That's close enough."
- The price of nonconformance (quality failures), not indexes, is the ***measurement*** of quality.

TQM is often thought to have been born from Japanese management practices, but, in reality, it was developed by two American management experts in the mid-1950s: Joseph M. Juran and William Edwards Deming. Finding their message about quality falling on deaf ears in the United States, they both agreed to accept extended engagements in Japan in 1954. Japan was looking for a way to gain a solid foothold in the global economy, and turned to TQM as a means of overcoming the perception that its products were of poor quality. Table 9.1 summarizes the key elements of Deming's and Juran's views on the essentials of effective quality management.[7]

TABLE 9.1 ESSENTIALS OF EFFECTIVE TQM, ACCORDING TO DEMING AND JURAN

Deming's Universal 14 Points	Juran's Steps to Quality Improvement
1. Create consistency of purpose with a plan.	1. Develop management commitment.
2. Adopt the new philosophy of quality.	2. Create a cross-functional quality improvement team.
3. Cease dependence on mass inspection.	3. Establish quality measurements for every process and activity.
4. End the practice of choosing suppliers solely on price.	4. Estimate the cost of quality to identify where to focus improvements.
5. Identify problems and work continuously to improve the system.	5. Take corrective action based on the information gained in 3 and 4.
6. Adopt modern methods of training on the job.	6. Raise quality awareness among employees.
7. Change the focus from production numbers (quantity) to quality.	7. Establish zero defects planning.
8. Drive out fear.	8. Establish a "zero defects" day.
9. Break down barriers between departments.	9. Conduct supervisory training at all levels.
10. Stop requesting improved productivity without providing methods to achieve it.	10. Teams and individuals should establish quality improvement goals.
11. Eliminate work standards that prescribe numerical quotas.	11. Encourage employees to communicate problems that prevent error-free work.
12. Remove barriers to pride of workmanship.	12. Give public, nonfinancial recognition.
13. Institute vigorous education and retraining.	13. Establish a quality council that meets regularly to share experiences and ideas.
14. Create a structure in top management that will emphasize the preceding 13 points every day.	14. Do it all over again.

5 Philip Crosby, *Quality Is Free*, New York: McGraw-Hill, 1979.
6 From *Quality*, a promotional brochure by Phillip Crosby Associates, Inc.
7 Juran developed a 10-step TQM approach that can be found in *Quality Is Free*, op.cit. from which we have developed "Juran's Steps to Quality Improvement" in Table 9.1.

As you can see, both authors view the tenets of TQM in much the same way. Both emphasize placing quality control in the hands of the workforce and using training to ensure that the right thing is done the first time, every time. You do not inspect quality in TQM; you build it in with every process and activity that takes place in the organization.

Measurement plays a key role in creating a TQM-driven organization. Operational measures, such as first-pass quality rates and defect rates per million parts produced, are used by most organizations to assess and track their quality improvement projects. Financial metrics, such as the **cost of quality,** *the price of defects, rework, and failure experienced as a result of a company's processes and external customers*, are also used to track the impact of TQM initiatives.

Henry Ford knew that waste was one of the biggest challenges facing business organizations. He wrote extensively about waste in his book *Today and Tomorrow,* which was published in 1926. What did Ford have to tell us?

LOOKING BACK ➤ Henry Ford and Learning from Waste

If one used nothing then one would waste nothing. That seems plain enough. But look at it from another angle. If we use nothing at all, is not then the waste total? Is it conservation or waste to withdraw a public resource wholly from use? If a man skimps himself through all the best years of his life in order to provide for his old age, has he conserved his resources or has he wasted them? Has he been constructively or destructively thrifty?

How are we to reckon waste? Usually, we count waste in terms of materials. If a housewife buys twice as much food as her family eats and throws the rest away, she is considered wasteful. But on the other hand, is the housewife who gives her family only half enough to eat thrifty? Not at all. She is even more wasteful than the first housewife, for she is wasting human lives. She is withdrawing from her family the strength which they need to do their work in the world...

A man cannot be paid much for producing something which is to be wasted....My theory of waste goes back of the thing itself into the labour of producing it. We want to get full value out of labour so that we may be able to pay it full value. It is use—not conservation—that interests us. We want to use material to its utmost in order that the time of men may not be lost. Material costs nothing. It is of no account until it comes into the hands of management...

Saving material because it is material, and saving material because it represents labour might seem to amount to the same thing. But the approach makes a great deal of difference. We will use material more carefully if we think of it as labour. For instance, we will not so lightly waste material simply because we can reclaim it—for salvage involves labor. The ideal is to have nothing to salvage.

Henry Ford, *Today and Tomorrow,* Garden City, N.Y.: Doubleday, Page & Company, 1926: pp. 89-91.

COST OF QUALITY REPORTING

One of the major innovations in management reporting resulting from the implementation of TQM is the **cost of quality report,** *an itemization of the various causes and costs of quality-related activities*. It is used to examine an organization's activities to determine whether or not it is focused on some element of the quality puzzle. Those that have something to do with quality are isolated in the activity-based management system to provide management with the information needed to determine whether or not quality is improving. Management is incentivized to provide high quality over poor quality by the marketplace, which seeks to find the best product at the best price. Anyone who goes online to shop understands the relationship between quality and price. Online shopping sites, such as Amazon.com, provide a comprehensive list of prices by product and providers' service rating. Success comes to the products and companies that receive the highest satisfaction ratings at a highly competitive price. The companies that trade on Amazon.com, along with the managers who run them, get very clear signals on their relative performance from the market in real time and real terms.

TABLE 9.2 COSTS OF QUALITY DEFINED

Cost	Definition
Prevention	Activities focused on eliminating quality problems before they start.
Detection, or appraisal costs	Activities designed to inspect or screen input and output to uncover problems.
Internal	Quality outlays associated with scrap and rework problems detected in a product or process.
External	Quality problems experienced directly by the customer.

A cost of quality report includes four basic categories of quality costs, which are explained in Table 9.2. Table 9.3 lists the categories and presents some examples of the causes within those categories.

TABLE 9.3 COST OF QUALITY: CATEGORIES AND EXAMPLES

Prevention	Detection	Internal Failure	External Failure
Process improvement	Raw material inspection	Scrap units	Warranty repairs
Product improvement	Packaging inspection	Rework units	Returns
Reengineering	In-process inspection	Repair costs	Customer complaints
Supplier certification	Final inspection	Rework cells	Lost sales
Pilot testing	Field testing	Scrap costs	Poor quality ratings
Training of workforce	Piece part inspection	Recalibration	Recalls
TQM training	Trial runs	Salvage	Short product life
Customer surveys	Burn-in tests	Design changes	Functional failure
Quality audits	First-pass parts	Quality-based downtime	On-site repair calls

A cost of quality report categorizes the spending that has taken place during a period based on what type of quality cost it is. The cost of quality metric that is often used is:

Cost of Quality = Cost of Good Quality + Cost of Poor Quality

Good quality costs are prevention and detection costs (also known as appraisal costs); poor quality costs are internal and external failure.

A typical report is illustrated in Table 9.4. As an examination of the table shows, this company has significant internal and external failure costs: the worst form of quality problems. These are the worst failure because the company has incurred all of the costs of production and have failed to meet, and perhaps even disappointed, final customers. It needs to spend more money on training and such things as supplier certification to head off many of the problems before they arise. Companies of all types and sizes are in the midst of a quality revolution. GE saved $12 billion over five years and added $1 to its earnings per share. Honeywell (AlliedSignal) recorded more than $800 million in savings.[8]

TABLE 9.4 COST OF QUALITY REPORT

Quality Category	Activity	Cost	Total cost
Prevention	Training	$25,000	0.98%
	Process improvement	$50,000	1.96%
	Customer workshops	$15,000	0.59%
	Supplier certification	$23,000	0.90%
Total Prevention Costs		$113,000	4.43%
Detection	Inspection	$75,000	2.94%
	Trial runs	$30,000	1.18%
	Burn-in tests	$45,000	1.77%
	Shewhart control charts	$10,000	0.39%
Total Detection Costs		$160,000	6.28%
Internal Failure	Scrap	$350,000	13.74%
	Rework	$250,000	9.81%
	Salvage	$175,000	6.87%
	Repair cells	$300,000	11.77%
Total Internal Failure		$1,075,000	42.19%
External Failure	Warranty work	$275,000	10.79%
	Repair cells	$500,000	19.62%
	Customer complaints	$250,000	9.81%
	Returns	$175,000	6.87%
Total External Failure		$1,200,000	47.10%
Total Cost of Quality		$2,548,000	100.00%

8 These figures were posted on March 30, 2014, at the website www.isixsigma.com/implementation/financial-analysis/six-sigma-costs-and-savings/.

In Table 9.4, the total cost of quality is $2,548,000. Of this, only $273,000 (10.7%) is the cost of good quality, while $2,275,000 (89.3%) is the cost of poor quality due to internal product or service failures (42.19%), and, worst of all, external failures that directly affect the customer (47.1%). It is clear that more money needs to be spent on prevention and detection if internal and external failure costs are going to be reduced. A company that incurs external failure costs of this magnitude will quite likely have problems keeping customers.

Once a customer is faced with a problem, the long-term impact on the company's reputation can spell disaster. This is increasingly true in today's electronic world where problems get aired on the internet long before a company has the chance to fix them. For instance, problems with the battery of the Chevrolet Volt became widely known, negatively impacting sales of this promising new technology. No amount of marketing can overcome major quality failures in the customers' eyes. People shop for information before they buy, and, if that information is negative, sales will suffer.

Cost of quality reports are not normally reviewed every day. Rather, they are part of the monthly, quarterly, and/or annual reviews of process performance. When an organization is seeking major improvements in quality performance, it will generate quality reports more often. Once quality is under control, attention can be directed to other measurements. In evaluating prior performance, management and the workforce teams get a better idea of where they need to focus their attention in the future. These reports are a useful tool, one that ties accounting to the shop floor in a valuable way. The information can be trended over time or analyzed as an annual event. The more intense the need to improve quality, the more likely quality information will be trended over time. Figure 9.5 illustrates some of the costs of quality in terms of their visibility to management.

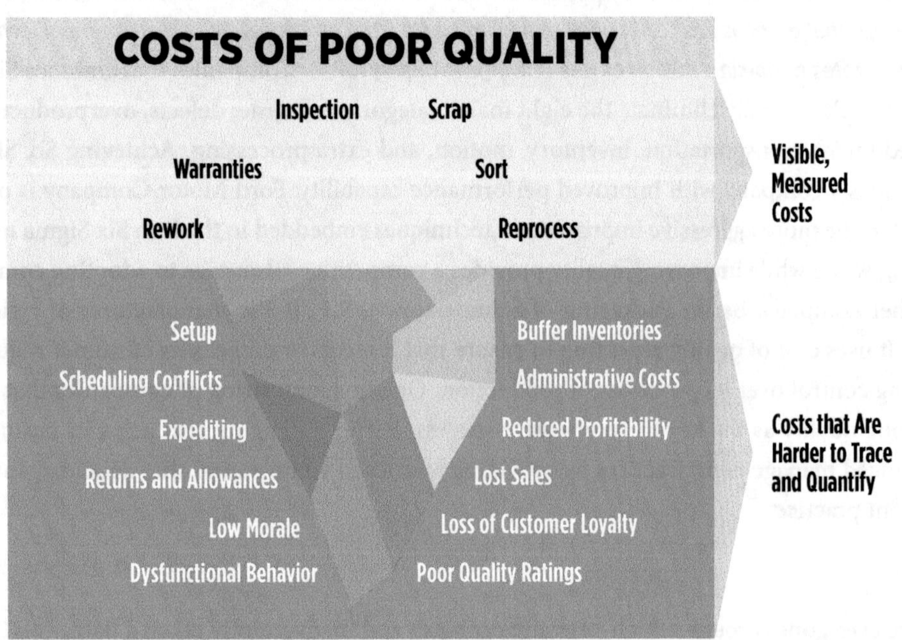

FIGURE 9.5 THE TIP OF THE ICEBERG ILLUSTRATES THOSE COSTS THAT ARE EASILY DISCERNIBLE. AS WE GO DEEPER AND DEEPER, THE COSTS ARE MORE DIFFICULT TO IDENTIFY AND QUANTIFY.

There are five basic steps needed to compile a cost of quality report:

1. Define the product(s) or process(es) being measured. This sets the scope for the study.
2. Identify components of the four measurement areas: prevention, detection, internal failure, and external failure. Some measures, such as customer impact, may be hard to quantify. If this occurs, look for the closest measurable event and use this information in the report.
3. Identify the costs attributable to each of the chosen measurements. This should include both direct costs and those indirect costs that can be reasonably attached to the activity. Waste of any form should always be included in the cost measures.
4. Compile the information into a cost of quality report.
5. Use the information to develop cost of quality metrics.

Xerox started its drive towards TQM in the 1970s with the opening of its Palo Alto Research Center. Launching the research facility was one of Xerox's ways of implementing TQM even while TQM was in its infancy in the United States. Now that TQM has become known in the marketplace, Xerox has established its own program to obtain it. Xerox focuses on benchmarking, a reduced supplier base, and leadership teams in its utilization of TQM principles. Xerox looks at what the competition is doing and sets a level of quality and value higher than what is currently available in the market for all of its products. These quality standards are often adopted by other companies because of Xerox's excellent standards. Once the standard that has been set is met, then a new and higher standard is set so that the company is continually striving to do better and have a higher-quality product.

Many companies are moving beyond the lessons contained in TQM to embrace **lean Six Sigma,** *a managerial concept that emphasizes continually removing waste from processes (lean management) while striving to reduce defect rates to one in a million or less (Six Sigma quality level)*. Companies that embrace Six Sigma as a guiding principle virtually eliminate the eight major categories of waste: defects, overproduction, waiting, nonutilized talent, transportation, inventory, motion, and extra processing. Achieving Six Sigma quality levels provides a company with improved performance capability. Ford Motor Company is one firm that has turned to the more aggressive improvement techniques embedded in the lean Six Sigma methodology. Eliminating waste while improving quality provides a competitive advantage to adopting companies.

Another company, Berlin Packaging of Saunderstown, R.I., is the manufacturer of rigid packaging materials. It uses cost of quality reporting to ensure that it meets or exceeds its customer requirements by maintaining control over its processes of production. One in a long string of companies that have turned to improving quality as the key to competitive success, Berlin Packaging also helps its customers implement advanced management practices by providing a series of white papers that detail key innovations in management practice.

THE TAGUCHI LOSS FUNCTION

If you have ever gone through a high-pressure car wash and inadvertently taken a bath, you have actually experienced the lessons taught by the **Taguchi loss function,** *a statistical tool that analyzes the impact of variation on overall customer satisfaction*. Basically, the probability of getting wet depends on whether the door and door frame of your car come into contact correctly. If the door meets specifications, but is a little on the small side, and the frame meets specifications, but is a little on the large side (and we mean very little here), you will get wet. If the door is a tad too large and the frame a bit too small, you will have trouble closing the door. Small variations make a big difference.

Emphasizing the impact of design and process variation on product reliability, the Taguchi loss function is a statistical approach to quality that stresses the need to hit the specification target, not simply to get close. It places more weight on errors that fall within our control limits than we have seen with our Shewhart control charts, suggesting that the cost of not meeting specifications grows quadratically rather than linearly. The formula for the Taguchi loss function is very straightforward. It is:

$$L(y) = k(y - T)^2$$

Where:

k = a proportionally constant cost related to the firm's external cost of quality
y = actual observed value of the quality characteristic
T = target, or correct, value for the quality characteristic
L = the quality loss

Let us use a simple example, such as that depicted in Table 9.5, based on the leaky door, to get a better understanding of how the equation works. First, let us assume a company has done a study of its external failure costs and determined that it costs the company $500 when a quality failure in the customer's hands occurred. So (k) = $500. On the plant floor, we observe the following results: If the cell makes the doors a bit too small, they leak; if the cell makes the doors a bit too big, they are hard to close. The target size is 28 inches.

TABLE 9.5 TAGUCHI LOSS FUNCTION CALCULATION

Unit	Actual Observation	Y - T	$(y - T)^2$	$k(y - T)^2$
1	28.1	0.1	0.01	$5.00
2	27.9	-0.1	0.01	$5.00
3	28.2	0.2	0.04	$20.00
4	27.8	-0.2	0.04	$20.00
Total			0.10	$50.00
Average			0.025	$12.50

As illustrated in Table 9.5, the loss on units 1 and 2 is $5 each; the loss on units 3 and 4 expands to $20 each because the deviation from the target (T) is larger. When we calculate the average of the four observations, we find that the average variation is 0.025, or a cost of $12.50 as the average loss. Note that the loss is taken as an average of the four observations, not as 0.025 times $50, which would only be $1.25. We average out the observations, not the application of the formula in this final cell. In other words:

$50 / 4 = $12.50 **average loss**

Companies that use lean Six Sigma rely on measurements such as the Taguchi loss function to help provide the justification for driving defects to zero and constantly pursuing continuous improvement in their processes and products.

IN THE NEWS ➤ Six Sigma at Caterpillar, Inc.

Caterpillar, Inc., the large manufacturer of heavy construction equipment, gas engines, locomotives, and other equipment, introduced Six Sigma processes in 2001. Its approach included what it called the "DMAIC methodology," which stands for Define, Measure, Analyze, Improve, and Control.

The goal was both to provide a structured approach for tackling needed cost improvements and to embed these concepts into all of its employees' thinking. The company reported record sales and profits from 2003 to 2008. Equally important, company management credits Six Sigma and related processes for helping the company implement its cost reduction plans, called "trough plans," to help it survive the severe recession that started in 2008. Caterpillar was well-positioned for the recession because it had explored what could be done to reduce non-value-added costs ahead of time.

Source: David G. DeFreitas, John W. Gillet, Ross L. Fink, and Whitney Cox, "Getting Lean and Mean at Caterpillar with ABM," *Strategic Finance*, January 2013, pp. 24-33.

THE MALCOLM BALDRIGE AWARD

The Malcolm Baldrige National Quality Award *is a national award given to companies that exhibit quality in their leadership, customer focus, process and workforce management, and related areas.* It is a highly prestigious award given for quality performance in the small business, healthcare, education, and nonprofit sectors of the U.S. economy. Companies receiving the Baldrige Award serve as role models and are active in best-in-class benchmarking activities. It is awarded by the president of the United States based on the recommendations of a board of examiners; the program is run by the National Institute of Standards and Technology, which is part of the Department of Commerce. Up to 18 awards can be given annually. The award was established by an act of Congress in 1987, and the first three awards were given in 1988. As of 2016, 109 organizations have received the award, including Memorial Hermann Sugar Land Hospital in Texas in 2016 and the Charter School of San Diego in 2015.

The Baldrige Framework for Performance Excellence, illustrated in Figure 9.6, focuses on these seven criteria as they apply to the healthcare industry:

1. **Leadership** looks at how well senior executives guide the organization and how well the organization reflects good citizenship principles.
2. **Strategic planning** emphasizes how the organization sets it direction and develops key action plans.
3. **Customer focus** is concerned with how well the company acquires, satisfies, and retains its customers.
4. **Measurement, analysis, and knowledge management** concentrates on how well the company uses data and information to support its processes and performance management systems.
5. **Workforce focus** examines how well the company deploys the full potential of its workforce and its alignment with company objectives.
6. **Process management** considers how key processes are designed, managed, and improved.
7. **Results** take into account both the performance metrics used by the organization (customer satisfaction, financial and marketplace performance, human resources, supplier and partner performance, operational performance, and governance and social responsibility) and how the organization performs against these metrics.

Baldrige Criteria Applied to Healthcare

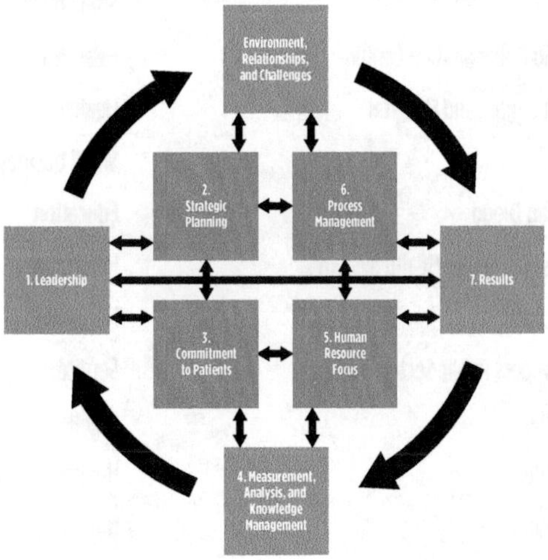

FIGURE 9.6 THE BALDRIGE FRAMEWORK FOR PERFORMANCE EXCELLENCE SHOWS INTERRELATIONSHIPS AMONG THE SEVEN CRITERIA.

The Baldrige Framework for Performance Excellence serves two main purposes: (1) to identify Baldrige Award recipients that will serve as role models for other organizations; and (2) to guide organizations in assessing their overall process performance and competitiveness. Baldrige Award recipients are considered to be "best practice" firms. Part of the award requirements is that recipients participate in benchmarking studies conducted by other organizations in order to provide a basis for overall improvement in business practices in the United States.

Sutter Davis Hospital (SDH) was the first organization in the greater Sacramento, Calif., area and the smallest hospital ever to receive the Malcolm Baldrige National Quality Award. Following Baldrige practices, SDH became a top performer in several areas, including ratings on readmission rates and the average length of hospital stays for pneumonia, heart failure, and acute myocardial infarction.

Moreover, SDH has constantly improved its emergency room wait time, reducing average door-to-door times from 45 minutes in 2008 to under 20 minutes in 2015. The average time for California emergency rooms is 58 minutes. Furthermore, the Hospital Consumer Assessment of Healthcare Providers and Systems (HCAHPS) has given SDH an overall hospital rating at or above 90% since 2011. SDH also ranks in the top 10% for communication with doctors and nurses, and discharge information. It has also ranked in the top 10% for physician satisfaction since 2008, and it has met and surpassed the goals of the entire Sutter Health Sacramento Region healthcare system for employee satisfaction and participation since 2009. Finally, its overall rating for inpatient services is in the 98th percentile. Constantly striving to improve the quality of and access to healthcare services, SDH embodies the Baldrige commitment to excellence.

TABLE 9.6 RECENT BALDRIGE AWARD WINNERS

Year	Baldrige Winners	Sector
2016	Don Chalmers Ford	Small business
	Momentum Group	Small business
	Kindred Nursing and Rehabilitation Center	Healthcare
	Memorial Hermann Sugar Land Hospital	Healthcare
2015	Midway USA	Small business
	Charter School of San Diego	Education
	Charleston Area Medical Center Health System	Healthcare
	Mid-America Transplant	Nonprofit
2014	PriceWaterhouseCoopers Public Sector Practice	Service
	Hill Country Memorial	Healthcare
	St. David's Healthcare	Healthcare
	Elevations Credit Union	Nonprofit
2013	Pewaukee School District	Education
	Sutter Davis Hospital	Healthcare

The Baldrige Award also supports the drive toward delivering increasing levels of value to customers and stakeholders throughout the various Baldrige industries. This contributes to organizational sustainability and competitiveness. It also supports improvements in the effectiveness and efficiency of participating firms, serving as a basis for both organizational and personal learning and growth. The program is relatively inexpensive to sustain and provides a wide range of benefits, such as improved reputation and profit margins to participating firms and organizations. Organizations that "go lean" by pursuing TQM gain added benefits when they pursue the Baldrige Award. It solidifies their learning and provides the impetus to continuously improve quality. Table 9.6 provides a list of recent winners of the Baldrige Award. As you can see, the winners span industries and are organizations of various sizes. What determines a Baldrige winner is the organization's dedication to ongoing performance excellence.

IN CONTEXT ➤ Implementing Lean at Kinkaid Cabinets

"Sam, we've been through all the reviews, and would like to try to implement some of the lean techniques we've discussed. We'd also like to let the teams manage themselves. It will be a real morale booster when they see how much trust we're placing in them!"

"I don't know, Brad. I've been managing in the same way for over 30 years, and you're telling me a bunch of new tools will eliminate the need for managers on the shop floor. I'll have to see it to believe it!"

"It's worked in a great many places, Sam. They've made the workforce responsible for setting the pace of their work and helping to design the flow so that it's balanced. Of course, they are cross-trained so everyone on the shop floor can help out on the line where needed. They are shown how to implement the TQM system; it's been shown to result in a neater, more organized plant floor and saves valuable time now spent looking for tools. You know how often that happens."

"Who is going to do all of this training, Brad? Shelley can't do it. I don't see how you can since you're still new to the idea. How much will it cost in training and consulting fees to make this new system work? Are the savings really worth it?"

"I've gotten several quotes. Here they are—take a look. It's really not that expensive, especially if we start by training only one work team. My thought is to focus on modular office furniture until we gain some expertise. My bet is that once the line starts working the way I believe it can, you're going to be one of the system's biggest cheerleaders!"

"I'll let you have a go at it, Brad, but just so you know, I'll also pull the plug if it doesn't come up to our production standards in six weeks. Experimenting with my plant floor makes me nervous!"

"Thanks, Sam—you won't be sorry!"

Capacity Analysis and Reporting

OBJECTIVE 3:
Develop a capacity variance analysis.

The continuous improvement model challenges many long-held views in cost management, including the method chosen to be "best." In traditional settings, the emphasis is placed on using standards that remain unchanged throughout the year, and that reflect the planned activity level established during the budget cycle. Engineered standard cost has been the method of choice in this "meet standard" world. In a continuous improvement worldview, a **capacity cost management system (CCMS)**—*a complete set of tools and measures for monitoring and managing process or machine capacity utilization*—measures cost and productivity for managers.

When continuous improvement is a company's manufacturing philosophy, management's emphasis shifts from identifying the "one best way" of doing work to the constant analysis of performance and a search for ways to improve performance. In this setting, the "best" cost estimate is, in fact, a **trended actual average cost**—*a rolling average of actual costs, where cost moves across time, and as one observation is added to the data set, the oldest is eliminated.* It is the trends in unit cost estimates and their underlying drivers that are managed. An information system that fails to capture these trends robs management of the ability to isolate problems, analyze both the operational and financial impact of proposed changes, and assess whether improvements are achieved.

In a continuous improvement world, there is also an expanded need to understand and manage capacity. Since the machines or bottlenecks ultimately end up governing output, the only way more can be produced without huge expenditures in resources is to figure out ways to get the most out of the equipment or processes already in place. Of course, we never want to produce solely to keep a machine busy, but, when faced with increased demand, management should seek to better utilize the capacity it has before purchasing new machinery. One of the ways we identify the available capacity is with **capacity variance analysis,** *a comparison between the actual performance on a machine or process and the standard set for its operation; both the productivity of a process as well as its costs are examined.*

CAPACITY VARIANCE ANALYSIS

A simple example illustrates what can happen when capacity is not optimally managed. A manufacturer of bottled beers has a high-speed bottling line that the manufacturer rates as being able to make 2,000 bottles per minute. Company engineers have set the rated speed at 1,400 bottles per minute to account for process irregularities. The plant currently operates 5.5 days per week for 16 hours per day. Last week's average output was 1,022 bottles per minute. Finally, the company currently makes $0.10 profit per bottle made. With this information, we can determine how the week's effort stacks up against the company's potential. Table 9.7 defines the various ways we can view capacity ranging from the theoretical to the actual.

TABLE 9.7 TYPES OF CAPACITY

Type of Capacity	Definition
Theoretical	Quantity a machine or process could produce if it performed continuously 24/7; the best a process could be.
Practical	Theoretical capacity reduced to reflect unavoidable downtime for maintenance and related issues.
Budgeted	Planned utilization of a machine or process for a given year.
Normal	The average use of a machine or process over three to five years.
Actual	Quantity a machine or process produces over a period of time.

If this firm used all of its available time on the machine, its *theoretical capacity* would be 20,160,000 bottles per week (10,080 minutes per week times 2,000 bottles per minute or BPM; see Figure 9.7). This is deemed *impractical* because of normal occurrences such as machine maintenance, and results in a rate adjustment of 30%, which brings its *practical capacity* down to 14,112,000 bottles per week or BPW (10,080 minutes per week times 1,400 BPM). The *normal* practice, based on management decisions, is to operate the machine only 5.5 days, 16 hours per day, resulting in only 7,392,000 BPW (5,280 minutes per week times 1,400 BPM), the machine's *normal capacity*. Because the projected demand for the beer is low this year, the machine's *budgeted capacity* is 6,500,000 BPW. But *actual capacity*, or yield, as a result of unanticipated problems is only 5,396,160 units (5,280 minutes per week times 1,022 BPM).

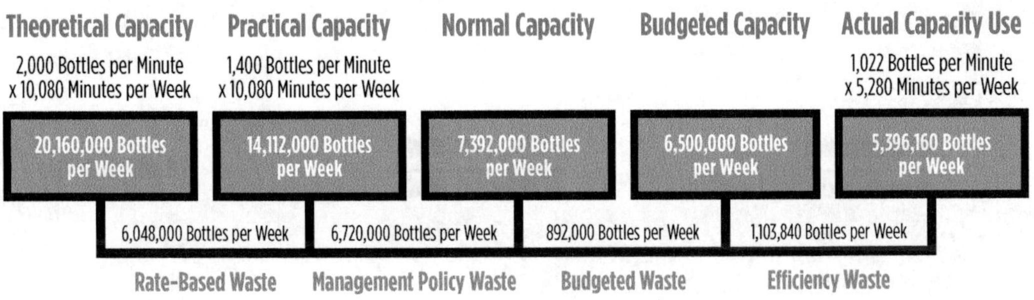

FIGURE 9.7 CAPACITY UTILIZATION CAN BE VIEWED AS A SERIES OF VARIANCES THAT MOVE A COMPANY AWAY FROM OPTIMAL OUTPUT TO ACTUAL USE.

As you can see, this analysis contains four variances:

1. **Rate-based waste:** The difference between theoretical capacity and practical capacity. This is considered waste because it is output that is sacrificed based on the assumption that the machine can operate effectively only 70% of the time.

2. **Management policy waste:** Management's decision about how many hours to staff the plant drives the potential output down to 7,392,000 bottles; 6,720,000 bottles are therefore wasted.
3. **Budgeted waste:** Management builds in another 892,000 wasted bottles.
4. **Efficiency waste:** Problems running the line result in 1,103,840 bottles lost.

All of these forms of waste have an implicit cost of 10 cents a bottle of foregone profit. In isolating this waste as well as the cost of good units, a CCMS provides two of the four desired metrics of performance: cost and productivity. A caution is in order, however. If we rely solely on capacity measurements to plan production, there can be a tendency to produce to inventory to use more capacity. This is not the goal. Instead, we should use this information to make sure that when demand increases, existing machines are utilized to their fullest before more capital investment is added to the business.

We can understand a great deal about why measurement assumptions matter when we compare the actual utilization of the bottle-filling machines with the view management is likely to take of the efficiency of the process; that is, it is likely to believe it is operating at 73% of capacity (5,396,160 BPW divided by normal volumes of 7,392,000 BPW) when it is only using 26.8% of available capacity (5,396,160 BPW divided by 20,160,000 BPW) on the machine. This means it is also foregoing $1.476 million in potential profit from this machine per week (20,160,000 BPW less 5,396,160 BPW times 10 cents profit per bottle). Table 9.8 shows the two calculations.

TABLE 9.8 CAPACITY UTILIZATION MEASURES

Actual Utilization / **Theoretical Capacity**	5,396,160 **BPW** / 20,160,000 **BPW**	26.8% **utilization**
Actual Utilization / **Normal Capacity**	5,396,160 **BPW** / 7,392,000 **BPW**	73.0% **utilization**

Management might feel compelled to improve utilization when the line is achieving only 73% efficiency, but it clearly would feel a much greater sense of urgency if it knew that capacity utilization was, in reality, only 26.8%. Management will only utilize the capacity it believes it has available—*what has been made visible by the capacity cost management reporting system.* If management believes that the best output it can get from the existing machine is 7,392,000 bottles (the normal capacity utilization rate), it will buy another machine if expected demand goes to 7,400,000 bottles. Management responds to the measures it is given.

We can see that the existing machine is more than capable of more production. A new machine is not needed until production approaches 20,000,000 bottles per week. Avoiding the costly acquisition of unnecessary fixed assets is sufficient justification for maintaining theoretical capacity limits within the CCMS. No company wants to buy equipment that it really does not need if present equipment could do the job if better utilized. The goal of the CCMS, as part of the overall cost management system, is to support continuous improvement; theoretical capacity-based committed cost estimates are crucial because *they are the best benchmarks for assessing improvements.*

A properly designed and implemented CCMS helps managers:

1. Understand the potential minimum and current total average cost of producing a good.
2. Analyze cost estimates for new products as well as existing products instantaneously.
3. Combine accountability and controllability at the process and product level.
4. Support rapid and accurate incremental analysis based on proposed cycle times.
5. Compare performance information *across diverse operations.*
6. Pinpoint areas where outsourcing would be beneficial by providing immediate information on current costs of production compared to those proposed by a potential trading partner.
7. Narrow the gap between strategic and operational analysis by providing a common language and methodology for analyzing problems.

So far, our discussion suggests that the CCMS is tied to the factory floor. In reality, CCMS can be used in other settings as well. The key factor that determines whether the CCMS approach can or cannot be used is whether the process has an identifiable "steady beat"—a reliable, repetitive, time-linked measure of process capability. In a bank, the processing of checks on its coding machine has a very steady beat—processing such transactions can be analyzed using a CCMS.

If a CCMS estimate cannot be developed, then activity-based management (ABM) becomes the tool of choice. The work done by a teller in a bank is an example of this situation. There are inherent variations in the type of work the teller completes, differences in the capability of individual tellers, and deviations in the flow of customers in this people-paced setting. Nevertheless, there are still ways to improve the capacity baseline measures in people-paced (for example, ABM) systems, such as benchmarking. The current output of the process can be compared to the speed, yield, and effectiveness of a best-in-class benchmark firm's performance. The benchmarked cost and performance estimate serves as a form of "competitive cost" for the activity.

A second method is a **cost containment strategy,** *an approach that sets limits on the amount of resources that management is willing to spend to perform certain types of work.* These limits serve as the baseline definition of capacity where management determines the maximum amount of resources it is willing to expend to complete an activity. This target activity cost can be compared to current process costs. The difference between the target activity cost and current actual cost is a summary of the nonproductive and idleness costs of the process. In our banking example, the time it takes to handle a deposit transaction for a customer could be compared either across tellers in one site or against best practice times gathered by the banking industry. Any excess cost can be targeted for reduction to reach the benchmark objective.

IN CONTEXT ➤ Measuring Results at Kinkaid Cabinets

Several months have passed, and the new manufacturing cell is up and running. While there have been a few problems, in general, the workforce has embraced the new approach to manufacturing modular furniture. The weekly production meetings, where all cell employees meet to discuss productivity and quality, have become quite lively as the team debates the best way to tackle problems.

"Brad, I have to give you credit. The new line is running well. How are we going to measure the effect of these improvements?" asked Sam.

"We're using cycle time, good output per day, and piece part per million defect rates as our starting point," replied Brad. "We also intend to add capacity utilization because the cell is machine-paced, so even though most of the work is done by people, we have instituted a machine-pace flow that lends itself well to capacity analysis."

"That's great. The quality metrics and the capacity reports can be used to compare the cell to the rest of the plant," noted Sam. "If we're going to transition operations to cells wherever we can, we first have to get buy-in on how we're going to hold people accountable."

"Actually, Shelley and I have found that the new cell is even easier to account for than the old production flow. If we can sustain the culture of improvement we've created in modular furniture in the rest of the plant, we're going to see major gains across departments!"

"I'm counting on you to take Kinkaid Cabinets to new heights, Brad. You're going to be one busy man! Glad I had the good sense to listen to you! Thanks!"

Measuring Delivery Performance

OBJECTIVE 4
Explain the four basic delivery metrics used to evaluate process performance.

A final metric used in evaluating process performance is on-time delivery. For any merchandising company, this would be the number of shipments that were received by customers on the promised date. For a manufacturing company, a useful metric for delivery performance would be the number of orders that ship complete on time. As you might imagine, there are a broad number of metrics that can be used to evaluate delivery performance. Several examples of delivery metrics are:

1. **On-Time Delivery to Commit:** This metric is the percentage of time that manufacturing delivers a completed product on the schedule that was committed to customers.
2. **Manufacturing Cycle Time:** Measures the speed or time it takes for manufacturing to produce a given product from the time the order is released to production, to finished goods.

3. **Time to Make Changeovers:** Measures the speed or time it takes to switch a manufacturing line or plant from making one product over to making a different product.
4. **On-Time Shipping Performance:** a calculation of the number of order lines shipped on or before the requested ship date vs. the total number of order lines.

Delivery takes the form of in-office delivery of a package through one of the primary delivery services in the country (United States Post Office, United Parcel Service or UPS, Federal Express or FedEx, or a wide variety of smaller organizations). The objective of delivery metrics is clear: to ensure that customer expectations for the timeliness of product or service delivery are met.

So how would we calculate a delivery metric? Let us start with a simple metric, number of complete orders shipped, in Table 9.9. Kinkaid Cabinets has managed to clear 80% of its daily orders on time, according to the percentages suggested. This means 20% of the company's customers are dissatisfied with Kinkaid's performance in this category.

TABLE 9.9 ON-TIME DELIVERY METRIC

1. Number of orders received for shipment today	125
2. Number of orders shipped complete today	100
3. On-time shipment percentage (2 / 1)	80%

We can get the manufacturing cycle time from the CCMS, underscoring the value of this system. Time to make changeovers is also charted in the CCMS as it robs the line of productive time. As long as that time is needed to fill orders, changeover time is a form of waste. When we can obtain multiple measures from a single system such as CCMS, management's efficiency and effectiveness is increased.

The example above focused on delivering the order on time. What about the efficiency of delivering a multiline order to the customer? What type of measure could we use here? Table 9.10 provides one approach. Here we compare the average lines in an order to the average lines shipped per order to get a daily complete on-time shipment result. This firm back-orders, on average, 1.5 out of every five line items ordered by a customer, for a complete shipment percentage of only 70%. Therefore, 30% of the firm's customers fail to get a complete order the first time. This performance can lead to high levels of customer dissatisfaction.

TABLE 9.10 LINE ITEMS SHIPPED ON TIME

1. Average number of line items per daily order	5
2. Average line items shipped per order	3.5
3. Complete on-time shipment percentage (2 / 1)	70%

The goal in developing delivery metrics is to isolate the most important factor for customer satisfaction and then drive performance as close to expectations as possible. Comparing the United States' two largest delivery firms, UPS handles more than 1 billion more packages per year (4.6 billion) than FedEx does (3.6 billion). UPS delivered approximately 93.1 percent of its ground-based packages on time, while FedEx delivered 96.2 percent of its ground-based packages on time. Both posted a 99% delivery rate for their express services. Despite handling significantly more package deliveries, UPS only earned $12 billion more in revenue, or $58 billion, than FedEx, at $46 billion dollars. Finally, UPS posted a $3 billion net income in 2015 compared to $2 billion for FedEx. These delivery metrics matter. These two companies actively compete for daily shipping volumes from a variety of companies and individuals. Every process needs to deliver, on time, a major portion of the time to be considered reliable and effective.

To make the chapter complete, let us now turn our attention to incentives and how they are used in the process domain to drive the continuous improvement philosophy over time.

Incentives and Behavior: A Process Perspective

OBJECTIVE 5

Assess the various ways incentives are used to generate and sustain continuous improvement.

While it would be great to think that everyone would just automatically embrace changes that make an organization perform better, there are always behavioral issues as we saw in the earlier chapters. People need to be rewarded in some way if a company is going to bring their employees' goals in line with what the company needs. No matter what perspective we take on the organization, establishing goal congruence is a challenge that has to be met.

USING INCENTIVES TO FOSTER IMPROVEMENT

The goal in the lean process environment is to find a way to create incentives that will make workers want to constantly improve. These incentives can be intrinsic in nature (for example, celebratory awards) or extrinsic (such as bonuses). In one respect, this is like constantly changing the target in a game. Once you reach a goal, it is ratcheted up. There have been many studies done on the **ratchet effect,** *resetting goals higher whenever a goal is met; in essence, rolling standards used to monitor and manage performance and build in continuous improvement*. They have shown that there are three conditions that have to be met for it to occur:[9]

1. Some kind of minimum standard has to be entrenched.
2. A principle that encourages innovation has to be implemented.
3. A feedback loop has to be created between each new innovation and the minimum standard, so that, with each new innovation, the minimum standard goes up (positive ratchet) or down (negative ratchet).

---

9 John Brathwaite and Peter Drahos, *Global Business Regulation*, Cambridge, UK: Cambridge University Press, 2000: p. 526.

Combating the behavioral problems that can be created when performance standards are continually changed upward requires some form of incentive system. One of the most common of these is an extrinsic reward called **gain-sharing,** *an incentive system that gives a portion of the profit that results from a process improvement to the workforce as a form of bonus.* In gain-sharing, the workforce receives part of the profit that comes from improving throughput, quality, or any other innovation on the plant floor. This money is channeled into a bonus pool that is distributed on a regular basis to the work teams responsible for the performance improvements.

Some companies use both a positive and negative approach to gain-sharing. Specifically, if there is a negative "ratchet" in performance, either no money is added to the pool, or in a worst-case scenario, funds are removed. It is not a good idea behaviorally to remove funds from the bonus pool, but if performance peaks and then falls back markedly, there needs to be some way to regenerate the continuous improvement goals in the team's culture. Sometimes, only a form of punishment can do this.

In intrinsic motivation, the focus is on making the employees feel positive about the company and its goals. Pizza lunches, awards, and recognition ceremonies have been found to be as effective as bonus pools in many companies. Figure 9.8 depicts some of the ways intrinsic rewards can be built into the structure of an organization.

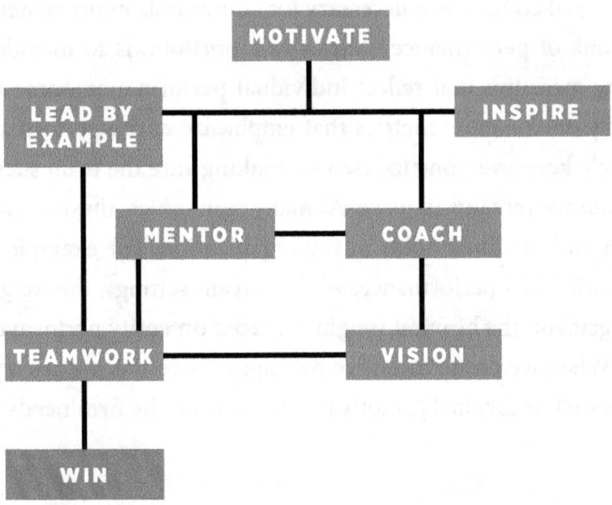

FIGURE 9.8 MANAGEMENT CAN BUILD POSITIVE MORALE IN ITS WORKERS USING THE VARIOUS TECHNIQUES DEPICTED HERE AS WELL AS OTHER INTRINSIC REWARDS TO REINFORCE THE POSITIVE FEELINGS GENERATED.

BUILDING A PORTFOLIO OF INCENTIVES

Relying solely on bonus pools to create the incentive to change has its limits. Many workers are just as motivated by a pizza party when a team reaches an improvement goal as they are by a financial reward. Companies need to build a portfolio of incentives so that employees benefit in many different ways when they participate in process improvement initiatives.

The types of rewards and recognitions that go into building a sound portfolio of continuous improvement awards include the following:

- Gain-sharing, or creating *continuous improvement* bonuses
- Team celebrations when improvement goals are reached
- Awards ceremonies where top performers are publicly recognized
- Employee of the month programs to instill the goal to improve across the organization
- Gift certificates that employees can use to dine out with their families or friends
- Thank-you cards to acknowledge extra effort
- Extra leave time
- Stock options

Clearly, the list could go on, but the point is that it normally takes a combination of incentives to keep the continuous improvement program working. Some incentives work for a time and then lose their impact. That is when management needs to find new ways to incentivize its workers to keep making gains.

It is also important to define the incentives across more than one or two performance measures, because it can be very difficult to keep improving if only one definition of success exists. Here, integrated performance measurement systems, such as the balanced scorecard mentioned earlier, are useful. By defining improvement that includes simply getting better on one measure while all the rest stay steady can help provide an opportunity for the workforce to succeed on an ongoing basis. The aim is to always find new ways to achieve the goal congruence necessary for continuous improvement processes to succeed.

Another way to think of performance metrics as a portfolio is to include in each individual's performance package some measures that reflect individual performance, some that reflect team or group performance, and finally one or more metrics that emphasize entity performance. This type of bundled performance metrics help keep everyone focused on making sure the team succeeds while ensuring individual motivation to improve remains in place. At many companies, these blended incentive packages are tailored to the position an individual holds in the organization. For example, for line employees, more emphasis is placed on individual performance, while in team settings, the weight is placed on team measures. For senior management, the heaviest weight is placed on entity performance, as that is where it has the greatest influence. When we create incentive packages, therefore, we are trying to find ways to blend measures to ensure that each individual is motivated to do what the firm needs them to do.

BEHAVIORAL ISSUES OR, WHO'S IN CHARGE?

The last issue we need to cover before leaving the process domain is that managing becomes a very different task when lean or continuous improvement methods are put in place. While it might seem that all of the impact of the change effort drops down to the workforce, it is actually management that has a much more difficult time adjusting to its new roles. Gone is the command-and-control structure that many managers mastered on their way up the corporate ladder. Instead of "controlling" the workforce, the management role shifts to enabling employees to improve, facilitating their change initiatives, and trusting them to know how to best structure and execute work plans.

Often managers require training programs for a continuous improvement program to work. Managers themselves have to be given incentives to support the new program and be encouraged to make the changes in their behavior necessary for the team-based environment to succeed. Managers who cannot let go of the reins of control can destroy even the best-planned improvement initiative, so some system needs to be devised that allows the workforce to "push back"' on heavy-handed managers.

This really places the question, "Who's in charge?," in a new light. Managers have become accustomed to setting standards and meting out rewards and punishments. For the team environment to work, it is often the manager who needs to be managed. This change places a strain on all layers of management, for top management can cause just as much trouble trying to discipline line managers as line managers can cause on the shop floor or in the back office. In a world of continuous improvement, everyone needs to adjust their worldview and learn new skills. The workforce is no longer the "muscle" that implements the plans the management "brain" has developed for them. It is a delicate cultural balance that revolves around the word "trust."

When we talk about team structures, we are in the arena of what is called "clans." As first described by William Ouchi,[10] clan-based forms of control look to shape the behavior of people using ritual, ceremony, and shared experiences. They rely on socialization techniques to integrate the interests of individuals and organizations. The most important thing about clan forms of control is that they depend totally on everyone trusting that the other members in the clan will behave in the prescribed manner. All it takes is one major situation where this trust is betrayed, and the clan form of control falls apart. For this reason, it is seen as a nonrobust form of control, and is why it is important for management to learn its new roles and to follow through on them with the workforce. It takes very little to destroy the pride and enthusiasm for improvement that lies at the heart of every successful lean management initiative.

If the team structure begins to disintegrate, management has to be able to put in place remedial actions that will isolate the problem and, using the team as a guide, eliminate the problem from the work unit. This has to be done with the team's support if trust is to be restored. At the end of the day, no one person is in control in a team setting. Effective teamwork requires a delicate balancing act of cooperation and trust, all focused on commonly agreed-upon goals and the organizational processes that support the attainment of these goals.

Summary

This chapter opened with a discussion of the kaizen, or continuous improvement philosophy. Taking a systems perspective, continuous improvement methods start with the recognition of a problem and then a reliance upon the efforts of everyone involved to find solutions. It focuses on making small changes to processes to generate constant performance gains. There are times when quantum leaps of improvement are pursued, but it is normally a slower process of incremental change with the goal to make things better, cheaper, on-time, and in the right place every time.

The Japanese word for waste is muda. Continuous improvement makes its gains by continuously identifying and eliminating waste from the organization. This waste can take many forms, including move,

10 William G. Ouchi, "Markets, Bureaucracies, and Clans," *Administrative Science Quarterly*, 25(1), 1980, pp. 129-141.

queue, and quality failures. It can also result from excess complexity, unfocused processes, excess variation, and redundancy, just to name a few common problems. Wherever waste occurs, there is an opportunity for improvement.

Total quality management (TQM) is one set of tools and techniques for managing the elimination of defects from a process. Quality, or the freedom from deficiencies in a product or process, is defined as conformance to requirements, not how good it is. The underlying belief is that the key to achieving quality is prevention, not detection. The goal is zero defects, and the measurement of quality is the cost of nonconformance (quality failures). Measuring the cost of quality is a major task performed by the business planning and analysis (BPA) professional in a TQM setting. Separating quality problems into four categories (prevention, detection or appraisal, internal failure, and external failure), the cost of quality should be part of the scorecard used in companies pursuing continuous improvement.

Lean Six Sigma is a major extension of the tenets of TQM to encompass all of the aspects of process performance. It is a customer-driven approach that emphasizes the elimination of waste and quality problems from processes. The voice of the customer is integrated into lean Six Sigma through **quality function deployment (QFD),** *a process that emphasizes integrating the voice of the customer into all product, process, and service design and improvement efforts*. Groups of customers are actually brought in to confer with the design engineers while a product is being designed for production. Customer input is used to identify what features are most important; technical specifications are then tailored toward ensuring that these product attributes are present in the designed product. It is one of many quality tools that are identified with the lean Six Sigma methodology.

Achieving higher levels of process performance is so important that a national award, called the Malcolm Baldrige National Quality Award, has been established. This award serves two purposes: (1) to identify organizations that can serve as role models for others, and (2) to support the drive toward delivering increasing levels of value to customers and stakeholders throughout the U.S. economy.

Capacity analysis plays a major role in managing processes in organizations. A capacity variance analysis was introduced that broke down capacity into one of five categories: theoretical, practical, normal, budgeted, and actual. Four variances were generated from these five categories: rate-based waste, policy waste, budgeted waste, and efficiency loss. We saw that if a company uses theoretical capacity limits (24/7 the best they can be), they gain significant power to analyze incremental business decisions and to compare performance throughout the organization. The stability, elegance, and information content of capacity cost management systems (CCMS) make them useful for crafting decisions ranging from the back office to the plant floor and senior management's strategic analysis of the future.

Delivery metrics are important for measuring process performance. The four dimensions of process performance—cost, quality, delivery, and productivity—are contained to some extent in the CCMS. We use complementary measures to keep attention focused on reaching organizational goals as set by customer expectations.

Incentives are used to drive and sustain continuous improvement efforts. In an attempt to avoid the negative behavioral problems that can come from the ratchet effect of performance measures, companies have to use a blend of incentives to keep the workforce's goals aligned with those of the company. These blends not only include different types of measurements but also measurements that focus on different structural elements of the organization (for example: individual, team, and entity performance). Finally, managers often have the most difficult time adjusting to the continuous improvement world because they lose their traditional command-and-control role, becoming facilitators and resource providers, not decision makers. Continuous improvement teams, like clans, require trust to remain effective. Keeping this trust alive between members and between the team and management is a critical job for a manager in a continuous improvement world.

Key Terms

Actual capacity: the quantity a machine or process produces over a period of time.

Balanced scorecard: a set of measurements that captures the key dimensions of performance in a decision domain.

Budgeted capacity: the planned utilization of a machine or process for a given year.

Capacity cost management system: a complete set of tools and measures for monitoring and managing process or machine capacity utilization.

Capacity variance analysis: a comparison between the actual performance on a machine or process and the standard set for its operation; both the productivity of a process as well as its costs are examined.

Cognitive bias: a pattern of deviation in judgment where projections about other people and situations may be drawn in an incomplete or illogical fashion.

Cost containment strategy: an approach that sets limits on the amount of resources management is willing to spend to perform certain types of work.

Cost of quality: the price of defects, rework, and failure costs experienced as a result of a company's processes as well as the total short- and long-term costs of failures experienced by external customers.

Cost of quality reports: an itemization of the various causes and costs of quality-related activities.

Detection: or appraisal costs, outlays for activities designed to inspect or screen input and output to discover problems.

External quality costs: quality outlays associated with problems experienced directly by the customer.

Gain-sharing: an incentive system that gives a portion of the profit that results from a process improvement to the workforce as a form of bonus.

Innovation: a far-reaching change to the status quo that often is the result of a large investment in new technology and/or equipment and/or process improvements.

Internal quality costs: quality outlays associated with scrap and rework of problems detected in a product or process.

Kaizen: the philosophy of continuous improvement that starts with recognizing problems and then looks to everyone in the organization to solve them.

Lean Six Sigma: managerial concept that emphasizes continually removing waste from processes (lean management) while striving to reduce defect rates to one in a million or less (Six Sigma quality level).

Learning curve: the ability of people to become better at a task through frequent repetition.

Maintenance: upkeep that reinforces existing practices and assumptions.

Malcolm Baldrige National Quality Award: a national award given to companies that exhibit quality in their leadership, customer focus, process and workforce management, and related areas.

Muda: the Japanese term for waste, the continuous process of eliminating waste from operations.

Normal capacity: the average use of a machine or process over three to five years.

Practical capacity: theoretical capacity reduced to reflect planned downtime.

Prevention costs: outlays for activities designed to stop defects in a process or product from occurring.

Productivity: the amount of output produced by a given set of inputs.

Quality: (1) a product or process that contains the most desired characteristics, and (2) the lack of flaws in a product or process.

Quality function deployment: a process that emphasizes integrating the voice of the customer into all product, process, and service design and improvement efforts.

Ratchet effect: resetting goals higher whenever a goal is met; in essence, rolling standards used to monitor and manage performance and build in continuous improvement.

Six Sigma quality initiatives: customer-driven approaches that emphasize the elimination of quality problems and waste from processes.

Taguchi loss function: a statistical tool that analyzes the impact of variation on overall customer satisfaction.

Systems perspective: a way of looking at an organization as a whole, not a set of parts.

Theoretical capacity: the quantity a machine or process could produce if it performed continuously 24/7; the best a process could be.

Trended actual average cost: a rolling average of actual costs, where cost moves across time, and as one observation is added to the data set, the oldest is eliminated.

Questions

1. What does it mean to take a systems perspective to process management? How does this affect how managers approach their work in organizations?
2. What does the term kaizen mean and how is it applied in the continuous improvement setting? How does the continuous improvement setting differ from traditional management approaches?
3. What is muda and what are some sources of it in organizations? How does muda impact the cost and quality of work done in an organization?
4. What are the basic tenets of TQM and how do they impact work in organizations? Please be sure to note some of the points made by Deming and Juran. Can you think of some examples in your school of places where TQM principles might improve performance?

5. What are the four categories used in cost of quality reports? How do they differ from each other? Why do we care about separating costs into these categories?
6. What is the Taguchi loss function? What is its primary concern? How do you think a company can use the Taguchi loss function to direct attention to its quality problems?
7. What does the term Six Sigma mean in the quality literature? What role does quality function deployment play in Six Sigma settings? How does Six Sigma impact how a company approaches quality?
8. What is the Malcolm Baldrige Award? Define the key points used to assess an organization seeking to gain this award. What benefits do you think a company obtains by winning the Baldrige Award?
9. What are the various types of capacity measurement used to define how much work a set of resources can do? How do they differ? What aspects of the production process does each measure emphasize and how would this emphasis change management decision making?
10. What are some of the benefits of capacity cost management for controlling and understanding the process domain? Do these benefits justify the cost of maintaining a capacity-related system?
11. In looking at the four dimensions of performance that make up the balanced scorecard in the process domain, how does delivery tie to the other measurements?
12. What are some of the different ways companies combine measurements to create incentives for goal congruence in a process setting? What are the benefits of each of these approaches?

Exercises

1. **COST OF QUALITY CATEGORIES.** For the following list of quality activities, note whether it is best categorized as Prevention (P), Detection (D), Internal failure (IF), or External failure (EF). Each activity should be given only one code.

Activity	Category	Activity	Category
Inspect materials		Rework cells	
Train workers		Poor quality ratings	
Process redesign		Field testing	
Customer complaints		Supplier certification	
Burn-in tests		Recalls	
Quality audits		Salvage	

2. **COST OF QUALITY CATEGORIES.** For the following list of quality activities, please note whether it is best categorized as Prevention (P), Detection (D), Internal failure (IF), or External failure (EF). Each activity should only be given one code.

Activity	Category	Activity	Category
Short product life		Customer surveys	
Trial runs		Quality function deployment	
TQM training		Scrap units	
Recalibration		Warranty repairs	
First-pass part rates		Repair costs	
Packaging inspection		Product improvement	

3. **SCRAP AND OUTPUT IMPROVEMENT.** Scalar Enterprises wants to calculate how much productivity improvement it could get if it eliminates scrap from its production process. The company provides you with the following information and asks you to give it the answer to the question, "What percentage improvement could we get in productivity if scrap is eliminated?"

- Current scrap rate: 15%
- Current good output: 100 units

4. **SCRAP AND OUTPUT IMPROVEMENT.** Goldstar Company wants to calculate how much productivity improvement it could get if it eliminated scrap from its production process. It provides you with the following information and asks you to give it the answer to the question, "What percentage improvement could we get in productivity if scrap is eliminated?"

- Current scrap rate: 12%
- Current good output: 240 units

5. **ANALYSIS OF CAPACITY UTILIZATION.** Brown Industries currently uses normal capacity as its baseline in analyzing capacity utilization. It has asked you to compare its numbers to those it would get using theoretical capacity to determine what degree of actual utilization it is getting from its machines. The data it provides you with for the current year is:

- Current actual capacity utilization 2,250,000 parts
- Normal capacity utilization 2,500,000 parts
- Theoretical capacity utilization 10,500,000 parts

What is its actual capacity utilization rate using theoretical capacity? Normal capacity? What different message would each of these measures send to senior management about process performance?

6. **ANALYSIS OF CAPACITY UTILIZATION.** Always Ready Manufacturing currently uses normal capacity as its baseline in analyzing capacity utilization. It has asked you to compare its numbers to those it would get using theoretical capacity to determine what degree of actual utilization it is getting from its machines. The data it provides you with for the current year is:

- Current actual capacity utilization 5,000,000 pieces
- Normal capacity utilization 4,500,000 pieces
- Theoretical capacity utilization 20,000,000 pieces

What is its actual capacity utilization rate using theoretical capacity? Normal capacity? What different message would each of these measures send to senior management about process performance?

7. **DELIVERY METRICS.** Just-in-Case, a manufacturer of party goods, often gets large orders requiring 10 to 15 line items of products for the order to be complete. Lately there have been a lot of complaints from customers about orders that were not delivered complete or on time. Tim Goodwin, managing director for shipping, compiled the following measures of shipping performance for last week.

Measure	Results
Number of orders received	250
Average number of lines per order	10
Orders shipped by promise date	210
Orders shipped complete	180
Average number of lines shipped per order	8

Develop several delivery metrics and then explain to management where it needs to make changes to existing methods and why. Be precise in noting these changes and reasons.

8. **DELIVERY METRICS.** Make-it-on-time, a wholesaler that buys a large variety of items and then combines them into one shipment for customers, has lately been experiencing

order fulfillment problems. Specifically, it has not been able to get complete customer orders out within the promised delivery window. The results for the last week compiled by Jack Bradley, VP of shipping and order fulfillment, are as follows.

Measure	Results
Number of orders received	300
Average number of lines per order	8
Orders shipped by promise date	260
Orders shipped complete	210
Average number of lines shipped per order	7

Develop several delivery metrics and then explain to management where it needs to make changes to existing methods and why. Be precise in noting these changes and reasons.

Problems

1. **COST OF QUALITY REPORTS.** Samstone Industries makes false stone facings that are used in a variety of residential and commercial building projects. It recently installed a cost of quality reporting system. The following is the list of its quality costs for 20x6.

Quality Activity	Cost
Recalls	$50,000
Rework	$102,500
Final inspection	$35,000
On-site repair calls	$47,500
TQM training	$10,000
Field testing	$32,500
Salvage	$16,500
Lost sales	$225,000
Raw material inspection	$35,000
Quality audits	$15,000
Scrap costs	$92,000

Quality Activity	Cost
Piece part inspection	$50,000
Supplier certification	$20,000
Returns	$75,000
Workforce training	$25,000
	$831,000

REQUIRED:

a. Develop a cost of quality report for the company for 20x6. State your amounts in both dollars and percent of the total.
b. The company's revenue for the year was $10,000,000. What percent of its total revenue are the quality costs?
c. Where should the company place its attention in the coming year to most improve its quality performance? Why?

---

2. **COST OF QUALITY REPORTS.** Thermaglass, Inc., makes a large number of products for use in the kitchen. The company advertises that its products can go from the freezer to the oven or the microwave and never crack. Over the past two years, however, there have been increasing problems with products failing to stand up to these rapid changes in temperature. With the company's reputation and future on the line, Randy Paul, the company's president, has decided to put in place a new cost of quality reporting system so management can see exactly where the problems are coming from. The company provides you with the following data.

Quality Activity	Cost
Recalls	$250,000
Design changes	$400,000
In-process inspection	$250,000
Pilot testing	$300,000
Recalibration	$125,000
Scrap costs	$175,000
Returns	$350,000
Kitchen burn-in tests	$75,000
Salvage	$125,000
Final inspection	$45,000
TQM training	$15,000

Quality Activity	Cost
Warranty claims	$250,000
Raw material inspection	$35,000
Supplier certification	$15,000
Quality-based downtime	$65,000
Customer complaints	$125,000
	$2,600,000

REQUIRED:

a. Develop a cost of quality report for the company. State the amounts in both dollars and percent of the total.

b. The company's revenue for the year was $25,000,000. What percent of its total revenue are the quality costs?

c. Where should the company place its attention in the coming year to most improve its quality performance? Why?

3. **TAGUCHI LOSS FUNCTION.** Good Practices Engineering Company (GPEC) makes a wide range of machine tools that are used by other companies to manufacture products of its own. When a machine tool fails, it results in significant cost and quality problems. Therefore, GPEC has decided it needs to understand the impact of variation on its customers' product failure costs. GPEC has determined that it costs $2,500 when a product fails in the customer's hands (represented by (k), the proportionally constant cost of failure). It tests 10 runs of one of its products; the results are given in the table below. The target value for the machined part is 35 centimeters in diameter.

Unit	Actual Observation
1	34.5
2	34
3	33.5
4	36
5	36.5
6	36
7	35.5
8	35
9	34.5
10	34

REQUIRED:

a. Compute the total quality loss for GPEC using the Taguchi loss function formula and solution approach given in the text.
b. What would you recommend to GPEC regarding its quality practices? Why?

4. **TAGUCHI LOSS FUNCTION.** Slipstream, Inc., makes slipcovers for furniture. If the slipcovers do not fit properly, customers are very upset. This is especially true if the slipcover is a bit too small, which can make getting the slipcovers on very difficult and leads to product returns. The company has determined a quality failure in the customer's hands (slipcovers that do not fit) costs the company $600 each time it occurs (this is (k), the proportionally constant cost of external quality failures). The company decides to randomly test one of its slipcover lines, which makes a slipcover that should be 36 inches wide. The results of the test are given in the table below.

Unit	Actual Observation
1	35
2	37
3	36.5
4	36
5	35
6	34
7	33.5
8	35
9	36
10	37

REQUIRED:

a. Compute the total quality loss for Slipstream, Inc., using the Taguchi loss function formula and solution approach given in the text.
b. What would you recommend to Slipstream, Inc., regarding its quality practices? Why?

5. **CAPACITY COST VARIANCE ANALYSIS.** Ames Beverage makes several different types of sodas in cans for distribution throughout the Midwest. To get the products into the cans, it uses a very expensive ($25,000,000) high-speed filling line. The company is considering buying another filling line because, according to its capacity analysis, which

is done by comparing actual utilization to budgeted utilization, it is running at an average of 85% of its existing capacity. Marketing has come up with a new, and quite large, customer that will cause the company to exceed its budgeted capacity numbers, a problem management is concerned about. Before managers do anything, however, Mark Watson, the VP of manufacturing, wants to get a better idea of how well the company is using its existing capacity. He provides you with the following information.

- The line is rated to run 1,500 cans per minute.
- Actual output is only 1,275 cans per minute.
- The plant is budgeted to produce 720,000 cans per day this year.
- The plant runs one, eight-hour shift, five days a week.
- The output of the plant per day over the last three years has been 750,000 cans, 850,000 cans, and 800,000 cans.
- For practical purposes, engineering lowered the run rate in the manufacturer specifications from 2,000 cans a minute to the current rated line speed of 1,500 cans a minute.

REQUIRED:

a. **Develop a capacity utilization variance analysis for Ames Beverage using the information above. Make sure to calculate all four variances.**
b. **Should Ames buy a new machine? Why or why not? Use a business case structure to make your arguments.**

6. **PROCESS BALANCED SCORECARD.** Janet Winthrop, VP of manufacturing for Able Systems, Inc. (ASI), has been asked to develop a set of balanced performance metrics for the company's just-in-time cell. Janet compiles a range of measures that could be combined into a balanced scorecard. She asks for your help in choosing the final set of measures. The information Janet obtains for the last month is in the following table.

Measure	Value
Theoretical capacity	6,000 units
Normal capacity	3,000 units
Actual output	2,000 units
Defects per 1,000 units	25
Units delivered on time	1,200
Standard cost per unit	$800.00
Current cost per good unit	$1,150.00
% of orders shipped complete	80%
Customer returns for quality or delivery problems	250 units

Using this information, develop a balanced scorecard for ASI. How would you describe its performance for this month? Make a formal report and suggest some ways that ASI might look to improve its performance.

7. **PROCESS BALANCED SCORECARD.** GoodTymes Beverages, Inc. (GTB), makes a variety of powdered drinks for the consumer market. GTB sells into the wholesale market, where high priority is placed on obtaining the right amount of product at the right time, in the right place, and definitely at the right price. Lately GTB has been experiencing a high number of complaints from its wholesale customers, who claim that the final customer is returning large quantities of GTB's product to their supermarket. When looking for replacement merchandise, the wholesalers are often met with stockouts—there simply is not any replacement stock. John Schilling, VP of manufacturing, has been tasked with getting a comprehensive look at how the company is performing. He compiles the following list of measurements.

Measure	Value
Theoretical capacity	500,000 packages
Normal capacity	250,000 packages
Actual output	180,000 packages
% of packages with inadequate fill	25%
Units delivered on time	120,000 packages
Standard cost per unit	$1.25
Current cost per good unit	$1.50
% of orders shipped complete	75%
Final customer returns for quality problems	30,000 packages

Using this information, develop a balanced scorecard for GTB. How would you describe its performance for the month? Make a formal report and suggest some ways that GTB might look to improve its performance.

Database Problem

For database templates, worksheets, and workbooks, go to MAdownloads.imanet.org

DB 9.1 COST OF QUALITY REPORT. For this problem, you are simply going to transfer data, by row, from the DB 9.1 Cost of Quality Data worksheet to the DB 9.1 COQ Report Template. The challenge is to decide what type of quality cost each item is (for example, prevention, detection, internal failure, or external failure).

Starting from Row 5 on the Data worksheet, highlight across Columns A thru F. Right click and choose Copy. Now go to the COQ Report Template worksheet, choose what quality category you feel best fits the activity/cost and choose the first available row under that category in Column A. Right click and choose Paste. Continue to do this for Rows 6-23. Then calculate totals and % in the designated rows.

REQUIRED:

Turn in the completed COQ Report Template to your instructor along with your answers to the following questions: What quality category is Prestige spending the largest amount of its quality costs on? What recommendations would you make to management to improve its quality performance?

Cases

CASE 9.1 TAGUCHI LOSS FUNCTION. Bright Lights, Inc., makes a variety of lamps. It is very important that the base of the lamp fits snugly to the body if the customer is going to be satisfied with the look of the lamp itself. While there is a tightening mechanism on top, if the base is not close to an exact fit for the body of the lamp, the product is a reject.

Juan Hernandez, president of Bright Lights, has been getting concerned about the number of customer complaints and product returns for the main line of the company, Quality Lights. This is a premium product where there is no room for error in design or production, but errors have been creeping in. The company keeps a tight control on its production facilities, but the engineers have designed each lamp to be made within specified parameters. The two main parameters are width and circumference. Both are critical for the lamp body to fill the frame properly.

To address this problem, Juan decides to pull together his quality team. This includes Barb Haverhill, VP of manufacturing; Frank Burns, VP of marketing; and Joel Dempski, director of quality. The meeting does not go well from the start.

Barb: We are making our products within specifications. We are constantly taking readings and we fill more Shewhart control charts in a day than any other company I've ever worked for. We're staying within spec, I swear.

Frank: If that's true, Barb, why are we getting so many units returned to us? My salespeople are ready to mutiny, because the brand image is getting tarnished. How can we ask a premium price for a product that just doesn't look right?

Joel: Wait, I have to agree with Barb here. We're meeting the specs set up by engineering, so if you want to blame someone, blame them.

Juan: I didn't call this meeting to pin blame. We have a problem. The base and body aren't coming together properly. Every return costs us anywhere from $150 to $250 directly, and at least four times that in lost reputation. I'd say this problem is costing us $1,000 every time it occurs. I don't want excuses or blame, I want solutions.

Joel: We could try something new. I just learned about Taguchi loss function in the last quality class I took. It looks at variation in a much more precise way. What it basically says is that variation costs money even when it's small. We could use that method instead of Shewhart charts to see what our quality picture looks like.

Barb: Are you telling me I have to send my crews to stat class to find a solution to Juan's problem? We're already measuring. How is this different?

Joel: It's different because we put a higher cost on variation the farther the problem is from the exact measure. We could be in spec on both the base and the body and still have huge gaps (in the customer's eyes) when we put the two together.

Frank: I think you should give this a try. Otherwise we may all be looking for new jobs as we lose our quality niche in the market.

Juan: I agree with Frank. Joel, you need to work with Barb and her teams to find the easiest way to implement this. Let's look at both parameters, width and circumference, to see where our problems are.

Joel: I'll assume you want to use $1,000 for the actual cost of a problem when we don't meet spec dead on? I need this number for the formulas to work. Then, Barb, your team will simply measure a bit more often and still chart the results. You and I can put our heads together to solve the actual underlying equation. It's simple once you have a target value, which we have, and actual observations.

Barb: I'll have to trust you, Joel. I'm not that comfortable with statistics, but this is important enough that I may have to learn something new. We'll start charting every fifth unit instead of every 20, and we'll measure both circumference of the body and the diameter of the base, since you say they both matter. We'll get some use out of those calipers you bought us, Juan.

Juan: Thank you all for working together on this. I'd like to hear back in a week to see how bad our problem really is. Frank, tell marketing to keep collecting information for us, too. We need to know what is going wrong here, and quickly.

The data Barb and her team collected for the first 20 observations of circumference of the body and diameter of the base are in the tables below. The target value for the lamp being studied is a diameter of six inches, and therefore, the target value for the circumference of the body is 15.7 inches.

Unit	Actual Observation—Diameter of Base	Actual Observation—Circumference of Body
1	6	15.54
2	6.4	15.7
3	6.25	15.44
4	6.25	15.42
5	6.3	15.41
6	5.75	15.4
7	6.3	15.39
8	6.25	15.37
9	6.2	15.36
10	6.15	15.34
11	6.4	15.2
12	6.25	15.15
13	5.7	15.1
14	6.15	15.2
15	6.3	15.44
16	6.4	15.45
17	6.7	15.42
18	6.55	15.41
19	6.04	15.4
20	6.25	15.51

REQUIRED:

a. Compute the Taguchi loss function for both key measurements of a lamp. What do your results tell you?

b. Looking at the numbers themselves, can you see a pattern of interaction that might be troubling? What is it?

c. What would you report back to Juan at the end of this trial run? Please be specific as to how you think the company should address its quality challenges using a business case structure to support your arguments.

CASE 9.2 COST OF QUALITY AND TAGUCHI LOSS FUNCTIONS. Radnor Industries makes a variety of small one- to four-cup automatic coffeemakers that are used by hotels and in some residential settings for people who just need that quick jolt of caffeine to get their day started. It is critical that the machines are durable and work properly as they are often situated on the same desk as someone's laptop computer in a hotel room. Nothing can make a hotel guest more frustrated than puddles of water everywhere and a mess to clean up before they even get their day going.

Even though quality is known to be critical, Jack Wallace, the company owner, has recently been receiving customer complaints that the machines are leaking and also making very weak and lukewarm cups of coffee, suggesting the water is not getting heated enough. The machines also seem to be breaking easily with use, making it very expensive for the hotels to offer their free coffee service in the guests' rooms.

Jack calls together his key managers to see if they can get to the bottom of the problem. The conversations do not go well.

Sam Sneed, VP of marketing: You guys in manufacturing are killing us! There's a lot of competition out there for small coffeemakers, and ours used to be one of the best. Now? We're getting a terrible reputation for leaky, easily broken machines that make awful coffee. It's not the coffee grounds that are the problem, believe me. It's our machines!

Rudy Gentry, VP of manufacturing: Sam, you're exaggerating once again. Our machines have a few problems, but we run a quality shop. I think our problem lies in poor design and poor pilot testing.

George Colby, director of product development: Come on, guys. Product development is not going to eat the problems on this one. We're using tried and true engineering standards for coffeemakers, good materials, and good designs. If they're leaking or not making coffee right, it's a materials or manufacturing problem, not design!

Judy Dean, director of purchasing: I'm not going to let this be blamed on my group! We purchase according to specifications. Sure, we try to find some materials that may be a bit cheaper, but that's how we're rewarded! We make sure the materials meet our buying criteria. So if the engineered specifications aren't tight enough, it's sure not our fault!

Jack: Whoa! I didn't call this meeting to set up a round robin blame game. I'm more concerned now than I was when we started as it seems no one has a clue as to why our units are failing in the field. If we're purchasing materials that don't work, this has to stop! Let's change our reward structure if that is where it's leading us. And design has to be more focused on setting tight, clear standards in place so purchasing and manufacturing can get the job done right.

Beth White, controller: Jack, I have a suggestion. Why don't we put together some cost of quality information and see if we can spot where the biggest problems appear to be in-house and with our customers? It won't be an answer to the problem, but at least it will help us see where the issues are coming up internally.

Jack: Thank you for putting in something positive, Beth. I want all of you in this room to cooperate with Beth while she tries to start putting some shape around this problem for us. I also want Engineering to look at other ways we can start measuring and managing quality here in the shop. We have to get a handle on this problem or we'll all be looking for a new job. And, I want you all to start working like a team. I mean it! I want team players and I intend to have them!

With that, the meeting broke up with everyone jostling to get out of the conference room door first. In the next week, Beth and her accounting analysis team set out to collect data. The information she gathered included both cost of quality information (see Table C9.2a) and some data from Engineering on the Taguchi loss function (see Table C9.2b). She now needs your help to compile this information into something useful for the next meeting with Jack.

For the Taguchi loss function, it was determined that a failure in the field would cost the firm 10 times the actual cost of the unit because of the reputation effect poor quality is having on sales. This means the constant cost of external failure is $100. The specifications that are determined to matter are the heating temperature of the coils and the size of the coffee "drawer" that holds the pod of coffee grounds (this is where the leaks are happening). The target value for the heating element is 190 degrees while the size of the coffee drawer is supposed to be 2.5 inches.

TABLE C9.2A COST OF QUALITY DATA

Customer returns	$50,000
Production problems due to poor materials	$75,000
Pilot testing	$10,000
Scrap	$60,000
Warranty claims	$100,000
Final inspection	$35,000

Raw material inspection	$30,000
Supplier certification	$12,000
Rework	$25,000
Customer complaints	$50,000
Employee training	$20,000

TABLE C9.2B TAGUCHI LOSS FUNCTION DATA

	Heating Element	Coffee Drawer
Unit 1	185	2.4
Unit 2	190	2.3
Unit 3	178	2.1
Unit 4	175	2.5
Unit 5	170	2.4
Unit 6	165	2.6
Unit 7	185	2.3
Unit 8	192	2.2
Unit 9	177	2
Unit 10	165	2.1

REQUIRED:

a. Prepare the cost of quality report for Radnor Industries. Make sure the report shows both total costs and percentage of total quality costs for each item in the report.
b. Calculate the Taguchi loss function for the two parameters given.
c. Where do you see the problems lying?
d. How is Jack going to get his team working together to solve these problems? Try to think of how incentives and performance evaluation can be used to sort out the team conflicts and get everyone working toward solving the company's problems.
e. Draft a short memo to Jack with the results of your analysis and your suggestions for management changes to help bring quality into line. Use a business case structure to organize your argument.

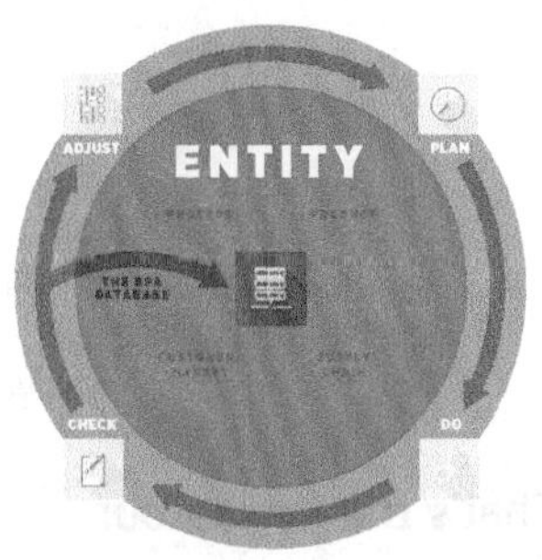

Setting Performance Expectations at the Entity Level

An intelligent plan is the first step to success. The man who plans knows where he is going, knows what progress he is making, and has a pretty good idea when he will arrive. Planning is the open road to your destination. If you don't know where you are going, how can you expect to get there?

BASIL S. WALSH [1]

CHAPTER ROADMAP

1. **Planning Prerequisites: Missions and Objectives**
2. **Three Organizational Archetypes**
   - ➤ *Small Organizations*
   - ➤ *Functional Organizations*
   - ➤ *Divisional Organizations*
3. **Planning in Small Organizations**
   - ➤ *Scenario Planning in Small Organizations*
4. **Planning in Functional Organizations**
5. **Budgeting in Functional Organizations**
   - ➤ *Forecasting Sales*
   - ➤ *Production Budget*
   - ➤ *Raw Materials, Labor, and Overhead Budgets*
   - ➤ *Finished Goods and Cost of Goods Sold Budgets*
   - ➤ *Sales and Marketing, Administrative, and Research and Development Budgets*
   - ➤ *Budgeted Income Statement*
   - ➤ *Cash Budget*
   - ➤ *Ending Balance Sheet*
   - ➤ *"Flexing" the Budget*
6. **Eliminating or Reducing the Planning Gap**
7. **Target-Setting Alternatives**

LEARNING OBJECTIVES

After studying this chapter, you should be able to:

1. **Compare and contrast small, functionally organized, and divisionalized organizations.**
2. **Describe the purposes of planning in the entity domain, and understand the mechanics of preparing an entity-level plan.**
3. **Explain the advantages of scenario planning, and apply the concepts of expected value to scenario planning.**
4. **Illustrate the benefits of planning in functional organizations.**
5. **Create a company budget for a medium- to large-sized organization.**
6. **Explain why a planning gap occurs and how to address it.**

---

1 *The Forbes Scrapbook of Thoughts on the Business of Life*, Chicago: Triumph Books, 1992: p. 410.

IN CONTEXT ➤ Focusing on the Customer Is Everyone's Business at Prestige Auto

"We have to keep our eyes on the customer. That's the key to our business success, one we can never forget regardless of what part of the business we're directly responsible for."

Jack Noble, president and owner of Prestige Auto, a car dealership specializing in high-end cars such as Mercedes and Jaguars, was holding his weekly management meeting. He had just received several letters from customers complaining about both the sales experience and interactions with the repairs department. To say that he was none too happy would be an understatement. The company was the only local supplier of the brands it offered, and it did a very good leasing and used car business in addition to selling new cars. Leases represented 35% of the business, new car sales 35%, and used cars 30%.

"We continually train our sales force in customer-based selling," said Judy Pierce, head of marketing and sales. "I know we have demanding customers. They're out to buy the best car they can get and they expect special treatment. I thought we were making progress."

"It's not just the sales force I'm concerned about. Part of buying a car is financing it. One letter said that the salesperson just dropped her off with the finance specialist, and returned to the showroom floor, where, the writer said, he simply chatted with the other salespeople. Even worse, the finance specialist took forever, seemed disorganized, and was rude."

"Whoa, Jack. I can't believe any of my finance specialists was rude. We all have bad days, but rude? I don't think so," Alice Long, head of Finance, jumped in.

"I don't know. Sometimes they can be a bit curt, Alice. I send one of my guys from repairs over to get some basic paperwork completed so we can send a customer on his way and they make us feel as if we're being too much trouble," said Tony Silvio, manager of repairs.

Bruce Robbins, manager of purchasing and acquisitions, agreed. "We run into problems when we're dealing with buybacks when cars come off of lease. We need numbers run for the customer, and Finance seems harried and out of sorts."

"That's enough piling on, but Alice, there does seem to be a consistent theme here. Is there a problem in your department?" asked Jack.

"It's true it's sometimes hard for us to keep up!" replied Alice. "Just think of all the transactions Bruce and Tony just mentioned, and that doesn't begin to cover everything we're responsible for. I'm always training my staff, but a new deal seems to come out of marketing almost every day."

"Well, there has to be some way for us to tackle the work flow. We're right at the benchmark figure for a medium-sized car dealership in terms of the number of finance specialists we have, so we shouldn't need to hire more staff. I want each of you to sit down with Alice this week and see if we can improve our internal communications and methods so that we keep our good customers happy and learn to identify those who simply ask too much of us! We also need to understand how this problem might affect our forecasts and budgets. Those are key tools for running our business."

Jack ended the meeting on his typical high note, waving his hands to signal it was time for everyone to leave.

WE HAVE SEEN WHY THE BUSINESS PLANNING AND ANALYSIS (BPA) process is critical to the product, process, customer, and supply chain domains. The BPA process is also critical for managing in the entity domain; that is, for managing entire organizations and the sub-entities of which they are composed. In this and the next chapter, we focus on the issues leaders face in planning and then measuring the results of their organizations and managers. This chapter focuses on small organizations, while Chapter 11 focuses on more complex organizations, which tend to be larger and organized into multiple business units.

Some basic management principles apply to entities of all types. All managers must direct their entity's resources toward the achievement of organizational goals, and all managers must plan their operations and measure their entity's performance. However, entities differ in many ways, and these differences necessitate some variation in their BPA processes. For example, some entities are severely cash-constrained, so their managers must carefully plan and monitor their entity's use of cash. An example is energy services contractor Halliburton which, while struggling in the low-oil-price environment, reduced its staff nearly 20% in the 2014-2015 time period. Other entities, such as Apple, which has had more than $200 billion in cash reserves, have considerable resources at their disposal, so their managers can focus on finding and sifting through opportunities for using those resources. Some entities, such as those in the pharmaceutical industry, must be creative to be successful. Others, such as T-shirt manufacturers, must merely be consistent in executing operating practices that have been in place for years. For some, finding new customers is the key. For others, it is getting quality products out the door on time. And, for still others, finding and retaining qualified employees is critical to success. Obviously, managers must adapt their entity's BPA databases and processes to correspond to the situations and challenges they face.

We begin this chapter by discussing one important planning prerequisite for managers of both large and small organizations: the need to understand the organization's mission and objectives. We then discuss the entity domain, which we base on an organizational stage-of-development framework, and consider how the planning and performance measurement elements of the management process work in relatively small, simple organizations. The smallest of these organizations are highly centralized, with an owner/founder making virtually all of the decisions. As an example, you might think of a small, local restaurant. The largest of these small organizations tend to be organized functionally, with specialists making decisions in at least some of the important functional areas, such as production (cooking), marketing, and finance. As the small restaurant grows, at some point the owner will see a need to add some managerial help, perhaps in the areas of the menu planning and food preparation, training and supervision of the waitstaff, facility design and maintenance, marketing, management of human resources, and finance and accounting.

As you will see in Chapter 11, most organizations that are even larger become divisionalized. The local restaurant might grow into a large restaurant organization with several lines of business, with multiple brands serving customers at different price points, and a general manager heading up each division. Darden Restaurants, for example, operates seven brands of restaurants: Olive Garden, LongHorn Steakhouse, The Capital Grille, Bahama Breeze, Seasons 52, Eddie V's and Yard House. Up until 2013, it also operated Red Lobster restaurants. The different brands of restaurants have different strategies and operating styles.

It is primarily within the entity domain that financial and management accounting intersect because organizational performance is often planned and evaluated using accounting measures that are used also for financial reporting purposes. However, managers often use special, nonfinancial BPA measures and analytical techniques to supplement the financial accounting measures and to make them more meaningful for managerial purposes.

The entity domain is also where we enter the arena of budgeting, which is where most organizations develop comprehensive plans for the coming year's activities. It is the domain in which managers set strategies, develop plans, and analyze results reflecting the performance of the whole business, not just its component parts.

Planning Prerequisites: Missions and Objectives

Before any organization or organizational subunit can develop plans and budgets, the board of directors and the key managers must agree on the organization's mission and objectives. An organization cannot be successful if it does not have agreement on its mission.

In profit-seeking organizations, agreement on mission is generally not a major problem. Managers of these organizations know that their primary objective is to generate a profit or, more precisely, to create value for their owners. Most not-for-profit organizations also understand their missions well. For example, managers of universities know that their primary objective is to help students learn, and hospital managers know that their mission is to heal the sick and injured. However, sometimes major confusion or conflict does exist. For example, some religious communities have debated the extent to which they should allocate their limited resources to provide services to their members, to missionary work, and/or to provide assistance to the poor, or some combination of these purposes.

If the key employees in an organization do not have general agreement about their organization's objectives, or if all employees do not agree on how best to balance conflicts among competing objectives, such as profits vs. responsibilities to employees and society, discussion of the objectives is a necessary first step in the planning process. Some level of agreement must be reached because objectives are a prerequisite for all purposeful activities. Without agreement as to missions and objectives, any claims that the organization was a success would be debatable.

While objectives can vary significantly across organizations of different types, *financial objectives* play at least some role in every organization. In profit-seeking organizations, financial objectives are paramount, but even in nonprofit organizations, finances are important. Managers of not-for-profit organizations must pay attention to their money inflows (revenues) and their money outflows (expenses) both to provide the resources to fulfill their primary missions and to ensure the long-term viability of the organization. Finances are not the primary objective in not-for-profit organizations, but they are an important facilitator and constraint.

Three Organizational Archetypes

OBJECTIVE 1

Compare and contrast small, functionally organized, and divisionalized organizations.

A long stream of research shows that managers of even quite diverse types of companies face remarkably similar sequences of problems and issues as their organizations grow and mature.[2] Here, we focus on three common archetypical organizations:

1. Small companies that use a centralized organizational structure, such as the local restaurant referred to previously. Many of these organizations are young and just have not had an opportunity to grow yet.
2. Organizations that use a functional organizational structure, as is found in larger companies that still operate in a single line of business, such as previously mentioned Darden Restaurants.
3. Large, decentralized companies that operate in multiple lines of businesses and, hence, use the relatively complex, but powerful, divisionalized organization structure. The conglomerate General Electric is a good example of this type of corporation.

Figure 10.1 illustrates the relationships among these three stages of business development.

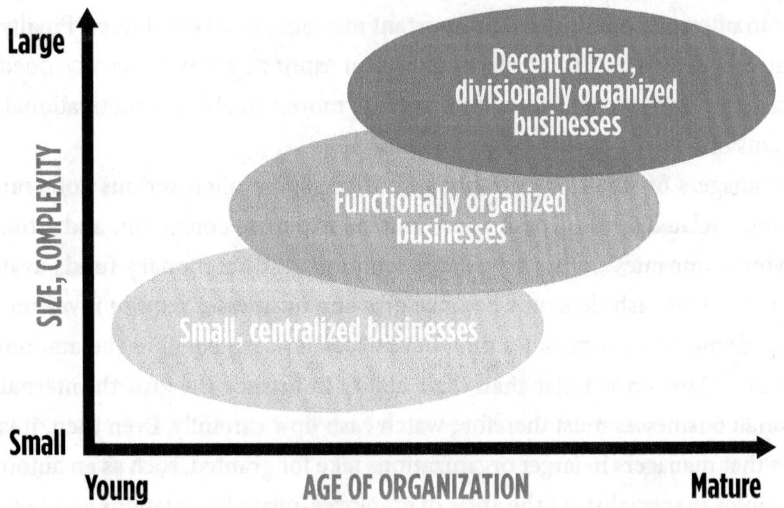

FIGURE 10.1 AS BUSINESSES AGE AND GROW, THEY TEND TO MOVE FROM A CENTRALIZED STRUCTURE—OFTEN FOUNDER-MANAGED—TO A FUNCTIONAL ORGANIZATION AND FINALLY TO A DECENTRALIZED STRUCTURE TO ACCOMMODATE THE DIFFERENT DEMANDS PLACED ON THEM.

---

2 In chapters 10 and 11, we have adapted insights from Theodore Cohn and Roy A. Lindberg, *How Management is Different in Small Companies,* New York: American Management Association, 1972; Larry E. Greiner, "Evolution and Revolution as Organizations Grow," *Harvard Business Review,* July-August 1972, pp. 37-46; Neil C. Churchill and Virginia L. Lewis, "The Five Stages of Small Business Growth," *Harvard Business Review,* May-June 1983, pp. 1-11; and Guy Geeraerts, "The Effect of Ownership on the Organization Structure in Small Firms," *Administrative Science Quarterly,* June 1984, pp. 232-237.

SMALL ORGANIZATIONS

Virtually all small companies, and particularly those that are still managed by their founders, employ a highly centralized management structure. An extreme example of this type of entity is a one-person start-up. These entities' founders—owners do almost everything—decide what to do, and then they personally do most of it. As entities of this type start to grow, the owners will add some employees, but those employees are given little or no authority or discretion. The owners tell them what to do, and then they supervise the actions taken to make sure the employees are doing what they were asked to do.

Small companies have some significant advantages over larger ones. The first is that their owners and managers (if the ownership and management roles are separated) are closer to the action. The managers can maintain "visual contact" with the operations, which means that they are either able to perform themselves or to observe directly most of the key company activities. A second advantage is that the organizational and operational simplicity makes it easier for the owner and managers to manage. They can easily focus their attention on the issues at hand and coordinate the organization's activities. And without multiple organizational subunits, sophisticated product costing analyses and allocation schemes are not necessary. A third advantage is that the small size and concentrated ownership structure make it easier for managers to adjust priorities and shift resources quickly. They do not have to call meetings to achieve a consensus; they can just send out the marching orders. And communication is often quite easy. The owner and managers can often personally deliver important messages to all employees. Finally, in a small organization, it is relatively easy to build a positive culture, an **esprit de corps,** *a common bond among a group; an organizational culture of teamwork*. This culture is often more valuable for motivational purposes than are the formal systems of rewards used in larger businesses.

However, managers of small organizations also face some often serious constraints, which we can describe in various, related terms: a cash constraint, an expertise constraint, and a time constraint. Most small-but-growing companies do not have large amounts of discretionary funds available to them; yet, many of them have great cash demands because growing businesses require investment before revenues are forthcoming. Some small companies only have access to cash equal to the amount of equity in their owners' residences. Many grow faster than their ability to finance the growth internally does. The managers of most small businesses must therefore watch cash flow carefully. Even then, it is rare that they can afford resources that managers in larger organizations take for granted, such as an automated record-keeping system or employee specialists in the areas of employee-related regulations and taxation. The necessity to manage an organization with no margin for error and without much help places great demands on the managers. Most report that they are constantly pressed for time and unable to devote the time they would like to the many important matters that present themselves daily.

FUNCTIONAL ORGANIZATIONS

In the second development stage are businesses that employ a **functional organization structure**—*the organizational sub-entities are structured around different processes or types of work*. These organizations are now large enough that their founders are unable to perform all of the management tasks themselves. They need help. New, key managers are responsible for business functions, such as marketing, production, and human resources, rather than responsible for specific projects, whole business units, or geographical territories. The founders still determine the business strategy, and they may stay heavily involved in the function that they consider their specialty, which are typically product development, sales, or both. But the founders do not have time to do everything, so they hire functional managers—perhaps eventually managers of marketing, production, finance/accounting, human resources, information technology, and perhaps legal—to take over some of the duties. At this point, the founders must learn to delegate decision-making authority to others, something that some find quite difficult to do.

These somewhat larger, functionally organized organizations have some significant advantages over small businesses. They have, by now, almost assuredly demonstrated their viability. Their survival should not be threatened, at least not on a daily basis. The managers can take advantage of the professional expertise—the functional managers—that the company can now afford. The functional managers also begin to track more specific measures that provide information about performance in their area of responsibility. Examples in the marketing area are market share, customer satisfaction, and customer retention. Measures commonly used in production and distribution areas assess throughput, capacity utilization, product quality, productivity, waste, and schedule attainment.

Cash flow is often still a constraint unless the company has either quite high gross margins or is not growing very rapidly, or if bankers or investors can provide a ready source of additional capital. But the growing organization's financial focus tends to shift toward getting a better understanding of the relationships between its revenues and expenses. For example:

- Which products are the most profitable, and which are losing money?
- Can business process efficiency be improved?
- Which of the various investment options could provide an adequate return?
- Where does the company create most of the value customers are willing to pay for?
- Where are wasteful or unnecessary activities beginning to occur?

However, increasing size presents its own set of challenges. As organizations move toward a functional organizational structure, the owners and managers start to lose visual contact with the organization as a whole. They must rely on other managers to make key operating decisions. As a result, they face challenges in staying informed and motivating and coordinating the efforts of these managers, who themselves may not always be aware of what actions other parts of the organization are taking.

Functional managers also tend to be parochial. Marketing managers, for instance, are often concerned with increasing sales without necessarily paying adequate attention to whether or not the additional sales are generating additional company profits. At the same time, production managers are concerned about reducing production costs, but often without adequate concern for the effects on the value provided to customers. These managers are therefore prone to produce products in long production runs that extend customer delivery times, and they may cut quality in order to squeeze a few more cents out of the production cost. Functional managers also face the issue of motivating all of their employees to take actions that are in the best interest of the business. Issues like these create additional demands on the organization's planning and budgeting processes and measurement systems, as we shall describe later in this chapter.

DIVISIONAL ORGANIZATIONS

Organizations in the third, most advanced, development stage are **divisionalized,** *composed of a number of business units*. The business units (often called divisions) operate relatively independently from each other. They are supported by centralized staff functions, such as finance, human resources, and legal. Some of the subunits of divisionally structured organizations can themselves be quite large, and can contain most of the functional elements of independent businesses.

Figure 10.2 shows an example of a divisionalized organization. Brown Industries is in the food business and has three major divisions: Asian Seafood, Farm-Raised Seafood, and Ever-Fresh Vegetables. Each division is supported by a variety of centralized staff functions, such as finance. Brown Industries' three divisions operate independently. However, it is not unusual for companies that are part of a large corporation to actually buy and sell each other's products and services. Most of the organizations we think of as mega-corporations, such as General Electric (GE), use a divisionally organized structure. GE's Aviation Division, which makes jet engines, among other things, almost certainly buys multiple products and services from GE's Power and Water Division. When they do so, they have to decide what internal ***transfer price*** to charge for the internal transfers of products and services.

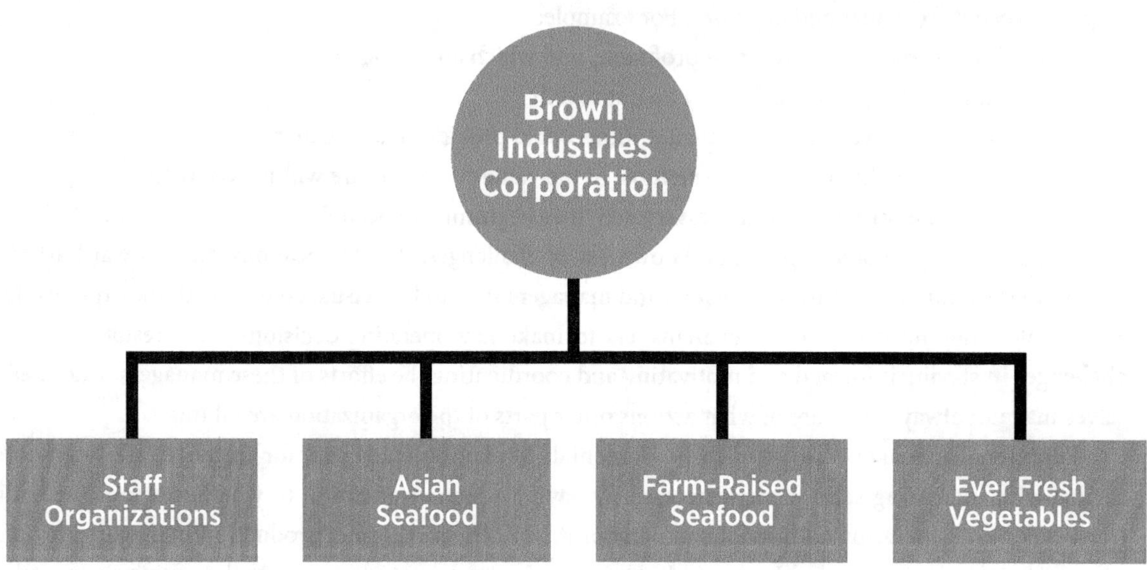

FIGURE 10.2 DIVISIONALLY STRUCTURED ORGANIZATIONS ARE MADE UP OF INDIVIDUAL DECENTRALIZED ENTITIES SUPPORTED BY CENTRALIZED SUPPORT GROUPS; THE GOAL IS TO RETAIN THE ADVANTAGES OF SMALLER SIZE—FLEXIBILITY, AUTONOMY, ENTREPRENEURISM, ETC.—WHILE AT THE SAME TIME GAINING THE BENEFITS OF A CENTRALIZED SUPPORT SYSTEM.

In divisionally organized organizations, inevitably, top managers cannot keep on top of the details of each subunit's business activities. They have to decentralize their operations, delegating to some employees additional **decision-making authority, or decision rights,** *which convey the ability, right, or power to make decisions*. **Decentralization**—*which is the delegation of authority and decision rights to managers in the organization*—is sometimes explained in terms of **autonomy or empowerment,** *which signify the freedom of a manager to make decisions without consulting upper management*. In decentralized organizations, lower-level employees have some autonomy; that is, they are empowered or have the freedom to make decisions in a specified operating area with no, or perhaps minimal, oversight from upper management before a decision is made. The goal of granting higher levels of autonomy is to retain the advantages of small size, including the flexibility of response and the entrepreneurial spirit.

After they decentralize and reorganize divisionally, the top managers must implement controls to ensure that their subordinates consistently act in the organization's best interest. Many of the controls, such as policies and procedures and incentive systems, either force or motivate employees to act in ways the company desires. At managerial levels of the firm, incentive systems involve the use of accounting measures. But accounting measures, by themselves, are not adequate. Divisionally organized entities need a performance measurement system that helps coordinate actions across the organization while integrating activities throughout the organization—from top to bottom. We discuss these controls and their functional, and sometimes dysfunctional, effects in Chapter 11.

Planning in Small Organizations

OBJECTIVE 2

Describe the purposes of planning in the entity domain and understand the mechanics of preparing an entity-level plan.

Planning is important even in the simplest of organizations. Consider a one-person entity. As an example, think of a vendor who sells ice cream at high school football games. Call the entity Joe's Ice Cream. Joe works alone. He sells ice cream at Central High School's football games. Central has four home games each season.

It is not difficult to understand the objective of Joe's Ice Cream. First and foremost, it is to earn a profit. Joe might also have some secondary goals. He might enjoy the work, and he might eventually want to provide jobs for his children. But his primary objective is to earn a profit.

1. Even though his entity is simple, to be effective, Joe needs to pay attention to all of the elements of the BPA process. Joe has to: ***Plan*** his operation; particularly how much ice cream to buy and carry to the stadium.
2. ***Do:*** purchase and sell the ice cream.
3. ***Check*** on what happened; tally his sales so that he can learn from the experience.
4. ***Adjust:*** decide how much ice cream to bring to the next event.

Before we examine how Joe prepares a plan, we need the following information about his business:

- ***Franchise cost***: Joe purchased the right to sell ice cream at the games from Central High School for $400 for the season.
- ***Products offered***: ice cream cones and ice cream sandwiches.
- ***Price charged to customers***: $3 apiece.
- ***Product cost:*** cones: $1.50; sandwiches: $1.
- ***Attendance:*** From ticket sale information the school gave him, Joe estimates that the average attendance per game is about 600, although he estimates it ranges from 200 to 2,000, depending on the weather, the time of the game, and the quality of the opponent.
- ***Percentage of fans that purchase ice cream***: Based on other years, Joe estimates that 25% of the fans in attendance will buy some ice cream from him, but he knows that the percentage can vary widely, depending on factors such as how hot the weather is on a particular day.
- ***Sales mix:*** Historically, roughly two out of three customers who buy something purchase cones.

Based on this information, how should Joe prepare a plan? Let us consider a plan for the first game of the year. Most plans start with a **revenue forecast,** *a projection of future sales for a period of time*. Joe has no reason to believe that game one on the schedule will be atypical, so Joe's **best-guess revenue forecast**—*a prediction based on the most likely outcome, a 50% probability of attainment*—is as follows:

Attendance at game	600
Number of attendees who will buy ice cream (25%)	150
Revenue from cones sold (100 units x $3.00)	$300
Revenue from sandwiches sold (50 units x $3.00)	$150
Total revenue	$450

This best-guess forecast takes into consideration all of the information Joe has at his disposal. Joe is aware that he is as likely to exceed this revenue forecast as he is to miss it.

Next, Joe has to prepare the rest of his plan for the game. He is likely to prepare his plan in financial terms, because monetary units provide nice summaries of all of the elements of performance. Although Joe may not know the jargon, what he is doing is preparing a **pro-forma financial statement, or profit plan,** *which shows the estimated, or forecasted, results of operations*. Pro-forma balance sheets and statements of cash flow are also important outputs of a planning process.

The profit plan for Joe's Ice Cream is shown in Table 10.1.

TABLE 10.1 PLAN UNDER A BEST-GUESS REVENUE FORECAST

	First game of the year
Revenue	$ 450
Cost of goods sold	200
Gross margin	250
Amortized cost of franchise	100*
Net profit	$ 150

Note:
* Straight-line amortization of the $400 franchise fee over the four at-home games.

As mentioned earlier, in many small businesses, cash flow planning is critical because the founders have limited capital to invest. Joe can easily change this profit plan into a pro-forma statement of cash flow. Joe's business has no receivables or payables. The only noncash item on his profit plan is the franchise cost. So Joe's expected cash flow from the first game of the year is $250.

This profit plan is a key element in what most companies refer to as a **budget,** *a quantitative (financial) expression of a plan of action for a specific short period of time*. At Joe's Ice Cream, it would be logical to prepare a budget for the entire football season, broken down by game. This information would help Joe make decisions about how much ice cream he should buy, as he might be able to obtain some quantity discounts with larger orders, how large a freezer he should rent, and, therefore, how much cash he needs. In larger organizations, budgets are typically prepared for a year, which is disaggregated into quarters and, often, months. Budgets provide managers with day-to-day operating guidance about the acquisition and use of resources under their control.

SCENARIO PLANNING IN SMALL ORGANIZATIONS

OBJECTIVE 3

Explain the advantages of scenario planning, and apply the concepts of expected value to scenario planning.

In an uncertain world, a best-guess revenue forecast is not the only possibility. Consider two other plausible possibilities, an optimistic and a pessimistic forecast. For Joe's Ice Cream, an optimistic forecast might assume that the attendance at the opening game will be 1,000 people and, because the weather will be warm, that 60% of the people will buy ice cream. A pessimistic forecast might assume that attendance will only be 400, and only 15% of the people will buy ice cream. (Obviously, scenarios can be prepared anywhere between, or even outside of, these extremes.) Table 10.2 shows three plausible plans: the best-guess plan shown in Table 10.1, an optimistic plan, and a pessimistic plan.

TABLE 10.2 THREE REVENUE SCENARIOS COMPARED

	Plans based on different revenue scenarios for the first game		
	Pessimistic	Best-guess	Optimistic
Revenue	$180*	$450	$1,800**
Cost of goods sold	80***	200	800****
Gross margin	100	250	1,000
Amortization of franchise cost	100	100	100
Net profit	$0	$150	$900

Notes:
* 60 ice cream items x $3.00
** 600 ice cream items sold x $3.00
*** 40 cones x $1.50 + 20 sandwiches x $1.00
**** 400 cones x $1.50 + 200 sandwiches x $1.00

Which is the best plan for Joe? That's a trick question: Joe really does not have to choose just one plan; the information contained in each of these scenarios might be valuable. Plans based on different revenue scenarios help us understand the risks and opportunities inherent in a business. Each of these plans provides information that can be useful in helping Joe shape what will happen and, then, after the performance period ends, understand what actually did happen. The pessimistic plan, if it is truly the most pessimistic, tells Joe something about what he should purchase. He should bring a minimum of 40 cones and 20 sandwiches to the game. If he does not, he will lose a sale that could have been made. It also shows Joe that he will not lose any money, even if attendance and ice cream consumption fall short of his expectations.

The optimistic scenario, if it is truly the most optimistic, tells Joe that if he brings fewer than 400 cones and 200 sandwiches to the game, he is risking the possibility that he will run out of inventory and lose the profits on sales he might have made. The optimistic plan should also force Joe to address the question of whether or not he can sell 600 items by himself. If he has to add an employee for the game, he will have to add a labor cost line item to his budget.

The best-guess scenario probably provides the best standard against which to compare actual performance. If actual performance is different from this best guess, as it almost inevitably will be, Joe can learn from this new information. With experience, Joe's forecasting ability should improve, and he will become better able to understand the impact of the various factors that affect attendance, ice cream consumption, and sales mix.

Joe could add a few statistics to his analysis to make the decision about how best to stock the coming game more concrete. While he currently has pessimistic, best-guess, and optimistic scenarios, he has not assigned probabilities to each of these possibilities. If he did, he could generate an **expected value,** *which takes into consideration the probabilities of occurrence of each of the scenarios.* Let us say Joe thinks the probability of the optimistic scenario is 20%, the probability of his best-guess scenario is 50%, and the probability of his pessimistic outcome is 30%. Using the net profits of the three scenarios from Table 10.2, what is the expected value, or probability-adjusted estimate, of the outcome?

Expected value = (.2 × $0) + (.5 × $150) + (.3 × $900) = $345.00

The expected value tells us that Joe should probably do slightly better than his best-guess scenario. Since his inventory is frozen and can be used at another game, he might want to increase quantities by 30% of his best-case scenario inventory of the goods he brings to the first game. If his best guess is right, he will have some leftover inventory. But if his optimistic version is closer to the truth, he will make $195 more in profit for the effort he puts in.

Some companies prepare multiple plans based on different plausible visions of the future. This is called **scenario planning,** *the preparation of multiple plans or budgets based on different plausible visions of the future*. The purpose of scenario planning is not to predict the future, but rather to show how different forces the organization might face in the future can affect it. Understanding the effects of these forces requires some thought about potential actions and improves the organization's ability to respond to those events.

IN THE NEWS ➤ World-Class Planning for the Unexpected

The Royal Dutch/Shell Group, the giant oil company, is long renowned for its scenario planning.* Shell managers prepare for the unexpected by developing strategies to safeguard the company against a broad range of possible risks defined in terms of scenarios.

In the mid-1980s, one of the company's scenarios, called "The Greening of Russia," predicted the opening of the Iron Curtain and estimated the consequent effects on world oil demand. This scenario helped the company avoid large investments in multibillion-dollar oil platforms in the Bering Sea.

Two other Shell scenarios, focused on a 20-year horizon, were called "Sustainable World" and "Global Mercantilism." The Sustainable World scenario assumed a resolution of the major international economic disputes, and, thus, greater attention would be paid to environmental issues, such as global warming trends, conservation, recycling, and emission controls. If this scenario happened, the major implication for Shell was an energy industry mix change toward more use of natural gas and less use of oil. The Global Mercantilism scenario assumed a gloomier future with numerous regional conflicts, a destabilized world, increased protectionism, and world recession. If this scenario happened, Shell managers thought there would be less regulation, less focus on environmental issues, and greater oil consumption.

*See, for example, Kees van der Keijden, *Scenarios: The Art of Strategic Conversations*, New York: John Wiley & Sons, 1996.

In some industries, it makes sense to base the scenarios on different assumptions about revenue, as illustrated by the scenarios we developed for Joe's Ice Cream. In others, the most important contingencies are cost-related. Airlines and plastics manufacturers, whose results are highly dependent on oil prices, might prepare multiple plans based on different assumptions about oil prices. And many organizations do **disaster planning,** *a form of scenario planning that assumes a major disaster occurs and establishes action plans to meet the resulting critical and unique demands placed on management*. Disasters include natural catastrophes, such as earthquakes and hurricanes, or man-made attacks, such as the sabotage of an organization's computer facility. Disaster planning allows managers to prepare and polish their response beforehand so that they can react quickly and with minimal stress should a disaster occur.

It is important to recognize that planning provides multiple benefits for even the simplest of organizations, such as Joe's one-person organization. Preparing a plan *forces Joe to consider the future*. To prepare a plan, Joe must think about how much ice cream he might sell at the various games and throughout the season. This will help him *determine the amount of resources*, both ice cream products and possibly salespeople, he should have in place at various times. Planning might also help Joe think about the *implications of various policy decisions*, such as pricing. He could easily alter the plan to consider, for example, the implications of raising the price of cones to $4. The plan provides a *standard against which to compare performance*. This can be useful to Joe in identifying possible problems, such as shortfalls in the sales of one or both products, and their implications. Comparing the standards with actual results can also help Joe improve his forecasting. More accurate forecasts will lead to better decision making and, hence, higher profits.

It is important to recognize that all plans are based on forecasts of the future. Forecasting and planning the responses to the forecasts are not exact sciences. They require management judgment, which improves with training and experience. The variances between plans and actual results (actuals) will be lower the more accurate the estimates are. But that does *not* mean that the benefits of planning are necessarily higher in situations where more accurate estimates can be made. The benefits of planning may actually be higher when the future is very uncertain. The planning processes and information can help managers cope with that uncertainty.

If Joe's activities at Central High School are successful, he might try to grow the business to other high schools. He could try to sell other types of products at Central High School football games and perhaps also at other events, or he could try to sell products at the events of other schools or organizations. Inevitably, the first employees he would add would be family members or friends whom he can trust. The addition of these employees would not change Joe's operations much. He would still be making all of the decisions and directing the others' actions.

Only if Joe's organization got considerably larger, or if Joe wanted to minimize his direct involvement in the business, could Joe's Ice Cream move to a later stage of business development. If Joe set up specialists to control the various functions of the business—purchasing, sales, finance—he would start to reap the advantages but face the problems of a functional organization.

Joe's business does not necessarily have to go through a functional organization stage to get to the divisionally organized stage. As the business becomes larger, Joe could create divisions by appointing "general" managers responsible for a geographic area (in this case, a school) or a product line (such as ice cream, hot dogs, souvenirs), granting them decision-making authority in their areas of operation, and providing rewards based on the results they generate. If he did these things, Joe would have to face the issues common to decentralized, divisionally organized businesses.

LOOKING BACK ➤ Mrs. Fields: Grew Big, Plans Like She Was Still Small

Mrs. Fields started small, with a single cookie store. Over the years, however, the company grew considerably. It now has nearly 1,000 cookie stores located across the United States and in several foreign countries, generates more than $100 million in annual sales, and has more than 3,500 employees.

The company has moved to a franchised structure. It plans and directs its activities with a sophisticated computer system. Using information about seasons, days of the week, and weather, the computer makes hourly sales projections and tells the managers what cookies to bake. If sales are slow, it prompts the manager with selling suggestions, such as distributing free samples outside of the store. It schedules the crew. It helps interview and screen job applicants by analyzing their responses to a fixed set of questions. It helps with personnel administration by printing out the needed forms. It helps with maintenance by telling the manager how to get service in the local area. And it provides direct contact with the company's founder/CEO, Debbie Fields. In fact, the purpose of the computer system is to leverage Debbie's time and expertise, enabling each store to run just as Debbie would run it if she were there.

Thus, while Mrs. Fields is now a reasonably large business, and one that is no longer young, it still operates like a small business. The computer system allows the business to run on a highly centralized basis, but Debbie still runs virtually everything.

Source: Lynda M. Applegate and Keri Pearlson, "Mrs. Fields, Inc.," *Harvard Business Review: Case Series*, June 2, 1994.

Planning in Functional Organizations

OBJECTIVE 4

Illustrate the benefits of planning in functional organizations.

As small organizations grow and add more employees, the vast majority of them evolve toward a functional organizational structure. As they add employees, top management gradually delegates responsibility for certain functions—production, sales, purchasing, finance, or research—and probably eventually all of them to subordinates. Each of these functions gradually gets more sophisticated using measures that reflect aspects of performance specific to each operating area. The goal is to develop a **balanced scorecard,** *a multidimensional set of* *performance measurements*. The set will eventually include measures focused on financial performance, the customer value creation, internal business processes, and employee learning and growth. These measures are related to one another, as is shown in Figure 10.3. Thus, for example, in the internal business process area, production managers track throughput, efficiency, waste, and schedule attainment, while purchasing managers track purchased item costs and trends, stockouts, and inventory levels. All of these measures can contribute to customer value, and pleasing customers will create value for the company.

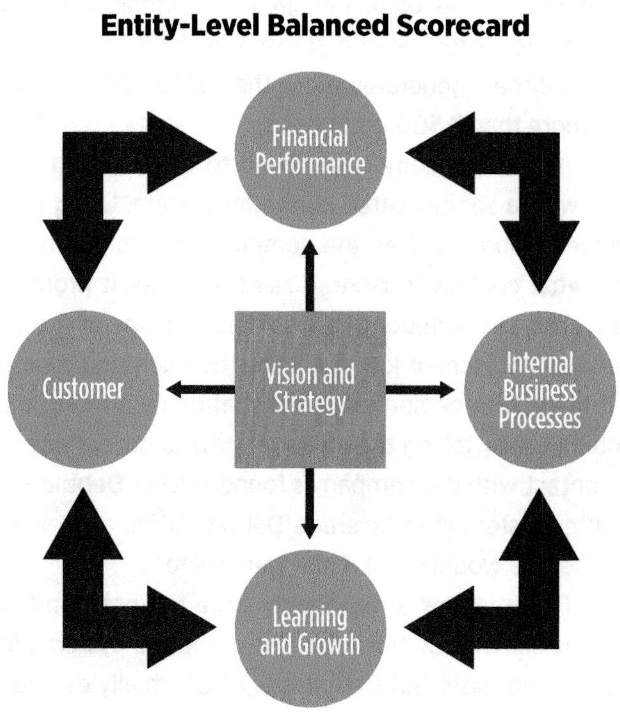

Entity-Level Balanced Scorecard

FIGURE 10.3 THE ENTITY-LEVEL BALANCED SCORECARD TAKES A TOP-DOWN APPROACH AND INVOLVES ALL FUNCTIONAL MANAGERS IN THE PROCESS OF CONTINUOUS IMPROVEMENT.

We have already discussed balanced scorecards from an operational perspective, in which we focused on productivity, delivery, quality and cost. The entity-level balanced scorecard, developed by Kaplan and Norton in 1992,[3] takes more of a top-down view to balancing performance, one that encompasses all of the functional managers in the organization in the process of continuous improvement. While clearly some of these metrics are more easily measured for one function, in reality, as we have seen, nearly everyone in the organization affects performance on all of these dimensions. What might be considered a customer by one manager can be another internal manager who interfaces directly with external customers,

3 Robert S. Kaplan and David P. Norton, "The Balanced Scorecard—Measures that Drive Performance," *Harvard Business Review*, January-February 1992: pp. 71-79.

such as an accounts receivable manager in Accounting. Everyone has a customer in the chain of activities and events who helps a company meet external customer expectations.

When organizational responsibilities are dispersed among many people, the planning processes employed must provide more benefits than those provided to managers of simple organizations like Joe's Ice Cream. One such benefit is *communication*. The planning processes provide a useful forum in which to communicate valuable information. Some of this information flows via a **top-down manner:** *from top management to functional managers*. Top managers can use the planning processes to communicate the organization's objectives and exigencies (for example, short-term cash flow needs), their predictions of the future (such as the impact of changes to government policies), and the effects of policy decisions they have made (for instance, average salary increases for the following year). But some of the information flows in a **bottom-up manner:** *from lower levels of the organization to upper management*. Lower-level managers can use the planning processes to inform upper-level managers about their plans, problems, and opportunities. These communications can result in *better-informed* decisions by all organizational parties and *better-coordinated* activities.

Another important benefit is *motivation* of the lower-level managers. Most people like a performance target to shoot for, rather than merely being told to "do your best"; thus, the plans become performance targets. Plans are also motivating because their achievement can be, and usually is, linked to various organizational rewards, such as salary increases, bonuses, promotions, and recognition.

As an example of planning in a functional organization, consider the case of Ionics, Ltd., a small firm that manufactures and sells household air purifiers. Ionics' income statement for the past year is shown in Table 10.3.

TABLE 10.3 INCOME STATEMENT OF FUNCTIONAL ORGANIZATION

Ionics, Ltd.		
Calendar Year 20x6	(in thousands)	
Sales		$1,000,000
Direct materials	$220,000	
Direct labor	$160,000	
Manufacturing overhead—variable	$80,000	
Manufacturing overhead—fixed	$40,000	$500,000
Gross margin		$500,000
Selling expenses—variable	$100,000	
Advertising expense—discretionary	$100,000	
Research and development expense	$40,000	
Administrative expense	$60,000	$300,000
Net income		$200,000

The company is organized functionally, as is shown in Figure 10.4, and planning at Ionics had been done on a centralized and informal basis. However, several significant uncertainties regarding 20x7 made Jill Maycock, Ionics' president and CEO, want to involve additional managers in a more systematic planning process. Although performance had lagged in the recession of 20x3–20x4, its performance had improved a bit in the following years, and Jill believed that economic conditions for 20x7 were favorable. She wanted the company to return to its historical growth rate of 20%. So she told her managers that the company's goals for 20x7 would be $1.2 billion in sales and $240 million in net income. She asked them to prepare a plan to produce that level of performance.

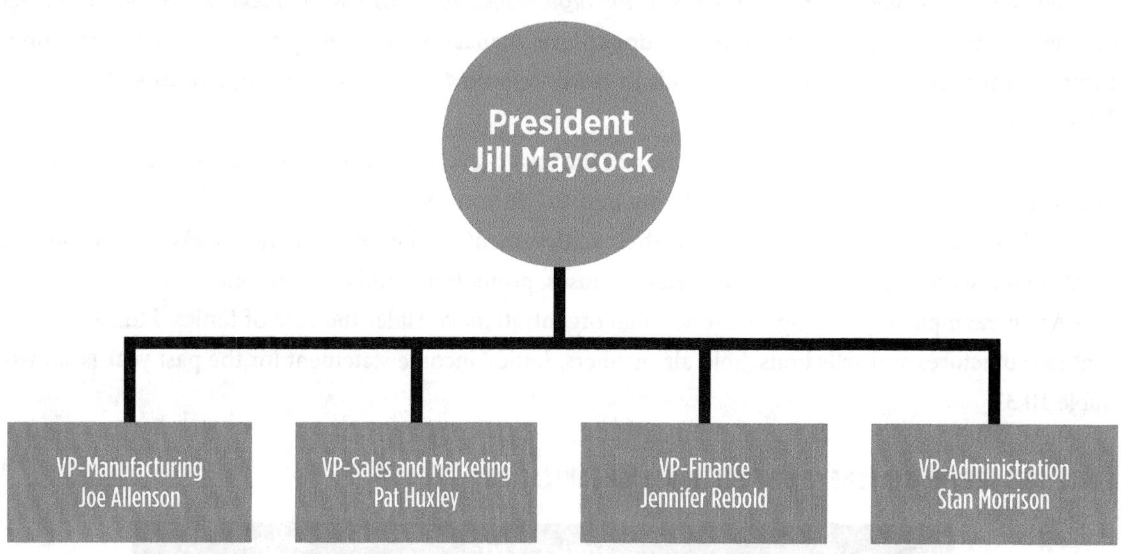

FIGURE 10.4. IN A FUNCTIONALLY ORGANIZED ENTITY, EACH GROUP OPERATES INDEPENDENTLY AND REPORTS UP THE CHAIN OF COMMAND, WHERE THE GOALS ARE SET. THE PLANS FOR ACHIEVING THOSE OBJECTIVES ARE DESIGNED WITHIN EACH SEPARATE DEPARTMENT.

In a series of planning meetings, Ionics' functional managers developed the following expectations for 20x7:

- Unit sales of purifiers will increase by 10%.
- The unit price will not change.
- Material prices will increase by 5%.
- Direct labor wages will increase by 5%.
- Fixed manufacturing expenses will not change unless unit sales growth exceeds 40%, in which case additional manufacturing space and equipment would be needed.
- Administrative expenses will increase by 5%.

Jennifer Rebold, Ionics' vice president of finance, used these expectations to assemble the profit plan shown in Table 10.4. This is a bottom-up plan because it was developed by employees lower in the organization, not top management, setting the plan. **Participation**—*the involvement of managers in the planning process and their subsequent influence over the final plan*—has two elements, *involvement* in the process and *influence* over the outcome. **Pseudo-participation** *is the involvement of subordinates, who actually have little or no influence over the plans and performance targets that are set*, in the planning process.

TABLE 10.4 BOTTOM-UP BUDGET PLAN: PROJECTED INCOME STATEMENT FOR A FUNCTIONALLY-ORGANIZED ENTITY

Ionics, Ltd.		
Year Ending December 31, 20x7		
Sales		$1,100,000
Direct materials	$254,100	
Direct labor	$184,800	
Manufacturing overhead—variable	$88,000	
Manufacturing overhead—fixed	$40,000	$566,900
Gross margin		$533,100
Selling expenses—variable	$110,000	
Advertising expense—discretionary	$10,000	
Research and development expense	$40,000	
Administrative expense	$63,000	$223,000
Net income		$310,100

IN CONTEXT ➤ Planning the Future at Prestige Auto

The management of Prestige Auto met to start formulating a plan for improving its customer relations. Jack kicked off the meeting.

"When we last met, I asked all of you to work with Alice to try to understand why we're having problems in the finance area. Alice's group works hard, so we may need to start sharing some of the load and improving our procedures so things go more smoothly for customers when it comes to financing."

"We have all shared information with Alice," Judy piped up. "If the financing part doesn't go well, we can lose the sale, so we're in this together. I think my salespeople can get the process started earlier by asking the potential customer a few questions at the outset, giving Alice's group a chance to start pulling together the paperwork. I know we can help make it look seamless if we try."

"We can do a better job in repairs, too," noted Tony. "As soon as we finish a job, we're going to get the information over to Finance so they can get the paperwork squared away. That way, when the customer comes in to pick up a car, all they have to do is stop in Finance and arrange payment so the process will go quickly; that is, if one of Alice's people is free."

"I'm going to assign one person dedicated to repair invoicing, Tony. That will simplify things on both ends. You'll know who to go to and they'll know how to handle everything so the customer never sees us stumble," Alice assured him.

"In Purchasing, we're going to work with Alice's group so she knows what cars we're looking at as soon as possible. Since we either buy directly from corporate managers for the new and leased cars or from customers who are right in front of us for used cars, we should be able to coordinate the process better," noted Bruce.

Jack said: "It looks like all of you are now on the same page. That's good. We can't let our communications break down because that directly impacts how our customer sees us. Now we can turn our attention to everyone's favorite topic—budgeting for next year. I want you to take special care, Alice, as you reorganize your workforce, because it may have resource implications.

"I don't just want financial estimates this year, I want each of you to suggest some performance measures I can use to keep better track of what is going on in the shop, on the sales floor, and in the back office. I've got my own set started, but I'd like your input on these. Okay? We'll meet next week with your first projections."

The meeting ended with quite a few groans and rolled eyeballs. His team had great functional managers, but they really hated the planning process. Since it was so critical to Jack's ability to keep track of his business, it had to be done. No way to avoid it.

Wait until they saw he wanted scenario planning from them as well!

Budgeting in Functional Organizations

OBJECTIVE 5

Create a company budget for a medium- to large-sized organization.

All organizations need to plan in some way, shape, or form. For very small organizations, such as Joe's Ice Cream, simple planning of what inventory may be needed at a specific time is enough. Once Joe chooses an inventory level, the goal is simply to make sure it is sold. There is no coordination between functions needed in Joe's situation. He is in charge and makes all of the decisions. Personnel in Ionics, Ltd., and in most organizations, however, need to communicate a common plan and find ways to keep everyone focused on its attainment. In most medium- to large-sized organizations, the communication tool of choice is the organizational budget.

Figure 10.5 shows that quite a few different stages or activities take place during the budgeting process at a company like Ionics, Ltd. First, the sales forecast needs to be made, like Joe did for his business. From this, the functional budgets flow. For a manufacturing firm, this includes the production budget, coupled with materials, labor, and overhead budgets. For a service firm, this would be a labor and overhead budget—materials become irrelevant. Once managers determine the cost of goods sold or cost of sales, they can determine and add the marketing, administrative and research, and development budgets to the mix. The result is the budgeted income statement.

Once the income statement is complete, attention turns to cash flows. Here, managers must take a more long-term focus, emphasizing the need to replenish capital assets in addition to keeping the company running from day to day. Once the cash budget is done and meets with general approval, the process closes with the creation of a budgeted balance sheet and statement of cash flows. Three pro forma statements, therefore, are key elements of the budget preparation process, one we will now look at in detail for Ionics.

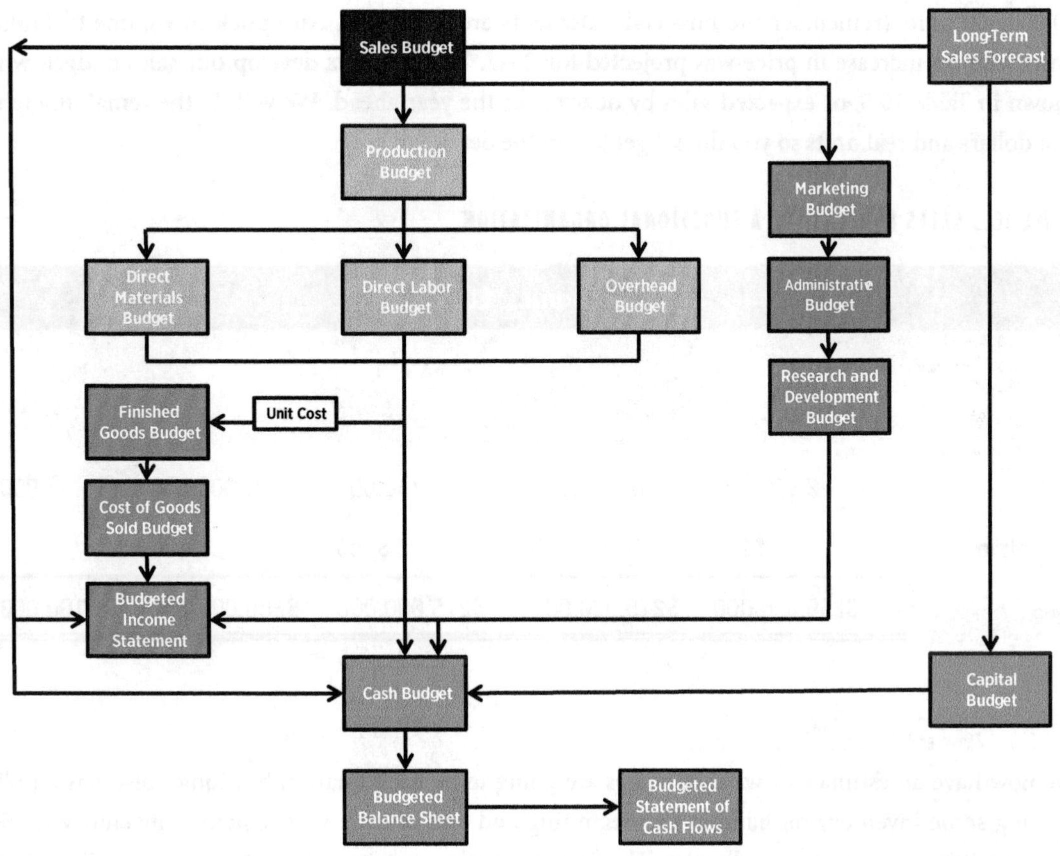

FIGURE 10.5 THE BUDGETING STRUCTURE OF A FUNCTIONAL ORGANIZATION FOCUSES ON DEPARTMENTS AND THE COST OF SALES ANALYSIS.

As we walk through each of the major stages of the budgeting process, our goal is not to make you an expert in budgeting, but it is important that you understand the basic flow of information that makes the budgeting process work. What we will do is recreate Ionics' budgeted income statement, Table 10.4, using information from 20x6 to support our analysis.

FORECASTING SALES

In most companies, one of the first steps in planning is to forecast the level of sales expected during the coming period. While this could be done weekly, monthly, quarterly, or annually, we will see things most clearly if we focus on one year's quarterly projections. A longer horizon adds considerable uncertainty and, hence, noise to the projections. Some companies, such as electric utilities, must plan decades in advance because of the lead time required to bring additional productive capacity online. For Ionics, an annual horizon allows us to show the budget calculations while not losing ourselves in excessive detail. Good budgets need to be communicated, and this starts with having numbers people understand.

Ionics, Ltd., sells its air-purifying units for $100 each. That means that actual unit sales in 20x6 were 10,000,000 units (remember the financial statements are in 1,000s). An uptick in volume to 11,000,000 units with no increase in price was projected for 20x7. This helps us develop our sales budget, which is shown in Table 10.5, or expected sales by quarter for the year ahead. We will do the remaining tables in real dollars and real units so you do not get lost in the detail.

TABLE 10.5 SALES FORECAST OF A FUNCTIONAL ORGANIZATION

Ionics, Ltd.					
20x7					
	Quarter 1	Quarter 2	Quarter 3	Quarter 4	Annual
Units	2,500,000	2,750,000	2,750,000	3,000,000	11,000,000
Selling Price	$100	$100	$100	$100	$100
Sales	$250,000,000	$275,000,000	$275,000,000	$300,000,000	$1,100,000,000

PRODUCTION BUDGET

We now have an estimate of what our sales are going to be each quarter, but Ionics also has a policy of keeping some inventory on hand at the beginning and end of each year. Opening inventory is 250,000 units, or 10% of the next period's sales. This is its normal inventory policy. We will keep 10% of the next quarter's sales on hand at the end of each quarter. Because we have to deal with inventory moving up and down, we need a production budget that allows us to accommodate not only those units we intend to sell but also those we need to keep on hand to ensure we can meet customer demand.

Whenever we have to reconcile inventory, we use the same formula:

Units needed to be produced (bought) =
Ending inventory units + Projected sales - Beginning inventory units

We clearly need to adjust inventory for the difference in ending and beginning inventory to ensure we keep our customers' needs in mind. Every time we deal with inventory in a budgeting problem, we need to use this formula. Therefore, let us develop a production budget for the coming year for Ionics, Ltd. We will need to *assume* that the desired ending inventory for Quarter 4 is 300,000 units as we do not have a budget for 20x8 to work from. There is another thing you need to keep in mind. When we look at the annual column, the desired ending inventory is Quarter 4's ending inventory, which is the end of the year, while Quarter 1's beginning inventory is the inventory for the beginning of the year. This is logical, right?

TABLE 10.6 PRODUCTION BUDGET FOR A FUNCTIONAL ORGANIZATION

Ionics, Ltd.					
	For the year ending December 31, 20x7				
	Quarter 1	Quarter 2	Quarter 3	Quarter 4	Annual
Projected sales	2,500,000	2,750,000	2,750,000	3,000,000	11,000,000
Plus: Desired ending inventory	275,000	275,000	300,000	300,000	300,000
Units needed	2,775,000	3,025,000	3,050,000	3,300,000	11,300,000
Less: Beginning inventory	250,000	275,000	275,000	300,000	250,000
Units to make	2,525,000	2,750,000	2,775,000	3,000,000	11,050,000

If we look at Tables 10.7, 10.8, and 10.9, we see that the production budget allows us to break down our spending on making items into materials, labor, and overhead budgets. The materials and labor budgets both face a 5% increase in cost, while the overhead budget has both fixed and variable components.

RAW MATERIALS, LABOR, AND OVERHEAD BUDGETS

Let us do the materials budget first because it also requires an adjustment for beginning and ending inventory. To make this simpler, we will assume for now that only one raw material—plastic—goes into our purifiers. The plastic is molded and shaped in all sorts of ways during production, but, in the end, it is all a light gray plastic. It takes two pounds of this magical plastic material to make one air purifier at a projected cost for the coming year of $11.55 per pound ($254,100,000 divided by 11,000,000 units equals $23.10 per unit, or two pounds of material). We will assume that 20% of the raw materials needed next period were kept on hand. Ending raw materials inventory will be *assumed* to be 20% of Quarter 4's sales. Using these figures, the raw materials budget would look like Table 10.7.

TABLE 10.7 RAW MATERIALS BUDGET

Ionics, Ltd.					
For the Year 20x7					
	Quarter 1	Quarter 2	Quarter 3	Quarter 4	Annual
Units to make	2,525,000	2,750,000	2,775,000	3,000,000	11,050,000
Raw materials per unit	2	2	2	2	2
Raw materials for production	5,050,000	5,500,000	5,550,000	6,000,000	22,100,000
Plus: Desired ending inventory	1,100,000	1,110,000	1,200,000	1,200,000	1,200,000
Raw materials needed	6,150,000	6,610,000	6,750,000	7,200,000	23,300,000
Less: Beginning inventory	1,010,000	1,100,000	1,110,000	1,200,000	1,010,000
Units to buy	5,140,000	5,510,000	5,640,000	6,000,000	22,290,000
Times cost per unit	$11.55	$11.55	$11.55	$11.55	$11.55
Total raw materials	$59,367,000	$63,640,500	$65,142,000	$69,300,000	$257,449,500
Materials Used in Production	$58,327,500	$63,525,000	$64,102,500	$69,300,000	$255,255,000

In preparing the materials budget, we have transformed our plan from quantity to dollar terms. We see that it is going to cost us $257,449,500 in total materials purchases for the upcoming year. We also are going to use $255,255,000 in materials for production (22,100,000 raw materials for production times the cost of $11.55 per unit). Given the arrangements we have with our suppliers, we can probably put off paying some of this until next year, but that means we probably have some accounts payable open from last year also. We will look at these issues when we do the cash budget. Having done the materials budget, we can now do the labor and overhead budgets for the coming year.

Our next budget is the labor budget. We know that we plan to pay a total of $16.80 for labor for the coming year, up 5% from the prior year ($184,800,000 divided by 11,000,000 units sold, or $16.80 per unit). To make this realistic, we will assume that it takes 1.5 hours to make one purifying unit. That means we pay direct labor $16.80 divided by 1.5, or $11.20 per hour. Table 10.8 shows how much labor we need to budget for. Here, we do not need to make adjustments for inventory because Ionics schedules labor just as we need it—remember that we cannot store labor like we can materials.

TABLE 10.8 LABOR BUDGET FOR FUNCTIONAL ORGANIZATION

Ionics, Ltd.					
	Calendar Year 20x7				
	Quarter 1	Quarter 2	Quarter 3	Quarter 4	Annual
Units to make	2,525,000	2,750,000	2,775,000	3,000,000	11,050,000
Times: Labor hours per unit	1.5	1.5	1.5	1.5	1.5
Direct labor hours needed	3,787,500	4,125,000	4,162,500	4,500,000	16,575,000
Times: Cost per hour	$11.20	$11.20	$11.20	$11.20	$11.20
Total labor dollars	$42,420,000	$46,200,000	$46,620,000	$50,400,000	$185,640,000

The overhead budget is a bit trickier because we have to deal with both the fixed and variable portions of the overhead. Variable overhead is $8 per unit ($88,000,000 divided by 11,000,000 units). We will assume the fixed overhead is incurred evenly throughout the year, which is a logical conclusion. Since this work goes on at a steady pace, it makes sense to assume that we will spend about the same amount per month every quarter unless volumes really spike. Table 10.9 shows what Ionics' overhead budget looks like.

TABLE 10.9 OVERHEAD BUDGET FOR FUNCTIONAL ORGANIZATION

Ionics, Ltd.					
	Calendar Year 20x7				
	Quarter 1	Quarter 2	Quarter 3	Quarter 4	Annual
Units to make	2,525,000	2,750,000	2,775,000	3,000,000	11,050,000
Times: Variable overhead per unit	$8.00	$8.00	$8.00	$8.00	$8.00
Total variable overhead	$20,200,000	$22,000,000	$22,200,000	$24,000,000	$88,400,000
Plus: Fixed overhead cost	$10,000,000	$10,000,000	$10,000,000	$10,000,000	$40,000,000
Total overhead budget	$30,200,000	$32,000,000	$32,200,000	$34,000,000	$128,400,000

Now that we have done the budget for the materials, labor, and overhead components of the budget, we can move on to the finished goods inventory budget and the cost of goods sold budget.

FINISHED GOODS AND COST OF GOODS SOLD BUDGETS

We have calculated the cost to actually make the product, now we need to assign a value to the ending finished goods inventory and to the cost of goods sold itself. First, we calculate the value of a unit in finished goods inventory; then we use this unit cost to calculate the value of the units we are keeping in inventory. Table 10.10 shows this calculation.

TABLE 10.10 YEAR-END FINISHED GOODS INVENTORY FOR FUNCTIONAL ORGANIZATION

Ionics, Ltd.	
Calendar Year 20x7	
Unit cost analysis:	
Materials per unit (2 pounds at $11.55 per pound)	$23.10
Labor per unit (1.5 hours at $11.20 per hour)	$16.80
Variable overhead per unit	$8.00
Fixed overhead per unit ($40,000,000 / 11,050,000 units)	$3.62
Total unit cost	$51.52
Finished goods (300,000 units at $51.52 per unit)	$15,456,000

Now that we have calculated finished goods inventory, we can complete the cost of goods sold budget. For this, we need to estimate the value of the beginning inventory. We know from Table 10.6 that the beginning inventory was 250,000 units. We also know that materials and labor were 5% less in 20x6, so they were $22 for materials ($23.10 divided by 1.05) and $16 for labor ($16.80 divided by 1.05). We assume variable overhead and fixed overhead are the same, so our unit cost is:

Materials	$ 22.00
Labor	16.00
Variable overhead	8.00
Fixed overhead	3.62
Total unit cost	$ 49.42

That means the value of our opening inventory is $12,405,000 ($49.62 times 250,000 units). We can now complete our cost of goods sold schedule, which is shown in Table 10.11.

TABLE 10.11 COST OF GOODS SOLD BUDGET

Ionics, Ltd.					
	20x7				
	Quarter 1	Quarter 2	Quarter 3	Quarter 4	Annual
Direct materials used (Table 10.7)	$58,327,500	$63,525,000	$64,102,500	$69,300,000	$255,255,000
Direct labor (Table 10.8)	$42,420,000	$46,200,000	$46,620,000	$50,400,000	$185,640,000
Overhead (Table 10.9)	$30,200,000	$32,000,000	$32,200,000	$34,000,000	$128,400,000
Budgeted manufacturing costs	$130,947,500	$141,725,000	$142,922,500	$153,700,000	$569,295,000
Plus: Beginning finished goods inventory	$12,405,000	$14,168,000	$14,168,000	$15,456,000	$12,405,000
Goods available for sale	$143,352,500	$155,893,000	$157,090,500	$169,156,000	$581,700,000
Less: Ending finished goods inventory (Table 10.10)	$(14,168,000)	$(14,168,000)	$(15,456,000)	$(15,456,000)	$(15,456,000)
Budgeted Cost of Goods Sold	$129,184,500	$141,725,000	$141,634,500	$153,700,000	$566,244,000

SALES AND MARKETING, ADMINISTRATIVE, AND RESEARCH AND DEVELOPMENT BUDGETS

Three general expense line items that originate outside of production—sales and marketing, administration, and research and development—fall into our budgeted income statement. With the exception of some variable selling expenses, most of these costs are fixed and occur fairly uniformly over the year, making preparing and understanding the budgets themselves quite straightforward. Table 10.12 illustrates what a sales and marketing budget—in this case, that of Ionics—looks like.

TABLE 10.12 SALES AND MARKETING BUDGET FOR FUNCTIONAL ORGANIZATION

Ionics, Ltd.					
	Calendar Year 20x7				
	Quarter 1	Quarter 2	Quarter 3	Quarter 4	Annual
Planned sales (Table 10.6)	2,500,000	2,750,000	2,750,000	3,000,000	11,000,000
Variable selling costs per unit	$10.00	$10.00	$10.00	$10.00	$10.00
Total variable selling expense	$25,000,000	$27,500,000	$27,500,000	$30,000,000	$110,000,000
Fixed Marketing Expense:					
Advertising	$25,000,000	$25,000,000	$25,000,000	$25,000,000	$100,000,000
Total Fixed Expense	$25,000,000	$25,000,000	$25,000,000	$25,000,000	$100,000,000
Total Sales and Marketing Expense	$50,000,000	$52,500,000	$52,500,000	$55,000,000	$210,000,000

Tables 10.13 and 10.14 are examples of administrative, and research and development budgets, again, from Ionics. As we see, the costs incur uniformly across the year, and the totals for both budgets equal our estimated beginning income statement amounts. These tables provide additional detail about where Ionic is spending its funds.

TABLE 10.13 ADMINISTRATIVE BUDGET FOR FUNCTIONAL ORGANIZATION

Ionics, Ltd.					
Calendar Year 20x7					
	Quarter 1	Quarter 2	Quarter 3	Quarter 4	Annual
Salaries	$6,500,000	$6,500,000	$6,500,000	$6,500,000	$26,000,000
Computers	$2,500,000	$2,500,000	$2,500,000	$2,500,000	$10,000,000
Depreciation	$1,500,000	$1,500,000	$1,500,000	$1,500,000	$6,000,000
Other expenses	$4,500,000	$4,500,000	$4,500,000	$4,500,000	$18,000,000
	$15,000,000	$15,000,000	$15,000,000	$15,000,000	$60,000,000

TABLE 10.14 RESEARCH AND DEVELOPMENT BUDGET FOR FUNCTIONAL ORGANIZATION

Ionics, Ltd.					
Calendar Year 20x7					
	Quarter 1	Quarter 2	Quarter 3	Quarter 4	Annual
Salaries	$4,500,000	$4,500,000	$4,500,000	$4,500,000	$18,000,000
Computers	$1,500,000	$1,500,000	$1,500,000	$1,500,000	$6,000,000
Research materials	$2,500,000	$2,500,000	$2,500,000	$2,500,000	$10,000,000
Other expenses	$1,500,000	$1,500,000	$1,500,000	$1,500,000	$6,000,000
	$10,000,000	$10,000,000	$10,000,000	$10,000,000	$40,000,000

BUDGETED INCOME STATEMENT

We are now ready to compute the budgeted income statement for the year 20x7. We construct this budget using the information in the earlier tables; in other words, we are keying in figures we have already calculated to arrive at the total. As you will see in Table 10.15, we now considered the changing inventory levels, which makes our final numbers slightly different than they were in the original plan for materials. The rest of the numbers track our original projections, so we know our budget is within the established parameters.

TABLE 10.15 BUDGETED INCOME STATEMENT FOR FUNCTIONAL ORGANIZATION

Ionics, Ltd.					
Calendar Year 20x7					
	Quarter 1	Quarter 2	Quarter 3	Quarter 4	Annual
Sales (Table 10.6)	$250,000,000	$275,000,000	$275,000,000	$300,000,000	$1,100,000,000
Less: Cost of Goods Sold (Table 10.11)	$129,184,500	$141,725,000	$141,634,500	$153,700,000	$566,244,000
Gross Margin	$120,815,500	$133,275,000	$133,365,500	$146,300,000	$533,756,000
Less: Selling and Marketing (Table 10.12)	$50,000,000	$52,500,000	$52,500,000	$55,000,000	$210,000,000
Administrative (Table 10.13)	$15,000,000	$15,000,000	$15,000,000	$15,000,000	$60,000,000
Research and Development (Table 10.14)	$10,000,000	$10,000,000	$10,000,000	$10,000,000	$40,000,000
Total SG&A	$75,000,000	$77,500,000	$77,500,000	$80,000,000	$310,000,000
Income Before Tax	$45,815,500	$55,775,000	$55,865,500	$66,300,000	$223,756,000
Less: Income Taxes (30%)	$(13,744,650)	$(16,732,500)	$(16,759,650)	$(19,890,000)	$(67,126,800)
Net Income	$32,070,850	$39,042,500	$39,105,850	$46,410,000	$156,629,200

CASH BUDGET

Since all companies must maintain an adequate, but not excessive, supply of cash, the cash budget is one of the most important budget elements—without cash, a company cannot operate. The cash budget requires knowledge of or assumptions about, for example, how fast our customers pay us for our goods and how quickly we have to pay all of our obligations. Here, we break this budget into three pieces—Table 10.16, the cash receipts budget; Table 10.17, the cash disbursements budget; and Table 10.18, our actual ending cash balance—to make it easier to track the various elements of our cash picture. That means we have to collect our cash from customers in a reasonable period of time if we are to be able to pay our bills to vendors and employees on time.

In preparing the cash receipts budget, we have to allow for the fact that not all of our customers pay us at the same rate. Some pay promptly, taking advantage of any terms we have offered for rapid payment, such as 2% off the invoiced amount if paid in 10 days or less from receipt of the goods (2/10, net 30). Other customers wait and pay us within the prescribed 30-day period. Still others stretch their payment terms to 60 or even 90 days! This is not good for our business in general, but there are always some customers that are slow to pay. If they become too difficult, we simply stop supplying them with merchandise or ask for it to be paid upon delivery (C.O.D., or cash on delivery terms). To put the cash receipts budget together, therefore, we need to know which customers pay us when. Those that have not paid us make up the accounts receivable total for the business.

Ionics, Ltd., has a long experience with its customers. Looking at its accounts receivable, it estimates that 25% will pay right away or soon enough that they will receive the 2% discount. Of the remaining 75% credit sales, 40% will be collected during the current quarter, and the other 35% the following quarter. The company has very few bad debts, so these are not factored into the plan. Given the selling price of $100, all we need to know to do the cash receipts budget is what the level of sales were in the fourth quarter of 20x6. Management informs us that it sold 2,250,000 units in the fourth quarter of 20x6. This gives us the information we need to complete the cash receipts chart. Note that Ionics, Ltd., plans a major capital acquisition in the fourth quarter of 20x7. It is going to take out a loan to pay for that acquisition, and those loan proceeds also enter into our cash receipts analysis, as you will see in Table 10.16.

TABLE 10.16 CASH RECEIPTS BUDGET FOR FUNCTIONAL ORGANIZATION

Ionics, Ltd.					
Calendar Year 20x7					
	Quarter 1	Quarter 2	Quarter 3	Quarter 4	Annual
Cash sales (25%)	$62,500,000	$68,750,000	$68,750,000	$75,000,000	$275,000,000
Collected this quarter (40%)	$100,000,000	$110,000,000	$110,000,000	$120,000,000	$440,000,000
Collected from last quarter sales (35%)	$78,750,000	$87,500,000	$96,250,000	$96,250,000	$358,750,000
Total cash collected	$241,250,000	$266,250,000	$275,000,000	$291,250,000	$1,073,750,000
Amount borrowed—loan	$-	$-	$-	$25,000,000	$25,000,000
Total cash receipts	$241,250,000	$266,250,000	$275,000,000	$316,250,000	$1,098,750,000

*Note: Ending Accounts Receivable is 35% of Quarter 4 sales, or $105,000,000

When dealing with cash disbursements, we need to remember that a small amount always remains from purchases made in the last month of the prior quarter even though we try to pay for all of our materials within the quarter. For example, an invoice might not have been received during the quarter. For budgeting purposes, we will assume that 25% of the prior quarter's purchases of materials are paid for in the next quarter. That means 75% of the quarter's purchases get paid right away and 25% sits in accounts payable at the end of the quarter. We pay all of our other bills as soon as they are received, so these amounts are not carried over from one quarter to the next. In the fourth quarter of 20x6, we purchased $60,000,000 of raw materials, so we need to account for 25% of this, as we forecast our cash disbursements for materials in the first quarter of 20x7. Ionics is also buying $35,000,000 in new assets in Quarter 4. Finally, depreciation is a noncash expense, so if we include depreciation in any of our other budgets, we need to remove that amount from the budgeted cost to get the cash disbursements. Table 10.17 is an example of a cash disbursements budget.

TABLE 10.17 CASH DISBURSEMENTS BUDGET FOR FUNCTIONAL ORGANIZATION

Ionics, Ltd.					
	Calendar Year 20x7				
	Quarter 1	Quarter 2	Quarter 3	Quarter 4	Annual
Raw materials payments:					
Current quarter	$44,525,250	$47,730,375	$48,856,500	$51,975,000	$193,087,125
From last quarter	$15,000,000	$14,841,750	$15,910,125	$16,285,500	$62,037,375
Direct labor	$42,420,000	$46,200,000	$46,620,000	$50,400,000	$185,640,000
Overhead	$32,220,000	$34,200,000	$34,420,000	$36,400,000	$137,240,000
Sales and marketing	$50,000,000	$52,500,000	$52,500,000	$55,000,000	$210,000,000
Administrative	$13,500,000	$13,500,000	$13,500,000	$13,500,000	$54,000,000
Research and development	$10,000,000	$10,000,000	$10,000,000	$10,000,000	$40,000,000
Income taxes	$13,144,643	$16,072,500	$16,099,649	$19,170,000	$64,486,792
New equipment	$-	$-	$-	$35,000,000	$35,000,000
Total cash disbursements	$220,809,893	$235,044,625	$237,906,274	$287,730,500	$981,491,292

With both the cash receipts and disbursement budgets completed, we can put together a simple cash statement, Table 10.18. Our opening cash balance is $20,000,000, which we will need to make the statement work.

TABLE 10.18 CASH BUDGET FOR FUNCTIONAL ORGANIZATION

Ionics, Ltd.					
	Calendar Year 20x7				
	Quarter 1	Quarter 2	Quarter 3	Quarter 4	Annual
Opening Balance	$20,000,000	$40,440,107	$71,645,482	$108,739,208	$20,000,000
Plus: Cash receipts	$241,250,000	$266,250,000	$275,000,000	$316,250,000	$1,098,750,000
Total cash available	$261,250,000	$306,690,107	$346,645,482	$424,989,208	$1,118,750,000
Less: Cash disbursements	$(220,809,893)	$(235,044,625)	$(237,906,274)	$(287,730,500)	$(981,491,292)
Ending cash balance	$40,440,107	$71,645,482	$108,739,208	$137,258,708	$137,258,708

As you can see, Ionics has a healthy cash flow. The ending balance includes the loan that was taken out to help finance the large capital investment in the fourth quarter of 20x7. We are now ready to put together the pro forma balance sheet for 20x7.

ENDING BALANCE SHEET

To generate a closing balance sheet for the year, we combine all of the information gathered in developing the budget. Here, we will find out if we made any errors, because the balance sheet only balances if all of the other numbers are correct. As Table 10.19 makes clear, our balance sheet does balance, so this planning cycle is done. Ionics is expected to do much better in 20x7 than it did in 20x6.

TABLE 10.19 ENDING BALANCE SHEET

Ionics, Ltd.		
Fiscal Year Ending December 31, 20x7		
ASSETS		
Cash	$137,258,708	
Accounts receivable	$105,000,000	
Raw materials inventory	$13,860,000	
Finished goods inventory	$15,695,973	
Total current assets		$271,814,681
Property, plant, and equipment		
Land	$25,000,000	
Building and equipment	$110,000,000	
Less: Accumulated depreciation	$(28,500,000)	
Total PP&E		$106,500,000
Total Assets		$378,314,681
LIABILITIES AND OWNER'S EQUITY		
Accounts payable	$17,325,000	
Loan payable	$25,000,000	
Total liabilities		$42,325,000
Stockholder's equity		
Common stock, no par	$125,000,000	
Retained earnings	$210,989,681	
Total stockholder's equity		$335,989,681
Total liabilities and stockholder's equity		$378,314,681

"FLEXING" THE BUDGET

As you probably noticed, we were careful to separate out the fixed from the variable costs in our budgets. In some situations, we also identified some step-function costs. Keeping the cost behavior expectations visible makes it easy to create a **flexible budget,** *one that can be adjusted to take into account the impact of changing volumes on variable costs*. The process itself is known as *"flexing" the budget.* As we will see in Chapter 12, flexing the budget becomes very important when doing the "check" function in the BPA cycle. If volume is greater or less than planned, we have to make adjustments to remove the "forecasting error" when evaluating how well managers have done.

Eliminating or Reducing the Planning Gap

OBJECTIVE 6

Explain why a planning gap occurs and how to address it.

A **planning gap** *is the disparity that occurs when top management's performance desires exceed the performance figures in a bottom-up plan.* It is caused, in part, by top-level managers endeavoring to push their organizations to the highest possible levels of performance by working toward stretch goals. They also often face pressures from the owners or shareholders for better performance.

Lower-level managers tend to be more informed about the details of their operations and the problems they face. They also tend to be conservative. Even if they are aware of some good news about the future, they tend not to want to share this **private information,** *knowledge line managers have but do not share with those above them*. Hiding this knowledge can create a cushion, which will protect them in the event of unforeseen contingencies or simply make their lives easier. They can achieve their performance targets even while not working hard. When they engage in this downward bias in the plans, they are said to be **sandbagging, or creating slack,** *the building of a downward bias in an operational plan*. This occurs when lower-level managers do not share their private information about their entity's prospects and submit a plan that is highly likely to be achieved. These two perspectives create an almost universal tension in organizations' planning processes: "stretch vs. realism."

When a planning gap exists, as it almost always does, managers must take steps to try to eliminate or reduce the gap, or at least to understand its causes. It is essential all managers be comfortable with and committed to achieving the company's plan. Eliminating the gap may involve sharing information. Perhaps, once top management becomes aware of all of the problems faced by its subordinates, it will lower its performance expectations. Conceivably new ideas, such as accelerating the introduction of a new product, can be developed to reduce or eliminate the gap. Or maybe, through a process of negotiation, top management can convince lower-level managers that their forecasts are too conservative, and that the company's goals are achievable.

Sometimes the gap can be eliminated in the short run. Other times, the planning focus is on eliminating, or just reducing, the gap over the long run. In the case of Ionics, Ltd., the discussions aimed at reducing the planning gap stimulated a new idea. The sales manager suggested that if advertising expenses were increased by $30,000, unit sales could be expected to increase by 30%. This led to a revision of the plan; the new numbers appear in Table 10.20.

Based on this new plan, the entire budget that we put together would need to be redone. This is why planning is such a major event at the entity level—every plan needs to be analyzed for its impact across the organization. When assumptions are changed, the budget has to change. It is not unusual for a company to run five, 10, or even 20 or more budgets before a final set of targets is agreed upon. In the age of computers, the budget preparation process is automated, so assumptions can be changed and a new set of budgets is easily calculated.

TABLE 10.20 REVISED PLAN

Ionics, Ltd.	
Projected income statement for the year ended December 31, 20x7	
Sales	$1,300,000
Direct materials	286,000
Direct labor	208,000
Manufacturing overhead–variable	104,000
Manufacturing overhead–fixed	40,000
	638,000
Gross margin	662,000
Selling expenses–variable	130,000
Advertising expenses–fixed	170,000
Research and development	40,000
Administrative expenses	66,000
	406,000
Net income before tax	$256,000

What if no new ideas had emerged and lower-level managers maintained their pessimistic view of future prospects? Should top management impose its top-down view on the operating managers? Possibly, if it believes that lower-level managers are being unrealistically conservative. But imposing a top-down budget is risky. Lower-level managers may not be committed to the plan and, consequently, lose motivation. Commonly, the negotiation processes lead to either new ideas or a compromise. Planning for the future involves a lot of subjective judgments, and gamesmanship, salesmanship, and politics usually affect the processes and outcomes.

While we have looked at only one planning period, you must remember that planning is a multiperiod "game." Lower-level managers who have a history of consistently exceeding their plans, which is indicative of slack, will likely be asked to increase their targets. On the other hand, lower-level managers, who top management believes are good managers but who fail to achieve their plans in prior months or years, may be given an easier, more achievable plan.

Target-Setting Alternatives

Because of the politics and gamesmanship that can affect budgeting processes, some organizations look for alternatives for setting performance targets. Some companies use a form of **ratcheting**—*the process of raising performance expectations annually*—to set performance targets, particularly those that are linked to organizational rewards. Ratcheting systems set performance targets based solely on historical performance. For example, managers who exceeded their performance target by 10% in the prior year may be given a target that is 5% higher than the prior period's actual results. Conversely, managers who fell 10% short of achieving their prior year's target may be given a target that is 5% lower than the prior period's actuals. The sensitivity of targets to prior periods' excesses or shortfalls can be varied.

Some companies choose to **benchmark**—*set performance targets based on external standards, generally the realized performance of comparable organizations*. By themselves, however, the performance targets are not plans. They are just a starting point for a planning process. Managers must then develop ideas and action plans to make achieving the performance targets likely, or at least possible.

Summary

This chapter is an introduction to the topic of planning in organizations, with the focus on businesses that use a centralized or functional organizational structure. As it is in all organizations, planning is an essential part of the management process. Planning provides multiple benefits. It forces managers to consider the future and to think about decisions they will make. It provides a standard against which to compare actual performance. It provides a forum in which useful employee communication can take place, thus producing more organizational coordination. Planning also includes goals that can motivate employees to work harder and in the organization's best interests.

Budgets are used to formalize the plans that management makes. Starting with a sales forecast, the budget can be broken down into specific pieces, which include the production budget, raw materials budget, labor budget, overhead budget, cost of goods sold budget, marketing budget, administrative budget, research and development budget, income statement, cash budget, and finally the projected balance sheet. We can make the budgets flexible by factoring in the impact of changes in volume (plan) on our variable, mixed, and stepped costs.

Planning processes are varied. For example, they can be organized to emphasize top-down or bottom-up communications, or to use both extensively. And the goals that become part of the plans can be negotiated, set by benchmarking the performances of like outside entities, or ratcheted, based on historical performance.

Key Terms

Autonomy, or empowerment: the freedom of a manager to make decisions without consulting upper management.

Balanced scorecard: a multidimensional set of performance measurements, which includes measures focused on financial performance, the customer, learning and growth, and internal business processes.

Benchmark: to set performance targets based on external standards, generally the realized performance of comparable organizations.

Best-guess revenue forecast: a prediction based on the most likely outcomes; it has a 50% probability of attainment.

Bottom-up planning process: the method in which information flows from employees lower in the organization to top management.

Budget: a quantitative (financial) expression of a plan of action for a specific short period of time.

Decentralization: delegation of authority and decision rights to managers in the organization.

Decision-making authority, or decision rights: the ability, right, or power to make determinations and assign accountability.

Disaster planning: a form of scenario planning that assumes a major disaster occurs and establishes action plans to meet the resulting critical and unique demands placed on management.

Divisionally organized entities: entities made up of a number of freestanding components.

Esprit de corps: a common bond among a group; an organizational culture of teamwork.

Expected value: the weighted probability; the result of analyzing various scenarios or outcomes.

Flexible budget: one that can be adjusted to take into account the impact of changing volumes on variable costs.

Functional organization entities: entities structured around different processes or types of work.

Participation: involvement in the planning process and influence over the outcome.

Planning gap: a disparity that occurs when top management's performance desires exceed the performance figures in a plan prepared in a bottom-up plan.

Private information: knowledge that line managers have but do not share with top management.

Pro forma financial statements, or profit plan: estimated, or forecasted, results of operations.

Pseudo-participation: the involvement of subordinates, who actually have little or no influence over the plans and performance targets that are set in the planning process.

Ratcheting: a system in which the performance targets are set only as a function of historical performance.

Revenue forecast: a projection of future sales for a period of time.

Sandbagging, or creating slack: the building of a downward bias in an operational plan.

Scenario planning: the preparation of multiple plans or budgets based on different plausible visions of the future.

Top-down planning process: opposite of a bottom-up process; it starts with top management and then is communicated to lower-level managers as a defined expectation.

Questions

1. How does the stage of development of a company affect the way it creates and uses plans?
2. Why is it important that key managers agree on the organization's missions and objectives before the planning process begins?
3. What are the three primary business archetypes, and how do they differ in terms of size and age?
4. How do functional organizations differ from divisionally organized entities?
5. What does the term autonomy mean in reference to organizations?
6. What is a "best-guess" revenue forecast and profit scenario?
7. What does the term "expected value" mean, and how do managers use it in scenario planning?
8. What is a budget and why is one completed? How are pro forma statements used in the budgeting process?
9. What is scenario planning, and why do managers use it?
10. What is disaster planning, and why do managers use it?
11. What is an entity-level balanced scorecard, and how can managers use it to coordinate activities in a functional firm?
12. What is a planning gap?
13. What is pseudo-participation, and how does it differ from normal participation?
14. What is the difference between slack and ratcheting effects? Who is in charge of each of these potentially problematic events?

Exercises

1. **TYPE OF ORGANIZATION.** For the following list of characteristics, place an "S" if it is most likely to be a small organization, "F" if it appears to be a functional organization, and "D" if the descriptor most accurately fits a divisionally organized entity. Some may belong to more than one category; if so, indicate that.

Descriptor	Type	Descriptor	Type
Small		Very large	
Many different entities		Owner-managed	
Managers accountable for functions		Multiproduct-based	
Managers accountable for outcomes		Mature	
High-risk		Cash-constrained	

2. **TYPE OF ORGANIZATION.** For the following list of characteristics, place an "S" if it is most likely to be a small organization, "F" if it appears to be a functional organization, and "D" if the descriptor most accurately fits a divisionally organized entity. Some may belong to more than one category; if so, indicate that.

Descriptor	Type	Descriptor	Type
Staff division		Functional orientation	
Talent-constrained		Top management makes all decisions	
Medium to large		Pseudo-participation	
Independent units		Medium age	
Managers set functional targets		Ratcheting prevalent	

3. **BALANCED SCORECARD MEASURES.** For each of the following set of measures, indicate whether it is financial (F), customer-focused (C), internal processes (P), or innovation/growth-oriented (I) in nature.

Measure	Type	Measure	Type
Productivity growth		Number of training hours	
Market share		Cycle time	
Net income		Profit per unit	
Number of new patents		New product sales	
Customer profitability		Value-added	

4. **BALANCED SCORECARD MEASURES.** For each of the following set of measures, indicate whether it is financial (F), customer-focused (C), internal processes (P), or innovation/growth (I) in nature.

Measure	Type	Measure	Type
Number of new customers		Product profitability	
Throughput time		Return on investment	
Gross margin		Customer retention rate	
Number of new skills learned		Quality training	
Scrap units		First-pass yields	

5. **PRODUCTION BUDGET.** Ratchet Now makes a ratchet set that is compact for ease of use and storage. It predicts it will sell 100,000 units in Quarter 1, 125,000 units in Quarter 2, 140,000 units in Quarter 3, and 150,000 units in Quarter 4. It expects that in Quarter 1 of the following year, it will also sell 150,000 units. Opening inventory is 20,000 units. The company wants to retain 20% of the next quarter's sales on hand as ending inventory. Using this information, develop a production budget for Ratchet Now.

6. **MATERIALS BUDGET.** Based on the production budget, Ratchet Now has a good idea of what it needs to manufacture. It now wants to develop its raw materials budget. It uses 1.5 pounds of steel for each ratchet set at a cost of $0.50 per pound. Opening inventory is 25% of the raw material needs for Quarter 1. The company wants to keep this inventory policy in place, so it plans to have 25% of its next quarter's needs on hand in ending inventory. Using this information and the information from Exercise 5, develop a raw materials budget. Make sure to note both the quantity of steel it needs to purchase and the amount it needs to use to arrive at the total dollars it needs to budget for in your analysis. Assume that production in Quarter 1 is equal to that of Quarter 4.

7. **LABOR BUDGET.** Ratchet Now would also like to develop a labor budget. It takes 0.25 hours to make one set of ratchets. Labor costs the company $16 per hour. Using this information and the information from Exercise 5, develop the labor budget for the company.

8. **OVERHEAD BUDGET.** Things are looking good for Ratchet Now. Next, it wants to prepare its overhead budget. Variable overhead cost per ratchet set is $0.50, and the fixed overhead costs are estimated to be $25,000 per quarter. Using this information and the information from Exercise 5, develop the overhead budget for Ratchet Now.

9. **ENDING FINISHED GOODS AND COST OF GOODS SOLD BUDGETS.** Now that you have completed these tables, Ratchet Now is ready to do its ending inventory

and cost of goods sold budget using the information you have developed in Exercises 5 through 8. Opening inventory is valued at $100,000. Develop these budgets.

10. **PRODUCTION BUDGET.** Clear Channels makes portable radios that can be used during storms. The radios do not require an outside source of power because the battery is charged with a crank. They are a highly prized item in people's home emergency kits. Sales are strong and growing each quarter. Opening inventory is 250,000 units. Quarter 1 sales are projected to be 1,000,000 units, Quarter 2 sales 1,250,000 units, Quarter 3 sales 1,500,000 units, Quarter 4 sales 1,750,000 units, and sales in the first quarter of next year are expected to top 2,000,000 units. The company's policy is to keep 25% of the next period's projected sales on hand at the end of each quarter. Using this information, please develop the production budget for Clear Channels.

11. **RAW MATERIALS BUDGET.** It takes two pounds of plastic and one receiving/charging unit to make each Clear Channels radio. The plastic costs $0.75 per pound (it is very high-quality), and the receiving/charging unit costs $7.50 each. The company keeps enough inventory on hand to make 30% of the next month's production. Opening inventory for the plastic is 500,000 pounds, and there are 200,000 receiving/charging units on hand. Using this information plus that developed in Exercise 10, prepare the materials budgets for Clear Channels. Increase ending inventory in Quarter 4 by 25% of Quarter 3's total. Note: You will need to develop a budget for each material separately.

12. **DIRECT LABOR BUDGET.** It takes 30 minutes (one half hour) to make one Clear Channels unit. Labor is paid $20 per hour as the work requires high technical skill. Using this information plus that developed in Exercise 10, develop a direct labor budget for Clear Channels.

13. **OVERHEAD BUDGET.** Clear Channels is really making progress! Now it wants to develop its overhead budget. Variable overhead per unit is $2.50. Fixed overhead is $150,000 per quarter. With this information plus that provided in Exercise 10, develop an overhead budget for Clear Channels.

14. **FINISHED GOODS INVENTORY AND COST OF GOODS SOLD BUDGET.** With the data developed in Exercise 10 through 13, you now have all of the information needed to complete a finished goods budget and a cost of goods sold budget for Clear Channels. Opening finished goods inventory is $5,250,000. Develop these budgets.

Problems

1. **SCENARIO PLANNING.** Sheila Felgood is the owner of a small dog-grooming business, Felgood Clippers. She would like to increase her sales over the last three years' actual results and is looking at a variety of alternatives for increasing business. Her results for the last three years are shown in the table below.

Felgood Clippers			
Income Statement for 20x4 to 20x6			
	20x6	20x5	20x4
Sales revenue	$182,000	$172,900	$160,797
Less: Cost of sales	$81,900	$76,076	$69,143
Gross Margin	$100,100	$96,824	$91,654
Advertising	$15,000	$12,500	$12,000
Marketing	$7,500	$7,000	$6,500
General office	$22,000	$21,000	$20,000
Total SG&A	$44,500	$40,500	$38,500
Net Income	$55,600	$56,324	$53,154

The alternatives Sheila is looking at include:

- **Scenario 1:** Place more ads in the local newspaper offering a 10% discount for dog grooming. The ads would cost $10,000. She believes 50% of the company's current customers would use the coupons and they would also attract 20% more customers. Sheila currently does 100 groomings a week at $35 per grooming. If she does more than 120 groomings, she would need to hire more help, so this would be a big decision for her. The costs of sales and revenue would decline 1% from last year because she now would qualify volume discounts on several key products. The rest of the costs of the business would remain relatively steady.
- **Scenario 2:** Open up a second location. She would be able to do 100 more groomings per week in the new location. Her cost of sales as a percentage of total sales would drop 5% from last year due to the huge increase in volume. Other business expenses would increase 20% due to the increased volume of customers and the complexity of maintaining two sites.
- **Scenario 3:** Do nothing and expect the revenue and cost of sales to be averages of the last three years. All other costs would be the same as 20x6.

REQUIRED:

a. Develop income statements for these three alternatives.
b. Based solely on the numbers, which alternative should Sheila pursue for the coming year?
c. What else would you like to know before making the decision?

---

2. **SCENARIO PLANNING AND EXPECTED VALUES.** Hydrangea, Inc., is a maker of silk floral arrangements that are sold in high-end flower shops. The company is thinking about expanding after a year of record sales that really stretched existing resources to their maximum. The results of the last three years of business are shown in the table below.

Hydrangea, Inc.			
Income Statement for 20x4 to 20x6			
	20x6	20x5	20x4
Sales revenue	$375,000	$356,250	$331,313
Less: Cost of sales	$180,000	$171,000	$159,030
Gross Margin	$195,000	$185,250	$172,283
Advertising	$20,000	$18,500	$17,000
Floral design	$22,500	$20,000	$17,500
Administrative	$34,000	$32,000	$30,000
Total SG&A	$76,500	$70,500	$64,500
Net Income	$118,500	$114,750	$107,783

The company is looking at four different ways to grow its business:

- **Scenario 1:** Buy an additional store. It would require a onetime investment of $50,000 to get the store ready for operation. The operating costs (cost of sales) would go up by 40% over 20x6. Revenues would increase 60%. All three SG&A costs would also go up. Advertising would increase $10,000, floral design $12,000, and administrative by $6,000.
- **Scenario 2:** Rent the building next to the existing store. This would require a onetime cost of $15,000 to get the space ready. Sales would increase 20%. Cost of sales would increase 15%. Advertising would go up $5,000. Floral design and administrative costs would remain the same.
- **Scenario 3:** Expand the existing business by adding hours and squeezing in another two coolers for flowers. This would require an outlay of $5,000 for the coolers. Advertising would increase $5,000. Sales revenue would increase 5%, and cost of sales would remain steady. Floral design and administrative costs would remain unchanged.

- **Scenario 4:** Do nothing. Next year's revenues and cost of sales would remain constant compared to 20x6. Advertising would increase $5,000 to ensure sales stay at the existing high level.

REQUIRED:

a. Develop income statements for the four scenarios.
b. What would you recommend that the company do? Why?

3. **SCENARIO PLANNING AND EXPECTED VALUE.** Blue Moon Taxi Service is a very busy local taxi service. Recently, a retirement village opened up in Blue Moon's area, driving up volumes to the point where Blue Moon is having trouble responding in a timely manner to requests for rides. The owner of Blue Moon, Charlie Owens, has to decide on a plan going forward; he has several options available to him. The results for last year are shown in the table below.

Blue Moon Taxi	
Income Statement for 20x6	
	20x6
Sales Revenue	$425,000
Less: Cost of Sales	$255,000
Gross Margin	$170,000
Advertising	$12,000
Accounting	$25,000
General office	$30,000
Total SG&A	$67,000
Net Income	$103,000

Blue Moon is weighing the following options:

- **Scenario 1:** Buy three new taxis at a cost of $120,000. They would be amortized over a four-year period and paid for in installments over that period of time. Each new taxi would increase sales revenue by 10%, for a total increase of 30%. Cost of sales, which is the drivers' cost and fuel, would remain steady at the 20x6 rate. Charlie feels he would need to do some initial advertising to get the sales revenue he needs to generate for the three new taxis. He estimates this would cost an additional $8,000 for the year. Accounting costs would increase 10%, while general office costs would remain unchanged.

- **Scenario 2:** Lease three new taxis at a cost of $50,000 per year. Again, each new taxi would increase sales revenue by 10%. Cost of sales would go up 3%, however, as the leased taxis require a higher insurance premium. Advertising would again go up $8,000 for the year. Accounting would again increase 10%, while general office costs would go up 5% because of the additional paperwork the leasing company requires. The leases would run annually, which means Charlie could drop the three additional taxis if they are not being used with minimal penalty.
- **Scenario 3:** Do nothing. Charlie could expect to increase his revenues 5% more before he had to start turning down business. Cost of sales would remain steady at 60%. All other costs would remain at their 20x6 level.

REQUIRED:

a. Develop income statements for the three scenarios.
b. What would you recommend that Charlie do? Why?

4. **FLEXIBLE BUDGETING AND COST OF GOODS SOLD SCHEDULES.** Damp Less makes room dehumidifiers. It buys the electronic parts to make the dehumidifiers in kits, so it only purchases metal for the casings and the electronic kitted parts. Assembly is done in its one plant located in the Midwest. The company wants to put together a cost of goods sold set of budget schedules so it can plan its labor and materials purchases for the year. The data the company provides you is:

   - Sales are expected to be 5,000 units in Quarter 1, 6,000 units in Quarter 2, 7,500 units in Quarter 3, and 6,000 units in Quarter 4. Quarter 1 sales for next year are expected to be 5,500 units.
   - The electronics kits cost $65 each. The metal for the outside casings costs $15. Each finished goods unit uses one kit and one casing.
   - The company likes to keep 20% of the next quarter's sales on hand in finished goods. It started out the year with 20% of Quarter 1's projected sales on hand. Each unit costs $100.
   - The company keeps 25% of its raw materials needs for the next quarter on hand at the end of each quarter. It started the year with 1,000 electronic kits and 1,200 metal casings. Costs per part are unchanged from last year.
   - It takes 20 minutes to assemble a finished unit. Labor is paid $18 per hour.
   - Overhead includes rent for the building at $5,000 per month, electricity at $1,200 per month, supervision at $4,000 per month, and general costs of $1,800 per month. Variable overhead is $8 per unit.

REQUIRED:

For each quarter of the year, prepare:

a. A production budget
b. A materials budget for the two materials
c. A labor budget
d. An overhead budget
e. A cost of goods sold budget
f. An ending finished goods inventory budget for the year
g. If the company considers its cost of goods sold to be 60% of sales price, what price does the company have to charge for a finished unit?

5. FLEXIBLE BUDGETING AND COST OF GOODS SOLD BUDGET SCHEDULES.

Harvest Beverages makes a full line of carbonated seltzer water in various flavors. Every can of seltzer is comprised of a can to put the liquid in, flavoring, and the carbonated water. The company is beginning to plan its production costs for the upcoming year and has asked you to help it prepare the various schedules needed to determine its cost of goods sold. It provides you with the following data:

- Projected sales are 500,000 cans in Quarter 1, 600,000 cans in Quarter 2, 750,000 cans in Quarter 3, and 600,000 cans in Quarter 4. Quarter 1 sales next year are expected to be 550,000 cans.
- The company likes to keep 25% of the next quarter's sales on hand in finished goods. It plans to start the year with that level of inventory for Quarter 1. The cost of beginning inventory is $28,000.
- Raw materials costs are $0.04 for each can, $0.05 per ounce of flavoring, and $0.005 per ounce for the carbonated water. Each finished can uses one metal can, 0.5 ounce of flavoring, and 12 ounces of carbonated water.
- The company keeps 20% of the next quarter's raw materials needs on hand at the end of each preceding quarter. It starts the year with this percentage of Quarter 1's projected sales on hand. Prices are unchanged from last year.
- Labor costs are $5 for 200 cans. This amounts to .005 labor hours per can produced.
- Monthly overhead is $6,000 for building rental, $2,500 for the canning machine, $3,500 for supervision, and $1,000 for miscellaneous costs. Variable overhead is $0.02 per can made.

REQUIRED:

For each quarter of the year, prepare:

a. A production budget
b. A materials budget for the two materials
c. A labor budget
d. An overhead budget
e. A cost of goods sold budget
f. An ending finished goods inventory budget for the year
g. If the company considers its cost of goods sold to be 70% of sales price, what price does the company have to charge for a finished can of seltzer?

6. **CASH BUDGETS.** Once Only produces various kinds of weed killers for commercial lawn applications. The company needs to watch its cash carefully in order to make sure that it can survive the busy summer months when there is a huge demand for the product, requiring large inventories. Unfortunately, not all of Once Only's customers pay right away, so the company ends up floating receivables at its busiest time. To keep its credit rating solid, however, Once Only pays all of its bills monthly. That means at the end of each month, it still owes half of the inventory purchases to its supplier for goods received after the 15th of the month. The information pertaining to Once Only's cash budget for the months of July through September is:

- Opening cash balance on July 1 is $25,000.
- Sales of fertilizer were:
  - » May: $125,000
  - » June: $175,000
  - » July: $250,000
  - » August: $200,000
  - » September: $300,000
- It projects sales in October of $250,000.
- Once Only's customers pay in the following way: 25% pay in the month of purchase, 50% pay the month following purchase, and the remaining 25% pay two months after purchase.
- The materials costs are 50% of the total sales price for each month.
- The company likes to keep 25% of its next month's sales on hand at the end of each month. It started the quarter with 25% of July's needs on hand.
- Direct labor costs are $18,000 per month.
- Overhead for the warehouse is $30,500 per month.
- Back office workers earn $27,500 per month.

REQUIRED:

For each month, prepare:

a. A purchases budget to determine how much fertilizer Once Only needs to buy
b. A cash receipts budget
c. A cash disbursements budget
d. A cash budget
e. At the end of September, what is the company's accounts receivable balance?
f. At the end of September, what is the company's accounts payable balance?
g. How does Once Only's cash position look to you each month? Provide specific details for your answer.

---

7. **CASH BUDGETS.** Wonder Products purchases granite cleaning products from a Midwestern manufacturer and sells the product under its own brand name. The company sells its goods to local hardware stores and granite suppliers. The product is very well-received, so the company does very well in terms of sales. Unfortunately, Wonder Products deals with retailers that often do not pay their bills on time. Wonder Products, on the other hand, has to pay for the goods it receives within 30 days. That means it carries only half of each month's purchases as accounts payable. The information pertaining to Wonder Products' business for the second quarter of the year (April through June) are:

- Opening cash balance is $30,000.
- Wonder Products sales were:
  - » February: $150,000
  - » March: $175,000
  - » April: $200,000
  - » May: $250,000
  - » June: $275,000
- It expects to sell $300,000 of product in July.
- Wonder Products' customers pay the following way:
  - » 20% pay in the month they receive the goods
  - » 40% pay the month following purchase
  - » 40% pay two months after receiving their goods
- The materials costs for the granite cleaner are 60% of the selling price.
- The company likes to keep 20% of its upcoming month's sales on hand at the end of the previous month. It started out this quarter with its inventory targets being met.
- Direct labor costs are $9,000 per month.
- Warehousing and shipping costs are $25,000 per month.
- Back office and other overhead costs are $30,000 per month.

REQUIRED:

For each month, prepare:

a. A raw materials budget to determine how much granite cleaner Wonder Products needs to buy
b. A cash receipts budget
c. A cash disbursements budget
d. A cash budget
e. At the end of September, what is the company's accounts receivable balance?
f. At the end of September, what is the company's accounts payable balance?
g. How does Wonder Products' cash position look to you each month? Provide specific details.

8. **COMPREHENSIVE BUDGET PROBLEM.** Highways End produces energy drinks that are sold in convenience stores and at rest stops along major highways. The drinks provide a burst of energy that can keep drivers alert for long distances. The company has been in business for three years and is experiencing growth due to an increase in demand for its energy drink from people who find their jobs draining. The company has launched a national advertising program that should boost its sales even more.

   As a wholesaler dealing directly with retail customers, Highways End needs to keep a careful eye on its cash flow to ensure that it meets future demand without lack of cash causing it to go out of business. The data you need to do a flexible budget for the year ahead for Highways End are in Highways End's opening balance sheet below:

Highways End		
Opening Balance Sheet		
Assets		
Cash	$25,000	
Accounts receivable	$137,500	
Raw materials inventory	$24,500	
Finished goods inventory	$48,600	
Total current assets		$235,600
PP&E	$250,000	
Less: Accumlated depreciation	$(50,000)	
Total fixed assets		$200,000
Total assets		$435,600
Liabilities and Owners' Equity		
Accounts payable	$58,500	

Highways End		
Opening Balance Sheet		
Assets		
Notes payable	$50,000	
Total liabilities		$108,500
Common stock	$200,000	
Retained earnings	$127,100	
Total owner's equity		$327,100
Total liabilities and owner's equity		$435,600

- Sales for the last quarter of 20x6 were $275,000. Budgeted sales for 20x7 are $300,000 in Quarter 1, $325,000 in Quarter 2, $350,000 in Quarter 3, and $375,000 in Quarter 4. Total sales for the first quarter of 20x7 are expected to hit $400,000, with the second quarter projected to reach $425,000. Each bottle of Highways End energy drink sells for $1.25.
- 50% of the company's customers pay in the quarter they buy the merchandise; 50% pay in the next quarter.
- The company keeps 25% of the next quarter's sales on hand in ending inventory.
- Raw materials are the container for the product, which cost $0.05 each, and the actual product, which costs $0.15 per fluid ounce. There are three fluid ounces in a bottle.
- Highways End pays for 50% of raw materials purchases in the quarter of production and 50% in the following quarter. It pays all other costs in the quarter in which they are incurred.
- It keeps ending raw materials inventory at 20% of the next quarter's production. It expects costs of raw materials to be stable in 20x7.
- It takes 0.010 hours to fill one bottle of energy fluid. Each labor hour costs the firm $22.
- Variable overhead is $0.05 per unit made. Fixed overhead includes rent for $9,000 per quarter, filling machine costs of $4,000 per quarter, supervision of $9,000 per quarter, and general overhead of $3,000 per quarter.
- Factory depreciation is $10,000 per quarter.
- Variable selling costs are $0.05 per unit. Fixed quarterly SG&A overhead costs are $4,000 for fixed selling costs, $5,000 for marketing costs, $6,000 for administrative costs, and $1,200 for general overhead costs.
- Income taxes are 30% of income before tax.

REQUIRED:

For the coming year, complete:

a. A sales budget
b. A production budget
c. A raw materials budget for each raw material used in the energy drinks
d. A labor budget
e. An overhead budget
f. An ending finished goods budget
g. A cost of goods sold budget
h. An SG&A budget
i. An income statement
j. A cash receipts budget
k. A cash disbursements budget
l. A cash budget
m. An ending balance sheet

---

9. **COMPREHENSIVE BUDGET PROBLEM.** Davros, Inc., makes tea kettles for kitchen and department store sales. Tony Davros, the president of the company, has decided it is time for him to begin budgeting as his business is growing by leaps and bounds due to Davros tea kettles' unique designs. Each tea kettle is made from stainless steel. It takes roughly two pounds of stainless steel to make each tea kettle as well as an accessories kit that includes the knob for the lid, the handles, and a spout whistle. The major cost comes from forming the tea kettles, so machining and labor are high. The company also employs one designer who develops all of the innovative products that Davros sells.

The opening balance sheet for Davros, Inc., is shown below.

Each tea kettle sells for $45.

Davros, Inc.		
Opening Balance Sheet		
Assets		
Cash	$ 40,000	
Accounts Receivable	$ 2,700,000	
Raw materials inventory	$ 186,875	
Finished goods inventory	$ 547,052	
Total Current Assets		$ 3,473,927
PP&E	$ 1,250,000	
Less: Accumulated Depreciation	$ (250,000)	

Davros, Inc.		
Opening Balance Sheet		
Assets		
Total Fixed Assets		$ 1,000,000
Total Assets		$ 4,473,927
Liabilities and Owners' Equity		
Accounts payable	$ 255,875	
Notes Payable	$ 350,000	
Total Liabilities		$ 605,875
Common stock	$ 2,000,000	
Retained earnings	$ 1,868,052	
Total Owner's Equity		$ 3,868,052
Total Liabilities & Owner's Equity		$ 4,473,927

Sales for last year's ending quarter and for the coming six quarters are in the table below.

Davros Inc. Sales and Sales Budget							
	Q4 20x6	Q1 20x7	Q2 20x7	Q3 20x7	Q4 20x7	Q1 20x8	Q2 20x8
Sales and Sales Forecast in Units	100,000	125,000	150,000	175,000	200,000	225,000	250,000

- 40% of the company's customers pay in the quarter they receive the goods. The other 60% pay in the following quarter.
- The company keeps 20% of the next quarter's sales on hand in ending inventory.
- The stainless steel, which is of the highest quality, costs $2.50 per pound. The accessories kits cost $0.75 each.
- Raw materials purchases are paid 60% in the quarter of purchase, and 40% in the next quarter.
- Raw materials ending inventories are kept at 25% of the next quarter's production demand.
- It takes 30 minutes to make one tea kettle. Labor is paid $30 per hour because they are fine metal workers, a dying trade.
- Variable overhead is $1.25 per unit. Fixed overhead for manufacturing per quarter includes $6,000 for rent, $12,000 for the metal-working machines (half of which is depreciation), $10,000 for supervision, and $2,500 for miscellaneous.

- Variable selling costs are $1 per unit. Fixed quarterly SG&A costs include $10,000 for the designer, $12,000 for marketing, $8,000 for administrative costs, and $4,000 for general overhead.
- Income taxes are 35% of income before taxes.

REQUIRED:

For the coming year, complete:

a. A sales budget
b. A production budget
c. A raw materials budget for each raw material used to make the tea kettles
d. A labor budget
e. An overhead budget
f. An ending finished goods budget
g. A cost of goods sold budget
h. An SG&A budget
i. An income statement
j. A cash receipts budget
k. A cash disbursements budget
l. A cash budget
m. An ending balance sheet

Database Problems

For database templates, worksheets, and workbooks, go to MAdownloads.imanet.org

DB 10.1 SCENARIO PLANNING. Prestige Auto's president, Jack Noble, is doing some planning for the coming year. The auto dealership faces both fixed and variable costs. For new and used cars, the variable selling costs are currently 15% of revenue (commissions), while the variable cost of the car itself averages 65% of the revenue earned. For repair services, the variable costs of running the repair facility are 20% of revenues. All of the fixed costs are as noted in the following income statement.

Prestige Auto				
Income Statement for the year ending 12/31/20x6				
	New Car Sales	Used Car Sales	Repairs	Company Total
Revenue	$25,000,000	$7,000,000	$3,125,000	$35,125,000
Less: Variable costs				

Prestige Auto				
Income Statement for the year ending 12/31/20x6				
	New Car Sales	Used Car Sales	Repairs	Company Total
Selling costs	$3,750,000	$1,050,000	$625,000	$5,425,000
Cost of cars	$16,250,000	$4,550,000	$-	$20,800,000
Total variable costs	$20,000,000	$5,600,000	$625,000	$26,225,000
Contribution margin	$5,000,000	$1,400,000	$2,500,000	$8,900,000
Less: Fixed costs				
Marketing costs	$500,000	$300,000	$100,000	$900,000
Customer service costs	$200,000	$75,000	$80,000	$355,000
Management costs	$250,000	$100,000	$50,000	$400,000
Overhead costs	$400,000	$200,000	$75,000	$675,000
Total fixed Costs	$1,350,000	$675,000	$305,000	$2,330,000
Income before taxes	$3,650,000	$725,000	$2,195,000	$6,570,000
Income taxes (30%)	$1,095,000	$217,500	$658,500	$1,971,000
Net Income	$2,555,000	$507,500	$1,536,500	$4,599,000

Starting with the income statement for 20x6, Jack decides to test the following assumptions:

- **Scenario 1:** Sales increase 25% due to a new line of Mercedes being released. Preliminary reports from the field are that the new line is exceptionally strong. Fixed sales and marketing would increase by 15% so that the showroom could handle the new volume. Variable selling costs would go up by 10% while the variable cost of the car itself would remain constant. Other new car fixed costs would go up 5%. Repair revenues and their variable costs will increase 10%. Used car sales would also increase 10% with a 5% increase in their variable costs. Neither repairs nor used cars would face any increase in fixed costs. Jack feels this scenario, the optimistic one, has a 30% chance of occurring.
- **Scenario 2:** Sales increase 15% as normally happens when Prestige introduces new models. One salesperson, who will be paid $30,000 in addition to the existing commission structure (variable selling costs), would be added. Variable selling costs would go up 5% with the new volume, but the variable cost of the car itself would remain a constant percentage. Repairs revenue and their variable costs would increase 5%. Repairs fixed costs would be unchanged. Used car sales would increase 5% with no increase in its fixed or variable cost percentage. Jack feels this scenario, the most likely one, has a 50% chance of occurring.
- **Scenario 3:** Sales only increase 5% because the new models fail to live up to their reputation. Therefore, Jack would not add another salesperson. All

costs remain static with variable costs staying at the same percentage of sales and fixed costs. Repairs and used car sales would remain steady with no relevant increase in revenues or costs. Jack feels this scenario, the pessimistic one, has a 20% chance of occurring.

REQUIRED:

a. Using the templates provided in the database for this problem, change the key assumptions as noted in each of the scenarios. Be careful when you come to the increase in variable costs as this is a percentage of existing variable costs. For instance, if variable costs are currently 5% and they increase 25%, you multiply 5% by 1.25 to get the new percentage, which is 6.25%.
b. What is the expected value of the options available to Jack?
c. What should Jack plan for? Why?

DB 10.2 CASH BUDGETS. Having decided to use his most likely scenario as the plan for 20x7, Jack decides to develop cash forecasts. The opening balance sheet is presented below.

Balance Sheet as of 12/31/20x6		
Assets		
Cash	$50,000,000	
Accounts receivable	$5,250,000	
Car inventory	$22,500,000	
Total current assets		$77,750,000
Property, plant, and equipment	$12,500,000	
Less: Accumulated depreciation	$(4,375,000)	$8,125,000
Total assets		$85,875,000
Total Liabilities and Owner's Equity		
Accounts payable	$14,625,000	
Notes payable	$7,500,000	
Taxes payable	$1,971,000	
Total current liablities		$24,096,000
Mortgage on building	$2,500,000	
Total liabilities		$26,596,000
Common stock	$200,000	
Retained earnings	$59,079,000	

Balance Sheet as of 12/31/20x6	
Assets	
Total owner's equity	$59,279,000
Total liabilities and owner's equity	$85,875,000

OTHER INFORMATION:

- The company pays its taxes quarterly on the prior quarter's income. That means the ending taxes payable is always the total taxes payable from the prior quarter. Prestige ends the year owing 25% of 20x6's income taxes, which must be paid in March of the first quarter of the following year. Assume 25% of 20x7's projected taxes are in taxes payable at the end of Quarter 1.
- Accounts payable are always paid the month following the cost. This is mostly the cost of acquiring the automobiles the company sells.
- The company plans to sell $9,000,000 of new and used cars over the first quarter of 20x7. It plans to sell $2,000,000 in January, $2,500,000 in February, and $4,500,000 in March. It will collect 75% of these sales in cash either from the customer directly or from the loan company servicing the customer. The remaining 25% of the sales are in Accounts Receivable in the form of a bridge loan collected according to the instruction below.
- The cars sold cost the company 65% of their selling price. The company pays for these purchases in the month following the purchase. This is the opening accounts payable balance.
- Repairs revenue is planned to come in evenly throughout the year, so one-twelfth of the annual total will be collected in cash (all repairs revenues are cash-based) in each month.
- The company pays for 50% of the cost of purchased cars in the month of sale and 50% the next month.
- All other variable and fixed costs are paid in the month they are incurred.

Remember: Under the most likely scenario, variable costs are 1.05 times 15%, or 15.75%. Used cars variable costs remain at 15% and repairs variable costs go up 5%, 20% times 1.05, or 21%. Prestige incurs repairs variable costs uniformly over the 12 months of operations.

- It also incurs fixed costs uniformly over the 12 months of operations.
- Annual depreciation, included in the overhead costs, comes to $200,000 of these fixed costs.
- The accounts receivable consists of short-term notes that are used to help some customers finance the original purchase of the cars from the dealership. Of the opening balance of $125,000, 70% will be collected in January, the remainder in March. Of the sales made, 25% require an accounts

receivable bridge loan, while the rest are cash sales. Customers who take the bridge loan pay 25% in the month of sale, 45% in the month after sale, and 30% two months after the sale.

- Prestige is scheduled to make a $10,000 payment on its notes payable every month. The note was originally valued to include interest, so no separate cash entry is required for the interest on the note.

REQUIRED:

Using the template provided for the first three months of 20x7, develop a cash receipts budget, a cash disbursements budget, and a total cash budget. Also calculate ending accounts receivable, ending taxes payable, and ending accounts payable. Place them in the box provided on the template. Finally, when you turn in your completed template, include a comment on how Prestige Auto's cash projections look for the first quarter of 20x7.

Cases

CASE 10.1 SCENARIO PLANNING AND BREAKEVEN ANALYSIS. Paul Knotts, president of Photo Swift, a website that allows sharing of photos, wants to expand his business to make other uses of the pictures that are posted on the host website. He calls together his marketing and development head, Rachelle Wright, and his BPA specialist, Susan McCoy, to talk about potential new products and their impact on the company.

Paul: Good morning, all! Thought we'd start off the week by brainstorming to come up with some new products for our product line. The sharing of photos is going so well, there has to be some other things we can offer to boost revenues and profits.

Rachelle: My team's been thinking about different options, Paul. We could offer photo albums with nice covers that could be given as gifts. We could add to that personalized calendars, which we'd print and ship from headquarters.

Susan: Wait a minute! We don't have the software or the hardware for doing these things. I thought we were concerned about costs this year. I think we could find some cost-cutting projects that would help raise profits without investing in new products and equipment.

Paul: I don't know if just cutting costs is enough. We can run very lean given our business model, but if we don't keep coming up with new products, we're going to eventually hit the wall.

Susan: Then I'd rather see us put some money into advertising. New products are risky, and the forecasts Rachelle's group put together make me a bit nervous. They show growth with no changes in our structure. Now they want to add bells and whistles to the site that will require outlays with no guarantee of inflows downstream. I'm nervous about the whole concept.

Rachelle: I don't know what you're talking about, Susan! My group does market research before we put forward any projections. Remember, our bonus is tied to hitting sales targets, not like yours, which is tied solely to profits. Without new products, we will have trouble making those sales targets in coming years. To be fair to my team, we need to start adding products to our line to give them something to sell!

Paul: It seems like the two of you have very different pictures of the future of this firm. I have trouble believing it's all because of the result of different incentive structures; you both bonus on company profits, just not in the same degree! I want a company that is growing. So, Rachelle, how do you see the new product lines shaping up?

Rachelle: Well, we've run some projections. We believe that an optimistic forecast would be sales of $2.5 million in photo albums and $2 million in calendars. Together, they would also increase our regular sales from their current $18 million to $20 million as people come back for additional photos.

Susan: That's very optimistic, Rachelle, and you know it. We ran the projections in BPA and found that it was more likely that we'd sell $1.5 million in photo albums and $1 million in calendars. And, the bump in regular sales would only be $500,000. We saw this as the likely scenario, with a 60% probability of occurring. When we add the $2.4 million in software and hardware that we'll need to offer these products, and the 50% variable costs that come with all of our products, it's hardly worth the risk!

Rachelle: We think our scenario is the likely one, with a 60% probability of occurring. I thought your group did some studies that dropped our variable cost down to 40%. Your scenario is very pessimistic. I'd say it isn't impossible, but that it has only a 20% chance of occurring. There is also a 20% chance that the actual outcome will be in the middle of our two plans. That would see $2 million in photo albums and $1.5 million in calendars, and $1.5 million in new sales. I agree it will take us $2.4 million to get the business up and running, but it leaves us open to other new products that use the same technology downstream. And, the equipment will be useful for three years, so that's really only an additional $800,000 per year in fixed costs. There's always a new twist we can put on photographs. I see T-shirts and hats, and all sorts of things downstream! We've got a great little business here!

Paul: I hate to see us so far apart, but I like the idea, Rachelle. Tell you what, Susan, why don't you and your group run the scenarios the way that Rachelle sees them. Change the probabilities if you'd like, so we get two perspectives. And, I'd like to see the plan include the option of getting variable costs down. Since our fixed costs are significant, every penny we get into contribution margin [revenues minus variable costs] increases our profitability. I want those cost savings and the new products!

Susan: I'll do it, Paul, but my instincts tell me that Marketing's projections are once again too rosy. Remember last year when we had to run sales to finally hit our sales goals? We can't count on sales, which are lower profit, to make sure they hit their target sales goals. If we add these two products, I hope you make midstream adjustments to the marketing goals for the year. The rest of us will be facing a bigger risk if the company's profit goals, and, hence, profit sharing, are negatively impacted by these plans!

Paul: Concerns noted, Susan. Why don't you run the scenarios? And since our fixed costs are currently sitting at $7.5 million per year, why don't you add in a bit of breakeven analysis on the most likely scenario so I can get a feeling for the riskiness of the project? See you both next week when we'll continue the discussion. Rachelle, keep working your group for new ideas and refinements of your projections, while Susan and her group start developing options for us, costed out, of course!

Paul tended to be optimistic, but he needed to get his two key managers on the same page. Maybe running the numbers would help. And he'd definitely have to make adjustments to Marketing's incentive plan to make sure they did not just come up with ideas to boost sales but that do not raise profits. Sales were okay, but profits were king.

REQUIRED:

a. Generate the profitability of the three scenarios using the current variable cost ratio of 50%.
b. Calculate the expected value of the plans given Rachelle's probabilities. Now redo the expected value with the optimistic plan being 20% likely, the midrange plan 50% likely, and the pessimistic option 30% likely.
c. Calculate the breakeven point for the company before and after adding the new business.
d. Calculate the payback using Rachelle's middle scenario (album sales $2 million).
e. Redo these four steps using the 40% variable cost ratio that is targeted for the year.

f. What recommendation would you make to Paul? Why?
g. How do you feel about the company dynamics? Is there some way to use incentives to bring the objectives of these two top managers into closer alignment?

CASE 10.2 CASH BUDGETS AND TREND ANALYSIS. Blue Sky Spas is a medium-sized franchisor of luxury spa facilities. It offers the full range of spa treatments, nail specialists, fitness specialists, swimming, aquatic exercise programs, and yoga classes. Franchisees pay $25,000 for the right to use the name and receive support in setting up their spas. They, in turn, agree to buy 75% of their merchandise from the franchisor. In addition, the franchisee pays Blue Sky 10% of its total sales to help support marketing programs for the entire chain. Blue Sky, the franchisor, provides top-notch products to the spas, counseling and business analysis support, and marketing for the national chain. Of the products sold, the purchase cost is 60% of the dollar amount it charges the spas. Since Blue Sky buys in large quantities, it actually can sell the marked-up goods to the local spas for less than they could negotiate a similar product's purchase on their own. Right now, Blue Sky has 2,500 franchisees that, on the average, buy $2,500 of product each month and book $30,000 in total revenues per month.

Blue Sky's biggest challenge is keeping the chain growing and managing its cash flow (it has to pay for products and store them until the spas order them). The spas usually take 60 days to pay Blue Sky for both regular sales revenue and product purchases. Bruce Compton, founder of Blue Sky Spas, watches his cash flow carefully from year to year. The cash flow information for the last six months is laid out in the tables below. The monthly sales and product information is updated for the new number of franchisees each month, as you can see in the income statement.

Blue Sky Spas						
Cash Receipts Summary						
	January	February	March	April	May	June
Total Franchisees	2500	2530	2570	2620	2680	2750
New franchisees	$750,000	$1,000,000	$1,250,000	$1,500,000	$1,750,000	$1,750,000
Monthly sales revenue	$7,290,000	$7,410,000	$7,500,000	$7,590,000	$7,710,000	$7,860,000
Product sales revenue	$6,075,000	$6,175,000	$6,250,000	$6,325,000	$6,425,000	$6,550,000
Total cash receipts	$14,115,000	$14,585,000	$15,000,000	$15,415,000	$15,885,000	$16,160,000

Blue Sky Spas						
Cash Dispursements Summary						
	January	February	March	April	May	June
For product sales	$3,795,000	$3,855,000	$3,930,000	$4,020,000	$4,125,000	$4,230,000

Blue Sky Spas						
Cash Dispursements Summary						
	January	February	March	April	May	June
Marketing	$5,125,000	$5,186,500	$5,268,500	$5,371,000	$5,494,000	$5,637,500
Franchise support	$3,000,000	$3,036,000	$3,084,000	$3,144,000	$3,216,000	$3,300,000
Customer service	$1,000,000	$1,012,000	$1,028,000	$1,048,000	$1,072,000	$1,100,000
General overhead	$1,250,000	$1,250,000	$1,250,000	$1,250,000	$1,250,000	$1,250,000
	$14,170,000	$14,339,500	$14,560,500	$14,833,000	$15,157,000	$15,517,500

Blue Sky Spas						
Cash Summary						
	January	February	March	April	May	June
Beginning balance	$75,000	$20,000	$265,500	$705,000	$1,287,000	$2,015,000
Plus: Receipts	$14,115,000	$14,585,000	$15,000,000	$15,415,000	$15,885,000	$16,160,000
Cash available	$14,190,000	$14,605,000	$15,265,500	$16,120,000	$17,172,000	$18,175,000
Less: Cash disbursements	$14,170,000	$14,339,500	$14,560,500	$14,833,000	$15,157,000	$15,517,500
Ending cash balance	$20,000	$265,500	$705,000	$1,287,000	$2,015,000	$2,657,500

Blue Sky Spas						
Income Statement						
	January	February	March	April	May	June
Product Sales	$6,250,000	$6,325,000	$6,425,000	$6,550,000	$6,700,000	$6,875,000
Less: Cost of Sales	$(3,750,000)	$(3,795,000)	$(3,855,000)	$(3,930,000)	$(4,020,000)	$(4,125,000)
Gross Margin from product	$2,500,000	$2,530,000	$2,570,000	$2,620,000	$2,680,000	$2,750,000
Franchise revenue	$750,000	$750,000	$1,000,000	$1,250,000	$1,500,000	$1,750,000
Service fees revenue	$7,500,000	$7,590,000	$7,710,000	$7,860,000	$8,040,000	$8,250,000
Total Gross Margin	$10,750,000	$10,870,000	$11,280,000	$11,730,000	$12,220,000	$12,750,000
Less:						
Marketing	$5,125,000	$5,186,500	$5,268,500	$5,371,000	$5,494,000	$5,637,500
Franchise support	$3,000,000	$3,036,000	$3,084,000	$3,144,000	$3,216,000	$3,300,000
Customer service	$1,000,000	$1,012,000	$1,028,000	$1,048,000	$1,072,000	$1,100,000
General overhead	$1,250,000	$1,250,000	$1,250,000	$1,250,000	$1,250,000	$1,250,000
Total SG&A	$10,375,000	$10,484,500	$10,630,500	$10,813,000	$11,032,000	$11,287,500
Income before tax	$375,000	$385,500	$649,500	$917,000	$1,188,000	$1,462,500
Taxes (30%)	$(112,500)	$(115,650)	$(194,850)	$(275,100)	$(356,400)	$(438,750)
Net Income	$262,500	$269,850	$454,650	$641,900	$831,600	$1,023,750

Bruce is considering a new marketing blitz that would increase the number of new franchisees by 250 per month for the next three months, at which point it would drop back to the normal 60 new franchisees per month. Bruce would need to buy product to support each of these franchisees the month before they come online (just as he does now), which he would pay for in the month of purchase (that is, one month before he actually sells the goods to the franchisee). He would need to wait 60 days to receive payment for the goods and services the franchisee books. Bruce would provide services to the franchisees at the same level as he does now, which is $2,050 for marketing on average per franchisee, $1,200 per month per franchisee for franchise support, and $400 per month for customer service per franchisee. The new marketing blitz would add another $2.5 million to Blue Sky's July cash budget requirements. Fixed general overhead would increase to $1.5 million due to the increase in volume of franchisees. The question is: Can Bruce support this level of cash outlay to gain the new franchisees?

REQUIRED:

a. Extend the cash flow tables to cover July through December. Remember that the payments received are delayed by 60 days, so sales and product receipts made in June are not collected until August. Also remember that Bruce buys product one month in advance, so he buys and pays for goods for the next month's level of franchisees.

b. Complete the income statement for the 12 months. Remember there is no lag here.

c. With your 12 months of cash data, do a trend analysis chart of cash receipts, cash disbursements, and ending cash balance on the same chart.

d. How do Blue Sky's cash flow projections look given these projections?

e. Does the new marketing plan look like a good idea? Why or why not?

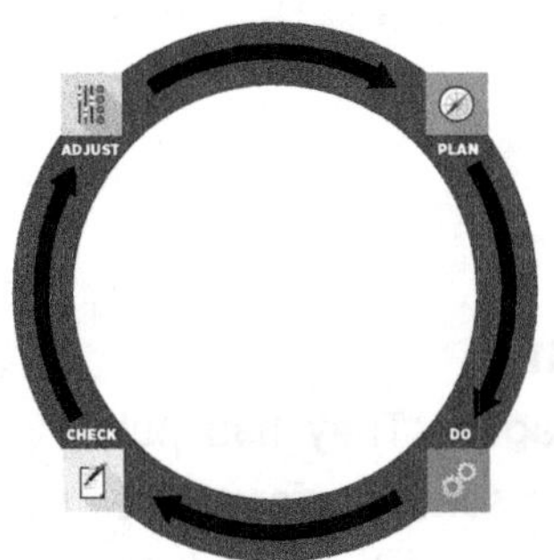

Setting Performance Expectations in Large, Complex Organizations

The "Sacred Obligations of Senior Leadership": Vision: What will we be? Goals: What four or five key things must we do to get there? Alignment: Translate the work of each person into an alignment with the goals.[1]

SOCHIRO HONDA,
FOUNDER OF HONDA MOTOR CORPORATION

CHAPTER ROUNDUP

1. **Organizing for Performance**
   - *Benefits of Decentralization*
   - *Costs of Decentralization*
2. **The Role of Responsibility Centers**
3. **Planning and Budgeting Systems in Large, Complex Organizations**
   - *Three Planning and Budgeting Cycles*
   - *Company-by-Company Variations in Practice*
4. **Performance Measurement Problems in Divisionally Organized Entities**
   - *The Primary Financial Objective: Maximizing Shareholder Value*
   - *Accounting Metrics as Surrogate Indicators of Value*
   - *The Congruence Problem*
   - *The Interdependency Problem*
   - *The Suboptimization Problem*

LEARNING OBJECTIVE

By the end of the chapter, you should be able to:

1. **Explain the costs and benefits of decentralization.**
2. **Describe the basic structure used to define responsibility centers in organizations.**
3. **Discuss the major elements and purposes of planning and budgeting systems.**
4. **Talk about why and how managers set performance targets of different types and with different levels of difficulty.**
5. **Explain why companies typically prepare their plans and track their performance in accounting measurement terms even though their primary objective is to maximize the value created.**
6. **Explain the common problems caused by lack of measurement congruence and how they can be addressed.**
7. **Suggest ways to mitigate the effects of four common measurement problems.**

1 Quoted in William Fonvielle and Lawrence P. Carr, "Gaining Strategic Alignment: Making Scorecards Work," *Management Accounting Quarterly*, Fall 2001, p. 5.

IN CONTEXT ➤ Prestige Auto: Decentralized Budgeting

The week had gone quickly for Prestige's managers. They had put together preliminary budgets and even developed some performance measurements, just as Jack had requested. The hardest part fell to Alice, who had to take all of the pieces that each manager gave her and develop a comprehensive, *balanced* budget for the company. While Alice was very skilled, balancing a budget was a challenge that often took her many hours. She had a preliminary balance for the meeting, but she was sure it still needed some tweaking.

"I've run the preliminary numbers," Alice loudly said to start off the meeting. "We're looking at roughly $42.4 million in sales for next year, an increase of 21% over last year. That's really good. The profit on these sales is roughly $5 million using the expected value of the three scenarios we decided to run. That makes for a very good year if everyone hits their projections."

"That sounds like a great start!" said Jack. "I was hoping we'd plan for an increase, and we did. It seems you've all gone the extra mile to make sure we have a bang-up year. That makes all our profit-sharing plans look very good! Outstanding!"

"What do you mean when you say you ran three scenarios, Alice?" asked Tony. "That's a new term for me. Can you explain it?"

"Sure. First, we took the preliminary estimates you gave us and developed some alternatives that questioned the assumptions that were made. This usually results in at least three potential outcomes. We call the first plan—the one based on the information you gave us—the optimistic plan. The remaining two are a middle-ground or likely scenario, in case your estimates are off in some way, and a pessimistic scenario, where sales grow much more slowly than anticipated. Next, we assign probabilities to each of these potential outcomes, and *voilà!*—we have three different estimates. We could run any number of options, but we only generated these three."

"Why do you do that?" asked Bruce, sounding a bit irritated. "Why don't you just take our numbers?"

"We want to be sure that if your numbers are off a little, the company still does fine. That's our job in Finance...to make sure the business remains solvent regardless of the plan's accuracy," replied Alice.

"I asked Alice to run some scenarios off of your numbers to make sure we had a robust plan this year," interceded Jack. "My biggest concern this year is that we convince the manufacturers to let us have more cars for new sales and leasing. We're not their biggest customer, so we don't have a lot of leverage. We'll need to figure out a way to make it in *their* best interest to help us out."

"I'll take that task on," said Bruce. "Judy, maybe you could work with me on it. I know you've met quite a few of the manufacturers' representatives at various marketing meetings. If we pull together, maybe we can find a way to make Prestige Auto's best interest their best interest."

"Sure," responded Judy. "Why don't we start working on this and use it to kick off the next meeting? We're making progress. No time to stop now!"

Organizing for Performance

AS WAS MENTIONED IN CHAPTER 10, WHEN BUSINESSES GET VERY LARGE, they have no choice but to decentralize. The top management team cannot make all of the important decisions that need to be made in a timely manner. In its typical form, decentralization involves the creation of largely autonomous operating units within the corporate structure. The managers of these operating units, which might be called companies, divisions, regions, or groups, have considerable discretion to set their business's strategy and to make sure that it is implemented properly.

To a large extent, the main challenge in managing a large corporation involves taking advantage of the benefits of decentralization while minimizing its costs. As a point of departure in this chapter, it is useful to review these benefits and costs.

BENEFITS OF DECENTRALIZATION

OBJECTIVE 1
Explain the costs and benefits of decentralization.

Decentralization can provide any of four main benefits. The first benefit is *better-informed decision makers*. No central manager or management group can know everything about a complex organization's many product (or service) markets and operational capabilities and constraints. Even wise, experienced top managers cannot be experts in every operating area of a complex organization. Decentralized organizations can employ specialists who are trained in, and who can focus on, specific functions (for example, human resource management), geographical areas (such as Japan), customers (for example, large building contractors), suppliers (like steel manufacturers), or technologies (such as digital signal processors). In many cases, these specialists can make better decisions than can less informed, generalist managers.

The second benefit of decentralization is *faster decision making*. Larger organizations, in which top-level managers do not delegate much decision-making authority, cannot respond very quickly to new business opportunities or changing business conditions. Even with staff support, it takes time for the top management group to direct its attention to each issue that arises, to become informed about the details of the issue, and then to reach a decision. The managers cannot work hard enough or long enough to gather and process all of the specialized information they would need to make good, informed decisions on a timely basis. And if they take a vacation or are away on a business trip, decision making might grind to a halt.

The decision-making capabilities of decentralized organizations are greatly expanded. The lower-level managers can gather and process the required information and make at least some decisions without involving the top-level managers. In this way, the decision-making bottleneck that can occur in centralized organizations is eliminated. The organization becomes more nimble and responsive. And top-level managers, freed of the obligation of making many of the operating decisions, can focus their attention on the few decisions of major strategic importance.

The third benefit is that decentralization tends to make subunit managers *more motivated and more entrepreneurial*. Most people are motivated by the challenge of controlling their own destiny. They like having the power to make decisions and then to be evaluated in terms of how well they made those decisions. It is energizing and also stimulates creativity. Because they will be rewarded for making improvements in their areas of responsibility, the lower-level managers are stimulated to seek new, better ways of doing things. As Richard Chandler, CEO of Sunrise Medical, a medical products company headquartered in Carlsbad, Calif., said in defending his company's decentralized organization and lucrative performance-based bonuses: "People want to be rewarded based on their own efforts. [Without accountability,] you end up with a system like the U.S. Post Office. There's no incentive ..."[2]

Finally, decentralization often *develops personnel better* and more quickly. The involvement of the lower-level managers in decision making helps these managers acquire useful experience. This experience benefits them in their current jobs as they learn to see more aspects of the decisions they are making. It will also benefit them as they move on to jobs at higher organization levels. Thus, it increases the organization's pool of experienced managers.

COSTS OF DECENTRALIZATION

OBJECTIVE 2

Describe the basic structure used to define responsibility centers in organizations.

Decentralization, however, is not without its costs, problems, and challenges. These costs are magnified by a poorly designed and implemented structure. But even decentralized companies with well-designed systems face some of these problems and bear some of these costs.

One pervasive and often large cost of decentralization is commonly referred to as **suboptimization,** *an act that is not as useful or effective as possible for the corporation*. It stems from the fact that lower-level managers are prone to make decisions or take actions that are in their subunit's best interest but that are not in the best interests of the corporation as a whole. One form of suboptimization, *behavioral displacement*, was introduced in Chapter 2. Where it occurs, the subunit managers are actually motivated to serve objectives that are not consistent with the overall organization's objectives because the performance measures for which they are held responsible are not congruent with the overall organization's objectives. For example, rewarding salespeople for bringing in sales revenue will motivate the salespeople to seek the largest sales that can be obtained with the least effort. However, these sales might not be the best—the most profitable—for the corporation. It might be better, more congruent, to make the salespeople

2 Quoted in Tom Petruno, "Sunrise Scam Throws Light on Incentive Pay Programs," *Los Angeles Times*, January 15, 1996, p. D3.

responsible for the total profits generated from sales. Other performance measurement congruence failures are described later in this chapter.

Gamesmanship, *the use of manipulation to gain an advantage*, is another common form of suboptimization. Gamesmanship occurs when a manager knowingly takes actions—for example, creates budget slack or manipulates performance measures—that are not intended to serve the organization's best interests but to achieve a preset personal or unit goal. In the extreme, gamesmanship can involve fraudulent behavior. These problems, which often stem from accuracy problems with performance measures, are discussed in more detail later in this chapter.

Finally, decentralization almost always leads to increased administrative and coordination costs. More communication is needed to link the activities of the large number of decision makers so that the organization can coordinate their efforts. Much of this communication takes place during the organization's formal planning and budgeting processes and its formal performance review processes. The performance-dependent incentives, such as bonuses, raise compensation costs because they are generally added onto base salaries, at least to some extent. And organizations take many steps, such as requiring upper management decision-making approvals or internal audit checks, to help minimize the costs of suboptimization and game playing. Each of these steps is costly.

Estimating the magnitude of each of these benefits and costs is difficult, but it is essential for managers who are designing the optimal structure for their organization. There are trade-offs to consider. Most organizations of any size have concluded that some degree of decentralization is desirable, but some organizations decentralize further than others.

The Role of Responsibility Centers

The management of decentralized organizations requires the establishment of **responsibility centers,** *subunits of the corporation that are held accountable for specified results*. Each subunit in a decentralized organization that has a manager is a responsibility center. Each responsibility manager has at least some decision-making authority and is held at least somewhat responsible, or **accountable**—*answerable for; obliged to report, explain, or justify certain outcomes or activities*, for the performance of that subunit. There are many different types of responsibility centers. Some are whole businesses; others focus only on narrow functions.

Accountability can be classified in terms of the breadth of *financial responsibility* given to managers. The basic types of financial responsibility centers are:

- **Cost centers**: entities that are held accountable for managing costs; their contributions to company profit are not measured in financial terms.
- **Revenue center**: entities that are responsible for selling products or services.
- **Profit center**: entities that generate both revenues and expenses and, hence, are held accountable for profits or losses.

- **Investment center**: entities with responsibility for their own revenue, expenses, and assets; their financial results are based on all three factors; they utilize capital to directly contribute to the company's profitability.

The managers of each of these responsibility centers—*cost center managers*—are held accountable for a specific set of financial statement line items, as well as some nonfinancial measures of the output produced by that expenditure of cost, such as units produced and product quality. *Revenue center managers* are held accountable for a specific set of revenue line items, as well as the expenses incurred to produce that revenue. Table 11.1 lists the major types of financial responsibility centers and provides examples of the results measures for which the managers of each might be held accountable.

TABLE 11.1 FINANCIAL RESPONSIBILITY CENTERS: ACCOUNTABILITY MEASURES

	Responsible for (examples)	Manager Accountable for (examples)
Cost center	Production department Assembly line	Cost per unit Schedule attainment Product quality
Revenue center	Sales department	Sales revenue Sales department expense
Profit center	An entity responsible for producing and selling a single product line	Prespecified profit goals; pretax profit.
Investment center	A subsidiary company	Return on net assets Return on investment Return on equity

One of the most important types of responsibility centers in a divisionally organized entity is that of the lowest level of profit center. As is shown in Figure 11.1, it is at this point in the organization in which most of the translations between financial and operating measures of performance occur. Managers of these profit centers tend to communicate upward in the organization (for example, with their superiors) in financial terms—in terms of profits and returns. But they tend to communicate downward in the organization (such as, with their subordinates) in operational terms—yields, schedule attainment, efficiency, inventory levels. Thus, they are involved in this important terminology-translation process.

Communication Patterns Regarding Financial and Operational Measures for Lower-Level Profit Center Managers

Top Management

Conversations in terms of:
- Return on Investment
- Net Income
- Return on Assets
- Sales Growth
- Return on Equity
- Cash Flow

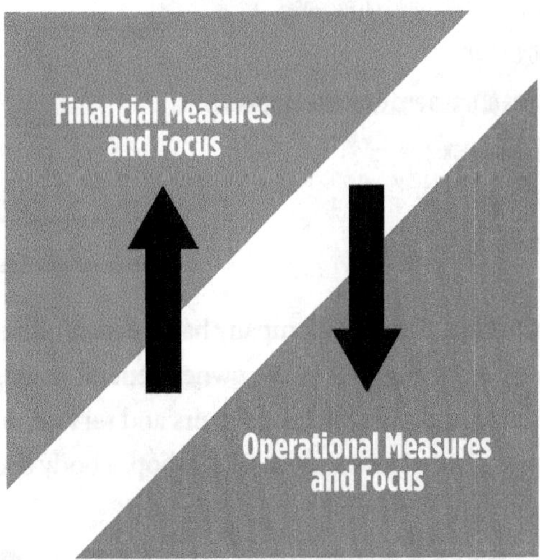

Conversations in terms of:
- Throughput
- Capacity Utilization
- Process/Product Quality
- On-time Delivery
- Cost per Unit
- Productivity
- Waste

The Day-to-Day Organization

FIGURE 11.1 MANAGERS OF LOWER-LEVEL PROFIT CENTERS USUALLY COMMUNICATE WITH THEIR MANAGERS ABOUT PROFITS AND RETURNS, WHILE THEY GENERALLY COMMUNICATE WITH THOSE REPORTING TO THEM ABOUT YIELDS, SCHEDULES, EFFICIENCY, INVENTORY LEVELS, AND OTHER OPERATIONAL GOALS.

A key concept underlying decisions as to what responsibility to give specific managers is that of **influence, or controllability,** *the ability to affect the measured outcomes*. That is, managers should be held accountable for all aspects of performance over which they have significant influence, but *only* those aspects over which they have significant control. For example, managers who have influence over some categories of costs but little influence over revenues are almost always set up as cost center managers. In addition, the specific line items of revenues, expenses, assets, and liabilities for which managers are held accountable can be refined depending on the manager's degree of influence over that line item. Production managers, who are typically considered cost center managers, are not held accountable for all of the company's costs; they are accountable only for the costs over which they have significant influence.

Table 11.2 shows a performance report for a division manager who has profit center responsibility. This report traces all of the division-related revenues and costs down to a bottom-line net-profit-after-tax figure. The manager of that division, however, is held accountable only for the line called controllable profit because he does not have significant influence on group and corporate expenses or income taxes. These other expenses are considered "below the line" on which the manager is being evaluated. **Responsibility accounting** *is a reporting system that holds managers accountable only for those aspects of performance over which they have significant influence.*

TABLE 11.2 PERFORMANCE REPORT: SEGREGATING CONTROLLABLE AND NONCONTROLLABLE ITEMS

	Stated in thousands
Revenue	$135,975
Less: Directly controllable division expenses	96,181
Controllable profit	39,794
Less: Allocations of group and corporate expenses	24,101
Net profit before tax	15,693
Less: Income taxes	6,277
Net profit after tax	$9,416

When Jack Noble took over Prestige Auto, the company had a decentralized, departmental structure that is traditional in the industry. Directly reporting to Art, the owner/general manager, were four department managers, those responsible for marketing and sales, finance, repairs and service, and acquisitions (see Figure 11.2). The service department was further divided into a mechanical shop, a body shop, and a parts department.

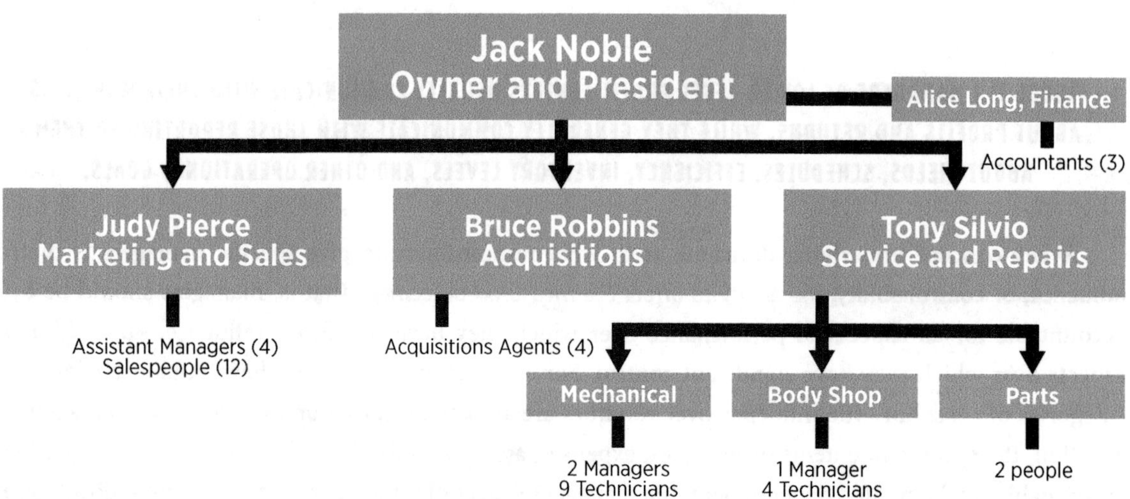

FIGURE 11.2 A DECENTRALIZED ORGANIZATION STRUCTURE ALLOWS MANAGERS TO STAY ON TOP OF THEIR DEPARTMENT'S EXTERNAL AND INTERNAL ACTIVITIES.

This organization makes sense because it provides many of the benefits of decentralization. The managers of each department can stay better informed about the details of their department's business than can a single general manager. Judy Pierce, as head of marketing and sales, will follow carefully the communications from the manufacturer, such as changes in prices, promotions, and product designs. The used car sales manager, one of the two assistant managers under Judy, will follow changes in the used car market and will establish personal relationships with the managers of auction houses so that he can quickly dispose of cars that are too old or not the right type to display on the dealership lot.

The second assistant manager makes sure the company stays on top of its leasing options. Since they all have the authority to make decisions, these managers can make decisions more quickly than could be done if Jack had to be involved in every decision. The managers are also more motivated than they would be if they were merely implementing Jack's directives. They have incentives to make good decisions and to come up with new ideas for doing things. And as they run their subunits, they are developing their management skills. Jack's career demonstrates the common progression through a car dealership hierarchy: salesman, manager of new car sales department, manager of used car sales department, then general manager, and finally owner.

Marketing and Sales, and Repairs and Service are run as profit centers as managers have control over both revenues and costs. Acquisitions and Finance are cost centers, although Acquisitions does indirectly influence revenue based on the cars Bruce Robbins is able to attain.

Is this the only way to design a car dealership responsibility structure? No, there are some options. One option is to combine the marketing and acquisitions departments into one sales department, and, in fact, many dealerships, particularly smaller ones, use that organization structure.

Another option is to manage the service department as a cost center. The dealership could hold the service department manager accountable for both controlling costs and for maintaining the quality of the work done, perhaps monitored through a customer satisfaction report. Work done for customers would still be charged at market rates, but for service work done internally, for the new car and used car subunits, the charges would be at cost. This would pass the value created by the service department onto the two sales groups. They would look more profitable, while the service department would look less profitable.

Even while managing the service department as a cost center, the parts department could be operated as a profit center within the service cost center. There are many precedents for this. Some nonprofit organizations, such as universities, operate profit centers, such as bookstores and restaurants, within their boundaries. There are many feasible responsibility center possibilities.

Planning and Budgeting Systems in Large, Complex Organizations

OBJECTIVE 3

Discuss the major elements and purposes of planning and budgeting systems.

Decisions about the degree of decentralization and responsibility center structure serve as prerequisites to implementation of a business planning and analysis (BPA) process. Planning, the first element of the BPA process, is particularly critical in organizations comprised of multiple financial responsibility centers. It includes all of the issues of planning in small organizations, as were discussed in Chapter 10. The complication is that in larger organizations, many more informed parties must be involved in the planning processes. More elaborate processes must be used in order to solicit and communicate information from these parties and to get everyone committed to implement the plan as designed.

THREE PLANNING AND BUDGETING CYCLES

Larger, more decentralized corporations often use planning and budgeting processes comprised of three distinguishable, sequenced planning cycles, which can be called strategic planning, programming, and operational budgeting. The typical ordering of these cycles and the timing of the involvement of managers at different levels is shown in Figure 11.3.

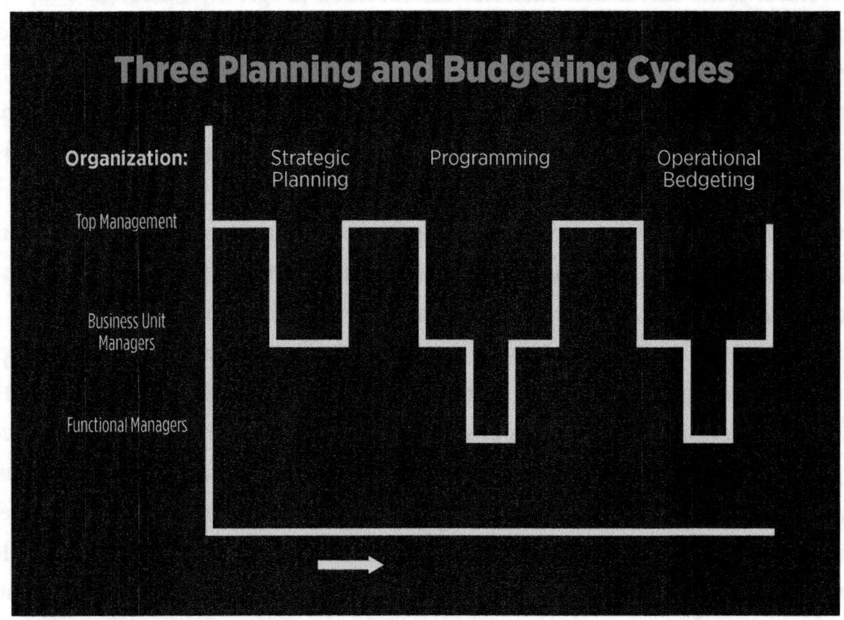

FIGURE 11.3 TYPICALLY, IN A DECENTRALIZED SYSTEM, THE STRATEGIC PLANNING PHASE IS CONFINED TO TOP AND MIDDLE MANAGEMENT. ONCE PLANNING MOVES ON TO THE PROGRAMMING AND OPERATIONAL STAGES OF PLANNING AND BUDGETING, FUNCTIONAL MANAGERS ARE BROUGHT INTO THE CONVERSATION.

➤ CYCLE 1: STRATEGIC PLANNING

Strategic planning *is a process designed to help an organization develop and communicate a corporate strategy and a strategy for each strategic business unit.* It usually involves four steps. First, it involves a further development of the corporate mission, vision, and objectives, if they have not been previously agreed upon. Second, it involves **SWOT analysis,** *a detailed examination of the corporation's as well as each business unit's strengths, weaknesses, opportunities, and threats.*

Third, managers must discuss and decide on strategies that are considered the best for moving the organization from its current position to one that best leads to the achievement of the organization's objectives. Larger organizations, because they usually have entities in multiple lines of business, must articulate two types of strategies.

1. **The corporate strategy** *is a plan that defines what types of businesses the organization will engage in.* For example, managers of the Goodyear Tire and Rubber Company understand that their company's relative expertise is in businesses involved in tire and rubber products. Therefore, they do not look for opportunities to run hotels or sell soap that would require skills and abilities that are not already part of the business's portfolio.
2. A **business strategy** *is an understanding as to how each strategic business unit within the corporation will compete*. Unless they are quite similar, **strategic business units (SBUs)** each have their own strategy that allow them to benefit from their own sets of comparative advantages. For example, at Goodyear, the business units for which strategies must be developed include those that sell tires into various markets (for example, automobiles, trucks, farm equipment, construction equipment, airplanes) and those that sell rubber products (such as belts and hoses). In developing its business strategies, each SBU must consider how best to take advantage of its relative strengths to be able to perform at its best. For example, will the business attempt to compete globally or focus its activities regionally? Will it take advantage of its highly efficient plants and leverage its cost advantages? Or, will it take advantage of its technical superiority and attempt to attain or maintain a reputation as a product innovator?

And fourth, strategic planning involves the preparation of a **strategic plan,** *a written description of the tactics to be followed to achieve the plan's goals*. The strategic plan is a written description of the strategies to be followed in the expected and other possible scenarios. It also includes an articulation of some long-term (for example, those generally for periods greater than one year in advance), summary performance targets. In some faster-moving (such as high technology) industries, the long-term targets might extend only for two or three years. In other industries (like utilities), targets may be set for the following 25 years, or even longer.

LOOKING BACK ➤ Long-Term Planning is a Continuous Process

Budgeting and planning became significant issues for study in the 1940s. The development of long-term profit plans quickly became part of the planning cycle. R.G. Lochiel, who was vice president and controller of Central Airlines Corporation, described the process this way:

One might define long-term profit planning as a series of economic actions taken or decisions made by management, based upon well-considered financial forecasts, to insure satisfactory profits and a sound financial condition. Sound and intelligent decisions can be made by management only after it has been provided with the tools of financial forecasts.

It is appropriate at this point to state the most important principle of profit planning, which is that neither the tools nor the plans can remain static and retain value...it cannot be too strongly emphasized that long-term planning is a continuous process. Every day *external and internal conditions are changing so as to affect the completed forecast. If such changes are not reflected in the forecast it quickly loses its value, and continued management reliance on outmoded forecasts is not only a waste of time, but extremely dangerous.**

As Lochiel's words so clearly state, long-term planning of a strategic nature is a continuous process, one that begins with projecting a sales forecast and ends with the development of pro forma financial statements that help management direct its attention to those areas of the company at greatest risk. Formal in nature, long-term strategic planning is as important today as it was more than 70 years ago.

*R.G. Lochiel, "Long-Term Profit Planning," *NACA Yearbook* 1946, reprinted in Vol. III *Relevance Rediscovered*, edited by Richard Vangermeersch, IMA® (Institute of Management Accountants), Montvale, N.J.: 1992: pp. 209-210.

➤ CYCLE 2: PROGRAMMING

Programming *is the identification of specific action plans and the allocation of scarce resources* (for example, capital, people) *to those programs.* Programs can be developed at different levels of detail. Some are relatively simple and short-term in duration, perhaps involving only the purchase of a single new machine. Others can be considerably more complex and long-term, perhaps involving the purchase or start-up of an entirely new business.

An important part of an organization's programming process involves the allocation of funds to capital programs. Capital programs involve the expenditure of resources on tangible assets, such as property, plant, and equipment, those items that are expensed as long-term assets for financial accounting purposes. The *allocation of funds to specific tangible assets* is commonly known as **capital budgeting**, much of which is structured in financial terms using discounted cash flow analyses.

But also important—in fact, even more important in some industries—are the processes used to allocate other scarce resources (for example, research scientists, space) to program alternatives. Many of these programs, including research and development and new product promotion ideas, involve the allocation of discretionary expense, not capital. While discounted cash flow analyses are the correct way to structure these discretionary expense decisions, the benefits and the costs of these programs can often be difficult to quantify. Thus, managers often make the allocation decisions based on their experience and intuition. Sometimes, however, the negotiating skills of the presenters as well as politics can affect these decisions—they are not always rational in nature.

➤ CYCLE 3: BUDGETING

Budgeting *is the process designed to help an organization develop and communicate a budget, the financial expression of the plan for a specific short period of time.* The planning horizon for an operating budget is typically one year, which is broken down into quarters and, often, months. Budgets provide managers with day-to-day operating guidance about the acquisition and use of resources under their control. Budgets are so important in guiding operations that many managers believe that the primary purpose of strategic planning and programming processes is to be able to develop a good budget.

In large companies, budgets represent both top-down and bottom-up organizational commitments. In the top-down sense, approved budgets include resource commitments from top management to each responsibility center manager. This means that the responsibility center managers can depend on having available the resources that they included in their budget. In the bottom-up sense, the budgets also represent performance commitments from the responsibility center managers to their superiors. The responsibility center managers are expected to perform within the constraints of their budgets. Cost center managers are expected *not* to spend more money than budgeted, and profit center managers are expected to produce at least as much profit as forecast in the budget, unless conditions change significantly from those assumed at the time of budgeting.

Budget targets define the line between acceptable and unacceptable performance for that performance period. The stakes are high. Budgets are common standards used in determining how much managers should earn in performance-dependent incentive schemes, such as making a predetermined profit target in order to earn a bonus. And if managers fail to achieve their budgets a couple of years in a row, without some good excuses, then it is likely that they will be replaced. Budgets serve as a primary tool for coordinating action and putting the accountability criterion into action.

IN CONTEXT ➤ Prestige Auto: Developing Specific Programs and Tactics

It is one week later. Judy and Bruce have been hard at work contacting the large auto manufacturers who would have a major impact on whether or not Prestige Auto would meet its aggressive strategic and operational goals. Their timing was good: The large automakers were also right in the middle of their planning cycles, so they were able to make an accurate assessment of whether or not they would be able to supply the number of cars Prestige planned to sell. Not all of the firms contacted were receptive to their request for more cars, because they used their own internal numbers of prior years' sales performance when allocating cars to specific dealerships.

"We've run into a few bumps along the road," said Bruce. "Several of our suppliers said they couldn't see how we could boost sales so much in one year. They want to see our strategic and operational plans so they can judge for themselves whether or not we can really move so much more merchandise. They said a five to 10% increase wouldn't be a problem, but over 20% certainly gave them pause."

"I can't see letting them have access to our strategy, Bruce. That's an internal document I don't want any of us sharing, let alone showing to our suppliers," Jack responded.

"That's what we thought you would say," said Judy. "But we need to have a sound idea of how we intend to reach our sales goals, and it has to be something that we *can* share. I know we can hit these targets, but we need to come up with a careful plan; for example, about when and what type of incentive programs we're going to use to pull consumers into our showroom. We really haven't developed these plans; we agreed on targets and even developed a budget and a few performance metrics, but we really haven't developed any specific programs or plans showing exactly *how* we're going to reach these goals. That's what made it hard for us to convince our suppliers that we could reach our target."

"I guess I understand their concern. And, you're right; we really need to do the operational planning to make our goals a reality," said Jack. "We need to develop specific programs and gauge the optimal time of the year to run them."

"What we thought, Jack," said Bruce, "is that we should have everyone come up with specific programs that they think would help us gain the sales we all feel we can achieve. Let's take the budget and strategic plan as a given and work on operational plans for each of our areas. I would include the support groups, like Finance, in this as well. They might, for example, come up with a special financing deal that we can use to lure more customers into the showroom. If we develop a good set of programs, we can share them with our suppliers to show them exactly how we intend to boost our sales."

"Sounds like a good plan," Jack said. "Sit down with your people and develop some creative operating plans and programs that will get us to our goals. Think of all of the different ways we can bring people in; maybe a new service plan in your group, Tony. We all need to put on our thinking caps if we're going to convince our suppliers that we can meet our new goals. See you next week, same time, same place!"

COMPANY-BY-COMPANY VARIATIONS IN PRACTICE

OBJECTIVE 4

Talk about why and how managers set performance targets of different types and with different levels of difficulty.

While the basic functions of planning and budgeting processes are the same across all organizations, companies' processes vary considerably in their length, style, complexity, and cost. In many smaller organizations, the three planning cycles—strategic planning, programming, and budgeting—take place concurrently. Some organizations use only a single, short planning process, one that might start in November and end in December. This type of simple process was described in the Ionics, Ltd., example described in Chapter 10. Within this single process, however, if the system is well-designed, managers are performing all of the planning functions. They are discussing strategies, identifying specific action programs to be funded, and preparing a short-term financial plan. This is what we see taking place at Prestige Auto as the company's managers begin to move from planning to action.

As companies mature and grow, their planning and budgeting systems tend to evolve toward having the three distinct process cycles. Some of the more elaborate processes may take place over the entire year. If the process takes the entire year, when the final cycle, typically budgeting, concludes, a new cycle, typically strategic planning, begins immediately. The company never stops planning.

One major cause of the variation among practices stems from the fact that planning and budgeting processes serve multiple purposes, and different companies emphasize different purposes. To summarize some of the material presented in this chapter and Chapter 10, the following are among the major purposes served by planning and budgeting systems:

1. Clarify and communicate the corporate objectives.
2. Force managers to think about the future and to develop strategies that take maximal advantage of their entities' strengths.
3. Provide a forum in which alternate allocations of scarce resources can be analyzed so that informed, well-considered decisions can be made.
4. Help coordinate the various activities of the organization, as they force managers of the various subunits to communicate their plans and wishes.
5. Provide performance targets that can be used both for motivating employees and for evaluating the performances of both entities and their managers.

These multiple purposes underscore the important role that strategic planning and budgeting systems play in modern organizations. While plans may not always come to fruition, the planning process is the key point where communication takes place and performance expectations are set. They guide behavior throughout the year, serving as the basis for evaluating progress and making adjustments to ensure that strategic objectives are met in the long term. Budgets are one of the key tools used by organizations to keep actions directed toward desired results.

Performance Measurement Problems in Divisionally Organized Entities

Planning is inextricably related to performance measurement. The quantitative representations of plans should be expressed in the same units in which performance will be measured. This matching facilitates the "check" and "adjust" elements of the BPA process. If we plan in one way and evaluate performance in another, managers will be confused, not knowing what really defines success. Since the maxim "You get what you measure and reward" underlies all planning and control processes, it is important that the goals clearly set out performance expectations and that the measurements of actual outcomes can be clearly tied to the objectives being pursued. Good communication and good results depend on consistency in purpose and meaning.

THE PRIMARY FINANCIAL OBJECTIVE: MAXIMIZING SHAREHOLDER VALUE

Up until now, we have implied that the primary objective of the for-profit companies on which we are focusing our discussion is to earn profits, and we described the financial aspects of planning as involving the preparation of pro forma financial statements. The key performance metrics, therefore, were profits and accounting returns. If the primary objective of for-profit organizations was, indeed, to earn

OBJECTIVE 5

Explain why companies typically prepare their plans and track their performance in accounting measurement terms even though their primary objective is to maximize the value created.

profits, then the financial plans would provide a perfect reflection of where managers want the organization to go, and the measures of performance, as included in the standard financial reports, would provide a perfect reflection of what the organization has accomplished.

While many managers and analysts talk as if a business's primary raison d'être is the creation of profits, that belief is not quite right. The primary purpose of for-profit organizations is to create wealth, which is sometimes expressed as **maximization of shareholder (or owner) value,** *the goal of wealth creation.*[3] Measures of profits provide only an imperfect reflection of the amount of value that has been created.

What is shareholder value? The value of any economic asset, which can be a piece of equipment, a financial investment, or an entire corporation, is the sum of the discounted future cash flows that stem from that asset. Value is calculated according to the following formula:

$$\textbf{Value} = \sum C_0 + \frac{C_1}{(1+r)} + \frac{C_2}{(1+r)^2} + \ldots$$

where: C = cash flow in period i

r = rate, which varies with the time value of money, the expected inflation rate, and a risk premium based on the asset's (or the company's) risk. An r of .10 (10%), for example, might reflect a 3% time value of money, a 2% expected inflation rate, and a 5% risk premium.

Let us take a simple example: Assume that a project is expected to generate a stream of four cash flows, as shown in Table 11.3. The discount rate will be the 10% we just discussed. What is the value of that stream of cash flows in today's terms?

---

3 This is the primary goal only for business enterprises in capitalist countries. Not-for-profit organizations typically have more complex sets of goals. In profit-seeking corporations in socialist societies, particularly in which the government owns the business enterprises, the primary objective is often to keep people gainfully employed, even if that means running an enterprise at a loss.

TABLE 11.3 COMPUTING DISCOUNTED CASH FLOW

(1) Cash Flow	(2) Term ("t")	(3) 1 Plus the "r" value	(4) = (1) / (3) Present Value
$100,000	Time zero	1.0	$100,000.00
$50,000	Period 1	1.10	$45,454.55
$80,000	Period 2	1.21	$66,115.70
$120,000	Period 3	1.331	$90,157.78
Total Present Value			$301,728.03

This means that this string of cash returns worth $350,000 in nominal terms is valued at $301,728.03 because of the discounting. If the investment made was $200,000 at time zero, then $101,728.03 in value was created by investing in this project. Only by discounting all of the cash flows to today's equivalent in dollars can we really judge whether a project is going to be worthwhile. This approach also allows us to compare different streams of cash from different projects to determine which creates the most value for shareholders in today's terms. It is a key decision tool used by managers when making any kind of investment in a firm.

The discounting, or present value, formula shows that managers can increase the value of their asset in any given performance period by doing any or all of three things:

1. Increasing the size of the cash flows that the asset will bring in.
2. Bringing those cash flows forward in time (such as closer to the present).
3. Decreasing the asset's risk, which means making the realization of those cash flows more certain and reliable.

The problem with the economic value concept, however, is that in the absence of a transaction, such as the sale of the asset, value cannot be measured objectively. Value is *subjective*; it is based on people's expectations of the future. Those expectations can vary across people, and they vary across time, as societies' and individuals' degrees of optimism ebb and wane. In other words, the future cash flows that the method relies upon are based upon judgments made by managers who have a vested interest in seeing their projects move forward. Unless we are doing the calculation after the fact, we are computing estimates of future value, not concrete amounts.

Can the value of an entity ever be measured directly? Yes, sometimes it can. It can be measured if the entity is sold. If a company is sold, the value of that entity at that point in time is the price at which it was sold. If, for example, a company was started in 2000 with an investment of $100,000, there were no further investments, and the company was sold in 2016 for $1 million, then the company created $900,000 in absolute dollar value during the period of its existence.[4]

4 This answer assumes that the size of the measurement unit has not changed. If inflation has caused the value of the dollar to diminish, the amount of this reduction in value has to be subtracted from the $900,000.

Value can also be measured directly if all of the entity's assets are converted to cash at the end of the measurement period. It is easy to measure the value of a company like Joe's Ice Cream, which was discussed in Chapter 10, because all of the business's assets are converted to cash at the end of the football season. Because Joe earns profits, he ends each season with more cash than with which he started. The incremental cash the business brings in is the amount of value created. But this is an unusual case—most businesses are ongoing.

Can stock prices provide useful indications of the value of a company? Yes, they can. Actively traded stock markets yield prices that can be used to value the companies traded on them. Changes in those valuations over time are useful indicators of the changes in value created by those companies in any given measurement period. This change in value, however, should be isolated from the general trends in the market itself. One of the primary tools you learn in finance is how to understand the value of the stock itself separate from the trends in the market at large. This is an advanced topic, but it is important for you to know that when we say the market reflects the value of the firm, it is a relative value—one linked to the marketplace as a whole.

However, market valuations are not perfect. Markets do not have access to all of the companies' confidential information, so a company's real intrinsic value may be hidden. Markets have "mood swings." Stock prices fluctuate up and down even when nothing has happened to affect companies' real values. Stock prices are affected by expectations about the future, and some of those expectations never come to fruition. Stock markets also make mistakes. They seem to have been slow, for example, to have recognized the massive problems that subsequently came to light in companies like Enron and WorldCom. Market valuations also have a significant limitation in that they cannot be used in measuring value changes in private companies, those whose shares are not traded, or of sub-entities (for example, subsidiaries) within publicly traded companies.

ACCOUNTING METRICS AS SURROGATE INDICATORS OF VALUE

Because of the problems in measuring entity values and changes in those values, almost all companies must use **surrogate measures** *of performance, those that move in approximately the same way as the underlying phenomenon.* What makes a good surrogate measure? First and foremost, it should go up when value is created and it should go down when value is destroyed. When this occurs, it is **congruent** with the corporate goal of value creation.

Virtually all companies use accounting profits and returns as their primary surrogate measures of value creation. There are good reasons for this. Accounting profits and returns are at least somewhat congruent with value changes; in most situations, they are positively correlated with value changes. While the relationship is not perfect, when accounting profits rise, shareholder values also tend to rise, and when they fall, shareholder values also fall. The correlation across all types of firms is not particularly high. For example, across a broad sample of firms, annual accounting profits measured are correlated approximately .20 with changes in stock prices.[5] These correlations are higher for periods longer than a year and lower

5 Baruch Lev, "On the Usefulness of Earnings: Lessons and Directions from Two Decades of Empirical Research," *Journal of Accounting Research,* 27, Supplement 1989: pp. 153-192.

for shorter periods. But the key point is that accounting profits are at least somewhat congruent with companies' primary goal—value maximization—because the correlations between accounting profits and shareholder returns are positive.

Accounting profits and returns measures also have other important advantages, which can be explained in terms of other measurement alternative evaluation criteria. Accounting profits and returns can be measured on a *timely* basis (that is, in short time periods) relatively *accurately*; for example, relatively precisely and objectively. Accounting rules are described in great detail by various accounting rule makers, and independent auditors check the application of the rules. They are relatively *understandable*, as most managers have studied accounting as part of their education. And the accounting measures of performance are *cost-effective* because preparation of the numbers is legally mandated for reporting to outside investors, creditors, and regulators.

THE CONGRUENCE PROBLEM

Managers must be aware, however, that the accounting performance measures are only imperfect, surrogate measures of performance, and they must take steps to minimize the effects of the imperfections, which vary significantly across settings. We will now discuss one of the most pervasive and important limitations of accounting performance metrics—the congruence problem.

OBJECTIVE 6

Explain the common problems caused by lack of measurement congruence and how they can be addressed.

➤ CAUSES OF THE CONGRUENCE PROBLEM

There are many reasons why we should not expect accounting profit and return measures to be perfectly reflective of, or totally congruent with, changes in value. Many things that affect economic values are not reflected, or are at least not quickly reflected, in accounting measures. This is not surprising. One of the basic principles underlying accounting is the **realization principle,** *which defines when revenues and profits can be recognized*. This principle requires that substantial evidence, such as in the form of a sales transaction, exists before profits are recognized. In this sense, accounting measures are providing a summary of events that have already happened. Economic values, on the other hand, are derived from future cash flows. They are, therefore, affected by expectations of the future; there is no guarantee that past performance is a reliable indicator of future performance. That is the problem we are seeing at Prestige Auto—it needs to find a way to communicate that future performance will exceed prior trends.

As one example, consider the effects of changes in the overall business climate, such as the stage a company is in in the business cycle. In boom times, many company assets, including buildings and equipment, increase in real economic value, but these increases are not reflected in the accounting figures. There has been no transaction that would cause an accounting entry to be made.

Another example is good ideas, such as the development of a promising new product in the laboratory, that increase a company's real value. When these ideas become publicly disclosed, stock valuations almost immediately increase. But the changes in value are not reflected in the accounting measures. The accounting rules for recognizing profits are conservative. Accountants are slow to recognize revenues and gains and quick to recognize expenses and losses.

Similarly, many things affect the accounting metrics even while there is no real change in value. For example, when a company depreciates its fixed assets, the company takes a charge against income, and its book value declines. But the real value of the fixed assets may actually be increasing. And the accounting measures themselves are affected by the choice of measurement method, such as straight-line or accelerated depreciation, but those choices have no effect on real economic values. That is why we often prefer units-of-production depreciation in BPA—it more accurately captures the way an asset is used up in the course of operations.

➤ EFFECTS OF THE CONGRUENCE PROBLEM

Because of the advantages described above of accounting metrics, most companies continue to use them as their primary indicators of performance. In doing so, they must understand that maximizing profits can be quite different from maximizing value.

One common problem induced by the use of accounting metrics is **myopia, or short-termism,** *an excessive focus on the short run at the expense of the long term*. To illustrate the problem, consider the example of a manager who is trying to keep alive his company's record of 18 consecutive years of increasing earnings per share (EPS), even as business conditions are deteriorating. Last year, his company's earnings were $2.60 per share. He can perhaps keep the improvement record going by cutting all discretionary expenses. This action could be programmed into the company's annual plan. One of the things that would have to be cut is a promising research program that will probably yield some new, highly profitable products in the coming years which, we assume, might be valued at $50 million. The financial effect, assuming the research program annual cost is $10 million and the company has 10 million shares outstanding, is illustrated in Table 11.4.

TABLE 11.4 EARNINGS/SHARE AND ECONOMIC VALUE: IMPACT OF ELIMINATING A PROMISING RESEARCH PROGRAM

	Maintain $10 million Research Program (in $ million)	Eliminate $10 million Research Program (in $ million)
Revenues	$100	$100
Expenses	80	70
Net income	$20	$30
Earnings per share	$2.00	$3.00
Company value	$400 million	$350 million

This is a case where the accounting metric, in this case EPS, is not congruent with the change in real economic value. The decision to cut a valuable investment in research would increase EPS, but with disastrous effects on real economic value. If the manager makes this decision, he would be said to be myopic, excessively focused on his company's short-term earnings, to the detriment of what is best for his company. This myopia problem is so pervasive that it has been cited by many critics as the most serious problem facing U.S. businesses (and those in some other countries).[6]

Another related consequence of the congruence problem is caused by generally **incomplete metrics,** *measures that do not capture all of the important information needed for assessing performance*. The accounting metrics provide a good measure of, particularly, short-term financial performance, the *realized accomplishments* of the company's existing businesses in the given measurement period. But they ignore other important factors that managers should pay attention to because they do or will affect company values. These can include factors like customer satisfaction, product quality, employee safety, or environmental performance. Like in the myopia example above, managers can improve their accounting performance in the short run by slighting any or all of these other important aspects of performance.

Conversely and equivalently, managers may have done many things to improve their entity's *future prospects* that are not reflected in the current period's profit and return measures. For example, they may have begun to create whole new products or business lines through their research and development activities. They may have made process improvements that will produce a valuable annuity of cost savings in future periods. Or they may have taken steps to improve product quality and customer satisfaction, both of which should produce increased sales in future periods. These things are said to be **value drivers**—*events or actions that increase the value of the business in the market's eyes.*

Because the effects of these important considerations are not reflected in the accounting measures, it can be said that the accounting metrics are incomplete and less than perfectly reflective of changes in value. This is a prominent cause of the congruence failure of accounting measures of performance. Since much of managers' pay is based on performance measured in accounting terms, what the managers earn does not reflect well the value they have created for shareholders. For example, a study by the corporate governance research firm MSCI answered the question: "Has CEO pay reflected long-term stock performance?" The answer, in a word, is "No."[7]

This problem must be dealt with, but the question is how? Can one system designed to keep track of transactions that are tightly defined in nature also be expected to incorporate value metrics? It is more likely that the financial reporting system needs to become just one part of the comprehensive set of measures that are used to determine value creation.

IN THE NEWS ➤ Rewarding the CEO of Coca-Cola

Critics of U.S. corporations' pay practices point to many examples where top-level managers were generously rewarded even while shareholders were not doing well. One such example is Coca-Cola.

In late 2000, Coke hired a new CEO, Douglas Daft. To attract and motivate Daft, the board granted him 1 million performance-based

6 For example, Michael T. Jacobs, *Short-Term America: The Causes and Cures of Our Business Myopia*, Boston: Harvard Business School Press, 1992.

7 Ric Marshall and Linda-Eling Lee, "Are CEOs Paid for Performance?," New York: MSCI, July 2016.

restricted shares, with a total value of nearly $50 million. He would earn the shares if Coke's earnings per share grew at least 20% per year over the five years beginning January 1, 2001. If growth was less than 15%, he would earn no shares. At exactly 15%, he would earn 500,000 shares. Between 15% and 20% growth, the share grant would be prorated between 500,000 and 1 million.

In early 2001, Daft realized that he could not reach the 15% benchmark. In May 2001, Coke's board of directors lowered the threshold to 11% and the targets for the maximum reward to 16%.

In 2001, Coke's stock lost 22.6% of its value (compared to a 12% loss for the S&P 500), and 6,000 Coca-Cola employees (21% of the company's workforce) were laid off just a year earlier.

Source: "Coke Rewrote the Rules, Aiding the Boss," *The New York Times*, April 7, 2001, and Arianna Huffington, *Pigs at the Trough*, New York: Crown, 2003: p. 40.

➤ ADDRESSING THE CONGRUENCE PROBLEM

OBJECTIVE 7

Suggest ways to mitigate the effects of four common measurement problems.

Managers who prepare their plans and measure their performance in terms of accounting metrics must take steps to reduce the congruence problem or they will be aiming their organizations in the wrong directions. They have two basic options: They can improve the congruence of the accounting metrics and/or they can supplement the accounting metrics with other performance indicators.

In measuring profit, managers can choose from among multiple, allowable measurement alternatives, such as straight-line vs. accelerated depreciation and aggressive vs. conservative revenue recognition. How should managers choose from among these alternatives?

Some managers choose accounting policies that provide a better matching of revenues and expenses based on their belief that better accounting provides better information for management decision-making purposes. For example, consider the two depreciation policy choices presented in Table 11.5. Would a firm be better off using straight-line or accelerated (double declining balance) depreciation on this new piece of equipment?[8] In this case, the less conservative straight-line depreciation appears to provide a better matching of revenues and expenses and, hence, a more meaningful profit pattern.

8 There is no tax effect. Both depreciation methods are allowable for tax purposes. Regardless of the company's choice for financial reporting and management accounting purposes, in its tax financial statements, the company can use whatever depreciation policy saves it the most cash. Generally, this will be accelerated depreciation.

TABLE 11.5 CHOOSING AN ACCOUNTING POLICY: DEPRECIATION

Asset: Electronic test equipment — Cost to acquire: $210,000 — Expected useful life: three years			
	Year 1	Year 2	Year 3
Profit before depreciation	$100,000	$110,000	$121,000
Straight-line depreciation	$70,000	$70,000	$70,000
Profit after SL depreciation	$30,000	$40,000	$51,000
Double declining balance depreciation	$140,000	$35,000	$35,000
Profit after DDB depreciation	$(40,000)	$75,000	$86,000

One consulting firm, Stern Stewart & Co., recommends use of a measure it calls economic value added (EVA™), which involves, potentially, depending on the setting, more than 150 modifications to standard accounting profit measures. These modifications include capitalization and subsequent amortization of intangible investments such as for research and development and advertising and promotion, standardization of accounting policies such as for depreciating fixed assets and costing inventory, elimination of goodwill amortization, and the elimination of successful efforts accounting in oil and gas exploration companies. Some of these modifications are not allowable under Generally Accepted Accounting Principles (GAAP), but Stern Stewart & Co. recommend them "to achieve higher correlations between the short-term measure (in this case, EVA) and share prices, which in turn can lead to more congruent goals for division managers and shareholders."[9]

A simple way to think about EVA is the following formula, which simply adjusts the operating income of the firm or subunit for a charge for the assets it had at its disposal during the time period in question. This is also called residual income, as we will see in more depth later in this chapter. The weighted average cost of capital (WACC) is basically an estimate of average combined cost the company incurs to finance its operations. It takes the amount of a specific funding source, such as bonds, and assesses how much it represents of the total financing base. So if we have $500,000 in 6% bonds that make up 25% of our long-term financing, bonds add 1.5% to the WACC. If common stock makes up another 50% of invested capital, and it costs the company 8%, its weighted value is 4%. Finally, the company has 25% preferred stock that requires a 10% return to its holders, adding another 2.5% to our weighted average. Our WACC would then be 8%.

EVA = Net operating profit after tax - (Weighted average cost of capital x Invested assets)

9 S. David Young, "Some Reflections on Accounting Adjustments and Economic Value Added," *Journal of Financial Statement Analysis,* 4(2), p. 8.

Continuing our example, we now have a division that has $250 million in invested assets at its command. It earns $80 million in after-tax profits. Its EVA would be $80 million, less 8% times $250 million ($20 million), or $60 million in estimated value created. This simplification of the calculations done by Stern Stewart are just to show you that the goal of the approach is to make adjustments to the accounting income that come closer to reflect the real economics of the business.

So that they do not have to rely solely on financial measures of performance, many companies have moved toward developing **integrated performance measurement systems (IPMS),** *a special type of balanced scorecard that links performance metrics both horizontally and vertically*. They attempt to address the measurement incompleteness problem by employing multiple performance indicators at each organization level (see Figure 11.4). This can be called **horizontal integration,** *the linkage of measures across a level in the organization*. They also attempt to provide measures that are causally linked from the top to the bottom of the organization. That is, the quantities being measured lower in the organization (such as efficiency, attendance, throughput, and reliability) are the drivers of the quantities being measured higher in the organization (for example, profits, returns, quality, and customer satisfaction). This can be called **vertical integration,** *the linkage of measures from the bottom to the top of the firm*.

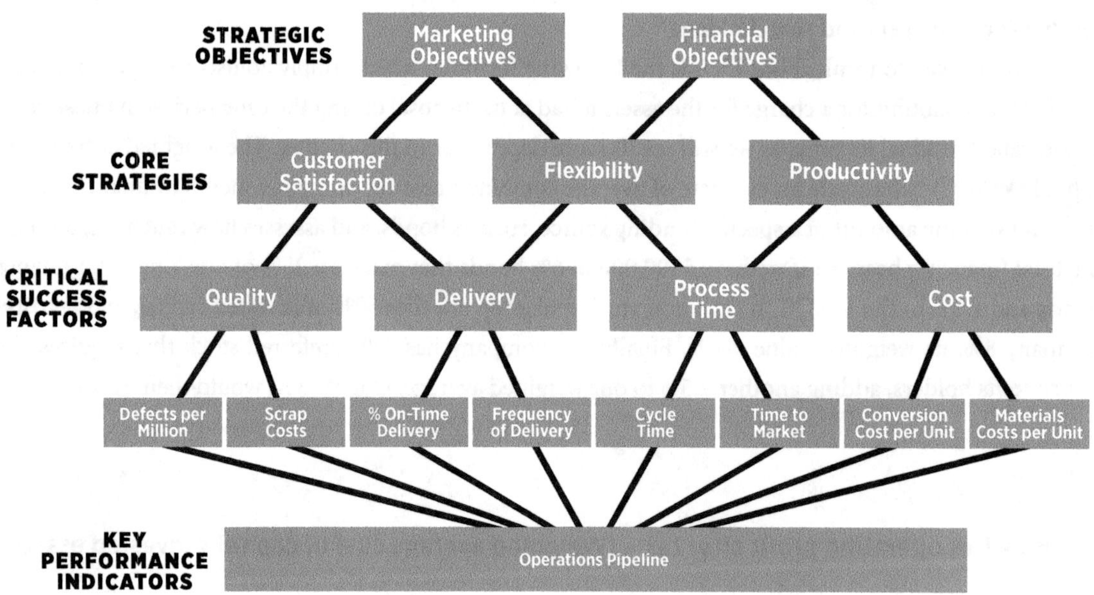

FIGURE 11.4 THIS SCHEMATIC OF AN INTEGRATED PERFORMANCE MEASUREMENT SYSTEM ILLUSTRATES HOW MULTIPLE PERFORMANCE INDICATORS ARE USED UP AND DOWN EACH LEVEL OF A DECENTRALIZED ORGANIZATION IN ORDER TO COMPENSATE FOR MEASUREMENT INCOMPLETENESS.

One stylized and well-publicized IPMS-like package is known as the **balanced scorecard (BSC)**.[10] We have already detailed elements of the BSC, but let us look at them again for completeness's sake. The BSC suggests setting performance targets, measuring performance, and developing initiatives using four perspectives:

1. The **External Financial Perspective** asks the question: "To succeed financially, how should we appear to our shareholders?" This perspective typically includes a set of bottom-line financial measures, such as accounting profits or returns, and possibly also measures of growth and/or risk.
2. The **Customer Perspective** asks the question: "To achieve our vision, how should we appear to our customers?" The measures assess performance in specific customer and market segments. They might include customer satisfaction, repeat purchases, and market share.
3. The **Internal Business Process Perspective** asks the question: "To satisfy our shareholders and customers, what business processes must we excel at?" The measures to be used are those that are indicative of the effectiveness and efficiency of the company's business processes, such as throughput, productivity, and responsiveness.
4. The **Learning and Growth Perspective** asks the question: "To achieve our vision, how will we sustain our ability to change and improve?" The focus is on three sources of organizational learning and growth: people, systems, and organizational procedures. Measures that might be used here include indicators of employee competencies, system reliability, and the appropriateness of reward systems.

By measuring performance in areas not well-addressed by short-term accounting performance measures, BSC clearly seems to address the completeness problem. And the BSC measures are designed to be linked causally in a web that defines the organization's strategy.

Many well-known companies, including Mobil, DuPont, Cigna, United Parcel Service, and ABB, have used BSC successfully in some periods of their history. However, only anecdotal evidence is available at this time to support the notion that the highly stylized BSC framework is superior to that of other IPMS frameworks, either generally or in any specific type of company. In addition, the larger companies typically face some additional measurement problems not faced in smaller companies. Two common problems—those caused by organizational interdependencies and potential problems of suboptimization—are discussed here.

THE INTERDEPENDENCY PROBLEM

Organizational **interdependency** *occurs when the results of one organizational entity are affected by the actions of employees of other entities within the organization.* Some interdependency occurs in the vast majority of multiunit corporations because few organizational sub-entities are totally independent from all other parts of the corporation. For example, virtually all line responsibility centers (for example, business units

10 See, for example, Robert S. Kaplan and David P. Norton, *The Balanced Scorecard: Translating Study into Action*. Boston: HBS Press, 1997.

and the revenue and expense centers of which they are comprised) benefit from the activities of many shared **service departments**, *entities that provide services on a shared basis to other entities within the organization*, such as facilities, human resources, accounting, finance, and legal departments. The costs of these service departments are known as **shared costs or common costs,** *expenditures for resources shared by two or more organizational entities*.

In addition, some responsibility centers often buy products or services from other organizational sub-entities. In a vertically integrated electronics manufacturer like Texas Instruments (TI), for example, an investment center that sells electronics equipment to consumers might buy a module subassembly from another TI investment center that, in turn, buys semiconductors from another TI investment center. And at an earlier point in the company's history, the TI semiconductor investment center bought its silicon chips from still another TI investment center.

These interdependencies often raise some difficult performance measurement issues. How should the service-using responsibility centers be charged for the products and services they use that are provided by other organizational sub-entities? Should it be an approximation of a market price or some function of the costs of providing them (such as variable costs, full costs, or perhaps even cost plus a markup)?

Cost assignments *are charges from a shared service department to any type of responsibility center.* Cost assignments can include both *tracings* of direct costs and *allocations* of indirect costs. Allocations of costs between responsibility centers are important because they directly affect both the costs of the entity for which the service is being provided and the net costs, after allocations, of the entity providing that service.[11]

Transfer prices *are charges from a profit or investment center to another profit or investment center.* Transfer prices can be based on marginal costs, full costs, market prices, or some combination of these including opportunity costs. Transfer prices are important because they directly affect both the costs of the entity purchasing the product or service and the revenues of the entity supplying that product or service.[12]

The primary reason for assigning common costs and/or charging transfer prices is to provide better information for decision making. Entities that consume products or services provided internally should understand that what they are consuming is not free. If the managers are shown the cost or price of what they are consuming, they can make proper decisions about how much to consume or, if given the freedom to source externally, whether they should purchase the product or service internally or externally. Cost assignments and transfer prices also remind responsibility center managers that their entities benefit from services provided by parties outside of their entity and that, therefore, their product markups must cover the costs of providing these services.

If responsibility center managers are allowed to purchase some of these services outside of the company, then these cost allocations provide information that the managers can compare with outside prices to decide where to do their sourcing. Even if outside sourcing is not allowed, assignments of common costs help corporate managers control these costs. The cost allocations remind the responsibility center

---

11 Like transfer prices, however, these intercompany cost allocations do not affect overall company profits.

12 They do not directly affect the profit of the company measured as a whole, however, because the effects of intercompany transfers are eliminated. This is a standard element of consolidation accounting, which is outside the scope of this textbook. The transfer prices can affect company profits indirectly through their effect on manager decision making, as is described in this chapter.

managers that the services they are consuming are not free and that, therefore, they should limit their consumption of them. Without the allocations of the costs of shared services, line profit centers will be measured only in terms of *operating profit.* Hence, almost all of them will look profitable. But the sum of the line profit centers' profits will exceed the total profits of the corporation.

The allocations also give the responsibility managers "jawboning power." In budget meetings, particularly, they can complain to corporate managers about the size of these allocations. These complaints put pressure on the service department managers to be efficient and to provide only the services and service levels that the other responsibility center managers want to use. And finally, allocations of common costs provide a signal to responsibility center managers that their entities are generating profits only after a fair share of the common costs is considered. Thus, they should price their products and control their costs accordingly.[13]

The cost allocations and transfer prices also provide better information for evaluating the performances of all the entities and managers involved. They show the full cost of the purchasing cost centers, and the total revenues of supplying profit centers or the net costs of supplying cost centers. Performance reports showing full cost information can be compared more easily with full stand-alone entities.

Finally, transfer prices and cost allocations can stimulate the managers of the purchasing responsibility center to exercise some control over the costs of the supplying responsibility center. If the transfer price from a profit center, or the allocations of costs from, say, the information systems department, seem too high in comparison to what would be paid for equivalent products or services received from an outside vendor, the purchasing responsibility center can bring pressure on the supplier to become more cost-effective.[14] But there are multiple ways to allocate the costs of shared services and multiple transfer pricing methods. Which should be used?

➤ ASSIGNING COSTS OF SHARED SERVICES TO LINE RESPONSIBILITY CENTERS

Deciding how to assign shared service department costs to line responsibility centers usually requires some choices. Some cost assignments, such as those dealing with costs that can be directly traced from one responsibility center to another, are easy. For example, sometimes responsibility centers "borrow" employees from another responsibility center. The cost of these borrowed employees is relatively easy to calculate. For example, calculating the cost of borrowing 10 employees for a week could be as simple as:

$$C = N \times W(1 + B)$$

---

13 Allocations of common costs are also essential in organizations that bill their work on a cost-plus basis, such as for billing on government contracts. If these costs are not allocated to projects, the company will not be reimbursed for them.

14 Transfer prices and cost allocations are also sometimes used to move profits between tax jurisdictions. Although laws limit companies' flexibility, companies try to earn greater profits in relatively low-tax localities (for example, countries, states).

Where	C	=	cost of borrowing employees
	N	=	number of employees borrowed = 10
	W	=	average weekly wage = $1,000
	B	=	average employee benefits cost = 30% of wage rate

In this case, C would be $13,000. This cost would be charged to the borrowing responsibility center and credited to the providing responsibility center.

A relatively easy cost assignment decision occurs where line responsibility centers are given the right to source the products or services they receive externally. In such cases, the responsibility center providing the product or service must compete for the business. The managers of the two responsibility centers would negotiate a mutually agreeable price. If they cannot agree on a price, the sourcing responsibility center would simply buy from an outside supplier.

The more difficult cost assignment decisions, however, occur when the products or services *must* be sourced from within the corporation. This can occur where the products or services provided are idiosyncratic—for example, nobody else could provide them. It can also occur where corporate management mandates internal sourcing because it is part of the overall corporate strategy. Generally, a market price for the exact mix of services provided is not available. Even if the exact services could be provided by an external supplier, in such cases it is difficult to know what price the external supplier would charge because, with no chance of getting the business, the external suppliers are not likely to venture a meaningful bid.

Generally, costs are assigned to responsibility centers in three steps. First, all the costs that can be traced to the service departments are assigned to those departments. Second, indirect costs, such as the costs of facilities, utilities, and insurance, are allocated to the service departments. The methods used to assign costs should be the methods that best reflect the consumption of resources required to provide the services. Chapters 3 and 4 discussed in detail the methods managers can use to determine good cost drivers. Finally, the service department costs are allocated to the line responsibility centers based on their relative share of the consumption of activities provided by the service departments. There are three methods of allocating service department costs to line responsibility centers in common use. These three methods, the direct, step-wise, and reciprocal allocation methods, are described and illustrated in an example later.

Generally, the costs assigned to the responsibility centers are the budgeted, not actual, service department costs. When budgeted costs are assigned, responsibility center managers know in advance exactly the cost rates they will be charged. If the actual costs were assigned, the responsibility center managers would not know the rates charged until after the measurement period is over. Budgeted rates also have the advantage of motivating the supplying responsibility center managers to improve cost efficiency. When the supplying responsibility center incurs excess costs but is allowed to charge only budgeted rates, unfavorable cost variances will occur and be quite visible to all.

Direct Allocation Method. The simplest method of allocating the costs of shared service departments is known as the **direct method**, *the allocation of shared costs directly from the service departments to the line responsibility centers based on the best set of knowledge about their consumption of these costs.*

To illustrate the application of the direct allocation method, consider a simple example of a company comprised of two divisions—X and Y—and two staff departments—Accounting and Administration. Table 11.6 shows the base situation, with the results of the two divisions measured only to the operating profit level (for example, before allocations), shown in Panel A. The two staff departments provide services to the other staff department and both divisions in the proportions shown in Panel B.

TABLE 11.6 ASSIGNMENT OF SHARED SERVICE DEPARTMENT COSTS ($ MILLIONS): BASE INFORMATION

Panel A:					
	Division		Service Department		Corporation
	X	Y	Accounting	Administration	Total
Sales	100	150			250
Cost of goods sold	50	80			130
Gross margin	50	70			120
Responsibility center expenses	43	30	6	12	91
Operating profit	7	40	(6)	(12)	29

Panel B:				
	To:			
Support provided by:	Accounting	Administration	Division X	Division Y
Accounting		20%	40%	40%
Administration	10%		30%	60%

The implementation of the direct method of assigning costs involves the allocation of the costs of each service department to the two divisions, ignoring the services provided to the other service department, as is shown in Table 11.7, Panel A. In this case, the $6 million of accounting department costs are allocated in equal proportions to the two divisions. The $12 million of administrative department costs are allocated $4 million (one-third) to X and $8 million (two-thirds) to Y.

TABLE 11.7 THREE METHODS OF ALLOCATING THE COSTS OF SHARED SERVICE DEPARTMENTS ($ MILLIONS) COMPARED

Panel A: Direct Allocation Method:					
	Division		Service Department		Corporation
	X	Y	Accounting	Administration	Total
Sales	100	150			250

Panel A: Direct Allocation Method:					
	Division		Service Department		Corporation
	X	Y	Accounting	Administration	Total
Cost of goods sold	(50)	(80)			130
Gross margin	50	70			120
Responsibility center expenses	(43)	(30)	(6)	(12)	91
Operating profit	7	40	(6)	(12)	29
Corporate allocations:					
Accounting dept.	(3)	(3)	6		
Administration dept.	(4)	(8)		12	
Net profit	0	29	0	0	29

Panel B: Step-Down Allocation Method:					
	Division		Service Department		
	X	Y	Accounting	Administration	Corp.
Operating profit	7.0	40.0	(6.0)	(12.0)	29.0
Corporate allocations:					
Accounting dept.	(2.4)	(2.4)	6.0	(1.2)	
Administration dept.	(4.4)	(8.8)		13.2	
Net profit	0.2	28.8	0	0	29

Panel C: Reciprocal Allocation Method:						
	Division		Service Department			
	X	Y	Accounting	Administration	Elimination	Corp.
Operating profit	7.0	40.0	(6.0)	(12.0)		29.0
Corporate allocations:						
Reciprocal alloc.			(1.4)	(1.5)	2.9	
Accounting dept.	(3.7)	(3.7)	7.4			
Administration dept.	(4.5)	(9.0)		13.5		
Net profit	(1.2)	27.3	0.0	0.0	2.9	29.0

While this direct allocation method is simple, it ignores a complication that is sometimes quite important. The complication is that service departments typically consume the services provided by each other.

Step-Down Allocation Method. The **step-down method,** *the sequential allocation of costs from one service department to another and then to line responsibility centers or other cost objects,* provides a partial recognition of the costs of services provided by service departments to each other. The actual allocation will depend somewhat on the sequence chosen.

The service department usually chosen as the first in the allocation sequence is the one that provides the largest proportion of its services to other service departments. The costs of the first department are allocated to all of the other service departments and the line responsibility centers. The allocation scheme then moves to the service department that provides the next-highest proportion of its services to other service departments and allocates its costs to all of the other service departments except the first service department (which has been zeroed out) and the line responsibility centers. Once a service department's costs have been allocated to other responsibility centers, it is not considered any further. You continue this sequential assignment of costs until all of the service department costs have been allocated to other responsibility centers.

In the simple example, the accounting department's costs would be allocated first. Using the proportions shown in Table 11.7, Panel B, \$1.2 million of the \$6 million in costs would be allocated to the administration department and \$2.4 million would be allocated to each of the operating divisions. Then in step two, the total administration department's costs, which are now \$13.2 million because they include the costs allocated from the accounting department, would be allocated to the two divisions. The proportions of support provided by the administrative department to X and Y are the same: one-third and two-thirds, respectively. Thus the administration department costs would be allocated \$4.4 million to X and \$8.8 million to Y.

The total costs that would be allocated to Division X would be \$6.8 million (\$2.4 million from Accounting and \$4.4 million from Administration). The total costs allocated to Division Y would be \$11.2 million (\$2.4 million from Accounting and \$8.8 million from Administration). If the allocations were sequenced in the opposite order, Administration first and then Accounting, the answers would have been different: \$7.2 million would have been allocated to Division X and \$10.8 million allocated to Division Y. (To test your understanding of the step-down allocation method, try to derive these numbers yourself.)

Reciprocal Allocation Method. The **reciprocal method,** *the allocation of the costs of services that organizational entities provide to each other*, recognizes all of the interdependence, the costs of services, that the service departments provide to each other, and, therefore, is the most accurate method of assigning the costs of service departments. But the method is somewhat complex because it necessitates the solution of a system of linear equations.

In the simple example with only two service departments, only two equations are needed. They are:

Accounting department costs = \$6 million + 10% x administration department costs
Administration department costs = \$12 million + 20% x accounting department costs

You need to substitute one of the equations into the other in order to start the solutions process. Let us substitute Accounting into Administration. We now end up with the equation:

Administration dept. costs = $12 million + 20% ($6 million + 10% administration dept. costs)

We then expand this equation and get the following:

Administration dept. costs = $12 million + $1.2 million + .02 administration dept. costs

Then:

.98 administration dept. costs = 13.2 million

And therefore, administration department costs equal $13.47 million (rounded). We can then substitute this amount into the equation for Accounting, getting the following:

Accounting dept. costs = $6 million + 10% ($13.47 million), or 7.35 million (rounded)

So, solving these two linear equations produces the following amounts to be charged from each support department to the producing departments.

Accounting department total costs = $7.35 million
Administration department total costs = $13.47 million

These total cost amounts are then allocated to the two divisions using the relative proportions of the services used, as is shown in Table 11.7, Panel C. Thus, Division X is allocated half of the accounting department total costs and one-third of the administration department costs, for a total of $8.2 million. Division Y is allocated half of the accounting department costs and two-thirds of the administration department costs, for a total of $12.7 million.

Because the reciprocal allocation method recognizes the costs of services that the service departments provide to each other, its solutions are conceptually the most correct (assuming the consumption proportions of each department's services are measured or estimated reasonably accurately). It is the only method that shows the full costs of each service department. These full costs can provide useful inputs into decisions as to whether or not the services of particular departments should be outsourced.

The reciprocal allocation method is not widely used in practice, however. Managers seem to be averse to its complexity, and it is true that in large corporations with, perhaps, hundreds of service departments, the reciprocal cost allocation method requires the solution of large sets of simultaneous equations. But even small personal computers can now solve these sets of equations, so the incremental solution cost of the reciprocal cost allocation method is minimal. The real cost of using the reciprocal allocation method is in defining the equations that describe the nature of the interdependencies.

Comparison of the Three Allocation Methods. Table 11.8 shows a comparison of the results of the three allocation methods using the Table 11.7 data. It shows the total amount of costs allocated to the divisions varies somewhat. The size of the variances between methods will increase with the size of the reciprocal services provided among the shared service departments and the differences in the line responsibility centers' usages of each of the shared services.

TABLE 11.8 THREE METHODS OF ALLOCATING THE COSTS OF SHARED SERVICES EFFECT ON NET PROFITS ($ MILLIONS) COMPARED

Method	Net profit		
	Division X	Division Y	Total Corporation
Direct allocation	0	29	29
Step-down allocation	0.2	28.8	29
Reciprocal allocation	(1.2)	27.3	29

The cost allocation variances across methods can sometimes be important. For example, look at the results of Division X, which showed an operating profit of $7 million. Depending on the method used to allocate the costs of shared departments, the "bottom-line" profit of Division X, after allocations, could be positive (if the step-down method is used), negative (reciprocal method), or breakeven (direct). These differences could determine, for example, whether the division is retained or divested or whether division personnel are evaluated favorably or negatively.

The "Non-Allocation" Approach. In some cases, it can be right not to assign some service department costs to line responsibility centers. If the responsibility center managers have no say in the incurrence of these costs, then assigning them violates the controllability principle (discussed earlier in this chapter). Further, in some cases, line responsibility centers do not clearly benefit from the activities of some service departments. Common examples are corporate contributions to charities and broad corporate image advertising. For example, some corporations, such as PSINet, Qualcomm, and Bank One, have provided donations each of more than $100 million to "name" athletic venues in, respectively, Baltimore, San Diego, and Phoenix. Should the responsibility centers in these corporations be assigned a proportionate share of the costs of these donations? Should the managers of their foreign subsidiaries be assigned a share even if their potential customers never come into contact with references to the venue? Because of the lack of a demonstrable link between the expenditures and forthcoming revenues and profits, many corporations do not assign these types of expenses to their line organizations.

➤ TRANSFER PRICING

Products and services provided from one profit (or investment) center to another are generally charged to the buying responsibility center and credited to the selling responsibility center. The issue is what the transfer price should be. Transfer prices can be charged based on *market prices*, or market prices less a discount that reflects the lower cost of doing business internally. They can reflect the *full cost* of providing the products or services. Sometimes companies charge the *full cost plus a markup*, which provides a crude approximation of a market price. Transfer prices can reflect the *variable (or marginal) costs* of providing the products or services. Sometimes companies just allow the managers of the responsibility centers involved to *negotiate* a suitable transfer price between themselves. Presumably the managers bring information about market prices and production (or service-providing) costs into these negotiations, but there is no guarantee that this happens.

Companies' transfer pricing methods vary considerably because no transfer pricing method is optimal in all situations. The only rule that seems to have wide applicability is the following: Set the *minimum* transfer price to be the *sum of the marginal (incremental) costs of producing the product (or providing the service) and the opportunity costs to the selling division (if any).*

To illustrate, consider a situation where the Alpha Division provides 100 units of an intermediate product, called X, to the Beta Division. The Alpha Division's unit costs are as follows:

Variable costs	$200
Fixed costs	100
Total unit costs	$300

Beta Division's managers have the freedom to source X externally if they deem it desirable to do so, and in this case, they determine that they could buy 100 units of product very close in quality to X for $40,000 from a competitor, Omega Corporation. What should the transfer price for these 100 units of X be? In this case, the marginal costs of production are $200 per unit, and no opportunity costs are indicated. Thus the minimum price for the transfer of 100 units should be at $20,000. Alpha will not willingly sell 100 units of X for less.

The $20,000 price, however, provides a huge, $20,000, savings for Beta. Sometimes in the transfer pricing negotiations, Beta will share some of that profit with Alpha, to provide the managers of Alpha some motivation to sell their product internally, or Alpha managers will scheme to capture some of the profit by not providing Beta managers with totally informative or accurate information about the true costs of production. The extent of the sharing of the profits varies with a number of factors, including the relative power of the two divisions and the extent to which the division managers have access to information about the other's economic situation. What we do know is that Beta will certainly not be willing to pay more than $40,000 for the 100 units of X. The $40,000 can be seen as the *maximum* transfer price possible in this example.

Change the situation slightly. Assume that Alpha is operating its plant at full capacity. To produce these additional 100 units, it will have to rent an additional facility and hire additional labor at a total additional cost of $15,000. In this case, this incremental cost would have to be added to the variable costs, and the minimum transfer price would be $35,000. The Beta managers would still want the 100 units of X at this higher price because it is still below what they would have to pay Omega.

Change the situation again. What if Alpha was operating its plant at full capacity but did not want to rent an additional facility or hire additional employees, but in order to satisfy Beta's demand for its product, it had to turn away an order from a customer who was offering to pay $32,000 for the 100 units of X? In this case, the incremental cost of production would be $20,000, which stems just from the variable cost of production. But the opportunity cost of turning down the outside customer's order would be $12,000, the contribution that would have been earned if this sale were made. Thus, applying the general rule described above, the minimum transfer price would be $32,000, the sum of the marginal costs of production plus the opportunity cost of turning down the outside order.

Why does this general rule work in many situations? Transfer prices that follow this rule provide the proper economic information about production and opportunity costs to Beta. The Beta managers are given good information about Alpha's, and, hence, the corporation's costs, and therefore they can decide whether or not it is economic to buy the units from Alpha. This set of transfer prices also provides the proper economic motivation to Alpha's managers. Alpha managers are allowed to recover their full marginal costs of production whether or not their division is at full capacity. They are compensated for the full profits on sales they have to relinquish in order to satisfy the internal demand for their product. And they can probably capture a share of the profits stemming from the savings Beta, and, hence, the corporation, will realize, because the costs of producing X are below the price that would have to be paid to source externally. Thus they retain their incentive to reduce their costs to enhance the profits.

What happens if Alpha's full cost of producing 100 units of X is greater than $40,000, the maximum transfer price Beta would be willing to pay? In such cases, Beta would prefer to buy from Omega. Sometimes in the short run, corporate managers do not allow this outsourcing because it will leave Alpha with significant excess capacity. In the long run, however, if Alpha cannot produce X at a competitive cost, corporate managers should force Alpha's exit from the business.

When does the general transfer-pricing rule not work well? If either marginal costs or market prices are not easily calculable or observable. As was discussed in Chapters 3 and 4, it is not always easy to measure accurately the costs of individual products and services. In addition, companies' management accounting databases often do not provide a clean break between variable and fixed costs. Poor cost systems can lead to poor transfer prices.

Similarly, many market limitations can cause problems. For example, suppose Alpha produces product X only for internal consumption by divisions like Beta. What market price should be used to determine Alpha's opportunity cost? X may be unlike any other product on the market. Still, Alpha should be compensated for making the investments in facilities and taking the risks needed to produce X.

In situations where good market prices for the intermediate products being transferred do not exist or cannot be observed, many companies use transfer prices based on full costs or full costs plus a markup. But this is a crude transfer pricing solution. In cases in which the selling division has excess capacity, full costs overstate the true incremental costs of production. The buying division will then choose to buy fewer units of product than is optimal.

In addition, full cost figures do not vary with market conditions. For example, in situations with significant industry excess capacity, which might lead to price wars where companies price their products below full cost, full cost transfer prices can be greatly overstated. In such a case, a transfer price based on full cost, combined with a corporate requirement to source internally, would penalize Beta significantly.

As we can see, therefore, the choice of transfer pricing has both an economic (what is rational) and behavioral (how will managers react) component. One of the most controversial decisions made by management revolves around its transfer pricing schemes. Even a company as small as Prestige Auto has to deal with these problems.

IN CONTEXT ➤ Prestige Auto: Tensions Over Transfer Prices

A week later, the managers met once again. Tony looked anything but happy. Jack immediately sensed that there was an issue brewing and decided to start the meeting by asking for Tony's input. He felt this would rapidly clear the air.

"Tony, did your group come up with any plans that will help us sell our new performance expectations to the suppliers' big guys?" he asked.

"Not really, Jack. I spent the whole week wrangling with my guys. As they see it, they do a lot of their work for Marketing and Sales and Procurement and get no credit for it. There's no customer to charge for getting cars ready to sell, so we have to eat the costs and do the best job we can. Now that we're going to have profit goals, my guys think we need a way to charge their time and effort to the other departments. They won't accept the new goals unless some changes are made. They think the problem will get worse if we're going to be busier. I can't say I disagree with them."

"Whoa, wait a minute, Tony," Bruce interjected. "We're all in this together. If you start charging me for your services, where am I supposed to get the money to pay for it? It's not in my budget, and I don't think I can meet those goals I promised earlier if I have to start adding costs to the cars before I even get them on the sales floor."

"Well, I don't know, Bruce," said Alice. "You charge us for the cars you acquire, which we carry until we sell them. If that's fair for your group, I think Tony has a point. After all, his group is doing work for you instead of for an outside customer. They should get some recognition for it."

Alice continued, "I've been wondering how long it would take for our personal motivations to become part of this conversation. We really don't have a complete transfer price system set up, and we don't assign all the costs for services used to the three profit centers—Acquisitions, Service, and Sales. If we're going to build the business and expect everyone to pull in the same direction, we have to even up the playing field so that when one group posts a profit, it recognizes all of the resources they've consumed." She paused and smiled.

"Alice, can you make some recommendations here? What did you call these things—transfer prices? Does that mean we recognize internal work as if it were done externally?" asked Jack.

"That's exactly right, Jack. I think we should start right away to reformat how we charge various internal services. We're small enough to use something called reciprocal allocation for the support departments, Finance, and General Administration; that's you and your group, Jack. And then we can use market prices for transferring goods and services between the profit centers because everything we need is available in our industry guidebooks. I'd like to take a crack at this before we move on to other things."

"Sounds like a good idea, Alice. I still want everyone else to be thinking about ways to promote our product lines this year, but let's pause our planning to take this kink out of our system. I want everyone to feel we're playing a fair game here. Short meeting, everyone! See you next week when we'll address these transfer pricing issues and then move on to creating incentive programs that work for us—and our customers." With that, Jack ended the meeting.

THE SUBOPTIMIZATION PROBLEM

Most large, divisionally organized companies base their performance measurement and control systems heavily on ratio-type financial return measures, such as return on investment (ROI), return on equity (ROE), and return on net assets (RONA). These measures are useful because the returns are *scaled*, divided by an indicator of the size of the organization, to facilitate comparisons of the performances of entities of different sizes. But use of them must be done with care because they tend to create a common form of organizational suboptimization. As was defined earlier, suboptimization occurs wherever managers take actions designed to make their entities look good, but those actions are not in the best interest of the corporation as a whole.

The suboptimization problem occurs because managers of divisions performing well are not likely to propose capital investments promising ROI returns below their division objectives, even if those investments are good ones from the company perspective. Figure 11.5 shows a simplified suboptimization example of this type. Assume the corporate cost of capital is 10%. If an investment opportunity arises promising a 15% return, corporate managers will generally want this investment to be made, assuming the opportunity is consistent with the corporate strategy and not too risky. Making the investment increases shareholder value. The manager of the poor-performing division, whose performance targets probably reflect the historical performance of 8%, would be willing to make this investment, but the manager of the well-performing division, which is operating with 20% ROI, would not. Since most new investments that will eventually provide satisfactory returns earn a low return at the outset, this form of ROI measure-induced suboptimization is highly likely. The opposite perverse incentive, namely motivating managers of unsuccessful divisions to invest in capital investments promising ROI returns below the corporate cost of capital, also occurs when ROI measures are used.

Corporate cost of capital: 10%

Base Situation:	**Poor-Performing Division**	**Well-Performing Division**
Profit before tax	$80,000	$200,000
Investment	$1,000,000	$1,000,000
Return on investment	8%	20%

Assume a good investment opportunity: Invest $100,000 to earn $15,000 per year.

New situation:		
Profit before tax	$95,000	$215,000
Investment	$1,100,000	$1,100,000
Return on investment	8.6%	19.5%
	WILL INVEST	**WILL NOT INVEST**

FIGURE 11.5 SUBOPTIMIZATION: IMPACT OF FAILURE TO INVEST IN A PROMISING PROJECT

ROI-type measures can also lead to suboptimization in financing decisions. ROE measures induce managers to use debt, rather than equity financing. Doing so increases their entities' ROE by decreasing the measure's denominator. This incentive can push their investment center's and the corporation's leverage to levels initially far in excess of the desired corporate leverage.

One solution to this suboptimization problem is to use a residual income measure in investment centers, rather than ratio measures such as ROI and ROE. **Residual income (RI),** *net income after tax less a charge for capital deployed*, is calculated by subtracting from profit a capital charge for the net assets tied up in the investment center. The capital is charged at a rate equal to the weighted average corporation's cost of capital.[15] This is clearly what the simplified EVA metric presented earlier in the chapter suggests. In fact, EVA is residual income with significant adjustments for the variety of income and expense items that can skew the reported results.

RI measures give all investment center managers incentives to invest in all projects that promise returns greater than the corporation's cost of capital. This is illustrated in Figure 11.6, which shows a modified version of Figure 11.5 with a row added for RI. In both divisions, RI is increased if the desirable investment is made.

SUBOPTIMIZATION PROBLEM: RESIDUAL INCOME SOLUTION

Assume: Corporate cost of capital = 10%

Base Situation:	**Poor-Performing Division**	**Well-Performing Division**
Profit before tax	$80,000	$200,000
Investment	$1,000,000	$1,000,000
Return on investment	8%	20%
Residual income	($20,000)	$100,000

Assume a good investment opportunity: Invest $100,000 to earn $15,000 per year.

New situation:		
Profit before tax	$95,000	$215,000
Investment	$1,100,000	$1,100,000
Return on investment	8.6%	19.5%
Residual income	$(15,000)	$105,000
	WILL INVEST	**WILL INVEST**

FIGURE 11.6 RESIDUAL INCOME MEASURES GIVE ALL INVESTMENT CENTER MANAGERS INCENTIVES TO INVEST IN ALL PROJECTS THAT PROMISE RETURNS GREATER THAN THE CORPORATION'S COST OF CAPITAL; HOWEVER, IT DOES NOT ALLOW FOR COMPARISONS BETWEEN CENTERS.

15 Conceptually, an argument can be made to adjust the capital charge rate for the investment center's risk, thus making the performance measurement system consistent with the capital budgeting system. However, this adjustment is made by only 19 percent of the firms that use residual income.

The main problem with RI measures, however—which accounts for their use in only a minority of companies—is that they are not scaled for size. For example, if you knew that in a single corporation one investment center reported RI of $100,000 while the other reported RI of $1 million, you still could not say which center was the better performer. A higher RI does not necessarily indicate a better performing entity; it may merely be indicative of a larger entity. Scaled measures, such as ROI, facilitate the use of the measures for comparisons of performances across investment centers. It makes sense to use multiple measures of performance when trying to gauge the relative performance of one entity over another. And, when it comes to investing in new assets, the key is to make sure that the entity is better off after the investment than it was before. That is the ultimate goal: to increase the value the firm creates with the assets its investors have entrusted to it.

Summary

This chapter focused on planning and measurement problems typically faced in larger, more complex organizations, which tend to adopt a divisionally organized structure. Some amount of decentralization is usually essential in these firms. However, managers must be careful to gain the benefits of decentralization—better-informed decision makers, faster decision making, more motivated and entrepreneurial employees, and better development of personnel—while minimizing the costs of gaining these benefits. The costs of decentralization can include suboptimization and increased administrative and coordination costs.

Choices about responsibility centers are closely related to the decentralization decisions. Choices must be made about what performance components to hold each manager accountable for in their annual evaluation. In financial terms, responsibility centers are categorized as cost centers, revenue centers, profit centers, and investment centers. But within each of these categories, many choices must be made as to which specific line items of revenues and expenses managers will be held accountable.

To establish plans for each of the responsibility centers, firms use planning and budgeting systems that accomplish strategic planning, programming, and budgeting. Some large firms separate these purposes into distinct planning cycles, while others combine the cycles.

Large, complex organizations face some special measurement problems. One such problem is that caused by organizational interdependency. Should the costs of entities that serve multiple responsibility centers be assigned to those responsibility centers? If so, how should it be done? The answers to these questions lead these firms into many questions regarding cost assignments and transfer prices. Cost assignments may be made using any of three methods: direct method, step-down method, and reciprocal allocation method. The reciprocal allocation method often yields the most accurate answers, but it is more complex and costly to implement. Transfer prices can be charged based on many different factors—including market prices, full costs (possibly with a markup), or variable costs. The managers of the affected responsibility centers can be allowed to negotiate an acceptable transfer price. No transfer pricing method is optimal in all situations.

A second common measurement problem is a danger of suboptimization caused by the use of accounting return measures of performance, such as return on investment (ROI). The accounting return measures do not motivate all responsibility center managers to propose and make all investments greater than the company's cost of capital. Residual measures, such as residual income (RI), provide a solution to this problem. But the residual measures cause another problem in that they complicate performance comparisons across responsibility centers. The optimum is to use a blend of performance measures that capture all of the key elements of performance and, in total, offset some of the tendency to engage in dysfunctional or suboptimal performance. It is a constant game of adjust and assess, one that top-performing firms have mastered.

Key Terms

Accountable: answerable for; obliged to report, explain, or justify certain outcomes or activities.

Budgets: the financial expression of plans *for a specific short period of time*.

Budgeting: the process designed to help an organization develop and communicate a short-term financial plan, typically for periods of one year or shorter.

Business strategy: an understanding as to how each strategic business unit within a corporation will compete.

Capital budgeting: allocation of funds to *specific* tangible assets.

Congruent measure: one that reflects well the organizational objective.

Conservatism: slow to recognize revenues and gains and quick to recognize expenses and losses.

Corporate strategy: a plan that defines understanding as to what types of businesses the organization will engage in.

Cost assignments: charges from a shared service department to any type of responsibility center.

Cost centers: entities that are held accountable for managing costs; their contributions to company profit are not measured in financial terms.

Direct method: the allocation of shared costs directly from the service departments to the line responsibility centers based on the best set of knowledge about their consumption of these costs.

Gamesmanship: the use of manipulation to gain an advantage.

Horizontal integration: the linkage of measures across a level in the organization.

Incomplete metric: measures that do not capture all of the dimensions of performance required for assessments.

Influence, or controllability: the ability to affect the outcomes in a significant way.

Integrated performance measurement system: links performance metrics both horizontally and vertically.

Interdependency: the actions of one organizational entity affect the results of other organizational entities.

Investment center: an entity with responsibility for its own revenues, expenses, and assets;

its financial results are based on all three factors; it utilizes capital to directly contribute to the company's profitability.

Maximization of shareholder value: the goal of profit-making corporations.

Myopia: an excessive focus on short-term results at the expense of the long term.

Profit center: an entity that generates both revenues and expenses and, hence, is held accountable for profits or losses.

Programming: the identification of specific action plans and the allocation of scarce resources to those programs.

Realization principle: a rule that defines when an event can be recognized in the accounting system.

Reciprocal method: the allocation of the costs of services that organizational entities provide to each other; involves the use of simultaneous equations that recognize that services are provided in multiple directions.

Residual income: net income after taxes less a charge for capital deployed.

Responsibility accounting: a reporting system that holds managers accountable (or responsible) only for those aspects of performance over which they have significant influence.

Responsibility centers: subunits of a corporation that are held accountable for specific results.

Revenue center: an entity that is responsible for selling products or services.

Service departments: entities that provide services on a shared basis to other entities within the organization.

Shared costs, or common costs: expenditures for resources shared by two or more organizational entities.

Strategic business units: freestanding entities that are part of a corporation but have their own distinct plans.

Strategic plan: a written description of the tactics to be followed to achieve the plan's goals.

Strategic planning: a process designed to help an organization develop and communicate both a corporate strategy and a strategy for each strategic business unit.

Step-down method: the sequential allocation of costs from one service department to another and then to line responsibility centers or other cost objects.

Suboptimization: an act that benefits an organizational entity but not the entire corporation.

Surrogate measure: one that moves in approximately the same way as the underlying phenomenon of interest.

SWOT analysis: a detailed examination of the corporation's as well as each business unit's strengths, weaknesses, opportunities, and threats.

Transfer prices: charges from a profit or investment center to another profit or investment center.

Value drivers: things that can be measured today that provide an early indication of the profits and returns that will be reflected in financial statements sometime in the future.

Vertical integration: the linkage of measures from the bottom to the top of an organization.

Questions

1. What are the benefits of decentralization?
2. What are some of the costs of decentralization?
3. What is a responsibility center?
4. What are the various types of responsibility centers found commonly in organizations and what are they held accountable for?
5. What is the controllability criterion?
6. How would you define responsibility accounting?
7. Please identify and define the three planning cycles that take place in most major corporations.
8. What is a strategic business unit and how does it function in an organization?
9. What are the major purposes served by planning and budgeting systems in organizations?
10. Provide an explanation of maximizing shareholder value and how the BPA system helps support this goal.
11. What is the congruence problem and how can accounting measures be modified to address this shortcoming?
12. Define some of the problems caused by accounting metrics.
13. Please describe the interdependency problem in organizations and note two key ways in which this interdependency needs to be dealt with.
14. What are the primary differences between direct, step-down, and reciprocal allocation methods?
15. Define the benefits of a market-based transfer price and note when it may not, or cannot, be used.

Exercises

1. **DISCOUNTED CASH FLOW.** A project has the following cash flows:

Period 0 Negative $100,000
Period 1 Positive $75,000
Period 2 Positive $50,000
Period 3 Positive $75,000

The firm has to pay 8% on its capital funds. What is the value of this stream of cash flows?

2. **DISCOUNTED CASH FLOW.** A project has the following cash flows:

Period 0 Negative $75,000
Period 1 Positive $50,000
Period 2 Positive $25,000
Period 3 Positive $30,000

The firm has to pay 9% on its capital funds. What is the value of this stream of cash flows?

3. **INTEGRATED PERFORMANCE MEASUREMENT SYSTEM.** For the following list of measurements, determine whether they take a strategic perspective (S), a core strategies perspective (C), critical success factors (F), or the key performance indicators (K) perspective.

Measurement	Symbol	Measurement	Symbol
Customer satisfaction		Market performance	
On-time delivery		Quality	
Defects per million		Scrap rate	
Flexibility		Productivity	

4. **INTEGRATED PERFORMANCE MEASUREMENT SYSTEM.** For the following list of measurements, determine whether they take a strategic perspective (S), a core strategies perspective (C), critical success factors (F), or the key performance indicators (K) perspective.

Measurement	Symbol	Measurement	Symbol
Financial performance		Productivity	
Cycle time		Quality	
Cost per unit		Process time	
Deliveries per day		Time to market	

5. **WEIGHTED AVERAGE COST OF CAPITAL.** Helter-Skelter makes various games. Its financial structure is made up of the following:

Long-term bonds—8% returns, 40%
Short-term bonds—6% returns, 20%
Capital stock—7% returns, 40%

What is the company's WACC?

6. **WEIGHTED AVERAGE COST OF CAPITAL.** Best Met makes baseball mitts. Its financial structure is made up of the following:

Long-term bonds—10% returns, 30%
Preferred stock—8% returns, 25%
Capital stock—9% returns, 45%

What is the company's WACC?

7. **COST OF BORROWING EMPLOYEES.** Sunwise Distributors has recently been very busy in its fruit juice bottling division. It has needed to borrow four employees from Packaging at a cost of $35,000 per employee with 30% benefits. It will be borrowing the employees for two months. What charge should Bottling receive for the use of these employees?

8. **COST OF BORROWING EMPLOYEES.** Teady Products has recently been very busy in its manufacturing division. It has needed to borrow five employees from Product Prep at a cost of $30,000 per employee with 35% benefits. Manufacturing will be borrowing the employees for three months. What charge should Manufacturing receive for the use of these employees?

9. **RESIDUAL INCOME.** Heaven's to Betsy produces kitchen aprons and potholders. It recently decided to treat each of these product lines as a specific division. Kitchen Aprons had a net operating profit after tax of $40,000. Its WACC is 7.5% on invested capital of $125,000. What is the RI for Aprons?

10. **RESIDUAL INCOME.** No Holds Barred produces shish kebab holders and rotisserie units. It recently decided to treat each of these product lines as a specific division. The shish kebab unit had a net operating profit after tax of $50,000. Its WACC is 8.2% on invested capital of $150,000. What is the residual income for the shish kebab division?

11. **DIRECT COST ASSIGNMENTS.** Real Life Productions has two major divisions, Filming and Distribution. It uses the work done by Accounting and Marketing in the following ways.

Providing Department	Cost	% to Filming	% to Distribution
Accounting	$ 150,000	40%	60%
Marketing	$ 200,000	50%	50%

Assign the costs of the supporting departments to the direct departments using direct allocation methods.

12. **DIRECT COST ASSIGNMENTS.** On Your Own has two major divisions, Internet Sales and Direct Sales. It uses the work done by Computing and Development in the following ways.

Providing Department	Cost	% to Internet Sales	% to Direct Sales
Computing	$ 200,000	70%	30%
Development	$ 150,000	40%	60%

Please assign the costs of the supporting departments to the direct departments using direct allocation methods.

Problems

1. **DISCOUNTED CASH FLOW.** Peterson Industries has three potential projects it could invest in for the coming year. Finances are tight, so it needs to choose the projects with the greatest benefit for the company. The company's WACC is 7%. The details on the three projects are:

Cash Flow Year	Project A	Project B	Project C
Cash flow year 0	($100,000)	($100,000)	($100,000)
Cash flow year 1	$60,000	$20,000	$25,000
Cash flow year 2	$50,000	$30,000	$35,000

Cash Flow Year	Project A	Project B	Project C
Cash flow year 3	$30,000	$50,000	$45,000
Cash flow year 4	$20,000	$60,000	$55,000

REQUIRED:

a. Calculate the present value of each of these projects using the 7% discount rate.
b. If the company can only afford to spend $250,000 this year to start projects, which two projects should the company choose? Why?

2. **DISCOUNTED CASH FLOW.** Randall Associates has three potential projects it could invest in for the coming year. Finances are tight, so the company needs to choose the projects with the greatest return for the company. The company's WACC is 8%. The details on the projects are:

Cash Flow Year	Project A	Project B	Project C
Cash flow year 0	($150,000)	($150,000)	($150,000)
Cash flow year 1	$90,000	$70,000	$85,000
Cash flow year 2	$80,000	$80,000	$75,000
Cash flow year 3	$70,000	$90,000	$65,000
Cash flow year 4	$60,000	$100,000	$55,000

REQUIRED:

a. Calculate the present value of each of these projects using the 8% discount rate.
b. If the company can only afford to spend $300,000 this year to start projects, which two projects should the company choose? Why?

3. **TRANSFER PRICING.** Cold Springs has four subunits: Filtering, Bottle Production, Bottling, and Distribution. They are run as independent units and can actually buy their inputs or sell their output either to the next subunit in line in the process or externally, depending on the path that maximizes their profit. The company currently has all four divisions cooperating in selling product to each other at cost plus a reasonable profit. Recently, Bottling has been approached by an outside customer who would like to buy time on the line. This customer would pay the going market price of $0.05 per bottle of water bottled. It would tanker the water into Bottling's holding tank and would pick up the bottled water at the end of the line. This outside customer would want 250,000 bottles filled. Bottling currently sells its services to Cold Springs for $0.04 a bottle because it is

very efficient. It costs the subunit $0.03 per completed bottle, so the subunit currently gets a 33.3% markup on its costs. If Bottling accepts the outside job, it would either need to run the compensating 250,000 units of internal work on overtime, driving the cost up to $0.045 per bottle leading to an internal price of $0.06 per bottle to keep the same profit margin. Bottling could also refuse the internal business and send the internal business out to a competitor. This competitor would charge the internal customer $0.05, the going market rate, so the company would end up paying market to another company.

REQUIRED:

a. What should the bottling subunit do in this case?
b. What impact will this have on company profits?
c. What transfer price should be used for Bottling under the circumstances presented here to keep the unit's interests aligned with what is best for the company?

---

4. **TRANSFER PRICING.** The bottle production department of Cold Springs has decided it would like to renegotiate its transfer price to Bottling now that it sees what advantages can be gained. Current transfer prices, market prices, and costs for the subunit are:

Market selling price per bottle	$0.075
Internal transfer price	$0.06
Unit variable cost	$0.03
Unit fixed cost	$0.015
Practical capacity in bottles	5,000,000

During the coming year, Bottle Production plans on making 4,000,000 bottles that it will sell to the bottling department. Bottling currently plans to buy an additional 1,000,000 bottles externally at the market price of $0.075. Frank Pearson, head of Bottle Production, has approached Janet Nielson, head of Bottling with an offer of $0.07 per bottle to supply the additional output needed. This production would need to be done on overtime, adding $0.01 to the variable costs of production. Frank sees this as a tremendous improvement for Bottling and a win for the corporation.

REQUIRED:

a. What is the minimum transfer price that Bottle Production would be willing to accept?
b. What is the maximum transfer price that Bottling would be willing to pay?
c. Should the internal transfer take place? What are the costs and benefits of this internal transfer for the corporation?

d. Suppose Janet knows that Bottle Production has idle capacity, so she wants to pay only $0.05 for the additional bottles. Should Frank be interested in the business at this price?
e. What if top management gets involved and decides to set everyone's transfer prices at full manufacturing cost. Would this transfer of an additional 1,000,000 bottles take place under these conditions?

5. **ALLOCATION METHODS.** Ajax Manufacturing has two support centers, Engineering and Accounting, and two production centers, Cutting and Milling. The overhead costs for the coming year for the four departments, and their share of usage of support services, is in the following table.

	Engineering	Accounting	Cutting	Milling
Overhead	$350,000	$250,000	$400,000	$600,000
% Engineering Used	-0-	10%	40%	50%
% Accounting Used	20%	-0-	35%	45%

REQUIRED:

a. Determine the amount of Engineering and Accounting to be charged to the two producing centers using direct allocation.
b. Determine the amount of Engineering and Accounting to be charged to the two producing centers using sequential allocation.
c. Determine the amount of Engineering and Accounting to be charged to the two producing centers using reciprocal allocation.
d. If Cutting works 4,000 hours a year and Milling 6,000 hours, what would be the overhead rate per hour worked under each of the three overhead charging schemes suggested above?
e. What allocation method should be used? Why?

6. **ALLOCATION METHODS.** Sunrise Development makes various types of modular homes for the housing market. The company has two support departments, Personnel and Finance, and two producing departments: Cutting and Assembly. The overhead costs for the coming year for the four departments, and their share of usage of support services, is in the following table.

	Personnel	Finance	Cutting	Assembly
Overhead	$ 250,000	$ 300,000	$ 450,000	$ 550,000
% Personnel Used	-0-	20%	30%	50%
% Finance Used	15%	-0-	30%	55%

REQUIRED:

a. Determine the amount of Personnel and Finance to be charged to the two producing centers using direct allocation.

b. Determine the amount of Personnel and Finance to be charged to the two producing centers using sequential allocation.

c. Determine the amount of Personnel and Finance to be charged to the two producing centers using reciprocal allocation.

d. If Cutting works 6,000 hours a year and Assembly 12,000 hours, what would be the overhead rate per hour worked under each of the three overhead charging schemes suggested above?

e. What allocation method should be used? Why?

7. **RETURNS AND RESIDUAL INCOME.** Parlance, Inc., has three divisions that it is trying to evaluate to determine which division should get the largest share of the capital available for new projects for the coming year. Sam Peabody, Parlance's CEO, believes it is best to evaluate how well the divisions have done with the money entrusted to them to this stage if he is going to make a good investment decision moving forward. He collects the following data on the three divisions, all of which is stated in millions of dollars.

Performance Metric	Division A	Division B	Division C
Net operating profit	$125.40	$250.60	$300.80
Invested capital	$150.80	$400.50	$500.40
Weighted average cost of capital	7.5%	8.0%	8.5%
Net assets	$1.095.40	$1,500.50	$1,950.60
Total equity	$759.60	$1,025.30	$1,325.40

REQUIRED:

a. Calculate the RI for each of the three divisions.

b. Calculate the ROI for each of the divisions.

c. Calculate the return on net assets (RONA) for each of the divisions.

d. Calculate the return on equity (ROE) for each of the three divisions.

e. Which division is doing the best (for example, should receive more capital this year)? Why?

8. **RETURNS AND RESIDUAL INCOME.** Kentucky Homes, a producer of various RVs and trailer homes, has three divisions that are always competing for funds: RVs, Trailer Homes, and Campers. Ken Williams, CEO of Kentucky Homes, has usually just looked at the projects the subunits wanted to invest in and used his own judgment as to which ones made the most sense. This year he has decided to put his recent MBA to work for him and evaluate the top projects based on how well the subunits have performed with their existing capital. The subunits that have performed the best will get the most funds. Ken will still use his discretion to make sure good projects are not overlooked in the process, but he wants to have a clean starting point for evaluating the projects. He collects the following data on the three divisions (stated in millions of dollars).

Performance Metric	RVs	Trailer Homes	Campers
Net operating profit	$375.80	$325.40	$272.60
Invested capital	$950.80	$895.40	$750.40
Weighted average cost of capital	8.0%	8.5%	7.5%
Net assets	$1,598.60	$1,700.90	$1,650.80
Total equity	$1,185.30	$1,230.50	$1,225.40

REQUIRED:

a. Calculate the RI for each of the three divisions.
b. Calculate the ROI for each of the divisions.
c. Calculate the RONA for each of the divisions.
d. Calculate the ROE for each of the three divisions.
e. Which division is doing the best (for example, should receive more capital this year)? Why?

9. **ACTIVITY-BASED COSTING AND COST ASSIGNMENTS.** Perkins Lumber has recently put in an activity-based costing (ABC) system. It wants to use it to assign the costs of its personnel and accounting departments to the two revenue centers, Lumber and Building Supplies. The personnel department is driven by number of employees while Accounting is driven by number of transactions. The following table summarizes the data for the company.

	Personnel	Accounting	Lumber	Building Supplies
Overhead	$200,000	$250,000	$300,000	$275,000
Number of employees	-0-	4	6	10
Number of transactions	10,000	-0-	45,000	45,000

REQUIRED:

a. Assign all of the support overhead to the revenue centers using direct cost assignment.
b. Assign all of the support overhead using sequential assignments.
c. Assign all of the support overhead using reciprocal assignments.
d. Develop overhead rates per direct labor hour for the revenue centers. Assume each employee works 2,000 hours per year.
e. Which method of assigning overhead is best? Why?

---

10. **ACTIVITY-BASED COSTING AND COST ASSIGNMENTS.** Grummond Engine Repair has recently adopted ABC for its two support groups, Engineering and Finance. Engineering is charged out on engineering hours (which includes computer support), while Finance is charged out on number of transactions. The following table summarizes key data for the company and its subunits.

	Engineering	Finance	Small Engine Repair	Large Engine Repair
Overhead	$600,000	$350,000	$500,000	$650,000
Number of engineering hours	-0-	800	2,400	2,800
Number of transactions	20,000	-0-	40,000	40,000
Repair hours	-0-	-0-	8,000	12,000

REQUIRED:

a. Assign all of the support overhead to the revenue centers using direct cost assignment.
b. Assign all of the support overhead using sequential assignments.
c. Assign all of the support overhead using reciprocal assignments.
d. Develop overhead rates per repair hour for the revenue centers.
e. Which method of assigning overhead is best? Why?

Database Problems

For database templates, worksheets, and workbooks, go to MAdownloads.imanet.org

DB 11.1 RESIDUAL INCOME AND RETURNS. You will be using three sheets for this problem—Corp Ten Year Income Statement, Corp Ten Year Balance Sheet, and DB Problem 11.1 Template. You will find the WACC for Prestige Auto on the solution template page.

Your task on this assignment is to calculate Prestige Auto's RI, ROI (invested capital, or the sum equity and long-term debt such as mortgages), RONA, and ROE. You will then make two graphs—one for RI for the 10 years and another for the combined results of your ROI, RONA, and ROE for the 10 years. This is a simple exercise once you key the correct formula into the right template cell.

Let us begin with RI. Here, we need to take net income and subtract the WACC times the invested capital, which is mortgage payable plus common stock and retained earnings.

Go to cell B7. Key in = then go to the 10-year income statement. Place your cursor over Cell B17. Left click. Key in -(in front of the DB Problem 1.1 Template'!B4 to note the subtraction you now need to do for the cost of invested capital. Now go back to your solution template sheet and place your cursor over cell B4. Left click. Then key in *(and go to your 10-year balance sheet. Place your cursor over cell B19. Left click. Key in + and place your cursor over cell B22. Left click. Key in + and place your cursor over cell B23. Left click. Key in) and hit Enter. Your resulting command should look like the following: ='Corp Ten Year Income Statement'!B17-('DB Problem 11-1 Template'!B4*('Corp 10 Year Balance Sheet'!B19+'Corp 10 Year Balance Sheet'!B22+'Corp 10 Year Balance Sheet'!B23).

Drag this formula across the entire row for RI. You will populate the entire 10 years with this formula.

Now let us move on to ROI (or invested capital). Here, we need to divide net income by the sum of long-term debt (mortgage payable) and equity (common stock and retained earnings).

Go to cell B10. Key in = then go to the 10-year income statement. Place your cursor over cell B17. Left click and then key in /(and move on to the 10-year balance sheet. Place your cursor over cell B19. Left click and then key in + and place your cursor over cell B22. Left click and then key in + and finally place your cursor over cell B23 and key in) and hit Enter. Your formula should look like: ='Corp Ten Year Income Statement'!B17/('Corp 10 Year Balance Sheet'!B19+'Corp 10 Year Balance Sheet'!B22+'Corp 10 Year Balance Sheet'!B23). Drag this formula across the entire row for ROI. You will populate the entire 10 years with this formula.

The next calculation is RONA. This is a simple calculation in which we divide net income by total net assets.

Go to cell B11. Key in = then go to the 10-year income statement. Place your cursor over cell B17. Left click then key in / and go to your 10-year balance sheet. Place your cursor over cell B12. Left click and then hit Enter. Your resulting formula should look like: ='Corp Ten Year Income Statement'!B17/'Corp 10 Year Balance Sheet'!B12.

Drag this formula across all of the cells to finish off this row of calculations.

The final calculation is ROE. Here we will need to divide net income by the sum of common stock and retained earnings. Go to cell B12. Key in = then go to the 10-year income statement. Place your cursor over cell B17. Left click then key in /(and go to your 10-year balance sheet. Place your cursor over cell B22. Left click and then key in + and place your cursor over cell B23. Left click and key in) finally hitting Enter. Your resulting command should look like: ='Corp Ten Year Income Statement'!B17/('Corp 10 Year Balance Sheet'!B22+'Corp 10 Year Balance Sheet'!B23).

Drag this formula to complete the last row of the table.

You are almost done. Now make two charts. First make a trend chart of the RI that you have calculated for the 10 years. Second, make a chart that contains all three of the returns you calculated in the steps above.

REQUIRED:

a. Turn in your sheet with your calculation and graphs.
b. Comment on the trends you see. Specifically, compare the WACC to the different returns earned by the firm. What does this comparison tell you?

DB 11.2 ACTIVITY-BASED COST ASSIGNMENTS FOR 20X6. In this exercise, you are going to do a simple allocation of the four support department costs to the operating groups Marketing, New Car Sales, Used Car Sales, and Repairs. You are only going to do direct and sequential allocation in this exercise. You will need the 10-year income statement worksheet, the Allocation Data for 20x6 worksheet, and your solution template for DB 11.2. To make this easier for you, the allocation grid has been copied onto your template sheet.

Direct Allocation. Here, you assign all of the costs directly from the support departments to the producing divisions. That means you can ignore the cross-usage detailed in the worksheet. Let us start by assigning marketing.

Marketing Assignment. Go to your solution template and place your cursor over cell F12. Key in =$ and then place your cursor over cell B10. Left click. Key in *(then place your cursor over cell F4. Left click then key in ($ and place your cursor over cell F4. Left click and then key in +$ then place your cursor over cell G4. Left click and then key in +$ and place your cursor over cell H4. Left click finally keying in)) and hitting Enter. Your command should look like: =$B10*(F4/($F4+$G4+$H4)).

Because we locked all of the cells that we need to keep constant by using our dollar sign (Why did we lock these? Make sure you know), we can now click and drag this formula across the rest of the row. Make sure not to wipe out your total. You will need to repeat this exercise, moving across the other three support departments. Use this type of command structure to fill in the Customer Service, Management, and Overhead assignments.

To complete this part of the exercise, you need to calculate support cost per car for new and used cars and by repair hour for the repairs department. This is set up in your grid. All you need to do is go to cell F18 and hit = and then place your cursor over cell F16. Left click then key in / and move to the Allocation Data for 20x6 worksheet, place your cursor over cell F9. Left click and hit Enter. Your formula should look like this: =F16/'Allocation Data for 2011'!F9.

Drag this formula across column G18. Now you need to do the repairs department. This is set up for you in cell H19. You follow the same logic, dividing the total overhead charged out to Repairs by the repair hours noted on the allocation worksheet.

Sequential Assignments. Now things become a bit more challenging. First, we have to determine in what order to do the assignments. The easiest way is to look at the driver quantities and see how much each group shares of its service with other service departments. Go to the column to the right of the active allocation section, namely cell J4. Now figure out how much the marketing department provides support to the other support departments by keying in =SUM(and then place your cursor over cell B4. Left click and key in : and place your cursor over E4. Left click and key in)/ and finally place your cursor over cell I4. Left click and hit Enter. Your command should look like this: =SUM(B4:E4)/I4. This is a good way to use the summation command. Now simply drag this formula down the rest of column J's departments.

Now you need to determine what order this information suggests you should allocate in. Take the largest percentage shared per your calculations and put a 1 in the sequence box. Then do the same based on magnitudes for allocation sequences 2, 3, and 4.

To allocate sequentially with four departments, you have to move very carefully. For these instructions, we are going to assume the sequence of assigning the support departments is Management, Customer Service, General Overhead, and then Marketing. Let us walk through charging out management (on people, correct?).

Go to cell B28 and key in =$ then place your cursor over the overhead amount for Management in cell D24. Left click then key in *(and place your cursor over cell B6. Left click then key in /$ and place your cursor over cell I6. Left click and then close the argument by keying in) and hit Enter. Your command should look like this: =$D24*(B6/$I6).

Now copy the command in cell B28 and paste it into cells C28, E28, F28, G28, and H28 to complete the rows. To make the grid work, now enter a negative $385,000 in cell D28 to zero out the row across and Management down. You will not charge anything else to Management.

Customer Service. We have added some dollars to Customer Service from Management, so now we have to be more careful in setting up our charging commands. Go to cell B27 to start the process and key in =($ and then place your cursor over cell C24. Left click then key in +$ and place your cursor over cell C28. Left click then key in)*(and then place your cursor over cell B5. Left click then key in /($ and place your cursor over cell B5. Left click then key in +$ and place your cursor over cell F5. Left click then key in +$ and place your cursor over cell G5. Left click and key in +$ and place your cursor over cell H5. Left click and then close the argument by keying in)) and hitting Enter. Your command should look like: =($C24+$C28)*(B5/($B5+$F5+$G5+$H5)).

What we have done is added the management charge to the original overhead charge and then created a ratio of the departments that use Customer Service's output. You will now copy this command and paste it in cells F27, G27, and H27 to complete the row. Enter the balance you started with in Customer Service as a negative amount in cell C27. This should zero out both the customer service column and the service calls row (the driver for Customer Service).

You will follow the same logic as above to complete the last two rows in the grid, first charging out ALL of General Overhead to the four departments that remain (Marketing, New Cars, Used Cars, and Repairs). You will end up by charging out Marketing to the three producing centers. Make sure you zero out every row and the four columns that go with the support departments. You are now ready to do the last calculations to complete the worksheet.

Go to cell F32 and key in = then move your cursor over cell F30. Left click then key in / and shift to worksheet Allocation Data for 2011 and place your cursor over cell F9. Left click and hit Enter. Your formula should look like: =F30/'Allocation Data for 2011'!F9. Drag this formula across to cell G30. Then repeat the same logic as before to fill in cell H31 for Repairs.

REQUIRED:

a. Turn in your worksheet with the direct and sequential allocations completed.
b. Does it make a difference which method you use? Why or why not?

Cases

CASE 11.1 TRANSFER PRICING. Arial Production makes movies and music videos. It has three divisions: Filming, Sound, and Editing. Sam Norwell, president and CEO of Arial, feels it is best to keep his divisions independent and lean, so he allows each division to go after its own business. Sound does not have to cooperate with Filming, nor Editing with Sound or Filming. Each division is freestanding and held accountable for its ROI. Over the last year, the three divisions have worked together less and less. While Sam has okayed these choices, he is beginning to feel that he is losing some economies of scale by not having the divisions work together more closely. The question is: How does he make this happen?

Sam decides to hold a meeting with the heads of the three divisions to see if they can come up with some way to make it in everyone's best interest to work together on projects. Bruce Walker, head of Filming, is first to arrive. He immediately begins lobbying Sam to make Sound and Editing work with him. Filming is having to purchase these services from the outside and the market is tight right now—everyone is very busy so the prices for these services keep going up. Filming's ROI is suffering as a consequence, leading Bruce to look toward his sister divisions to help shore up the filming part of the business. Their conversation goes like this:

Sam, nice to see you. I was wondering about something, if you have a few minutes to chat before the meeting begins. We in Filming are getting our clocks cleaned by having to buy our sound and editing services outside the corporation. Wouldn't it be in everyone's best interest to work together? We'd keep the costs on a film down and keep the profits inside!

I don't know, Bruce. I think it would be great to see the divisions working together more, but I really don't want to interfere too directly in decision making. I like seeing everyone strive to do the best with the assets I've entrusted to them. With the market as busy as it is, Sound and Editing are doing very well. They probably would want to be paid the going market price for any work they do for you.

I don't see why they need market. If they work with us in Filming, they don't have the same costs. We can cooperate and make the workload lighter for them. And the profits would all stay in the corporation, so everyone wins.

I'm not sure they'll see it that way, Bruce. They are doing very well selling at market prices. If I tell them they have to work with your group at reduced prices, it's going to directly impact their ROI, and, hence, their performance evaluation.

Well, Sam, what if you credited their income statement at market, but allowed us to be charged only cost on internal transactions? Since the profit is a wash for the corporation, wouldn't we be better off keeping more of the work internal?

That's a novel idea, Bruce, but how would it be fair to the other division heads if you get the equivalent of an internal price break on basic services? You'll look better than you would if you had to pay market.

But we need to work together, Sam. It only makes sense to put our focus on making money on our movies and music videos, not on our basic services. Isn't there some other way you can structure our incentive system so we still strive to do our best but we have the incentive to work together?

Let's see what we come up with during the meeting, Bruce. I'll float a few ideas and we'll see if there isn't something that can be done to keep more of our internal services available for Filming. My guess is you're going to have to pay close to market, though, perhaps with a discount for not having to pay commissions to salespeople and other marketing cost reductions. Let's see what can be done.

REQUIRED:

a. What do you think about Bruce's plan to use market prices for the supplying divisions and cost for the using division (Filming)? What are the pros and cons of this approach?

b. Are there other incentives or measurements that might lead to more cooperation between the divisions? Please try to be specific.

c. Is the corporation better off as it is currently run or would it be better off if the divisions worked together? Please explain your answer.

CASE 11.2 SUBOPTIMIZATION PROBLEM. Manson's Payroll Service consists of two primary divisions—Payroll Services and Tax Services. The payroll services division does very well, earning on average 18% ROI. Tax services, on the other hand, struggles earning on average only 8.5% ROI. The company's WACC is 8%. It is year-end, and both divisions are faced with deciding whether or not to invest in new computers and software support systems. The details of the options the two divisions are looking at are in the following table.

Manson Payroll Services				
Payroll Services Division	**Initial Investment (Year 0)**	**Cash Flow Year 1**	**Cash Flow Year 2**	**Cash Flow Year 3**
Project A—New Hardware	$1,500,000	$700,000	$600,000	$500,000
Project B—New Software	$1,000,000	$550,000	$300,000	$300,000
Tax Services Division				
Project A—New Hardware	$1,800,000	$900,000	$700,000	$500,000
Project B—New Software	$1,200,000	$600,000	$500,000	$400,000

Sam Houston, head of the payroll services division, is hesitant to take on any more investments because he likes to keep his ROI high. The problem is, however, that if the division does not keep current on its hardware and software, it could start losing business to competitors who stay more abreast of the situation.

Dave Brown, head of Tax Services, knows that he has to keep current if he is going to stay in the business at all. Tax laws change constantly, so keeping up to date with all of the latest changes and incorporating them in the packages it offers to customers is essential if the division is going to continue to survive in its highly competitive marketplace.

Jim Manson knows both divisions are being run well, but they just face very different markets. He would like to keep the company on the edge of technology because he knows that's what ultimately spells success or disaster in the payroll industry. He does not like to interfere with his managers, however, instead preferring to allow them to make the decisions they feel are best for their division.

REQUIRED:

a. Compute the discounted value of the cash flows for the four projects presented in the table. Use the company's WACC as your discount rate. Do the projects yield a positive discounted cash flow?

b. Recompute the discounted cash flow values of the various projects using the division's separate average ROI. Do the projects yield a positive discounted cash flow now?

c. The net operating profit after tax for the payroll services division before the investment in new assets is projected to be $2.5 million. The comparative number for Tax Services is $850,000. Using RI focusing only on Year 0 cash investments, what would these two divisions do? Specifically, would they invest in the new assets using the corporation's required 8% WACC? Without the new investment, net operating profit before tax for Payroll Services would be $2 million. Without the investment, net operating profit for Tax Services would be $750,000. Invested capital before the new investments was $8.5 million for the payroll division and $2.5 million for the tax division. To do these calculations, combine the two projects' costs for each division into one project to simplify the cash flow calculations.

d. What would you recommend that Jim do to motivate Payroll Services to keep abreast of current technology? Why?

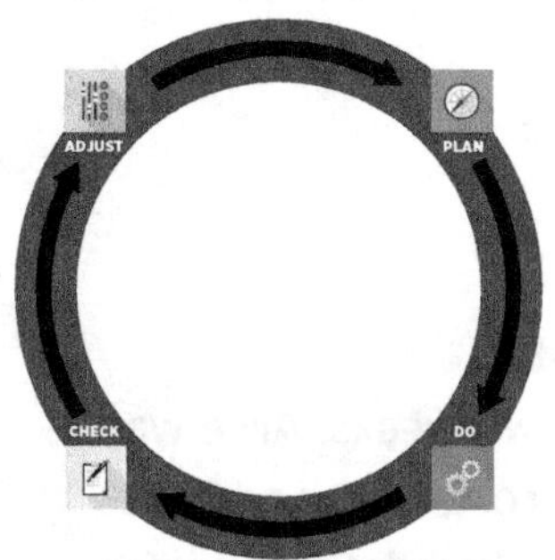

Evaluating and Improving Entity Performance

Satisfactory results are the basic objectives of all business activity. It was left to me to determine what would constitute satisfactory results at ITT.[1]

HAROLD GENEEN

LONGTIME CHIEF EXECUTIVE AT ITT CORPORATION

CHAPTER ROADMAP

1. Evaluating Performance
2. Comparing Measured Results with a Performance Target
3. Profit Variance Analyses
   - ➤ *Disaggregating Profit Variances by Line Item*
   - ➤ *Disaggregating Profit Variances by Responsibility Center*
   - ➤ *Disaggregating Profit Variances by Profit Driver*
4. Relative Performance Evaluations
5. Subjective Performance Evaluations
6. Designing an Incentive Program
   - ➤ *Performance Rewards: Individual vs. Group Performance vs. a Combination*
   - ➤ *Determining the Shape of the Function Linking Rewards and Performance Measures*
   - ➤ *Determining the Amount of the Incentive*
   - ➤ *Determining the Form of Incentives*

LEARNING OBJECTIVES

After studying this chapter, you should be able to:

1. **Explain the benefits of comparing actual performance with a performance target and how those comparisons differ depending on what kind of target is used as the comparison standard.**
2. **Discuss the reasons managers perform variance analyses.**
3. **Describe how to perform profit variance analyses by responsibility center, by line item, and by profit driver.**
4. **Put the concept of relative performance evaluations into plain English and explain how they can be used as a substitute for some types of variance analyses.**
5. **Explain why managers sometimes evaluate performance subjectively, rather than basing evaluations solely on objective performance measures.**

---

1 Harold Geneen, *Managing*, Garden City, N.Y.: Doubleday, 1984: p. 34.

IN CONTEXT ➤ Prestige Auto—Allocating Internal Costs

The team had been hard at work for more than two weeks. Alice was busy putting together allocation estimates of the costs of the administrative functions that Management and Finance shared and transfer prices for the three operating units—Marketing, Acquisitions, and Service. She had some concern that Acquisitions might not really be a profit center; on the other hand, it did buy cars from individuals and large manufacturers, which it transferred to Sales and Marketing. The question she faced was whether this transfer should be done at cost—which would mean Acquisitions was a cost center, not a profit center—or whether it should be allowed to earn a profit on each transfer of new or used cars to the showroom floor. This was the point of contention as the team got together on a sunny Monday morning.

"Jack, if you make me pay for the repairs and other work done on the cars I bring in, I've got to be able to add that charge to the amount I charge Sales and Marketing. That'll raise the price of our cars, sometimes even higher than the market price. I need a profit margin if I'm going to make the goals you set, but that's going to put the pinch on the sales staff," Bruce said emphatically.

"I think we should treat Acquisitions as one of those shared administrative cost centers Alice has been talking about," said Judy, defending her turf. "It doesn't make sense to mark up the cars internally. I agree that the service department deserves credit for the work they do, and we should be aware of how much work they have to put into the cars we buy before we can put them in the showroom. That makes sense. I think Bruce's group should be held accountable in some way for the margin Sales and Marketing can get; otherwise they may not drive the hard bargains we need them to on the Acquisitions side. It's a difficult problem!"

"If you make us a cost center, then I would imagine we'd have to transfer our cars to Sales and Marketing at cost, or perhaps at wholesale Blue Book prices. If we use Blue Book, Acquisitions can remain a profit center, but we won't hit the goals we set earlier in the year if I have to pick up the cost of repairs and other work to get the cars ready to sell. I'm willing to live with new goals if they make sense for the company," Bruce said, still looking worried.

"I think transferring at market from Acquisitions with the 'get ready' charges included as part of the cost makes sense. That leaves the incentives in place for your group to work to get good prices on the cars we bring in, Bruce, but also rewards Service for being there to support us all when we need it. Can we do it that way, Alice?" asked Jack.

"We can certainly do it that way. The only question is whether we charge the service work that's done at cost or market. You can argue either way. If we're going to hold Tony accountable for profitable repairs, then it's only fair to use the same repair prices as an outside person would pay him. If we're only going to hold him accountable for profits on outside sales, then I'll need to be a bit fancier in my accounting, but I think we can keep the two types of businesses separate. That would leave Bruce and his group with more profitable transactions and not penalize Tony's group for doing internal work," Alice explained.

"Why not charge Bruce market prices, Alice?" asked Tony.

"We can certainly do it, Tony; it just changes the way the numbers roll out. Bruce's group might find an outside repair service that would get the cars ready for less than our full cost. I'm not sure we want to see our profits going out the door to another firm. We have to leave some incentive for Bruce's group to work internally unless we really want to see changes in this company, some that may not work in our best interests! We already need to deal with the fact that our residual income trends aren't good. We need to focus on moving more cars with less investment all the way around. Don't you agree, Jack?" asked Alice.

"I definitely agree. I want all of us to continue working together to get the most bang for our buck. I want to keep the business in-house, and want everyone to work together to help get our performance back to where it was three years ago. That means moving more cars, which also means doing a great job in Acquisitions and Sales and that Service must always be ready to pitch in when needed. We may all end up as profit centers, but I don't want us to lose the feeling that we're partners, which has worked so well up to now," responded Jack.

After further discussion, the team decided to keep the three profit centers and two cost centers. Crediting the service department at market rates while charging Bruce's group at cost would provide a "false" profit for internal work, but Alice could zero out the difference in the monthly books. With everyone on board, attention could now return to the key question—how to generate more sales and improve company performance.

FTER PERFORMANCE HAS BEEN MEASURED IN A GIVEN OPERATING period, managers move into the "check" and "adjust" elements of the business planning and analysis (BPA) process. They have to evaluate the measured performance and decide whether or not to make changes going forward.

The measures do not mean anything without a standard against which to compare them, so the first step in the evaluation process involves comparing actual performance with one or more performance targets. Almost inevitably, performance will not be exactly in line with the targets, so the second step in the evaluation process involves analyzing the sources and reasons for the differences. Managers have to answer questions such as: Was last period's performance satisfactory? If not, where did the performance shortfalls come from, Division A or Division B, sales or production? Were the shortfalls due to a lack of effort, poor decision making, or bad luck? Only after questions like these are answered can managers decide what adjustments to make, if any.

The adjustments can involve any of a broad range of decisions. They might involve, for example, changing organization structures, business strategies (for example, allocations of scarce resources), operating tactics (such as pricing), personnel, and/or reward systems. These changes can make a big difference on the performance evaluations of the organization's managers, so they have to be made with care and an eye toward their behavioral effects.

This chapter describes the process of evaluating the performances of whole business entities and the managers of those entities, the challenges managers face in performing those evaluations, and some approaches they can use to improve their evaluations. It then discusses how performance evaluations can be improved through variance analyses, subjective adjustments, and relative performance evaluations.

Evaluating Performance

OBJECTIVE 1

Explain the benefits of comparing actual performance with a performance target and understand how those comparisons differ depending on what kind of target is used as the comparison standard.

Suppose you were told that in the recently completed year the Petrochemical Division of a large chemical company earned $12.4 million in profit, and you were asked if you thought that this division performed well in that year. How would you answer this question?

If this is the only information you have, then you cannot answer the question very accurately. The $12.4 million is above zero, but it still might represent quite poor performance. Performance measures, no matter how good they are, do not have any meaning unless they are compared with some type of performance target or standard. So before you venture an answer, you might ask for information about a potentially useful performance standard. You might ask: "What was the Petrochemical Division's profit budget for the year? What profit did the division report in the prior year or years? How did the division's profit, perhaps as a percent of sales, compare with its closest competitors' return-on-sales figures?"

Suppose you were told that this division's profit budget was $20 million, so it missed its budget target by 38%. Then you were asked if you thought this meant that performance was poor and, hence, that the division general manager should be fired, or at least reassigned.

You are not yet in a position to give a good answer to this question. It is impossible for you to know if the budgeted profit target was a meaningful performance target, given the actual business conditions the division faced last year. For example, did business conditions weaken significantly after the budget target was set? Did a large competitor start a price war after the new year had begun? Did the prices of oil (a significant factor of production) rise significantly during the year? Or, after the budget was set, did the division manager make a large investment, which was approved by top management and was expected to pay large dividends in future years, even at the expense of profits in the current year? If the answer to any of these questions is yes, then missing the budget target might be excusable and not something for which the division's managers should be reprimanded.

This little example illustrates three critical points about performance evaluations. First, no evaluations are possible without a performance standard. Second, good evaluations often require some analysis and judgment to look behind the cold, objective comparison of measures with standards. And third, the evaluation of the division can be quite different from that of the manager of the division. A judgment that the $12.4 million profit is poor might lead to the conclusion that petrochemicals is not a good business to be in, while, at the same time, top management might conclude that the manager of the Petrochemical Division performed quite well last year in difficult operating conditions.

Analyses of results can remove some "noise," perhaps caused by the effects of uncontrollable factors that distort the performance measures. They can also be used to adjust the performance target based on the conditions actually faced during the performance period. Thus, the adjustments make for better performance evaluations and better decisions that are dependent on those evaluations, such as changes in business strategies and tactics, allocations of salary increases and bonuses, and promotions.

Comparing Measured Results with a Performance Target

OBJECTIVE 2
Discuss the reasons managers perform variance analyses.

Managers usually start their performance evaluation processes by comparing actual measured results with a performance target. A **variance** *is the difference between actual results and the targeted, or planned, performance*. A **favorable variance** *indicates that actual performance was better than the performance standard*; that is, what was expected. For example, sales or profits exceeded the target or costs were lower than target. An **unfavorable variance** *indicates that actual performance was worse than the performance standard.*

Variances provide information to managers about how to allocate their attention. Variances, particularly large, unfavorable ones, suggest a high likelihood of problems that should be addressed. A common management style, called **management-by-exception,** *focuses primarily on areas with unfavorable variances*; that is, those having performance problems. It is management's implementation of the common sense adage, "If it ain't broke, don't fix it." If a company's Malaysian subsidiary reports very significant negative variances, it is likely that the managers in Malaysia are having problems. At a minimum, top management should investigate the cause of the variances. If the variances stem from **controllable performance**—*areas or activities over which managers have significant influence*, they should probably offer help to the Malaysian management team or, if they reach a conclusion that the team is not effective, replace some or all of the managers.

LOOKING BACK ➤ Variance Analyses—Still Relevant after All These Years

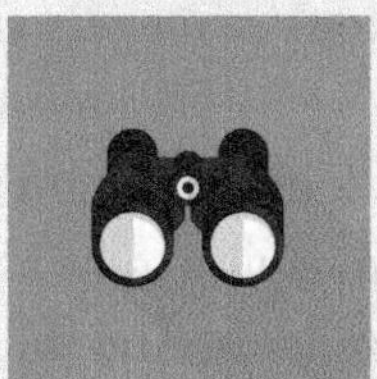

By 1925, management accountants were preparing detailed statements that contained a wide variety of variances. F. Brugger, who worked for General Electric, described its system of variances in the following way:

The Summarized Manufacturing and Efficiency Statement differs from the Summarized Manufacturing Statement in that columns are added to the former to show the reasons for the increase of decrease in cost; i.e., whether the increase or decrease is due: (1) to quantity of material consumed or time taken; or (2) to changes in prices or rates of wages. It also separates burden into direct departmental burden and general burden and indicates the amount of fixed burden applicable to idle equipment.

*Efficiency statements may be prepared along similar lines for each of the departments. Such statements might show labor segregated by machine groups and burden by main groups or even individual accounts. Departmental statements would show only items over which the department has control to a major degree. General burden would be omitted from such statements but the non-productive departments would be furnished with special statements showing comparisons of the actual and standard cost of the operation of their respective department.**

Although written close to 100 years ago, it is clear that standard costs and variances were understood well and that the controllability principle was firmly in place. It was deemed best practice to separate out idle time charges, another practice that has only recently been rediscovered by management accountants.

*Excerpted from "Standard Costs—Their Development and Use," *N.A.C.A. Bulletin*, Vol. 6, No. 13, March 2, 1925. It was reprinted in Richard Vangermeersch, ed., *Relevance Rediscovered*, Montvale, N.J.: IMA® (Institute of Management Accountants), 1990: p. 223.

The size, and sometimes even the sign and, hence, the interpretations to be made of the variances depends on the targets used for the comparisons. As was described in Chapter 10, managers make use of many different kinds of targets, including budgets, past performance, and competitive benchmarks. This point is illustrated in Table 12.1. What is this company's variance from target? It depends on the target. If the budget is deemed to be the best performance target, then performance for the year looks good. However, if the comparison of results is made against stretch targets, those with a low likelihood of achievement, then most variances will probably be unfavorable. These unfavorable variances, however, do not necessarily reflect badly on the managers involved. Everybody should have known when the targets were set that their achievement was more a hope than an expectation. Similarly, comparison of actual performances with those of the company's best-performing competitors will also lead, almost inevitably, to unfavorable variances. The comparisons are intended to be interpreted as quantitative expressions of opportunities for improvement; in essence, gaps between the organization's current state and an ideal.

TABLE 12.1 THE EFFECT OF DIFFERENT PERFORMANCE STANDARDS ON VARIANCES

Golden Industries, Inc.								
Yearly figures ($ million)	Actual	Budget	Variance from Budget	Stretch Target	Variance from Stretch Target	Performance of Closest Competitor	Variance from Performance of Closest Competitor
Sales	950	1000	(50)	1050	(100)	1701	(751)
Profit before tax	119	130	(31)	142	(23)	223	(104)
Return on sales	12.5%	13.0%	(0.5%)	13.5%	(1.0%)	13.1%	(0.6%)

If the targets used for the performance comparisons are not meaningful, the variances based on them will not have much meaning. Examples of targets that are not good and, hence, not useful as standards for performance comparisons, are budgets that are not carefully thought out or sloppily put together and benchmarks that stem from companies or operations that are not comparable with those whose performances are being evaluated.

Profit Variance Analyses

OBJECTIVE 3

Describe how to perform profit variance analyses by responsibility center, by line item, and by profit driver.

A simple comparison of overall entity results as measured against a target, such as a budget, provides a global indication as to whether performance was good or bad. It does not, however, provide managers with any insight as to what caused performance to be good or bad. For example, were profits up because sales were up, or costs down, or both? For a bank, the question might be: Was the good performance due to the retail banking or the commercial banking side of the business, or both? Did the good performance stem from the performance of certain domestic subsidiaries, international subsidiaries, or both?

To answer these questions, to develop some insight as to what happened, why, and what should be done next, managers must disaggregate the overall variance. Earlier chapters discussed disaggregation of cost and revenue performances. This chapter will focus on evaluations of profit and investment centers. To understand the reasons underlying profit variances, managers can perform **profit variance analyses,** *a study designed to assess the causes for missing or exceeding profit targets*. To understand the reasons underlying variances, in accounting returns, managers can perform **accounting return variance analyses,** *studies designed to assess the reasons for missing accounting return targets*, such as return on investment (ROI).

Variances can be usefully disaggregated to serve either or both of two important purposes. The first purpose is to *fix responsibility*. This is done by tracing the variances to responsibility centers. The second purpose is to *determine the variances' underlying causes.* Uncontrollable variances can be separated from controllable variances, and the specific factors that caused the controllable variances can be identified and analyzed.

Top-level managers often manage by monitoring global performance indicators about subsidiary company and division performance and overall sales and costs, so variance reports prepared for their purposes need not be greatly detailed. Lower-level managers, however, need more detailed information about smaller organizational segments and smaller aspects of the overall business and, hence, require greater levels of disaggregation of the performance variances. For example, in consumer products firms like Proctor & Gamble, ConAgra, and Nestlé, division managers need detailed information about the actual sales and cost performances of specific brands and plants as compared to plan. Brand managers need detail on the sales of specific products within brand categories. And production managers need information about the performance of specific production lines and processes.

Effectively done, variance analyses can lead to modifications in any of a number of operating decisions, such as changes in strategy, the divestment of a business line or the acquisition of a new line, alterations of price schedules, process redesigns, or a renewed pledge to focus on certain aspects of performance, such as inventory control or quality. The variances could lead to suggestions to replace a poor-performing manager or to promote a top performer. Or they could lead primarily to a sense of satisfaction, based on a conclusion that things are proceeding about as well as possible.

The evaluations based on variance analysis are also a prerequisite to the assignment of organizational rewards, such as salary increases, bonuses, and recognition awards. The assignment of organizational rewards should generally be based on controllable performance; for example, considering only those aspects of performance over which the managers have significant influence. The uncontrollable factors provide noise in the performance measures that subjects the employees to greater risk of unfair evaluations. Variance analyses provide one common way to isolate and remove the effects of some uncontrollable factors.

As mentioned earlier, managers should make distinctions between their evaluations of responsibility centers as entities and their evaluations of the responsibility center managers. This is because judgments as to whether or not an event or a line item of revenue or expense is controllable are irrelevant in evaluating the financial performance of an entity, while they are often quite relevant for evaluating the manager's performance.

The disaggregation of profit (and return) variances can be done in many ways. Managers commonly analyze variances, for example, by revenue and expense line items, by responsibility center, and by the effects of various profit drivers.

DISAGGREGATING PROFIT VARIANCES BY LINE ITEM

One common and easy, but often not particularly useful, way to disaggregate variances is by income statement line item. The standard variance report includes the entity's income statement for the period in one column, with a performance target, most commonly, a budget, in another column, and the difference between the two columns, the variance, in a third column. An example is shown in Table 12.2.

TABLE 12.2 A PROFIT VARIANCE ANALYSIS BY LINE ITEM

Golden Industries, Inc.			
Yearly figures ($ million)	Actual	Budget	Variance*
Sales	950	1,000	(50)
Cost of goods sold	674	720	46
Gross margin	276	280	(4)
Selling, general, and administrative expenses	137	150	13
Net profit before tax	139	130	(9)

* Positive numbers are favorable variances.

This approach to variance analysis is common in published annual reports, typically with a comparison of this year's to last year's performance.[2] Maybe this type of information is of use to investors, but it is of limited use to managers. Most of the variances are not detailed enough to be actionable, and they actually can be quite misleading. Table 12.2 does show that sales were below budget, and this unfavorable sales variance undoubtedly caused some of the profit shortfall. However, this analysis does not tell how much of the profit shortfall was due solely to the sales shortfall. The variance might also have been affected by good or bad cost performance. For example, the actual selling, general, and administrative (SG&A) expenses were below budget. Was this a direct result of the sales shortfall, a reduction in a significant discretionary expenditure category that will cause problems in later years, good cost control, or some combination of factors? Or was the causality in the opposite direction? Did a cutback in selling and advertising expenses cause the sales shortfall? This type of report, which treats the income statement line items as independent, makes answering these questions quite difficult.

However, profit variances disaggregated by line item can be informative if the line items happen to match up with specific concerns managers have. For example, a detailed line item variance analysis might show that the company's power or medical benefit costs are significantly higher than budget. This could provide a cue to management to look for unforeseen rate increases, or other causes of the company-wide variances.

2 This observation was made by Vijay Govindarajan and John Shank, "Profit Variance Analysis: A Strategic Focus," *Issues in Accounting Education,* Vol. 4, No. 2, Fall 1989, p. 399.

DISAGGREGATING PROFIT VARIANCES BY RESPONSIBILITY CENTER

Another common, easy, and often more useful way to disaggregate profit variances is by *responsibility center*. Figure 12.1 shows how this process works conceptually. Disaggregating variances by responsibility center is an essential part of responsibility accounting. Because these types of variance reports are so useful, reflecting the performances of specific entities in the corporation and their managers, they are a standard part of virtually all companies' financial reporting packages.

Profit Variance Disaggregation by Responsibility Center

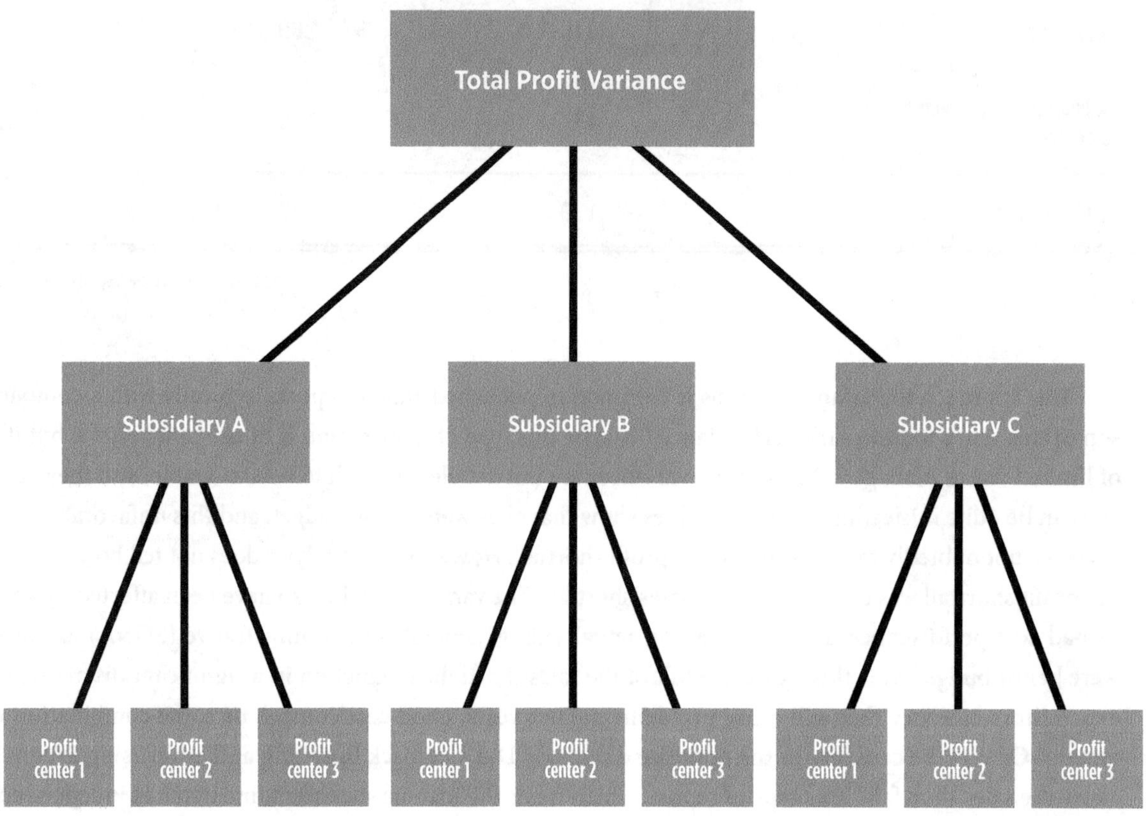

FIGURE 12.1 DISAGGREGATION BY RESPONSIBILITY CENTERS ALLOWS MANAGEMENT TO SEE AT A GLANCE WHICH CENTERS ARE MEETING, EXCEEDING, OR MISSING THEIR GOALS.

The disaggregation of profit variances can continue downward in the organization, into revenue centers and cost centers. A numerical example illustrating the usefulness of this type of variance disaggregation is shown in Table 12.3. This example disaggregates the line item variance report shown in Table 12.2 into Golden Industries' four divisions. This disaggregation shows that while the total corporation failed to achieve its budget targets, all of the news is not bad. Three of the four divisions actually exceeded their targets. Using the management-by-exception philosophy, top management should focus its attention on Division D, the only division that missed its targets. Significant problems that need to be solved are most likely there.

TABLE 12.3 PROFIT VARIANCE ANALYSIS BY LINE ITEM AND RESPONSIBILITY CENTER

Golden Inustries, Inc.															
Annual figures ($ million)*	Division A			Division B			Division C			Division D			Golden Industries, Inc.		
	Actual	Budget	Variance	Actual	Budget	Variance	Actual	Budget	Variance	Actual	Budget	Variance	Actual	Budget	Variance
Sales	$419	$390	$29	$97	$80	$17	$294	$330	$(36)	$140	$200	$(60)	$950	$1,000	$(50)
Less: Cost of Goods Sold	340	325	(15)	39	36	(3)	164	209	45	131	150	19	674	720	46
Gross Margin	79	65	14	58	44	14	130	121	9	9	50	(41)	276	280	(4)
Less: SG&A	34	48	14	30	29	(1)	48	43	(5)	25	30	5	137	150	13
Income Before Tax	$45	$17	$28	$28	$15	$13	$82	$78	$4	$(16)	$20	$36	$139	$130	$9

*Positive numbers in the variance column indicate favorable variances.

DISAGGREGATING PROFIT VARIANCES BY PROFIT DRIVER

A variance analysis by responsibility center is not the final answer, however. The responsibility center variance reports shown in Table 12.3 are still arrayed by independent line item. Managers need to disaggregate the profit variances in each profit center according to the *drivers* of profit. For each profit driver identified, these analyses provide a quantification of the effect on profits of having the driver deviate from target.

As a first step in this type of analysis, it is logical to isolate the *revenue* effects on profits from the *cost* effects on profits. Then the analysis can proceed to disaggregate the factors that caused revenues to deviate from target. The target can include erroneous assumptions about the size of the overall market, prices, or the mix of items sold (for example, high-margin vs. low-margin sales). When analyzing cost variances, manufacturing costs that are associated with inventories that are held across accounting periods should be analyzed separately from the categories of costs that are expensed during the period. Then the cost variances should be disaggregated into more specific categories that are analyzed into variances caused by (sales or production) volume, efficiency, and price effects. This type of variance analysis is illustrated diagrammatically in Figure 12.2.

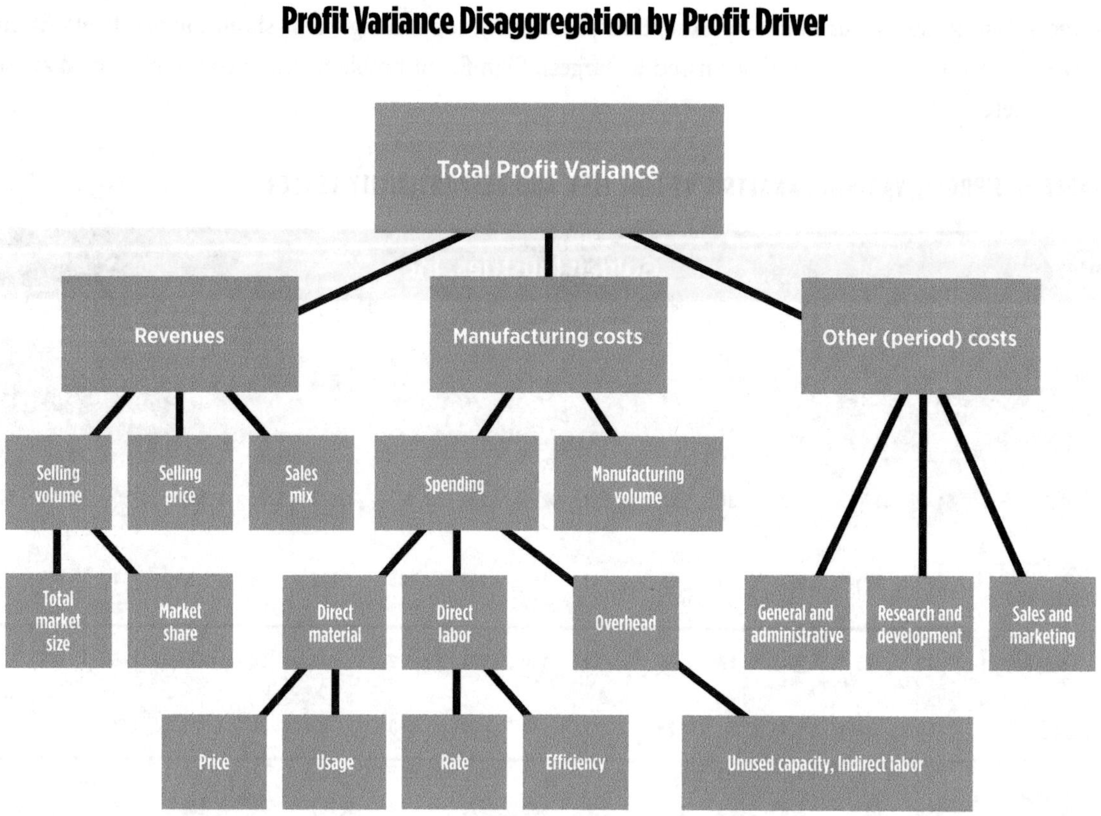

FIGURE 12.2 THE FIRST STEP IN THE DISAGGREGATION PROCESS IS TO SEPARATE REVENUE DRIVERS FROM COST DRIVERS IN ORDER TO ASSESS THE IMPACT EACH HAS ON PROFITABILITY.

Let us illustrate this profit variance analysis process with a numerical example. Suppose a corporate manager or analyst in Golden Industries wanted to understand why, in the just-concluded year, Division D reported a loss of $16 million, when it was budgeted to show a $20 million profit. (These are the same numbers as shown in Table 12.3.)

To illustrate a first cut at a more meaningful profit-driver variance analysis, let us analyze performance in terms of four factors: sales in units, price per unit, cost of goods sold (which in this case equals manufacturing costs for the period because there is no inventory change), and SG&A. To make the profit-driver analysis more transparent, however, we will divide the manufacturing costs and SG&A costs into their variable and fixed components.

In this simple example, we will assume that managers have previously prepared a budget based on a target for each of these profit drivers, and this budget is used as the performance standard. During the performance period, the "do" phase of the management process, the managers made a number of decisions, and, inevitably, things did not turn out exactly as expected. The actual profits earned result from the real outcome of each of these factors during the performance evaluation period.

The conceptual process that we will use to organize our analysis of the effect on the profit of each of these six factors is illustrated in Figure 12.3. The first step involves changing one profit driver from the value assumed in the performance target (here, the budget) to its actual value. We leave all of the other factors constant and see what the effect is on profits. That is the profit variance caused by the fact that that profit driver deviated from its budgeted amount. Then we repeat this step with the second profit driver; then the third, and so on. The sum of the variances calculated will equal the total profit variance between the budget and the actual results. So that the analysis does not become too complicated, we will assume that Division D produces and sells only one (type of) product. By doing so, we avoid the necessity of considering sales mix issues.

Profit Driver—Profit Variance Analysis: Conceptual Framework

		Analysis					
Factors that affect profit:	**Budget**	**1**	**2**	**3**	**4**	**5**	**Actual**
Sales in units (U)	U_b	U_a	U_a	U_a	U_a	U_a	U_a
Price per unit (P)	P_b	P_b	P_a	P_a	P_a	P_a	P_a
Manufacturing costs—variable per unit (MV)	MV_b	MV_b	MV_b	MV_a	MV_a	MV_a	MV_a
– fixed (MF)	MF_b	MF_b	MF_b	MF_b	MF_a	MF_a	MF_a
SG&A costs—variable per unit (SV)	SV_b	SV_b	SV_b	SV_b	SV_b	SV_a	SV_a
– fixed (SF)	SF_b	SF_b	SF_b	SF_b	SF_b	SF_b	SF_a
	V_1	V_2	V_3	V_4	V_5	V_6	

Key: $_b$ indicates budgeted value.
$_a$ indicates actual value.

Variance labels:

V_1 = sales unit (or volume) variance
V_2 = sales price variance
V_3 = variable manufacturing cost variance
V_4 = fixed manufacturing cost variance
V_5 = variable SG&A cost variance
V_6 = fixed SG&A cost variance

FIGURE 12.3 BY CHANGING ONE PROFIT DRIVER FROM ITS PROJECTED TO ITS ACTUAL VALUE AND MAKING NO OTHER CHANGES, WE CAN ASSESS THE IMPACT OF THAT CHANGE ON PROFIT (OR LOSS).

The data needed for this profit variance analysis is shown in Table 12.4. How could this additional information be used in a profit variance analysis? Following the conceptual scheme outlined in Figure 12.3, the corporate managers would do their analysis in six steps (see Table 12.5). In what is traditionally (but arbitrarily) the first analysis, change the number of units sold (and in this case produced) from the budgeted amount to the actual amount. Leave all the other factors at their budgeted amounts. This adjusted budget, shown as analysis #1 in Figure 12.3, is often referred to as a **flexible budget,** *one where variable costs have been adjusted for actual sales volume, without any activity forecasting variance.*[3] The key question in calculating a flexible budget is: If at the time we prepared the budget we had known exactly how many units we would sell during the period, what would our budget have looked like? The flexible budget is contrasted with the original budget, sometimes called a **static budget,** *one prepared before the performance period; based on activity volume projections; not adjusted for the impact of actual sales volume; potentially includes a forecasting variance.*

TABLE 12.4 PROFIT DRIVER–PROFIT VARIANCE ANALYSIS (WITH INFORMATION NEEDED FOR PROFIT-DRIVER PROFIT VARIANCE ANALYSIS)

Golden Industries, Inc.		
Division D		
	Budget	Actual
Sales		
Sales in units	2 million	1.545 million
Avg. price per unit	$100	$90.60
Cost of goods sold		
No change in inventory levels. Actual sales volume = actual production volume		
Variable manufacturing costs per unit of production	$.0675	$.0757
Fixed manufacturing costs (million)	$15.0	$14.0
SG&A		
Variable SG&A costs per million units sold	$10.0	$11.0
Fixed SG&A costs (million)	$10.0	$12.0

Since the only difference between the original budget and the flexible budget is in the sales volume, the difference between the bottom line in the original budget and the bottom line in the flexible budget is the *sales volume variance.* Here, the sales volume variance is $10.2 million unfavorable, as is shown in Table 12.5. This sales volume variance is caused by a sales forecasting error. That is, the sales forecast included in the original budget did not turn out to be totally accurate.

3 If units sold does not equal units produced, two of the sets of figures in the adjustment columns can properly be labeled flexible budgets. One is a *sales volume-driven flexible budget,* which is useful for evaluating the extent to which a sales and marketing department controlled its costs effectively. The other is a *production volume-driven flexible budget,* which is useful for evaluating the extent to which a sales and marketing department controlled its costs effectively.

TABLE 12.5 PROFIT DRIVER–PROFIT VARIANCE ANALYSIS

Golden Industries, Inc.							
Division D							
		— Analysis —					
$ millions	Budget	1	2	3	4	5	Actual
Sales	200.0[4]	154.5[5]	140.0[6]	140.0	140.0	140.0	140.0
Cost of goods sold	150.0[7]	119.3[8]	119.3	132.0[9]	131.0[10]	131.0	131.0
Gross margin	50.0	35.2	20.7	8.0	9.0	9.0	9.0
SG&A	30.0[11]	25.4[12]	25.4	25.4	25.4	27.0[13]	25.0[14]
Net profit before tax	20.0	9.8	(4.7)	(17.4)	(16.4)	(18.0)	(16.0)

Sales volume var.	Sales price var.	Variable mfg. cost var.	Fixed mfg. cost var.	Variable SG&A cost var.	Fixed SG&A
10.2U	**14.5U**	**12.7U**	**1.0F**	**1.6U**	**2.0F**

Total variance = 36.0 Unfavorable

Key: F = favorable variance
U = unfavorable variance

Order of analysis:

Analysis #1: Adjust sales in units from budget to actual
Analysis #2: Adjust sales price from budget to actual
Analysis #3: Adjust variable manufacturing costs from budget to actual
Analysis #4: Adjust fixed manufacturing costs from budget to actual
Analysis #5: Adjust variable SG&A costs from budget to actual
Analysis #6: Adjust fixed SG&A costs from budget to actual

In many situations, general managers and sales/marketing managers are held accountable for the sales volume variance, or some elements of it. (This variance will be disaggregated further below.) However, since most functional managers (for example, production managers) are not involved in the preparation of the *sales* forecast, for them this variance is considered uncontrollable and, hence, something for which they should not be held accountable. Note that this variance has now been isolated in the analysis. The rest of the analysis proceeds as if there was no sales forecasting error and, hence, no sales volume variance.

---

4 2 million units x $100/unit
5 1.545 million units x $100/unit
6 1.545 million units x $90.60/unit
7 2 million units x $.0675 + 15 million
8 1.545 million units x $.0675 +$15 million
9 1.545 million units x $.0757 +$15 million
10 1.545 million units x $.0757 + $14 million
11 2 million units x $10/million units + $10 million
12 1.545 million units x $10/million units + $10 million
13 1.545 million units x $11/million units + $10 million
14 1.545 million units x $11/million units + $8 million

The information given in Table 12.4 can be used to disaggregate the total variance further. Perform analysis #2 as shown in Figure 12.3. In other words, change the sales price from its budgeted amount to the actual average price of products sold during the period. Leave all of the other factors unchanged; for example, leave the sales units at their actual amount and all of the other factors at their budgeted values. As in all variance analysis, therefore, we are changing just one variable at a time so we can isolate its impact on reported results.

The only difference between analyses #1 and #2 is caused by the difference between the sales price assumption included in the original budget and the prices actually realized. This variance is called the **sales price variance,** *the difference between actual price and budgeted price on reported sales*. This must be true because the flexible budget uses actual sales volumes, so any profit differences can only be caused by differences in the sales price. Thus, this variance is $140 million minus $154.5 million equals $14.5 million unfavorable. This variance can also be calculated by formula. It is:

Sales price variance = actual units sold x (actual sales price - budgeted sales price)
= 1.545 million x ($90.60 – $100.00)
= $14.5 million unfavorable

The third step in the analysis (analysis #3) involves the changing of the variable manufacturing costs from the budgeted to actual amounts, leaving all other factors alone. This yields a **variable manufacturing cost variance**—*the difference between actual and planned variable cost*—of $12.7 million unfavorable. Continue this approach of changing one variable at a time to go through the analyses of the profit effects of each of the three other factors in the profitability equation, namely the fixed *manufacturing cost variance*, the *variable SG&A cost variance*, and the *fixed SG&A cost variance*. The sum of all six variances calculated explains the total division profit variance of $36 million unfavorable.

Does the order in which the analyses are done matter? The answer is: yes and no. The variance numbers *will* change depending on the order in which the factors are adjusted from budget to actual. This is because of the placement of the so-called joint variances, the effects of all of the factors deviating from their budgeted amounts at the same time. Including the joint variances with one factor emphasized rather than another is arbitrary. Importantly, however, the *sign* on each of the variances will not change depending on the ordering of the inclusion of the factors in the analysis. If the actual sales price is below the target, the sales price variance will always be unfavorable, regardless of when this factor is introduced into the analysis.

If they have more information available, managers can further disaggregate the variances shown in Table 12.5. For example, with the information shown in Table 12.6, managers can also disaggregate the sales volume variance into an **industry volume variance,** *the difference between actual and budgeted industry volume*, and a market share variance, if they wish to do so. If industry volume is the first factor considered, the industry volume variance is calculated as follows:

the difference x budgeted market share x budgeted profit per unit (for example, leaving all other factors at their budgeted values), which is: (15 million – 20 million) x 10% x 22.50 = $11.25 million unfavorable

The **market share variance,** *the difference between actual and budgeted market share*, is:

actual industry volume x the difference between the actual and budgeted market share x budgeted profit per unit, which is: (10.3% – 10%) x 15 million x 22.50 = $1.0125 million favorable

TABLE 12.6 FACTORS AFFECTING PERFORMANCE XYZ DIVISION

(additional information)	Budget	Actual
Industry volume (million)	20	15
Market share	10%	10.3%

This disaggregation of the sales volume variance can be useful because most general managers are held accountable for the profit effects of changes in market share, both positive and negative. Unless these managers have the authority to allocate resources from one industry to another, which is generally true only for general managers of whole corporations or large, diversified investment centers, they are not held accountable for the effects of increases and decreases in total industry volume. Eliminating the effects of this uncontrollable factor from the sales volume variance eliminates some "noise" in the measurement of controllable performance and provides better information for evaluating the managers' performances.

At this point in the analysis, the total original profit variance of $36 million unfavorable can be explained as follows:

	($ millions)
Industry volume variance	$(11.2)
Market share variance	1.0
Sales volume variance	$(10.2)
Selling price variance	(14.5)
Manufacturing cost variances	(11.7)
SG&A expense variances	0.4
Total profit shortfall	(36.0)

(Positive signs, those without parentheses, indicate favorable variances. Negative signs, shown with parentheses, indicate unfavorable variances.)

If the information is available, the manufacturing and SG&A cost variances can also be disaggregated using similar techniques, as we saw earlier in this book. Managers can conceivably calculate a price and usage (efficiency) variance for each variable cost line item and a spending variance for each fixed cost line item. If production volumes did not exactly equal sales volumes, thereby causing a change in inventory levels, then a volume variance can also be calculated.

Calculating accounting return variances for investment centers is identical conceptually to the method used for calculating profit variances. The only difference is that the total variance will be explained in units of return—for example, ROI, return on net assets (RONA), return on equity (ROE)—rather than in units of profit (such as dollars). Just add additional analyses (columns in Figure 12.3) that sequentially adjust the various categories of investment (or assets or equity) from their budgeted amounts to their actual amounts, and note the effect on returns. In other words, change one variable at a time to isolate the impact of price and volume differences on profitability and returns.

Managers can disaggregate their variances as far as their information allows. For example, if the Printed Circuit Board Division had multiple products and a good cost accounting system that traced costs effectively down to the product level, the managers could replicate this type of analysis for each product line and each product. They might find, for example, that:

- Some product lines sold quite well, and the sales shortfall is limited to one or a few specific areas.
- The cost of goods sold per unit increased only for certain products. In such cases, the gross margin and profits generated might have decreased even in areas where sales increased.

In actual practice, variance analyses can become very complex. A large corporation might include hundreds of profit centers at five different organization levels; they might sell thousands of products in each of 150 different countries (and currencies); they might produce those products in scores of plants located around the world, and each with a different cost accounting system. But the conceptual process of performing a variance analysis is the same in every setting. The causes of the variances just need to be isolated one at a time to untangle the complex web of performance variances.

LOOKING BACK ➤ An Example of a Complex Variance Analysis

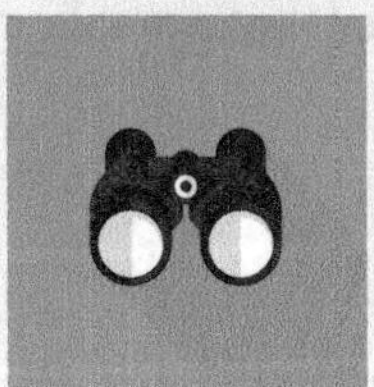

Before its merger with Phillips Petroleum Co., Conoco, the large oil producer and retailer, regularly made publicly available a corporate profit variance analysis. An example showing and explaining the factors that affected performance in the second quarter of 2002 using the second quarter of 2001 as the comparison standard is presented in Figure ITN. This analysis broke the variance down by the company's upstream (exploration and production) and downstream (retailing) activities, geographical locations, and other (emerging businesses, corporate administrative expenses, currency gains and losses). While this variance analysis looked complex and, indeed, is fully understandable only by people with considerable industry experience, Conoco managers actually did a lot of summarization of the data, and this analysis only told a partial story.

CONOCO EARNINGS VARIANCE ANALYSIS 2002Q2 vs. 2001Q2

	Earnings before special items			
	2002Q2	2001Q2	Variance	Variance
SEGMENT	($mm)	($mm)	($mm)	(%)
United States	57	249	(192)	-77%
International	216	244	(28)	-11%
Total Upstream	273	493	(220)	-45%
United States	(16)	221	(237)	-107%
International	47	6	41	683%
Total Downstream	31	227	(196)	-86%
Emerging Businesses	(30)	(17)	(13)	-76%
Corporate	(32)	(31)	(1)	-3%
Non-operating	(101)	(66)	(35)	-53%
TOTAL CONOCO	141	606	(465)	-77%

UPSTREAM	2002Q2	2001Q2	Variance	Dollar Variance ($mm)	Remarks
Important variances this Quarter				$(220)	Total variance
Realized crude oil prices [$/bbl] (including equity companies, excluding syncrude):					
United States	$22.37	$24.21	$(1.84)		Corresponds to a 6% decline in WTI.
International	$22.46	$23.74	$(1.28)		Corresponds to a 8% decline in Brent, and a 26% increase in Maya
Worldwide	$22.45	$23.81	$(1.36)	$(12)	Includes about $(2)MM in 2002Q2 of production-related hedge gains.
Realized natural gas prices [$/mcf] (including equity companies):					
United States	$3.18	$4.47	$(1.29)		Corresponding to a 30% decline in NYMEX.
International	$2.68	$3.33	$(0.65)		
Worldwide	$2.83	$3.89	$(1.06)	$(109)	Includes about $5MM in 2002Q2 of production-related hedge gains.
Realized NGL prices [$/bbl]	$14.46	$18.22	$(3.76)	$(5)	
Crude oil volume changes [000b/d] (including equity companies, excluding Syncrude):					
United States	36	53	(17)		Almost all U.S. production declines are associated with dispositions for the 2001 debt reduction plan.

UPSTREAM	2002Q2	2001Q2	Variance	Dollar Variance ($mm)	Remarks
International	357	310	47		Increases in Canada, Venezuela, Norway, and Indonesia, partially offset by declines in the U.K. and Russia.
Worldwide	393	363	30	$6	
Natural gas volume changes [mmcf/d] (including equity companies):					
United States	717	831	(114)		Primarily due to dispositions for the 2001 debt reduction plan and reduced Lobo rig count.
International	1,609	885	724		Increases in Canada, Norway, Netherlands, and Indonesia offset by declines in the U.K.
Worldwide	2,326	1,716	610	$71	
NGL volumes [000b/d]	35	21	14	$9	Associated with Gulf Canada acquisition in July 2001.
Timing of lifts				$11	Additional U.K. lifts.
Production overhead and operating costs (Excludes Can. Syncrude)				($45)	Additional costs associated with Gulf Canada acquisition
DD&A (excludes Can. Syncrude)				($58)	Additional DD&A associated with Gulf Canada acquisition.
Exploration expense				($27)	Primarily due to Mackenzi Delta and Canada foothills seismic programs, and increased Russia and Indonesia activity.
CG&P (U.S. only)				($42)	Mainly due to higher natural gas and NGL prices, LIFO gains, and transportation settlement in 2001 Q2.
Equity companies				$24	Addition of Canada Petrovera with Gulf Canada, plus Russia Polar Lights and Venezuela Petrozuata price improvements.
Syria				($21)	Project completed 2001.
Syncrude				$9	Associated with Gulf Canada acquisition.
Hedging mark-to-market associated with Gulf Canada acquisition				($28)	Mark-to-market portion of hedge; the remainder is in price. This reflects a 2002Q2 loss of $4.5MM and a gain of $23.9MM in 2001Q2.
Mark-to-market on 2001 put options				$9	Crude puts in 2001Q2 had a cost of $9MM as prices rose.
U.K. gas contracts				($14)	Mostly from application of FAS133 to certain U.K. gas contracts.
All other				$2	

DOWNSTREAM	2002Q2	2001Q2	Variance	Dollar Variance ($mm)	Remarks*
Important variances this Quarter				$(196)	Total variance
U.S. Gulf Coast Light Oil Spread [$/bbl]	$3.71	$6.90	$(3.19)		
WTI/Maya Differential [$/bbl]	$4.29	$10.54	$(6.25)		
WTI/LLB Differential [$/bbl]	$5.88	$10.49	$(4.61)		
Total U.S.				$(152)	
Brent Cracking Margin [$/bbl]	$0.08	$2.10	$(2.02)		
N.W. Europe Light Oil Resid Spread [$/MT]	$87	$142	$(55)		
Singapore 3-2-1 Spread [$/bbl]	$3.88	$5.26	$(1.38)		
Total International				$(21)	
Co-product margins				$5	Due to a decrease in WTI prices by 6%.
Inland advantage (the difference between Gulf Coast and inland prices)				$(58)	Inland differentials down 70% vs. 2001Q2.
Marketing margins				$(7)	Impaired U.S. wholesale margins.
Crude market factors				$(7)	Includes the impact of backwardation and contago.
Volume changes (including yield and product mix):				$26	Humber incident occurred in early 2001Q2.
Overhead and operating costs				$6	Primarily lower energy costs.
Tax impacts				$12	Primarily recovery of deferred tax credit against capital gain on upstream disposition
All other				$-	

EMERGING BUSINESSES/CORPORATE/NON-OPERATING	Dollar Variance ($mm)	Remarks
Important variances this Quarter	($49)	Total variance
Emerging Businesses	($13)	Construction (which is being expensed) of the GTL plant.
Corporate administrative costs	($1)	A variety of small increases.
Exchange gains and losses	($35)	Primarily Norway
All other	$-	

FIGURE ITN

In the age of computers, the computational costs of such an analysis do not provide any limitations. If managers have a performance model in a computer spreadsheet program, they can easily perform a variance analysis by changing one factor in the model at a time from standard to actual. For example, they could ask, "What would performance have been if we had sold as many units as we had planned to sell, everything else being equal?" The answer to that question would yield a sales volume variance. This *type of variance analysis used in the planning process, which questions the impact a specific change would have on various aspects of the business* is known as a **what-if analysis**. In comparing actuals with standards, it is a variance analysis.

When should the disaggregation of variances be stopped? Managers should stop their analysis when they run out of useful, accurate information. They can analyze variances only down to the lowest level of responsibility center, geographical region, or product category for which data is traced effectively.

Managers should also stop their analysis when the factors they are attempting to analyze are so interdependent that trying to isolate the effects of each factor independently is not meaningful. For example, it might not always make sense to disaggregate a material spending variance into a material price variance and a material usage variance. The two profit drivers may be highly interdependent. A favorable price variance and a negative usage variance might both result from a decision to purchase and use cheaper but inferior quality materials. Similarly, it may not always make sense to calculate a sales (unit) volume variance and a sales price variance. If customers are at all price-sensitive, raising prices often leads to a favorable sales price variance at the same time it is causing an unfavorable sales volume variance. If the causal factors are highly interdependent, then it does not make sense to attribute separate profit impacts to each of them.

The calculation of the variances is only the first step in completing an evaluation of subunit performance, however. Managers must interpret the variances. Even these focused intricate variance analyses do *not* explain *why* the factors deviated from their standards or *what should be done* to minimize unfavorable variances or to take better advantage of favorable variances in the future. Managers have to decide if and how to use the information stemming from the variance analyses.

Perhaps the only general rule that managers should follow is that they should pay particular attention to the factors that are strategically critical. For example, a business following a "harvest" strategy, which emphasizes production efficiency and cash flow, should be trying to be a cost leader. Its managers probably should not be making long-term investments and sacrificing current gross margins in order to build market share. Conversely, a business following a "build" strategy should be spending its full marketing budget and increasing market share, perhaps even at the expense of current margin levels. With an effective variance analysis, the effects of these behaviors, both good and bad, should be apparent in the pattern of performance variances.

IN CONTEXT ➤ Prestige Auto—Restructuring to Gain Greater Control

Once the team decided how it would handle transfers of work between profit centers, it returned to the challenge of increasing sales volume by 20% without losing sight of profitability. The company had to turn around its negative RI and low ROI by making sure every sale was profitable. Having separated the company into three specific divisions, Jack was considering splitting used car sales from new car sales. It seemed important since the sales goals were based on selling the new model. This was the focus of the next meeting.

"Good to see all of you looking so perky today," said Jack. "I want to continue our discussion and float an idea I'd like you to consider. We've made progress on changing our structure so we can focus on holding managers accountable for the things they can control. I'm wondering if we shouldn't go one step further and split our sales department into new cars and used cars. They're very different markets with very different drivers. What do you think?"

"I'm not sure, Jack. We currently have one sales force that sells both new and used cars. If we're going to set up separate divisions, then I'm going to need to assign salespeople to one or the other. That could leave us stretched pretty thin at times. I don't think we want to hire a lot of new people; that would hurt profits," Judy responded.

"I think the salespeople could sell both, Judy, and still evaluate the profitability of each type of car sale separately. We pay commissions, which are variable costs, and the salespeople receive only a small base salary, which we can handle as a fixed cost in our analyses. I think they're very different types of businesses, and, if we're going to understand how to reach our new sales goals, we have to separate out the two biggest factors driving profits," replied Jack.

"In the repairs area, it would be useful to separate the two because the work we do on used cars is very different from the cleaning and prep we do on new cars. I need my best technicians to handle the used cars, but I can have one of the younger guys handle new car prep. This would change the costs charged to Acquisitions significantly," pitched in Tony.

"Acquisitions is already broken into new and used cars because I need the sales staff to have expertise in one area or the other in order to find the best buying options, ones that will increase the potential for profit. Acquisitions would have no problem supporting the split," added Bruce.

"I guess we can make this work," said Alice. "I'll have to develop some new variances, but I see the logic behind separating the two. It would give us a better idea of where the profits are coming from. With our new transfer price program and by separating new and used cars, we should be able to get a better handle on where things are going right and where they're going wrong."

"Let's consider it a done deal, then," noted Jack. "Can Bruce and Judy work together this week and separate out the sales and profit goals for the two types of sales? Then we can tailor the reports we need to convince the major suppliers to provide us with more cars."

"Sounds good, Jack," they all responded in unison. They all agreed to work out the kinks of the new structure and have adjusted sales goals ready the following week.

"Great! Thank you all for coming on board with the idea. If we keep at it, we'll gain much better control over profits and sales, making it easier to plan the future and keep the present on track to meet those plans," said Jack, ending the meeting on a high note.

Relative Performance Evaluations

OBJECTIVE 4

Put the concept of relative performance evaluations into plain English and explain how they can be used as a substitute for some types of variance analyses.

A second alternative for evaluating the performance of specific responsibility centers and their managers is with **relative performance evaluations,** *assessments of a unit's outcome against the performance of like units, which become the performance standard*. When they use relative performance evaluations, managers evaluate their subunits as *compared to each other*, or compared to benchmarks derived from the performances of other like units facing the same environmental circumstances, rather than as compared to a budget target. These standards control for the effects, positive and negative, of many factors that influence all of the subunits being compared.

Professors who grade "on a curve" are using relative performance evaluations. In their classes, students are not judged based on an absolute scale (for example, a 90 is an A and an 80 is a B). Instead, students are judged on their performance as compared to others in their class: those who completed the same set of assignments and faced the same exams and projects. The "best" students get As, regardless of their absolute scores on exams and projects. For example, an absolute overall score of 80, or perhaps even 50, points out of a maximum score of 100 might earn a student an A. One advantage of relative performance evaluations is that it filters out the uncontrollable effects in the environment. In the students' situation, it does not matter how difficult the final exam was. In a managerial situation, it does not matter how deep the recession was. The managers who are evaluated as best are those that performed the best in the conditions that they, and all others like them, faced.

Relative performance evaluations provide at least a partial substitute for variance analyses. For example, managers of a national chain of travel agencies could perform a variance analysis to isolate and remove the nationwide effect of the terrorist activities of September 11, 2001, on the profit performance of each of their outlets. Equivalently, evaluating the performances of the individual agencies relative to each other would filter out effects of this uncontrollable factor that is common to all of the outlets. It would control for the national effects of the terrorist activities just as effectively as would the calculation and elimination of an unfavorable "terrorist variance."

Where relative performance evaluations are used, no static budget targets need be set for performance evaluation purposes. (One might still be useful for motivational purposes.) The managers of the travel agencies can be told merely that their performance will be evaluated in comparison with that of other like units. This performance target is flexible and dynamic.

A relative performance evaluation system can be harmful, however, if it is desirable for managers to cooperate with each other by, for example, sharing good ideas for performance improvements. Since managers' performance evaluations are based on comparisons with other managers' performances, they have no incentives to make the other managers look better because it will harm their own performance evaluations.

The major constraint in using relative performance evaluations, however, is feasibility. It is rare that multiple operating units, even seemingly like units, face exactly the same operating conditions. For example, comparing McDonald's locations with one another might lead to flawed conclusions if some of the locations being compared are situated right off of a superhighway in an affluent community and others are situated in an older urban area undergoing construction. In such cases, the use of a relative performance evaluation would have to be based on a finer partitioning of units, perhaps based on virtually identical transportation and demographic characteristics, so that only like units are compared.

Subjective Performance Evaluations

OBJECTIVE 5
Explain why managers sometimes evaluate performance subjectively, rather than basing evaluations solely on objective performance measures.

Sometimes managers do not perform elaborate, formal, objective variance analyses, such as would be done with formal variance analyses or relative performance evaluations. Instead, they perform a **subjective performance evaluation,** *an informal assessment that relies exclusively, or heavily, on the personal judgment of the evaluator*. Some of these evaluations are totally subjective, based on the "feel" or intuition of the evaluator; others are just partially subjective.

A partially subjective performance evaluation might involve an informal variance analysis, rather than the formal, detailed analysis illustrated previously. Evaluators might base their evaluations on the formal actuals vs. budget comparisons, but only after an additional "back of the envelope" variance analysis to eliminate the effect of one or more factors deemed uncontrollable. For example, suppose an evaluator had ordered the division manager to make a significant research and development investment during the year, and this investment had not been factored into the budget for the year. This R&D expenditure would have to be expensed. It might, without an adjustment, cause the division not to achieve its annual budget profit target. The evaluator could solve this problem by subjectively "eliminating" the effect of this investment from the performance results. This elimination would not be apparent in the corporation's formal performance reports, but the subjective elimination would lead to the same end.

Another common use of subjectivity in performance evaluations involves evaluators considering objective comparisons of measured performance vs. targets, but also considering some other aspects of performance that are not as easy to measure, such as employee morale, employee development, teamwork, or social responsibility. When considering more than one performance indicator, the evaluators then have to weigh the importance of each of the multiple indicators in order to come to a conclusion about overall performance. This weighting is often done subjectively.

In extreme cases, the evaluators do not base their subjective evaluations heavily on any objective performance measure vs. target comparisons. For example, suppose in evaluating the manager of Division D, Golden Industries' COO concluded, for whatever reason, that the performance measures did not reflect the effectiveness of the management team or, equivalently, that the original budget was not a good performance standard. (Without good performance measures *and* a good evaluation standard, variances will not be meaningful.) Accounting measures of performance are notoriously inadequate in start-up businesses, for example. These young businesses show huge accounting losses because they are making (presumably value-creating) investments that will pay off in later accounting measurement periods.

Division D, however, appears to be a more mature entity, so, in this case, we have to assume that something else, something large and unforeseen had occurred—perhaps a hurricane damaged the factory so that the division was unable to satisfy customer demand for its products. In such a case, the COO might ignore the actual results vs. budget comparison. He might base his evaluation of the division manager for the year solely on his judgment as to how effectively the division recovered from the disaster.

These totally subjective judgments can work for or against the manager being evaluated. For example, sometimes in divisions that achieve all of their objective targets (such as sales, profits, and returns), managers are not evaluated favorably because they failed in other important performance areas about which the evaluator has knowledge. Perhaps the division failed to participate effectively in a cross-division initiative that the evaluator considered important.

Performance evaluations with subjective elements have some significant advantages. Importantly, they allow evaluators to adjust for limitations in the performance measures and targets. In addition, the vagueness of the evaluation standards makes it more difficult for the subordinates to play games. As has been discussed in earlier chapters, game playing involves taking actions that make the subordinate look good but that are not in the best interest of the corporation. Examples include padding budgets, smoothing income, and taking actions to keep assets off of the balance sheet (for example, by leasing instead of purchasing the asset or by passing the debt onto off-balance-sheet partnerships and joint ventures).

However, subjective evaluations are not a panacea; they also have some significant disadvantages. One is that the vagueness of the performance targets can hinder motivation. Most people like to know how their performance will be evaluated, and they like a specific target for which to strive. They do not respond well if evaluators tell them something like, "Do your best; I'll judge your performance after the period is over."

Second, allowing subjectivity in performance evaluations can add personal biases to the evaluation process. One is a **favoritism bias,** *a subjective evaluation resulting in preferential treatment or a review being given to an employee on the basis of personal affinity rather than actual performance*. Another is a **hindsight bias**, *a subjective evaluation based on knowledge gained after the fact and/or that was not available to the person being evaluated*.

Third, allowing subjectivity in performance evaluations can increase costs to the organization. These costs are due to the need to add bureaucratic rules and procedures, such as reviewing of performance evaluations at multiple organization levels, to protect against the incidence and effects of the risks of the evaluation biases.

And fourth, subjective evaluations usually result in ambiguous, or even no, feedback to those whose performances are being evaluated. Sometimes evaluators who are allowed to add their judgments to the evaluation process base their conclusions on vague feelings about the performance that was achieved in the specific situation. They might not really know what factors they took into consideration in reaching their overall judgment about performance. When this happens, they cannot provide much performance-related feedback to subordinates. This can hinder organizational learning.

Designing an Incentive Program

To motivate employees to do what the organization wants them to do, performance evaluations should be linked to one or more things that the employees like or dislike. These are called **incentives, or rewards,** *motivational tools intended to enhance employee performance, inspire greater effort, increase productivity, and so on*. There are many possible incentives, including cash, stock options, raises, promotions, recognition, and autonomy. **Disincentives, or punishments,** *are motivational tools used to induce employees to change their poor performances*. Examples are criticism, public embarrassment, and failure to give rewards (such as raises, promotions) that the others are getting.

Since the primary purpose of incentive systems is to motivate employees, the power of incentives is best understood by analyzing them in terms of a model of motivation. Here is one common motivational model, called expectancy theory, which has been tested in many settings. The formula for motivation is expressed as follows:

$$M = IV_G + P_1 \left(IV_P + \sum_{i=1}^{n} P_2 EV_i\right)$$

where:

M = motivation

IV_G = (intrinsic) value associated with goal-directed behavior. (People like to have a purpose in life.)

IV_P = (intrinsic) value associated with successful performance. (People who achieve goals feel good about themselves.)

EV_i = (extrinsic) value associated with the ith reward contingent on goal accomplishment. (People prefer more rewards to less, and they value some rewards more than others.)

P_1 = expectancy that the individual's behavior will accomplish the goal. (If the employee performs effectively, is it more likely that the goals will be accomplished?)

P_2 = expectancy that achievement of the goal will lead to the reward. (If the goal is achieved, will the company provide the reward?)

This model allows us to analyze many incentive system design choices. We will use the motivation formula described above to analyze four important questions. First, should performance be rewarded based on individual performance, group (like division, corporate) performance, or both? Second, what should be the shape of the function linking the rewards and performance measures? Third, how much incentive is enough? And fourth, what form(s) of incentives should be provided?

PERFORMANCE REWARDS: INDIVIDUAL VS. GROUP PERFORMANCE VS. A COMBINATION

Many companies provide significant incentive payments to employees based on group or shared performance. These group rewards come in many forms. Some companies provide stock options to a broad class of employees, and these options increase in value depending on the corporation's overall performance. Some companies offer even lower-level managers all or a portion of bonus payments based on division or corporate performance. Profit-sharing plans are an extreme example of this form of bonus. Also common are bonus plans that provide bonuses to lower-level managers, such as a division-level production manager, based as follows:

Division performance	40%
Corporate performance	40%
Individual performance	20%

And some companies offer production employees "gain-sharing" rewards, based on improved factory performance.

Are these group rewards effective? The expectancy theory formula suggests that they usually do *not* provide good incentives. The problem is in the P1 term. It can be zero, or near zero, when the size of the group is larger than just a few employees. To illustrate, consider the example of the division-level production manager whose incentive plan is described above. This manager works in one division of a corporation with 100 divisions. If that production manager works exceptionally hard, say 100 hours per week in a given year, and has a very productive year, will those efforts have a material effect on the results of the overall corporation? Probably not. Corporate performance is often not controllable from the perspective of this individual manager. The second term of the expectancy theory motivational formula will be essentially zero. The 40% of the rewards that are based on corporate performance will have no effect on this manager's motivation.

Why do companies provide rewards based on group performance? These rewards can have a positive cultural effect. That is, they provide a wealth-sharing function by giving employees a feeling that they are all fighting the same battles. As a consequence, they may monitor each other's behaviors. They provide a smoothing function, as the company's compensation expense and required cash outflows are lower in periods when its profits and, probably, cash flows, are lower. And group rewards are popular where managers do not have well-developed measurement systems, systems that can track performance down to the individual level of performance. These managers believe that they must provide incentives for something, so they base their incentives on what they can measure—corporate performance.

DETERMINING THE SHAPE OF THE FUNCTION LINKING REWARDS AND PERFORMANCE MEASURES

Designing the shape of the performance/reward function in an incentive plan requires many choices, as is shown in the typical bonus plan function illustrated in Figure 12.4. The performance measure on which the rewards are based is shown on the *x* axis. The size of the incentive, which is paid in cash, is shown on the *y* axis. Many companies provide no extra reward—only base salary—for performance below some threshold level of performance. For financial measures, this might be the budgeted level of performance. They do not want to reward performance they consider mediocre.

Similarly, many companies cap their incentive awards—provide no extra incentives—for results above a level of performance considered outstanding. Their managers are worried that if actual performance was that high, it must have been because the target level was not set appropriately, or perhaps the manager benefited from a "bluebird," a stroke of good luck that was uncontrollable.

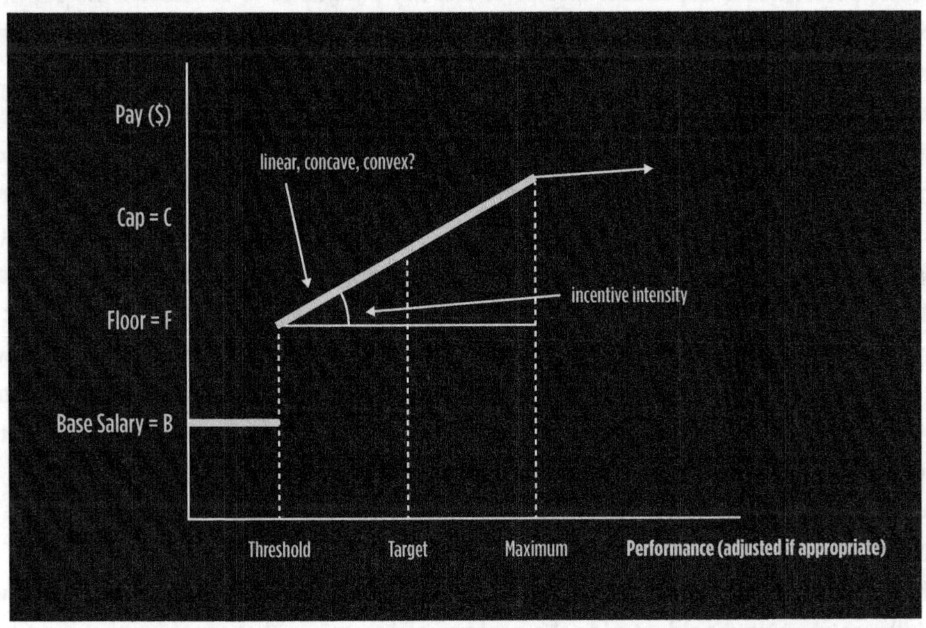

FIGURE 12.4 A TYPICAL PAY-PERFORMANCE FUNCTION

Should companies use these upper and lower limits on the performance/reward function? The danger of using them can clearly be seen by using expectancy theory to consider the implications. Below the threshold and above the outstanding performance level, EV is zero. Therefore, in these ranges, extrinsic motivation is also zero. Further, these functional constraints will cause managers to be prone to game playing. If their entity's performance is below the threshold, they will either be motivated to boost performance in the current period in order to earn a bonus or to "take a bath," getting all of the bad news out of the way in the current performance period, thus making it easier to earn a bonus in the subsequent period. Similarly, if their entity's performance is above the outstanding performance level, they will be motivated to "save" some of that good performance for a subsequent period in which they will be rewarded for it. In these ways, these constraints on the performance-reward function are dangerous.

What is likely to happen in the range of performance for which rewards are provided? It is traditional for companies to define a linear function because the payoffs are easy to explain and calculate. But some companies define a convex function—much higher rewards for higher performance—to stimulate extra effort and perhaps creativity to find new ways of doing things.

DETERMINING THE AMOUNT OF THE INCENTIVE

Another parameter in the Figure 12.4 function is the slope of the reward-performance line. How much of the incremental improvement in performance should be allocated to the employees who produce those gains? Is it possible to pay incentives that are too high?

The expectancy theory formula suggests that motivation will be higher the more someone is paid a controllable performance-dependent incentive. The key parameter to consider is EV_i. If the ith reward is valued, then the more that is promised to an employee, the more motivation should be produced. However, managers must be aware that most rewards produce diminishing amounts of utility and, hence, motivation. Take, for example, office size as the reward. Employees who perform well get bigger offices. At some point, however, a larger office ceases to become a motivator. Offices can even become too large. So managers must be aware that the EV of every reward diminishes as the size of that reward increases.

Clearly, however, most employees never get to the point where they are totally indifferent (satiated) to more of some forms of reward, such as cash. Should managers promise extraordinarily high cash reward potentials in order to induce even more motivation? Here, managers must consider a cost constraint. Every employee should be paid only a competitive compensation rate. So the real choice is between paying variable, performance-dependent compensation or a guaranteed fixed salary, keeping the total compensation level roughly fixed.[15] Most employees need to have some fixed salary in order to meet their fixed living expenses, so the amount of performance-dependent incentive must be bounded.

DETERMINING THE FORM OF INCENTIVES

Although motivation is the benefit of incentive systems, managers also have to be concerned with system costs. Ideally, companies should provide the package of incentives that provides the most motivational value at the least cost. Since all employees value cash, cash rewards are common. Some employees might respond better to grants of recognition or various forms of perquisites, such as a larger office or better parking space, things that the company could provide at lower cost. Older employees tend to value job

15 Employees who are paid with performance-dependent compensation generally have to be promised a little extra, to compensate them for bearing some risk.

security; younger employees tend to place a premium on training and promotion opportunities. But many companies do not know their individual employees' reward preferences very well, and in any case, administration of a system that tailors rewards to the individual employee level is difficult, at best.

IN CONTEXT ➤ Prestige Autos—Rewarding Performance

Jack began the next meeting by finally asking his managers for the details about how they were going to reach the coming year's stretch goals. He had to decide how he was going to reward his managers for their performance, so he wanted to get a good handle on what their assumptions were before making a decision about how to reward their performance.

"Okay, I'll start with you, Judy. How is your sales team going to move 20% more units than last year in order to meet the budget you gave me? What types of promotions and specials are you planning?" asked Jack.

"Okay. We're going to give special deals on trade-ins—the 'if you can get it to us even on a flatbed, we'll take it in trade.' We're also going to offer special financing on the new model, with zero money down and extended terms to keep the payments reasonable. Of course, we will only offer these to customers with great credit," replied Judy with gusto.

"Have you checked with Bruce on the impact your special will have on used car sales, Judy? If we're taking in a bunch of clunkers, we may have to pay someone to take them off our hands. Perhaps they're worth something as parts, but that's a big if! And the special financing, has Alice approved this? We'll need to partner with a bank if this is going to work," responded Jack.

"I've checked with Alice and she thinks the local bank will go along as long as the customers have good credit. I have to admit I didn't run the used car issue past Bruce. Since we sell both the new and used cars, I assumed I could just make this work," Judy noted.

"Selling junk cars is not as easy as it sounds, Judy," replied Bruce. "We're going to have to line up some buyers for the cars we can't refurbish to sell, or we will have to take them to an auction. I can do this. Now that I know about it in advance, I can get working on finding out what type of money we can expect to get for junkers. Let me get back to you on this next week."

"Thanks, Bruce. I'm also open to other ideas on how to move cars. I know if we can get good financing deals, it makes it easier to move cars. With our new structure, I don't feel as comfortable offering great trade-in prices because we have to pay going rates to get them ready to sell. This is another one for you, Bruce. And perhaps Tony needs to have a say in it also. How much can we afford to spend to fix a car before it doesn't make sense for us to keep it?" asked Judy.

"My shop can fix anything," said Tony emphatically. "But that doesn't mean it makes good financial sense. Maybe we can arrange special billing during the weeks you run your specials so we keep the price of repairs down and the profit for the company up. Would that work? We could do cost-based repairs, maybe even a little below charging rates... closer to actual pay rates for the labor. I don't want to do this on everything, because my guys will grumble, but we could help out during the weeks you run those specials."

"That would be great, Tony. I'll let you know what weeks we're talking about so we can limit the repair shop's exposure to just those weeks in which we're running a special. Don't want my salespeople to take advantage of such a generous deal!" replied Judy.

"I think you're making progress in sales. You might want some specials on used cars, too, Judy. Just think about it. Now what are we going to do in Service to make customers want to come in more often?" asked Jack.

"Our incentives are to bring in profitable business, so I want to focus on seasonal specials and 'creature comfort.' In other words, make it easy to do business with us. I want a drop-off van or car so people can leave their cars on the way to work and then we'll pick them up again in the evening. We need to streamline paperwork so they're not kept waiting. And, I want to spruce up the waiting lounge, have TV and fresh coffee for them plus a decent selection of magazines and newspapers. Make it feel like home, only better!" replied Tony.

"I think making it better for the customers is a good idea, but I would like more details on specials you're going to run. Customers need to have a reason to come in in the first place!" said Jack. "Tell you what, let's finish up for today. I want Judy and Bruce to continue working together on both getting and selling cars. Your bonus is in many respects tied together, so let's see if we can come up with a few more ideas. Tony, I'd like you to be more specific about the special events you're going to run so I know how to evaluate your performance come year-end. Make sense to everyone? Great! See you next week."

Summary

This chapter discussed the "check" and "do" functions of the management process in the entity domain. The basic problem is in evaluating performance, both of whole business entities and their managers. These entities are controlled as either profit centers or investment centers. The evaluations are important in making any of a broad range of decisions, such as those regarding organization and responsibility structures, business strategies, operating tactics, personnel assignments, and the allocation of organizational rewards.

Like in the other domains, formal, quantitative performance evaluations involve, first, comparing actual performance with a performance target, and second, calculating the size of the variance. But entity performance measures, such as accounting profits and returns, typically aggregate many aspects of performance into one summary indicator. Thus, the profit or return variance needs to be disaggregated to identify the causes of the variances and to separate the controllable from the uncontrollable causes. These variance analyses can disaggregate variances in different ways: by line item, by responsibility center, and/or by profit driver. Each can provide useful insights.

Finally, the variances need to be interpreted. The variances and their interpretation will vary depending on the specific performance standards used. Variances from easy targets will generally result in variances that look "favorable," while variances from stretch targets will look "unfavorable," yet the two analyses perhaps should lead to identical conclusions about performance.

Some managers use quite formal, quantitative variance analyses, while others rely more on subjective judgments. Subjectivity has its advantages. It is quite flexible and can be used to take into consideration important factors that are not well-captured in the quantitative performance measures. But it also has some disadvantages. It can leave the evaluation bases vague; it can add personal biases to the evaluation processes; and it often consumes significant management time.

In designing a complete incentive system, managers must make many judgments, such as the types of incentives that are linked to the performance evaluations and the shape of the function linking the two. As motivation is a key consideration in performance measurement and evaluation systems, motivational theories, such as expectancy theory, can be useful in understanding the effects of various system design choices.

Key Terms

Accounting return variance: an analysis study designed to assess the reasons for missing accounting return targets.

Controllable performance: areas or activities over which the managers have significant influence.

Disincentive, or punishment: a motivational tool used to induce employees to change their poor performances.

Favorable variance: an indication that actual performance was better than the performance standard.

Favoritism bias: preferential treatment or review given to an employee on the basis of personal affinity rather than actual performance.

Flexible budget: one in which variable costs have been adjusted for actual sales volume, without any activity forecasting variance prepared at the activity volume level at which the entity actually operated during the performance period.

Hindsight bias: subjective evaluation based on knowledge gained after the fact and/or that was not available to the person being evaluated.

Incentive, or reward: a motivational tool intended to enhance employee performance, inspire greater effort, increase productivity, and so on.

Industry volume variance: the difference between actual and budgeted industry volume.

Management-by-exception: the primary focus is on areas with unfavorable variances.

Market share variance: the difference between actual and budgeted market share.

Profit variance analysis: a study designed to assess the causes for missing or exceeding profit targets.

Relative performance evaluation: the assessment of a unit's outcome against the performance of like units, which become the performance standard.

Sales price variance: isolates the difference between actual prices and budgeted prices on reported sales.

Static budget: one prepared before the performance period; based on activity volume projections; not adjusted for the impact of actual sales volume; potentially includes an activity forecasting variance.

Subjective evaluation: an informal assessment that relies exclusively, or heavily, on the personal judgment of the evaluator.

Unfavorable variance: an indication that actual performance was worse than the performance standard.

Variable manufacturing cost variance: isolates the impact of differences between actual and planned variable costs in manufacturing.

Variance: the difference between actual results and the targeted, or planned, performance.

What-if analysis: a type of variance analysis typically used in the planning process that questions the impact a specific change would have on various aspects of the business.

Questions

1. Why is it dangerous to evaluate a subunit's performance with one simple number, such as its profit, during a particular period?
2. What does it mean to have favorable variances? Unfavorable variances?
3. What does the term "management-by-exception" mean and how is it used?
4. Define profit variance analysis and describe when it is used.
5. Define accounting return variance analysis and describe when it is used.
6. What are the pros and cons of disaggregating profit variances by line item?
7. What does it mean to disaggregate profit variances by responsibility center, and why would we do this?
8. When we speak of disaggregating variances by profit driver, what are we trying to accomplish?
9. What is the primary difference between a static and a flexible budget?
10. Identify and define the various variances that we use to disaggregate the revenue and profit variance. Please be specific as to the type of variance and why it is used.
11. What do the terms "industry volume variance" and "market share variance" mean?

12. What does it mean to use relative performance evaluations when assessing the performance of a subunit?
13. Define subjective performance evaluations and identify when they may be used.
14. What is the difference between a favoritism bias and a hindsight bias?
15. What is expectancy theory and how can it be used in evaluating subunit performance?

Exercises

1. **PROFIT VARIANCES BY LINE ITEM.** Lemon Enterprises reports the following actual vs. budgeted performance for the year.

Line Item	Actual	Budget
Sales	$ 2,525,000	$ 2,252,000
Less: Cost of Goods Sold	1,136,250	1,080,960
Gross Margin	$ 1,388,750	$ 1,171,040
Less: Selling, General, and Administrative	833,250	761,180
Net Income Before Tax	$ 555,500	$ 409,860

REQUIRED:

Compute the variances by line item for Lemon Enterprises.

2. **PROFIT VARIANCES BY LINE ITEM.** Hughes Industries reported the following actual vs. budgeted performance for the year.

Line Item	Actual	Budgeted
Sales	$ 3,250,500	$ 3,500,750
Less: Cost of Goods Sold	1,657,750	1,767,880
Gross Margin	$ 1,592,750	$ 1,732,870
Less: Selling, General, and Administrative	796,400	831,800
Net Income Before Tax	$ 796,350	$ 901,070

REQUIRED:

Compute the variances by line item for Hughes Industries.

3. **PROFIT VARIANCES BY LINE ITEM AND RESPONSIBILITY CENTER.** Pierce Enterprises has four operating divisions that reported the following results for 20x6.

Pierce Enterprises (stated in millions)										
Line Item	Division A		Division B		Division C		Division D		Pierce Enterprises	
	Actual	Budget	Actual	Budget	Actual	Budget	Actual	Budget	Actual	Budget
Sales	$54.5	$58.3	$65.8	$62.3	$38.5	$34.2	$98.9	$86.5	$257.7	$241.3
Less: Cost of Goods Sold	$26.2	$27.4	$33.6	$34.4	$18.1	$16.4	$44.5	$40.7	122.3	$118.9
Gross Margin	$28.3	$30.9	$32.2	$27.9	$20.4	$17.8	$54.4	$45.8	$135.4	$122.4
Less: SG&A	$15.0	$15.8	$15.5	$13.1	$10.6	$9.1	$26.7	$21.1	$67.8	$59.0
Income Before Tax	$13.3	$15.1	$16.8	$14.8	$9.8	$8.7	$27.7	$24.8	$67.6	$63.4

REQUIRED:

a. Compute the variances by line item for Pierce Enterprises' four divisions and company total.
b. Which divisions are performing better than expected?

4. **PROFIT VARIANCES BY LINE ITEM AND RESPONSIBILITY CENTER.** Doggone, Inc., has four operating divisions that reported the following results for 20x6.

Doggone, Inc. (stated in millions)										
Line Item	Division A		Division B		Division C		Division D		Doggone, Inc.	
	Actual	Budget	Actual	Budget	Actual	Budget	Actual	Budget	Actual	Budget
Sales	$37.3	$39.4	$88.5	$82.3	$46.5	$42.8	$86.5	$74.2	$258.8	$238.7
Less: Cost of Goods Sold	$17.9	$18.5	$45.1	$45.4	$21.9	$20.5	$38.9	$34.9	$123.8	$119.4
Gross Margin	$19.4	$20.9	$43.4	$36.9	$24.6	$22.3	$47.6	$39.3	$135.0	$119.3
Less: SG&A	$10.3	$10.6	$20.8	$17.3	$12.8	$11.4	$23.3	$18.1	$67.2	$57.4
Income Before Tax	$9.1	$10.2	$22.5	$19.5	$11.8	$10.9	$24.3	$21.2	$67.8	$61.9

REQUIRED:

a. Compute the variances by line item for Doggone, Inc.'s four divisions and company total.
b. Which divisions are performing better than expected?

5. **SALES PRICE AND VOLUME VARIANCES.** Jameson Industries reported the following results for 20x6 for its three operating divisions.

Jameson Industries						
	Division A		Division B		Division C	
	Budgeted	Actual	Budgeted	Actual	Budgeted	Actual
Sales volume	1,000,000	950,000	450,000	500,000	800,000	900,000
Sales price per unit	$10.00	$9.75	$14.50	$14.25	$16.25	$16.50

REQUIRED:

a. Compute the sales volume and sales price variances for the three divisions of Jameson Industries.

b. Which division performed best? Why?

6. **SALES PRICE AND VOLUME VARIANCES.** Best of Luck, Inc., reported the following results for 20x6 for its three operating divisions.

Best of Luck, Inc.						
	Division A		Division B		Division C	
	Budgeted	Actual	Budgeted	Actual	Budgeted	Actual
Sales volume	800,000	825,000	375,000	350,000	650,000	675,000
Sales price per unit	$9.25	$9.50	$10.25	$10.00	$14.25	$14.00

REQUIRED:

a. Compute the sales volume and sales price variances for the three divisions of Best of Luck, Inc.

b. Which division performed best? Why?

7. **INDUSTRY VOLUME AND MARKET SHARE VARIANCES.** Hansen Industries reported the following results for 20x6.

Hansen Industries		
	Budget	Actual
Industry Volume (millions)	18.5	17
Market Share	12%	11%
Budgeted Profit per Unit	$15.75	

REQUIRED:

Calculate the industry volume variance and market share variance for the year.

8. **INDUSTRY VOLUME AND MARKET SHARE VARIANCES.** Candice, Inc., reported the following results for 20x6.

Candice, Inc.		
	Budget	Actual
Industry Volume (millions)	22.5	25.4
Market Share	13%	15%
Budgeted Profit per Unit	$8.25	

REQUIRED:

Calculate the industry volume variance and market share variance for the year.

9. **EXPECTANCY THEORY.** Sunset Industries is thinking about putting in a new incentive system that incorporates individual, group, and corporate performance in setting bonuses. Tom Grady believes he only has a minimal impact on corporate performance and only a 15% impact on group performance. How motivating will this system be for Tom? Why?

10. **EXPECTANCY THEORY.** Harrold Enterprises is thinking about putting in a new incentive system for its top management team that balances individual, divisional, and corporate performance in setting bonuses. John McIntosh, head of Division B, the firm's largest division, knows he has a 30% impact on corporate performance and an 80% impact on divisional performance. His individual performance is judged as outstanding. How successful will this new system be in motivating John to do his best? Why?

Problems

1. **RESPONSIBILITY CENTER LINE ITEM VARIANCES.** Blue Spruce is a large wholesale gardening operation that sells trees, shrubs, and a variety of perennials and other bedding plants to small retail garden shops throughout New England. The company is split up into three major responsibility centers: Trees, Shrubs, and Bedding Plants. Tim Conway, president of Blue Spruce, has decided he would like to start comparing the performance of his responsibility centers so he knows where he needs to spend his management time. He collects the following information about the three responsibility centers.

Blue Spruce Actual vs. Budget

	Budget	Actual	Budget	Actual	Budget	Actual	Budget	Actual
	Trees		Shrubs		Bedding Plants		Company Totals	
Sales Revenue	$1,200,500	$1,189,200	$995,800	$1,020,800	$853,400	$900,600	$3,049,700	$3,085,600
Less: Cost of Goods Sold	$588,245	$564,870	$497,900	$494,846	$401,098	$463,809	$1,487,243	$1,526,579
Gross Margin	$612,255	$624,330	$497,900	$525,954	$452,302	$436,791	$1,562,457	$1,559,021
Less: SG&A Expenses	$360,150	$374,598	$278,824	$289,765	$273,088	$263,876	$912,062	$917,298
Income Before Tax	$252,105	$249,732	$219,076	$236,189	$179,214	$172,915	$650,395	$641,723

REQUIRED:

a. **Develop a line item variance analysis for the three divisions of Blue Spruce.**
b. **Plot the variances on a bar graph.**
c. **Using percentages, develop an analysis of the percent of cost and profit for the three divisions. Use the budget as your divisor in this exercise.**
d. **Which division looks like it is performing the best? Why?**
e. **Where should Tim spend his management time?**

2. **FLEXIBLE BUDGET VARIANCES.** Silverado, Inc., produces a wide range of silver utensils for use in buffet serving settings. Its buffet spoons are valued for their size, balance, and durability, as are its other serving pieces. The company wants to understand where it did well in the last year and where it needs to put more attention. To gain this information, Ralph Anders, president of Silverado, has asked the accounting group to pull together some basic cost information. What they provide him is in the exhibit below.

Silverado Inc.		
	Budgeted	Actual
Sales volume	2,500,000	2,750,000
Selling price	$10.00	$10.50
Manufacturing cost-variable	$3.50	$3.78
Manufacturing cost–fixed	$3,750,000	$4,620,000
SG&A expenses–variable	$2.000	$1.995
SG&A expenses–fixed	$3,250,000	$3,465,000

Ralph decides that he is going to run a series of variances to see better where things are going well vs. where they are going poorly. He is most concerned with the overall impact on profitability. He asks for your help in developing the following variances.

REQUIRED:

a. Develop a sales volume variance for the company.
b. Develop a sales price variance for the company.
c. Develop a variable manufacturing cost variance.
d. Develop a fixed manufacturing cost variance.
e. Develop a variable SG&A cost variance.
f. Develop a fixed SG&A cost variance.
g. Where should Ralph put his time? Why?

3. **FLEXIBLE BUDGET VARIANCES.** Bent Rods, Inc., repairs engine rods of various types for diesel motors. The company is one of the few in its industry to do these repairs, so it has a fairly stable customer flow. That said, the number of bent rods the company has to repair can vary greatly from one year to the next. Since a bent rod can wreck an engine, there is little downward pressure on price. Tom Peters, owner of Bent Rods, has decided it would be a good idea to examine his company's performance for the last year, taking into account actual vs. planned volumes of sales. His accountant provides Tom with the following information.

Bent Rods, Inc.		
	Budgeted	Actual
Sales volume	1,125,000	1,120,000
Selling price	$75.00	$76.50
Manufacturing cost–variable	$26.25	$27.54
Manufacturing cost–fixed	$14,343,750	$13,708,800

Bent Rods, Inc.		
	Budgeted	Actual
SG&A expenses—variable	$15.000	$14.535
SG&A expenses—fixed	$10,968,750	$10,281,600

REQUIRED:

a. Develop a sales volume variance for the company.
b. Develop a sales price variance for the company.
c. Develop a variable manufacturing cost variance.
d. Develop a fixed manufacturing cost variance.
e. Develop a variable SG&A cost variance.
f. Develop a fixed SG&A cost variance.
g. Where should Tom put his time? Why?

---

4. **SALES VARIANCES.** Better Products, Inc., buys electronic games wholesale and then sells them retail via the internet. It is a highly competitive business that Better Products has to carefully manage to remain profitable. Over the last year, it has seen the following results.

Better Products, Inc.		
Line Item	Budget	Actual
Industry volume	450,000,000	500,000,000
Market share	12.50%	12.75%
Selling price	$9.99	$9.50

Glen Landry, owner of Better Products, would like to understand exactly how well his company performed against its budget and in the industry in general. He has asked for your help in analyzing performance.

REQUIRED:

a. Develop the industry volume variance.
b. Develop the market share variance.
c. Develop the selling price variance.
d. How would you describe Better Products' performance over the past year? Please be specific.

5. **SALES VARIANCES.** Andrews Chicken is a producer of poultry products that sells directly both to the wholesale market that serves restaurants and to large grocery chains. The chicken market is a solid one, with only minimal growth from one year to the next but steady demand. The competition for share, therefore, is quite rigorous, with price often being the only way to change share and hopefully profits. Price wars have broken out, much to the benefit of the grocery chains that use the items as loss leaders on a weekly basis. Sam Andrews, president of Andrews Chicken, has decided he needs to analyze actual sales performance against plan. He recruits you from your accounting class to come in and help him do the analysis, for which he will pay you generously. You accept, and Sam provides you with the following data.

Andrews Chicken		
Line Item	**Budget**	**Actual**
Industry volume	500,000,000	500,250,000
Market share	10.90%	11.12%
Selling price	$2.49	$2.25

REQUIRED:

a. Develop the industry volume variance.
b. Develop the market share variance.
c. Develop the selling price variance.
d. How would you describe Andrews Chickens' performance over the past year? Please be specific.

A HELPING HAND

When we calculate ROI, ROE, and RONA variances, we are comparing actual results (the return) against planned results. We run the percentages at the top of the "forks" or variance figures, looking at how the percentages change as we move from actual profit against actual investment (equity, net assets), then budgeted profit divided by actual investment (equity, net assets) to get the variance due to profit. Finally, we divide budgeted profit by budgeted investment (equity, net assets) to get the final investment (equity, net asset) variance. They are simple to do and help us understand what element of the equation did not turn out as planned. Let us try a few.

6. **RETURNS VARIANCES.** Southview Medical is a medium-sized general practice clinic that has invested in its own radiology and laboratory departments, which are run as profit centers. The clinic has three profit centers—Clinical Practice, Radiology, and Laboratory. It budgeted profits and invested capital, equity, and net assets for the three divisions and now wants to compare actual results to plan. It has enlisted your help to run the variances using the following information.

Southview Medical						
	Clinical Practice		Radiology		Laboratory	
	Budget	Actual	Budget	Actual	Budget	Actual
Profit	$875,000	$900,000	$1,200,000	$1,190,000	$750,000	$775,000
Invested capital	$4,800,000	$5,000,000	$6,500,000	$6,900,000	$5,900,000	$5,750,000
Equity	$3,900,000	$4,000,000	$5,600,000	$5,400,000	$4,750,000	$4,900,000
Net assets	$5,250,000	$5,500,000	$7,250,000	$7,500,000	$6,540,000	$6,430,000

REQUIRED:

a. Calculate the ROI, ROE, and RONA variances for Clinical Practice.
b. Calculate the ROI, ROE, and RONA variances for Radiology.
c. Calculate the ROI, ROE, and RONA variances for Laboratory.
d. Where are the major problems for the medical practice? Where does it look strongest? Be specific, using the numbers from your analysis.

7. **EXPECTANCY THEORY.** Fiskar, Inc., has conducted a study of its managers' motivations. It used the expectancy theory framework and a questionnaire that asked the managers to quantify their expectations on a 10-point scale for intrinsic and extrinsic values and then assign a probability to whether or not they felt they could accomplish their goals and whether or not they felt a reward would be forthcoming if they reached their goals. The survey came up with the following results for three of its top managers.

Fiskar, Inc.				
	IV_G	IV_P	$\Sigma P_2 EV_1$	P_1
Sam Johnson	8	9	6	0.85
Bill White	9	10	8.55	0.9
Susan Breyer	7	8	3.75	0.75

REQUIRED:

a. Calculate the motivation of each of the three top managers.
b. Where should top management be concerned? Why?

8. **EXPECTANCY THEORY.** Carlisle Enterprises has three managers it is considering for promotion to a top spot in the corporate hierarchy. These three managers have performed at relatively the same level throughout the two years preceding the promotion decision, making it very difficult for management to gauge which one is most deserving of a promotion. It decides to try expectancy theory, which looks at motivation, as the basis for making the decision. The company uses a companywide survey to determine where its managers are really promoting positive behavior and where they might be using hard-handed techniques to reach their divisions' goals. The results for the general population for the three managers' divisions are stated in the table below.

Carlisle Enterprises				
	IV_G	IV_P	$\Sigma P_2 EV_i$	P_1
Division 1 average	6	7	5.2	0.75
Division 2 average	5	8	6.75	0.8
Division 3 average	8	8	7.65	0.85

REQUIRED:

a. Calculate the motivation of each of the three top divisions.
b. Which divisional manager should top management promote? Why?

Database Problems

For database templates, worksheets, and workbooks, go to MAdownloads.imanet.org

DB 12.1 LINE ITEM VARIANCES. In the database, you will find a worksheet named Annual Performance Comparison (APC). It will serve as the basis for doing your analysis of the line item variances for Prestige Auto for the year 20x6.

Open up the Template for DB 12.1 worksheet. You are going to need to use data from the APC to fill in this worksheet. For cell B4 under New Cars, left click, then key in = and then go to the APC worksheet and place your cursor over cell C4, left click, enter – and then place your cursor over cell B4 on the APC worksheet, left click, and hit Enter. You can drag this formula down the entire B column in your template worksheet. Follow the same logic and fill in columns D and F with the actual vs. budgeted results for the company. The grid already contains the allocated overhead totals from DB Problem 11.2, so you don't need to go back in and regenerate these numbers.

You now need to assign F and U for favorable and unfavorable for your variances on your template worksheet. This will fill columns C, E, and F. Remember that this is the rule: For revenues, actual less than budgeted is unfavorable, while for expenses, actual less than budgeted is favorable. Use this rule to assign favorable or unfavorable variance notations. Be careful with the contribution margin, income before tax, and net income numbers. Try to remember that more income is better than less, and less taxes is better than more. They are following the same cost and revenue rules as above; you just need to be careful in applying them.

REQUIRED:

a. **Complete the worksheet Template DB 12.1 and turn it in to your instructor.**
b. **Add an essay that notes which part of Prestige Auto is doing the best, and which is doing the worst. Please be specific, using the results of your analysis to justify your opinion.**

DB 12.2 RETURNS VARIANCES. For this exercise, you will need your DB 12.2 template sheet and the Annual Performance Comparison (APC) worksheet. You are going to populate the template based on the titles at the top of each section.

First, you need to fill in the data grid so you can do your returns analysis. Go to cell B4 and hit = and then go to the sheet APC cell B18 and hit Enter. Your command should look like this: ='Annual Performance Comparison'!B18.

Drag this formula across the profit line in your template to capture the various actual vs. budgeted profits for the three divisions on your template. Now you need to gather the investment data for your template. Go to cell B5 and hit = then go to APC worksheet and place your cursor over cell B20. Left click and then hit Enter. Your command should look like this: ='Annual Performance Comparison'!B20. Drag this command down the B column for cells B6 and B7 and across the columns B, C, D, E, F, and G to complete the data element part of your worksheet.

Now you are ready to compute the returns and their variances. First go to cell B10. Hit = and then place your cursor over cell E4. Left click and key in the / sign, and place your cursor over cell E5. Left click and hit Enter. Your command should look like this: =E4/E5. You cannot click and drag this formula because each cell requires its own calculation. Using the key that is on top of each cell, key in the = sign and then place your cursor over the correct numerator, enter the / sign, and then place your cursor over the correct denominator and hit Enter. You will populate this template one cell at a time, placing answers in cells B, C, and D 10, 14, and 18; Cells I, J, and K 10, 14, and 18; and Cells B, C, and D 24, 27, and 31. Be careful to enter each formula so it matches the description for that cell.

Now you need to put on your thinking cap. You will need to note whether the variance is favorable (F) or unfavorable (U) in the space below each two-cell row. Here, the rule is simple. If the number to the left (actual) is larger than the number to the right (some form of budget), then the variance is favorable. If it is less than the actual, it is an unfavorable variance. This holds for the two cells that contain half actual and half budget against the pure budget cells, also. If the cell with the actual component is larger than budget to budget, then the variance is favorable. If not, it is unfavorable. Think carefully and you should be fine. Enter the amount of the favorable or unfavorable variance followed by the terms U or F and the type of variance to complete filling in these cells. For instance, your response for cell B-C11 should look like this:

0.21% Unfavorable Profit Variance

REQUIRED:

a. Complete the worksheet DB 12.2 Template and turn it in.
b. Which division looks best now? Why?

Cases

CASE 12.1 SUBJECTIVE EVALUATIONS. Holy Cow is a producer of milk products, including an entire line of frozen ice cream. In fact, the company has three major product lines: milk, creams, and ice cream products. There is a manager in charge of each product line. While they all sell into the same grocery stores, they call on the stores separately, causing some confusion for the customer who ends up with three sales calls and three invoices for the Holy Cow products. It would be better if the divisions worked together to pool their selling resources, but the incentive system rewards them for individual performance.

Harry Dugan, president of Holy Cow, does not believe in keeping a lot of numbers around. He trusts his managers to do the right thing and increase sales for the company. As long as the bottom line keeps growing, Harry is happy. He does not really know which product line is the best performer or the worst performer; he just knows that the company keeps growing. That being said, Harry does have favorites. Jim Rutman, head of ice cream products, is actually Harry's son-in-law. So when performance bonus time comes around, Jim always gets more than his fair share. This is a point of friction between the managers. Andy White, head of milk sales, has been keeping track of company sales on his own and knows that his volume is up while ice cream products are flat. Cream products are struggling, with the latest fads in health foods causing people to veer away from the heavier cream products for substitutes that are lower in fat and cholesterol.

Andy has been trying to get Harry to pay attention to his sales numbers, but Harry simply is not interested. He says he gauges who is working the hardest and pays out the bonus money based on this subjective judgment. Andy is getting frustrated because it seems he always ends up on the short end of the bonus pool. Even though he is Holy Cow's only professional salesperson, he is thinking of leaving the company for a competitor that uses more modern management methods. This would leave Holy Cow in terrible shape because Andy has been the driving force behind company growth. Andy tries one more time to have a conversation with Harry.

Harry, can I have a moment of your time?

Sure, come on in, Andy. What do you have for me today?

I wanted to share the sales volume and profit numbers with you that I've been keeping for the company. They show that milk products are responsible for the profit we've been earning. Ice cream sales are flat and cream products are hitting new lows due to healthy-eating trends. I just wanted to know if this information could be factored into this year's evaluations and bonus decisions.

You know I don't like those fancy number games you play, Andy. It's one of the things that really bothers me about you. I want you guys to cooperate. Like Jim always says, we're in this together. Your numbers show that you're doing the best, but if Jim put the numbers together, I bet you wouldn't look so good. You don't seem to be as busy as Jim, or Pete in cream products for that matter. If you could only work harder, maybe your bonus would grow.

I am working hard, Harry, I just also work smart. I even try to help out ice cream and cream products when I'm in the stores if I know they are running a special that they haven't told the store manager about. It does me no good to be a team player around here, though, because it doesn't seem to matter what I do, I don't do well at bonus time.

I've told you that you need to work harder, look busy when I walk by to check things out. You're always out and about, not sitting at your desk making sales calls like the other guys. You work in the field instead of leaving the field to your sales associates. You're a manager, not a doer, at least in my book. So act like one!

I have a feeling I'm going to have to tender my resignation, then, Harry, because I do work hard. That's why the milk products numbers are the best. I don't believe in sitting behind a desk when there is sales work to do. Guess I need to find a company where I fit in better. Consider this my two weeks' notice, Harry.

You can leave today, Andy. I'll promote one of your guys to your position and we'll keep on growing because I have Jim keeping track of things for me. Sorry to see you go, but I wish you the best.

With that, Andy turned away and trudged back to his office to collect his personal belongings. He had tried his best, but without any rewards. He'd get on the phone to Holy Cow's competitor as soon as he got home. He had a standing offer of employment there, so things would not be too bad. He might even take that vacation he had kept putting off to put in more hours in sales. Andy turned out his lights for the last time and left the building quietly.

REQUIRED:

Comment on the situation at Holy Cow, using some of the terms and concepts from the chapter.

CASE 12.2 FLEXIBLE BUDGETS AND PERFORMANCE EVALUATION. Fine Metals, Inc., is a wholesaler of precious metals. The company maintains two key product lines: gold and silver. The company keeps the metals in both coins and bars and sells to both the investing market and the various industries that use silver in their manufacturing process. Keith Bolton, president of Fine Metals, Inc., has assigned responsibility for sales to three managers, one in charge of gold sales to investors (Joy Barnes), one in charge of silver sales to investors (Pete Blake), and one in charge of industrial sales of silver (Joey Michaels). Each subdivision of the business develops its own budget, which is then "flexed" to develop variances once a sales period has ended. This variance analysis is used to judge the performance of the three managers. The following table contains the key information for the three branches of the business for the latest year. No inventory changes have taken place as the company buys only what it sells in an arbitrage market—it does not really hold any inventory on hand. The results are:

Fine Metals, Inc.						
	Gold Investment Data		Silver Investment Data		Silver Industrial Data	
	Budget	Actual	Budget	Actual	Budget	Actual
Sales in ounces	1,200,000	1,150,000	2,500,000	2,850,000	3,425,000	3,500,000
Average price per ounce	$1,580.00	$1,490.00	$26.25	$26.50	$26.25	$26.50
Variable acquisition costs per ounce	$35.00	$38.75	$10.00	$11.00	$9.00	$9.25
Fixed acquisition costs	$250,000,000.00	$257,500,000.00	$10,500,000.00	$12,000,000.00	$20,500,000.00	$19,500,000.00
Variable SG&A costs per ounce	$40.50	$42.00	$12.00	$12.50	$10.00	$9.50
Fixed SG&A costs	$40,000,000.00	$45,000,000.00	$3,750,000.00	$3,500,000.00	$4,250,000.00	$4,500,000.00

The company does not have enough sales to really influence the trends in the marketplace. Individual managers, however, can be more or less successful at moving their products, using marketing pitches on major television networks and radio programs to move the product into the marketplace. Silver industrial sales are an exception to this type of marketing. Here, the marketing dollars need to go into trade shows and trade publications, including the buyers' guides that purchasing agents use when making purchases for their company. It is a very different business from the investing side of the house, facing different types of competition. Market demand is much steadier for industrial sales, also, as companies that make products using silver are fairly large and reliable consumers of the silver ingots. Industrial sales can buy in larger quantities, driving down its acquisition costs as compared to the other two products.

The gold market is volatile, with annual price swings being significant. When economies get in trouble, investors flock to gold, driving the prices up. When economies are stable, then investors tend to put their money in the stock market and gold prices plummet. Again, Fine Metals, Inc., is not a market mover or price setter—it is definitely a price taker. It also takes a lot more marketing to move gold because of its high price per ounce. Where almost any investor can afford to buy silver coins, gold coins are much more difficult for people to acquire. That means the customers demand more and the acquisition costs of moving the gold are much higher than they are for silver.

REQUIRED:

a. Prepare a budgeted vs. actual income statement for each of the business segments.
b. Compute the flexible budget variances for the three segments of Fine Metals' market. Remember that if cost variances show positive in this analysis, they are actually unfavorable, while revenue variances are unfavorable if they are negative. In other words, if actual sales are less than planned, it will show up as a negative which makes sense as less sales is not good (unfavorable). If actual costs are lower than plan, this will also show up as a negative, but is actually a favorable outcome.
c. Which set of numbers do you feel is a better indicator of segment performance? Why?

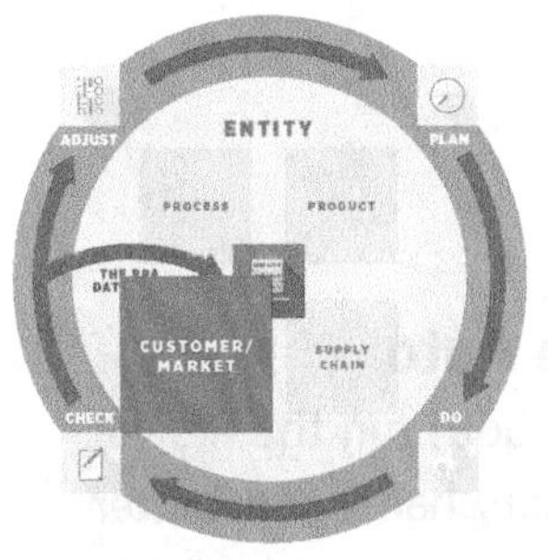

CHAPTER THIRTEEN

Setting and Achieving Targets in the Customer Domain

Achieving the full profit potential of each customer relationship should be the fundamental goal of every business.

ALAN W.H. GRANT AND LEONARD A. SCHLESINGER[1]

CHAPTER ROADMAP

1. **Measuring Customer Profitability**
2. **The Customer Value Perspective**
3. **Planning in the Customer Domain**
   - *Acquiring Customers of the Right Type*
   - *Making Existing Customers More Profitable*
   - *Retaining Existing Customers*
4. **Measuring Performance and Making Adjustments**
   - *Customer Profit Variance Analyses*
   - *Nonfinancial Performance Measures in the Customer Domain*

LEARNING OBJECTIVES

After studying this chapter, you should be able to:

1. **Describe how to compute the profitability of a customer or customer type.**
2. **Explain how firms create value for their customers.**
3. **Discuss the ways companies identify which customers to acquire, how they increase the profitability of each, and how they retain them.**
4. **Perform a customer profit variance analysis at multiple levels of aggregation and use nonfinancial measures to assess performance.**

1 Alan W.H. Grant and Leonard A. Schlesinger, "Realize Your Customer's Full Profit Potential," *Harvard Business Reivew*, September-October, 1995: p. 59.

IN CONTEXT ➤ Success and Its Challenges at Prestige Auto

A month had passed and Sales and Service had both run the first of their special customer sales programs. The results had been better than expected: The new car group sold 40 units of the new model in addition to older models. Since the sale only ran for four days, this was a major accomplishment. Many of the customers had bought from them before, trusted the sales force and the company, and knew they would get good service from the repair department.

"We have solid customer loyalty!" noted Judy with some excitement at the first management meeting following the sales event. "They came out in droves, former customers as well as friends and family of existing customers. I'd say 80% of our sales resulted from this loyalty, which means only great things for the future!"

"I agree," said Jack. "Tony, how did your service special go?"

"There was a major influx of customers who decided now was a good time to get their service work done. I'd say 50% of the additional service jobs came from existing customers taking advantage of the special. The other 50% were new customers, who, I hope, we made so happy they will become regular customers!" replied Tony.

"I've been running our flex budget with the new sales and service results and things are looking up. I think we'll finally turn around some of those negative returns if we can keep moving cars and selling service at this rate. I'd love to see us have a great year!" announced Jack.

"Well, we're going to run another new car campaign in two months, and we are actually in the process of planning a promotion for used cars for next week. With the huge uptick in new car sales, we have a lot more good used cars that we need to move. I'm hoping we can lure people in to take advantage of some of the mint condition cars that were turned in because people were so excited about the new model," Judy piped up dramatically.

"We did a record business, that's for sure," agreed Alice. "We're still clearing some of the paperwork from the sales; the results overwhelmed us. I hope this doesn't cause anyone problems, but we just couldn't handle everything that came at us last week. I don't want Finance to be the reason a customer is unhappy with us."

"How did you manage the load and leave it with our customers, Alice?" asked Jack.

"Well, it often took us two days to completely process the purchase request. We worked hard to get preliminary financing arranged so the customer knew the sale was going through, but we cleaned up a lot of the paperwork as the car was heading out the door. Service also overwhelmed us. The one analyst who handles that work is awfully fast, but I know there were a few delays because she had to handle multiple requests at once. Did you get any negative feedback, Tony?" asked Alice.

"A couple of customers got a tad impatient, but we offered them free coffee and sweet rolls, and that seemed to calm them down. I did have our odd jobber run a few people around to do their errands so they wouldn't feel that they had lost the whole day around the shop. It isn't a fix we can use all the time; maybe we can find a way to expedite the paperwork so we can avoid these small glitches in the future," Tony suggested.

"Well, I have nothing more to say except keep up the good work, everyone! I'll see you next week!" Jack said.

EARLIER CHAPTERS HAVE DISCUSSED THE VALUE OF BUILDING AND ANALYZ-ing the management accounting database along product/service, process, and entity domains. This chapter discusses a fourth useful domain—the customer domain. The importance of this domain is obvious—serving customers is the only reason that organizations exist. Organizational revenues stem almost exclusively from the value delivered to customers. Consequently, many firms are striving to become more "customer-savvy."

Management accounting data, tools, and techniques can help managers to understand better which customers to serve and how to serve them better than the competition. Only by evaluating the relative profitability of the various customers that are using the company's services can managers choose the best portfolios of customers to serve and the mix of product and service features to provide to them. These are vital decisions that affect the long-term profitability of the firm.

The application of management accounting in the customer domain is a relatively recent, but important, development. Its advancement stems both from an increasing awareness of the importance of good performance in the customer domain and as a result of recent technological developments that make these analyses easier to complete. Faster computers and cheaper storage devices enable the building of populated data warehouses, and the development of new "customer intelligence" software applications facilitates the analysis of the customer information contained within them.

This chapter details all of the "Plan-Do-Check-Adjust" management process elements as they apply to making customer-oriented decisions. It describes how to measure customer profitability, how to understand what customers value, how to plan in the customer domain, and how to measure performance and make adjustments in this critical domain. As you make your way through this discussion, you will gain a better understanding of how companies manage their customer portfolios for maximum profitability.

Measuring Customer Profitability

OBJECTIVE 1

Describe how to compute the profitability of a customer or customer type.

The measurement of short-term customer profitability is the basic analysis in the customer domain. At first glance, it might seem that the customer domain represents just a higher level of aggregation of the data in the product/service dimension because customers purchase a specific and determinable mix of products and services. However, this is not exactly correct. Customers also consume many company resources, the costs of which are not reflected in the product/service cost data. Examples are promotional materials, salespeople's time, and post-purchase product support. The costs of these resources consumed must be considered in calculating customer profitability.[2]

Traditionally, few firms have measured customer profitability well because Generally Accepted Accounting Principles (GAAP) do not require the tracing of costs to customers or customer groups. Until relatively recently, most firms have measured the profits by customer only down to the gross margin level. Revenues and cost of goods sold are the basic elements of sales transactions, so measuring gross margin by customer is easy and inexpensive to do. However, judging customer profitability based on gross margins earned is often misleading. Almost all sales are profitable at the gross margin line, but many sales are unprofitable when the full costs of the activities needed to make and support the sale are considered.

The costs of any particular sale include not only the cost of making the product, but typically also a variety of other costs, including:

- the presale costs necessary to induce the customers to buy (for example, advertising, promotional displays, sales calls, catalog mailings, inventory carrying),
- order processing costs (for example, written sales order vs. electronic submission),
- distribution costs (for example, handling and delivery charges),
- customer service costs (for example, required entertainment, cost of an on-site employee),
- environmental and litigation costs,
- order collection costs (terms, required follow-up), and
- post-sale service costs (for example, training, parts inventory costs, field support, warranties).

These costs all fall in the traditional financial accounting category of selling, general, and administrative expenses (SG&A). In some industries, SG&A expenses, in total, can be quite large, often 50% to 100% of a company's total manufacturing costs and sometimes even more. SG&A expenses tend to be larger in companies that are more customer-focused.

SG&A costs are sometimes also referred to as downstream costs because they occur late in the value creation process, after production has finished. Understanding the downstream costs and tracing them to cost objects, such as customers, is an important part of the life cycle approach to costing. Customers are sometimes charged for some of these services (for example, shipping, extended warranties) but not others (such as basic warranties, advertising, comfortable waiting lounges, some technical support). But in either case, the costs of these other services need to be considered in any complete customer-oriented profitability analysis.

Table 13.1 shows a simple customer profitability report for Omega Products, Inc., a company that has only three customers: Arnold, Inc., Hakes, Ltd., and Johnson Industries. The total annual revenue of Omega is the sum of its revenues from these three customers. As you can see, there is a significant amount of unassigned cost using the current costing method. This cost includes many of the organizational costs, such as payroll processing and senior management salaries that are not caused by a specific customer, order or product/service.

---

2 This section has been adapted from Carol J. McNair, Lidija Polutnik, and Riccardo Silvi, "Cost and the Creation of Customer Value," *Handbook of Cost Management.* New York: Warren, Gorham and Lamont, 2001.

TABLE 13.1 CUSTOMER PROFITABILITY STATEMENT

Omega Products					
For the year ending December 31, 20x6 (in millions)					
Costs Traceable to Customers					
	Arnold, Inc.	Hakes, Ltd.	Johnson Industries	Unassigned	Total
Revenues	$100	$300	$600	$-	$1,000
Cost of goods sold	$75	$180	$300	$-	$555
Gross margin	$25	$120	$300	$-	$445
Sales and marketing expense	$10	$15	$25	$20	$70
Order processing expense	$5	$7	$8	$-	$20
Order collection expense	$5	$5	$10	$5	$25
Post-sale support expense	$10	$15	$5	$10	$40
General and administrative expense	$10	$30	$60	$50	$150
Total selling, general, and administrative expenses	$40	$72	$108	$85	$305
Operating income	$(15)	$48	$192	$(85)	$140

Tracing expenses to customers is harder than tracing revenues to them, however. Normally it is not possible to trace or assign all of a company's expenses to customers. Some companies just allocate them based on crude allocation bases, such as a percentage of revenue. Since it is impossible to allocate all of the SG&A expenses to customers, one column in every customer profitability report will show all the unassigned expenses. It is also likely that the company has unassigned expenses because it may be trying to penetrate new markets and therefore incurs some costs that are not caused by current customers. Leaving some costs unassigned is better than forcing costs onto specific customers that do not cause those costs.

Some assignments of expenses to customers are appropriate and, hence, they yield good customer profitability analyses. But some assignments are bad. The good ones trace as many expenses to customers as can meaningfully be done, but they do not go too far and assign them arbitrarily. Through better cost systems, managers might be able to shrink the size of the unassigned expenses. They might conduct a study, for example, to determine how many accounting department resources are caused by activities necessitated by specific customers (for example, credit analyses and collections). But there will always be some expenses that cannot be traced, or even allocated in a meaningful way, to customers.

LOOKING BACK ➤ True Then, True Now—It's the Customer, Stupid

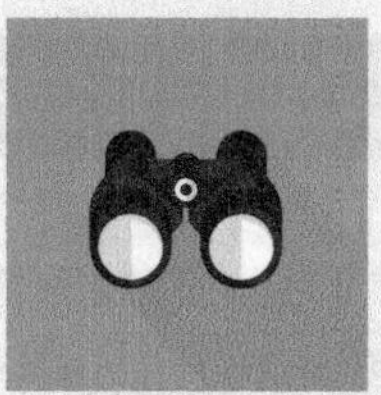

As we noted earlier, Peter Drucker provided great insights into the basic functioning of corporations. One of his key points was the central role played by the customer in defining a business. He notes:

What is our business is not determined by the producer but by the consumer. It is not defined by the company's name, statutes, or articles of incorporation, but by the want the consumer satisfies when he buys a product or a service. The question can therefore be answered only by looking at the business from the outside, from the point of view of the customer and the market. What the consumer sees, thinks, believes, and wants at any given time must be accepted by management as an objective fact deserving to be taken as seriously as the reports of the salesman, the tests of the engineer, or the figures of the accountant—something few managements find it easy to do. And management must make a conscious effort to get honest answers from the consumer himself rather than attempt to read his mind.

From Drucker's point of view, there was no doubt that consumers drive the very definition of what a business is. Today, meeting customers' demands is viewed as a basic business necessity. Nevertheless, it is a fact that often gets overlooked.

Excerpt from Peter Drucker, *The Practice of Management*, New York: Harper & Row, 1954: p. 50.

The Omega Products example (Table 13.1) shows how the profitability of a customer can change when the pre- and post-sales expenses are considered. At the gross margin line, Arnold, Inc., looks like a profitable customer, with a not insignificant gross margin of 25% of sales. But after all of the expenses of doing business with Arnold are considered, the analysis shows that Omega would actually be better off not dealing with Arnold, at least in the short run. Or perhaps Omega management just needs to find less expensive ways to support Arnold, Inc. While not every customer is a good customer, a company should always look first to its expenses before arbitrarily abandoning a customer.

When managers analyze their customer profitability, they typically find that relatively few customers provide the firm with a high proportion of its profits. In most cases, reality is quite close to the oft-cited 80/20 rule. In other words, 20% of the customers yield 80% of the firm's total profits. Sales to the other 80% of customers are quite often unprofitable due to heavy servicing costs and related problems.

Figure 13.1 shows a typical cumulative effect on total company profits of a company's entire set of customers. In this example, the top 20% of the customers account for approximately 80% of the corporation's total profits. If all of the unprofitable customers were abandoned, total company profits would be about 25% higher than they actually are.

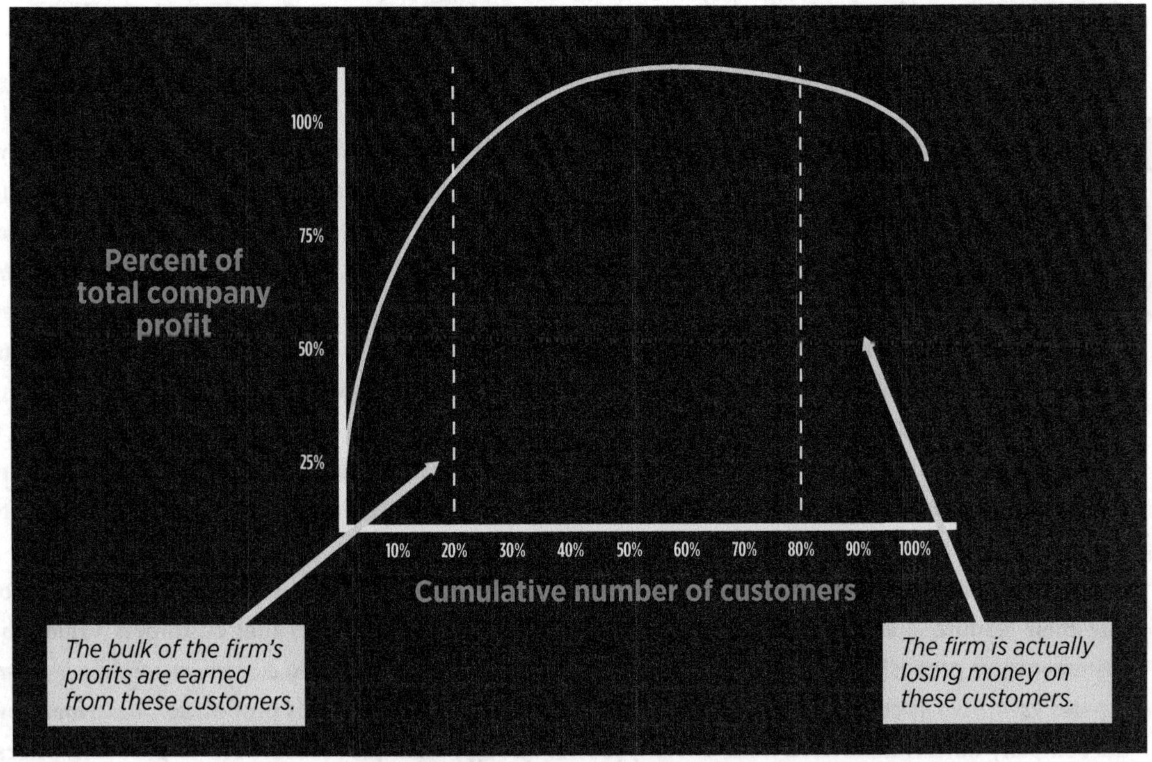

FIGURE 13.1 NOT ALL CUSTOMERS ARE EQUAL WHEN IT COMES TO PROFITABILITY; IN SOME CASES—IN THIS CASE, THE LAST 20—COMPANIES LOSE MONEY ON SUCH CUSTOMERS.

This distribution may seem extreme at first glance, but in many industries, it is more typical than unusual. For example, one bank-consulting firm estimated that the top 20% of typical bank customers produced as much as 150% of the bank's final overall profit, while the bottom 20% reduced the overall profit by about 50%.[3] A senior vice president at Bank of America said, bluntly, that "the top 20% of our customers is our franchise."[4] Knowing what these customers value is the key to enhancing firm profitability.

Once the profitability of specific customers or customer segments is understood, decisions can be made whether to drop them, increase the price paid by unprofitable customers to make them profitable, or find ways to reduce the number or cost of services provided. In other words, once the information about the total profitability of a customer or segment is known, management can take a range of actions to improve overall company profitability by addressing in a specific way the problems caused by unprofitable customer relationships.

3 Rick Brooks, "Alienating Customers Isn't Always a Bad Idea, Many Firms Discover," *The Wall Street Journal*, January 7, 1999: pp. A1, A12.

4 Rick Whiting, "Profitable Customers," *Informationweek.com*, March 29, 1999, p. 1.

The Customer Value Perspective

OBJECTIVE 2

Explain how firms create value for their customers.

How do companies earn profits from their customers? They earn revenues and their associated profits because they supply products and services that the firm's customers value. Customers know the value that they place on specific value attributes. A **value attribute** *is a characteristic or feature of a product or service that is directly valued by the customer.* It could be a specific product or service, a specific add-on feature (such as antilock braking systems, chrome wheels), or an element of sales or post-purchase support (for example, comfortable waiting lounges, prompt and effective customer service, extended warranties). The values customers put on a value attribute sets an upper limit on the price they are willing to pay for that attribute. Customers are certainly willing to pay less than the value they place on a particular item, but they are not willing to pay more.

A company's revenues are based solely on the value delivered to customers. Companies allocate their resources, and thus incur costs, by creating products or services that customers value. The **customer value proposition**—*the strategy used by a company to attract its desired customers and how it differentiates itself from its competitors*—is at the core of all business strategies. This proposition describes how the company differentiates itself from its competitors, through a unique combination of products, prices, services, and image. Companies that provide value for customers better than their competitors do are able to charge higher prices, usually satisfy their customers better, and earn customer loyalty.

Only the resources that create customer value create firm revenue. All remaining resource usage creates costs that are not revenue-generating and therefore reduce profit. This point is illustrated in Figure 13.2. The innermost black circle represents the costs of everything that the firm does that customers value, which includes the product features and supporting services. The size of the outer yellow circle reflects the firm's total revenue—what customers are willing to pay for the company's products and services given the amount of value they contain compared to their current market price. If the value-adding core of activities becomes larger, the outer circle will also become larger because both existing and new customers will perceive the added value and will be willing to pay more for it.

Figure 13.2 has three other rings besides the value-added core. The first of these, the gray ring, is labeled "Business Value-Added Activities and Costs." This category includes all of the activities a firm has to undertake to stay in business, like issuing invoices, even though customers do not place any direct value on them. A company's research and development program falls into this layer, because today's customers are not interested in paying for tomorrow's innovations. They pay only for the value they receive from the company's products and services. While there are some industries, such as pharmaceuticals, in which tomorrow's breakthroughs are valued by all customers, current and future, in most industries a new product released to the market tomorrow will quite likely make the items purchased by customers today obsolete. This is often the case in technology-intensive industries such as cell phones and computers.

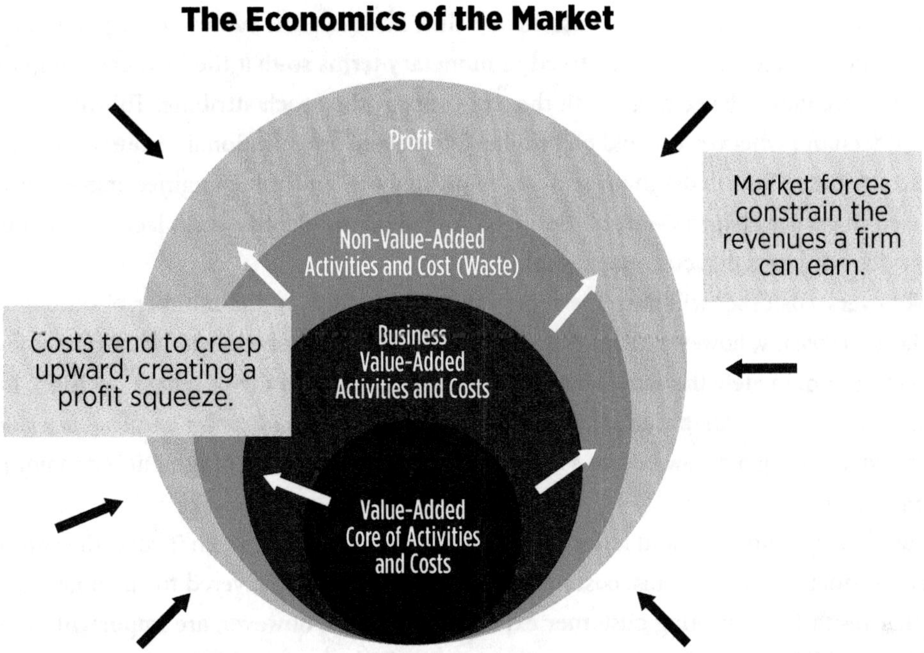

The Economics of the Market

Profit

Non-Value-Added Activities and Cost (Waste)

Business Value-Added Activities and Costs

Value-Added Core of Activities and Costs

Market forces constrain the revenues a firm can earn.

Costs tend to creep upward, creating a profit squeeze.

FIGURE 13.2 WHAT CUSTOMERS ARE WILLING TO PAY FOR A PRODUCT OR SERVICE IS BASED ON ITS PERCEIVED VALUE, NOT THE AMOUNT OF MONEY A COMPANY EXPENDS ON OTHER ACTIVITIES LIKE GENERAL OVERHEAD, WASTE, AND SO ON.

The two outermost rings are labeled "Non-Value-Added Activities and Cost (Waste) (the orange ring) and "Profit" (the yellow ring). We discussed waste at some length in the process domain. Waste occurs everywhere in the organization and definitely is not valued by customers. Eliminating waste helps improve profits. Profit is what is left over if the value-add, business value-add, and non-value-add/waste activities do not consume all of the firm's revenue. Profit is not guaranteed—it only results if the company does enough things right to earn the revenues it needs from its customers and then does not spend all of these vital resources running the business itself. One of the primary reasons companies need good management and planning systems is so they can remain profitable.

It is important to note that firms must earn much more than one dollar of revenue for each dollar of value-added cost. If this did not happen, all firms would lose money. So the value-adding core of activities provides **leverage,** *the multiplier effect of one more dollar of value-added work on the company's revenue line*. The wise spending of a dollar that creates customer value will yield much more than one dollar in price. The amount of leverage varies widely across industries. Firms in highly competitive industries, such as grocery stores, have relatively little leverage because they face the risk that a competitor will be willing to take a sale at a lower price. Firms that are innovative and build a competitive advantage, however, such as Apple, have a large amount of leverage available. Many customers are willing to pay more for the newest innovation. Leverage is one of the key factors influencing a company's ability to make a profit.

It is not enough to know what customers value, however. The values of the potential attributes of the products and services must be quantified in monetary terms so that the firm can compare the value created—the revenues to be earned—with the costs of providing each attribute. This information helps managers understand whether it would be profitable to devote organizational resources to create or support a specific attribute. Target cost management, value analysis, and value engineering—techniques that were discussed in earlier chapters—are all designed to help firms identify and place a value upon the product and service attributes that customers want.

Not every customer will have the same value profile. In fact, the number of different profiles can be quite large. Typically, however, firms can identify clusters of customers who want the same set of attributes and place approximately the same amount of weight on them in the purchase decision. Identifying these clusters is known as **value-based segmentation,** *the clustering of customers because they have a similar value proposition*. Figuring out how best to serve each value-based customer segment is a major purpose of strategic planning.

Customers do not care, and in fact probably do not know, how much it costs the company to produce a given product or service. Thus, cost has no effect on the value delivered to customers or the firm's revenues that result from meeting customer expectations. Costs, however, are important because companies should add additional product features and services, which require additional costs, only to the extent that their customers value these features and services. If the feature is valued, customers will quite likely be willing to pay for it.

IN THE NEWS ➤ Shifting Focus at Hewlett-Packard

Hewlett-Packard is known for its high-quality printers. But how do customers define quality, and what are they willing to pay for it? Roughly 10 years ago, one HP executive thought that some of the quality the company was building into its printers was non-value-added. To prove his point, the 200-pound manager stood on a printer and asked the other managers attending the meeting whether customers needed to use the printers as step stools. The group concluded that no, the printers did not have to be that strong.

Customers valued other things, such as print quality, speed, reliability, small size, and low cost. The HP managers concluded that if HP did not spend its limited resources wisely to give customers what they wanted, they would gradually lose their low-end printer business to more aggressive competitors, like Canon and Epson. So HP managers launched a major effort to build a more cost-effective machine, one that would sell for under $49—$30 less than HP's least expensive model at the time. The effort cost more than $2 billion before the first revenues were realized, but the newly developed, smaller printer produced a higher-quality image at a faster speed. After the scaled-back model was introduced, HP gained both market share and profitability.

In today's highly competitive computer printer market, features are constantly being added while price points continue to drop. Through this early decision to shift the definition of value-added from durability to features and price, HP was able to take a formidable lead in the market, one that continues today.

Planning in the Customer Domain

OBJECTIVE 3

Discuss the ways companies identify which customers to acquire, how they increase the profitability of each customer, and how they retain them.

Planning in the customer domain involves deciding which customers to serve and how to serve them. The customer profitability analyses and the customer value perspective just discussed are critical in making these decisions. If managers understand how they are earning profits from specific customers and customer classes, then they can decide how to improve these profits and set performance targets to reach these new sales and profit goals.

Using a customer perspective, firms can earn greater profits in three basic ways. First, they can acquire new customers of the right type. Second, they can enhance the profitability of existing customers. And third, they can do things to improve the retention of their desirable customers and thereby earn a longer, and more valuable, stream of profits from them. Each of these ways of improving performance can be viewed from both a tactical and a strategic perspective, as illustrated in Table 13.2.

TABLE 13.2 TACTICS AND STRATEGIES THAT INCREASE PROFITABILITY PER CUSTOMER

Method	Tactic	Strategy
Acquire new customers (of the right type)	Offer a new promotion for new customers	Determine the type(s) of customer to focus on
Enhance profitability of existing customers	Raise prices for customers who demand a lot of attention	Change focus; for example, determine whether to focus marketing efforts on retail of wholesale customers

Method	Tactic	Strategy
Improve retention of desirable customers	Waive customer service fees or other fees for good customers	Improve customer service; for example, create a new customer service hotline

Tactical decisions are those that employees in the firm face every day. In the customer domain, managers considering tactics might be thinking about whether or not to place a newspaper advertisement this weekend, whether to raise prices for customers who demand a lot of attention, or whether or not to give a specific customer a discount. The strategic perspective is longer-term. It might involve answering questions about what lines of business to be in, what distribution channels to use, what promotional methods to employ, what types of customers to serve, and what general pricing policies to follow.

ACQUIRING CUSTOMERS OF THE RIGHT TYPE

The customer perspective helps managers understand who their target customers are. Obviously, firms would like to serve customers that are profitable, or those that can be made profitable in the not-too-distant future. Customer profitability analyses are a key tool in performing value-based customer segmentations.

Which customers can be expected to be most profitable? Customer profits are affected by four characteristics descriptive of the customer and the corporation's position in the market.[5] First are the customer's *economics*, particularly their price and service sensitivity. Second is the customers' *buying power*, their ability to extract concessions from their suppliers. Third is the customers' *purchase decision-making person*. Purchasing personnel are generally more price-sensitive, and engineering and technical personnel are more sensitive to product and service features. And finally, the *buyer-seller relationship* is important. Long-standing relationships, particularly where friendships have built up, make buyers less apt to pressure suppliers for price and service concessions.

The effects of these four factors can be arrayed in a chart using two key dimensions: the volume and mix of purchases that the customers make and the costs required to serve them, as shown in Figure 13.3, which identifies four archetypal customer categories. The most profitable customers are "passive customers." Because they are not price-sensitive, they buy relatively high-margin products, and they are easy to do business with. They consume relatively less of the indirect services that the firm is willing to provide. Being the most profitable, these passive customers should be protected and nurtured.

---

5 Shapiro et al, 1987.

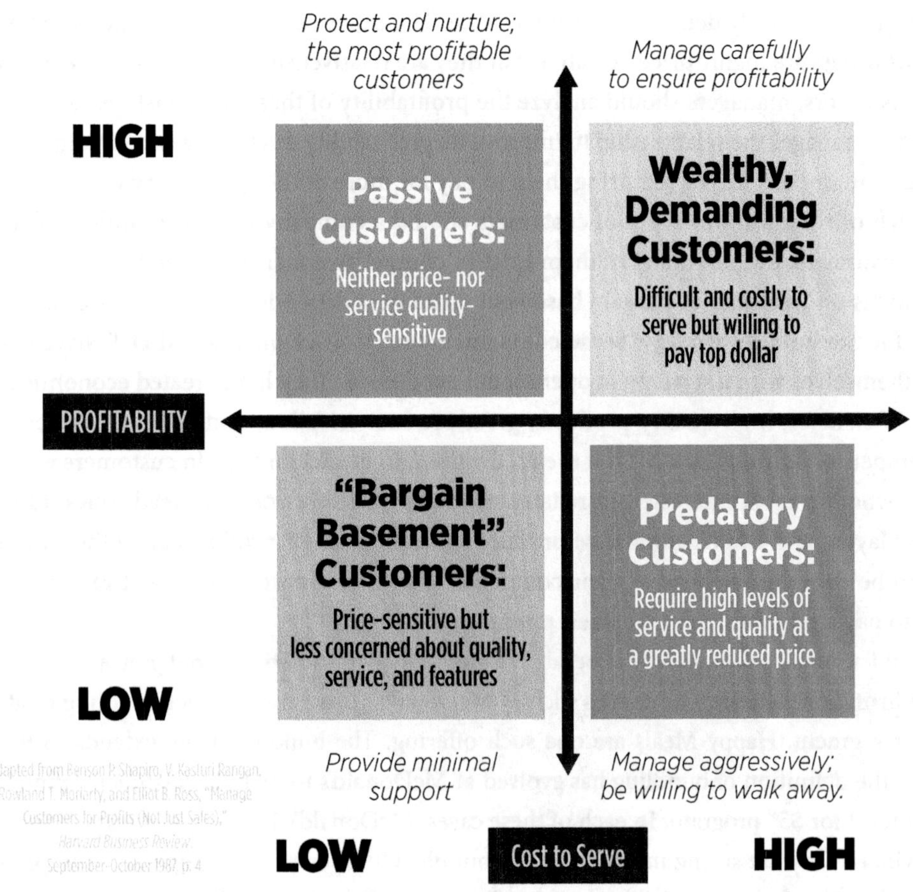

FIGURE 13.3 BASED ON THESE FOUR ARCHETYPES, COMPANIES CAN DETERMINE THE CUSTOMERS THEY WANT TO ATTRACT AND THOSE THEY WANT TO STAY AWAY FROM, OR, IF THAT IS NOT POSSIBLE, HOW TO MANAGE THEM TO INCREASE THE PROFITABILITY OF THE GOOD CUSTOMERS AND MINIMIZE THE DRAIN ON PROFITABILITY OF THE QUESTIONABLE ONES.

The least profitable customers are either small, not worth the effort to serve, or, more likely, are "predatory customers"—they require huge price concessions and extra service components in order to get their business. Predatory customers leverage their buying power to demand low prices, yet they also demand special features (for example, product customization) and/or special services (such as on-site customer service, longer warranties). Many people see companies such as Walmart as predatory customers because the company demands significant price concessions from their suppliers. The customers of Walmart benefit from lower prices, but the companies that provide the goods and services are squeezed and might not be around in the long run to gain the benefits of having satisfied customers.

In between these two extremes are two types of customers that might be worthwhile serving. One category is the "wealthy, demanding customers," who are willing to pay good prices for their products but who simultaneously demand superior service. The other category is "bargain basement" customers. These customers are highly price-sensitive, but they are relatively inexpensive to serve. With these categories of customers, managers should analyze the profitability of these relationships carefully. They should also try to "manage" the relationship to improve its profitability, such as by encouraging customers not to demand so many services or requiring them to pay for more of the special services they require.

Which of these various types of customers should a company seek? Certainly all firms should seek passive customers, but not many of them exist in competitive markets. Whether a firm or business unit should focus on wealthier or bargain basement customers depends on the entity's customer-value proposition; for example, its strategy. Some companies, such as McDonald's and Dell, have chosen to differentiate themselves with a strategy of operational excellence. They have created economies of scale, operational efficiencies, high-quality products, great product selection, and reliable business processes that their competitors cannot match. So it is easy for them to attract and retain customers who are price-sensitive or who are most interested in reliable products and short delivery lead times. Other companies, such as Maytag and BMW, emphasize product leadership. Their products are either unique or are perceived to be superior to those of their competitors, so it is easy for them to attract customers who are willing to pay a premium price for their products.

Should unprofitable customers be abandoned? This is sometimes, but not always, the best option facing a firm. For instance, companies such as McDonald's often use product bundling to attract a specific customer segment. Happy Meals are one such offering. The bundling logic extends to its "Meal Deals." Recently, the definition of bundling has evolved at McDonald's to include customer-defined bundles, such as the "Pick 2 for $5" program. In each of these cases, McDonald's is trying to attract more customers who are convinced they are saving money with the bundle. Other customers, however, may prefer to just have a sandwich and soft drink and skip the fries. For the McDonald's bundling strategy to work, therefore, it still has to offer each menu item as a freestanding purchase. Clearly, these bundled meal packages are profitable for McDonald's, but they do reduce profitability vs. the customers who pay a higher price for specific menu items.

First Chicago Corp., part of Chase Bank, took a different approach in dealing with unprofitable or difficult customers. It imposed a teller fee on some of its money-losing customers. Approximately 30,000 customers, close to 3% of the bank's total customers at the time, closed their accounts, and the bank's managers were pleased to be rid of them. Whether a company chooses a bundling strategy that stabilizes profits and service, raises fees for customers that are unprofitable, or abandons a market, the driving force is the same: to find a way to make every customer segment profitable by providing the right service, at the right quality, at the right time, and at the right price.

Before they chase away customers, however, managers should keep in mind that short-term customer profitability reports sometimes present a misleading picture, for two basic reasons. First, not all costs assigned to a customer can be reduced if the customer is abandoned. Sometimes the customer's revenue is lost, but with no coincident cost savings. And second, customers that are not profitable today might become profitable in the near future. Firms must look at the customer value over the life of the relationship. Young consumers who buy low-profit, entry-level automobiles after multiple test drives and considerable soul-searching might prove to be outstanding customers in the future. They have potential for moving into larger, more profitable vehicles; they might be relatively easy to retain as customers; and they might be a good source of new ideas for product improvement. Many firms operate with this notion of lifetime customer value in mind, often intuitively. But lifetime customer value is often difficult to estimate at the time a new customer comes to the company.

To facilitate communications within the firm, these customer categories are typically given memorable labels. Some descriptors rank customers from "platinum" to "lead" based on their impact on company profitability. Federal Express labels its customers as "the good," "the bad," and "the ugly."[6] First Union, which was part of Wells Fargo, coded its customers by color. The bank was quite open to requests, such as a fee waiver or a lower credit card interest rate, from "green" customers. "Red" customers, those whose accounts lost money for the bank, had no chance of having such a request approved. "Yellow" customers might have had some chance to negotiate.[7] The importance of paying attention to factors such as these are captured in the following statement by Sir Colin Marshall, chairman of British Airways:

> *Even in a mass-market business, you don't want to attract and retain everyone. As far as we're concerned, the key is first to identify and attract those who will value your service and then retain them as a customer and win the largest possible share of their lifetime business.*[8]

MAKING EXISTING CUSTOMERS MORE PROFITABLE

From a company perspective, ideal customers—those whose value proposition closely matches the firm's value creation profile—have three basic traits. First, ideal customers sole-source. That is, they satisfy all of their needs for the products sold by the firm from the firm. For example, if we operate a catering company, our ideal customers satisfy all of their needs for catering by using us. Second, ideal customers pay the full price we need to maintain our desired profit margins. We do not have to give discounts to get their business. And finally, ideal customers demand no special services. We can satisfy their needs in our normal course of business. For this reason, it is highly beneficial for the firm to treat ideal customers well.

Obviously, not many customers approach this ideal. Keeping the ideal in mind is important, however, because the difference between ideal and actual performance on each of these dimensions defines a "customer profit opportunity." If managers can move their customers closer to the ideal, then they will have increased their firm's profits.

The actions that firms can take to move customers closer to the ideal can be divided into two categories: (1) those that focus on getting additional revenue, and (2) those that focus on reducing costs. To improve customer profitability, firms can consider any of a number of actions designed to increase revenue. First, they can sell their customers more products. Many firms have customers who satisfy some of their needs for the products they sell from competitors. Some of them buy products from only one of the

---

6 These examples are taken from Valerie A. Zeithaml, Roland T. Rust, and Katherine N. Lemon, "The Customer Pyramid: Creating and Serving Profitable Customers," *California Management Review*, 43(4), Summer 2001, pp. 118-142.

7 Brooks, 1999, op cit.

8 Steven E. Prokesch, "Competing on Customer Service: An Interview with British Airways' Sir Colin Marshall," *Harvard Business Review*, November-December, 1995: pp. 101-116.

firm's product lines but not others. Capturing a better share of each customer's business, such as through better cross-selling of products, will increase revenues and profits.

The Limited, Inc., operator of such well-known retailers as Express, New York & Company, Lane Bryant, The Limited stores, Bath & Body Works, and Victoria's Secret, maintains a customer database that provides a "360-degree view" of the company's customer interactions.[9] It often finds customers who buy some products from one retailer in stores and other products from another retailer through catalog purchases. Armed with that knowledge, The Limited's managers can design programs to increase customer profitability or to improve customer satisfaction. They can design marketing campaigns aimed at inducing customers to buy from more channels, to buy higher-margin products, or to use less-expensive channels. Or they can provide more personal service or higher credit limits to their best customers.

Second, firms can sometimes shift their customers' mix of purchases toward more profitable items. For example, the Chevrolet salesman who convinces a customer who came in to buy a Cruze to instead buy an Impala with custom chrome wheels and adaptive cruise control, has earned his company many thousands of dollars of additional profit.

Third, firms can raise prices. This can be done in many ways. They can increase their prices across the board (for example, their list prices), they can lessen their reliance on discounting; or they can add fees for performing extra services. When First Chicago Corp. imposed a teller fee on low-balance customers, it chased a lot of unprofitable customers away, as described previously. At the same time, some other customers changed their behaviors and became profitable. These customers either raised their account balances or began completing their transactions at ATMs, instead of tellers, to avoid the fee.[10]

Price changes should generally only be made with a good understanding of the values customers place on given products or services and their specific attributes, the costs of providing that product or attribute, and the competitive environment (for example, what competitors are charging). Higher prices can alienate customers and drive them off.

Firms can also improve customer profitability by taking any of a number of actions designed to reduce costs. Managers can use the understanding of what their customers value and how they consume firm resources to make decisions about how best to serve the various categories of customers. The ultimate benefit is in eliminating or reducing the costs of non-value-added activities, those that provide value neither to customers nor to the firm. Non-value-added costs could stem from unproductive advertising, inefficient invoicing processes, and customer service activities that customers do not value. Activities that do not provide as much value to customers as they cost to provide should also be eliminated, although eliminating activities that have some value to customers may require some pricing adjustments.

---

9 This example taken from Center for Customer Relationship Management, "Case Studies: The Limited Inc. Channel Management and Customer Profitability," 2002, p. 1.

10 Brooks, 1999, op cit.

IN CONTEXT ➤ Meeting Customer Expectations at Prestige Auto

A month later, the dealership found itself struggling with some of the customers who had responded to their special offers on the new model and with problems in the service department. More customers than Tony could remember returned, complaining that their repairs had not been properly done. He knew they had been busy, but assumed that the quality of the mechanics' work had been maintained, and some buyers of the new model claimed the car had not been fully prepared before it was delivered. It seemed that the specials had stretched Tony's shop beyond its breaking point.

Judy started the management meeting off by hitting directly on the problems: complaints from new car buyers that the cars were not as clean as they should have been. Stickers and sticker glue were still on the windshield in many cases, and the natural dirt that came from transporting the car to the dealership had not been fully cleaned off. Judy was not a happy camper.

"I don't think we should run any more specials in the service department, at least not when we're trying to sell more new and used cars. Our reputation gets tarnished when a new car doesn't feel and look new to the buyer. Service just didn't take the time they usually do detailing each new car, and when you combine that with the fact that they were late delivering the cars, we really had a serious customer service problem!"

"Tony, what happened?" asked Jack.

"We were just too busy. I'm going to have a long talk with my guys about the fact that quality always has to come first. But we got slammed. I've had complaints on my end, too, so I know the problems weren't isolated to one or two guys. Everyone started working too fast to pay attention to the details that we all know are so important. No excuses, though... we should have kept the quality up!"

"Judy, were the cars we delivered really in such bad shape? If so, will offering customers free detailing to be redeemed any time in the next year appease them?" asked Jack.

"Free detailing will probably solve the problem for most of the customers, but there are some you just can't please. Those are the ones I'm worried about. They would be difficult even if everything went right. But with the shortfall in service on top of the delays in Finance we spoke about before, well, some customers just didn't get the type of service they had come to expect from us, and I don't know what will change those folks' minds," replied Judy.

"We're going to have to do more planning in the future if we're going to run specials. Service specials certainly shouldn't run at the same time we're doing special deals on new and used cars. We should have seen that problem coming. But, we also need to get ready in Finance before we offer any more specials. It doesn't serve us well to have unhappy customers," noted Jack. "Let's reconvene next Monday and have a focused discussion on the role of special sales campaigns in our annual strategy."

RETAINING EXISTING CUSTOMERS

The final customer-focused method to increase profits is by improving the retention of desirable customers. In many, if not most, cases, improved customer retention improves profits both by increasing revenues and by reducing costs. Managers can properly view customers as providing annuities, a stream of cash flows, into the firm. The value of these annuities is greater the longer the cash flow stream persists. Hence, retention is valuable just for that purpose.

In addition, however, firms derive other benefits from retaining customers. Many customers actually become more profitable over time, for any number of reasons. On the revenue side, as customers become more comfortable with the relationship, they may buy more products. Where there are long-standing buyer-seller relationships, particularly where friendships have built up, buyers are less apt to pressure suppliers for price and service concessions. And existing customers sometimes provide referrals to new clients.

On the cost side, extending the duration of customer relationships can reduce many non-value-added costs. Generally the costs of finding and then making the first sale to a new customer are far greater than the costs of maintaining and servicing existing customers. A general rule of thumb that applies in many industries is that it is five times more costly to acquire a new customer than it is to retain an existing customer. With existing customers, the initial advertising or promotional burst is not necessary, less sales time is required because the buyers have already learned about the product, and the accounts are already set up on the computer.

How should managers improve customer retention? They should endeavor to get to know their customers well so that they know what the customers value. They should try to keep their good customers happy, as satisfied customers are less likely to look for supplier alternatives. And they should look to create unique competitive advantages that increase the barriers or costs to switching suppliers.

When managers focus on retention, they are taking a perspective that is longer-term than just the current accounting period. Improving customer retention will have relatively little effect on current period profits, but it can have a significant effect on future periods' profits and, hence, the value of the firm as measured at any particular point in time.

For instance, banking customers who maintain small balances in their accounts are almost always unprofitable. On a checking account with an average balance of $1,000, a bank will earn only about $40 per year, assuming it earns a 4% spread on the money. But look at the costs! The preparation and distribution of each statement costs about $1, so that is $12 per year. Suppose the customer makes one visit per month to the branch, with the average cost of each visit about $5. That is another $60 per year, so the bank is already losing money. And it will lose even more for each phone call the customer makes asking for information, each use of an ATM, each "free" cup of coffee consumed, and any special marketing costs incurred to bring this customer into the bank.

It is important to allocate costs correctly. For example, only 11% of the customers of most banks ever enter a bank building after they have set up their accounts, and less than 30% use drive-up windows.[11] If

---

11 J.M. Floyd, "Five Steps to Customer Profitability," BankersOnline.com, May 27, 2002.

the expenses needed to operate the bank building and to employ its staff are allocated to the entire customer base, the resulting profitability analyses will show that the customer group(s) that uses only ATMs is less profitable than it actually is. They will show the opposite for the groups of customers that take up the time of the lobby staff. That makes it important for us to use such tools as activity-based costing to identify the cost drivers and to trace the costs of specific customer segments so that their profitability can be determined before decisions are made to adjust the services offered to them.

Measuring Performance and Making Adjustments

OBJECTIVE 4

Perform a customer profit variance analysis at multiple levels of aggregation and use nonfinancial measures to assess performance.

As you have seen in the decision-making domains discussed in earlier chapters, the "check" and "adjust" elements of the management process involve the comparison of actual results with targets. In this domain, the goal of the analyses should be to explain in as much detail as possible why the results attributable to specific customers and to the corporation as a whole were better or worse than expected.

The factors that might account for differences in customer profitability include a range that can affect revenues, including sales volume, sales mix, and prices. They can also include the cost factors that are related to customers, which, as was discussed previously, could include advertising and promotional expenses, customer support expenses, and warranty expenses.

Performance analyses in the customer domain can be done in one of two ways. One is a customer profit variance analysis approach. The other is a key performance indicator approach. Both of these approaches should be guided by strategic concepts, including an understanding of what the firm must do to be successful.

CUSTOMER PROFIT VARIANCE ANALYSES

If you remember, variance analyses are structured approaches to explaining the difference between two numbers. Typically the most important differences to explain are between actual profits earned and a useful comparison standard such as plan or last period's actuals. In the customer domain, the goal of the variance analysis is to disaggregate the company's overall profit variance, by customer (or customer type) and by the key factors that drive performance.

Customer profit variance analyses can be structured in different ways, depending on managers' purposes and the information they have available. One straightforward and useful way to explain why the profitability of one or more customers was different from that expected involves merely following the format of the customer profitability reports. If plans or budgets are prepared by customer, then the actuals can easily be compared with those plans. Table 13.3 shows how this type of variance analysis might be done for Omega Products, an organization introduced earlier in this chapter.

TABLE 13.3 CUSTOMER PROFITABILITY ANALYSIS BY CUSTOMER AND LINE ITEM

Omega Products															
For the year ending December 31, 20x6 (in millions)															
	Customer														
	Arnold, Inc.			Hakes, Ltd.			Johnson Industries			Unassigned			Total		
	Plan	Actual	Variance	Plan	Actual	Variance	Plan	Actual	Variance	Plan	Actual	Variance	Plan	Actual	Variance
Revenues	$120	$100	$(20)	$270	$300	$30	$720	$600	$(120)				$1,110	$1,000	$(110)
Cost of good sold	$90	$75	$15	$162	$180	$(18)	$360	$293	$67				$612	$548	$64
Gross margin	$30	$25	$(5)	$108	$120	$12	$360	$307	$(53)				$498	$452	$(46)
Sales and marketing expense	$11	$10	$1	$19	$15	$4	$30	$25	$5	$20	$20	$-	$80	$70	$10
Order processing expense	$6	$5	$1	$8	$7	$1	$12	$8	$4			$-	$26	$20	$6
Order collection expense	$5	$5	$-	$4	$5	$(1)	$10	$10	$-	$5	$5	$-	$24	$25	$(1)
Post-sale support expense	$9	$10	$(1)	$18	$15	$3	$6	$5	$1	$10	$10	$-	$43	$40	$3
General and administrative expense	$10	$10	$-	$28	$30	$(2)	$66	$60	$6	$52	$50	$2	$156	$150	$6
Total selling, general and administrative expenses	$41	$40	$1	$77	$72	$5	$124	$108	$16	$87	$85	$2	$329	$305	$24
Operating income	$(11)	$(15)	$(4)	$31	$48	$17	$236	$199	$(37)	$(87)	$(85)	$2	$169	$147	$(22)

NOTE: Positive numbers are favorable variances; negative numbers are unfavorable variances.

What does Table 13.3 tell the managers of Omega Products? It tells them that their profits shortfall stemmed primarily from a failure to meet the sales targets set for their largest customer: Johnson Industries. Cost control looks good, as the company's actual costs were below plan in almost all areas. Managers should also look at the sales and, hence, the profit shortfall from Arnold, Inc. But since Arnold is a much smaller customer, its effect on Omega's overall profits is relatively small.

Omega managers should push the analyses beyond that shown in Table 13.3. They should probe more deeply into the reasons for the sales shortfalls, particularly to their largest customer. This can be done casually, by talking with the marketing and sales managers and, possibly, the salespeople assigned to Johnson Industries. But if the right information can be collected, the probing can also be done in a more structured way using the variance analysis approach.

The information that is available dictates what kind of variance analysis can be done. Table 13.4 provides more information about the assumptions that were impounded into Omega's 20x6 profitability plan for Johnson Industries and about some of the results that actually occurred.

TABLE 13.4 PROFITABILITY ANALYSIS

Johnson Industries		
For the year ending 12/31/20x6		
Omega Product Line A:	Plan	Actual
Johnson's overall purchases of A units (estimated)	$45 million	$40 million
Omega's share of Johnson's A purchases (%)	10%	11%
Average price	$100	$110
Average manufacturing cost	$50	$50
Omega Product Line B:	Plan	Actual
Johnson's overall purchases of B units (estimated)	$27 million	$25 million
Omega's share of Johnson's B purchases (%)	20%	11.6%
Average price	$50	$40
Average manufacturing cost	$25	$25
Cost Behavior for SG&A Expenses		
50% Variable with Revenue	Sales and Marketing Expenses	
	Post-sale Support Expenses	
	Order Processing Expenses	
100% Fixed	Payment Collection Expenses	
	General and Administrative Expenses	

Table 13.5 shows a plan for using the information provided in Table 13.4 to analyze the profitability of Johnson Industries. Here, as in all variance analyses, the analysis should proceed by isolating the effects of one factor at a time. The four factors being considered are shown in the left column of Table 13.5. Omega's plan was originally prepared by making assumptions about each of these factors. This is indicated in Table 13.5 by showing a P in the Plan column for each of the four factors. The actual results came about because each of the four factors came in at some actual level, which was different from the planned level, as is typical. This is indicated by showing an A for each factor in the Actual column in Table 13.5. The variance analysis is done by changing one factor at a time from the planning assumption to the actual amount, leaving all of the other factors alone, and then computing the effect on profits. Thus, for example, changing the assumption about Johnson Industries' overall volume of purchases to the actual amount but leaving all other items at their planned level will yield an amount that can be called the customer purchase volume variance.

TABLE 13.5 PROFITABILITY VARIANCE ANALYSIS

Johnson Industries					
For the year ending 12/31/20x6					
	Plan	Analysis #1	Analysis #2	Analysis #3	Actual
Johnson's overall purchases of product line in units (estimated)	P	A	A	A	A
Omega's share of Johnson's purchases of product line (%)	P	P	A	A	A
Average price	P	P	P	A	A
Costs	P	P	P	P	A

P = assumption or forecast in plan

A = actual results in 20x6

The results of this variance analysis are shown in Table 13.6. The variance summary shows that the negative operating income variance of $37 million for Johnson Industries (see Table 13.3) is due to two primary factors. First, Johnson scaled back its purchases of product lines A and B (the customer purchase volume variance). It did not buy as much from any source as Omega managers had forecasted in their plan. This difference alone accounts for a $33 million negative effect on Omega's bottom line. The finding in the second analysis has more serious implications: Omega failed to meet its planned share of Johnson's total purchases of A and B (the customer market share variance). This, by itself, had a negative $32 million effect on Omega's profits. The sum of the customer purchase volume variance and the customer market share variance results in the sales volume variance.

TABLE 13.6 VARIANCE ANALYSIS

Johnson Industries					
For the year ending 12/31/20x6 (in millions)					
	Plan	Analysis #1	Analysis #2	Analysis #3	Actual
Revenue—Product Line A	$450.0	$400.0	$440.0	$484.0	$484.0
Revenue—Product Line B	$270.0	$250.0	$145.0	$116.0	$116.0
Total Revenue	$720.0	$650.0	$585.0	$600.0	$600.0
Cost of Goods Sold—Product Line A	$225.0	$200.0	$220.0	$220.0	$220.0
Cost of Goods Sold—Product Line B	$135.0	$125.0	$73.0	$73.0	$73.0
Total Cost of Goods Sold	$360.0	$325.0	$293.0	$293.0	$293.0
Gross Margin—Product Line A	$225.0	$200.0	$220.0	$264.0	$264.0
Gross Margin—Product Line B	$135.0	$125.0	$72.0	$43.0	$43.0
Total Gross Margin	$360.0	$325.0	$292.0	$307.0	$307.0
Sales and Marketing Expense—Product Line A	$19.0	$18.0	$19.0	$20.0	$16.0

Johnson Industries					
For the year ending 12/31/20x6 (in millions)					
	Plan	Analysis #1	Analysis #2	Analysis #3	Actual
Sales and Marketing Expense—Product Line B	$11.0	$10.0	$8.0	$8.0	$9.0
Total Sales and Marketing Expense	$30.0	$28.0	$27.0	$28.0	$25.0
Order Processing Expense—Product Line A	$8.0	$8.0	$8.0	$8.0	$5.0
Order Processing Expense—Product Line B	$4.0	$4.0	$4.0	$4.0	$3.0
Total Order Processing Expense	$12.0	$12.0	$12.0	$12.0	$8.0
Order Collection Expense—Product Line A	$6.0	$6.0	$6.0	$6.0	$6.0
Order Collection Expense—Product Line B	$4.0	$4.0	$4.0	$4.0	$4.0
Total Order Collection Expense	$10.0	$10.0	$10.0	$10.0	$10.0
Post-Sale Support Expense—Product Line A	$4.0	$4.0	$4.0	$4.0	$3.0
Post-Sale Support Expense—Product Line B	$2.0	$2.0	$2.0	$1.0	$2.0
Total Post-Sale Support Expense	$6.0	$6.0	$6.0	$5.0	$5.0
General and Administrative Expense—Product Line A	$41.0	$41.0	$41.0	$41.0	$38.0
General and Administrative Expense—Product Line B	$25.0	$25.0	$25.0	$25.0	$22.0
Total General and Administrative Expense	$66.0	$66.0	$66.0	$66.0	$60.0
Total Customer—Related Expenses	$124.0	$122.0	$121.0	$121.0	$108.0
Operating income	$236.0	$203.0	$171.0	$186.0	$199.0

NOTE: Operating income is the difference between the total gross margin and the total customer-related expenses.

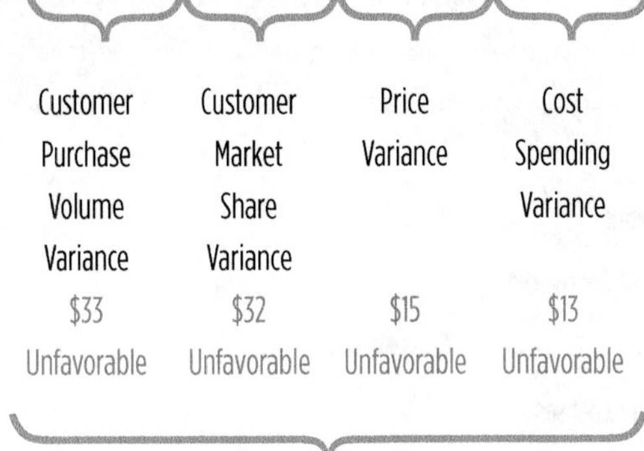

Total variance $37 Unfavorable

The variance analysis shown in Table 13.6 also shows a favorable price variance of $15 million. This is a quantification of the effect caused by the fact that the prices paid by Johnson Industries on the units they bought from Omega were higher than Omega's managers forecasted in the plan. The favorable price variance could be interpreted as good news, as Omega more than maintained its margins on the units it sold to Johnson. However, the higher prices could also be the cause, or one of the causes, of the unfavorable customer market share variance. This is something that Omega's managers should investigate further.

The final analysis of the cost spending variances shows a favorable variance. Even after adjustments for the declining sales volumes are factored in, Omega managers spent less than plan in servicing the

Johnson account. The total positive effect on Omega profits was $13 million. This is generally good news unless it can be determined that the failure to spend money in certain areas had some adverse effects. It is possible, for example, that the decrease in Sales and Marketing Expense caused part of the decline in sales to Johnson Industries. This might be revealed if a nonfinancial performance measure such as customer satisfaction was included in the management monitoring reports. The cost variance could also be separated into fixed and variable pieces. Since half of the total costs for sales and marketing and post-purchase support vary with revenue, the spending variance could be split into fixed and variable spending differences. This would require changing the variable portion of the total SG&A first, and then the fixed portion.

Managers may not want to stop with the report shown in Table 13.6. They could easily disaggregate the variances by product line. This analysis is shown in Table 13.7. The product line variance report shows more clearly that the performance problems relating to Johnson Industries in 20x6 stemmed exclusively from Product Line B. Johnson Industries did not buy as much of B; they particularly did not buy B from Omega; and what they did buy from Omega was at a lower price than Omega managers had planned for. Omega managers should probably focus their attention on understanding and fixing the problems with the B product line.

TABLE 13.7 VARIANCE ANALYSIS: CUSTOMER PROFITABILITY BY PRODUCT LINE

Johnson Industries					
For the year ending 12/31/20x6 (in millions)					
Product Line A:	Customer Purchase Volume Variance	Customer Market Share Variance	Price Variance	Spending Variance	Total Variance
Revenue	$(50.0)	$40.0	$44.0	-	$34.0
Cost of Goods Sold	$25.0	$(20.0)	-	-	$5.0
Gross Margin	$(25.0)	$20.0	$44.0	-	$39.0
Other Expenses	$1.0	$(1.0)	$(1.0)	$11.0	$10.0
Total Variance—A	$(24.0)	$19.0	$43.0	$11.0	$49.0
Product Line B:					
Revenue	$(20.0)	$(105.0)	$(29.0)	-	$(154.0)
Cost of Goods Sold	$10.0	$52.0	-	-	$62.0
Gross Margin	$(10.0)	$(53.0)	$(29.0)	-	$(92.0)
Other Expenses	$1.0	$2.0	$1.0	$2.0	$6.0
Total Variance—B	$(9.0)	$(51.0)	$(28.0)	$2.0	$(86.0)
Total Customer-Related Variance	$(33.0)	$(32.0)	$15.0	$13.0	$(37.0)

Note: Positive numbers indicate favorable variances; negative numbers indicate unfavorable variances.

Omega managers might also want to push their formal variance analysis even further. For example, they might find it useful to disaggregate the product line variances all the way down to the individual product level. This would require knowledge about Johnson Industries' total purchases of individual products. The point of this discussion is to show the power of variance analysis. If you have the information required to analyze the reasons for a sales or profit shortfall, there is almost no limit to the analysis that can be done. The goal is to analyze the variances until causes can be determined. When Omega determined it was poor performance on Product B that caused the profitability problem, it really did not need to look much further. Variance analysis is a tool to be used to gain an understanding of trends and to decouple as many effects from each other as possible.

IN CONTEXT ➤ Linking Special Sales to Strategy at Prestige Auto

A week has gone by and every manager at Prestige Auto has had one key question in mind: What role should special sales campaigns play at Prestige Auto?

"Well, the next special runs next week," said Judy. "We're going to offer some trade-in promotions to go with the used car sales. Tony, can you set some people aside to detail the used cars that are purchased? I know we detail them when they come in, but a bit of extra care when they are sold would make a good impression. I'd like to be able to put 'certified' on the used cars so the customers know that we'll stand behind the reliability of the cars. That means we should also be sure they don't have any mechanical problems."

"This is the first I've heard about the used car special sale," Bruce exclaimed. "Acquisitions needs to be front and center here; we could have spent time bringing in really great used cars. At this late date, there's only so much we'll be able to do to support the sale."

"And Finance is going to need to get ready for a deluge of used car financing deals. They are more complex than new car and service work because we have to certify to the lending agency that the car will function for the life of the loan. They are always hesitant about quality, and in addition they are concerned because many used car buyers aren't as credit-worthy as new car buyers tend to be. I'll get started at reassigning my people so we avoid some of the problems we had, but it would have been great to know earlier so we could have trained some more people," said Alice.

"Well, the special has been promoted on radio, local television, and the newspapers, so we have to go with it," Judy responded. "But I hear what everyone is saying. We need to communicate better internally and learn more in advance about our likely customers so we can be sure to meet their expectations. I suggest that from now on we give each other at least a one-month warning on any special sale or event we want to run. That way I won't run a sales event at the same time Tony is doing one in Service. We're learning the hard way that meeting customer expectations takes a lot of planning."

Jack said: "Why don't the four of you get together and hammer out a plan for the used car sale? Bruce, see if your guys can pull some rabbits out of their hats to bring in the highest-quality used cars they can find, preferably high-end cars coming off leases. Tony, find out what the demand is going to be on your group, and then let me know if we need to get you some more help in the shop. Alice, same goes for you. We need Finance ready to go when we run these specials. Finally, Judy, I want you to get a report to me by Friday that summarizes the plans that have been made to deal with the surge in used car sales. Bruce's group will also need to be available to put a value on any trade-ins, so let's not forget that detail. OK, group: Let's get busy pleasing our customers by being the best car dealership around!" With that, Jack ended the meeting, hoping his managers could rapidly find a way to focus resources where they needed to be to make the next sales event a smooth, customer-pleasing experience.

NONFINANCIAL PERFORMANCE MEASURES IN THE CUSTOMER DOMAIN

Many companies use any of a number of customer-related nonfinancial measures, such as customer satisfaction, market penetration, number of complaints, and customer referrals to provide a more complete reflection of performance in the customer domain than the financial performance measures alone can provide. These nonfinancial measures allow managers to pay extra attention to some of the key customer-related determinants of organizational success. Some of these nonfinancial measures also have the advantage of being leading indicators of success. Better performance in some of these areas today should lead to better financial performance in the future.

The corporate frameworks that provide the links between the nonfinancial and the financial performance measures vary considerably in their specificity and completeness. Some companies use a few key performance indicators that are thought to reflect aspects of performance that are "obviously" important. For example, it is hard to argue with the notion that managers should be concerned if customer satisfaction is declining.

Other companies have attempted to build more complete models of the strategies they want to follow to create customer value and, hence, shareholder value. Sometimes these are referred to as balanced scorecards, which are guided by strategy maps.[12] A strategy map specifies the critical elements in an organization's strategy and their linkages. Since creating value for customers is the central mission for all organizations, strategy maps usually cut across all aspects of an organization. For example, customer satisfaction can be affected by production quality, sales force knowledge, pricing policies, delivery promptness, and accounting (for example, billing) procedures.

A customer value proposition, which delineates how the firm's focus on customers will create value, is clearly visible inside some strategy maps. Figure 13.4 shows the customer value proposition for a

12 Robert D. Kaplan and David P. Norton. *The Strategy-Focused Organization,* Boston: Harvard Business School Press, 2000.

diversified service company.[13] One of the themes in this company's strategy was to grow its high contribution margin business. In order to remain viable, its managers knew that the business needed to remain competitive in three basic performance areas: on-time delivery, competitive quality, and competitive pricing. But to grow a high-margin business, managers knew they needed also to differentiate their company from its competitors. **Differentiators** *are aspects of performance valued by the firm's target customers; areas where the firm can outperform its competitors.*

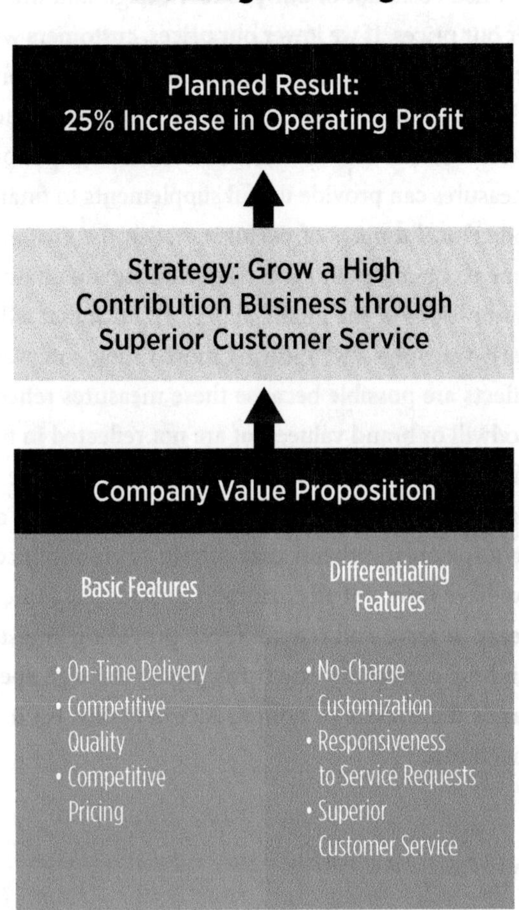

FIGURE 13.4 THIS STRATEGY MAP ILLUSTRATES HOW THE FIRM'S FOCUS ON CUSTOMERS WILL CREATE THE VALUE THAT LEADS TO SUPERIOR PROFITS FOR THE COMPANY.

13 Michael Contrada, "Using the Balanced Scorecard to Manage Value in Your Business," *Balanced Scorecard Report,* January 15, 2000, pp. 3-6.

This firm's managers identified three differentiators: no-charge customization, responsiveness to service requests, and superior customer service. Performance in each of these areas could be measured in nonfinancial terms. Then managers focused on what was necessary for the organization to be able to perform well in these areas of differentiation. This led them to identify needed improvements in their production and sales organizations and to develop nonfinancial measures that were used to monitor performance in those areas of the company.

Other companies' customer value propositions involve other foci and measures. For example, a customer value proposition for a company that competes for price-sensitive customers might proceed as follows: "If we cut non-value-added costs out of our product design and improve our production efficiency, then we will be able to lower our prices. If we lower our prices, customers will perceive that they are receiving more value from our products. If customers perceive that they are receiving more value, then they will buy more of our products." These strategic statements help employees to understand the business's strategy. They also suggest specific measures that should be tracked to monitor performance in the critical areas.

Clearly, nonfinancial measures can provide useful supplements to financial measures of performance. They can provide a focus on critical aspects of performance in the customer domain, such as those that deal with customer requirements or competitors' actions that are not obvious in the financial results. They often also provide leading indications of the financial performance that will be realized in the future, thus providing managers with early warnings and allowing more timely interventions to solve potentially burgeoning problems. These effects are possible because these measures reflect the value of some intangible assets, such as customer goodwill or brand value, that are not reflected in financial statements.

When we examine issues in the customer domain, therefore, we have to deal with a variety of issues and challenges. From the time the firm's value proposition for its products and services is defined through the completion of the order-to-payment process that culminates in profits or losses, customer preferences need to be considered. As we have seen, not all customers provide the same level of profitability for a company. Some customers are easy to serve and remain loyal, providing long-term, stable profitability. Other customers are highly demanding, consuming the firm's profits through special services and price concessions. A firm that understands the impact of nonproduct demands on its bottom line will have greater control over its profits and its future.

Summary

The customer domain provides a different, but also valuable, way to organize the information about how a corporation or one of its business units earns its profits. The customer perspective is obviously valuable because serving customers, and earning profits from them, is the primary purpose for the existence of corporations. If managers can improve customer profitability, they can improve firm profitability. Both managers and finance professionals must become conversant with the customer domain issues and the tools that can be applied to them.

The application of business planning and analysis data, tools, and techniques to the customer domain is relatively recent. At the present time, most firms do not do a good job of measuring customer profitability; they track it down only to the gross margin level. But many marketing, administrative, and post-sale customer service costs can be traced to customers, and this tracing can greatly alter the customer profitability picture. Activity-based costing can help with this tracing task, so it is a tool that has value beyond the manufacturing floor.

However, the standard customer profitability analyses are short term-oriented. They do not provide managers with good measures of lifetime customer value, which is what the firm's managers should be most interested in when they decide which customers to serve. To get a long-term perspective, firms must focus on customer loyalty and their tendency to buy products over a period of years, not just in one month or year. Customer loyalty is the linchpin to long-term profitability and growth, a measure that is just beginning to be understood in measurable terms in the management literature.

Once they are able to measure customer profitability effectively, managers can use that information to decide better which customers to serve and how to serve them. They can also disaggregate customer profitability reports to understand better where they are doing a good job and where they need to improve their performance. Nonfinancial measures of performance can also provide a useful supplement to the financial performance measures because some of them are indicators of the drivers of success. They provide more timely leading indicators of future performance, which is always the concern of the management team because only the future can be changed.

Key Terms

Customer value proposition: the strategy used by a company to attract its desired customers; how it differentiates itself from its competitors.

Differentiators: aspects of performance valued by the firm's target customers; areas where the firm can outperform its competitors.

Ideal customers: those whose value proposition closely matches the firm's value creation profile.

Leverage: the multiplier effect of one more dollar of value-added work on the company's revenue line.

Predatory customers: those that require significant price concessions and extra service components in order to get their business.

Value attribute: the characteristic or feature of a product or service that is directly valued by the customer.

Value-based segmentation: the clustering of customers because they have a similar value proposition.

Questions

1. Name some of the costs, outside of producing the product, that customers cause in organizations that serve them.
2. What is the measurement of short-term customer profitability?
3. What defines a good customer profitability analysis vs. a bad one?
4. Define the term "value attribute" and give several examples of them.
5. What is a customer value proposition?
6. Describe the economics of the market in terms of what each ring in Figure 13.2 represents.
7. What is value-based customer segmentation? Why is it used?
8. What are the three ways a company can earn greater profits from customers?
9. Identify the four basic types of customers and describe how each affects the costs of a firm trying to serve them.
10. What are the three basic traits of an ideal customer?
11. What is customer retention and why is it important to a firm?
12. Describe a customer profitability report.
13. What are some of the variances we can run on customer profitability?
14. What is the difference between basic features of a firm's value proposition and its differentiators? Please give examples of each.

Exercises

1. **ACTIVITY-BASED CUSTOMER COSTS.** The following table contains information about several activity-based customer costs and the use of these activities by customers.

Activity	Cost	Use by Customer A	Use by Customer B	Use by Customer C
Order processing	$250,000	1,000	5,000	4,000
Invoicing	$175,000	2,500	12,500	5,000
Customer service calls	$300,000	600	4,400	1,000

REQUIRED:

Using the information provided, please develop an ABC rate for each activity and use it to charge costs to the firm's customers.

2. **ACTIVITY-BASED CUSTOMER COSTS.** The following table contains information about several activity-based customer costs and the use of these activities by the firm's customers.

Activity	Cost	Use by Customer A	Use by Customer B	Use by Customer C
Sales call hours	$500,000	1,500	3,500	5,000
Number of sales made	$350,000	5,000	10,000	2,500
Post-purchase support hours	$600,000	6,000	5,000	1,000

REQUIRED:

Using the information provided, please develop an ABC rate for each activity and use it to charge costs to the firm's customers.

3. **CATEGORIZE ACTIVITIES.** For the list of activities in the following table, note whether they are value-add (VA), business value-add (BVA), or waste (W).

Activity	Type	Activity	Type
Fill customer order		Take customer order	
Type invoice		Make product	
Hold meeting		Queue product in line	
Scrap part		Create report	

4. **CATEGORIZE ACTIVITIES.** For the list of activities in the following table, note whether they are value-add (VA), business value-add (BVA), or waste (W).

Activity	Type	Activity	Type
Provide service to customer		Ship order to customer	
Process purchase order		Close accounting books	
Rework part		Prepare annual report	
Hire employee		Expedite materials	

5. **A BASIC CUSTOMER PROFITABILITY REPORT.** Using the following information, determine which customer is more profitable to serve. Calculate both total profit and profit percentage (of revenue) for each customer.

Line Item	Customer A	Customer B	Customer C
Revenue	$10,000.00	$15,000.00	$20,000.00
Cost of goods sold	$5,000.00	$8,250.00	$12,000.00
Order processing	$750.00	$1,250.00	$1,500.00
Order shipment	$500.00	$1,000.00	$2,000.00
Sales support	$250.00	$500.00	$1,000.00

6. **A BASIC CUSTOMER PROFITABILITY REPORT.** Using the following information, determine which customer is more profitable to serve. Calculate both total profit and profit percentage (of revenue) for each customer.

Line Item	Customer A	Customer B	Customer C
Revenue	$150,000.00	$20,000.00	$250,000.00
Cost of sales	$72,000.00	$102,000.00	$135,000.00
Sales calls	$5,000.00	$10,000.00	$15,000.00
Service support	$25,000.00	$30,000.00	$50,000.00
Post-purchase training	$18,000.00	$25,000.00	$35,000.00

7. **PROFITABILITY VARIANCE REPORT.** Calculate the following variances for Customer X of Easy Speed Printing Services. Mark each variance as favorable or unfavorable. Remember that if the variance of actual minus budget is negative for revenues, it is unfavorable, but would be favorable for expenses. If need be, just think through the relationship.

Customer X Profit Analysis		
Line Item	**Budget**	**Actual**
Revenue	$10,000.00	$9,500.00
Less: Cost of goods sold	$4,800.00	$4,465.00
Gross margin	$5,200.00	$5,035.00
Selling expenses	$750.00	$600.00
Support services	$1,200.00	$1,000.00
Invoicing	$250.00	$350.00
General overhead	$1,800.00	$1,750.00
Total SG&A costs	$4,000.00	$3,700.00
Customer profitability	$1,200.00	$1,335.00

8. **PROFITABILITY VARIANCE REPORT.** Calculate the following variances for Customer Z of Tom's Limo Services. Mark each variance as favorable or unfavorable. Remember that if the variance of actual minus budget is negative for revenues, it is unfavorable, but would be favorable for expenses. If need be, just think through the relationship.

Customer Z Profit Analysis		
Line Item	**Budget**	**Actual**
Revenue	$2,800.00	$2,600.00
Less: Cost of sales	$1,344.00	$1,222.00
Gross margin	$1,456.00	$1,378.00
Pickup orders	$250.00	$300.00
Limo downtime	$250.00	$150.00
Invoicing	$125.00	$160.00
General overhead	$500.00	$600.00
Total SG&A costs	$1,125.00	$1,210.00
Customer profitability	$331.00	$168.00

9. **LEVERAGE EFFECT.** For each of the following value attributes, the revenue it earned for the company is stated alongside the cost to provide that attribute. For each attribute, determine its leverage or multiplier effect. Note it in the column provided.

Value Attribute	Revenue	Cost	Leverage
Ease of use	$250	$150	
Length of useful life	$200	$100	
Post-purchase support	$150	$100	
Appearance	$50	$20	

10. **LEVERAGE EFFECT.** For each of the following value attributes for a car, the revenue it earned for the company is stated alongside the cost to provide that attribute. For each attribute, determine its leverage or multiplier effect. Note it in the column provided.

Value Attribute	Revenue	Cost	Leverage
Durability	$8,000	$5,500	
Appearance	$8,000	$4,500	
Acceleration	$2,500	$1,000	
Post-purchase service	$4,500	$2,500	

Problems

1. **ABC COSTING AND CUSTOMER ANALYSIS.** Chopsticks, Inc., makes chopsticks that are used in Chinese restaurants and in households across the Midwest. It has several different types of customers, including restaurants, department stores, and grocery stores. Restaurants order the chopsticks one to two cases at a time from a distributor that buys in large quantities and resells the chopsticks to the restaurants. Department stores buy directly from Chopsticks, Inc., and usually buy partial cases that are delivered directly to the stores. Finally, grocery stores buy for their entire chain so they order several cases at a time directly shipped to their distribution center, where they are broken down into smaller

quantities. Chopsticks charges the same price to all three channels of distribution. Each channel marks up the chopsticks about 40%, so the price the ultimate customer faces is about the same regardless of where they buy the product.

The data for the three channels is in the table below. It details the work done to support the various channels.

Chopsticks, Inc.					
Activity	**Cost**	**Driver**	**Distributors**	**Department Stores**	**Grocery Stores**
Sales	N/A	N/A	$2,000,000	$750,000	$1,500,000
Cost of goods sold	N/A	N/A	$960,000	$375,000	$720,000
Order processing	$300,000	Orders	20,000	4,000	16,000
Case breakdown	$50,000	Breakdowns	-	4,000	1,000
Shipping packing slips	$150,000	Packing slips	20,000	16,000	16,000
Delivery	$200,000	Deliveries	20,000	16,000	16,000
Invoices	$350,000	Invoices	40,000	50,000	40,000
Returns	$175,000	Returns	100	500	150

REQUIRED:

a. **Develop ABC charging rates for each of the activities.**
b. **Use this rate to charge out the cost of the various services to the customers.**
c. **Develop customer profitability statements for each type of customer.**
d. **Calculate the percentage profit for each type of customer.**
e. **Which customer class is the best for Chopsticks, Inc.? Which is the worst? Why?**

2. **ABC COSTING AND CUSTOMER ANALYSIS.** Sparkle, Inc., makes paper towels that it sells to several different types of customers: wholesale distributors, warehouse stores, and grocery stores. The wholesale distributor requires smaller cases that it can deliver to convenience stores and other small users, such as office buildings. This specialty pack-out requires Sparkle to use a different packaging machine and changes the configuration of the pallets it uses to ship out goods (it gets more cases on a pallet, but fewer actual paper towels because of the bulky boxes). The company has compiled the following information on its customers and the services they use from Sparkle.

Sparkle, Inc.					
Activity	**Cost**	**Driver**	**Distributors**	**Warehouse Stores**	**Grocery Stores**
Sales	N/A	N/A	$10,000,000	$20,000,000	$15,000,000
Cost of goods sold	N/A	N/A	$4,900,000	$9,600,000	$7,350,000
Order processing	$750,000	Orders	100,000	25,000	75,000
Cases	$2,500,000	Cases packed	2,000,000	1,250,000	800,000
Palletizing	$1,500,000	Pallets made	250,000	125,000	80,000
Delivery	$2,000,000	Deliveries	100,000	25,000	100,000
Invoices	$1,250,000	Invoices	250,000	50,000	1,500,000
Returns	$350,000	Returns	500	100	400

REQUIRED:

a. Develop ABC charging rates for each of the activities.
b. Use this rate to charge out the cost of the various services to the customers.
c. Develop customer profitability statements for each type of customer.
d. Calculate the percentage profit for each type of customer.
e. Which customer class is the best for Sparkle, Inc.? Which is the worst? Why?

3. **VALUE-BASED SEGMENTATION.** Sub-tropics makes a variety of clothing for use in very hot climates. Its special fabrics wick moisture away from the body of the wearer, without becoming sodden because it has rapid-drying characteristics. The result is clothing that actually helps keep the customer cooler and drier even on the hottest, most humid days. The line of clothing has become increasingly popular with athletes, too, who find that the clothing helps keep them from sweating through their running shorts and T-shirts quite so fast. The various types of customers vary greatly in terms of how much value they place on the style of the clothing vs. its durability. Sub-tropics has compiled the following value attributes for 10 of its largest retail outlets.

Sub-tropics, Inc.										
Value Attribute	**Jack's Trading Company**	**Benny's Sporting Goods**	**Ralph's Clothing Store**	**Frank's Clothiers**	**Evertyhing Casual**	**Outfitters, Inc.**	**Trudy's Designer Wear**	**Family Values**	**Blue Glass Clothiers**	**Phantom Suppliers**
Style	7	4	10	9	8	4	10	8	10	5
Durability	7	9	4	5	8	10	6	8	7	10

REQUIRED:

a. Create a chart that captures these two value attributes.
b. Place an X with the initials of the store on your chart to position each according to its value preferences.
c. Draw a circle around groups that seem to cluster together. These are your segments.
d. How many segments did you derive? What are their primary differences?
e. What would you recommend to Sub-tropics regarding its product lines? Should it focus on one segment or does it need to develop marketing strategies that are different for each segment with one consistent quality product? Why?

---

4. **VALUE-BASED SEGMENTATION.** Grillmasters makes a variety of gas and charcoal grills for customers across the United States. While the grills vary in a number of ways, the primary differences are features (special functions) and price. Joe Blake, president of Grillmasters, has asked its marketing department to do some value-based segmentation analysis of its primary 10 customers. The study results in the following information.

Grillmasters										
Value Attribute	Martin's Hardware	Big Box Stores	Sam's Outdoor Furniture	Janus Outdoor Supplies	Everything Grilling	Outdoor Living	Alice's BBQ Shop	Homestyle Hardware	Red Goose BBQ Supplies	Garbo's Hardware
Price	7	10	8	10	8	4	4	8	10	5
Features	7	4	7	5	8	10	10	8	7	10

REQUIRED:

a. Create a chart that captures these two value attributes.
b. Place an X with the initials of the store on your chart to position each according to its value preferences.
c. Draw a circle around groups that seem to cluster together. These are your segments.
d. How many segments did you derive? What are their primary differences?
e. What would you recommend to Grillmasters regarding its product lines? Should it focus on one segment or does it need to develop marketing strategies that are different for each segment with one consistent quality product or develop different products for each market segment? Why?

5. **PRODUCT LINE PROFITABILITY VARIANCE ANALYSIS.** McGregor Electronics makes wireless handheld telephones and answering machine units for use in the home. It makes two models, a three-phone set with answering machine and a six-phone set with answering machine. It also sells freestanding phones that can be added to any one of the existing systems. The company is trying to understand the profitability of its product lines, so it develops the following information.

McGregor Electronics						
Line Item	Three-Phone Sets		Six-Phone Sets		Single Phones	
	Budget	Actual	Budget	Actual	Budget	Actual
Revenue	$25,000,000	$24,750,000	$85,000,000	$92,000,000	$55,000,000	$62,500,000
Less: Cost of goods sold	$11,250,000	$12,500,000	$36,550,000	$39,560,000	$26,400,000	$28,750,000
Gross margin	$13,750,000	$12,250,000	$48,450,000	$52,440,000	$28,600,000	$33,750,000
Order processing	$1,500,000	$1,800,000	$5,200,000	$6,400,000	$4,500,000	$5,000,000
Packing	$3,800,000	$3,600,000	$12,500,000	$13,800,000	$9,300,000	$10,000,000
Invoicing	$1,800,000	$1,900,000	$4,500,000	$5,400,000	$4,500,000	$5,400,000
General overhead	$4,200,000	$4,400,000	$15,420,000	$17,500,000	$6,300,000	$7,500,000
Total SG&A	$11,300,000	$11,700,000	$37,620,000	$43,100,000	$24,600,000	$27,900,000
Profit before tax	$2,450,000	$550,000	$10,830,000	$9,340,000	$4,000,000	$5,850,000
Profit percentage	9.80%	2.22%	12.74%	10.15%	7.27%	9.36%

REQUIRED:

a. Prepare a line item variance report for the three product lines at McGregor's. Remember that positive variances for revenues are favorable (actual larger than budget) and positive variances for expenses are unfavorable.

b. Convert everything in the tables into percentages.

c. Prepare a line item variance report using your percentages.

d. Compare the variances when using absolute dollars to those using percentages, focusing on line items where the percentage variance gives a different picture of performance than the absolute variances. Do they give the same information? Why or why not?

6. **PRODUCT LINE PROFITABILITY VARIANCE ANALYSIS.** Outdoor Life makes three different product lines of outdoor furniture: recliners, chairs, and table sets. The company is known for its distinctive materials, so all three product lines offer the same options for materials and colors. They clearly vary in the amount of material used. Also, the freestanding chairs are exactly like the table chairs for each fashion grouping, so they

can be used as additional seating or as freestanding chairs. That means there is some cross-selling that takes place between table sets and chairs. Management has decided it would like to compare the performance of the three lines against its budget. Managers have prepared the following information for you and have asked that you do the analysis.

Outdoor Life						
Line Item	Recliners		Chairs		Table Sets	
	Budget	Actual	Budget	Actual	Budget	Actual
Revenue	$30,000,000	$27,850,000	$45,000,000	$48,000,000	$60,000,000	$62,500,000
Less: Cost of goods sold	$14,400,000	$13,500,000	$20,250,000	$20,160,000	$28,800,000	$28,750,000
Gross margin	$15,600,000	$14,350,000	$24,750,000	$27,840,000	$31,200,000	$33,750,000
Sales calls	$2,500,000	$2,400,000	$2,400,000	$3,000,000	$4,800,000	$5,000,000
Order processing	$4,600,000	$4,200,000	$3,500,000	$3,800,000	$4,600,000	$4,800,000
Shipping	$1,500,000	$1,300,000	$1,600,000	$1,800,000	$3,000,000	$3,500,000
General overhead	$3,600,000	$3,400,000	$4,800,000	$5,000,000	$6,300,000	$6,800,000
Total SG&A	$12,200,000	$11,300,000	$12,300,000	$13,600,000	$18,700,000	$20,100,000
Profit before tax	$3,400,000	$3,050,000	$12,450,000	$14,240,000	$12,500,000	$13,650,000
Profit percentage	11.33%	10.95%	27.67%	29.67%	20.83%	21.84%

REQUIRED:

a. Prepare a line item variance report for the three product lines at McGregor's. Remember that positive variances for revenues are favorable (actual larger than budget) and positive variances for expenses are unfavorable.
b. Convert everything in the tables into percentages.
c. Prepare a line item variance report using your percentages.
d. Compare the variances when using absolute dollars to those using percentages, focusing on line items where the percentage variance gives a different picture of performance than the absolute variances. Do they give the same information? Why or why not?

---

7. **LINE ITEM CUSTOMER PROFITABILITY VARIANCE ANALYSIS.** Safe at Home produces several lines of ant traps for commercial and domestic use. It sells its products to three major wholesalers, which then distribute them to the retail market. Recently new management took over the company and it would like to get an idea of the profitability of these three wholesalers: Bennie's Wholesale, Pickens Wholesaling, and Rogers Products, Ltd. It provides you with the following information for the last year.

Safe at Home						
Line Item	Bennie's Wholesale		Pickens Wholesaling		Rogers Products, Ltd.	
	Budget	Actual	Budget	Actual	Budget	Actual
Revenue	$12,000,000	$11,500,000	$10,000,000	$11,500,000	$15,000,000	$16,500,000
Less: Cost of goods sold	$5,760,000	$5,462,500	$4,500,000	$4,830,000	$7,200,000	$7,590,000
Gross margin	$6,240,000	$6,037,500	$5,500,000	$6,670,000	$7,800,000	$8,910,000
Sales calls	$1,500,000	$1,800,000	$1,200,000	$1,500,000	$1,800,000	$2,300,000
Order processing	$1,000,000	$900,000	$850,000	$900,000	$1,200,000	$1,500,000
Shipping	$750,000	$700,000	$600,000	$650,000	$800,000	$850,000
General overhead	$1,800,000	$1,850,000	$1,600,000	$1,400,000	$1,900,000	$2,200,000
Total SG&A	$5,050,000	$5,250,000	$4,250,000	$4,450,000	$5,700,000	$6,850,000
Profit before tax	$1,190,000	$787,500	$1,250,000	$2,220,000	$2,100,000	$2,060,000
Profit percentage	9.92%	6.85%	12.50%	19.30%	14.00%	12.48%

REQUIRED:

a. Create a customer profitability variance report by line item for Safe at Home's three major customers.
b. Translate the results in the above table into percentage terms.
c. Create a customer profitability variance report by line item using the percentages derived in (b).
d. Which customer looks best? Why? Does your answer change any if you use percentages instead of absolute dollars?

---

8. **LINE ITEM CUSTOMER PROFITABILITY VARIANCE ANALYSIS.** Lucky Foods produces a variety of dog treats that it sells through three major wholesalers, BJ's Pet Foods, Anderson Pet Products, and Nielsen, Inc. There has been some debate over the last few years about which customer is best for the firm. To answer this question, management has decided to do a customer profitability analysis for the prior year to see what it can find out. The information it gathers to do this analysis is in the following table.

Lucky Foods						
Line Item	BJ's Pet Foods		Anderson Pet Products		Nielsen, Inc.	
	Budget	Actual	Budget	Actual	Budget	Actual
Revenue	$18,000,000	$20,100,000	$15,000,000	$13,500,000	$20,000,000	$16,500,000
Less: Cost of goods sold	$9,000,000	$9,748,500	$7,200,000	$6,210,000	$9,600,000	$7,590,000
Gross margin	$9,000,000	$10,351,500	$7,800,000	$7,290,000	$10,400,000	$8,910,000
Order processing	$2,000,000	$2,200,000	$1,500,000	$1,500,000	$2,500,000	$2,600,000

Lucky Foods						
Line Item	BJ's Pet Foods		Anderson Pet Products		Nielsen, Inc.	
	Budget	Actual	Budget	Actual	Budget	Actual
Packaging	$3,000,000	$3,500,000	$2,500,000	$2,300,000	$3,500,000	$3,000,000
Shipping	$900,000	$1,100,000	$800,000	$650,000	$1,300,000	$1,500,000
General overhead	$2,250,000	$2,500,000	$2,000,000	$1,800,000	$2,200,000	$1,800,000
Total SG&A	$8,150,000	$9,300,000	$6,800,000	$6,250,000	$9,500,000	$8,900,000
Profits before tax	$850,000	$1,051,500	$1,000,000	$1,040,000	$900,000	$10,000
Profit percentage	4.72%	5.23%	6.67%	7.70%	4.50%	0.06%

REQUIRED:

a. Create a customer profitability variance report by line item for Lucky Foods' three major customers.
b. Translate the results in the above table into percentage terms.
c. Create a customer profitability variance report by line item using the percentages derived in (b).
d. Which customer looks best? Why? Does your answer change any if you use percentages instead of absolute dollars?

9. **DETAILED CUSTOMER VARIANCE ANALYSIS.** Susie Goodman's Products makes several lines of women's handbags. While it sells to many customers, it has recently become concerned over the performance of one specific customer, Neon Lights. Neon Lights buys two specific types of purses that come in a variety of colors. Since all that changes when the color changes is the color of the material, the company pays little attention to this detail. Instead, it focuses on whether the product is a handbag or a clutch purse. The information the company has collected on Neon Lights is in the tables below.

	Plan	Actual
Revenues	$865,500.00	$826,200.00
Less: Cost of goods sold	$447,000.00	$528,000.00
Gross margin	$418,500.00	$298,200.00
Variable SG&A	$82,500.00	$101,000.00
Fixed SG&A	$147,500.00	$147,500.00
Total SG&A	$230,000.00	$248,500.00
Income before tax	$188,500.00	$49,700.00

	Plan	Actual
Susies Groodman's Handbags		
Neon Lights overall purchase of handbags	50,000	60,000
Goodman's share of Neon Lights handbag purchases (%)	20%	25%
Average price	$50.00	$45.00
Average manufacturing cost	$30.00	$28.00
Susie Goodman's Clutch Purses		
Neon Lights overall purchase of clutch purses	35,000	30,000
Goodman's share of Neon Lights clutch purses purchases (%)	15%	12%
Average price	$40.00	$42.00
Average manufacturing cost	$28.00	$30.00
Cost Behaviors:		
Variable cost of SG&A as percent of revenue	9.53%	12.22%
Fixed cost of SG&A	$247,500	$247,500

REQUIRED:

a. Calculate the following variances:

Total available market variance
Market share variance
Sales price variance
Manufacturing cost variance
Variable SG&A spending variance
Fixed SG&A spending variance

b. How does the Neon Lights account look? What recommendations would you make to Susie Goodman's management?

10. **DETAILED CUSTOMER VARIANCE ANALYSIS.** Fresh Scents makes a variety of candles that it sells to retailers across the Western part of the country. It sells scented candles in a jar and tapers of various colors to one of its major customers, Wickers Candle Works. Since the only thing that changes when a different scent or color is used is a small amount of scent and a change in dye color, Fresh Scents treats all sales for the

type of product as the same because its cost to produce any scent or any color is basically the same. The following is the information Fresh Scents has obtained for Wickers Candle Works.

	Plan	Actual
Revenues	$362,500.00	$491,625.00
Less: Cost of goods sold	$164,250.00	$230,625.00
Gross margin	$198,250.00	$261,000.00
Variable SG&A	$30,812.50	$43,017.19
Fixed SG&A	$150,000.00	$150,000.00
Total SG&A	$180,812.50	$193,017.19
Income before tax	$17,437.50	$67,982.81
Fresh Scents Scented Candles		
Wickers Candle Works overall purchase of scented candles	250,000	300,000
Goodman's share of Wickers Candle Works scented candles sales (%)	20%	25%
Average price	$5.00	$4.80
Average manufacturing cost	$2.25	$2.10
Fresh Scents Tapered Candles		
Wickers Candle Works overall purchase of tapered candles	300,000	325,000
Goodman's share of Wickers Candle Works tapered candles sales (%)	15%	18%
Average price	$2.50	$2.25
Average manufacturing cost	$1.15	$1.25
Cost behaviors:		
Variable cost of SG&A as percent of revenue	8.50%	8.75%
Fixed cost of SG&A	$150,000	$175,000

REQUIRED:

a. Calculate the following variances:

Total available market variance
Market share variance
Sales price variance
Manufacturing cost variance
Variable SG&A spending variance
Fixed SG&A spending variance

b. How does the Wickers Candle Works account look? What recommendations would you make to Fresh Scents' management?

Database Problems

For database templates, worksheets, and workbooks, go to MAdownloads.imanet.org

DB 13.1 ANALYSIS OF VALUE-ADDED COSTS. The worksheets you need to review and use to complete this exercise are:

- Marketing Value Analysis
- Customer Service Value Analysis
- Repairs Value Analysis
- Management Value Analysis
- Acquisitions Value Analysis
- Total ABCM Analysis Template
- % ABCM Analysis Template

The last two sheets are the ones you are going to fill in using the data that was developed for you in the Value Analysis worksheets. You are simply going to capture all of the totals from the bottom of the value analysis worksheets and place them in the summary template sheets. You will need to do the Total ABCM Analysis Template before you can do the % ABCM Analysis Template as the latter one uses the results of the former to get its percentages.

Make sure you find the correct cells in the Value Analysis worksheets that correspond to the department you are bringing across. When you are done, your total at the bottom of column G should be $2,250,000, the budget for the year 20x6 for the company. Now do the second part of the worksheet, focusing this time on the value attributes themselves. When you are done, the total at the bottom of column I should be $737,932, the total value added from the top portion of your worksheet.

To do the % ABCM Analysis Template, you are going to divide everything in the Total ABCM worksheet upper portion by the total budget amount, filling in cells B8 through G12. Then do the same basic calculation for the value-added activities alone. When you are done, if you have done it all correctly, cell I35 should show 100%.

REQUIRED:

a. Turn in your completed worksheets along with answers to the two following questions.
b. Look at your percentage totals. What department provides the most value-add to customers? The least value-add to customers?
c. Again, looking at your percentages, which attribute is most served by the company (has the highest percentage of cost)? Does this make sense for a car dealership? Why or why not?

DB 13.2 ACTIVITY-BASED COSTING. In this exercise, you are going to "cut and paste" costs and driver frequencies and then use this information to develop activity-based costs. The worksheets you will need for this exercise are:

- Marketing Value Analysis
- Customer Service Value Analysis
- Repairs Value Analysis
- Management Value Analysis
- Acquisitions Value Analysis
- ABCM Driver Information
- DB 13.2 Template.

The template already has all of the categories of cost you are going to develop ABC rates for noted already. What you need to do is capture the total cost data for that attribute and then obtain the driver frequency from the ABCM Driver Information worksheet so that you can calculate your rates. Now add the frequency data to the driver description and then calculate the ABC rates.

REQUIRED:

a. Turn in your completed template worksheet along with your answer to the following question.
b. What activities are the most expensive? Just note the top two or three most costly activities.

DB 13.3 CUSTOMER PROFITABILITY ANALYSIS. In this exercise, you are going to take the answers you derived for DB 13.2 and use this information to cost out the work done for individual customers during the year. You will need the following worksheets:

- Database Problem 13.2 Solution
- Database Problem 13.3 Template

First, fill in all of the activity costs from your DB 13.2 template worksheet onto your DB 13.3 Template worksheet. Now attach costs to customers and total these costs for each customer. Finally, calculate the profitability for each customer. Note that all service is under warranty for the first year of ownership, whether the car is new or used, so there is no service revenue to be reported.

REQUIRED:

a. Turn in your completed worksheet.
b. Which customer is the most profitable in absolute terms?
c. Which customer is most profitable in percentage terms?

Cases

CASE 13.1 ABCM AND CUSTOMER PROFITABILITY. Bright Forever Flowers is a producer of silk flowers used in all forms of arrangements. It sells its products to retail stores, through a catalog supported by an internet website, and floral shops. While the company makes a wide variety of flowers, they all come down to a few basic materials—the silk, some beads, and a cloth-wrapped "stem" made of wire. The results of the last year's operations are in the income statement below.

Bright Forever Flowers Income Statement by Segment				
	Retail Stores	Catalog and Internet	Floral Shops	Total
Revenue	$25,000,000	$35,000,000	$30,000,000	$90,000,000
Cost of goods sold	$12,000,000	$16,450,000	$15,000,000	$43,450,000
Gross margin	$13,000,000	$18,550,000	$15,000,000	$46,550,000
Less: SG&A	$7,500,000	$8,000,000	$8,500,000	$24,000,000
Income before tax	$5,500,000	$10,550,000	$6,500,000	$22,550,000
Income percentage	22.00%	30.14%	21.67%	25.06%

The president of Bright Forever Flowers, Cheryl Bedford, is not comfortable with the way SG&A is currently being charged out. She decides to enlist the help of her business planning analysts to conduct an activity-based study of SG&A activities and trace them to specific customers. The results of the study are in the two tables below.

Activities for SG&A				
Activities	Cost	Driver	Driver Frequency	Activity Cost
Take orders	$2,500,000	Orders taken	1,000,000	$2.50
Handle customer inquiries	$1,500,000	Customer calls	500,000	$3.00
Process invoices	$2,000,000	Invoices sent	1,200,000	$1.67
Process payment	$2,000,000	Payments processed	2,000,000	$1.00
Maintain customer database	$3,000,000	Customers	500,000	$6.00
Develop and print catalogs	$8,000,000	Catalogs printed	2,500,000	$3.20
Mail catalogs	$1,500,000	Catalogs mailed	1,800,000	$0.83
Make sales calls	$1,200,000	Sales calls	250,000	$4.80
General overhead	$2,300,000	Sales Revenue	$90,000,000	2.56%
	$24,000,000			

Activity Drivers	Retail Stores	Catalog and Internet	Floral Shops	Total
Orders taken	250,000	600,000	150,000	1,000,000
Customer calls	75,000	300,000	125,000	500,000
Invoices sent	400,000	-	800,000	1,200,000
Payments processed	750,000	600,000	650,000	2,000,000
Customers	75,000	300,000	125,000	500,000
Catalogs printed	400,000	1,400,000	700,000	2,500,000
Catalogs mailed	150,000	1,400,000	250,000	1,800,000
Sales calls	100,000	-	150,000	250,000
Sales Revenue	$25,000,000	$35,000,000	$30,000,000	$90,000,000

What was left was to calculate the profitability of the various types of customers using the ABCM analysis. What would make this analysis tricky is the managers of each segment currently got a bonus dependent on their income before tax results. If these went up or down significantly, there could be trouble, especially since it would be a zero sum game with some winners and some losers in the costing scheme. This did not deter Cheryl, who wanted the numbers to reflect the realities of the business. It would just have to be dealt with.

REQUIRED:

a. **Calculate the profitability of each customer segment using the information derived from the ABCM study.**

b. **Which divisions benefit from the new costing scheme? Which lose?**

c. **How would you explain the shift in profitability? What seemed to be the cause?**

d. **How would you approach implementing this new scheme knowing that individual managers may not be overly excited by the results? Would you change your incentive system or simply let the chips fall where they may?**

CASE 13.2 CUSTOMER PROFITABILITY ANALYSIS. Happy Kitchen, Inc., produces several lines of dish towels and pot holders that are sold through department stores, grocery stores, and through wholesalers to smaller kitchen shops throughout the United States. The company has traditionally kept track of its sales by product line, but lately has begun to feel it should pay some attention to the different demands of customer segments on its profitability. Department stores and wholesalers are normally content with the prices Happy Kitchen charges, but the grocery store buyers are more demanding. Recently, the company has also started selling product to the wholesale warehouses, such as Sam's Club. Here, price has really become an issue, with the customer demanding small shipments to each of its stores but at a much lower price for a bundled package of goods (such as three dish towels in one sale).

Pete Bayou, president of Happy Kitchen, decided to hire a team of consultants to investigate the profitability of each of its customer segments. The study results were broken down by dish towels and pot holders to give the company more information about where things were going well and where attention might need to be paid. The consulting team also used internal information to develop the "as is" budget for each segment of business so the results could be compared with plan. It did not address fixed overhead because it was felt to be out of the control of the product lines. The results of the consulting team's study are in the following tables.

Happy Kitchen, Inc.
Customer Profitability Analysis—Kitchen Towels

	Department Stores		Wholesalers		Grocery Stores		Warehouse Stores		Company Total	
	Budget	Actual	Budget	Actual	Budget	Actual	Budget	Actual	Budget	Actual
Units sold	$20,000,000	$19,000,000	$25,000,000	$30,000,000	$18,000,000	$15,000,000	$2,000,000	$25,000,000	$65,000,000	$89,000,000
Revenue	$25,000,000	$24,700,000	$31,250,000	$39,000,000	$20,700,000	$16,500,000	$2,000,000	$23,750,000	$78,950,000	$103,950,000
Less: Cost of goods sold	$12,000,000	$12,103,000	$15,000,000	$19,110,000	$10,350,000	$8,415,000	$1,300,000	$16,150,000	$38,650,000	$55,778,000
Gross margin	$13,000,000	$12,597,000	$16,250,000	$19,890,000	$10,350,000	$8,085,000	$700,000	$7,600,000	$40,300,000	$48,172,000
Less: SG&A										
Order processing costs	$1,750,000	$1,800,000	$2,500,000	$3,000,000	$1,600,000	$1,500,000	$200,000	$2,000,000	$6,050,000	$8,300,000
Sales calls	$1,200,000	$1,100,000	$1,300,000	$1,500,000	$900,000	$800,000	$80,000	$800,000	$3,480,000	$4,200,000
Invoicing	$1,500,000	$1,750,000	$1,800,000	$2,000,000	$1,200,000	$1,500,000	$30,000	$800,000	$4,530,000	$6,050,000
Customer service	$1,600,000	$1,500,000	$2,000,000	$2,200,000	$2,400,000	$2,600,000	$125,000	$1,300,000	$6,125,000	$7,600,000
General overhead	$3,000,000	$3,000,000	$3,500,000	$3,500,000	$2,070,000	$2,070,000	$200,000	$200,000	$8,770,000	$8,770,000
Total SG&A	$9,050,000	$9,150,000	$11,100,000	$12,200,000	$8,170,000	$8,470,000	$635,000	$5,100,000	$28,955,000	$34,920,000
Income before tax	$3,950,000	$3,447,000	$5,150,000	$7,690,000	$2,180,000	$(385,000)	$65,000	$2,500,000	$11,345,000	$13,252,000
Profit percentage	15.80%	13.96%	16.48%	19.72%	10.53%	-2.33%	3.25%	10.53%	14.37%	12.75%

Happy Kitchen, Inc.
Customer Profitability Analysis—Pot Holders

	Department Stores		Wholesalers		Grocery Stores		Warehouse Stores		Company Total	
	Budget	Actual	Budget	Actual	Budget	Actual	Budget	Actual	Budget	Actual
Units sold	10,000,000	12,000,000	15,000,000	14,000,000	8,000,000	9,500,000	1,500,000	8,500,000	34,500,000	44,000,000
Revenue	$13,000,000	$15,000,000	$19,500,000	$17,500,000	$9,200,000	$10,450,000	$1,500,000	$8,075,000	$43,200,000	$51,025,000
Less: Cost of goods sold	$6,110,000	$6,900,000	$9,165,000	$8,050,000	$4,508,000	$5,016,000	$825,000	$4,845,000	$20,608,000	$24,811,000
Gross margin	$6,890,000	$8,100,000	$10,335,000	$9,450,000	$4,692,000	$5,434,000	$675,000	$3,230,000	$22,592,000	$26,214,000
Less: SG&A									$-	$-
Order processing costs	$1,250,000	$1,400,000	$1,400,000	$1,500,000	$1,000,000	$1,200,000	$100,000	$750,000	$3,750,000	$4,850,000
Sales calls	$1,400,000	$1,500,000	$1,750,000	$1,700,000	$900,000	$1,000,000	$150,000	$800,000	$4,200,000	$5,000,000
Invoicing	$1,500,000	$1,750,000	$1,500,000	$1,400,000	$1,200,000	$1,450,000	$125,000	$1,200,000	$4,325,000	$5,800,000
Customer service	$750,000	$800,000	$1,100,000	$1,050,000	$800,000	$875,000	$50,000	$475,000	$2,700,000	$3,200,000
General overhead	$1,500,000	$1,500,000	$1,800,000	$1,800,000	$750,000	$750,000	$125,000	$125,000	$4,175,000	$4,175,000
Total SG&A	$6,400,000	$6,950,000	$7,550,000	$7,450,000	$4,650,000	$5,275,000	$550,000	$3,350,000	$19,150,000	$23,025,000
Income before tax	$490,000	$1,150,000	$2,785,000	$2,000,000	$42,000	$159,000	$125,000	$(120,000)	$3,442,000	$3,189,000
Profit percentage	3.77%	7.67%	14.28%	11.43%	0.46%	1.52%	8.33%	-1.49%	7.97%	6.25%

What surprised the president of Happy Kitchen was the fact that profitability on pot holders was so much lower than had originally been thought. The addition of ABCM costs to the analysis had really made a difference. What was also of concern was the fact that the warehouse stores were not carrying their fair share of general overhead yet. If that had been raised to be equivalent to the other segments, it is doubtful it would have shown any profits at all.

Pete really wants to dig a bit further into this analysis and has asked you to come in and give a hand. What Pete needs you to do is the following.

REQUIRED:

a. Prepare a variance analysis report for the two products across their four customer segments.

b. Analyze the results and note where Pete should place his attention and where things are going okay.

c. What should Pete do about the warehouse store sales? They have added a lot of volume to the business, leading to the need to put on another shift in both products and add staff to the back office. If the volume is eliminated, quite a few employees will have to be laid off.

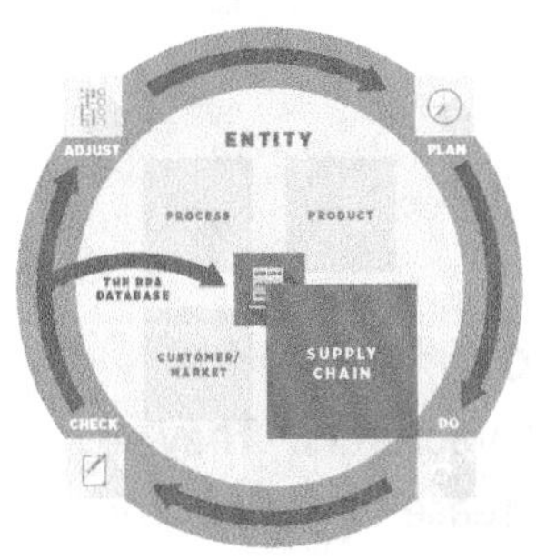

Strategic Cost Management and the Supply Chain Domain

Facts do not cease to exist because they are ignored.
ALDOUS HUXLEY[1]

CHAPTER ROADMAP

1. **Key Issues in the Value Chain Domain**
   - *Basic Features of Value Chains*
   - *Strategic Cost Management*
   - *Value Chains and Competitive Advantage*
2. **Beyond the Basics**
   - *Identifying and Measuring Current Performance*
   - *Return on Equity and a Firm's Basic Economic Structure*
   - *Channel Analysis*
   - *Value Chain Patterns*
   - *Value Migration*
3. **Integrated Supply Chain Management**
   - *The Basics of ISCM*
   - *Aligning the Supply Chain with Business Strategy*
   - *Measuring and Controlling Supply Chain Performance*

LEARNING OBJECTIVES

After studying this chapter, you should be able to:

1. **Define the basic features of a value chain; explain the basic tenets of strategic cost management and the structural, executional, and perceptual cost drivers.**
2. **Complete a basic analysis of value chain performance; identify and describe major value chain patterns; and explain the concept of value migration within industry value chains.**
3. **Discuss the basic concepts of integrated supply chain management within the value chain domain.**

1 Aldous Huxley, *Proper Studies*, New York: Doubleday, Doran & Company, Inc., 1928.

IN CONTEXT ➤ Gearing Up for Growth at Prestige Auto

"We've finally heard from the large auto manufacturers. They've agreed to let us have more cars! Not the 20% increase we asked for, but 15%. This is great news, everyone! Now we have to figure out how we are going to sell so many more cars!" Jack was pumped.

"That is great news, Jack," Judy piped in. "And we should be ready to handle the additional sales volume. We've been working out some of the kinks between Marketing and Service. The used car program went great last week! We moved more cars than we anticipated; inventory is way down, isn't it Bruce? Service kept up with the detailing and preparation work and even provided some 'show and tell' spots for us that helped convince used car buyers that they could count on us for good, reasonably priced service."

"Thanks for the compliment, Judy," said Tony. "We worked hard last week; we wanted to make sure we had enough time set aside to support the sales event. We had to postpone a few scheduled oil changes for regular customers, but, because we gave them notice, they didn't seem to mind the two- or three-day delay. They said they appreciated that we were on top of things and hadn't inconvenienced them and caused them to hang around waiting for the work to be done."

"Now we need to get to the point where we can handle extra sales *and* our regular workload. I know you're putting a lot of effort into doing exactly that, Tony. Thanks. And Bruce, when can we expect to start seeing the additional cars? Also, what are you doing about our short inventory in used cars?" Jack was on a roll.

"We'll start getting shipments in the next two weeks," replied Bruce. "After that, we'll see a 15% increase in our regular shipments. We may accumulate a bit of inventory in between sales events, but evenly paced delivery was the only way we were going to get the additional volume. I've talked with Alice, and although the extra inventory will stretch our cash flow a little, if we keep up the current volume of sales, we should do all right."

"You're right, Bruce," noted Alice. "We will be stretched until we get our sales up and running. I'm assuming we already have plans for increasing our sales. We can only stretch our cash flow so far, and Tony has already said that, if we keep the levels up permanently, he will probably have to hire a few more technicians and customer support people. That will mean more cash out every week. I know I'm a worrywart, but, actually, I'm sure those sales will come in."

"We have every intention of selling everything we get, and quickly," replied Judy. "My salespeople are already on the phone lining up customers for the new model. I can have them expand their calls to include cold calls of potential customers, those with older model cars that we service, and maybe even some people that have not done business with us before. Right now, we're calling folks on our used car customer list to see if we can interest them in buying new cars in the future. Get them to trade up!"

"I'm convinced we're all going to be ready," said Jack. "This is a big moment for us. Our growth hasn't been what I would have liked the last few years. It's time to take on new ventures, to take a little more risk to earn better returns. Alice, make sure you keep me up to date on the cash flow situation. I can infuse a little more capital if it is needed. If we need the cash, you just have to let me know."

"Then I'll worry a bit less," Alice sounded relieved. "With that, I have repair invoices that need filing and other work to catch up on after everything all of you have been doing. So, may I be excused for now, Jack?"

"I think there's plenty for all of us to do. This meeting felt more like a celebration than a working meeting," Jack said. "You deserve it. Next week, we'll dig into how to gear up and make sure we don't neglect our existing customers as we take on more business. So thinking caps on, everyone. Let's be ready to handle all those new cars and buyers!" With that, Jack ended the meeting, sending his managers scurrying to deal with the repercussions of having won the support of their supply chain partners.

THE COMPETITIVE CHALLENGES FACING ORGANIZATIONS TODAY REQUIRE innovative strategies and structures. Assets and relationships need to be leveraged, whether these exist within the traditional boundaries of the company or within the industry **value, or supply, chain,** *the linked set of companies that participate in the design, development, provision, and support of a product or service*. A value chain includes the entirety of the linked set of companies that participate in the design, development, provision, and support of a product or service. Just as many people have to work together to create and maintain effective processes, companies have to cooperate in many different ways to ensure that customer demands are met.

A typical value chain for the paper industry is detailed in Figure 14.1. As you can see, the value chain encompasses everything from the tree farmer who plants the tree that ultimately is used to make paper through to the retail store that sells you a ream of copy paper. The raw material, a tree, is harvested by the logger, who brings it to the pulp facility where it is reduced to slurry, a mix of chemicals, water, and wood fibers. The pulp is then transformed to paper at the paper mill by pouring the pulp on a moving conveyer that vibrates the wood fibers into place while removing the liquefied chemicals and water. At the end of the paper machine, a roller winds the paper into rolls of various widths and lengths (all quite large). These rolls, often weighing in excess of one ton each, are then shipped to the converter, which cuts them down into smaller sheets and then packages them in standard quantities (for example, 500-sheet reams).

The next steps in the value chain focus on the distribution of the now-completed ream of paper. In most traditional value chains, the distribution activity has at least two unique steps: wholesale distribution and retail distribution. The wholesaler orders large quantities from the manufacturer of various goods and services, storing them until an order is received from a specific retail customer. While the distributor holds a relatively limited set of goods in its inventories in large quantities, a retailer (for example, Office Depot or Staples) holds a large variety of different items in small quantities. Consumers buy quantities as small as a single ream of paper from the retailer, completing the flow of goods through the value chain.

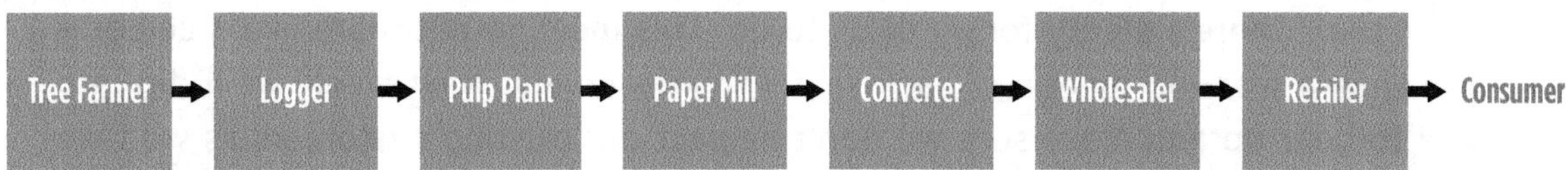

FIGURE 14.1 THE VALUE CHAIN STARTS WITH RAW MATERIALS AND FOLLOWS THE PROCESS EVERY STEP ALONG THE WAY TO THE CONSUMER.

Michael Porter was one of the earliest management writers to develop techniques and concepts focused specifically on the industry value chain.[2] One of his primary ideas was the concept of **five forces of competition:** *suppliers, customers, new entrants, substitutes, and the group of competitors that comprise the market* (see Figure 14.2). Each firm, therefore, faces not only its competition for business, but the demands of suppliers and customers and the threat embodied in the potential for new entrants and substitute products. These five different groups vie for power and the ability to influence prices, profits, and performance requirements. The more power one of these groups has, the more demands it can place on other value chain participants. More power can also mean more profits, as the key value chain firm forces price concessions and no-charge service enhancements onto its trading partners.

Walmart is a good example of a company that uses its position of power in its value chain to drive supplier prices down, while requesting ever greater levels of service. This is reflected in one of Walmart's advertising themes—the ongoing drive to "roll back" consumer prices. To achieve this goal, Walmart places significant pressure on its suppliers, earning it the dubious connotation of a predatory customer within its value chain. While an individual company can decide that it will not do business with Walmart directly, the erosion of consumer prices created by Walmart's strategy impacts every company in the industry. Why? Because prices are ultimately based on the market's perceptions of the value of a product or service, not on the product's or firm's cost and profit requirements. As long as one company in an industry concedes to the price reduction, the price points for the entire industry will be negatively affected.

---

2 Michael Porter, *Competitive Strategy*, New York: The Free Press, 1980. Michael Porter, Competitive Advantage, New York: The Free Press, 1985.

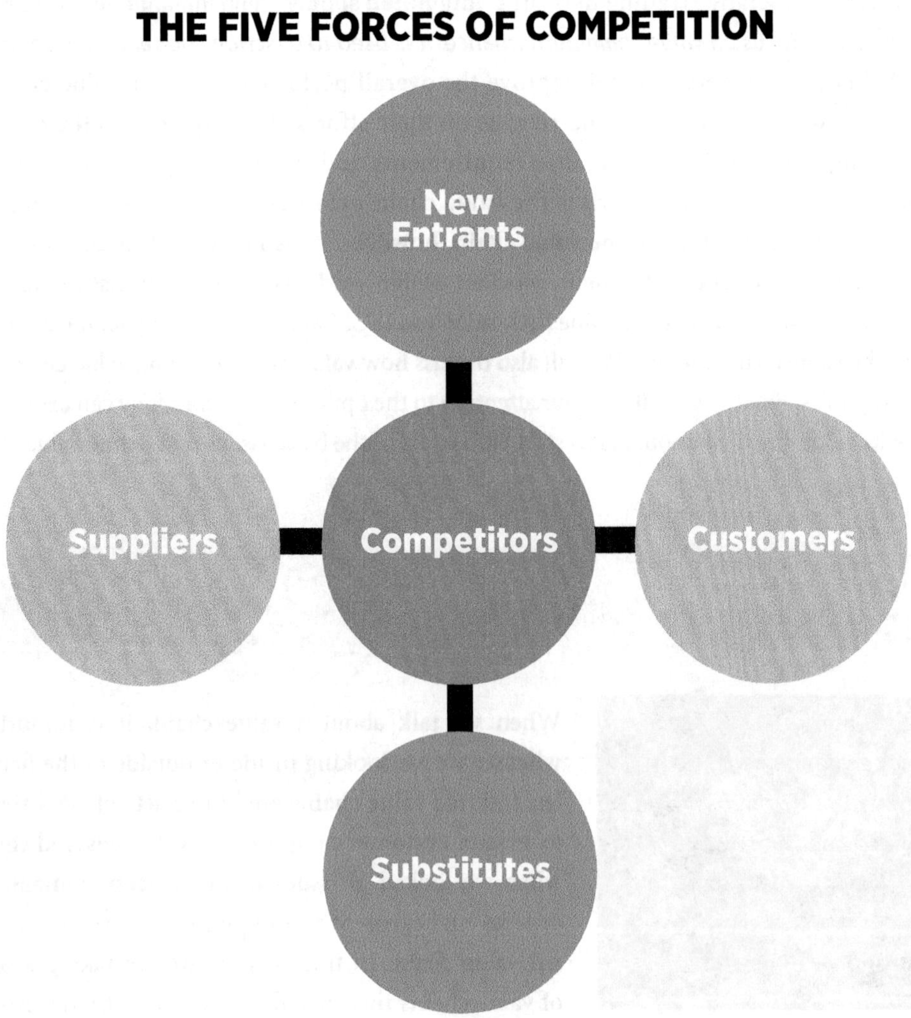

THE FIVE FORCES OF COMPETITION

New Entrants

Suppliers

Competitors

Customers

Substitutes

FIGURE 14.2 THESE GROUPS CHALLENGE ONE ANOTHER FOR POWER AND THE ABILITY TO INFLUENCE PRICES, PROFITS, AND PERFORMANCE REQUIREMENTS.

Porter's five forces, and the underlying competitive analysis that it reflects, are the basis for one of the two primary planning tools we will look at in the value chain domain—**strategic cost management (SCM),** *a planning tool that focuses on the relative profitability of different members of an industry value chain.* Developed by John Shank and Vijay Govindarajan in the mid-1990s, SCM focuses on the relative profitability of different companies within a value chain, as well as each firm's return on investment, return on assets (ROA), and sales turnover. As we will see shortly, several different basic financial ratios are used in SCM to define and measure the relative performance and, by inference, the relative power of value chain participants. A company can use any of several strategies to attempt to change its competitive position and degree of influence within a value chain.

There is no question that different groups or companies within an industry have varying degrees of power over their trading partners. That said, more and more companies are deciding to use this power to create cooperative trading networks. **Integrated supply chain management (ISCM)** *is the tactical and operational focus on value chain performance. It is used to describe cooperative trading networks.* It reflects a belief that cooperation will improve the overall performance of the value chain, providing every company with higher profits and returns on their efforts. The customer is the central figure in ISCM, defining value chain performance requirements and determining the market clearing price for the bundle of products and services the value chain provides. ISCM does more than change the nature of trading relationships in the value chain, however. It also extends this cooperative structure into the realms of product development, product design, and customer relationship management.

In this chapter, we will briefly examine both SCM and ISCM and how they impact the management process within the value chain domain. We will also discuss how value migrates along value chains, taking with it power and profits. Finally, we will turn our attention to the options that a company can exercise to improve or leverage its value chain position. Let us start with some of the basic issues that define value chain analysis.

Key Issues in the Value Chain Domain

OBJECTIVE 1

Define the basic features of a value chain; explain the basic tenets of strategic cost management and the structural, executional, and perceptual cost drivers.

When we talk about a value chain, it is important to note whether we are looking inside or outside of the firm's boundaries. Internal value chains are linked sets of activities performed to meet a customer's requirements. We covered these concepts when we looked at issues in the process domain. Specifically, process management techniques emphasize a company's internal value chain. In this chapter, we are taking a broader view of value chains that includes all of the activities from basic raw material sources to component suppliers through to the ultimate end-use product delivered into the customer's hands.[3] So, what are the key features of these industry value chains?

BASIC FEATURES OF VALUE CHAINS

Value chains knit together different organizations in the ongoing quest for the customer's dollars and loyalty. That said, they are inherently structured by both the natural flow of the product or service they support as well as the nature of the competitive landscape within which they exist. The **natural flow** *is the sequence of steps required to complete the product or service and the resources consumed in its production.* As shown in Figure 14.3, industry value chains exist in two basic structures: **divergent** and **convergent**.

---

3 This definition of value chains was first suggested by John Shank and Vijay Govindarajan in their book, *Strategic Cost Analysis*, Homewood, Ill.: Richard D. Irwin, 1989.

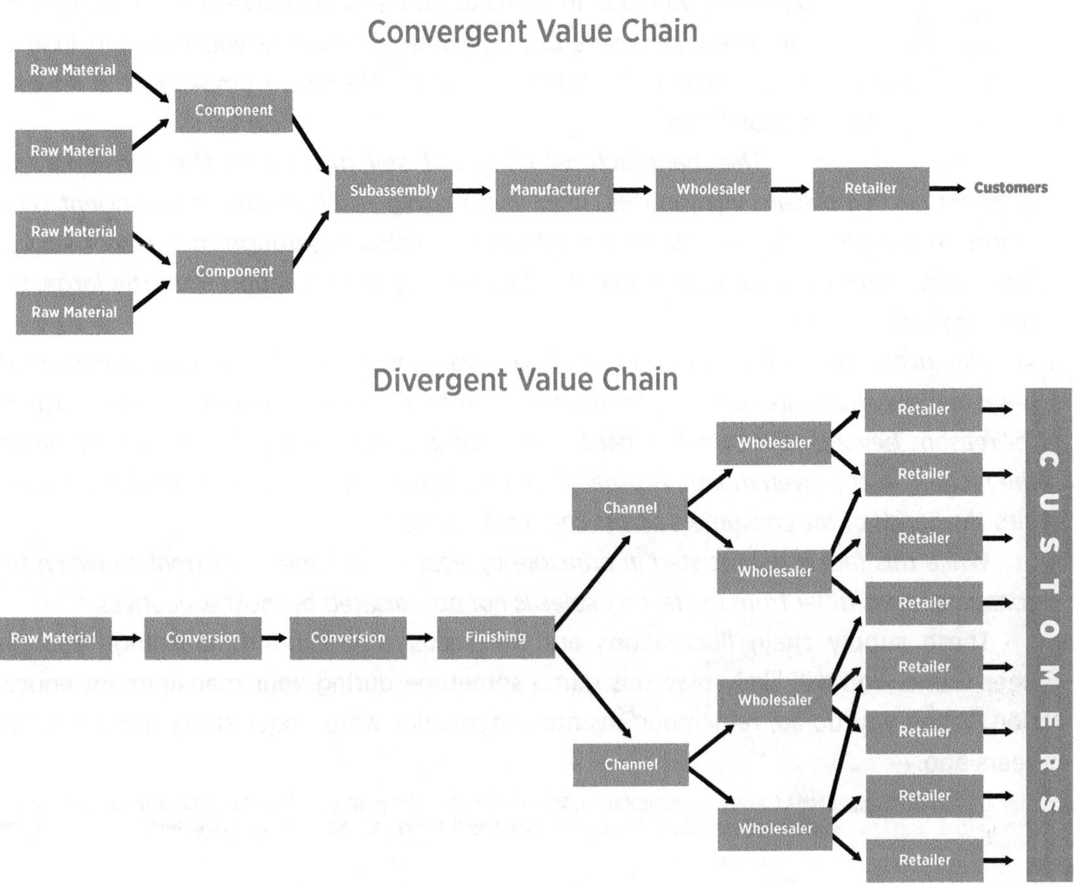

FIGURE 14.3 THE TWO VALUE CHAIN STRUCTURES—CONVERGENT AND DIVERGENT—ARE ALMOST REVERSE IMAGES OF ONE ANOTHER.

As the figure suggests, a **convergent value chain**—*one where multiple steps (players) converge to one final channel to the consumer*—starts with many different suppliers and raw materials, which are then funneled into a unitary pipeline of product that passes through to the final consumer. Original equipment manufacturers (OEMs) and automobile manufacturers are two types of companies that operate within convergent industry structures. On the other hand, a **divergent value chain** *is one where a small number of suppliers support an array of channels, final products, and customers*. This type of structure exists in the paper industry. Clearly, some value chain structures have both convergent and divergent characteristics. In addition, each company is itself part of an industry structure that may have unique structures. When we talk about value chains in this chapter, we will use a simple linear flow of product to make it easier to understand the key concepts. But, as is nearly always the case, the "real world" is far more complex than our simple examples suggest.

LOOKING BACK ➤ Fluctuations in the Supply Chain

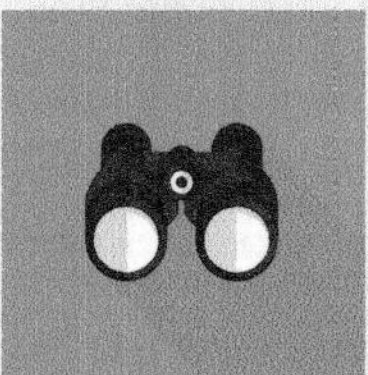

The different players in a value chain have long been recognized as a source of variation in demand patterns that have little to do with the ultimate consumer's buying patterns. This fact was noted in 1936 by A.C. Nielsen, president of A.C. Nielsen Company, the market research firm:

The manufacturer does not sell directly to the consumer but to chain and wholesale warehouses, who in turn ship to chain and independent retail stores. These retailers then sell to the ultimate consumers through markets of various types and stores of various types and in cities ranging in population from the largest to the smallest.

The inventories in the chain and wholesale warehouses and in the retail stores are so great and they fluctuate so widely from month to month and from season to season (usually for reasons beyond your control), that the amount of orders received or goods shipped at the factory, in any given month, is usually quite different from the amount of goods moved into the hands of the consumers across the retail counters.

*While this fact is appreciated in principle by nearly everyone, the extent to which the consumer sales differ from the factory sales is not appreciated by most executives.**

These supply chain fluctuations are the focus of a modern teaching tool: the Beer Game. You will likely play this game sometime during your management education. When you do so, remember inventory dynamics were under study more than 80 years ago.

*Excerpted from A.C. Nielsen, "Continuous Marketing Research—A Vital Factor in Controlling Distribution Costs," *N.A.C.A. Yearbook*, 1936, reprinted in Richard Vangermeersch, ed., *Relevance Rediscovered*, Vol. II, Montvale, N.J.: IMA® (Institute of Management Accountants), 1991: p. 289.

Why do we care about whether a value chain is divergent or convergent? Because the structure can influence the distribution of power within a value chain and limit the options available to a company to leverage its position to gain a competitive advantage. Clearly, when only one supplier of a product or service exists, then that firm will have greater power than a company that is one of many suppliers to a large corporation that assembles parts to make finished goods (for example, Boeing, Apple). While other factors contribute to the power structure within a value chain, the natural flow of the product and how the industry has responded to these features is a primary definer of power and profits in a value chain.

The second main influence on value chains is the competitive nature of an industry. Specifically, a number of relationships within value chains arise over time. One company may develop a unique material, or have such a large share of the market, that it defines the standard for the industry and controls the performance of the value chain. The antitrust laws in the United States were designed to prevent these types of competitive situations, but it is often difficult to prove that a company is a **monopoly,** *the only supplier of a product or service*, in the marketplace.

Other industries are dominated by **oligopolies,** *industries where only a few large companies serve the market*. They tend to mirror each other's behavior and decisions. The airline industry and the auto industry are oligopolies. In oligopolies, aggressive competitive behavior, such as a radical redesign of a value chain, tend to be avoided because it can set off a bitter competitive battle in which every firm loses. Finally, **competitive industries**—*ones in which many different companies vie for the customers' business*—normally have a more divergent value chain structure in which many companies vie for the same consumer dollar with comparable products.

Industries develop structures in response to the resource demands of a product or service. For instance, if there are **high barriers to entry**—*a significant investment in fixed assets is required to compete in an industry*—new companies find it difficult to enter into competition with existing players. In other cases, a product or service can be provided by a company with little or no investment in assets at all. Mortgage brokers only need a phone, a desk, a computer, and an office to begin operations. As one might expect, there are many more companies in the mortgage brokerage business than in the airline industry. Industry concentration, therefore, mirrors the fixed asset demands of the product.

When an industry is in its infancy, typically no one company dominates. The value chain for a product that is early in its life cycle will be fluid, dynamic in nature, and often unstable in structure, as new entrants come into the industry, and new methods and materials are introduced. Over time, the product becomes more stable, leading to a more rigid value chain structure. Prior practices become engrained, often blinding companies to opportunities to leverage or modify the value chain to improve their performance. Changing mind-sets requires changing the management models that a company has relied upon to compete.

STRATEGIC COST MANAGEMENT

Strategic cost management (SCM) was developed to draw attention to the competitive issues that define an industry and to identify ways to create a competitive advantage within existing value chain structures. The value chain methodology that underlies SCM consists of three primary steps:

1. Identify the industry's value chain and assign costs, revenues, and assets to value activities.
2. Diagnose the cost drivers regulating each value activity.
3. Develop sustainable competitive advantage, either by controlling cost drivers better than competitors or by reconfiguring the value chain.[4]

The value chain is built around a series of **value activities,** *those things a company does that a customer values and is willing to pay for*, which are the building blocks by which firms in an industry create a product or service that the customer desires. If a customer does not recognize the value, or worth, of an activity, it is not value-creating. Only those activities valued by customers generate demand and revenues. Other activities may be essential, but they do not lead to improved profits—they instead create costs that erode the profitability of a value chain. This is a lesson that was emphasized in Chapter 13, where we discussed the value-added concept and its impact on customer decision making.

---

4 John Shank and Vijay Govindarajan, *Strategic Cost Management*, New York: The Free Press, 1996.

Within SCM, four different criteria are used to isolate and emphasize value activities that have the potential to create a competitive advantage for a firm:[5]

- They represent a significant percentage of operating costs; or,
- The cost behavior of the activities (or the cost drivers) is different; or,
- They are performed by competitors in different ways; or,
- They have a high potential for creating differentiation.

Let us return to Easy Air and the airline industry in general to gain a better understanding of these issues. If we were to define the value activities for the airline industry, they would probably include:

1. Providing reservation information and ticketing services.
2. Operating the aircraft from point A to point B.
3. Providing service to the passenger before the flight, during the flight, and after arrival (for example, baggage handling).

As we discovered in the early pages of this text, Easy Air emphasizes low fares and no frills as its core value proposition to its customers. In other words, it focuses on the basic value activity—operating the aircraft—with much less attention paid to special services. Of course, it has to provide the basic services (take reservations, check in customers, handle bags, and so on), but it does not seek to differentiate itself on these dimensions.

Once the core value activities have been identified, attention turns to attaching costs, revenues, and assets to them (see Figure 14.4). In this example, the profit per sales (P/S), sales per asset dollar (or asset intensity, S/A), and ROA are used to analyze the linkages in the wine industry.

Chalice Wines, the subject of the analysis, is a specialty wine producer that is trying to make inroads into the wine value chain. It is faced with fierce competition from a winery that buys its wine already made (the excess wine from other wineries during a season), blends it, and bottles it. It will be difficult for Chalice, with its Cimarron Meritage White, to enter the wine industry value chain from the very beginning (growing the grapes) and use the existing channels for marketing wine (distributors to retailers) to gain market share.[6]

---

5 Ibid, pp. 58-59.

6 This discussion is based on the Chalice Wines case in John Shank's *Cases in Cost Management: A Strategic Emphasis*, 3rd Edition, Cincinnati: South-Western College Pub, 2006.

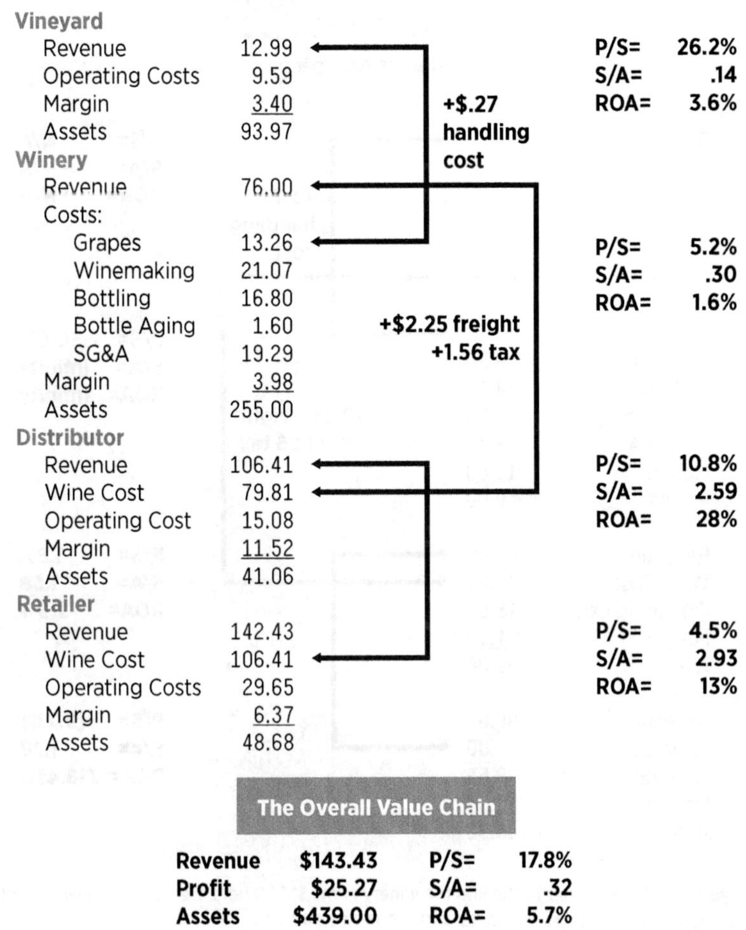

FIGURE 14.4 IN THIS EXAMPLE OF A VALUE CHAIN ANALYSIS, THE PRODUCER—CHALICE WINES—WHO WANTS TO ENTER THE VALUE CHAIN HAS THE LOWEST ROA; THE DISTRIBUTOR OF THE WINE, THE HIGHEST, AND THEREFORE THE GREATEST LEVERAGE.

What we see is that the most profitable position in the value chain for wine is the distributor, which gets a 28% ROA for simply moving the wine from the producer (the winery) to the retailer. Remember that a distributor collects case quantities from a variety of different companies and then provides smaller quantities to retailers. Its role is to consolidate inventory in the value chain and then, in a divergent value chain setting, move the product out to the marketplace in the small quantities that an independent wine merchant could actually plan to move in a reasonable period of time. The power in this value chain, therefore, rests with the distributor, which chooses the wines to carry and negotiates price with the winery. The retailer is a price taker, using the price passed on by the distributor for setting its retail price.

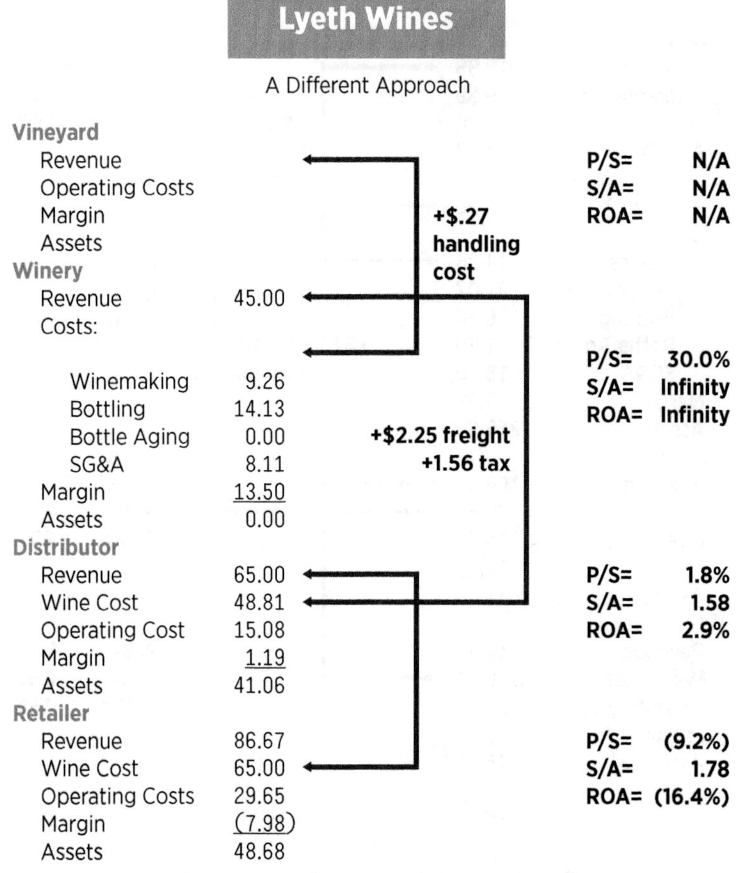

FIGURE 14.5 LYETH WINES IS SIMPLY A BOTTLER, ELIMINATING THE COSTS ASSOCIATED WITH THE FIRST TWO STEPS IN THE VALUE CHAIN, RESULTING IN THE HIGHEST ROA, AND THE GREATEST LEVERAGE.

The approach taken by Chalice Wines is usefully compared with that of its competitor, Lyeth Wines. Lyeth buys its blended wine directly from the wholesale market and simply bottles it and places it in the distribution channel. The company has basically eliminated the first two links in the value chain—growing the grapes and making the wine. It picks up the chain with the bottling process and then moving the wine through the distributor to the retailer, where it has already set a market price of $7.25 per bottle. Its profitability is excellent, while its supply chain partners do not do very well, as illustrated in Figure 14.5.

Lyeth is a "virtual" winery. It does not make wine. Rather, it purchases excess wine from other wineries. Its expertise, or **core competency**—*an aspect of doing business, or providing value to customers, that a firm is better at than its competitors*—comes in blending the wines it is able to obtain to get a uniform product at the end. The blended wine made by Lyeth is well-received in the market for several reasons. First, it is a reasonably priced alternative to more traditional wines such as those sold by Chalice. Second, it has a consistent flavor, which is unlikely in a winery that is subject to seasonal differences in its grapes that affect the final taste of the wine significantly. Finally, Lyeth's has a unique marketing pitch. Its wines are advertised as "fine wine for the ordinary person." The results of this unique approach to the value chain are striking. Lyeth has a 30% profit margin on each dollar of sales, and because it is a virtual winery (for example, it owns only a negligible amount of assets), its ROA is nearly infinite in mathematical terms.

The results of the SCM analysis suggests that Lyeth owns the strongest position in its value chain, while Chalice has the weakest. This fact is not only evident in the financial performance of the two firms, but also in the results of downstream trading partners. The distributor and retailer both use a "mark-up" approach to pricing the wine as it makes its way to the final consumer. Specifically, both mark up the cost of the wine by 33% as a basis for setting their prices (for example, the $65 price charged by the distributor to the retailer is 133% of $48.81, the price charged by Lyeth).

Because Chalice's wine is a high-priced wine ($76 per case when leaving the winery), the markup provides a reasonable profit for the distributor and retailer. Lyeth, on the other hand, is relatively inexpensive at under $49 per case. The mark-up method leaves the retailer with less profit than the cost it incurs to run the business, resulting in an $8 loss for every bottle of Lyeth wine it sells. Of course, we have to be careful at this point. Since most of the costs incurred by the distributor and retailer are fixed, or at least general to the entire business, a decision to drop Lyeth would not be a good one. Why? Because dropping Lyeth from its line will not change the costs of running the distributor's or retailer's business, but will instead reduce the revenue available to these firms. In fact, someone buying a case of Lyeth wine is also quite likely to buy one or more bottles of a more expensive wine.

What the example does show is how a different approach to the value chain can have a significant impact on the profits earned by a firm in an industry. Chalice and Lyeth are competitors, but with very different approaches to the market. Lyeth clearly has less control over its future because it is dependent on the availability of excess wine from other vineyards, but it also has little business risk because it has a low fixed asset position. If things change radically, Lyeth can easily exit from the market. Chalice, on the other hand, has a more stable business structure, but less flexibility.

VALUE CHAINS AND COMPETITIVE ADVANTAGE

What we see in Figures 14.4 and 14.5 is the heart of an SCM analysis. SCM looks at the profitability and returns for the entire value chain, looking for areas where a specific company is able to leverage its position in the value chain to basically "take" profit and returns from its trading partners. This result is the primary concern of SCM—how to use the planning cycle, and information from the structure of the industry, to find a way to gain a competitive advantage in an industry.

To gain this advantage, SCM suggests that three different types of cost drivers—**structural**, **executional**, and **perceptual**—can be leveraged by an organization. A **structural cost driver** *is a strategic choice a firm makes about the size and scope of its operations and the fundamental technologies it employs; it affects the cost of any given product or service.*[7] The five structural drivers of strategic performance are:

- *Scale*: How big an investment to make in manufacturing, research and development, marketing, and related areas of the business.
- *Scope*: The degree of vertical integration; how much of the value chain to encompass in the firm's structure.
- *Experience*: How many times in the past the company has done what it is doing right now. How many repetitions of the same actions and programs the firm has conducted to gain expertise in a specific area.
- *Technology*: The level of advanced technology used at each vital step in the firm's value chain. For instance, does the entire value chain use bar-coding technology to identify parts and suppliers?
- *Complexity:* How wide a line of products or services to offer to customers. Unless this variety can be provided at close to zero cost, the complexity of a business will increase as the number of choices it allows customers to make increases.

An **executional cost driver** *is a strategic choice a firm makes about how its assets, including individuals, are deployed to complete value-added work.* Here we start to see many of the tools and techniques that you have learned in earlier chapters of the book starting to come into play in a strategic sense. What are some of the key executional drivers of strategic performance?

- *Workforce involvement:* Participation, or the commitment of the workforce to the continuous improvement philosophy, can have a major impact on how well a company deploys its resources.
- *Total quality management*: As we have seen, the beliefs and attitudes of the workforce and management toward product and process quality can have a major impact on how well assets are used to create value for customers.
- *Capacity utilization*: Not only having the right assets, but using them productively, is a critical element of competitiveness. A firm that has assets that lie idle is not going to be able to compete as effectively as one that deploys its assets to create value for customers.
- *Plant layout efficiency:* As we saw in just-in-time, or cellular, manufacturing, how the plant floor is configured can have a marked impact on the efficiency and effectiveness of the work flow. Plants that are designed to maximize throughput will be able to favorably compete with less well-designed competitors.
- *Product design*: Is the product itself designed to be easily produced and flexible enough to be adapted to customers' specifications at minimal cost or work? Putting ample time into ensuring a sound, effective, flexible design can save companies a lot of money. This is one of the keys to success for Dell.

---

7 The information in this section is based on John Shank and Vijay Govindarajan, *Strategic Cost Management: The New Tool for Competitive Advantage*, New York: The Free Press, 1993: pp. 20-22.

- *Exploiting value chain linkages*: As we saw with Lyeth Wines, there is an opportunity to change the way the value chain is organized to gain a competitive advantage. This places the firm in the driver's seat to achieve superior performance gains over competitors by eliminating unnecessary or wasteful links in the industry value chain.

Executional drivers provide a way for two firms with the same asset base to perform very differently based on how those assets are used. Many of the tools and techniques you have learned about in earlier decision domains provide executional cost driver advantages to the firm that uses them effectively.

Perceptual cost drivers *are the known relationships between members of the value chain—a company, its trading partners—and the products they support.* This is the land of psychology, beliefs, and opinions, which might or might not be directly based on hard facts. What are some examples of perceptual cost drivers? They might include:

- *Perception of cost to value:* Customers have a perception of the amount of value a specific product or service provides for them vs. the price being paid. Lyeth Wines provided a perceived equal or better quality wine than Chalice for a much lower price, hence having a favorable cost to value perception in the marketplace.
- *Suppliers' perception that customers will not pay for a specific attribute:* Here, we have the situation where the supplier of a product or service foregoes a product or service enhancement because it thinks the customers will not care about it. It may be right, saving the firm money, but if it is wrong, it is sacrificing a competitive advantage for the firm. Packaging of a product is one where a firm believes that how the product appears to customers will drive their perception of the quality of that product.
- *Perception of poor quality:* This is the barrier that Japanese cars faced in the late 1950s and early 1960s. Japanese cars were widely perceived to be of inferior quality, so the cars could not command a price that was equal to those being charged by U.S. manufacturers. This relationship, or perception, has flipped 180 degrees today, with U.S. car manufacturers striving to be perceived as having quality that matches their Japanese competitors.
- *Perception that the supplier is not reliable:* If you need to know that your product will be available when you need it, your perception as to the reliability of different suppliers becomes important. This is the driving perception behind the Amazon.com supplier ratings and services such as Angie's List that rate the reliability of service providers.

Many perceptions might be relevant. What is important to remember is that a company has to pay as much attention to how it is perceived in the marketplace as to how it actually performs from day to day. A bad reputation can destroy a good company. Once earned, a bad reputation is hard to undo, and can cost significant outlays of advertising and marketing dollars to overcome. When companies hire public relations firms, they are attempting to influence the perceptual drivers of their strategic performance.

We have now dealt with the basic logic that underlies strategic planning in the value chain/supply chain domain, so it is time to turn our attention to defining some measureable points in the analysis so that we can determine how well we are doing in executing our strategy and meeting customer expectations.

Beyond the Basics

OBJECTIVE 2

Complete a basic analysis of value chain performance; identify and describe major value chain patterns; and explain the concept of value migration within industry value chains.

As we have seen, management accounting always comes down to ultimately measuring some aspect of performance to ensure that what is being done meets the goals that were set for it. We have already seen some basic measurements that can be used in SCM—profit on sales, sales per asset deployed, and return on assets. Let us look a little deeper now and see what else can be measured and analyzed.

IDENTIFYING AND MEASURING CURRENT PERFORMANCE

We have learned many different ways of identifying and measuring current performance. When we take a value chain perspective, these tools break down into five basic categories:

- *SCM:* This can be expanded to include returns on equity, broken down into its component parts, as we shall see shortly.
- *Target costing:* A tool we learned about in the product chapter has significant impact on the planning dimension of strategic analysis in the value chain. During target costing, the various options open to the firm in terms of suppliers, value chain structures, and a host of customer-oriented features, such as those that fall into the perceptual drivers category, are explored.
- *Life cycle costing:* Touched on briefly earlier, life cycle costing deals with the total costs incurred over a product's life. It can be looked at from the firm's perspective as the total costs to develop, produce, and retire a product, or from the customer's perspective that is concerned with the total lifetime cost of ownership.
- *Customer, segment, and divisional profitability:* We have spent significant time dealing with these issues in the entity and customer domain chapters. They are part of the strategic analysis and "check" portion of actions in the value chain domain.
- *Channel analysis:* Here, we deal with the specific costs of offering a product in one channel vs. another. For instance, companies that maintain retail storefronts but also have a heavy presence on the internet are firms that are deploying a dual-channel strategy. They are hoping to appeal to customers with very different buying habits. Each channel brings with it both costs and benefits, as we will soon see.

Because we have dealt with many of these issues in depth earlier, we will concentrate on just a few of these concepts in this chapter. We will expand SCM to include return on equity and undertake a brief excursion into channel analysis. For the other topics, you should refer to your notes from earlier chapters.

RETURN ON EQUITY AND A FIRM'S BASIC ECONOMIC STRUCTURE

When we add return on equity (ROE) to SCM analysis, it helps us round out the picture about the basic economic structure of a firm. Let us first look at how to calculate ROE in an expanded way that gives us more insight into the strength of the firm's value chain. We will then use this logic to complete the picture of the basic economic structure of a firm.

ROE is net income divided by the firm's total equity. We have done this type of calculation numerous times. How do we change it to gain more insight into the functioning of the firm? We expand it into three component pieces:

ROE = Profit Margin x Asset Intensity x Degree of Leverage

or

ROE = (Profit / Sales) x (Sales / Net Assets) x (Net Assets / Equity)

Let us do a simple example.

Sales	$1,000,000
Profit	$150,000
Net assets	$1,800,000
Equity	$900,000

We can now calculate ROE in its three component parts:

Profit margin:	$150,000 / $1,000,000,	or	15%
Asset intensity	$1,000,000 / $1,800,000,	or	55.556%
Leverage:	$1,800,000 / $900,000,	or	200%

So ROE equals:

0.15 × 0.55556 × 2, **or** 16.67%

This is the same as dividing net profit by equity, or $150,000 divided by $900,000 equals 16.67%. We know more now, however. We know the firm makes 15% on its sales, has a moderate asset intensity (it takes one dollar in assets to generate $0.55 in sales), and the firm is reasonably leveraged, with its financial structure being one-half equity and one-half debt (the only two ways to finance the firm, correct?). The company in this example is earning a very strong ROE due to a low asset intensity and solid use of leverage to make the most out of its asset base.

We can now combine this with a series of other metrics to get a complete picture of the firm's performance: What are the components of a firm's economic structure? They are:

- Contribution margin per unit
- Annual fixed cost base: manufacturing and SG&A
- Breakeven point in sales units or sales dollars
- Profit earned in a period (usually one year)
- Asset investment:
    - » Days of inventory on hand (average inventory / (COGS / 365)
    - » Accounts receivable days (average accounts receivable / (sales / 365)
    - » Fixed asset turnover (net sales / average fixed assets)
- Fixed cost percentage of sales, which can be broken down into manufacturing and SG&A
- Gross margin percentage
- Selling and administrative cost percentage

If we know all of this information about a firm, we can understand how it is performing and why it is (or is not) reaching its sales and profit goals. This information comes from an income statement and balance sheet of BlueTooth Equipment, illustrated in Table 14.1.

TABLE 14.1 INCOME STATEMENT AND BALANCE SHEET

BlueTooth Equipment		
Income Statement for the Year Ending 12/31/20x6		
	Dollars	Percentage
Sales	$10,000,000	100.0%
Less: Variable Costs		
Manufacturing	$3,100,000	31.0%
Selling, General, and Administrative	$1,400,000	14.0%
Total Variable Costs	$4,500,000	45.0%
Contribution Margin	$5,500,000	55.0%
Less: Fixed Costs		
Manufacturing	$2,400,000	24.0%
Selling, General, and Administrative	$1,700,000	17.0%
Total Fixed Costs	$4,100,000	41.0%
Income Before Tax	$1,400,000	14.0%

BlueTooth Equipment		
Income Statement for the Year Ending 12/31/20x6		
	Dollars	Percentage
Less: Income Tax (35%)	$490,000	4.9%
Net Profit	$910,000	9.1%
Note: The Cost of Goods Sold amount for the year is:		$5,500,000

BlueTooth Equipment			
Balance Sheet for the Year Ending 12/31/20x6			
Assets		Liabilities and Owner's Equity	
Cash	$800,000	Accounts Payable	$850,000
Accounts Receivable	$950,000	Salaries Payable	$250,000
Inventory	$460,000	Short-Term Notes Payable	$275,000
Total Current Assets	$2,210,000	Total Current Liabilities	$1,375,000
Property, Plant, and Equipment	$5,250,000	Long-Term Debt	$1,700,000
Less: Accumulated Depreciation	$1,837,500	Total Liabilities	$3,075,000
Net Property, Plant, and Equipment	$3,412,500	Common Stock	$550,000
Total Assets	$5,622,500	Retained Earnings	$1,997,500
		Total Equity	$2,547,500
		Total Liabilities and Equity	$5,622,500
At the beginning of the year:			
Accounts Receivable were $ 850,000			
Inventory was $ 500,000			
Net Property, Plant, and Equipment was $3,800,500			

What does the economic structure of BlueTooth Equipment look like? Let's review Table 14.2 together. BlueTooth Equipment sells 1,000,000 units per year.

TABLE 14.2 ECONOMIC STRUCTURE

BlueTooth Equipment		
For the year ending 12/31/20x6		
Measurement	Calculation	Result
Contribution margin per unit	$5,500,000 / 1,000,000 units	$5.50
Annual Fixed Cost Base		$4,100,000
Breakeven Point	$4,100,000 / $5.50	745,455
Profit earned FY 20x6		$910,000
Asset Investment:		
Inventory on hand—# of days	(($460,000 + 500,000) / 2) / ($5,500,000 / 365)	31.85 days
Accounts receivable—# of days	(($950,000 + 850,000) / 2) / ($10,000,000 / 365)	32.85 days
Fixed asset turnover	$10,000,000 / (($3,412,500 + 3,800,500) / 2)	2.77 turns
Fixed Cost Percentage of Sales:		
Manufacturing	$2,200,000 / $10,000,000	22%
SG&A	$1,900,000 / $10,000,000	19%
Gross margin percentage (using COGS)	$5,500,000 /$10,000,000	55%
SG&A Percentage*	$3,100,000 / $10,000,000	31%
*Note: $10,000,000 – $5,500,000 COGS – $1,400,000 income before tax = $3,100,000 SG&A		

So, how does the company look? Clearly, we would need information on the industry to do a complete analysis, but simply looking at these numbers, BlueTooth Equipment earned 9.1% net profit on $10,000,000 worth of sales, which is reasonable given that it operates in a competitive industry. Its breakeven point leaves it with a 254,545 unit margin of safety (1,000,000 units sold minus the 745,455 breakeven units), or 25% above its breakeven sales (254,545 divided by 1,000,000). It keeps low inventory and accounts receivable days, with reasonable turns on its fixed assets. In general, therefore, we see a company that is currently operating in a stable way in a competitive industry. It has good management of its assets and reasonable returns on overall investment. Its ROE is very high at 35.7% ($910,000 profit divided by $2,547,500 total equity), with a return on net assets (RONA) of 16.2% ($910,000 divided by $5,622,500 net assets). These two critical performance measures indicate a quite good performance.

We could also do a quick calculation of the expanded ROE that we worked with earlier, resulting in the following:

- Profit margin: $910,000 / $10,000,000, or 9.1%
- Asset intensity: $10,000,000 / $5,622,500, or 1.778
- Leverage: $5,622,500 / $2,547,500, or 2.21

BlueTooth Equipment is not using leverage as effectively as our first example, having $2.21 in assets for every dollar of equity. But it is earning high returns on equity, so its investors are probably quite happy with the firm's performance. In general, BlueTooth shows a strong economic structure with good returns for its investors.

CHANNEL ANALYSIS

BlueTooth Equipment sells its products through two channels: direct sales via its internet website and sales through electronics stores (retail channel). What costs are incurred in each channel? When we think about channel costs, we need to consider the following:

- Cost to manage the channel
- Costs to maintain the channel
- Advertising, promotion, and marketing costs to the general marketplace by channel
- Product liability costs by channel
- Trade show costs by channel
- Marketing staff costs by channel

The analyses of BlueTooth Equipment's two channels are in Table 14.3. In it, we have broken down the SG&A costs of $3,100,000 into two components: general management expenses of $500,000 and sales and marketing costs (channel costs) of $2,600,000. Where does the $2,600,000 go?

TABLE 14.3 CHANNEL COSTS

BlueTooth Equipment		
For the year ending 12/31/20x6		
Type of Cost	Internet Channel	Retail Channel
Channel Management	$450,000	$300,000
Channel Maintenance	$500,000	$125,000
Advertising, Promotion, and Marketing	$175,000	$350,000
Product Liability	$75,000	$100,000
Trade Shows	$25,000	$125,000
Marketing and Sales Staff	$175,000	$200,000
Total Channel Costs	$1,400,000	$1,200,000
Total Channel Revenues	$4,000,000	$6,000,000
Channel Costs as Percentage of Revenue	35%	20%

We can see that, while close in total costs, the two channels spend their money in very different places. The internet channel uses $950,000, or 67.9% of its total channel costs, managing the channel and maintaining it. This cost is due to the high ongoing costs of keeping a website up and running efficiently and effectively. While $300,000 goes into managing the retail channel, its largest cost is in advertising and marketing at $350,000. These two costs combine to be $650,000, or 54.2%, of its total channel costs. The two channels are very different. To totally understand these numbers, however, we should compare them to the revenue each channel generates. Here we see that the market breaks up into 40% internet sales and 60% retail sales. This makes the channel costs as a percentage of revenue 35% for the internet channel and only 20% for the retail channel. Clearly, the retail channel is the more efficient of the two channels being served by BlueTooth Equipment.

Having analyzed the firm's economic structure and channel patterns, let us turn our attention to the various patterns value chains can take.

VALUE CHAIN PATTERNS

The concept of value chain patterns and supply channel patterns was introduced into the management literature by Slywotzky and Morrison in 1999 in the context of the game of business.[8] It is a useful way to think about how companies compete in value chain settings. The four major ways competition breaks out in value chains are illustrated in Figure 14.6.

De-integration, a term coined by Slywotzky and Morrison, is *the point at which firms begin to outsource major parts of and increasingly concentrate on only a small segment of the industry value chain*, that is, they stop trying to be totally vertically integrated. It ends finally with a splintered value chain in which firms operate only in very small segments of the total value chain.

In the computer industry, for example, some key value chain players, such as Intel, focus only on supplying processors. They leave the rest of the manufacturing of the computer to other firms, who tout their Intel processors as part of their marketing strategy. Dell buys all of its component parts, emphasizing the assembly of the computer and strong interactions with its customers. Dell started in only one channel, the internet channel, and has expanded in the retail sector, but remains focused on assembly, not manufacturing. Microsoft only does programming, offering both operating system and application software products. Each company has taken up only a small stage in the computer industry value chain, but each can provide nice returns.

The computer industry, therefore, has changed from the days of IBM and Texas Instruments—which made many of their parts, assembled the equipment, wrote software, and sold products in multiple channels—to a situation in which many companies need to cooperate and coordinate their activities to meet the ever-changing, ever-growing demands of the computer customer. To succeed in the computer value chain of today, therefore, a company needs to specialize in and dominate an important link in the new, fragmented value chain.

---

8 *Profit Patterns: 30 Ways to Anticipate and Profit from Strategic Forces Reshaping Your Business*, by Adrian Slywotzky and David Morrison, with the support of Ted Moser, Kevin Mundt, and James Quella, New York: Times Business Press, 1999.

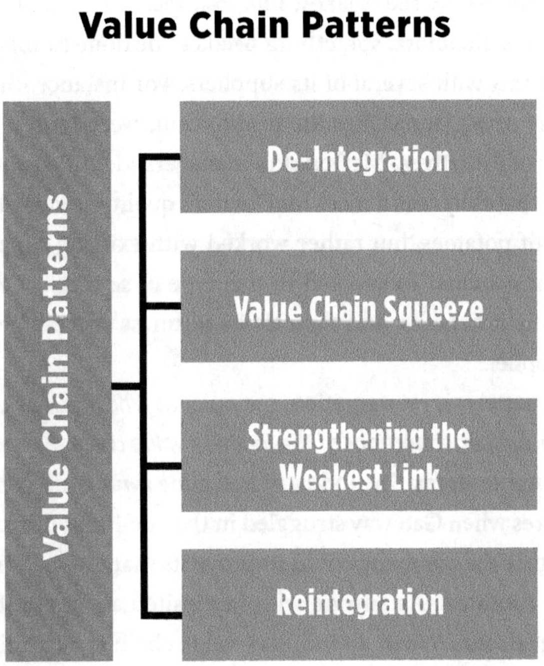

Value Chain Patterns

Value Chain Patterns

- De-Integration
- Value Chain Squeeze
- Strengthening the Weakest Link
- Reintegration

FIGURE 14.6 THE FOUR WAYS VALUE CHAIN PATTERNS EVOLVE

This pattern is in contrast to the **value chain squeeze,** *the point at which a company's place within a value chain is absorbed by other firms in that chain, making it redundant*. It is left with minimal or no profit and nowhere to turn. Three reasons lie behind the tendency of a value chain to go into "squeeze mode": 1) relative scarcity of some key resource, such as talent; 2) a faster rate of performance improvement by trading partners; or 3) a consolidation of players in a segment, which gives them more power over the events that take place in the value chain.

An example of this pattern are the major television networks: NBC, CBS, ABC and Fox. They face increased pressure from two sides. The local TV affiliates have considerable control over the local market and take most of the value created by the networks for themselves. On the other side are content providers, such as the NFL, which demand greater and greater premiums for participating with a specific network. The large networks, therefore, are stuck in the middle. The development of the market has continued, however, with firms such as MSNBC, CNN, and Fox starting up freestanding cable networks that are focused more on news, an area in which they face no consolidated power base, with less emphasis on traditional programming. To compete successfully in this environment, a firm has to improve its performance faster than its value chain partners and also to encourage the entry of new players to more evenly distribute the power in the value chain network.

In the pattern **strengthening the weakest link,** *a firm's trading partners work together to improve its performance*. This is done because those firms do not want to undertake vertical integration, or absorption, of the place in the chain dominated by the weakest link, but recognize that it can limit the amount of value they can create for customers; therefore, something needs to be done to support it.

McDonald's has done this with several of its suppliers. For instance, the suppliers of the fries, which make up such a large part of McDonald's value proposition, were fragmented and lacked quality standards. Through a number of initiatives, McDonald's managers identified some viable french fry suppliers and worked with them so that they could meet McDonald's quality standards reliably. McDonald's did not try to become a supplier of potatoes, but rather worked with existing suppliers to strengthen both their products and their control systems. To succeed in this type of setting, a company has to fix the weakest link in such a way that only it benefits, and then tie its business success (its business model) to the new, higher standard of the supplier.

The final value chain pattern is **reintegration,** *the point at which value chains that fragmented over time begin to reconsolidate to secure larger portions of the industry value chain*. An example of this in the computer industry is Apple with its Apple stores. The industry had gone away from computer developers and assemblers having their own stores when Gateway struggled in the late 1980s during the industry de-integration. Apple managers decided that the company could improve its market position if it developed retail outlets dedicated solely to Apple products. As anyone who has visited an Apple store knows, this reintegration attempt has been a raging success. When an industry value chain is beginning to reintegrate, therefore, it is essential that a firm reabsorb those elements of the value chain that matter because of profitability, customer information, or strategic control. If possible, it may be better to use contracts or minority interests in other firms to accomplish the reintegration with minimal risk.

VALUE MIGRATION

What we saw with the various value chain patterns is that there are dynamics in play in any industry. One of the key dynamics is called **value migration,** *the flow of market value from one firm or business model to another*. The reason for this flow of value is that one firm or business model does a better job of serving customers than another. **Market value, or capitalization,** *the sum of a company's stock value and long-term debt* (shares outstanding times stock price plus long-term debt), captures a firm's ability to create and capture value in the marketplace. Market value is the primary constraining factor for growth in a company. Without long-term capitalization, a company cannot start new businesses or find innovative ways to grow existing businesses because it simply does not have the funds to do so.[9] The power of a company inside its value chain is a function of its market value relative to its size.

Migration of value takes place in three phases. The first phase is *value inflow*, which takes place in the early phase of a company's development. Value is driven by a superior **business design, or model,** *the core aspects of a business, including purpose, offerings, strategies, infrastructure, organizational structures, trading practices, and operational processes and policy*. Value flows into a company that is perceived to have superior economics and the strong ability to satisfy its customers. Apple changed its business design by

9 The discussion of value migration is based on comments made in Adrian Slywotzky, *Value Migration: How to Think Several Moves Ahead of the Competition*, Boston: Harvard Business School Press, 1996.

opening up the Apple stores. This has greatly enhanced its competitiveness and has been responsible for value flowing into Apple from its competitors, such as Dell.

The second phase of value migration is *stability*. Here, we see business designs that are well-matched to customer desires and priorities. The stability phase is also a period of relative competitive equilibrium because what is being done by firms, and how it is done, matches well with the expectations of their customers. A stability phase can last varying lengths of time, depending on whether consumer tastes change or whether a new business model once again enters the market, causing value to flow away from existing competitors. The auto industry is in a relative state of stability at this point in time. This has been in place for many years. Some might argue that firms like CarMax or AutoTrader.com are threatening the existing structure of at least the retail marketplace, but, to date, they have not taken a significant share from the existing players in the auto market. While consolidation and mergers continue unabated in the auto industry, and there are some new market entrants (e.g., Tesla, Fisker) and exits (e.g., Suzuki from the U.S. market), key players remain intact and operate much the same way as they have for decades.

The third phase of value migration is *value outflow*. Here, we see market value start to leave companies that have more traditional structures toward innovative new business models that are more effective in meeting customers' changing priorities. The book marketplace is one area of the economy in which we see value flowing out of traditional bookstores and into electronic books that can be read on Amazon's Kindle devices or Barnes & Noble's Nook. While many people still prefer a real book with paper pages, the number of people switching to digital editions is having a major impact on the viability of retail bookstore chains in the United States.

What are some of the reasons that value flows away from the large corporations to smaller, more nimble competitors? Adrian Slywotsky provides the following reasons for this value migration pattern:[10]

- Customers are becoming more knowledgeable, and are increasingly unwilling to pay premium prices when good, cheaper alternatives exist.
- The competitive circle has expanded as globalization becomes an issue in almost all industries. New competitors from new countries often offer innovative business models.
- Advances in technology make it easier to produce low-cost substitutes for many goods. E-books are an example of this effect.
- Many businesses are becoming less scale-dependent, which reduces the barriers to entry in a field. The mini-steel mill is an example of this phenomenon.
- Improved customer access to information has reduced switching costs.
- New competitors have easier access to capital, as venture capitalists and other investors provide capital that is not dependent on having an established, healthy cash flow.

The result is a change in the basic assumptions of what defines and drives business success, as suggested in Figure 14.7.

10 Ibid, pp. 8, 10.

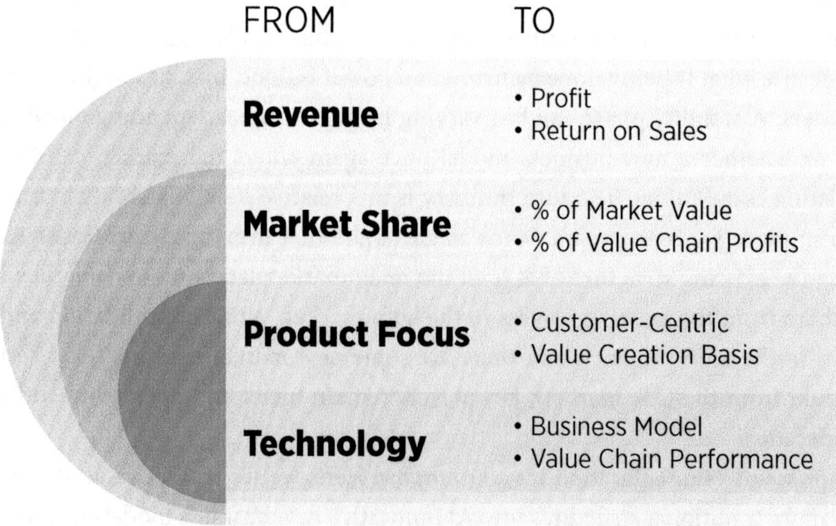

FIGURE 14.7 WITH THE CHANGE IN EMPHASIS ON WHAT CONSTITUTES A SUCCESSFUL ENTERPRISE COMES MORE POWER FOR THE CONSUMER WHOSE PREFERENCES HAVE ALSO CHANGED.

What is critical in this process of changing assumptions is the increased power of the customer, who ultimately forces the migration of value through a change in preferences and expectations. As customers' wants change, space opens up for new business models that will meet these wants even better than before. Notice that the shift in customer power is present in the simple change of words from customer needs driving the market to customer wants. The internet is one of the great enablers of this shift in customer power.

Having talked about the different dynamic patterns an industry value chain can take, let us now turn our attention to the management of the supply chain as it is structured, the tactical and operational aspects of value chain management, by taking a brief look into integrated supply chain management.

IN CONTEXT ➤ Gaining a Competitive Edge at Prestige Auto

The new cars were rolling onto the lot at Prestige Autos, and the company was poised for a new bout of growth. Jack's final concern was finding new ways to please its customers, so he could open up a competitive edge in the local auto market. He decided he would like to support a "virtual" test drive of the new model in an attempt to provide new value to increasingly internet-savvy buyers.

Who should he turn to? No one in the company had the expertise to create a realistic driving simulation, so Jack started to shop around for someone who could do the work he needed. One Friday afternoon, Brady Noel, a young entrepreneur whom an associate recommended, came in to see him. Brady specialized in virtual reality games, so Jack was skeptical at first, but was soon enthralled with what he saw.

"You see, Jack, we can put the interior of your cars right into the module and then allow the customer to 'take it for a spin' on a variety of roads. They'll be able to feel the acceleration and smooth ride, especially as your new model hugs those corners. We can add whatever sound effects you'd like; we can even let customers select the music they want to listen to while they test-drive the car. That will help to shape the car's image," said Brady.

"Can you really make it feel like an actual test drive?" asked Jack, still a bit dubious.

"Sure can!" replied Brady enthusiastically. "Today, especially, your customers are very computer- and internet-savvy and have played a lot of action games that use virtual reality technology. What we'll do is film one of your employees, or you, driving the car and putting it through its paces, and then build a game module with a variety of road conditions that allows the customer to test the car out. The music will make the experience much more personal."

"You've sold me," exclaimed Jack. "Can you also help us set up internet ordering so customers can actually shop from the comfort of their home? I'd really like to take greater advantage of the technology. That will make a great impression on the customer, and, combined with the changes we're making in the way we run our physical shop, should help us grow. That means taking sales away from our competitors. If you can help us do that, you'll be a hero around here!"

"Why don't we film the virtual test drive later this week? You choose a driver and a set of road conditions, and we'll be ready to do our bit. Give us two weeks and we should have a demo for you and your people to try out. The sales support tool is an easy application. I've got someone I can put on that right away, so we should be able to demo that when we come back later this week to start the virtual test drive modeling," noted Brady.

"You're going to help us gain an edge, I can feel it," said Jack. "We can't just sit back and do the same old things and expect new sales to come bustling through the door. We can offer specials, but being able to reach out to the customer 24 hours a day, 7 days a week is great. There should even be a way to give an estimate of trade-in value to help the process along. We can deliver the new car to their door with the paperwork already completed online. Simple, no-stress, no-hassle car buying! That's our new goal!"

With that, Jack rose from his desk, and shook Brady's hand. He decided he would surprise his management team with this last innovation. They would be blown away by the changes taking place—Prestige Autos was going to take value away from its competitors and find new ways to service...no, not service, to *please* customers. It was time for change in the auto industry, and Jack intended to be on the leading edge, not the tail end, of these changes.

Integrated Supply Chain Management

OBJECTIVE 3
Discuss the basic concepts of integrated supply chain management within the value chain domain.

When we enter the topic of integrated supply chain management (ISCM), we are really simply making the transition from the strategic domain of the value chain, where we have been spending our time, to the tactical and operational side of value chain management. ISCM is the "how" in getting to the goals set up during strategic planning—taking plans and making them into reality. A supply chain really is a value chain. It consists of a company and all of the suppliers and customers of the company. That is how we defined a value chain earlier, so do not be confused by the addition of this term. What has changed is the focus of our discussion, not the emphasis on the value chain itself.

THE BASICS OF ISCM

In ISCM, the chief concern is managing the interactions of responsiveness vs. efficiency. Responsiveness means being able to meet unexpected customer demand rapidly, which often requires keeping excess resources on hand. As detailed in Figure 14.8, five major elements drive supply chain performance: production, inventory, location, transportation, and information. As with the Theory of Constraints (TOC) discussed earlier, the goal of the design of a business is to maximize throughput, or the revenue generated by selling a company's products and services. This is done by balancing the needs for responsiveness and efficiency in each of these five activity domains. More inventory can make a company much more capable of meeting a sudden uptick in demand, but that inventory brings with it many new costs that reduce the efficiency of the firm. For each trade-off, therefore, the goal is to find that balance of features that will allow the firm to compete efficiently and effectively.

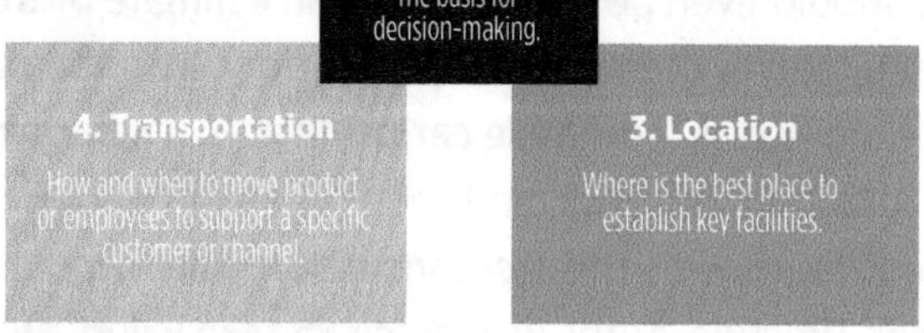

The Five Major Supply Chain Drivers

1. Production What, how, and when to build product or supply service.	**2. Inventory** How much product to make and how much to store, or number of employees retained to provide a specific service.
5. Information The basis for decision-making.	
4. Transportation How and when to move product or employees to support a specific customer or channel.	**3. Location** Where is the best place to establish key facilities.

FIGURE 14.8 TO MAXIMIZE REVENUE, A COMPANY MUST BALANCE THE NEEDS FOR RESPONSIVENESS AND EFFICIENCY IN EACH OF THESE FIVE DOMAINS.

One of the key trade-offs made by organizations within a supply chain is between responsiveness vs. efficiency. The ultimate goal is to improve the productivity—both in terms of quantity and velocity (for example, speed) of work completed—of the supply chain so that responsiveness is improved without incurring major expenses in terms of inventory, transportation, or redundant locations. Working together, supply chain partners pursue improvement from the inception of a new product or service until it is withdrawn from the market. During product design and development, input is sought from every participant in the supply chain in order to identify the optimal materials, services, and production methods. This active collaboration early in the product or service life cycle eliminates unnecessary activities and optimizes the utilization of resources.

As we saw with the value migration discussion, the marketplace faced by many companies today is evolving, and evolving rapidly. Whereas in the past, companies could vertically integrate and lock in specific models for reaching a stable mass market, today, companies use **virtual integration,** *the combination of businesses that takes place through contracts rather than ownership*, to give them flexibility in the face of fragmented, fast-moving markets. Companies seek to understand their core competency and build internal structures to build and protect that core competency. Honda's core competency is not in making cars or motorcycles, it is in making engines. It defines its products and businesses around its superior engine designs. Yes, the company makes cars, but it outsources the production of most of the major components and focuses on providing reliable engines as its primary source of competitive advantage.

ALIGNING THE SUPPLY CHAIN WITH BUSINESS STRATEGY

Who are the participants in an ISCM? They include suppliers of goods and services to a producer, who then works with distributors, who sell to retailers, who then sell to customers. This traditional chain of participants is part of what makes up a company's business design or model. Figure 14.9 is an example of an extended supply chain. Here, we see several service providers all interacting in various ways with other companies in the supply chain. In this manner, the supply chain brings the business strategy to life, looking for the optimal combination of insourcing and outsourcing of goods and services to provide a competitive advantage in the marketplace.

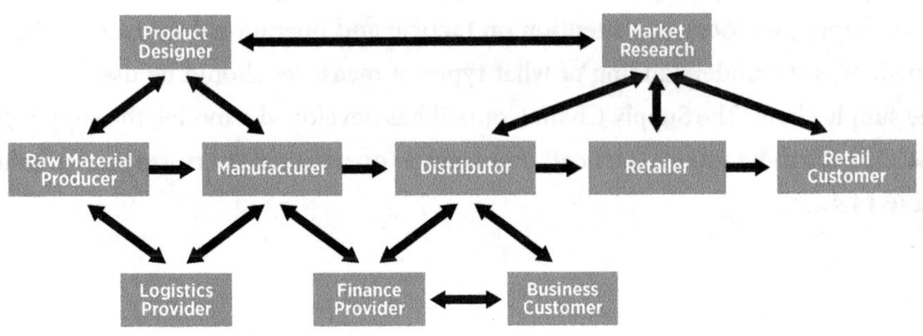

FIGURE 14.9 THE INTERACTIONS AMONG SEVERAL SERVICE PROVIDERS WITH OTHER COMPANIES IN THE SUPPLY CHAIN PERMITS THE BEST MIX OF INSOURCING AND OUTSOURCING OF GOODS.

Three steps are required to align a supply chain with the company's business strategy:[11] 1) Understand the markets the company serves; 2) Define the strengths or core competencies of the business and the role the company can play in serving its markets; and 3) Develop the needed supply chain capabilities to support the marketplace roles the company has chosen. The first point is where a company comes to grips with whether responsiveness or efficiency is more important for satisfying customer wants. Chopra and Meindl[12] developed the following list of attributes to help a company better understand its markets:

- The quantity of the product needed in each lot, or order;
- The response time customers are willing to tolerate;
- The variety of products needed;
- The service level required;
- The price of the product;
- The desired rate of innovation in the product.

The role played by responsiveness vs. efficiency cannot be overstated. It impacts every decision in building the ISCM and in managing the supply chain from day to day. By modifying the nature of the five drivers of ISCM performance, a company can radically shift its flexibility or narrow down on efficiency. It is simply important to match these choices to the strategy the firm has decided to pursue. If a firm is attempting to be the low-cost provider, it will need to choose the most efficient business design possible. It will not carry large amounts of inventory or keep excess capacity to handle swings in demand. If it faces seasonal demand, it may be forced to produce at a higher rate throughout the year, building as little inventory as possible but making it capable of handling expected demand surges. Unexpected demand surges will simply not be met by a company emphasizing efficiency over responsiveness.

In this way, therefore, we execute strategy in the choice of a business design, or infrastructure of our firm and its relationship with trading partners, through ISCM. Since ISCM is execution-focused, measurement and control are important.

MEASURING AND CONTROLLING SUPPLY CHAIN PERFORMANCE

We have already looked at strategic measures of performance for value chains. As we turn to the last section of this chapter, we focus our attention on tactical and operational measures. The field of ISCM is well-developed, as is the understanding of what types of measures should be used to control the performance of the supply chain. The Supply Chain Council has developed a model, the supply chain operations reference (SCOR) for these level 2 (tactical) and level 3 (operational) performance measures. It is reproduced in Table 14.4.

---

11 Ibid, pg. 28-29.

12 Sunil Chopra and Peter Meindl, *Supply Chain*, 2nd edition, Upper Saddle River, N.J.: Prentice-Hall, Inc., 2003.

TABLE 14.4 SUPPLY CHAIN PERFORMANCE METRICS (SCOR MODEL)

	TACTICAL Metrics	OPERATIONAL Metrics		
	Performance Metrics	Complexity Measures	Configuration Measures	Practice Measures
PLAN	Planning costs Financing costs Inventory days of supply	Percentage of order changes Number of SKUs carried Production volume Inventory carrying costs	Product volume by channel Number of channels Number of supply chain locations	Planning cycle time Forecast accuracy Obsolete inventory on hand
SOURCE	Material acquisition costs Source cycle time Raw materials days of supply	Number of suppliers Percentage of purchasing spending by distance	Purchased material by geography Percentage of purchasing spending by distance	Supplier delivery performance Payment period Percentage of items purchased by their associated lead times
MAKE	Number of defects or complaints Make cycle time Build order attainment Product quality	Number of SKUs Upside production flexibility	Manufacturing process steps by geography Capacity utilization	Value-add percentage Build-to-order percentage Build-to-stock percentage Percentage of manufacturing order changes due to internal issues WIP inventory
DELIVER	Fill rates Order management costs Order fulfillment lead times Line item return rates	Number of orders by channel Number of line items and shipments by channel Percentage of line items returned	Delivery locations by geography Number of channels	Published delivery lead times Percentage of invoices containing billing errors Order entry methods

Source: The Supply Chain Council, www.apics.org/apics-for-business/products-and-services/apics-scc-frameworks/scor, January 24, 2017.

As Table 14.4 illustrates, many of the things being measured are those we discussed either in this chapter or earlier chapters. We now know that capacity utilization is an important concern in the "make" step of the supply chain configuration. Once again, we see the trade-off between responsiveness and efficiency. If we want a responsive supply chain, we are going to have much more idle capacity, ready to produce, than if we want to focus on efficiency.

You also see a major role played by geography in the configuration metrics. This is because where you place your business with respect to its suppliers and customers will dictate how responsive you can be to changes in value chain (for example, supply chain) demand. As we can see from these measures, therefore, they are very focused on how the supply chain is going to achieve its objectives, not in the setting of the objectives themselves. Companies that have a lot of SKUs (different types of products) are probably focusing on a responsiveness approach, because efficiency would call for a limited number of SKUs serving a broad range of customers. We will work with these measures a bit more in the exercise and problem sections of the chapter.

In the end, therefore, the value chain domain is the home of two complete management models, both of which reflect the "Plan-Do-Check-Adjust" business cycle that has underlain this book. Strategic cost management emphasizes the development and constant evaluation of strategies. Its measures are business-level metrics such as ROE. When we shift our attention from strategy to execution, the models fall under the integrated supply chain literature, which is concerned with everything from planning through doing and evaluating, but at the tactical and operational level. Both models are focused on the value chain's performance, just from a different perspective. In the end, the company that does the best job of creating an innovative business design that matches the wants of its customers will win in the competitive wars. It is a constantly changing puzzle requiring innovation and change in all elements of the business.

Summary

The focus of this chapter was on the various tools and techniques used to plan, do, check, and act in the value chain domain. Reflecting Michael Porter's five forces of competition (suppliers, customers, new entrants, substitutes, and direct competitors), analysis in the value chain domain has to constantly be aware of other firms. It is an external perspective on firm performance and is very concerned with the relative market power of various players in the linked set of activities that start with the attainment of raw materials and ends up with product in the customers' hands. Value chains can be either divergent (one supplier splitting into many channels) or convergent (many suppliers converging on one or just a few channels).

Strategic cost management (SCM) is most concerned with comparing the economic structures of firms competing in the same industry. The three steps in completing a strategic cost analysis are: 1) Identify the industry's value chain and assign cost, revenues, and assets to value activities in the value chain; 2) Diagnose the cost drivers regulating each value activity; and 3) Develop sustainable competitive advantage either by controlling cost drivers better or reconfiguring the value chain. Cost drivers reflect the overall causes of cost patterns in an industry. They can be structural, executional, or perceptual in nature. Structural cost drivers are ones that emanate from how the industry is configured and reflects the choices a company makes in how to structure its economics. Executional cost drivers are the tools and techniques used by a firm to manage the flow of value creation. Perceptual cost drivers are beliefs held by companies in the industry or their customers regarding the firm, its products, and its services.

The four value chain patterns that reflect the dynamics of the value chain are de-integration, value chain squeeze, strengthening of the weakest link, and reintegration. These patterns describe how value migrates across value chains, moving from one player to another as one firm finds superior ways to add value to products and services for customers, gaining a power position in the value chain.

Integrated supply chain management (ISCM) is the tactical and operational side of value chain management. While still driven by strategy, ISCM is most concerned with how strategic goals are going to be obtained. Reflecting a constant trade-off between responsiveness and efficiency, ISCM focuses on five elements, or drivers, of supply chain performance: production, inventory, location, transportation, and information. The choices a company makes on these five dimensions have to match the demands of either a responsive or efficiency-driven strategy. In maximizing their value-creating potential, firms seek to gain and manage a core competency, some value-creating activity that they perform better than the competition. Many different performance metrics are used in ISCM. The choices are based on whether the focus is on planning, sourcing, making, or delivering a product or service.

In the end, therefore, these two models of value chain performance—SCM and ISCM—are complementary, not competitive. SCM emphasizes understanding the economics of the firms in the industry and finding a strategy that provides a sustainable competitive advantage. ISCM takes this strategic position and builds a business design, or model, that provides maximum assurance that strategic goals are met. Working together, they provide a comprehensive set of tools and techniques for managing in the value chain domain.

Key Terms

Business design, or model: the core aspects of a business including the purpose, offerings, strategies, infrastructure, organizational structures, trading practices, and operational processes and policies of a firm.

Competitive industries: ones in which many different companies vie for the customers' business.

Convergent value chain: one where multiple steps converge to one final channel to the customer.

Core competency: some aspect of doing business, or providing value to customers, that a firm is better at than its competitors.

De-integration: the point at which firms begin to outsource major parts of and increasingly concentrate on only a small segment of the industry value chain.

Divergent value chain: one in which a small number of suppliers support an array of channels, final products, and customers.

Executional cost driver: a strategic choice a firm makes about how assets, including individuals, are deployed to complete value-added work.

Five forces of competition: the suppliers, customers, new entrants, substitutes, and direct competitors a firm faces in the market.

High barriers to entry: a significant investment in fixed assets that is required to compete in an industry.

Integrated supply chain management: the tactical and operational focus on value chain performance; used to describe cooperative trading networks.

Market value, or capitalization: the sum of a company's stock value and long-term debt.

Monopoly: the only supplier of a product or service in the marketplace.

Natural flow: the sequence of steps required to complete the product or service and the resources consumed in its production.

Oligopolies: industries in which only a few large companies serve the market.

Perceptual cost driver: the known relationships between members of the value chain—a company, its trading partners—and the products they support.

Reintegration: the point at which a value chain that fragmented over time begins to reconsolidate to secure larger portions of the industry value chain.

Strategic cost management: a planning tool that focuses on the relative profitability of different members of an industry value chain.

Strengthening the weakest link: the point at which a firm's trading partners work together to improve its performance.

Structural cost driver: a choice a firm makes about the size and scope of its operations and the fundamental technologies it employs; it affects the cost of any given product or service.

Value activities: those things a company does that a customer values and is willing to pay for.

Value chain: the linked set of companies that participate in the design, development, provision, and support of a product or service.

Value chain squeeze: the point at which a company's place within a value chain is absorbed by other firms in that chain, making it redundant.

Value migration: the flow of market value from one firm or business model to another.

Virtual integration: the combination of businesses that takes place through contracts rather than ownership.

Questions

1. What is an industry value chain?
2. What are the five forces in a market and how do they affect how a firm competes in the marketplace?
3. Describe the key differences between SCM and ISCM.
4. What is the key difference between a divergent and a convergent value chain?
5. Describe the three key steps that make up SCM analyses.
6. Define the three different types of cost drivers and give examples of each.
7. What are the five basic financial tools we can use to analyze performance of a value chain?
8. What are the components of a firm's economic structure?
9. Identify the six elements of a company's channel costs.

10. What are the four value chain migration patterns and what does it mean to say value migrates within the value chain?
11. What are some of the reasons value migrates in an industry value chain?
12. Describe the five basic components of ISCM and how they respond to a shift between a responsiveness and an efficiency focus in the firm.

Exercises

1. **LIFE CYCLE AND TARGET COSTING.** StillWaters, Inc., is a producer of plastic bottles for various beverages. Recently, it was approached by a customer who wanted a quote on a new type of beverage bottle that would be much more complex to develop because of its special top. StillWaters' management determined that the customer would pay $0.30 per bottle. It normally earns a 25% profit margin on its products. The costs it estimates it would incur to develop the bottle are:
   - $50,000 development costs. The company would ultimately sell 2,500,000 of these bottles to the new customer.
   - $150,000 in machine purchases. The machines would be able to produce the entire 2,500,000 without replacement.
   - $0.08 in raw materials costs
   - $0.04 in direct labor costs
   - $0.05 in shipping and distribution costs
   - $25,000 in fixed costs for maintaining the relationship with the customer over the entire 2,500,000 units of sale

REQUIRED:

a. **What is the target cost for this product?**
b. **If the firm produces the way it intends, can it make its target margin?**

2. **LIFE CYCLE AND TARGET COSTING.** Smith Industries produces bicycle tires. It has just been approached by a major producer of bicycles to have a new type of tire produced that would be branded by the customer, who would sole-source the tire. It is estimated that the firm would use 300,000 tires over three years. The customer is willing to pay Smith $10 per tire because of its added features. Smith would like to earn 30% on this order. It projects the following costs:

- Development costs: $120,000 for the entire sale
- Machine acquisition: $300,000 for the entire sale
- Raw materials: $3 per tire
- Direct labor: $1.50 per tire
- Overhead: $0.75 per tire
- Shipping and distribution costs: $1 per tire
- Customer service costs: $75,000

REQUIRED:

a. What is the target cost for this product?

b. If the firm produces the way it intends, can it make its target margin?

3. **SEGMENT PROFITABILITY.** Simpson Enterprises provides computer maintenance services to a broad range of customers, from local schools to small businesses to residential customers. It obtains the following information about the costs to maintain these segments.

Simpson Enterprises				
	Schools	Small Businesses	Residential	Company Total
Revenues	$750,000	$1,250,000	$500,000	$2,500,000
Less:				
Direct labor costs	$360,000	$562,500	$255,000	$1,177,500
Computer equipment costs	$125,000	$200,000	$75,000	$400,000
Customer service costs	$50,000	$125,000	$75,000	$250,000
Travel costs	$20,000	$30,000	$50,000	$100,000
Entertainment costs	$-	$25,000	$-	$25,000
General overhead costs	$90,000	$125,000	$75,000	$290,000

REQUIRED:

a. Compute the segment profitability in dollars and percentages for each segment.

b. Based on these results, which segment is best for Simpson to serve? Which is worst?

4. **SEGMENT PROFITABILITY.** Anskar Industries makes computer modems that are used in a broad range of channels. Its three largest customer segments are large businesses, small businesses, and retail stores. The costs and revenues associated with these three segments are noted in the table below.

Anskar Industries				
	Large Businesses	Small Businesses	Retail Stores	Company Total
Revenues	$10,000,000	$4,500,000	$12,000,000	$26,500,000
Less:				
Direct material costs	$4,700,000	$2,160,000	$5,760,000	$12,620,000
Direct labor costs	$800,000	$360,000	$1,200,000	$2,360,000
General overhead costs	$1,800,000	$1,000,000	$2,000,000	$4,800,000
Distribution costs	$275,000	$550,000	$400,000	$1,225,000
Customer service costs	$150,000	$250,000	$-	$400,000
Warranties and repairs	$100,000	$150,000	$275,000	$525,000

REQUIRED:

a. **Compute the segment profitability in dollars and percentages for each segment.**

b. **Based on these results, which segment is best for Simpson to serve? Which is worst?**

5. **COMPONENTS OF RETURN ON EQUITY.** Falstaff, Inc., gives you the following information from its last year of performance.

Falstaff, Inc.	
Sales	$25,000,000
Profit	$7,000,000
Net assets	$21,000,000
Equity	$15,750,000

REQUIRED:

a. Calculate profit margin, asset intensity, and leverage for Falstaff, Inc.
b. Calculate the return on equity (ROE) using the three figures you derive in (a).
c. Compare this to a direct calculation of ROE. Are they the same (with rounding errors)?

6. **COMPONENTS OF RETURN ON EQUITY.** NuCastle Industries gives you the following information from its last year of performance.

NuCastle Industries	
Sales	$30,000,000
Profit	$7,500,000
Net assets	$28,000,000
Equity	$19,600,000

REQUIRED:

a. Calculate profit margin, asset intensity, and leverage for NuCastle Industries.
b. Calculate the ROE using the three figures you derive in (a).
c. Compare this to a direct calculation of ROE. Are they the same (with rounding errors)?

7. **CHANNEL PROFITABILITY.** Standish, Inc., serves the following three channels with its products. It only collects a limited amount of data on these channels, but wants you to calculate its profitability given what is known. The data provided is:

Standish, Inc.			
	Catalog Sales	Internet Sales	Retail Store Sales
Revenues	$10,000,000	$8,000,000	$25,000,000
Channel management	$1,000,000	$600,000	$4,500,000
Channel maintenance	$2,500,000	$3,000,000	$1,500,000
Advertising costs	$3,000,000	$750,000	$2,000,000

REQUIRED:

Calculate the channel costs in total and as a percentage of revenues.

8. **CHANNEL PROFITABILITY.** HighFive Industries serves the following three channels with its products. It only collects a limited amount of data on these channels, but wants you to calculate its profitability given what is known. The data provided is:

HighFive Industries			
	Direct to Business	Direct to Consumers	Retail Store Sales
Revenues	$25,000,000	$17,500,000	$30,000,000
Channel management	$1,200,000	$1,000,000	$1,500,000
Marketing staff costs	$4,000,000	$5,000,000	$3,500,000
Advertising costs	$2,500,000	$3,000,000	$1,850,000

REQUIRED:

Calculate the channel costs in total and as a percentage of revenues.

9. **SCOR MODEL.** You are given the following information about TeleCorp. Based on the numbers given, in your opinion, is the company following a responsiveness of efficiency strategy? Use the industry norm as an indication of a balanced strategy.

Measure	TeleCorp	Industry
Number of SKUs carried	3,000	2,000
Number of channels	5	3
Inventory days of supply	60	30
Capacity utilization	40%	60%

10. **SCOR MODEL.** You are given the following information about Huston, Inc. Based on the numbers given, in your opinion, is the company following a responsiveness of efficiency strategy? Use the industry norm as an indication of a balanced strategy.

Measure	Huston	Industry
Number of SKUs carried	1,000	1,500
Number of channels	2	3
Inventory days of supply	20	40
Capacity utilization	70%	50%

Problems

1. **TARGET COSTING AND VALUE CHAIN STRUCTURE.** MidRange, Inc., is considering entering the potato chips market with its new product, TastyChips, which in taste tests has beaten the competition available in the U.S. The potato chip market is a 4.5 million bags-a-year market, which MidRange thinks it could secure 15% of with reasonable marketing. Each bag would sell direct from MidRange at $2, to wholesalers for $1.50, and sell retail in the grocery stores for $2.79. Since this is a new market for MidRange, it has to make both sourcing and channel decisions.

   It could source its chips internally, buying a machine to make and bag the chips for $250,000. The machine would last for five years. It would take $0.35 in materials to make the chips, $0.20 in labor and machining costs, and $0.20 in overhead to make the chips. MidRange could also contract with a large manufacturer of salty snacks. This would cost $0.80 per bag but it would need to purchase in lot sizes of 50,000 bags to get this price. This would represent 1.4 months of supply, which would need to be stored at 25% carrying costs. Since chips have a fairly short shelf life, this would also put the firm at increased risk for returns of 10% of sales due to chips going out of date. A third option would be to rent the machine for making the chips, which would cost the company $60,000 a year, but it could return the machine at any time. It would cost the same to operate as a purchased machine.

   Once sourced, MidRange would need to determine how best to distribute its product. It currently does not have a sales force for salty products, so this would require hiring a product manager for $75,000 per year and a sales force of five people at $50,000 per year plus 10% commission each. Since the company would then have to ship to multiple store warehouses, it would take three picker/packers each at $30,000 per year plus $0.10

in shipping per bag due to multiple drop sites of small unit quantities. It would also require a new person in accounts receivable to process all of the paperwork, which would cost $40,000 per year.

If MidRange decided to use an existing wholesaler, it would only need the product manager but would face the lower price for its product. Shipping would be one drop, however, so it would only cost $0.05 per bag. The company would not need to add anyone to the back office to handle this business.

Finally, MidRange could use a jobber to distribute its product. Jobbers work for 15% of the total revenue (price to stores) that an item represents. MidRange would need to break the orders down into small lot sizes to ship to the jobbers. This would take two additional picker/packers in the company warehouse at a cost of $30,000 per year each plus $0.10 in shipping per bag due to the small lot sizes and multiple drop sites. It would also take a new person in accounts receivable to process the invoices at $40,000 per year.

Regardless of the choices made, the company will need to invest $100,000 in marketing to launch the product. This will be an annual charge to keep market share.

REQUIRED:

Given the information provided here, develop the value chain options that face MidRange. Specifically:

a. First look at the sales aspect of the value chain. Should MidRange rely solely on a sales force, a wholesale approach, or jobbers? Which would be most efficient (cost less)? Which would be most responsive or flexible? Make sure to include all of the costs, both sales and home office, in your analysis.

b. Calculate the target cost for the manufacturing operation. Use 20% as the target profit.

c. Look at the three options for sourcing the product. Which approach seems to be best for the firm financially (efficiency-based)? Which would be best for responsiveness? Make sure to include carrying costs for outsourced inventory using a calculation of number of days of sales the inventory represents at the 25% carrying cost noted.

d. Should MidRange enter this market if its target profit is 20%? Why or why not?

---

2. **TARGET COSTING AND VALUE CHAIN STRUCTURE.** Good Grains is a producer of breakfast cereals. There are 2.8 billion boxes of breakfast cereal sold each year in the United States at an average retail price of $3 per box. The company is trying to decide whether or not to launch a new type of cereal, which it thinks would garner 2% of the total market in its first year of launch, or 56 million boxes. To do so, it has to make several production and distribution decisions. It has no excess capacity, so the new product requires new capability.

On the production side, Good Grains has three options for sourcing the cereal. First would be to buy a new machine and produce it in-house. This would cost $250,000 for a machine that would make the flakes and another $200,000 for the machine that would blend the cereal with the other fruits and nuts and finish the packaging of the cereal. These machines would have a useful life of five years each. Raw material costs would be $0.60 per box (including packaging), labor would be $0.15 per box, and general overhead would be $0.25 per box. The company would be able to produce to meet demand so inventory on hand would be minimal.

Good Grains could also outsource the production in one of two ways. It could go to another large producer of cereals that would charge Good Grains $1.15 per box. The purchases would need to be made in large lot sizes of 2.5 million boxes, which would need to be stored for 30 days at a cost of 25% carrying costs for inventory. There would be a four-week lead time for an order, so Good Grains would need to factor this into its analysis. Shipment of the boxes to Good Grains' warehouse would cost $0.05 per box.

The cereal could also be outsourced overseas, where production costs are lower. Good Grains has received a quote of $0.85 a box from a foreign producer. The cereal would need to be bought in lot sizes of 5 million boxes to garner this price. There would be a four-week lead time for production and another four weeks for delivery, so Good Grains would need to keep eight weeks of buffer stock on hand, or 9 million boxes with a carrying cost of 25% of inventory value. It would also own the inventory once it left the dock at the manufacturer, creating another 5 million boxes of inventory that would have to be charged the 25% carrying cost for the company. Shipping itself would be $0.10 a box using a container ship. Damage could occur during shipping, with up to 10% of the boxes being damaged in shipment. This would be cost borne by Good Grains. This means Good Grains would need to order 10% more product if it uses this channel.

Once the manufacturing decision is made, Good Grains has to determine the best way to get the product on grocery store shelves. It could expand its existing sales force by three people at $60,000 per year plus a 5% commission on sales. The sale price to the grocery store would be $2. If it added this volume to its existing sales by its sales force, it would need to hire one customer service representative at $45,000 per year and one additional accounts receivable clerk for $40,000 per year. Since it would have to ship to multiple store locations, it would require an additional person in the warehouse at $35,000 per year. Shipment from the warehouse to customers would cost $0.05 per box.

Good Grains could also use a wholesaler to handle the new product. It uses wholesalers for several of its products. A wholesaler would only pay Good Grains $1.50 per box in order to make its own profit on the sale. It would not need to hire any additional support staff if it took this option. It would incur shipping costs of $0.05 per box.

Good Grains could also use the jobber network. This was something it has not done in the past but has been considering as the cost of its own internal sales force keeps mounting. A jobber would take the box of cereal at $1.60, but would also require a commission of 2% of the price paid by the grocery stores as a commission. Since the jobber network is quite spread out, it would require a customer service representative to handle its business at $45,000 per year and an additional accounts receivable clerk at $40,000 per year. It would also need an additional person in shipping to handle the increased demand, at $35,000 per year. Given the smaller lot sizes, shipping costs would be $0.07 per box.

Regardless of the channel used to move the product out to grocery stores, Good Grains would need to hire a product manager at $80,000 per year and incur marketing costs of $5 million per year in coupons and other discounts plus television and magazine advertising to gain and maintain its market share.

REQUIRED:

Given the information provided here, develop the value chain options that face Good Grains. Specifically,

a. **First look at the sales aspect of the value chain. Should Good Grains rely solely on a sales force, a wholesale approach, or jobbers? Which would be most efficient (cost less)? Which would be most responsive or flexible? Make sure to include all of the costs, both sales and home office, in your analysis.**
b. **Calculate the target cost for the manufacturing operation. Use 20% as the target profit.**
c. **Look at the three options for sourcing the product. Which approach seems to be best for the firm financially (efficiency-based)? Which would be best for responsiveness? Make sure to include carrying costs for outsourced inventory using a calculation of number of days of sales the inventory represents at the 25% carrying cost noted.**
d. **Should Good Grains enter this market if its target profit is 20%? Why or why not?**

3. **STRATEGIC COST MANAGEMENT.** Fancy Clip is a producer of hair clips and related types of hair accessories. Its value chain partners and information as it relates to the hair clips market is contained in the following table.

Measure	Plastic Supplier	Fancy Clip	Jobber	Retailer
Sales	$11,250,000	$25,000,000	$35,000,000	$43,750,000
Profit	$1,012,500	$3,000,000	$7,500,000	$3,500,000
Assets	$28,125,000	$50,000,000	$10,500,000	$75,000,000

REQUIRED:

a. Calculate the profit on sales, sales per assets, and return on assets (ROA) for each of these players.
b. Who has the best position in the value chain? Why?

4. **STRATEGIC COST MANAGEMENT.** Brighton Papers is a producer of a variety of papers. One of its biggest markets is for plain white 8½ x 11 paper used in printers and copiers. It sells the paper in cases of 10 reams of 500 sheets. Its value chain partners and information based on a case of paper sold is in the table below.

Measure	Tree Farmer	Pulp Mill	Brighton Papers	Wholesaler	Retailer
Revenue	$3.30	$13.20	$26.39	$43.99	$69.90
Paper cost	N/A	N/A	N/A	$26.39	$43.99
Operating costs	$2.25	$10.00	$23.20	$8.53	$15.55
Margin	$1.05	$3.20	$3.19	$9.07	$10.36
Assets	$7.00	$22.50	$52.75	$12.54	$69.00

REQUIRED:

a. Calculate the profit on sales, sales per assets, and ROA per case of paper sold for each of these players.
b. Who has the best position in the value chain? Why?

5. **CUSTOMER, SEGMENT, AND DIVISIONAL PROFITABILITY WITH ABC COSTING.** Yankee Spices is a medium-sized manufacturer of a wide variety of spices sold into two main segments of the market: direct to grocery store chains and to restaurants through a wholesaler network. The size of the bottle of spices is the main difference in the two markets, with larger containers made of plastic used for restaurants, and smaller bottles made of glass for the retail market. While prices vary for a bottle of spices, the average price is $4.79 for the retail market and $17.25 for the wholesale market. In each segment, Yankee Spices has four major customers that account for 80% of its sales and then a collection of smaller customers that make up the remaining 20% of its sales. The operating costs for the retail segment are $2,750,000 with an asset base of $7,500,000. The operating costs for the wholesale segment are $4,800,000 with an asset base of $10,400,000.

The two spice segments combine to make up the spice division of the parent company. The spice division's operating costs are $4,575,000 per year with a total asset base of $20,600,000.

The company has adopted activity-based costing (ABC) for its customer analysis. The data the company makes available to you is in the table below.

Yankee Spices

Customer Profitability Data

	Retail Segment					Wholesale (restaurant) Segment					
	ShopWell Markets	ABC Food Stores	McCarthy's Markets	TideWell Stores	Other 20%	Jones Wholesale	Spices Wholesaling	Quan Spices	Tompkins Wholesale	Other 20%	Totals
Revenue	$1,197,500	$1,341,200	$2,706,350	$2,155,500	$2,874,000	$1,759,500	$2,760,000	$3,018,750	$4,623,000	$6,900,000	$29,335,800
Raw Materials	$574,800	$643,776	$1,299,048	$1,034,640	$1,379,520	$791,775	$1,242,000	$1,358,438	$2,080,350	$3,105,000	$13,509,347
Orders placed	3,250	4,250	4,850	5,050	6,000	6,500	5,500	6,000	5,500	3,100	50,000
Orders picked/packed	3,900	4,500	4,800	5,430	6,600	7,200	7,500	8,700	6,900	4,470	60,000
Orders shipped	5,100	5,400	6,375	6,075	6,750	9,375	8,400	11,700	9,600	6,225	75,000
Invoices sent	8,375	9,375	10,250	9,500	10,875	15,625	17,000	18,125	14,000	11,875	125,000
Calls made	2,450	2,275	2,520	2,730	3,535	4,375	5,285	4,375	5,250	2,205	35,000

Yankee Spices

Activity-Based Data

Activity	Cost	Driver	Driver Frequency
Moving materials	$375,000	Raw material $'s	$13,509,347
Taking orders	$250,000	Orders	50,000
Picking and packing	$120,000	Orders picked	60,000
Shipping	$300,000	Orders shipped	75,000
Invoicing	$350,000	Invoices	125,000
Customer service	$200,000	Calls	35,000
General overhead	$500,000	Revenue $'s	$29,335,800

REQUIRED:

a. Do a customer profitability analysis using the ABC data to derive the nonmaterials costs for each customer.

b. Given the results of your customer profitability analysis, complete the segment profitability analyses. This should include an ROA calculation.

c. Given the results of your segment profitability analysis, complete the profitability analysis for the division. This should include an ROA calculation.

d. What does this information tell you about the spices division? Is it making a sufficient ROA?

6. **CUSTOMER, SEGMENT, AND DIVISIONAL PROFITABILITY WITH ABC COSTING.** Italian Favorites is the producer of an entire line of canned tomato products. It sells in two segments: retail grocery chains in a 28-ounce can, and a wholesale segment that sells #10 cans of product to various restaurants. The average price for the 28-ounce can to grocery stores is $2.85, and the average price to the wholesaler for the #10 can of tomatoes is $16. In each major segment, Italian Favorites has four customers who make up 80% of its sales with the remaining 20% being much smaller orders. The retail segment's operating costs are $2,150,000 per year on net assets of $6,500,000. The wholesale segment's operating costs are $3,500,000 per year on net assets of $8,000,000. The tomato division has operating costs of $3,750,000 on net assets of $18,500,000.

The company has adopted ABC for its customer analysis. The data the company makes available to you is in the table below.

Italian Favorites

Customer Profitability Data

	Retail Segment					Wholesale (Restaurant) Segment					
	Trudy's Italian Mart	Yagoo Supermarkets	Johnson's Markets	Goodtimes Markets	Other 20%	Nunzio Wholesale	Tomatoes International	TrueRed Wholesale	Brady's Wholesale	Other 20%	Totals
Revenue	$1,282,500	$1,083,000	$1,610,250	$1,282,500	$1,710,000	$1,632,000	$2,560,000	$2,800,000	$4,288,000	$4,800,000	$23,048,250
Raw materials	$609,188	$514,425	$764,869	$609,188	$812,250	$744,192	$1,167,360	$1,276,800	$1,955,328	$2,188,800	$10,642,400
Orders placed	3,900	5,100	5,820	6,060	7,200	7,800	6,600	7,200	6,600	3,720	60,000
Orders picked/packed	4,875	5,625	6,000	6,788	8,250	9,000	9,375	10,875	8,625	5,587	75,000
Orders shipped	6,800	7,200	8,500	8,100	9,000	12,500	11,200	15,600	12,800	8,300	100,000
Invoices sent	8,375	9,375	10,250	9,500	10,875	15,625	17,000	18,125	14,000	11,875	125,000
Calls made	3,500	3,250	3,600	3,900	5,050	6,250	7,550	6,250	7,500	3,150	50,000

Italian Favorites			
Activity-Based Data			
Activity	Cost	Driver	Driver Frequency
Moving materials	$425,000	Raw material $'s	$10,642,400
Taking orders	$350,000	Orders	60,000
Picking and packing	$240,000	Orders picked	75,000
Shipping	$500,000	Orders shipped	100,000
Invoicing	$400,000	Invoices	125,000
Customer service	$250,000	Calls	50,000
General overhead	$600,000	Revenue $'s	$23,048,250

REQUIRED:

a. Do a customer profitability analysis using the ABC data to derive the nonmaterials costs for each customer.

b. Given the results of your customer profitability analysis, complete the segment profitability analyses. This should include an ROA calculation.

c. Given the results of your segment profitability analysis, complete the profitability analysis for the division. This should include an ROA calculation.

d. What does this information tell you about the tomato division? Is it making a sufficient ROA?

7. **ECONOMIC STRUCTURE OF A FIRM.** Angie's Pies is a producer of a wide variety of pies that sell in the Midwest in grocery stores and convenience stores. Each pie retails for $8.79. Angie's sold 1 million pies in the last year. The income statement and balance sheet for the company are in the tables below.

Angie's Pies		
Income Statement for the Year Ended 12/31/XX		
Sales	$8,790,000	100.0%
Less: Variable Costs		
Manufacturing	$2,461,200	28.0%
SG&A	$1,054,800	12.0%
Total Variable Costs	$3,516,000	40.0%
Contribution Margin	$5,274,000	60.0%
Less: Fixed Costs		
Manufacturing	$2,500,000	28.4%
SG&A	$1,200,000	13.7%
Total Fixed Costs	$3,700,000	42.1%
Income Before Tax	$1,574,000	17.9%
Taxes at 30%	$472,200	5.4%
Net Income	$1,101,800	12.5%

Angie's Pies			
Balance Sheet for the Year Ended 12/31/XX			
Assets		Liabilities and Owner's Equity	
Cash	$275,000	Accounts Payable	$744,450
Accounts Receivable	$439,500	Salaries Payable	$248,150
Inventory	$293,000	Taxes Payable	$472,200
Total Current Assets	$1,007,500	Total S/T Liabilities	$1,464,800
		Long-Term Debt	$1,240,750
Property, Plant, and Equipment	$5,274,000	Total Liabilities	$2,705,550
Less: Accumulated Depreciation	$1,318,500	Common Stock	$496,300
Net PP&E	$3,955,500	Retained Earnings	$1,761,150
		Total Owner's Equity	$2,257,450
Total Assets	$4,963,000	Total Liabilities and Owner's Equity	$4,963,000
*Opening Inventory	$229,300		
*Opening Accounts Receivable	$496,500		
*Opening PP&E (net)	$4,218,500		

REQUIRED:

a. What is the profit margin in dollar terms and as a percentage?
b. Compute asset intensity.
c. Compute leverage.
d. Compute ROE.
e. Compute contribution margin per unit.
f. Compute annual fixed cost base.
g. Compute breakeven point in sales units.
h. What is the profit earned in one year?
i. What are the days of inventory on hand?
j. What are the accounts receivable days?
k. What is the fixed asset turnover ratio?
l. What is the fixed cost percentage of sales for manufacturing?
m. What is the fixed cost percentage of sales for SG&A?
n. What is the gross margin percentage?
o. What is the selling and administrative cost percentage?
p. Is this firm doing well or not? Why?

8. **ECONOMIC STRUCTURE OF A FIRM.** Sydney's Pizza is a national brand that sells frozen pizzas in grocery stores and convenience stores. Last year, it sold 2,000,000 pizzas at an average price of $6.25. The income statement and balance sheet for the firm are in the tables below.

Sydney's Pizza		
Income Statement for the Year Ended 12/31/XX		
Sales	$12,500,000	100.0%
Less: Variable Costs		
Manufacturing	$3,350,000	26.8%
SG&A	$1,862,500	14.9%
Total Variable Costs	$5,212,500	41.7%
Contribution Margin	$7,287,500	58.3%
Less: Fixed Costs		
Manufacturing	$3,000,000	24.0%
SG&A	$2,320,000	18.6%
Total Fixed Costs	$5,320,000	42.6%
Income Before Tax	$1,967,500	15.7%

Sydney's Pizza		
Income Statement for the Year Ended 12/31/XX		
Taxes at 30%	$590,250	4.7%
Net Income	$1,377,250	11.0%

Sydney's Pizza			
Balance Sheet for the Year Ended 12/31/XX			
Assets		Liabilities and Owner's Equity	
Cash	$878,000	Accounts Payable	$2,253,100
Accounts Receivable	$950,000	Salaries Payable	$675,930
Inventory	$1,562,500	Taxes Payable	$590,250
Total Current Assets	$3,390,500	Total S/T Liabilities	$3,519,280
		Long-Term Debt	$3,379,650
Property, Plant, and Equipment	$11,250,000	Total Liabilities	$6,898,930
Less: Accumulated Depreciation	$3,375,000	Common Stock	$1,351,860
Net PP&E	$7,875,000	Retained Earnings	$3,014,710
		Total Owner's Equity	$4,366,570
Total Assets	$11,265,500	Total Liabilities and Owner's Equity	$11,265,500
*Opening Inventory	$1,496,500		
*Opening Accounts Receivable	$850,000		
*Opening PP&E (net)	$8,215,000		

REQUIRED:

a. What is the profit margin in dollar terms and as a percentage?
b. Compute asset intensity.
c. Compute leverage.
d. Compute ROE.
e. Compute contribution margin per unit.
f. Compute annual fixed cost base.
g. Compute breakeven point in sales units.
h. What is the profit earned in one year?
i. What are the days of inventory on hand?
j. What are the accounts receivable days?
k. What is the fixed asset turnover ratio?

l. What is the fixed cost percentage of sales for manufacturing?
m. What is the fixed cost percentage of sales for SG&A?
n. What is the gross margin percentage?
o. What is the selling and administrative cost percentage?
p. Is this firm doing well or not? Why?

9. **CHANNEL COSTS.** Touhy Tires makes a broad range of tires for the automotive and truck markets. It sells its products directly to the original equipment manufacturers (OEMs; like Ford Motors), to wholesalers for delivery to small garages, and to large warehouse stores for mass consumption. The market Touhy sells to includes 68 million units sold to new car producers and 17.5 million in replacement tires for existing automobiles, 65% of which are sold through wholesalers and 35% through large warehouse stores. Touhy has a 15% market share in both markets. The tires sell for an average of $100 each.

Touhy has all of the channel costs of a large company. The distribution of these costs is detailed in the table below:

Touhy Tires				
Channel Cost Category	Channel Cost	% to OEM's	% to Wholesalers	% to Warehouse Stores
Channel management	$40,000,000	30%	40%	30%
Channel maintenance	$60,000,000	50%	35%	15%
Advertising, promotion, and marketing	$80,000,000	40%	40%	20%
Product liability	$50,000,000	35%	40%	25%
Trade show costs	$25,000,000	50%	30%	20%
Marketing staff costs	$12,000,000	30%	50%	20%

REQUIRED:

a. Calculate the channel costs by category and channel.
b. What are the total channel costs for OEMs? Wholesalers? Warehouse stores?
c. Calculate the revenue by channel.
d. What is the channel cost as a percentage of revenue for OEMs? Wholesalers? Warehouse stores?
e. Which channel seems the best for Touhy? Why?

10. **CHANNEL COSTS.** Absorbent Paper Towels is a producer of paper towels that are sold through three channels: direct to large grocery chains; through wholesalers to small convenience stores; and direct to large warehouse stores where the products are sold in very large bulk packages. The total market for paper towels in the United States is 13 billion pounds of paper towels, which at an average weight of 12 ounces per roll makes the total market in rolls of paper towels roughly 17.4 billion rolls that sell at approximately $0.75 per roll on average for the manufacturer. Absorbent has 20% of this total market.

Absorbent sells 30% of its product to large grocery stores, 30% to the wholesale market, and the remaining 40% to large wholesale warehouse stores. The channel costs in total and as a percent by channel are detailed in the table below.

Absorbent Paper Towels				
Channel Cost Category	Channel Cost	% to Large Grocery Chains	% to Wholesalers	% to Warehouse Stores
Channel management	$50,000,000	30%	40%	30%
Channel maintenance	$75,000,000	40%	30%	30%
Advertising, promotion, and marketing	$100,000,000	50%	30%	20%
Product liability	$2,500,000	50%	30%	20%
Trade show costs	$15,000,000	40%	30%	30%
Marketing staff costs	$25,000,000	40%	35%	25%

REQUIRED:

a. Calculate the channel costs by category and channel.
b. What are the total channel costs for large grocery chains? Wholesalers? Warehouse stores?
c. Calculate the revenue by channel.
d. What is the channel cost as a percentage of revenue for large grocery chains? Wholesalers? Warehouse stores?
e. Which channel seems the best for Absorbent? Why?

Database Problems

For database templates, worksheets, and workbooks, go to MAdownloads.imanet.org

DB 14.1 PARTIAL ECONOMIC STRUCTURE OF THE FIRM. In this exercise, you are going to calculate the following ratios for the three segments of Prestige Auto's business—new cars, used cars, and service:

Net profit margin percentage
Asset intensity
Leverage
Return on equity
Breakeven point in sales
Profit earned
Fixed cost percentage of sales
Gross margin percentage
SG&A percentage of sales

The numbers needed for this have all been incorporated in the spreadsheets that hold the segment's contribution for 10 years. Your calculations will be done on the worksheet titled Database Problem 14.1 Template. Do the calculations for each of the ratios requested.

REQUIRED:

a. **Turn in the worksheet when you have completed all of your analysis along with your answer to the following question.**
b. **Which segment looks best for Prestige Auto? Why?**

DB 14.2 CHANNEL COSTS. You will be using the Database Problem 14.2 Template and the same contribution margin worksheets for the three segments of Prestige Auto's business: new cars, used cars, and service. Your assignment is to sum up channel costs and calculate the percentage of sales the total channel costs represent.

To complete the exercise, determine the percentage of revenue the channel costs represent.

REQUIRED:

a. **Turn in your worksheet with the solution to the problem along with your answer to the following question.**

b. Which segment has the highest channel costs? Does this make sense? Why or why not?

Cases

CASE 14.1 TARGET COSTING AND VALUE CHAIN STRUCTURE. TruGreen Products is looking at developing a new product: plastic pill bottles for use by pharmacies. There is a huge market for both custom and generic-topped bottles. TruGreen estimates it could get $0.30 per bottle for custom bottles and $0.25 per bottle for generic-topped bottles. The market in total is estimated to be 4 billion bottles per year. TruGreen thinks it could secure a 5% market share (200 million bottles) if it keeps its prices within the target range, of which 50% would be custom tops and 50% generic tops.

TruGreen has several options available for both producing and distributing the product. For instance, it can make the bottle itself using some equipment that is sitting in storage. It would need to be updated, but the machinery is otherwise in good shape and could handle the new demand (and it is fully depreciated). The update would cost $3,600,000 and would be charged to product over three years. It would then cost the company $0.06 in materials and $0.04 in machining to produce custom-topped bottles. Overhead would be $0.06 per bottle. Production could be done within two days of receiving an order to build either to the stock in the distribution center or directly for customers. Shipping direct to customers would be via truck, taking one to two business days and cost roughly $0.01 per bottle. The company would make to order, so there would be minimal storage costs.

It could outsource the bottle production to a U.S. firm for $0.24 per bottle (either customized or generic top) which could produce orders within five days of receiving them and ship via truck in one to two business days at a cost of $0.01 per bottle. The minimum order size to get this price would be 1 million bottles, and TruGreen would probably have to store the custom-top bottles at 25% carrying cost for 12 weeks. Generic tops would only be in the warehouse for a few days at most so no carrying cost would be applied.

TruGreen could also take a slower route and have the bottles made overseas. The cost would only be $0.15 per bottle, but the cap could not be customized, which would reduce sales by 40%, and it would take four weeks' lead time to make the order and then another four weeks to ship the bottles via container ship to a U.S. port, where they would have to be off-loaded and trucked to the TruGreen distribution site. Shipping costs for overseas production would be $0.05 and the company would have to order a minimum of 10 million bottles at a time to get a reasonable price. The company would be charged inventory carrying costs at 25% from the time the order is completed and placed on the sourcing company's loading dock until it is sold, which, if only generic tops were sold, would take roughly 24 days to sell on average.

On the distribution side, TruGreen could rely on its own sales force to open this new market. It would need to hire four more sales representatives at a cost of $50,000 each per year plus a 10% bonus on all sales. TruGreen could also rely on catalog and internet sales, which would probably reduce its market share to 4% if done alone, or boost it by 1% if done in conjunction with a sales force. Getting an internet site up and running with full support and constant updating would cost the firm $48,000 per year for one in-house web maintenance employee. TruGreen could also deal directly with a wholesaler and avoid its own marketing costs. This would reduce the price to $0.25 for a custom top and $0.21 for a plain top so the wholesaler could make its profit.

Some marketing costs would be incurred no matter which channel the product is sold through. A new product manager would need to be hired at headquarters for $70,000 per year. Catalogs would need to be produced at a cost of $100,000 per year. If a sales force or internet approach is used, a new employee would need to be added to customer service at a cost of $40,000 per year and a new employee in accounts receivable for $45,000 per year. These last two employees would not be needed if the company used a wholesaler. The company would also need to ship the product to customers, which would cost $0.01 per bottle (which is included in the description for self-sourcing the bottles) no matter which channel it uses.

REQUIRED:

Given the information provided here, develop the value chain options that face TruGreen. Specifically,

a. **Look at the three options for sourcing the product. Which approach seems to be best for the firm financially (efficiency-based)? Which would be best for responsiveness? For this part of the analysis, assume the market is 200 million bottles. Make sure to include carrying costs for outsourced inventory using a calculation of number of days of sales the inventory represents at the 25% carrying cost noted.**
b. **Now take a look at the sales aspect of the value chain. Should TruGreen rely solely on a sales force, sales force plus internet site, or solely a wholesale approach? Which would be most efficient (cost less)? Which would be most responsive or flexible? Make sure to include all of the costs, both sales and home office, in your analysis.**
c. **Should TruGreen enter this market if its target profit is 20%? Why or why not?**

CASE 14.2 RETURN ON EQUITY AND THE SCOR MODEL. Novelty, Inc., makes several lines of customized novelty items, including T-shirts and sweatshirts that are made in two facilities. One facility makes the large runs of T-shirts and sweatshirts ordered by large amusement parks and related large tourist destinations. The other facility runs small custom orders, even having the capability to custom-embroider various designs into the product. Both factories use the same raw materials in terms of the T-shirts and sweatshirts themselves, so their major differences are in how they use their machines.

Bob Halvorsen is the head of Novelty, Inc. He believes in managing by the numbers, so he has been trying to compare the performance of the plant managers for the two T-shirt and sweatshirt plants. He knows their raw materials are the same, but, after that, they are very different. He decides to use two sets of numbers to evaluate the two plants. He plans to promote whichever manager is doing the better job. The approach Bob takes is to compare their ROE, decomposed into parts, their return on sales, and a number of SCOR metrics that he has recently learned about. The information Bob gathers about the two factories is in the tables below.

Novelty, Inc.		
Basic Financial Performance		
	Mass Plant	Custom Plant
Sales	$25,000,000	$25,000,000
Profit	$6,250,000	$5,000,000
Assets	$50,000,000	$75,000,000
Equity	$25,000,000	$20,000,000

Novelty, Inc.		
SCOR Metrics		
Metric	Mass Plant	Custom Plant
Raw materials days of supply	15	45
% of order changes	10%	20%
Production volume	5,000,000	3,125,000
# of channels	2	5
Forecast accuracy	75%	50%
# of defects or complaints	50	250
Make cycle time	1 minute	3 minutes
# of unique products made	100	500
Capacity utilization	60%	30%
Order fulfillment lead times	4 weeks	3 days
# of shipments by channel	5,000	25,000

REQUIRED:

a. Calculate the ROA, ROE, profit margin, asset intensity, and leverage for the two factories. When you are done, make sure that your profit margin times asset intensity times leverage equals the same number you got when you calculated ROE directly.

b. Which segment looks the best on these basic numbers? Why?

c. Now look at the SCOR metrics. What do they tell you about the two factories? Specifically, which one looks more efficient? Which one looks more responsive?

d. Given your answer to the above questions, which manager do you think Bob should consider promoting? In other words, which one is managing his plant most effectively given the strategy it is pursuing?

978-0-996-7293-5-2-CMAN